D1218401

Automatic Fingerprint Recognition Systems

Springer
New York
Berlin
Heidelberg
Hong Kong
London
Milan
Paris
Tokyo

Nalini Ratha   Ruud Bolle
Editors

Automatic Fingerprint Recognition Systems

With 135 Figures

 Springer

Nalini Ratha
IBM T.J. Watson Research Center
19 Skyline Drive
Hawthorne, NY 10532
USA
ratha@us.ibm.com

Ruud Bolle
IBM T.J. Watson Research Center
19 Skyline Drive
Hawthorne, NY 10532
USA
bolle@us.ibm.com

Library of Congress Cataloging-in-Publication Data
Automatic fingerprint recognition systems / editors, Nalini Ratha, Ruud Bolle.
    p. cm.
  Includes bibliographical references and index.
  ISBN 0-387-95593-3 (hc. : alk. paper)
    1. Fingerprints—Identification.   2. Fingerprints—Data processing.   I. Ratha, Nalini K.
(Nalini Kanta)   II. Bolle, Ruud.

  HV6074.A98 2003
  363.25'8–dc21   2003044593

ISBN 0-387-95593-3   Printed on acid-free paper.

Printed in the United States of America.

9 8 7 6 5 4 3 2 1   SPIN 10893934

www.springer-ny.com

Springer-Verlag   New York Berlin Heidelberg
A member of BertelsmannSpringer Science+Business Media GmbH

Preface

Advances in automatic fingerprint recognition are driven by improved fingerprint sensing and advancements in areas such as computer architecture, pattern recognition, image processing, and computer vision. In addition to the new developments in science and technology, several recent social and political events have increased the level of interest in fingerprint recognition for the purpose of positive person identification. This heightened interest in fingerprint technology and its promise to deliver cost-effective solutions have prompted us to undertake the endeavor to edit this book. And indeed, we have been lucky to convince top experts in the world to write 21 chapters on a wide variety of fingerprint topics, ranging from the history of fingerprints to evolving fingerprint standards in a networked society.

The chapters are loosely arranged according to the stages of a pattern recognition system; in other words, following the typical processing steps of automated fingerprint recognition systems.

Chapter 1 by Simon Cole summarizes the history of fingerprint recognition and its social significance. Inkless fingerprint sensing has greatly contributed to the automation efforts; Dale Setlak, in Chapter 2, presents new developments in inkless fingerprint sensing with specific emphasis on RF (radio frequency) imaging techniques. Once the fingerprint has been acquired, the signal often needs to be enhanced (preprocessed) based on automated assessment of the image quality. Chapter 3, written by Michael Yao, Sharath Pankanti, and Norman Haas, describes an approach to quantify the quality of a fingerprint image. A related issue in fingerprint image acquisition is to detect distortion of the fingerprint; in Chapter 4, Chitra Dorai, Nalini Ratha, and Ruud Bolle describe a method of detecting fingerprint image distortion using streaming fingerprint images.

The next three chapters deal with automatic enhancement of fingerprint images to remove as much as possible the noise and distortions, which are an unavoidable byproduct of fingerprint acquisition. In Chapter 5, Barry Sherlock gives a detailed description of an enhancement technique that uses anisotropic nonstationary Fourier domain filters. Toshio Kamei presents a filter design approach to fingerprint enhancement using fingerprint ridge frequency and orientation estimations in Chapter 6. In

Chapter 7, Lin Hong and Anil Jain present an enhancement technique using Gabor filters.

Fingerprint recognition inherits a rich history of manual methods used by human experts to compare fingerprints. Fingerprint recognition using minutia features is a popular method adapted by many research and commercial systems. In Chapter 8, Weicheng Chen and M. Eshera review the state of the art in fingerprint feature extraction and present an approach to minutiae extraction. In addition to using local minutia features, fingerprints can also be distinguished into broader classes using a global ridge pattern. Two chapters have been devoted to this interesting problem that researchers have attempted to solve for several decades. In Chapter 9, Raffeala Cappelli and Dario Maio survey the main approaches in the literature; they further introduce a fingerprint classification method based on a multispace generalization of the Karhunen–Loève transform (MKL). Combining hidden Markov models and decision trees, Andrew Senior and Ruud Bolle demonstrate classification results on large public databases in Chapter 10.

The discussion then switches to fingerprint matching and higher-level issues. Chapter 11 by Salil Prabhakar and Anil Jain reviews matching techniques for fingerprint authentication and explains the advantages of combining classifiers. Often in extremely noisy and poor fingerprint images, minutiae-based matching does not work well; Craig Watson and David Casasent, in Chapter 12, show how using distortion-tolerant filters can significantly improve correlation fingerprint matchers.

Fingerprint identification systems have been successfully deployed in many countries, in diverse applications, and in large-scale systems. It is useful to preselect fingerprints that fall in the same group as a query fingerprint for reasons of computational efficiency. In Chapter 13, Toshio Kamei presents an algorithm for fingerprint preselection using Eigen features of the fingerprint direction fields. Quantitative fingerprint system evaluation requires measurement of false reject and false-alarm error rates. Chapter 14, by Rajiv Khanna, introduces two parameters based on those error rates, *reliability* and *selectivity*, and describes their impact in designing large-scale fingerprint identification systems. Often multiple fingers are used in large-scale identification systems. In Chapter 15, James Wayman estimates penetration rates for single-finger systems based on thumb, index, middle, and ring fingers, and multifinger systems for two thumbs, two index fingers, and combined four thumb-index finger systems.

Fingerprint technology has contributed to forensic science via technologies to positively identify criminals from latent scene-of-crime fingerprints. Both automatic systems as well as manual systems that involve human experts exist. In Chapter 16, Mario Pattichis and Alan Bovik describe a novel image enhancement algorithm, suitable for latent fingerprint processing based on an AM-FM model. In Chapter 17, Lyn Haber and Ralph Haber present error rates of latent fingerprint matching by the human fingerprint expert.

Testing of fingerprint systems is a very time-consuming process dominated by the data collection process. Davide Maltoni, in Chapter 18, addresses this problem with a novel synthetic fingerprint generation techniques.

Often large-scale fingerprint systems need to store and transmit fingerprints. The FBI recommends a wavelet scalar quantization (WSQ) method for fingerprint image compression and decompression. In Chapter 19, Rem Onyshczak and Abdou Youssef introduce this WSQ fingerprint image compression and decompression standard. The early fingerprint systems did not involve much sophisticated information security, as the systems mostly operated in highly secure buildings with closed networks. With the Internet, this scenario is changing rapidly; in Chapter 20, Colin Soutar analyzes different types of attacks. Finally, with the large number of vendors in the automatic fingerprint recognition area, standardization is extremely important for interoperability. R. Michael McCabe looks at the history and development of fingerprint standard development in Chapter 21.

Through this wide variety of chapters, we have attempted to convey to readers the challenges in automating fingerprint recognition and in building practical, useful systems. This book is equally useful to researchers, scientists, practitioners, and students who are fascinated by these challenges and wish to advance the field of research in automated fingerprint recognition.

We thank all contributors for their cooperation and sharing their excellent research; we would like to thank our wives, Meena and Sylvia, for their continued love and patience.

Hawthorne, New York, USA   *Nalini Ratha*
                                                                  Ruud Bolle

Contents

20. Security Considerations for the Implementation of Biometric Systems

21. Fingerprint Interoperability Standards

Contributors

Ruud Bolle
IBM T. J. Watson Research Center
19 Skyline Drive
Hawthorne, NY 10532, USA
bolle@us.ibm.com

Alan Bovik
Department of Electrical Engineering
and Computer Engineering
The University of Texas at Austin
Austin, TX 78712-1084, USA

R. Cappelli
BIOLAB-DEIS
Faculty of Engineering
Viale Risorgimento 2
University of Bologna
40136 Bologna, Italy
cappelli@csr.unibo.it

David Casasent
Department of ECE
Carnegie Mellon University
Pittsburg, PA 15213, USA

Simon A. Cole
Department of Criminology,
    Law and Society
School of Social Ecology
2357 Social Ecology II
University of California, Irvine
Irvine, CA 92697-7080, USA
scole@uci.edu

Chitra Dorai
IBM T. J. Watson Research Center
19 Skyline Drive
Hawthorne, NY 10532, USA
dorai@us.ibm.com

M.A. Eshera
ARGTEC, Inc.
5513 Twin Knolls Rd.
Columbia, MD 20145, USA

Lyn Haber
Human Factor Consultants
730 Rimrock Dr.
Swall Meadows, CA 93514, USA
haberhfc@telis.org

Ralph Norman Haber
Human Factor Consultants
730 Rimrock Dr.
Swall Meadows, CA 93514, USA
haberhfc@telis.org

Norman Haas
IBM T. J. Watson Research Center
19 Skyline Drive
Hawthorne, NY 10532, USA

Lin Hong
One Exchange Place
Identix, Inc.
Jersey City, NJ 07302, USA
lin.hong@visionics.com

Anil Jain
Department of Computer Science
    and Engineering
Michigan State University
East Lansing, MI 48824, USA

Toshio Kamei
Multimedia Research Laboratories
NEC Corporation
4-1-1, Miyazaki, Miyamae, Kawasaki
Kanagawa, 216-8555, Japan
t-kamei@cb.jp.nec.com

Rajiv Khanna
Mitretek Systems
3150 Fairview Park Dr. South
Falls Church, VA 22042-4519, USA
Rajiv.Khanna@ieee.org

D. Maio
BIOLAB-DEIS
Faculty of Engineering
Viale Risorgimento 2
University of Bologna
40136 Bologna, Italy
dmaio@deis.unibo.it

Davide Maltoni
BIOLAB-DEIS
Faculty of Engineering
Viale Risorgimento 2
University of Bologna
40136 Bologna, Italy
maltoni@csr.unibo.it

R. Michael McCabe
National Institute of Standards
    and Technology
100 Bureau Dr., Stop 8940
Bldg. 225/Room A-216
Gaithersburg, MD 20899, USA
mccabe@nist.gov

Remigius Onyshczak
National Institute of Standards
    and Technology
Gaithersburg, MD 20899, USA
rjo@nist.gov

Sharath Pankanti
IBM T. J. Watson Research Center
19 Skyline Drive
Hawthorne, NY 10532, USA
sharat@us.ibm.com

M. Pattichis
Department of Electrical Engineering
    and Computer Engineering
The University of New Mexico
Albuquerque, NM 87131-1356, USA
pattichis@eece.unm.edu

Salil Prabhakar
Digital Persona, Inc.
805 Veterans Blvd., Suite 301
Redwood City, CA 94062, USA
salilP@digitalpersona.com

Nalini Ratha
IBM T. J. Watson Research Center
19 Skyline Drive
Hawthorne, NY 10532, USA
ratha@us.ibm.com

Andrew Senior
IBM T. J. Watson Research Center
19 Skyline Drive
Hawthorne, NY 10532, USA
aws@watson.ibm.com

Dale R. Setlak
Authentec
709 S. Harbor City Blvd., Suite 400
Melbourne, FL 32902-2719, USA
Dale.Setlak@authentec.com

Weicheng Shen
Science Applications International Corp.
1710 SAIC Dr., Mail Stop 2-6-9
McLean, VA 22102, USA
WEICHENG.SHEN@saic.com

B.G. Sherlock
Department of Electrical
    and Electronic Engineering
University of North Carolina at Charlotte
9201 University City Blvd.
Charlotte, NC 28223, USA
sherlock@uncc.edu

Colin Soutar
Bioscrypt, Inc.
5450 Explorer Dr., Suite 500
Mississauga, Ontario L4W 5M1, Canada
colin.soutar@bioscypt.com

Craig Watson
National Institute of Standards
    and Technology
Gaithersburg, MD 20899, USA
Craig.Watson@nist.gov

James L. Wayman
National Biometrics Test Center
College of Engineering
One Washington Square
San Jose, CA 95192-0080, USA
JLWayman@aol.com

M.Y. Yao
IBM T. J. Watson Research Center
19 Skyline Drive
Hawthorne, NY 10532, USA

Abdou Youssef
Department of Computer Science
The George Washington University
Washington, DC 20052, USA

Chapter 1

History of Fingerprint Pattern Recognition

Simon A. Cole

Abstract. This article summarizes the major developments in the history of efforts to use fingerprint patterns to identify individuals, from the earliest fingerprint classification systems of Vucetich and Henry in the 1890s through the advent of automated fingerprint identification. By chronicling the history of "manual" systems for recording storing, matching, and retrieving fingerprints, the article puts advances in automatic fingerprint recognition in historical context and highlights their historical and social significance.

1.1. Introduction

The modern history of fingerprint identification begins in the late 19th century with the development of identification bureaus charged with keeping accurate records about individuals indexed, not according to name, but according to some physical attribute. Only in the 19th century were modern states bureaucratic enough to presume to maintain organized criminal records that extended beyond a single parish or locality [81]. Early criminal records indexed by name were vulnerable to subversion by the simple expedient of adopting an alias. Hence there developed the idea of indexing records according to some bodily feature. An early, extremely cumbersome, effort was the British Register of Distinctive Marks, which listed convicts according to some distinctive feature like a birthmark, scar, or tattoo [82]. The demand for criminal histories was in large part driven by changes in jurisprudence. A shift of focus from the criminal act to the criminal individual demanded more complete and more accurate knowledge about each offender's criminal history. This would enable individualized penal "treatment" and differential punishment of first-time offenders and recidivists [30, 60].

Although there is a long and murky prehistory of uses of fingerprints to *authenticate* the identity of individuals, principally in Asia [8, 51, 91], it was not until the late 19th century that efforts were made to use fingerprints for the more technically demanding process of *identification*—that is, rather than merely verifying whether or not an individual is claiming the correct identity, selecting the correct identity of an unknown individual from a large database of possible identities.

The cradle of the modern fingerprint system was colonial India, where British administrators were concerned about maintaining social control over the native population. A workable identification system was desired for numerous purposes, including combatting fraud through impersonation in the disbursement of what today would be called "entitlements," such as pensions; resolving disputed identities in civil legal disputes over land deeds or contracts; monitoring the movement of targetted population groups, such as the so-called criminal tribes; and maintaining criminal histories of persons convicted of crimes [68].

Sir William Herschel, grandson of the Astronomer Royal William Herschel and son of the polymath John Herschel, a colonial administrator in the Hooghly district of Bengal, helped bring fingerprints to the attention of British scientists and bureaucrats. Although Herschel recorded his first inked handprint on a road-building contract with Rajyadhar Kōnāi in 1858, it was not until 1877, after two decades of dallying with fingerprints, that he formally proposed that "sign-manuals," as he called them, be used to identify individuals. Herschel tried to characterize his 1858 print as an inventive act, but it seems more likely that it was inspired by *tip sahi*, a Bengali practice of signing documents with a fingertip dabbed in ink [15, 40].

British awareness of the potential utility of fingerprint patterns was further stimulated by Henry Faulds, a Scottish physician doing missionary work in Tokyo. Faulds wrote a letter to *Nature* describing how he happened upon fingerprint patterns on ancient Japanese ceramics and proposing that their use be investigated for criminal identification purposes. Faulds also described some brief research establishing that Gibraltar monkeys and the various human races all shared the same basic pattern structure and an episode in which he actually used a "greasy finger-mark" to solve a petty crime at the embassy [24]. Herschel hastily answered Faulds' letter with one of his own, asserting his priority in the "discovery" of fingerprints, if not in publication [39]. This set off a priority dispute between Herschel and Faulds that would last more than 50 years [7, 89]. In fact, Thomas Taylor, a microscopist at the U.S. Department of Agriculture, had beaten both men to publication by three years [22, 79]. Faulds' claim to have made the earliest forensic fingerprint identification, meanwhile, turns out to have been anticipated, though quickly forgotten, more than two decades earlier by John Maloy, a constable in Albany, New York [16].

1.2. The Development of Fingerprint Classification Systems

As a means of individual identification, fingerprints faced a formidable rival, the anthropometric system of identification, devised by Alphonse Bertillon, a Paris police official and son of the famous demographer Louis–Adolphe Bertillon [9, 64]. Although the Bertillon system required strenuous efforts to ensure consistency between operators in taking delicate measurements of "osseus lengths," it enjoyed a crucial advantage. Since Bertillon's system was indexed according to easily quantifiable anthropometric measurments, he was able—for the first time—to devise a feasible system for indexing individualized records according to physical attributes rather than names. Fingerprint patterns did not possess any such inherent mechanism

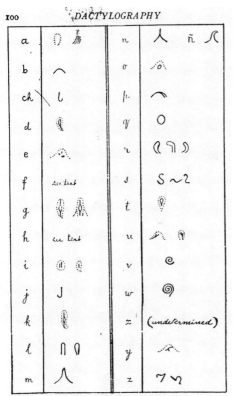

Fig. 1.1. H. Faulds' "syllabic" system for classifying fingerprint pattern types. (*Source*: Faulds, H., *Dactylography, or, The Study of Finger-Prints*, Halifax: Milner, 1912.)

for putting them into some sort of rational order. Rather, a fingerprint was much like a photograph: a rich source of qualitative data, but possessing no inherent characteristic by which it could be indexed. Bertillon had solved this problem by reducing the body to a set of numbers. In a sense, the analog nature of fingerprint data stymied efforts to index criminal records according to fingerprint patterns. In order to use fingerprint patterns as the basis for indexing criminal records, some sort of classification system would have to be imposed upon fingerprint patterns.

Faulds mounted the earliest attempt to devise such a system. He devised a "syllabic" classification scheme (Fig. 1.1), by which consonants represented a general pattern type and vowels represented the characteristics of the "core" (the center of the print). The print of each finger might, therefore, be represented by a "word," and these words might be kept in "a syllabic index arranged in alphabetical order" [25]. Faulds' efforts to interest Scotland Yard in this system were met with little success.

The problem was next taken up by the polymath Francis Galton. Galton had been alerted to fingerprints by his cousin, Charles Darwin, to whom Faulds had sent a copy of his 1880 letter. Fingerprints were of interest to Galton as potential markers of individuals' heredity and, secondarily, as a means of criminal identification. Galton

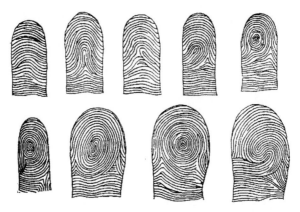

Fig. 1.2. J.E. Purkyně's nine fingerprint pattern types. (*Source*: Purkyně, J.E., A physiological examination of the organ of vision and the integumentary system, University of Breslau, 1823; trans. by H. Cummins and R.W. Kennedy, *American J. of Police Science*, 1.)

discovered an 1823 dissertation by Jan Purkyně, a Czech physician and anatomist, which noted the presence of friction ridges on human fingertips. Although Purkyně did not propose that these ridges be used for identification, he did make the earliest attempt to classify the pattern types, sorting them into nine categories, which today would correspond to the arch, tented arch, two types of loop, four types of whorl, and a twinned loop (Fig. 1.2) [61].

Finding Purkyně system unsatisfactory, Galton set out to devise his own classification system. Devising ever finer-grained categories of pattern type, Galton eventually ended up with 60 types. With so many pattern types to choose from, Galton found it extremely difficult to be consistent about assigning new samples to categories. With an assistant classifying as well, it became even more difficult to maintain consistency. It was at this point that Galton made his crucial contribution to the development of fingerprint classification. He realized that the key to a workable classification system lay in reducing, rather than expanding, the number of pattern types, deciding that all fingerprints could broadly be characterized as one of three basic pattern types: arch, loop, or whorl (Fig. 1.3). It should be noted that these are not "natural" types; what Galton called "transitional" patterns blur the distinction between, say, an arch and a loop. Therefore, in order to make the system work, arbitrary rules must be devised to govern the assignment of ambiguous patterns into in one category or another [27]. All classifiers must adhere to these rules consistently in order to avoid misclassification.

Because loop patterns comprised around 60% of the total, Galton proposed that they be divided into "inner" (today "radial," opening toward the thumb) and "outer" (today "ulnar," opening toward the little finger) loops. Because a single letter was assigned to each of these four pattern types (A for arch, I for inner loop, O for outer loop, W for whorl), each individual could be characterized by a word, usually 10 characters in length, comprising the pattern types of all of his or her fingers [32].

This proposal was hampered by the fact that pattern types were not evenly distributed in the human population. Instead, a sampling of sets of 10 fingerprint patterns

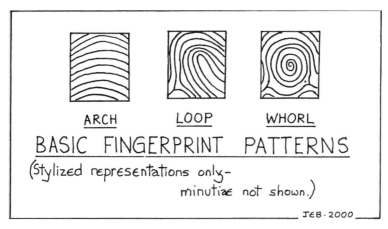

Fig. 1.3. Francis Galton's three basic fingerprint pattern types. (*Source*: Drawing by John E. Berry. Reproduced by permission of John E. Berry.)

from any population tended to cluster in certain common categories. For example, more than 6% of Galton's population had the pattern OOOOOOOOOO: outer loops on all 10 fingers. As a method of subdividing a large database of records into a small, searchable group of records, Galton's system was greatly inferior to Bertillon's, as Galton himself conceded [82].

Two research groups took up the problem where Galton left off, and, almost simultaneously, they came up with remarkably similar solutions. The first was headed by Juan Vucetich, head of the police statistical bureau in La Plata, Argentina. The second was composed of Edward Henry, another colonial official stationed in Bengal, and his mathematically trained subordinates, Azizul Haque and Chandra Bose. Both groups were dissatisfied with anthropometric identification. Both devised solutions based primarily on subdividing loops and whorls into a secondary set of categories. Both systems subdivided loops by *ridge counting*, which involved counting the number of intervening ridges between two designated points on the fingerprint patterns, the *delta* and the *core* (Fig. 1.4). The Indian group subdivided whorls by *ridge tracing*, which involved tracing a ridge from the delta and determining whether it passed inside, passed outside, or met the core. Vucetich devised subpattern types for whorls. Thus, both systems relied upon a process of *serial categorization*.

1.2.1. The Henry System

The rules of fingerprint classification under the Henry system are quite complex, but a brief summary may be instructive: The first two steps in the Henry system were based on Galton's three basic pattern types: arch, loop, and whorl. To these, Henry added a fourth group, called "composites," which consisted of rare patterns including "central pocket loops," "lateral pocket loops," "twinned loops," and "accidentals." The "primary classification" involved examining each finger and noting where whorls

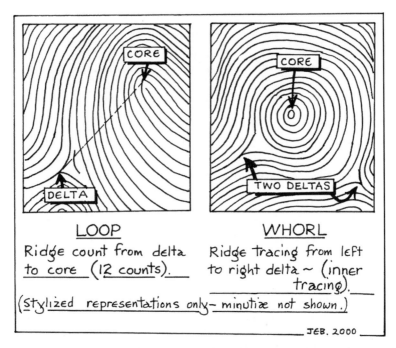

CORE

CORE

DELTA

TWO DELTAS

LOOP

WHORL

Ridge count from delta to core (12 counts).

Ridge tracing from left to right delta ~ (inner tracing).

(Stylized representations only – minutiæ not shown.)

JEB. 2000

Fig. 1.4. Core and delta. (*Source*: Drawing by J.E. Berry. Reproduced by permission of J.E. Berry.)

appeared. The fingers were numbered 1 through 10, beginning with the left little finger and proceeding from left to right across both hands. The primary classification was expressed as a fraction with odd-numbered fingers over even-numbered fingers. A given value was added to the numerator if a whorl appeared in a odd-numbered finger, and a given value added to the denominator if a whorl appeared in an even-numbered finger. These values were determined by the finger. The values were squares of one another: 1, 2, 4, 8, 16 (Table 1.1). Henry then added 1 to both the numerator and the denominator in order to avoid having zeroes. The primary classification could, therefore, range from 1/1 (zero whorls) to 32/32 (10 whorls). With a range between 1/1 and 32/32, there were 32^2, or 1024, possible primary classifications. The fingerprint cards were stored in a filing cabinet with 32 rows and 32 columns of pigeonholes. A fingerprint card with a primary classification 20/11, therefore, would be found in the 20th pigeonhole on the 11th horizontal row.

The secondary classification went on to characterize the fingers of the right hand (in the numerator) and the left hand (in the denominator). Because whorls had already been described in the primary classification, they were omitted in the secondary classification. The patterns of the fingers were characterized as arches (A), tented arches (T), radial loops (R), or ulnar loops (U).

Further subclassification was performed by ridge tracing. Whorl patterns originate in two *deltas*, where the transverse ridges divide (like a river delta) to form the whorl.

Table 1.1. Basis for Primary Classification under Henry System of Fingerprint Classification

1	2	3	4	5	6	7	8	9	10
Left little	Left ring	Left middle	Left index	Left thumb	Right little	Right ring	Right middle	Right index	Right thumb

Note: The numbering of the fingers for the Henry system. With palms facing down, fingers are numbered from left to right, beginning with the left little finger.

Numerator	Left little 1	Left middle 2	Left thumb 4	Right ring 8	Right index 16
Denominator	Left ring 1	Left index 2	Right little 4	Right middle 8	Right thumb 16

Note: Schematic for determining primary Henry classification. Odd-numbered fingers count for the numerator. Even-numbered fingers count for the denominator. If a whorl appears on a finger, the value in the box is added to either the numerator or the denominator. The primary classification is calculated using these values and then adding 1 to both numerator and denominator. The values for the primary classification may then range from 1/1 (zero whorls) to 32/32 (10 whorls).

Examiners would trace the lower ridge of the left delta and see whether it passed inside, passed outside, or met the right delta. If the ridge passed inside the right delta, the pattern was classified as an "inner" whorl, designated by I. If it passed outside, the pattern was classified as an "outer" whorl, designated by O, and if it met the core it was classified as a "meeting" whorl, designated by M. These letters were then added to the secondary classification.

Loops were subclassified by ridge counting. The examiner counted the number of ridges between the delta and the core, and these values were appended to the secondary classification. Ridge counts from 1 to 9 in the index finger (1 to 10 in the middle finger) were characterized by I, counts above these threshold by O. The third term of the equation was the actual numerical ridge count of each little finger if it was, as was typical, a loop. A typical Henry classification might look as follows:

$$\frac{15 \ R \ OO \ 19}{17 \ U \ II \ 8}$$

(Whorls in both thumbs, high-ridge-count radial loops in the right index and middle fingers, low-ridge-count ulnar loops in the left index and middle fingers. Nineteen-ridge-count loop in the right little finger. Eight-ridge-count loop in the left little finger.) After this there were even more subclassifications. With all this subclassification, the Henry system was able to sort fingerprint cards into finer groups than Galton's rudimentary system. Even common primary classifications, like 1/1, could be subdivided using ridge tracing and counting. So a properly classified fingerprint card would have to be searched against only a small number of fingerprint cards bearing the same classification. Henry's finer-grained classification system, therefore, greatly sped up the process of checking whether a suspect's fingerprint had already been registered with the police, perhaps under an alias.

Here it is worth quoting at length Henry's own description of the working of the Indian classification system:

A man charged with housebreaking and theft is convicted under the name of John Smith, sentenced to a term of imprisonment and sent to jail, where his finger print, together with the finger prints of other prisoners received, are taken by a prison warder. On the back of each slip is recorded the prisoner's name, with dates and full particulars of the case, and the slip thus filled up is forwarded to the Central Office. On receipt there, they are classified by one officer, and his work is tested by another, before they are filed in their respective collections and groups…

After a lapse of a year or two, the Central Office receives from police or Governor of a jail a slip, containing the finger prints of man on trial for theft, who has given the name of William Jones, and other information concerning himself, which the inquiries locally made show to be false…

On receipt of the slip one officer draws up the search form containing the full formula, viz.

$$\frac{13U}{18U}\left(\frac{IO}{IO}\right)14,$$

and makes over the slip and the search form to the searcher, who first verifies the correctness of the formula, and then proceeds to search. The type in all the impressions is unmistakable, so there can be no doubt as to the correctness of the Primary Classification number

$$\frac{13}{18}$$

—the subclassification

$$\frac{U}{U}\left(\frac{IO}{IO}\right)$$

of index and middle of the two hands is also obviously correct—but there may be divergence of opinion as to there being exactly 14 *counts* in the right little finger. To eliminate the possibility of error arising from this, he decides to search through the subgroups of

$$\frac{13}{18}\frac{U}{U}\left(\frac{IO}{IO}\right),$$

which have from 12 to 16 *counts* in the right little finger…If the slip he is looking for is in the Criminal Record, he knows it must be among subgroups 12 to 16 of

$$\frac{13}{18}\frac{U}{U}\left(\frac{IO}{IO}\right),$$

which file he picks out, and he concerns himself no further with ridge *counts*, but concentrates attention upon the salient features of the slip. The right thumb is a Lateral Pocket, the left thumb a Twinned Loop. He turns the slips of subgroups 12 to 16 over rapidly, much in the same way as a pile of bank notes are looked through, and delays only when he comes to a slip the right thumb impression of which is a lateral pocket, and his eye then glances at the left thumb. If it is not a Twinned Loop, he passes on to the next slip, and finally stops at one which has the right thumb a Lateral Pocket, the left thumb a Twinned Loop, and the two ring fingers Central Pockets. He then compares the ridge *characteristics* of one or two impressions on the slip in his hand with the corresponding impressions of the slip in the Record, and if they agree he knows that his search has been successful. The Central Office then inform the requisitioning police that the so-called Wm. Jones was, on a specified date, convicted under the name of John Smith, of housebreaking with theft, and give all information concerning him recorded on the back of their slip, which is sufficient to enable the local police to prove, in the manner prescribed by law, the previous criminality of the *soi-disant* Wm. Jones. [38]

1.2.2. The Vucetich System

Like Galton, Vucetich simplified his scheme to four basic pattern types: arch, loop with "internal inclination," loop with "external inclination," and whorl. For the thumbs, each of these patterns was designated with a letter: A, I, E, or V. For the fingers, they were indicated with the numbers 1–4. Vucetich's *primary classification* was given by the pattern types of the fingers in order, from thumb through little finger, expressed as a fraction with the right hand over the left. For example, the primary classification

$$\frac{V\,1211}{E\,1311}$$

indicated a whorl on the right thumb, an external loop on the left thumb, arches on both index fingers, an internal loop on the right middle finger, an external loop on the left middle finger, and arches on the remaining fingers.

So far, Vucetich's system was no more discriminating than Galton's original four-letter alphabetical system. But Vucetich used a *secondary classification* to further subdivide sets of fingerprints. For secondary classification, each of the primary pattern types was classed as one of five subtypes, denoted by the numbers 5–9. For example, loops were divided as follows:

5 = loop with plain pattern
6 = loop with adhering ridges
7 = internal loop approximating a central pocket
8 = external loop approximating a central pocket
9 = irregular loops like none of the above

One of these numbers for each finger was then placed in an adjoining fraction in the same manner as the primary classification.

Like Henry, Vucetich further subdivided patterns by ridge counting. Ridge counts for the index and little fingers, rounded to increments of five, were added in parentheses following the secondary classification. Thus, a complete Vucetich classification might look as follows:

$$\frac{A\,2142\ \ 85687\ \ (5)(15)}{V\,3413\ \ 76678\ \ (25)(25)}$$

where the first term indicates an arch on the right thumb, internal loops on the right index and little fingers, arch on the right middle finger, whorl on the right ring finger, whorl (*V* in Spanish) on the left thumb, external loops on the left index and little fingers, whorl on the left middle finger, and arch on the left finger (primary classification); the second term indicates various subdivisions of the pattern types described in the first term; and the third term indicates ridge counts (rounded to increments of 5) for the loop in the right index finger (5), the right little finger (15), the left index finger (25), and the left little finger (25) (tertiary classification). Within highly populated categories, even further classification processes would be applied. As with the Henry system, this processs of subdividing enabled classifiers to narrow down a search to a searchable number of records, even in a large database [9, 13, 65].

Both systems, the "Vucetich system" and the "Henry system" as they were called, were completed almost simultaneously. The Indian group completed its system around 1895. Vucetich appears to have had a completed system earlier, around 1893, but his superiors took it out of action. It was reinstated in 1896. With these classification systems, databases indexed according to fingerprint pattern types could seriously rival, and eventually surpass, those indexed according to anthropometric measurements, in terms of searching speed and ability to deal with large numbers of individualized records. Argentina and India became the first countries to replace identification systems indexed according to anthropometric measurements with systems indexed according to fingerprint patterns [65]. Britain switched to its colony's system in 1900.

1.3. Forensic Fingerprint Identification

The main impetus behind the development of fingerprint identification was using fingerprint patterns to index large databases of criminal records in order to prevent recidivists from evading their past crimes by adopting an alias. Early innovators quickly realized, however, that another application of fingerprint patterns was possible: forensic investigation of crimes, using friction ridge impressions the perpetrator inadvertently left at a crime scene. As noted above, John Maloy actually performed a forensic identification in the late 1850s, but the innovation was lost to history, and Thomas Taylor suggested that fingerprints left at crime scenes might identify perpetrators. Faulds also used a "greasy finger-mark" to link a suspect to a crime in the late 1870s [24]. Wilhelm Eber, a Prussian veterinarian, in 1888 suggested "developing" prints left in bodily secretions—what today would be called "latent" prints—by dusting with a fine powder [36], and Vucetich solved a crime using a bloody fingerprint in 1892 [14, 65].

The challenges of forensic fingerprint identification are quite different from those of 10-print identification. While 10-print identification requires complicated systems of pattern classification in order to hone in on a likely set of potentially matching cards, once the set of candidate matches has been produced, the examiner has a great deal of information available to make the comparison. Ten-print identification involves comparing *inked* impressions of a complete set of (usually) 10 fingers. An obvious lack of matching ridge characteristics between the finger impressions of any of the

10 fingers of different persons eliminates the possibility that the two sets of prints derive from the same hands. When the task is forensic identification, the situation is quite different. Latent prints typically do not have the clarity of information of inked prints; are limited in area compared to inked prints, which are *rolled* on the card in order to maximize area; contain background noise, impressions of foreign particles, and other artifacts that somehow must be distinguished from true ridge detail; and suffer from greater pressure distortion than inked prints.

In order to use fingerprint patterns for forensic purposes, three basic steps are necessary:

1. Establish the relative permanence of fingerprint patterns.
2. Establish the variability of fingerprint patterns.
3. Develop a method, process, and confidence measure for attributing a crime-scene impression to a known finger.

Anecdotal evidence for permanence was provided by Herschel, who took prints from the same individual at intervals of up to 57 years [40]. While this was hardly a comprehensive study, the idea that fingerprint patterns were relatively permanent was so intuitively plausible that there was little reason to dispute Herschel's conclusions.

The question of the variability of fingerprint patterns was for the most part answered with the assertion that all human fingerprint patterns were unique. Declarations of the uniqueness of fingerprint patterns had accompanied even some of the earliest observations of friction ridges. The Persian historian Rashid-eddin, in 1303 [51], the German anatomist J.C.A. Mayer, in 1788 [19], and Purkyně [61], in 1823, all asserted, based merely on intuition, that all fingerprints were unique. In the modern era, the American physician John S. Billings accompanied a report on Faulds' work with the assertion that no two fingerprints were exactly alike, and this assumption was repeated continually [26].

1.3.1. Statistical Models

Galton made the earliest attempt to actually measure the variability of human fingerprint patterns. Galton estimated that the smallest possible square that could be dropped onto an inked, rolled fingerprint and yield a 1 in 2 chance that he could correctly guess the underlying ridge path was a square 6 ridges wide on each side. The average rolled print consisted of 24 of these 6-ridge squares, thus giving him a chance of $1/2^{24}$ of a correct composite guess. Galton then estimated that the chances of two fingerprints having the same general pattern type was 1 in 16. He then estimated the chance of correctly guessing the number of ridges entering and leaving each square as $1/2^8$. By this method, he generated an estimate that the chances of two exact duplicate fingerprints existing was

$$\frac{1}{2^{24}} \times \frac{1}{2^8} \times \frac{1}{2^4} = \frac{1}{2^{36}}$$

Given a world population of approximately 16 billion fingers, the odds of two duplicate fingerprints patterns existing were around 1 in 4. Galton's statistical model has been criticized by later statisticians, such as Stoney and Thornton, though mostly for *under*estimating the variability of fingerprint patterns [76]. On the other hand, Stigler contends that Galton's work "can be rigorously defended as correct and conservative" [57, 71]. After Galton, around ten different statistical models of fingerprint variability have been proposed. In a review of the first seven, Stoney and Thornton conclude that "None of the models are free from conceptual flaws" [76]. More recently, reviewing all ten, Stoney has praised the work of Champod [12] but still concludes that "from a statistical viewpoint, the scientific foundation for fingerprint individuality is incredibly weak" [75]. Interestingly, these statistical models have had little impact on the practice of forensic fingerprint identification, at least until recently [71]. To the extent that fingerprint examiners did cite statistical models, they tended to cite the first two: Galton's or Balthazard's [5]. The reason is that, historically, fingerprint identifications have not been understood as being probabilistic in nature. Instead, fingerprint examiners have followed an experiential model of vouching for their conclusions. The individuality of fingerprint patterns is vouched for by the profession's collective failure to find any two exact duplicate fingerprint patterns on two different fingers. The validity of a declared match, similarly, has rested upon the fingerprint examiner's experiential familiarity with fingerprint patterns. Very recently, there has been renewed attention within the fingerprint community to the question of whether the foundation of forensic fingerprint identification should be shifted onto some kind of statistical basis [13]. But this proposition has proven highly controversial [54, 84].

1.3.2. Fingerprint Matches

No matter what the statistical basis, or lack thereof, of the variability of underlying fingerprint patterns, the question remains of how two impressions of these supposedly unique patterns might be matched to one another. That is, how can we vouch for the conclusion that two impressions derive from the same source pattern?

Galton and the French anatomist René Forgeot were probably the first to try to articulate a matching process. Forgeot suggested that photographs of two impressions to be compared be enlarged and that the ridgelines be traced—that is, visually enhanced [28]. From this enhancement it would be easier to make a visual determination of whether the two impressions matched. Galton's suggestion was somewhat more systematic. He proposed that the analyst focus on locations where the ridgelines either ended abruptly or bifurcated (Fig. 1.5). Galton called these locations "minutiae," and they were later variously termed "Galton points," "Galton details," or "ridge characteristics." By ascertaining that minutiae were located in the same locations relative to one another, Galton argued, one could conclude that two impressions derived from the same source finger [31, 32].

Police officials applied Galton's method in a homicide case in India in 1897 [38, 87, 88] and a burglary case in England in 1902 [48, 58], and Bertillon matched a bloody fingerprint the same year [64]. Galton's method of matching latent and inked prints naturally begged the question of *how many* matching minutiae were necessary to warrant the conclusion that two prints were from the same source. On the one hand, it seemed obvious that there would be some (small) number of minutiae that might be shared by two impressions of different fingers. On the other hand, there

Fig. 1.5. "Furrow-heads" and "bifurcations of furrows" through which Galton proposed different impressions might be linked to a common source. (*Source*: Galton, F., Personal identification and description II. *Nature*, 38(974):201–202, 1888.)

must also be some (large) number of minutiae that probably could not be shared by two impressions of different fingers. But what were these numbers? Where could the line be drawn?

In the earliest cases, police officials answered these questions based on their personal experience. For example, at the Deptford murder trial in Britain, Scotland Yard's fingerprint expert, Charles Collins, testified that four matching points would be sufficient to warrant a conclusion of identification since he had seen prints showing three common points but none showing four. Since the latent print at trial showed 11 matching points with the print of the suspect, Collins believed he was safe in declaring a match [7, 45, 52, 89].

The French criminalist Edmond Locard made the earliest attempt to articulate a specific number of matching minutiae required to establish a conclusion of identification in 1914. Locard's "tripartite rule" stated that positive identifications could be made with more than 12 matching minutiae, that positive identification was possible in latent prints showing between 8 and 12 points depending on the quality of the print, and that latent prints showing fewer than 8 matching points could not provide positive identification—they could only provide what would today be called a "probabilistic identification" (an identification that is less than certain). Locard's standard of 12 became the standard in some jurisdictions, while others adopted other numbers. Still other jurisdictions hewed more to Locard's second rule, deciding that the precise number of points necessary to warrant a match should be a question of judgment by the examiner. Locard's third rule—the idea of probabilistic identification—was almost entirely discarded, as fingerprint examiners developed norms of practice that mandated that an identification be either "positive" or not made at all. Thus, probabilistic identifications would eventually be banned by governing bodies and professional fingerprint organizations [11]. Recently, some have argued that banning probabilistic identification is unscientific [13].

Fingerprint matching was an intuitive process by which an examiner with extensive experience in looking at fingerprint patterns made a judgment about whether two impressions showed sufficient similarity to warrant a conclusion that they derived from the same source. The training ground upon which this experience was acquired began with the laborious task of assigning Henry- or Vucetich-type classifications to thousands of 10-print cards. Through this process, classifiers acquired an intuitive visual grasp of fingerprint patterns and minutiae. It was this visual skill, a skill that laypersons clearly lacked, that fingerprint examiners used to make judgments about latent prints [33]. What was lacking, however, was any empirical basis for knowing either the underlying variability of fingerprint patterns or when an examiner was warranted in making a conclusion of identification. Fingerprint examiners claimed that conclusions were warranted by their collective experience, but even their collective experience had not sought to put the question of when to declare a match to the test.

1.4. Diffusion of Fingerprint Systems

A myth has arisen and long been perpetuated that the technical superiority of fingerprint systems of identification over anthropometric systems was readily apparent and that fingerprint identification immediately displaced anthropometry as soon as identification bureau chiefs became aware of it. In fact, many identification bureaus stubbornly resisted retiring the anthropometric systems and were deeply suspicious of fingerprinting. For at least two decades, these identification bureaus regarded fingerprint systems as cheap expedients for agencies and institutions that could not afford the expense of "more scientific" anthropometric systems [1, 62, 86]. A 1907 survey by the French Academy of Science found fingerprint systems in place in England, the British Indies, Egypt, Argentina, Brazil, Uruguay, and Chile (note the close relationship of these countries to either the British Empire or Argentina); anthopometric systems in France, Russia, Belgium, Switzerland, Romania, Spain, and Mexico; and hybrid systems in Germany, Austria, and Portugal [20]. Fingerprint identification found early niche applications in areas that anthropometric systems had left unoccupied. These included "civil" (as opposed to criminal) identification, such as the identification of military personnel [46, 53, 78], or the identification of petty offenders in police departments and courts [21]. Anthropometric identification was reserved for serious felons and took place in prisons.

After proving themselves in these less crucial settings, fingerprint systems gradually began to chip away at anthropometric systems' dominance. Whereas anthropometric systems demanded that skilled operators input data into the system (that is, meticulously record physical measurements according to a precise set of instructions), fingerprint data could be input by low-skilled operators, who merely needed to ink the fingerprints and roll them on the fingerprint card. Fingerprint systems shifted skilled operators to the "back end" of the process: the classification of the cards according to the Henry or Vucetich system. Fingerprint systems eventually proved themselves cheaper and faster than anthropometric systems, and the prejudicial view of them as "less scientific" than anthropometry gradually eroded [29, 69, 77]. By 1920, the tide had noticeably turned in favor of fingerprinting, although identification databases filed according to anthropometric measurements were still large enough to engender strenuous resistance to switching systems [23].

The fingerprint systems adopted around the world between 1890 and 1930 were all based on either the Henry or the Vucetich system or a hybridization of the two. Most identification bureau chiefs, however, modified the systems somewhat as they adopted them and renamed them after themselves. Thus, Italy had the Gasti system, Denmark the Jørgensen system, Norway the Daae system, Austria-Hungary the Windt–Kodiek system, Indochina the Pottecher system, Germany the Klatt and Roscher systems. As a result, the world's fingerprint identification systems differed slightly from country to country and jurisdiction to jurisdiction. The idea of a single identification systems crossing national and linguistic boundaries remained, like Esperanto, a frustrated ideal [10, 20, 23, 42].

1.5. Demand for Automation

The demand for automated fingerprint pattern recognition was largely a product of the success of manual classification systems. As fingerprint files grew ever larger, cards bulged the categories established by the Henry and Vucetich systems. At the U.S. Federal Bureau of Identification in Leavenworth, Kansas, for example, it was necessary to extend the Henry system, by creating further subdivisions, as early as 1919 [83]. Many other bureaus had to extend their existing manual classifications systems with further subclassifications.

Although extending classification systems kept files manageable for the purposes of verifying criminal histories (that is, 10-print to 10-print comparisons), the more fingerprint files expanded, the less useful they were for forensic identification. This was because fingerprint files were indexed according to the aggregate pattern types on all 10 fingers. For example, as we have seen, the primary Henry classification was based on the total number of whorls in the complete set of 10 fingers. Crime scenes, however, often yield single latent prints, and even these are often incomplete to the point that the pattern type may not be determinable. An investigator with a single unidentified latent would have little idea where to begin searching a Henry file because, even if it were possible to determine the basic pattern type of the latent, it would be impossible to determine what pattern types appear on the perpetrator's nine other fingers.

Of course, if one or more suspects were identified, a forensic investigator need not use the card file at all. He or she could simply compare the latent print to inked prints taken from the suspect(s). Alternatively, if investigators recovered a complete set of 10 latent fingerprints, they could relatively search them in their proper Henry classification. Similarly, if investigators recovered several latent prints, appearing to come from the same hand, they could make educated guesses about the patterns on the absent fingers and thus narrow the search process somewhat. Finally, if by placement of the latent it was possible to determine or guess what finger the latent derived from, the search could be narrowed somewhat. In general, however, "cold" searches of unidentified latent prints—that is, "blind" searches of the database in which no suspect had been identified—became increasingly prohibitive, in terms of labor costs, as fingerprint files grew in size [90].

1.5.1. Single-Print Classification

For this reason, the ease of searching unidentified latent prints in fingerprint files diminished rapidly. The proposed solution to this problem was a "single-print classi-fication system." Such a system would classify not the complete set of 10 fingerprint patterns, but each finger of each individual separately. Since, as we have seen, 10-print classification systems relied so heavily on the variability of the combinations of 10 pattern types, the technical challenges in devising a single-print system were obviously much more daunting.

The earliest single-print systems were published simultaneously in 1914, one by the Belgian criminalist Eugene Stockis [73], the other by Hakon Jørgensen, head of the Copenhagen Identification Bureau [44]. Additional single-print systems prolifer-ated widely during the 1920s and 1930s. By 1935, there were more than 20 different single-print systems [10]. There were two general schools of thought in developing single-print systems. The first involved creating finer categories of pattern type than those used in 10-print systems [6, 17, 18, 44]. Rather than calling a pattern a loop, therefore, the single- print system would categorize the pattern as one of many differ-ent types of loop. Often these subtypes were defined according to ridge counts, as in 10-print systems. In other cases, a measured distance between delta and core would be substituted for the ridge count. These systems utilized magnifying glasses, often etched with either a grid or concentric circles, and hence their critics dubbed them "counting and glass methods." The second school of thought pointed out that latent prints were often so small in area that not enough information was visible to clas-sify the pattern type. Moreover, measured distances could be thrown off by pressure distortion. This school endorsed a "morphological approach." These approaches clas-sified prints according to detailed analysis of core and delta charactertistics (Fig. 1.6). Advocates of this approach argued that it would be possible to search a latent print, based on the core and delta characteristics it showed, even if not enough area of the latent was visible to determine the specific detailed pattern type [43, 49].

Single-print systems based on either approach were cumbersome and laborious. They required that classifiers make such fine distinctions that they sacrificed the ben-efits of the simplicity of Galton's tripartite division of almost all patterns into arches, loops, and whorls. In this way, they reintroduced the same difficulty encountered ear-lier by Galton: the problem of maintaining consistency between individual classifiers

LOOPS

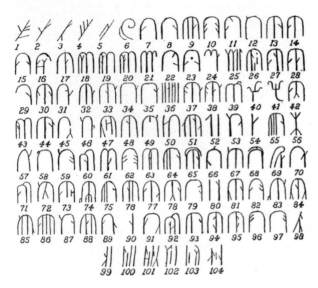

Fig. 1.6. Fine-grained classification of core types of loop patterns for J.A. Larson's single-print classification system. (*Source*: J.A. Larson, *Single Fingerprint System*. New York: D. Appleton, 1924.)

called upon to make extremely fine distinctions of pattern type. As such, they squandered the principal advantages of fingerprint systems in a maze of classification [50]. For this reason, single-print systems were seldom actually used [48, 56]. However, the enormous labor and energy put into developing single-print systems show how great was the demand for enhanced searching capability of 10-print files. It was this demand that automated fingerprint pattern recognition would ultimately fulfill.

1.6. Automation of Fingerprint Systems

The earliest applications of automation to fingerprint identification involved the use of IBM punch-card sorters. By assigning a punch card encoded with information such as the individual's gender, age, race, and Henry-type classification to each fingerprint card, operators could then do a card sort searching for certain parameters. The card sorter would produce a set of cards fitting the given parameters, and operators could then retrieve the matching fingerprint cards. This would somewhat streamline the manual searching process, but not much [10, 37, 72].

This, of couse, was mere data processing, not automated pattern recognition. The earliest experiments with optical recognition of fingerprint patterns appear to have been conducted around 1963 by John Fitzmaurice of Baird-Atomics [63] and Joseph Wegstein and Raymond Moore of the U.S. National Bureau of Standards [72]. During the late 1960s and early 1970s, General Electric [41], McDonnell Douglas, Sperry Rand, and the KMS Technology Center all conducted research on holographic imaging. Although holography was an attractive technology, these early forays suggested that a holographic identification system would be extremely expensive and also exceedingly sensitive to inevitable noise contained even in inked, not to mention latent, fingerprint impressions [63, 72].

In 1972, the U.S. Federal Bureau of Investigation (FBI) installed a prototype Automated Fingerprint Identification System (AFIS) using a fingerprint scanner built by Cornell Aeronautical Laboratory and fingerprint reader built by North American Aviation. The FBI began testing automatic searching in 1979, and automated searches became routine by 1983. During this period, smaller law enforcement agencies installed analog automated search-and-retrieval systems, which utilized microfilm or videotape. These analog systems did not actually search fingerprint images; they searched Henry-type classifications. If this search produced a close match, the system would retrieve the fingerprint image for the human examiner to compare [63, 72].

Around 1986, AFIS had become sophisticated and cheap enough to justify procurements by local law enforcment agencies in the United States. In the United States, there were three principal vendors: Printrak (United States), NEC (Japan), and Morpho Systems (France) [47, 72]. Great Britain installed an IBM system [2].

AFIS stored individual fingerprints as relational data between minutiae, much in the way that Galton had proposed. Early systems based the relational data on measured distances between minutiae; since measured distances were subject to pressure distortion, later systems used topological relationships between minutiae. Important work on topological coding was contributed by Sparrow [70]. Since AFIS did not use Henry- or Vucetich-type codes, the maturing of AFIS enabled identification bureaus to begin phasing out Henry- and Vucetich-type classification and manual searching. Inked fingerprint cards could be scanned into the computer systems, the image stored, and relational data extracted for automated searching. With the development of live-scan, or inkless, fingerprint scanning technology, 10-print data could be scanned directly into the system, without ever creating an inked card. For 10-print to 10-print searches, the known print could simply be input into the AFIS and the searching routine run. There was no need for a fingerprint examiner to code the known print's Henry- or Vucetich-type classification, and there was no need for the fingerprint examiner to then search for matching 10-print cards in the corresponding Henry or Vucetich classification. Latent prints also could be scanned into the system, relational data extracted, and these data searched against the relational data of all prints in the system. This enormously enhanced the identification bureau's ability to search a single or partial latent print against its databases. "Cold" searches, which once would have been performed at great cost in labor, were now routine. The AFIS would produce "candidate matches," and a human examiner would determine whether any of the candidates matched the latent print. Since AFIS are considered good at producing candidate matches but not good enough to make final determinations of a match, all final determinations are currently made by human examiners.

In short, AFIS has already had an enormous impact on fingerprint identification, by retiring manual Henry- and Vucetich-type classification systems and speeding up the 10-print search and identification process; by enormously enhancing the capability to search unidentified latent prints against a large database; and by increasing the potential for the internetworking of hitherto separate fingerprint databases. AFIS has justly been placed alongside DNA typing as "one of the two most important advances in forensic science in the 20th century" [80].

1.7. Considerations for the Future

Two parallel consequences of the development of automated fingerprint pattern recognition suggest that great changes may be in store in the near future. The development of automated systems has eliminated the necessity of manual classification of fingerprint patterns. Manual classification has long been the principal training ground for latent fingerprint examiners. Through years of experience classifying inked prints, examiners gained the visual acuity at looking at fingerprint patterns—understanding of ridge flow, orientation, distinguishing signal from noise, and so on—that is so necessary to perform latent fingerprint analysis [33, 85]. Since AFIS has eliminated the traditional training ground, the next generation of latent print examiners will require a new training routine. The FBI, for one, has responded to this gap by placing recent college graduates directly into a two-year training course focused directly on latent print identification. While FBI trainees are still taught to recognize basic pattern types, Henry-type classification is no longer a foundation of latent print training [55]. It is not known how crucial the years of manual classification experience have been in developing intuitive pattern recognition skills. Whether the current generation of trainees will match, exceed, or fail to reach the skill level of current senior examiners is unclear. At the same time, automated fingerprint pattern recognition is advancing rapidly. If human pattern recognition skills atrophy while automated pattern recognition improves, the longstanding assumption that final determinations should be delegated to human examiners rather than to automated systems may soon be questioned.

1.7.1. Questioning Human Fingerprint Pattern Recognition Skill

This question has been rendered all the more acute by recent pointed questioning of human pattern recognition skill, especially in the United States and Great Britain. North American fingerprint examiners opened the debate in the 1970s by complaining that the "point counting" methodology that followed the dictates of Galton and had persisted as the articulation of fingerprint matching methodology for most of the century misrepresented the pattern recognition process [3]. North American examiners lobbied instead for resting the conclusion of identification on the expert judgment of the examiner, rather than a set number of points. This begged the question of how that judgment was formed and invited some sort of articulation of the formation of opinions of identification by fingerprint examiners. Olsen offered perhaps the earliest attempt at articulating latent fingerprint identification as a psychological pattern recognition process: "*Latent print evaluation and comparison is primarily a visual information-processing system. It is visual discrimination based on geometrical data and pattern recognition and the application of cognitive analysis*" [59]. Ashbaugh later offered a more fleshed-out account of the pattern recognition process with reference to psychological processes of visual perception.

> The identification process is synonymous with sight. Even though friction ridge prints are physical evidence, the comparison of this evidence is a mental process. Physical data concerning friction ridge configuration is taken from the physical realm, and through the eyes, is relocated in the mental realm of the brain. . . .
>   A friction ridge comparison would therefore be comprised of an analysis of the latent print and the storage of this data in memory. Then a viewing of the exemplar print, which would also cause that data to travel to the brain. When the data of the exemplar print arrives in the brain, it causes an immediate comparison to the data from the latent print to take place. Even though the latent print was viewed a fraction of a second before the exemplar print, as soon as the eyes leave the latent print, the brain is depending on its memory for the comparison to take place. [4]

Both Olsen's and Ashbaugh's are *internal* attempts to articulate the human pattern recognition process. That is, Olsen and Ashbaugh are fingerprint examiners attempting to describe what they do by mapping their experience onto what they know of the psychological literature. Lacking to date have been actual attempts by psychologists to model or measure the human pattern recognition process. Psychologists have taken little interest in studying human fingerprint pattern recognition since the process was assumed to be simple, highly accurate, and therefore of little interest. Just recently, this situation has begun to change in reponse to renewed interest in forensic fingerprint identification spurred by litigation over its admissibility in the United States, a number of well-publicized erroneous identifications in Britain and the United States, unflattering comparisons with DNA typing [74], and the continuing battle between advocates of Galtonian "point standards" and proponents of "nonnumerical" identification standards. Criticisms began to appear in the literature that argued that the human fingerprint pattern recognition process had not had its accuracy measured [16, 67, 74]. What measuring had been done suggested that human fingerprint pattern recognition may not be as accurate as has widely been assumed [34]. Of course, this would not be difficult since the widespread assumption has long been that fingerprint identification is infallible.

Haber and Haber suggest that several different approaches to complex pattern matching might be applicable to human forensic fingerprint identification, including template matching, distinctive feature analysis, configurational perception, and higher-level heuristic analyses. They conclude, however, that "Little is known about the application of these approaches to human fingerprint examiners making fingerprint comparisons," and they regard Ashbaugh's efforts as only a beginning. Moreover, they conclude, the accuracy of the human fingerprint matching process, however it is to be characterized, has not been measured [35].

1.7.2. Man Versus Machine

If human fingerprint pattern recognition accuracy is lower than has been assumed, it is quite possible that automated fingerprint pattern recognition may surpass it in accuracy already, or may do so in the near future. If this is so, we might expect a reversal of the longstanding tradition of bestowing greater trust on humans than on machines. At this point, however, too little is known about the accuracy of rate of either human examiners or automated systems. Haber and Haber point out that AFIS vendors' accuracy claims are based on unpublished, proprietary data derived from benchmark tests that may not faithfully reflect actual casework, and are probably inflated. Based on the little published data available, they suggest that AFIS accuracy—both in terms of reporting the matching print as a candidate if it is in the database and in terms of ranking it highly among candidates—may actually be rather poor [35]. If the burgeoning interest of scientists and engineers in the process of fingerprint pattern matching by both man and machine is sustained, we may soon learn more about how these processes actually work and how accurate they are. Interestingly, the challenge from automated fingerprint pattern recognition systems may be the stimulus that finally forces the gathering of data about the accuracy of human fingerprint pattern recognition. What shape the future will take is still not yet clear, but there can be no question that the maturing of automated fingerprint pattern recognition has ushered in a new phase in the history of the identification of individuals by fingerprint patterns.

Acknowledgments

I am grateful for the generous support of the National Science Foundation (Award #0115305) during the writing of this chapter. During this period, I also had the honor and pleasure of being a scholar-in-residence at John Jay College of Criminal Justice, City University of New York. I am grateful to the faculty of the College and especially the members of the Department of Law, Police Science, and Criminal Justice Administration for their hospitality and the camaraderie during my time there. John Berry and Martin Leadbetter offered helpful comments on a draft of this chapter, while not necessarily endorsing it. The opinions expressed, and any errors, are mine.

References

1. The Bertillon System of Identification, *Scientific American*, 432–434, 1904.
2. Prints Fiasco Hinders Battle Against Crime, *Computing*, 8, 1996.
3. Ashbaugh, D.R., The premise of friction ridge identification, clarity, and the identification process, *J. Forensic Identification*, **44**(5):499–516, 1994.
4. Ashbaugh, D.R., *Quantitative-Qualitative Friction Ridge Analysis: An Introduction to Basic and Advanced Ridgeology*, Boca Raton, FL.: CRC Press, 1999.
5. Balthazard, V., De l'identification par les empreintes digitales, *Comptes Rendus des Academies des Sciences*, **152**:1862–1864, 1911.
6. Battley, H., *Single Finger Prints: A New and Practical Method of Classifying and Filing Single Finger Prints and Fragmentary Impressions*, London: His Majesty's Stationary Office, 1931.

7. Beavan, C., *Fingerprints: The Origins of Crime Detection and the Murder Case that Launched Forensic Science*, New York: Hyperion, 2001.
8. Berry, J., The history and development of fingerprinting, in *Advances in Fingerprint Technology*, H.C. Lee and R.E. Gaensslen, eds., New York: Elsevier, 1991, pp. 1–38.
9. Bertillon, A., Instructions for taking descriptions for the identification of criminals and others by the means of anthropometric indications, Chicago: American Bertillon Prison Bureau, 1889.
10. Bridges, B.C., *Practical Fingerprinting*, New York: Funk and Wagnalls, 1942.
11. Champod, C., Edmond Locard—numerical standards and "probable" identifications, *J. Forensic Identification*, **45**:136–163, 1995.
12. Champod, C., Reconaissance automatique et analyse statistique des minuties sur les empreintes digitales, Ph.D. diss., University of Lausanne: Switzerland, 1995.
13. Champod, C. and I.W. Evett, A probablistic approach to fingerprint evidence, *J. Forensic Identification*, **51**(2):101–122, 2001.
14. Chapman, C.L., Dr. Juan Vucetich: His contribution to the science of fingerprints, *J. Forensic Identification*, **42**:286–294, 1992.
15. Chatterjee, S.K. and R.V. Hague, *Finger Print or Dactyloscopy and Ridgeoscopy*, Calcutta: Srijib Chatterjee, 1988.
16. Cole, S.A., *Suspect Identities: A History of Fingerprinting and Criminal Identification*, Cambridge, MA: Harvard University Press, 2001.
17. Collins, C.S., A telegraphic code for finger-print formulae and a system for sub-classification of single digital impressions, London: Office of the Police Chronicle, 1921.
18. Crosskey, W.C.S., *The Single Finger Print Identification System: A Practical Work upon the Science of Finger Printing*, San Francisco: Crosskey Single Finger Print System, 1923.
19. Cummins, H. and C. Midlo, *Finger Prints, Palms and Soles: An Introduction to Dermatoglyphics*, Philadelphia: Blakiston, 1943.
20. Dastre, A., Des empreintes digitales comme procédé d'identification, *Comptes Rendus des Séances de l'Academie des Sciences*, **145**:28–47, 1907.
21. Deuel, J.M., *Finger-Prints*, New York: M. B. Brown, 1917.
22. Dillon, D.J., Finger print as evidence first proposed by Thomas Taylor—1877, in *Identification News*, 1972, pp. 11–12.
23. Dilworth, D.C., ed. *Identification Wanted: Development of the American Criminal Identification System, 1893–1943*, Gaithersburg, MD: International Association of Chiefs of Police, 1977.
24. Faulds, H., On the skin furrows of the hand, *Nature*, **22**(574):605, 1880.
25. Faulds, H., *Dactylography, or, The Study of Finger-Prints*, Halifax: Milner, 1912.
26. Faulds, H., The dawn of dactylography, in *Dactylography*, 1921. p. 29.
27. Federal Bureau of Investigation, *The Science of Fingerprints: Classification and Uses*, Washington, DC: United States Government Printing Office, 1985.
28. Forgeot, R., *Des Empreintes Digitales Étudiées au Point de Vue Medico-Judiciaire*, Lyon, 1892.
29. Fosdick, R.B., The passing of the Bertillon system of identification, *J. American Institute of Criminal Law and Criminology*, **6**:363–369, 1915.
30. Foucault, M., *Discipline and Punish: The Birth of the Prison*, New York: Vintage, 1979.
31. Galton, F., Personal identification and description II, *Nature*, **38**(974):201–202, 1888.
32. Galton, F., *Finger Prints*, London: Macmillan, 1892.
33. Grieve, D.L., The identification process: Traditions in training, *J. Forensic Identification*, **40**:195–213, 1990.
34. Grieve, D.L., Possession of truth, *J. Forensic Identification*, **46**(5):521–528, 1996.

35. Haber, L. and R.N. Haber, The accuracy of fingerprint evidence, this volume.
36. Hammer, H.-J., On the contribution made by German scientists to the development of dactyloscopy, in *Fingerprint Whorld*, 1986, pp. 13–15.
37. Harling, M., *Origins of the New York State Bureau of Identification*, Albany: New York State Division of Criminal Justice Services, 1996.
38. Henry, E.R., *Classification and Uses of Finger Prints*, 1st ed., London: H. M. Stationary Office, 1900.
39. Herschel, W.J., *Skin furrows of the hand*, Nature, **23**(578):76, 1880.
40. Herschel, W.J., *The Origin of Finger-Printing*, London: Oxford University Press, 1916.
41. Horvath, V.V., J.M. Holeman, and C.Q. Lemmond, Holographic technique recognizes fingerprints, *Laser Focus Magazine*, 1967.
42. Institute of Applied Science, *Directory of Identification Bureaus of the World*, 12th ed., Chicago, 1945.
43. Jaycox, T.H., *Classification of Single Fingerprints*, Wichita, KS: Wichita Police Department, 1931.
44. Jörgensen, H., *Distant Identification*. Copenhagen: Arnold Busck, 1922.
45. Joseph, A., Anthropometry, the police expert, and the Deptford murders: The contested introduction of fingerprinting for the identification of criminals in late Victorian and Edwardian Britain, in *Documenting Individual Identity: The Development of State Practices since the French Revolution*, J. Torpey and J. Caplan, eds., Princeton: Princeton University Press, 2001.
46. Kean, J.R., The system of personal identification by finger prints recently adopted for the U.S. Army, *J. American Medical Association*, **47**:1175–1177, 1906.
47. Klug, D.J., J.L. Peterson, and D.A. Stoney, *Automated Fingerprint Identification Systems: Their Acquisition, Management, Performance, and Organizational Impact*, Washington: National Institute of Justice, 1992.
48. Lambourne, G., *The Fingerprint Story*, London: Harrap, 1984.
49. Larson, J.A., *Single Fingerprint System*, New York: D. Appleton, 1924.
50. Larson, J.A., Review of Battley, "Single fingerprints", *American J. Police Science*, 361–365, 1931.
51. Laufer, B., *History of the Finger-Print System*, Washington: Government Printing Office, 1912.
52. Leadbetter, M., Rex v. Stratton and Stratton, *Fingerprint Whorld*, **2**(7):32–38, 1977.
53. McClaughry, M.W., Finger prints, *J. U.S. Cavalry Assoc.*, **17**:512, 1907.
54. McKasson, S., I think therefore I probably am., *J. Forensic Identification*, **51**(3):217–221, 2001.
55. Meagher, S. and E. German, Basic fingerprint technology, presented at the annual meeting of the *American Academy of Forensic Science*, Atlanta, GA, 2002.
56. National Police Conference. *Proceedings, National Police Conference*, New York, 1922.
57. National Research Council Commission on DNA Forensic Science, *The Evaluation of Forensic DNA Evidence*, Washington: National Academy Press, 1996.
58. Olsen, R.D., Sr., First instance of fingerprint evidence presented to a jury in a criminal court in Great Britain, in *Fingerprint Whorld*, 53–55, 1988.
59. Olsen, R.D., Sr., Identification of latent prints, in *Advances in Fingerprint Technology*, H.C. Lee and R.E. Gaensslen, eds., New York: Elsevier, 1991, pp. 39–58.
60. Pasquino, P., Criminology: The birth of a special knowledge, in *The Foucault Effect: Studies in Governmentality*, G. Burchell, C. Gordon, and P. Miller, eds., London: Havester Wheatsheaf, 1991, pp. 235–250.
61. Purkynê, J.E., *A Physiological Examination of the Organ of Vision and the Integumentary System*, University of Breslau, 1823.

62. Ramakers, L., A new method of identifying criminals, *Scientific American*, 264, 1905.
63. Reed, B., Automated fingerprint identification: From Will West to Minnesota Nine-Fingers and beyond, *J. Police Science and Administration*, **9**(3):317–326, 1981.
64. Rhodes, H.T.F., *Alphonse Bertillon: Father of Scientific Detection*, New York: Abelard-Schuman, 1968.
65. Rodriguez, J.E., Encoding the criminal: Criminology and the science of "Social Defense" in modernizing Argentina (1881–1920), Ph.D. diss., New York: Columbia University, 2000.
66. Rogers, S.L., *The Personal Identification of Living Individuals*, Springfield, IL: Charles C. Thomas, 1986.
67. Saks, M., Merlin and Solomon: Lessons from the law's formative encounters with forensic identification science, *Hastings Law Journal*, **49**:1069–1141, 1998.
68. Sengoopta, C., *Imprint of the Raj: The Emergence of Fingerprinting in India and Its Voyage to Britain*, London: Macmillan, 2002.
69. Shepstone, H.J., The finger-print system of identification, *Scientific American*, 256–257, 1910.
70. Sparrow, M.K., Topological coding of single fingerprints, Ph.D. diss., University of Kent at Canterbury, 1985.
71. Stigler, S.M., Galton and identification by fingerprints, *Genetics*, **140**:857–860, 1995.
72. Stock, R.M., An historical overview of automated fingerprint identification systems, in *International Forensic Symposium on Latent Prints*, Washington: Government Printing Office, 1987.
73. Stockis, E., One finger classification and the search for criminals by the identification of their finger prints, *Archives Internationales de Médecine Légale*, 164–185, 1914.
74. Stoney, D.A., Fingerprint identification: Scientific status, in *Modern Scientific Evidence: The Law and Science of Expert Testimony*, Vol. 2, D.L. Faigman et al., eds., St. Paul: West, 1997, pp. 55–78.
75. Stoney, D.A., Measurement of fingerprint individuality, in *Advances in Fingerprint Technology*, 2nd ed., H. C. Lee and R. E. Gaensslen, eds., Boca Raton, FL: CRC Press, 2001, 327–387.
76. Stoney, D.A. and J.I. Thornton, A critical analysis of quantitative fingerprint individuality models, *J. Forensic Sciences*, **31**(4):1187–1216, 1986.
77. Talbot, C.K., The influence of the popular press on criminal justice policy (The competition between the French Bertillonage system and the British fingerprinting system in New York State, 1890-1914), *International J. Comparative and Applied Criminal Justice*, **7**(2):201–208, 1983.
78. Taylor, J.H., The Navy's identification system, *The Fleet Review*, **4**(1):5–12, 1913.
79. Taylor, T., Hand marks under the microscope, *American J. Microscopy and Popular Science*, **2**, 1877.
80. Thornton, J.I. and J.L. Peterson, The general assumptions and rationale of forensic identification, in *Science in the Law: Forensic Science Issues*, D.L. Faigman, et al., eds., St. Paul: West, 2002, pp. 1–45.
81. Torpey, J. and J. Caplan, eds. *Documenting Individual Identity: The Development of State Practices since the French Revolution*, Princeton: Princeton University Press, 2001.
82. Troup, C.E., A. Griffiths, and M.L. Macnaghten, Report of a committee appointed by the Secretary of State to inquire in the best means available for identifying habitual criminals, in *British Sessional Papers. House of Commons*, London: Eyre and Spottiswoode, 1894.
83. United States Criminal Identification Bureau, *Annual Report*, Leavenworth, KS: U.S. Penitentiary Press, 1919.

84. Vanderkolk, J.R., Class characteristics and "could be" results, *J. Forensic Identification*, **43**(2):119–125, 1993.
85. Wertheim, P.A., The ability equation, *J. Forensic Identification*, **46**(2): 149–159, 1996.
86. Wilder, H.H., Palms and soles, *American J. Anatomy*, **1**:423–441, 1902.
87. Wilton, G.W., Finger-prints: The case of Kangali Charan, 1898, *Juridical Review*, **49**:417–427, 1937.
88. Wilton, G.W., *Fingerprints: History, Law and Romance*, London: William Hodge, 1938.
89. Wilton, G.W., *Fingerprints: Fifty Years of Injustice*, Galashiels: A. Walker and Son, 1955.
90. Works Progress Administration, *Installation of a Single Fingerprint File*, Washington, DC: Division of Women's and Professional Projects, 1937.
91. Xiang-Xin, Z. and L. Chun-Ge, The historical application of hand prints in Chinese litigation, *Fingerprint Whorld*, **14**(55):84–88, 1989.

Chapter 2

Advances in Fingerprint Sensors Using RF Imaging Techniques

Dale R. Setlak

Abstract. This chapter describes recent developments in fingerprint sensor technology aimed specifically at attaining the low cost, high reliability, and high usability needed for fingerprint identification to become a ubiquitous part of our everyday information and communication devices. The topic is introduced with a brief review of the many techniques available for acquiring fingerprint images and then reviews the history of direct electronic fingerprint sensing. Specifically we focus on semiconductor-based integrated fingerprint sensors using RF array imaging techniques.

2.1. Introduction

At the beginning of the 21st century it has become increasingly clear that our information and communication systems infrastructure would be unable to achieve its full potential until methods of reliably verifying the identity of the individuals using that infrastructure can be developed. Biometrics in general, and fingerprint identification in particular, appears capable of filling this gap in the infrastructure. For several decades, fingerprint image acquisition has been a research challenge and continues to be so. The inked method of acquisition has been mostly used by law enforcement agencies. The inkless method of acquisition is more interesting as it opens new avenues for use of fingerprints in automated systems. If this technology is to become an integral part of our everyday lives, though, it will have to mature. To reach this objective, fingerprint sensors will have to be

Inexpensive enough to integrate into user information and communication devices while allowing these devices to remain within cost constraints

Small enough to fit into these devices

Able to operate reliably on essentially everyone's fingers

Able to operate reliably across a wide range of skin conditions such as dry, sweaty, hot, cold, healthy, and ill

Able to operate reliably in a wide range of environments such as office, home, car, and outdoors

Able to work with fingers that are dirty or contaminated with foreign material

Viewed in this light, the design of a good fingerprint sensor becomes quite challenging. This chapter describes fingerprint sensor technology aimed specifically at meeting these requirements. We introduce the topic with a taxonomy of the many fingerprint acquisition methods available and a brief discussion of the key aspects of each in Section 2.2. We then review the history of direct electrical fingerprint sensing technologies, and some of the strengths and weaknesses of these approaches in Section 2.3. We discuss the structure of the finger skin and its electrical properties in Section 2.4 and then introduce the physics behind capacitive sensors and the recently developed radiofrequency (RF) sensors in Section 2.5. Finally, we investigate the ways that the RF sensors take advantage of the electrical properties of the finger skin to reliably capture high-quality fingerprint images in Section 2.6. We conclude the chapter with observations about the future of fingerprint sensing. The RF fingerprint imaging technology described in this chapter has been commercially realized [1]. Most of the data, observations, and concepts presented in this chapter originated from research performed in that process.

2.2. A Taxonomy of Fingerprint Sensing Methods

There are many different ways of imaging the ridge-and-valley pattern of finger skin, each with its own strengths, weaknesses, and idiosyncrasies. A brief listing would include the following:.

Mechanical
    Ink deposition
    Pressure sensing
    Vibration damping
Optical
    Direct illumination imaging
    Frustrated Total Internal Reflection
    (FTIR)
    Dispersion image

Electrical
    Conductive
    Capacitive
    RF imaging
Ultrasonic
    Reflection
Thermal
    Heat flux

2.2.1. Mechanical Methods

The earliest known methods of capturing fingerprints were impressions in clay and later in wax. In the late 19th century and throughout the 20th century, fingerprint images were captured by coating the finger with ink and pressing the inked fingers on paper or cards. Today inked cards remain popular as an inexpensive image capture mechanism. The fingerprint images may be transferred into a computer by scanning the cards with a high-resolution page scanner and processing the page images to extract the individual fingerprint patterns. The majority of the fingerprints in government law enforcement databases have been captured in this fashion. Ink-based systems are considered too slow, cumbersome, and messy for widespread use in electronic systems.

Mechanical methods can be used to convert the finger ridge and valley patterns directly into electronic signals. Arrays of tiny pressure-sensing pixels with micro strain-gage transducers can detect the pressure applied by the fingerprint ridges. Devices of this type have been fabricated in the laboratory using MEMS technologies [2]. An elaboration of this approach incorporates micropneumatic channels between the transducers and the finger. In another proposed variant, the pixels each contain tiny vibrating structures. Pressure from the finger damps the vibrations of pixels in contact with ridges, changing those pixels' signal output.

2.2.2. Optical Methods

The earliest method of converting fingerprint patterns directly into electronic signals used optical means. A picture of the finger was taken using an electronic camera. Difficulties arose immediately because finger ridges and valleys are generally the same color and must be differentiated by shadows cast under oblique illumination. FTIR optical scanners were a major improvement over simple cameras. In Frustrated Total Internal Reflection (FTIR) devices, light is focused on a glass-to-air interface at an angle exceeding the critical angle for total reflection. When the skin on a fingerprint ridge contacts the glass-to-air interface, reflection of the light at that spot is disrupted. The reflected light beam is focused on an electro-optical array, where the areas of skin contact will now appear dark. The principle is used today in many commercially available optical fingerprint scanners. In another method sometimes called dispersion imaging, optical energy is introduced into the finger skin (usually from the side) so that it diffuses throughout the finger. The finger is placed in contact with an electro-optical imaging array. More light is transmitted to the array in areas where a ridge contacts the array surface; less light is transmitted through the air spaces in the valleys, generating a light-intensity difference on the electro-optic array [3].

2.2.3. Electrical Methods

Electrical fingerprint sensing methods use electrical energy to detect the fingerprint pattern. Three mechanisms have been used: conductivity measurements, capacitance measurements, and RF (radiofrequency) field measurements. RF-based sensors can be configured to generate images of the internal layers of the skin. A major portion of this chapter focuses on electrical methods of fingerprint sensing, so discussion here will be deferred.

2.2.4. Ultrasonic Methods

Ultrasonic fingerprint sensing methods use ultrasonic energy to detect the fingerprint pattern. Ultrasonic systems can be based on differences in ultrasonic absorption between the ridges and valleys or on echo reflection techniques. Ultrasonic systems based on echo reflection can be configured to generate images of the internal layers of skin. Ultrasonic sensors built with currently available technologies are large devices with motor-driven mechanical scanning. Ultrasonic fingerprint sensors are commercially available [4].

2.2.5. Thermal Methods

Thermal energy flux can be used to detect the ridge and valley pattern. Since the temperature of the ridges and valleys is essentially the same, direct temperature measurements are typically not employed. However, when a ridge is in thermal contact with a sensor surface of a different temperature, heat will flow between the ridge and the sensor surface. This heat flux can be measured by an array of tiny differential temperature transducers and converted into an electrical signal. In these sensors the heat flux is maximized when the ridge first contacts the sensor surface. The heat flux decays rapidly as the region of contact approaches thermal equilibrium. The transient nature of the heat flux means that the finger must be in constant motion with respect to the sensor for good signal generation. Therefore, thermal flux sensors are usually constructed as narrow strips that the user slides his or her finger across [5].

2.3. Intrinsic Advantages of Electric Sensing

Systems that use electrical mechanisms to sense the fingerprint patterns have several intrinsic advantages over those that use other mechanisms. As most current applications are in electronic systems, compatibility with these systems is a key issue. When used in electronic systems, sensors based on electrical phenomenon generally have simpler structures than other systems because there is no need to convert a nonelectrical form of energy into an electrical form. In electrical sensing systems, the transducer is usually a simple conductive spot. Mechanical, optical, thermal, and ultrasonic sensing methods require specialized transducers that convert these various forms of energy into electrical signals. Electrical sensing systems are also the most easily incorporated into the silicon integrated circuits that are required to process the transducer signals, yielding a small, low-cost integrated device that is readily mass-produced using existing microelectronics technologies.

These advantages have led to the development of a wide variety of fingerprint sensor concepts and designs, driven by a growing understanding of the challenges involved in reliable fingerprint sensing.

2.4. History of Electrical Fingerprint Sensing

2.4.1. The Early Concepts

The benefits of electric fingerprint sensing were evident by the middle of the 20th century. In the late 1960s, several inventors proposed methods of capturing information about fingerprint patterns using conductive sensing elements arranged in a two-dimensional array. Killen describes such a device in a 1973 patent [6]. Figure 2.1 is a drawing from that patent, illustrating an array of conductance sensing spots.

Rapid advances in the early 1980s led to the development of several new sensing concepts. Figure 2.2 shows several drawings from a 1982 patent by Tsikos that illustrate the basics of electrical capacitive sensing [7]. The drawings show the concept of

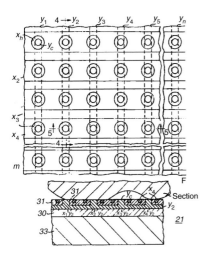

Fig. 2.1. Drawing from a 1973 patent [6].

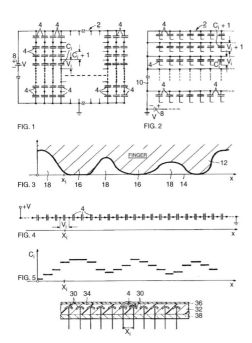

Fig. 2.2. Drawings from a 1982 patent [7].

a capacitive pixel whose capacitance to a local ground reference depends on whether the plate is near a ridge or a valley of the fingerprint being imaged. The last illustration in this group illustrates the fringing fields (shown as flux lines) between two sensors that define the active sensing region of these pixels. The patent shows a variety of ways to wire the capacitive sensing plates so that instrumentation external to the array can read the capacitance values.

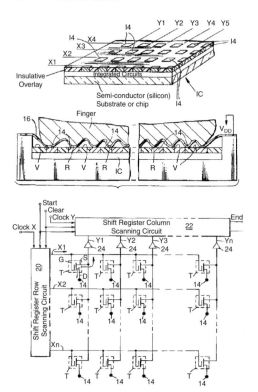

Fig. 2.3. Drawings from a 1986 patent [8].

The concepts described to this point propose methods of detecting electrical variations that do not rely on implementation in an active integrated circuit. Without the tremendous benefits of active electronics under pixel (available today in integrated circuit sensors) signal amplification, routing, and scanning were real problems for these devices. Low signal levels and difficulty in amplifying these signals also caused signal-to-noise ratio issues that reduced sensor performance. Figure 2.3 shows several drawings from a 1986 patent by Abramov [8]. These drawings show a sensing array built as an integral part of a monolithic semiconductor integrated circuit. The device illustrated measures local conductivity at each pixel using an active array of under pixel electronics. Electronic switches under each pixel allowed the signals to be multiplexed onto column buses for readout. This device also illustrates the use of a flexible membrane conforming to the ridges and valleys of the finger, an approach common to many early sensors. Constructing such a membrane to be simultaneously flexible enough to follow the ridges and valleys and rigid enough to be robust in use has proven to be a difficult challenge indeed.

2.4.2. Fingerprints from Memory Chips

An interesting sidelight to these early fingerprint sensor concepts is the connection to memory chips. In the late 1980s researchers working on memory devices discovered (undoubtedly by accident, as the touching of a semiconductor chip usually contaminates it beyond recovery) that a finger placed on top of the memory array caused data errors that followed the spatial pattern of the fingerprint. Recall that dynamic random access memories (DRAM) use a periodically refreshed charge stored on a small capacitor in the memory cell; clearly, the differences in capacitance between a ridge or valley and the individual memory cell caused bit flips in some cells. These were, in a sense, the forerunners of the capacitive fingerprint sensors introduced commercially 10 years later.

2.5. Commercial Capacitive Sensor Implementations

In the mid and late 1990s, the first commercial fingerprint sensors based on integrated capacitive sensors became available. All capacitive sensors are constructed using a two-dimensional array of small conductive plates covered by a thin dielectric protective layer. The finger is placed above the array such that the ridges and valleys affect the electrical capacitance of these plates. Two classes of capacitive fingerprint sensors have evolved: the single-plate capacitive sensors and the double-plate (or differential) capacitive sensors. We will discuss each of these implementations. In single-plate sensors, each sensor plate corresponds to a single pixel of the final image. The capacitance of each of the sensor plates to its global environment (predominantly ground) is measured. The sensor plates beneath the ridges of the fingerprint have a larger capacitance than those beneath valleys because the skin composing the ridge generally has a higher electrical permittivity than the air in the valleys.

An example of this class of sensor is illustrated in Figure 2.4, taken from a 2000 patent by Dickinson et al. [9]. Typically, the very small sensor capacitance is measured by depositing a fixed charge onto each sensor plate and then measuring the voltage developed by that charge. Each pixel is charged and measured separately and in sequence to generate a complete image.

In double-plate sensors, two adjacent conductive plates correspond to one pixel. The capacitance between these two plates is measured to generate the pixel value. An example of this class of sensor is illustrated in Figure 2.5 taken from a 2001 patent

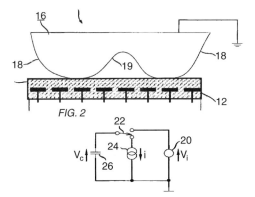

FIG. 2

Fig. 2.4. Single-plate capacitive sensor.

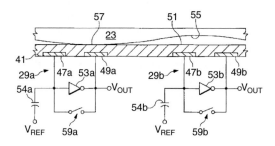

Fig. 2.5. Double-plate capacitive sensor.

by Kramer and Brady [10]. A variation of this technique measures the differential capacitance between each two adjacent plates in an array such that the image pixels correspond to the boundaries between the conductive plates in the physical array.

2.6. Capacitive Fingerprint Sensor Performance

The approaches described above demonstrate the basic feasibility of electronic fingerprint sensing, and several products based on these designs have been introduced into the commercial market. These products gave the industry its first commercial field experience with semiconductor fingerprint sensors and pointed the way toward future developments based on actual biometric performance data. While capacitive sensors work well with young, healthy, clean fingers—preferably in clean office environments—the devices proved difficult to use outside these ideal conditions. Outside this envelope, people whose skin is dry, sweaty, callused, or damaged, and people who are elderly, under stress, or on various kinds of medication often found capacitive fingerprint sensing devices unreliable and difficult to use. It was soon realized that these devices were unlikely to achieve the high reliability and usability needed to become an integral part of our information and communication infrastructure.

All the above fingerprint sensing approaches attempt to capture the ridge and valley pattern of the print as it is expressed at the exposed surface of the skin. Under anything less than ideal conditions, however, this exposed surface is subjected to wear, damage, and contamination, all of which inevitably tend to distort, damage, or obfuscate the pattern. From the signal analysis viewpoint, the image on the surface of the skin has a poor mechanical signal-to-noise ratio. It was soon realized that a better way to capture fingerprint patterns is to measure the pattern at a tissue boundary of sufficient depth beneath the surface of the skin that surface damage is not evident. The result would be a fundamentally better signal-to-noise ratio right at the source of the pattern.

The challenge then was to find a structure beneath the surface of the skin that has the shape of the fingerprint pattern, is deep enough in the skin that it is unlikely to be damaged, and can be detected remotely by some form of electrical sensing system. This is the challenge that drove the development of the RF antenna array imaging system that is discussed in detail in the rest of this chapter.

2.7. RF Imaging

The impetus for the use of RF imaging for fingerprint sensing comes from the desire to measure a higher-quality representation of the ridge pattern from beneath the surface of the skin.

2.7.1. The Basic Physics: Physiology of Finger Skin

Figure 2.6 is a microscopic image of a stained cross section of human skin. The surface layer of the skin (referred to medically as the stratum cornium) is composed of dry, dead cells. This region has a relatively low conductivity compared to that of the live layers of cells underneath. The live layer of cells constantly replenishes the dead layer of cells as they wear away. The structure of the live layer is the source of the ridge and valley pattern that is evident at the finger surface. This highly conductive layer of live cells is protected from most day-to-day damage, as it is well below the skin surface, and the boundary between it and the dead skin layer appears to be a much better source for the basic ridge and valley pattern. It is the structure of the boundary between the live cell layer and the dead cell layer that RF fingerprint imaging seeks to capture to generate a high signal-to-noise ratio image of the fingerprint pattern.

2.7.2. An Electrical Model of the Finger Skin

In Figure 2.7 we show a simplified structural model of the human skin that contains the elements essential to modeling the electrical behavior of the skin for purposes of RF fingerprint imaging. Note that the skin in Fig. 2.7 is upside down with respect to the photograph in Fig. 2.6. The orientation of Fig. 2.7 is typical of a fingerprint-sensing situation and will be used in subsequent diagrams. Starting from the external

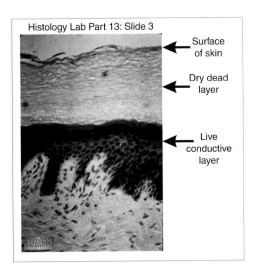

Histology Lab Part 13: Slide 3

← Surface of skin

← Dry dead layer

← Live conductive layer

Fig. 2.6. Image of a strained cross section of human skin. (Image from the Lumen database, Loyola University, Chicago, 1996.)

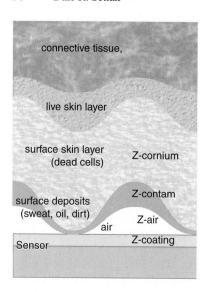

Fig. 2.7. Simplified model of the human skin's structure.

surface adjacent to the sensor, air gaps usually exist in the valleys. The surface of the skin may be coated with various types of surface deposits including water, salt, oil, dirt, grease, chalk, etc. In contaminated fingers, the valleys may be completely filled with deposits, eliminating the air gap entirely. This is typically seen when people with dirty hands simply wipe their finger before presenting it to the sensor, as is very common in commercial fingerprint sensor use. Surface deposits can range from highly conductive to highly insulating.

The dead skin layer, discussed in detail ahead, can have a wide range of electrical properties depending primarily on the moisture and salt concentrations in the layer. In contrast, the live skin layer appears highly conductive and is believed to be the limit of penetration into the finger of the RF signals during fingerprint imaging.

2.7.3. Characteristic Impedances of Finger Skin

Estimates of the bulk characteristic impedance of the low-conductivity layer of the skin (represented in Fig. 2.7 as Z-cornium) can be obtained from laboratory measurements and from computer models. This impedance spans a huge range when viewed across the entire population (see Grimnes and Martinsen [11].) For the average uncontaminated finger without sweat accumulation or high moisture content, we have found the impedance to be dominated by the capacitive component. The relative permittivities range between about 1 and 200, for excitation frequencies in the range of 100 kHz to 2 MHz. Very low relative permittivities appear in very dry skin, especially skin exposed to chemical solvents that damage the skin's ability to hold both moisture and oils. In these cases very dry skin may have very little conductivity and a permittivity that is close to that of air. Moisture and saline can be captured within the dead skin material, in which case it affects the permittivity of the skin and contributes to displacement currents and dielectric losses. Significantly higher permittivities appear

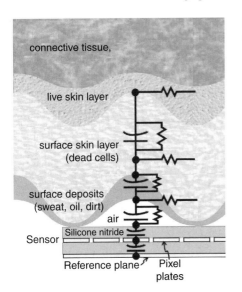

Fig. 2.8. A lumped-parameter representation of the complex skin impedances.

in demographic classes such as athletes and in children, whose skin may hold more trapped electrolytes. Oil in the skin can also affect the permittivity of the skin. In our computer models used to design RF imaging sensors, we usually assumed the relative permittivity of the normal skin layer to be about 20. In finger skin characterized as moist or sweaty, the conductive component of the complex impedance becomes more significant. In many of these cases, both the real and imaginary components of the skin impedance contribute to the signal seen at the sensors. In some of these cases, the conductivity appears to occur primarily along the surface of the finger. Sweaty fingers may have conductivities that are several orders of magnitude greater than a nominal finger, due to the very high conductivity of highly saline perspiration, and permittivities that are significantly higher as well.

Figure 2.8 illustrates a lumped-parameter representation of the complex skin impedances. This representation is useful in later discussions of RF phase-sensitive behaviors.

2.7.4. Physical Dimensions of the Layers of Finger Skin

We do not have direct measurements of the thickness of the low-conductivity surface layer of the finger skin. Our observations suggest that it varies from person to person and that the thickness might range from values as small as 0.002 in. for children up to values in excess of 0.050 in. for heavily callused adult fingers.

2.7.5. The Basic Structure of RF Sensor Arrays

This section develops a simplified view of the approach used in RF array sensors to generate images of the live skin layer's ridge and valley pattern. Subsequent sections refine the basic concepts and discuss the implications of this imaging method.

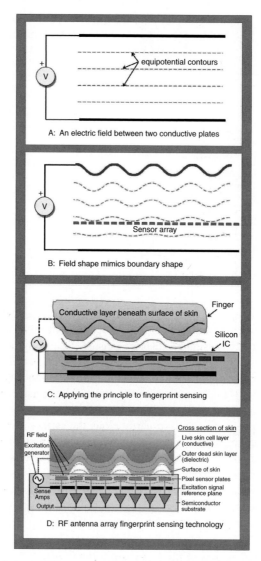

A: An electric field between two conductive plates

B: Field shape mimics boundary shape

C: Applying the principle to fingerprint sensing

D: RF antenna array fingerprint sensing technology

Fig. 2.9. Simplified view of RF array sensors used to generate images of the live skin's ridge and valley pattern.

To illustrate the basic concept, start with a simple DC electric field experiment. Take two flat parallel conductive plates (shown in edge view in Fig. 2.9a) and connect an electrical potential between the two plates. An electric field will be created between the plates, as illustrated by the equipotential contours shown in Fig. 2.9a. Now corrugate one of the plates as shown in Fig. 2.9b. We know from basic field theory that the equipotential contours in the field between the plates will mimic the shape of the corrugated boundary, as illustrated in Fig. 2.9b. If an array of tiny electric field sensors could be placed between the plates as shown in Fig. 2.9b, the relative voltages on those sensors could be interpreted spatially as mimicking the shape of the corrugated plate. Sensors in areas where the top plate is closer would have higher voltages than those in areas where the top plate is more distant. The sensor plates need to be small with respect to the average feature size of the corrugated plates in order to provide sampling of at least the Nyquist interval. Now take this basic concept and apply it to fingerprint sensing. Let one of the previously discussed conductive plates be the second metal layer below the surface of a silicon IC. The top layer of IC metallization will become the field sensing plates, as shown in Fig. 2.9c. The corrugated conductive plate is replaced by the live conductive layer of skin beneath the surface of the finger. Instead of a DC voltage we will use an RF signal to energize the conductive boundaries. The RF excitation frequency is chosen low enough that the wavelength is much longer than the distances involved in the sensor geometry. As a result, the field structure can be treated as a quasi-static AC electric field with no significant magnetic-field component and hence no appreciable electromagnetic radiation. The frequency is also chosen high enough that the signal driving the conductive layer of skin can be capacitively coupled into that layer from a reasonably sized electrode, external to the sensor array area. The resulting system, illustrated in Fig. 2.9c, operates such that the relative amplitude of the RF signal on each sensor plate in the array is an indication of the relative distance from that plate to the conductive layer of skin directly above the sensor plate.

As the sensor plates are extremely high impedance nodes, the final step in building our conceptual RF fingerprint sensor is to connect the pixel sensor plates to ultrahigh input impedance sense amplifiers. The sense amps are located deeper in the silicon IC beneath the active electric field sensing area, as indicated in Fig. 2.9d. The sensor plates can be viewed as having characteristic impedances in the range of a few femtofarads. This means that the interconnects between the plate and the sense amplifier have to be as short as possible; in practice, the sense amplifiers have to be located directly below the sensor plate in order to avoid signal contamination. The sense amplifiers provide gain and signal conditioning, and their much lower impedance outputs can then be multiplexed out of the sensor array by conventional scanned multiplexing techniques. Further signal processing can then be performed in more conventional circuitry. Figure 2.10 is a diagram from a 2000 patent by Setlak and Gebauer illustrating the key elements of an RF imaging system [12], including the RF drive system. In a practical application, the single pixel shown in the figure is replicated many times into a two-dimensional array with the pixel pitch sized to allow sampling in excess of the Nyquist rate for an average fingerprint.

2.7.6. An Example Physical Implementation

Figure 2.11 is a photograph of three different size fingerprint sensors that embody the RF array imaging technology and are commercially available. In use, the finger is simply placed directly on top of these devices. The square center region of each device (an exposed portion of the silicon chip) contains the active pixel array that reads the signals from the finger. The white ring around the outside, called the finger

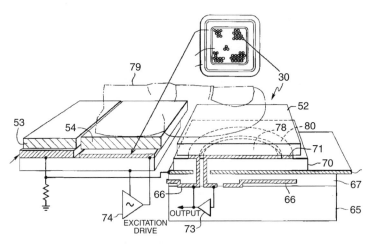

Fig. 2.10. Diagram from a 2000 patent [12].

Fig. 2.11. Three commercially available fingerprint sensors that embody the RF array imaging technology.

drive ring, is a conductive surface connected to the excitation signal generator. It is used to couple the small RF signal into the finger skin.

The finger drive ring is positioned far enough away from the sensor pixel array that fringing fields between these two structures are minimized. The sensor chip integrates all the analog electronics needed to perform the sensing function, as well as signal conditioning, scanning, analog to digital (A/D) conversion, and digital interface functions. The sensing arrays may contain in excess of 16,000 RF sensitive pixels.

2.7.7. Elaborating the Conceptual Model

The simplified model developed above shows conceptually how a system can be constructed to remotely sense the ridge and valley shapes of the live conductive layer of skin that resides beneath the surface of the skin. However, building a fingerprint sensor that works reliably in the real world imaging real fingers requires a somewhat deeper understanding of the physiology of the finger skin and the behavior of the fields and circuits involved in the sensing process. Subsequent sections of this chapter look at these issues in more detail.

The analysis examines the various electrical properties of the finger skin, the skin surface, and the air spaces often present in the valleys of the fingerprint. As noted above, the skin can have a wide range of electrical properties that must be understood to design sensors that operate reliably over a broad range of conditions. Finally, it is useful to examine the imaging system from both the electric field and electric circuit perspectives. These views emphasize different aspects of the system and help decompose the complex behavior of these systems into manageable, understandable components.

2.8. The RF Electric Field Model

2.8.1. Basic Field Model

In this section we take the RF fingerprint-sensing model developed above and elaborate it into a basic electric field model. The first elements we add to the concept model are

The characteristic impedances of the dead skin layer
The physical dimensions of the sensor and finger skin structures
Variations in the air space inside the fingerprint valleys

The electric field illustration developed earlier in this chapter is simplified in several ways. It ignores the differences in characteristic impedances between the dead skin layer and the air spaces typically trapped in the valleys during imaging. As noted previously, the impedance difference between air and the surface skin may range from negligible to several orders of magnitude. The air space itself may or may not be present, depending on the depth and stiffness of the surface ridge structure, contamination, surface wear, and amount of pressure applied by the finger to the sensor surface.

An indication of the effects of the air spaces in the valleys was investigated in a series of computer simulations of the electric fields in a ridge/valley structure representing typical ridge amplitudes, with and without air spaces in the valley. For these simulations we assumed a relative impedance (permittivity) of 20 for the surface layer of skin. The sensor plates were modeled as 96 by 96-μm squares arrayed at a 100-μm pitch. The surface coating of the sensor was assumed to be silicon nitride deposited 2 μm thick and having a relative permittivity of 4. The simulation output generated sensor plate signal amplitudes only and assumed that phase variation over this small region of dry finger skin was negligible. With the air space present, the average difference in signal amplitudes between sensors adjacent to the ridges and those adjacent to the valleys was 70 mV for an excitation voltage of 1 V. When the air space was removed (i.e., filled with material having the same dielectric coefficient as the dead skin layer), the average difference in signal amplitudes between the ridges and valleys sensors was 25 mV. Figure 2.12 shows the signal amplitude profiles at the sensors for a simulation of five pixels shown in cross section. Clearly the ridge/valley pattern can be differentiated by the sensor electronics in both cases. Generalizing the

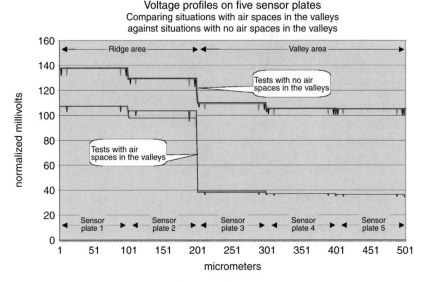

Fig. 2.12. Signal amplitude profiles at five pixels shown in cross section for various conditions.

behavior illustrated here, we see that as the skin impedance approaches that of the air, or as the air spaces become smaller, the behavior approaches that of the "no air space" examples.

2.8.2. Coherently Driven Sensor Array

One important consequence of driving the entire sensing array simultaneously, and essentially coherently, from the live skin layer is that the fields are relatively planar with flux lines that are substantially orthogonal to the sensor plane. Fringing effects are minimal everywhere except at the edges of the array, and the pixel target areas tend to be more focused than in technologies that do not provide simultaneous coherent field excitation of the array. This subtle difference allows the sensor array to maintain spatial resolution equal to the physical sensor plate resolution, even when imaging relatively distant targets. This is in sharp contrast to the behavior of capacitive sensor pixels, as discussed below.

2.8.3. Comparing the Field Structures of Capacitive and RF Imaging

It is instructive to compare the electric field structures in traditional capacitive sensor imaging to the equivalent structures in RF imaging devices.

2.8.3.1. Capacitive Fingerprint Sensor Electric Fields

A typical capacitive fingerprint system measures the electrical capacitance between each sensor plate and the local ground (which is a composite of the adjacent pixels

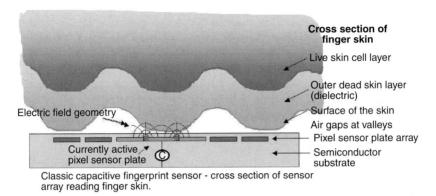

Classic capacitive fingerprint sensor - cross section of sensor array reading finger skin.

Fig. 2.13. Classic capacitive fingerprint sensor—cross section of sensor array reading finger skin.

and the chip substrate). The measurement is performed sequentially, one pixel at a time. A typical capacitive sensing method places a fixed charge on the sensor plate and measures the voltage developed on the sensor plate by that charge. The voltage is directly related to the capacitance of the plate. The electric fields associated with this capacitance measurement are illustrated in Fig. 2.13. Note that the fields penetrating the finger are actually the fringing fields around the edge of the active sensor plate and that the sensor actually measures the difference between the dielectric constant of the immediate finger ridge surface and the dielectric constant of the air spaces in the valleys. If the air space is missing for any reason, the sensor cannot generate an image. The air spaces can be lost by several mechanisms. Strong pressure on the finger can compress the ridges and eliminate the air spaces. Perspiration or other surface contaminants can fill the air spaces. Dry or elderly skin may have a dielectric constant so close to that of air that an image of an adequate contrast cannot be obtained. In all of these cases capacitive sensors cannot generate reliable images of the fingerprint pattern.

2.8.3.2. Pixel Crosstalk and Spatial Resolution

In traditional single-plate capacitive sensors, the sensitive area of the pixel's spherical fringing field is significantly wider than the pixel itself; hence each pixel's target spot is proportionally larger than the pixel plate. The result is significant crosstalk between adjacent sensors, which reduces the effective spatial resolution of classic capacitive sensor arrays to about one half of the physical pixel pitch. That is, a capacitive sensor array with 500 physical pixels per inch (ppi) generates an image with an information content of only 250 dots per inch (dpi). In contrast, the planar coherent fields in RF sensors do not have significant fringing except at the edge of the entire array. As a result, RF pixels have very little crosstalk between adjacent pixels and the image resolution captured is equal to the physical pixel pitch. For example, a 250-ppi RF imaging sensor generates images with true 250-dpi information content.

2.8.3.3. Allowable Protective Coating Thickness

The fringing fields used for imaging in classic capacitive sensors are confined to a region close to the sensor surface and do not penetrate into the finger skin very deeply. The pixels are most sensitive to materials right at their surface; the sensitivity falls off drastically with distance above the surface. As a rule of thumb, fringing capacitance fields become insignificant as the distance above the sensor approaches the diameter of the pixel. For typical capacitive sensors with a 50-μm (0.002 in.) pixel plate size, the fields will generally not penetrate to the depth of the live layer. The shallow penetration of capacitive sensor fields limits the thickness of the protective surface coating that can be placed on the top of the sensing structures, placing an upper bound on mechanical ruggedness. In double-plate capacitive sensors, the field is confined between two adjacent plates, and the electric field penetration can be even smaller than in single-plate designs, imposing similar or worse constraints on the protective coating thickness that can be used. In contrast, RF array fingerprint sensors have electric field structures that originate beneath the skin surface on the live layer of the skin and span the distance between that layer and the sensor surface. This nearly planar field eliminates the drastic fall-off in sensitivity with distance to the sensor surface that is seen in capacitive sensors with their spherical fringing field geometry. Therefore, RF sensors can function through a much thicker protective coating than capacitive sensors, and thicker coatings produce more robust sensors.

Figure 2.14 shows an extreme example of an RF sensor imaging through a thick protective coating. Capacitive sensors are limited to coatings of silicon nitride (or a similar substance) typically less than 1 μm thick. In Fig. 2.14 images of a dry finger are shown taken using RF imaging sensors, first through a sensor coating of 2-μm silicon nitride and second through 100 μm of a high-permittivity epoxy composite deposited on top of the 2 μm of silicon nitride. While some image degradation is noticeable, the sensor has clearly captured a usable image of a difficult finger, through the 100-μm coating.

Imaging dry fingers through protective coatings

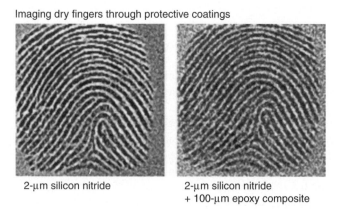

2-μm silicon nitride   2-μm silicon nitride
                              + 100-μm epoxy composite

Fig. 2.14. An extreme example of an RF sensor imaging through a thick protective coating.

2.8.3.4. Sensitivity to Finger Surface Damage and Surface Contact Quality

The capacitive sensor's very shallow region of sensitivity causes the images to degrade if the finger skin lifts slightly off the sensor surface. In many fingers the skin is stiff enough that it is difficult to maintain solid ridge contact with the sensor surface. Elderly, dry, and callused skin all tend to be stiff. These fingers typically generate "dotted-line" type ridge images on capacitive sensors. RF imaging sensors with their deep penetrating fields are much less sensitive to minor loss of contact between the sensor and the ridges. Figure 2.15 is an example comparing the behavior of a capacitive sensor and an RF array sensor [13]. This figure illustrates tests performed on two consecutive days for two people: a 45-year-old male and a 73-year-old male. The figure includes both the raw images from the sensor and binarized images produced by image optimization software for each test image instance. The binarized images make it easier to see the information that can actually be extracted from the somewhat weak capacitive sensor's raw images. The results from the capacitive sensor are highly inconsistent, especially for the older person, while the results from the RF array sensor are clearer and more consistent for both subjects.

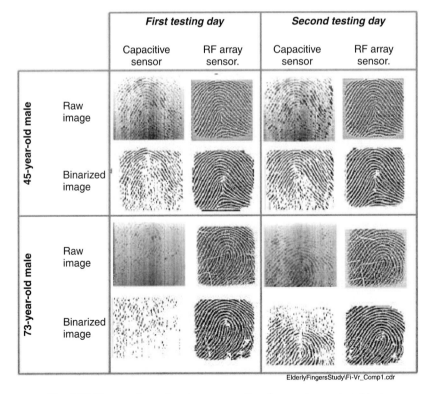

ElderlyFingersStudy\Fi-Vr_Comp1.cdr

Fig. 2.15. Tests performed on two consecutive days on two male subjects.

Similar behavior can be seen in fingers with very small cracks and abrasions on the skin surface. These wear-and-tear artifacts typically degrade capacitive sensor images more than RF sensor images.

2.8.3.5. Sensitivity to Finger Pressure Differences

A similar effect to the "dotted-line" ridge image can be observed in capacitive sensors when the finger pressure applied to the sensor is light. In this case the finger may be very slow to flatten against the sensor, leaving voids in the ridge image where there is insufficient contact. In such cases the system may have to wait for 15 to 20 seconds for the finger ridges to actually lay down against the sensor, a time lag that is much too long for successful live fingerprint recognition. RF sensors, with their reduced sensitivity to loss of surface contact, can produce unbroken ridge images from this type of finger presentation much faster than capacitive sensors.

2.8.3.6. Sensitivity to Surface Contamination

Minor contamination of the surface of the finger or of the sensor can prevent the finger from adequately contacting the sensor surface, or displace the air in the valleys. Either of these situations can also cause poor imaging in capacitive sensors. RF sensors can typically image through minor contamination with very little image degradation.

2.9. The Circuit Model

Some of the behaviors of RF array-based fingerprint sensors can be most easily understood by studying a lumped-parameter circuit representation of the finger/sensor system. The circuit models are intended to help develop a more intuitive understanding of these behaviors without the complexity of a detailed electric field model.

2.9.1. Basic Circuit Model

A generalized finger/sensor model is illustrated in Fig. 2.16. It is intended to represent the most significant current paths in the system. Different current paths will become more or less significant in different types of skin and in different situations. In this model tissues are represented as a resistor and capacitor in parallel. These elements represent the conductive currents and the displacement currents that the tissue can support.

The signal path starts with injection of a low-level excitation signal from the signal source via the finger drive plate. From the drive plate, the signal couples to the skin both conductively and capacitively. Depending on the specific character of the skin being imaged, the signal may disburse via several different mechanisms, eventually providing signal to the sensor pixel plates.

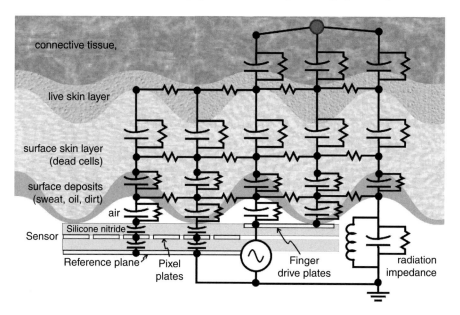

Fig. 2.16. A generalized finger/sensor system.

A key observation is that at optimal operating frequencies there will be a phase difference between components of the sensor signal that arrive via conductive surface paths and components of the signal carried by displacement currents from the underlying live skin layer.

2.9.2. Phase Synchronous Detection

The currently available commercial RF sensors [14] exploit this phase difference by the use of a phase synchronous demodulation scheme. This allows the sensor to differentiate the real and imaginary components of the complex sensor signals. The sensor circuitry allows the system to set the phase shift between the excitation signal and the demodulation clock with a high degree of accuracy. When the sensor's excitation frequency is set appropriately for the particular finger conditions, this mechanism allows the sensors to emphasize the subsurface component of the signal and minimize the surface conducted component. The result is significantly improved images of sweaty fingers and some contaminated fingers.

The phase and frequency adjustability of RF imaging sensors allow them to adapt to widely varying finger conditions. The entire concept of using frequency and phase sensitivity to enhance fingerprint imaging does not exist in traditional capacitive sensing systems. It is instructive to look at some examples of commonly encountered skin conditions to see how the skin behaves and how the RF array sensor can adapt to take advantage of these behaviors.

2.10. Types of Fingers

2.10.1. Normal/Dry Fingers

Figure 2.17 is a model with the elements limited to those appropriate for normal to dry skin. There is very little surface conduction. The signal is coupled via displacement currents to the live layer of skin, where it is distributed across the finger. When no surface contamination is present, coupling to the sensors is via displacement currents that pass through the dead surface layer of skin, possible air pockets in the valleys, and then through the silicon nitride protective coating of the sensor. Finger conditions like those described here are similar to those modeled in the electric field simulations described earlier in this chapter.

The quality of the signal at the sensors can be studied by following the signal back from the sensors, as illustrated in the diagram. The electric field produced by the signal on the live skin layer is attenuated at the sensors depending on the ratios of the permittivities of the dead skin layer, the air spaces, and the sensor coating. The voltage on the live skin layer is determined by the impedance of the excitation source generator, the impedance at the drive ring to skin contact, the permittivity of the dead skin layer, and the loading impedance from the live skin layer to ground (both through the sensors and through external paths such as radiation). The wide range of permittivities seen in finger skin suggests the use of automatic gain control techniques to keep the signals within the dynamic range of typical analog signal processing circuitry. Clearly a large-area, low-impedance contact between the finger skin and the excitation drive ring is essential to maintaining good excitation signal levels on the live skin layer, and hence at the sensors.

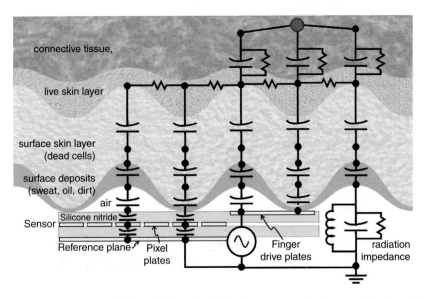

Fig. 2.17. The elements in this model are limited to those appropriate for normal to dry skin.

The permittivity of the dead surface skin layer depends to some degree on small amounts of saline fluid trapped in the keratinized tissue. This structure can exhibit impedances that vary considerably with frequency. It is sometimes possible to enhance an RF array fingerprint image considerably by changing the frequency of the excitation signal. This has been most noticeable in our experiments with dry fingers outdoors, and with very elderly fingers that may be very dry, wrinkled, and cracked. Research is ongoing in this area, but there is not yet a reliable understanding of which finger conditions will be most affected by operating at different frequencies, other than to note that some dry fingers perform better at higher frequencies and some damp fingers perform better at lower frequencies.

2.10.2. Nonconductive Surface Contamination

When nonconductive surface contamination is present, the model is similar to the normal/dry finger model except that the surface deposit layer may have a lower relative permittivity than typical skin. If this layer has significant thickness, it may attenuate the electric fields between the finger drive plate and the skin and again between the skin and the sensor pixels. The result is reduced signal levels at the sensors. Thick enough dielectric surface contamination with a low enough permittivity will reduce the signal to undetectable levels. Higher excitation drive voltages and higher pixel gains are needed to overcome thick dielectric contamination either on the surface of the skin or on the surface of the sensor.

2.10.3. Fingers with Surface Perspiration

Now we extend the model to include normal to dry fingers that have a fairly conductive layer of perspiration at the surface of the finger. Figure 2.18 extends the model used above for normal/dry fingers to account for conduction through a sweaty surface layer.

As the model illustrates, there are now two types of signal paths from the excitation source to the pixel sensor plates: the capacitive path via the live skin layer, and a conductive path along the sweaty surface of the skin. This condition can be represented by an electric fields model in which both real and imaginary components of the material impedance and surface effects contribute both real and imaginary currents to the system. In our simplified circuit model, the voltage at the sensors is now a combination of the surface conducted signal and the signal originating from the live skin layer (the subsurface signal).

It is useful to note that the surface signal path is composed primarily of conduction currents, while displacement currents dominate the subsurface path. When the excitation frequency is adjusted appropriately for the impedance values encountered, the surface signals will have a different phase angle than the subsurface signals. Phase-sensitive demodulation methods such as synchronous detection or other methods of complex signal processing can be used to enhance the subsurface signal and attenuate the surface signal, in effect helping the sensor "see through" a layer of surface sweat to the signal from the live layer beneath.

In mildly sweaty cases, on fingers with strong wide surface ridges, the moisture adheres to the skin and follows the ridge and valley pattern, making the ridges appear

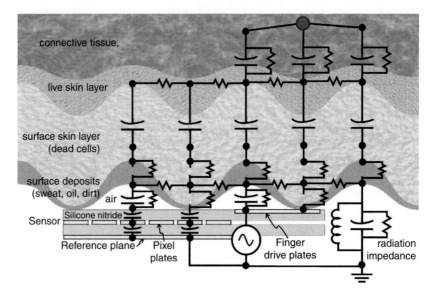

Fig. 2.18. An extension of the model in Fig. 2.17; this one accounts for conduction through a sweaty surface layer.

wider and the valleys narrower. In this case the surface conduction signal generally strengthens the subsurface signal without significantly degrading the fingerprint image. However, in extreme cases, the sweat collects in the valleys of the fingerprint and fills them. In that case the signal component from the surface conduction is flat against the sensor and no longer contains ridge and valley information. In this case, the ridge and valley information from the subsurface signal is in danger of being swamped by the flat surface signal. The relative strength of the two signal components (surface and subsurface) at the sensor depends on the ratios of the path impedances. In practice, the ratio can range anywhere from complete dominance by the deep signal (slightly damp finger) to complete dominance by the surface signal (dripping wet finger).

2.10.4. Fingers Saturated with Perspiration

In some situations, the model of a sweaty surface film over a dry dead skin layer appears inadequate. This is sometimes the case with young children, adults after extended exercise, and certain adults with extremely sweaty hands. In these cases there appears to be sufficient moisture in the dead skin layer that conductive currents become a significant component of the total complex current flow in that region of skin. This is illustrated in the model in Fig. 2.19 by the resistive elements in the dead skin layer.

  As a result, the phase difference between the subsurface and surface signals becomes smaller, and it becomes more difficult to emphasize the subsurface signals using phase-sensitive methods. In some cases it is possible to optimize the excitation frequency to enhance the phase selectivity. In some cases youthful fingers have

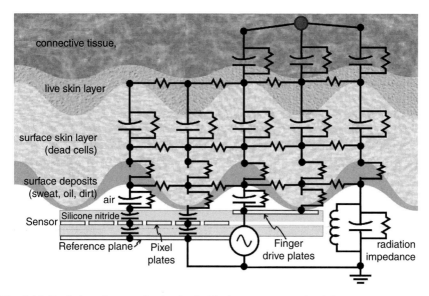

Fig. 2.19. Resistive elements in the dead skin layer are a result of fingers saturated with perspiration.

strong surface patterns; if the surface accumulation of sweat has not filled the valleys, it is sometimes adequate to optimize for the surface image. RF imaging sensors with phase-sensitive demodulation means can readily switch to surface imaging when desirable.

2.11. Conclusions and Future Directions

In practice, RF array fingerprint sensors are typically designed to work in close coordination with a fairly powerful microprocessor. The microprocessor analyzes the images produced by the sensor and exploits the flexibility inherent in the sensor by adjusting the sensor's operating point to adapt to the current condition of the finger and its environment. The same processor may perform the pattern matching operation or the image may be sent to a second (often networked) processor for pattern matching. In information and communication devices that already have a powerful CPU—such as personal computers (PC) and personal digital assistants (PDA)—it is most economical for the sensor to work with that pre-existing CPU. A detailed discussion of fingerprint sensor integration into mobile communications systems is included in Chapter 13 of the book The Application of Programmable DSPs in Mobile Communications [15].

The RF array-based fingerprint sensor technology, with its ability to capture fingerprint images beneath the skin surface, its ability to adapt to different finger skin conditions and environments, and its ability to image through minor surface contamination, is enabling a much wider range of applications than was possible with earlier fingerprint sensors. These sensors, when coupled with the higher-performance CPUs now being incorporated into many of our information and communications devices, have the potential to make convenient and reliable identity verification commonplace in our information and communications devices.

Several new trends are already evident in fingerprint sensor technology. They include a drive for smaller-size, lower-power sensors, as well as early work to identify lower-cost fabrication methods for situations that require full-size sensors. For personal identification systems in computing and communications gear, the prerequisites for adoption are low-cost and small panel footprint. In silicon sensors, cost is mostly a function of the size of the silicon chip. Therefore, both the cost and size constraints can be addressed by reducing the size of the imaging array. A significant effort is being devoted to development of smaller-size sensors. At the root of this work is the realization that high-quality imaging makes it possible to capture more detailed and more repeatable data from a smaller area of skin; hence it is possible to obtain match accuracies from the smaller high-quality images that are as good as or better than that achieved with the older, larger, lower-quality images. This development activity includes sensor work to further enhance the clarity and repeatability of the images, and matching algorithm work to develop effective ways of utilizing this detailed and highly repeatable image data. The smaller sensors are likely to be applied first to personal identification situations where one-to-one or one-to-several ID verification is used.

For criminology applications, security background checks, and double enrollment rejection applications, full-size sensors may remain the standard. If the size of these sensors is fixed, their cost cannot be reduced by the typical size reductions that continually drive costs lower in standard semiconductor process technology. The search is already on for fabrication methods with lower costs than traditional CMOS integrated circuit technology [16].

Finally, the academic community has been studying the design of integrated silicon devices that contain both the fingerprint sensor and the computing elements that perform image optimization and matching [17, 18]. While these concepts are interesting, they have not yet penetrated the commercial market. Currently, the mixed-signal silicon fabrication processes needed to construct good-quality fingerprint sensors are too expensive to devote to digital processor functionality. It is currently most cost effective to build sensors and computational structures separately in different silicon processes, and then integrate them at the board or module level.

References

1. The RF imaging technology has been commercialized by AuthenTec, Inc., Melbourne, Florida, in its TruePrint[TM] technology-based sensors. Its web site is www.authentec.com.
2. Thin film MEMS-based fingerprint sensors have been demonstrated by Fidelica Microsystems. Its web site is www.fidelica.com.
3. Optical fingerprint scanners using direct contact methods are available from several manufacturers. One such producer is Delsy Electronic Components AG, at www.Delsy.de.

4. Ultrasonic fingerprint scanners are available from Ultra-Scan Corporation. Its web site is www.Ultra-Scan.com.

5. Thermal flux-based fingerprint scanners are commercially available from Atmel Corporation. Fingerprint scanners on its web site can be found at www.atmel.com/atmel/products/prod42.htm.

6. Killen, Donald E., U.S. Patent #3,781,855, Fingerprint identification system and method, 1973.

7. Tsikos, Constantine, U.S. Patent #4,353,056, Capacitive fingerprint sensor, 1982.

8. Abramov, Igor, U.S. Patent #4,577,345, Fingerprint sensor, 1986.

9. Dickinson, Alexander George et al., U.S. Patent #6,016,355, Capacitive fingerprint acquisition sensor, 2000.

10. Kramer, Alan and James Brady, U.S. Patent #6,317,508, Scanning capacitive semiconductor fingerprint detector, 2001.

11. Grimnes, S. and O.G. Martinsen, *Bioimpedance & Bioelectricity Basics*, Academic Press, 2000.

12. Setlak, Dale and Dave Gebauer, U.S. Patent #6,067,368, Fingerprint sensor having filtering and power conserving features and related methods, 2000.

13. The capacitive sensor used in this study was the Veridicom FPS-110 sensor with the Veridicom SDK. The RF imaging sensor used in this study was the AuthenTec AFS1 sensor with the AuthenTec SDK.

14. The TruePrint technology-based sensors from AuthenTec, Inc. use the phase synchronous detection methods discussed here.

15. Setlak, Dale and Lorin Netch, Chapter 13: Biometric systems applied to mobile communications, in *The Application of Programmable DSPs in Mobile Communications*, Alan Gatherer and Edgar Auslander, eds., London: Wiley & Sons, Ltd., 2002.

16. Hashido, R., A. Suzuki, A. Iwata, T. Ogawa, T. Okamoto, Y. Satoh, M. Inoue, A capacitive fingerprint sensor with low-temperature poly-Si TFTs, Solid-State Circuits Conference, 2001. Digest of Technical Papers. ISSCC. 2001 IEEE International, pp. 250–251, 452.

17. Shigematsu, S., K. Fujii, H. Morimura, T. Hatano, M. Nakanishi, T. Adachi, N. Ikeda, T. Shimamura, K. Machida, Y. Okazaki, H. Kyuragi, A 500 dpi 224/spl times/256-pixel single-chip fingerprint identification LSI, with pixel-parallel image enhancement and rotation schemes, Solid-State Circuits Conference, 2002. Digest of Technical Papers. ISSCC. 2002 IEEE International, 1:354–473.

18. Shigematsu, S.; H. Morimura, Y. Tanabe, T. Adachi, and K. Machida, A single-chip fingerprint sensor and identifier, *IEEE J. Solid-State Circuits*, 34(12):1852–1859, Dec. 1999.

Chapter 3

Fingerprint Quality Assessment

Michael Yi-Sheng Yao, Sharath Pankanti, and Norman Haas

Abstract. For a particular biometric to be effective, it should be universal: Every individual in the target population should possess the biometrics, and every acquisition from each individual should provide useful information for personal identity verification or recognition. In other words, everybody should have the biometrics and it should be easy to sample or acquire. In practice, adverse signal acquisition conditions and inconsistent presentations of the signal often result in unusable or nearly unusable biometrics signals (biometrics samples). This is confounded by the problem that the underlying individual biometrics signal can vary over time due, for example, to aging. Hence, poor quality of the actual machine sample of a biometrics constitutes the single most cause of poor accuracy performance of a biometrics system. Therefore, it is important to quantify the quality of the signal, either for seeking a better representation of the signal or for subjecting the poor signal to alternative methods of processing (e.g., enhancement [9]). In this chapter,[1] we explore a definition of the quality of fingerprint impressions and present detailed algorithms to measure image quality. The proposed quality measure has been developed with the use of human annotated images, and tested on a large number of fingerprints of different modes of fingerprint acquisition methods.

3.1. Introduction

Because of adverse and/or hostile signal and image acquisition situations, a biometrics system performance suffers from random false rejects/accepts. In a deployed system, the poor acquisition of samples perhaps constitutes the single most important reason for high false reject/accept rates. There are two solutions to this. One can either probabilistically model and weigh all the adverse situations into the feature extraction/matching system, or one can try to dynamically and interactively obtain a desirable input sample.[2]

Automatic implementation of either strategy entails algorithmically characterizing what one means by *desirable* pattern samples and by quality of pattern samples. The term "quality" is then somehow related to "processability" of the sample. That

---

[1] Parts of this work previously appeared in IEEE AutoID 2002 [10]. Reproduced here with permission from IEEE. © IEEE.

[2] This is only possible in interactive overt online systems involving cooperative users.

is, the system faces difficulty in analyzing poor-quality samples and performs well when presented with good-quality samples. It is important to quantify the concept of quality so that consistent actions can be applied to samples having different degrees of undesirability. It is equally important to recognize the specific reasons why a sample is undesirable (e.g., partial face view) so that an appropriate corrective action can be suggested or taken by the system (e.g., apply enhancement) or by the subject (e.g., presents the biometrics in a different, "better" way). Finally, it is desired that assessment of quality be fast, and not require actually matching the given sample either with its mates or with its nonmates. Often, one single best sample is desired.

Gracefully and conveniently handling biometrics samples of diverse quality is of great significance to any practical biometrics identity system. However, in theory, for almost all applications it is possible to compromise some convenience (ease of use) by accepting only a certain quality of input. Therefore, it comes as no surprise that almost all operational biometrics systems have an implicit or explicit strategy for handling samples of poor quality. Some of the simplest measures for quality control include provision for presenting multiple samples to the system. In such systems, it is hoped that multiple opportunities to present a sample may alleviate the problem of overcoming the occasional poor-quality sample. In other schemes, the system provides a user with a live visual display of the biometrics that has been sampled (which is, of course, not practical for all biometrics). It is expected that this feedback to the user will provide an opportunity to self-correct some of the simple mistakes such as improper placement of a finger, or coughing during a speech sample. This feedback is, of course, especially important during the enrollment process. Enrolling undesirable samples can cause a lasting, more serious impact on system accuracy.

The rest of this chapter concentrates on fingerprints. Section 3.2 presents quality problems specific to the fingerprint domain. Sections 3.3 and 3.4 describe in detail our quality assessment algorithms, relying on two distinct types of criteria. Section 3.5 presents some quality assessment empirical results. Finally, Section 3.6 provides conclusions and ideas for further research.

3.2. Assessing Fingerprint Quality

Precise fingerprint image acquisition up to minutiae has some peculiar and challenging aspects [1], many because of contact[3] problems. Specifically, (i) *inconsistent contact:* The act of sensing distorts the finger. Determined by the pressure and contact of the finger on the imaging surface (e.g., 2D glass platen), the 3D shape of the finger is mapped onto the 2D surface. Typically, this mapping is uncontrolled and results in different, inconsistently mapped regions across impressions. (ii) *Nonuniform contact:* The ridge structure of a finger would be completely captured if the ridges of all imaged parts of the finger were in complete optical contact with the glass platen. In practice, for various reasons, this is not the case. (iii) *Irreproducible contact:* Manual work, accidents, etc. inflict injuries to the finger, thereby changing its ridge structure either

---

[3] The term "contact" does not necessarily mean physical contact and needs to be appropriately interpreted according to sensing modality.

permanently or semipermanently. This may introduce additional spurious minutiae or "minutiae-like" features. (iv) The act of sensing itself adds noise to the image; for example, residues left over from the previous fingerprint capture. Additionally, (v) a typical imaging system distorts the image of the sensed finger due to imperfect imaging conditions. All these factors contribute to poor samples and feature extraction artifacts during image processing and hence increase false accept/reject rates.

Many commercial-quality assessment systems detect the amount of the print area and the relative placement/orientation of the finger; these systems can provide simple feedback to the user about proper placement of the finger to the image acquisition device but cannot quantify the quality of the fingerprint image itself. More sophisticated systems have an explicit method of quantifying the quality of the fingerprint being captured. Although quality assessment is a critical part of any practical biometric system, the quality assessment ideas have not received much attention in the mainstream published literature. While some of the practical ideas have been patented [2–6], practical quality assessment ideas have mostly remained as some sort of black-art know-how shared among the biometric practitioners. Here, we briefly summarize a couple of recent publications that have addressed quality assessment ideas that have appeared in the mainstream research literature.

Ratha and Bolle [17] present a method of quality estimation from wavelet-compressed fingerprint images. They observe that a significant fraction of the normalized cumulative spectral energy is within the first few subbands of a WSQ-compressed good-quality fingerprint image. Accordingly, they design rotation-invariant criteria to distinguish smudged and blurred fingerprint images from good-quality fingerprint images.

Lim et al. [18] present a three-pronged attack to fingerprint quality assessment. First, they use strength and directionality of the ridge orientation information to assess the contrast of fingerprint image and the clarity of the ridge information. They further verify that the fingerprint possesses sufficiently clear ridge-valley structure by analyzing the gray-level profile of the fingerprint image. Finally, they assess the continuity of the ridge by analyzing the change in the ridge direction information.

We observe that poor-quality prints are predominantly due to nonuniform and inconsistent contact, and we make them the focus of this chapter. In the following two sections (Sections 3.3 and 3.4), we describe our approach to assessment of poor-quality fingerprints due to nonuniform contact and inconsistent contact.

3.3. Nonuniform Contact

Dryness of the finger skin, skin disease, sweat, dirt, and humidity in the air all contribute to a nonuniform and nonideal contact situation: Some parts of the ridges may not come in complete contact with the platen, and regions representing some valleys may come in contact with the glass platen. Nonuniform contact manifests itself in dry prints (too little ridge contact) and smudgy prints (neighboring ridges touching each other, obliterating the intervening valleys) or in prints with combinations. Nonuniform contact may result in "noisy," low-contrast images and could lead to many feature extraction artifacts, for example, spurious minutiae or missing minutiae. For instance, in a dry fingerprint (see Fig. 3.2b), the ridge is in intermittent contact with the platen, resulting in significant variation of pixel intensities along a dry finger ridge. In extreme situations, there is no particularly dominant direction of a very dry ridge because too small a fraction is in contact with the platen.

On the other hand, in a smudgy portion of the fingerprint (see Fig. 3.2d), variation in pixel intensities across the ridge direction is significantly lower than the typical expected variation across an ideal ridge. In extreme situations, the directionality of the ridges is obliterated due to a large number of ridges touching each other (this is analogous to image saturation).

For the pattern recognition task of fingerprint representations, prints have been (implicitly or explicitly) modeled as smoothly flowing directional textures (ridges) that can be extracted by typical fingerprint feature extraction algorithms [1, 7]. Since directionality of the finger ridges is an essential attribute of its image texture, we propose that this anisotropy constitutes a basis for assessing the overall quality of the fingerprint.

Below we summarize an algorithm for fingerprint quality assessment based on the directionality of its texture.

Subsampling and Blocking

For efficiency reasons, the quality analysis uses a subsampled image. The analysis samples the image at rate s in x- and y-directions. The subsampled image is further divided into square blocks of size B.

Direction and Foreground Estimation

This step determines if a given block depicts a portion of a fingerprint and extracts a nominal direction from a foreground block. Any number of existing strategies can be adopted [1, 7, 11]. For efficiency reasons, we use the method proposed by Mehtre [12]. At each pixel in a given block, a number of pixels are selected along a line segment of an orientation (d) and prespecified length (l) centered around that pixel; variation in the intensities of the selected pixels is then determined by computing the sum of intensity differences $D_d(i, j)$ between the given pixel and the selected pixels,

$$D_d(i, j) = \sum_{(i', j')} |f(i, j) - f_d(i', j')| \qquad (1)$$

with $d = 0, \pi/n, \ldots, \pi$ and where $f(i, j)$ is the intensity of pixel (i, j) and $f_d(i', j')$ are the intensities of the neighbors of pixel (i, j) along direction d. This indicates the summation of differences between the given pixel of interest, pixel (i, j), and a number l (say 6) of neighboring pixels along each of the directions. The variation in intensities is computed for n discrete orientations; the orientation at a pixel $\hat{d}$ is the orientation of the line segment for which the intensity variation thus computed is minimal.

Regions of background and portions of impressions having a faint residue left over from previously captured prints usually exhibit small intensity variation around their neighborhoods. To determine if an image pixel belongs to the background, the intensity variation $D(i, j)$ at the pixel (i, j) of interest is subsequently obtained by summing up the differences in the n directions with $D(i, j) = \sum_d D_d(i, j)$; when D is less than a background threshold τ for each d, the pixel is classified as a background pixel. When more than a fraction of pixels in a block are background pixels, the block is regarded as a background block.

Using connected component analysis, foreground components smaller than a certain threshold fraction of the total image area τ_a are considered spurious. A print with no legitimate foreground area is of poorest quality.

Dominant Direction

After the foreground blocks are marked, it is determined if the resulting direction for each block is prominent. The idea is that a block with a prominent direction should exhibit a clear ridge/valley direction that is consistent with most of the pixel directions in the block. Existence of a dominant direction can be assessed by computing a histogram of directions D_d [Eq. (1)] at each pixel in a given block. If the maximum value of the histogram is greater than a prominent threshold T_1, the block is said to have a dominant direction and is labeled as prominent. Bifurcations of ridges may often result in two dominant directions in a block. Therefore, if two or more directions of the direction histogram are greater than a bifurcation threshold, $T_2 < T_1$, the corresponding block is labeled as such. A postprocessing step removes blocks that are inconsistent with their neighbors. If a "directional" block is surrounded by "nondirectional" blocks, it is relabeled as a nondirectional block. Similarly, a nondirectional block surrounded by neighboring directional blocks is changed to a directional block. Finally, using connected component analysis, components having fewer than a threshold number of blocks β are discarded. The result is that the fingerprint foreground image is partitioned into (i) regions of contiguous blocks with direction and (ii) regions of blocks without direction or noncontiguous blocks with direction.

Quality Computation

Since regions (or accordingly, minutiae) near the centroid are likely to provide more information for biometrics authentication, the overall quality of the fingerprint image is computed from the directional blocks by assigning a relative weight w_i for foreground block i at location x_i, given by

$$w_i = e - \frac{||x_i - x_c||^2}{2q^2} \tag{2}$$

where x_c is the centroid of foreground, and q is a normalization constant.

The overall quality Q of a fingerprint image is obtained by computing the ratio of total weights of directional blocks to the total weights for each of the blocks in the foreground, $Q = \sum_{\mathcal{D}} w_i / \sum_{\mathcal{F}} w_i$. Here $\mathcal{D}$ is the set of directional blocks and $\mathcal{F}$ the set of foreground blocks. The quality Q is used as a measure of how much reliable directional information is available in a fingerprint image. If the computed Q is less than the quality threshold, T, the image is considered to be of poor quality.

Dryness and Smudginess

If it is determined that a fingerprint is of poor quality, it is desirable to be able to identify a more specific cause of the low quality. We describe a method of distinguishing smudged poor-quality prints from dry poor-quality prints based on simple statistical pixel intensity-based features. The idea is that, for a smudged impression, there are a relatively large number of blocks whose contrast is very small, while for a dry impression, there are a relatively large number of blocks where the contrasts of their neighbors vary significantly.

First, the mean intensity of pixels within each foreground block is computed. The pixels whose intensities are smaller than the mean intensity of all the pixels in their block are considered pixels on a ridge, that is, ridge pixels.[4] Let μ be the true mean intensity of ridge pixels. For each block, the mean intensity (μ) is estimated using pixels whose intensities are smaller than the mean intensity of all pixels within the block. Further, the standard deviation (σ) of intensities of all pixels within the same block is determined. For a block with good contrast, μ is small and σ is large; for a block with low contrast due to smudginess, μ is small and σ is small. The contrast within a block is measured using the product ($\delta c_s = \mu \sigma$). If the contrast measure c_s is smaller than a threshold ρ_1, the block is classified as a smudged block. Last, the smudginess measure is determined as the ratio of the number of smudged blocks to total number of foreground blocks. If the resulting ratio is larger than a threshold, ρ_2, a smudged impression is reported.

For a block with good contrast, on the other hand, μ is small and σ is large. For a block with low contrast due to dryness, however, μ is large and σ is small. Consequently, to measure the contrast within a block, we compute the ratio of corresponding μ to corresponding σ, that is, $c_d = \mu/\sigma$, where c_d is the contrast measure. A block is considered to be dry if c_d is greater than a dryness threshold, δ_1. Alternatively, the fingerprint is considered dry if the contrasts of its neighboring blocks vary significantly. Specifically, let the c_{max} (c_{min}) be the maximum (minimum) value of contrast difference between the contrast of the given block and those of its neighboring blocks. If the difference between c_{max} and c_{min} is larger than a dryness threshold δ_2, then the block is a dry block. The dryness measure of the image is computed as the ratio of the total number of dry blocks to the total number of foreground blocks. If the resulting measure is greater than a threshold, δ_3, it is reported that a dry impression causes the quality problems.

3.4. Inconsistent Contact

Inconsistent contact is one of the significant practical problems in matching fingerprints because it tends to decrease the similarity betweeen mated pairs of prints. The inconsistent contact may be due to either presentation of differently distorted finger-

---

[4] Assume that the finger imaging depicts ridges as darker pixels.

prints or presentation of different portions of the finger to the sensor. The former type of inconsistent contact is primarily due to application of different pressure on the finger while presenting it to the sensor. In situations where the sensor is explicitly equipped with force sensors, the differently distorted fingerprints can be recognized [6], and in such situations, undistorted (or consistently distorted) prints can be actively acquired during the acquisition phase using a feedback loop. There is also some research reported in algorithms used for processing differently distorted prints so that they can be transformed into a *canonic* distorted form [19]. Such an approach hypothesizes that such canonical (mated) fingerprints are easier to match, while not signficantly affecting the discrimination of nonmates. Typically, however, it is very difficult to assess differently distorted fingerprints without actually matching the prints.

Presentation of different portions of the finger is a practical problem because it decreases the magnitude of invariance among different impressions of the same finger. Many commercial fingerprint matching systems ensure that the different impressions have some signficant overlap by ascertaining that the prints are not *partial* images of fingers. This may typically be achieved by explicit detection of the features that typically reside near the central portion of the finger as the fingerprint is being acquired. Failure to detect such features within the print being captured, or failure to detect a significant print region surrounding the "central" finger portion causes the system to prompt the user to present the finger again to the sensor, possibly in some different way. Typically, "core" features signify the central portion of the finger; however, reliably detecting the core is a difficult problem, especially in some accidental finger categories. More importantly, complex algorithms used for detecting the core may not be easily amenable to real-time implementation.

Our approach for ensuring an imaging-consistent portion of fingers relies on ridge orientation information. We observe that, typically, a fully imaged upright finger will reveal a characteristic smooth inverted "U"-shaped ridge flow on the periphery (e.g., noncentral portion) of the print (see Fig. 3.1). Failure to find a sequence of oriented blocks to realize an inverted "U" implies that the finger is only partially imaged; such a

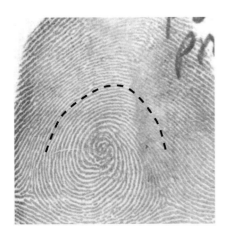

Fig. 3.1. Partial fingerprint assessment relies on detection of inverted "U"-shaped ridge flow orientation sequence.

print depicts either the predominantly left or predominantly right portion of the finger. The extent of "U"-shape realization required to qualify an image to be classified as a full print depends on application requirements. We observe that detection of partial prints based on this ridge flow information is more reliable than detecting localized features such as the core or the detection of ridges.

3.5. Experiments

The algorithms described above have been implemented and tested on a large number of the fingerprints captured in the laboratory and in the real world using inked prints and optical live scans, as well as solid-state live-scan fingerprint scanners. The quality assessment is extremely fast (e.g., less than 100 ms on a 933 MHz Pentium III processor on a 512×512 image). Typical operational parameters for the proposed quality assessment algorithm for an 8-bit, 512-dpi 512×512 gray-scale images are $s = 4$ and $B = 8$. Figure 3.2 illustrates results of fingerprint quality assessment for a few representative optically scanned fingerprint images. The results of the quality assessment typically appear consistent with visual human assessment. Figure 3.3 depicts some of the partial prints detected by the algorithm outlined in Section 3.4.

We use the fingerprint image quality assessment to compare fingerprints in three data sets: NIST-9, FVC-2000, and IBM-99. NIST-9 [14] is a public database of 8-bit gray-scale inked fingerprint images scanned from mated fingerprint card pairs. The database contains 90 mated card pairs of segmented 8-bit gray-scale fingerprint images (900 fingerprint image pairs per CD-ROM). Each segmented image is 832 by 768 pixels, and is classified using the National Crime Information Center (NCIC) classes given by the FBI. Only the first 600 images have been arbitrarily sampled from the entire data set for quality assessment. FVC-2000 is another public database. It is one of the databases used in a recent fingerprint verification contest [13] and was collected using optical sensing techniques. The prints in this database were possibly preselected by the test administrators to include somewhat challenging impressions ("visual preselection"). This database contains impressions of 110 fingers with 8 impressions per finger. This set was acquired from a set of 19 volunteers in the 5–73 age range (55% male). Without interleaving, two images of six fingers were taken from each volunteer per session. Each volunteer attended four sessions, with no more than two sessions per day, and depending on the volunteer, over a span of three days to three months. Much care was given to cleaning the sensor and the fingers between acquisitions. Some visual inspection of the data set was performed to ensure minimal overlap and not too much rotation between impressions. Database IBM-99 is a private database. This database was acquired from a group of 57 subjects in two sessions five weeks apart. There were approximately the same number of adult males and females, and the age group is 22–65 years old. During each session, five prints of both the left and right index fingers were obtained for each subject. Hence, the database contains a total of 1140 impressions, 10 prints of 114 fingers. All prints in data set IBM-99 were collected using the same optical fingerprint scanner with a 512-dpi image resolution.

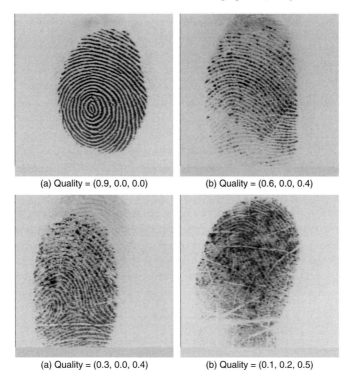

(a) Quality = (0.9, 0.0, 0.0)   (b) Quality = (0.6, 0.0, 0.4)

(a) Quality = (0.3, 0.0, 0.4)   (b) Quality = (0.1, 0.2, 0.5)

Fig. 3.2. A fingerprint quality assessment measure. Quality (x, y, z) indicates print of overall quality x, smudginess y, and dryness z.

Fig. 3.3. A partial fingerprint assessment. Three partial prints detected at a fingerprint scanner installed at an access control installation.

Histograms of fingerprint qualities for the fingerprints in the data sets are presented in Fig. 3.4. It can be clearly seen that the inked prints taken under careful supervision of trained personnel (e.g., NIST-9) appear to be of significantly better quality than the live-scan prints acquired under less supervised conditions. It is also interesting to note that the optical live-scan fingerprints in FVC-2000 and IBM-99 data sets appear to be of approximately comparable quality. However, FVC-2000 may contain

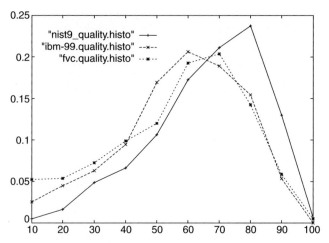

Fig. 3.4. Image quality histograms for three fingerprint data sets: NIST-9, FVC-2000, and IBM-99.

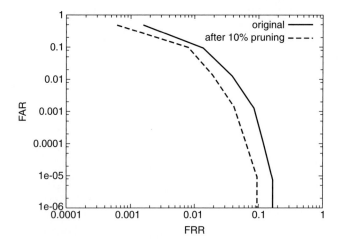

Fig. 3.5. Effect of quality pruning on fingerprint verification accuracy performance.

slightly poorer overall quality prints than IBM-99 (note the higher frequency of lower-quality prints with quality value between 0–40 in FVC-2000) possibly due to visual preselection used by the FVC-2000 designers ("three bears rule" [20]). Even though the absolute values of quality measurements are somewhat arbitrary, their rank order can be used to assess/compare biometric data sets [16].

Does the quality as computed by the quality assessment algorithm really reflect on the desirability of the print to be processed by an automatic fingerprint verification system? To investigate this issue, we plot ROC curves showing accuracy performance of a fingerprint matcher [15] for the IBM-99 data set. Subsequently, using the proposed quality assessment algorithm, some of the worst-quality prints (10%) from the IBM-99 data set were culled from the data set; the ROC curve was recomputed using the remaining prints of IBM-99. Figure 3.5 presents effect of culling fingerprints of poor quality from IBM-99. As expected, the accuracy of the matcher did indeed significantly improve.

3.6. Conclusions and Future Research

Automatically and consistently determining suitability of a given input measurement (biometrics sample) for automatic identification is a challenging problem. This chapter proposed a method of assessment of quality of a fingerprint based on a simple ideal fingerprint image model. We presented an algorithm for overall quality assessment. We further proposed a basis for categorizing a poor-quality fingerprint into either "dry" or "smudged" prints using simple local statistical measures of the pixel intensities. Algorithms for assessment of dryness and smudginess indices were also presented. The qualities of images in a few databases have been computed. The quality assessment results appeared to be mostly consistent with visual quality assessment. A more objective evaluation of the quality assessment is a topic of our future research.

There are a number of limitations to the impression quality measure. Most significantly, the proposed quality assessment algorithms are based on an intuitive domain-specific strategy, and it appears that a more generic framework for quality assessment would be a more useful tool for realizing quality assessment strategies for different representations of fingerprints and for different biometric identifiers. The proposed algorithms are meant to present an overall judgment of the quality of the fingerprint and are incapable of providing pointers to the most problematic portions of the finger. Finally, it is to be noted that the test for fingerprint quality does not imply existence of a fingerprint. The present model is sufficiently naive (for efficiency reasons), and many nonfingerprint images may successfully pass the fingerprint quality test.

Matcher-representation-independent description of complexities of biometric data sets has not received much attention in the literature. We hope that objective assessment of the quality assessment through careful ground-truth marking, development of generic frameworks for data modeling and of the quality assessment will be open not only to new approaches to comparing/assessing biometric data sets but also to characterizing the different categories of patterns [8]. For any specific applications, regulating the sample quality in effect results in artificially increasing the failure to enroll (FTE) rate. For applications where convenience is the motivating factor, this may not be a problem because increasing the FTE rate only decreases the pool of subjects that can "smoothly" use the installation. Enforcing quality control while maintaining a low FTE rate, for security-specific applications, on the other hand, inevitably will imply that the application becomes less convenient for many subjects. This is compounded by the fact that enrollment of poor samples will result in higher false-accept and false-reject rates caused by these samples.

References

1. Jain, A., L. Hong, S. Pankanti, and R. Bolle, Identity authentication using fingerprints, Proc. *IEEE*, 1365–1388, 1997.
2. Bolle, R. M., S. Pankanti, and Y-S. Yao, System and method for determining if a fingerprint image contains an image portion representing a partial fingerprint impression, U.S. Patent No. 6,005,963, Dec. 21, 1999.
3. Bolle, R. M., S. Pankanti, and Y-S. Yao, System and method for determining the quality of fingerprint images, U.S. Patent No. 5,963,656, Oct. 5, 1999.
4. Bolle, R. M., S. Pankanti, and Y-S. Yao, System and method for determining if a fingerprint image contains an image portion representing a dry fingerprint impression, U.S. Patent No. 5,995,640, Nov. 30, 1999.
5. Bolle, R. M., S. Pankanti, and Y-S. Yao, System and method for determining if a fingerprint image contains an image portion representing a smudged fingerprint impression, U.S. Patent No. 5,883,971, Mar. 16, 1999.
6. Levine, J. L., M. A. Schappert, N. K. Ratha, R. M. Bolle, S. Pankanti, R. S. Germain, and R. L. Garwin, System and method for distortion control in live-scan inkless fingerprint images, U.S. Patent No. US06064753, May 16, 2000.
7. Ratha, N. K., S. Chen, and A. K. Jain, Adaptive flow orientation based texture extraction in fingerprint images, *Pattern Recognition*, 28(11):1657–1672, Nov. 1995.
8. Pankanti, S., N. Ratha, and R. Bolle, Structure in errors: A case study in fingerprints, ICPR 2002, Quebec City, Canada, 2002.
9. Ghosal, S., R. Udupa, S. Pankanti, and N. K. Ratha, Learning partitioned least squares filters for fingerprint enhancement, Workshop on the Application of Computer Vision (WACV2000) Dec. 4–6, 2000, Palm Springs, CA.
10. Yao, Y. S., S. Pankanti, N. Haas, N. Ratha, and R. Bolle, Quantifying quality: A case study in fingerprints, IEEE AutoID Conference, March 14–15, 2002.
11. Maio, D. and D. Maltoni, Direct gray-scale minutiae detection in fingerprints, *IEEE Trans. Pattern Analysis and Machine Intelligence*, 19(1):27–40, Jan. 1997.
12. Mehtre, B. M., *Fingerprint Image Analysis for Automatic Identification, Machine Vision and Applications*, Springer-Verlag, Vol. 6, 1993, pp. 124–139.
13. Maio, D., D. Maltoni, R. Capelli, J.L. Wayman, and A.K. Jain. FVC2000: Fingerprint verification competition. Technical report, Univ. of Bologna, Sept. 2000.
14. Watson, C. I., NIST Special Database 9, Mated Fingerprint Card Pairs, National Institute of Standards and Technology, 1993.
15. Ratha, N., K. Karu, S. Chen, and A. K. Jain, A real-time matching system for large finger-print database, *IEEE Trans. on PAMI*, 18(8):799–813, 1996.
16. Bolle, R., N. Ratha, and S. Pankanti, Evaluating authentication systems using bootstrap confidence intervals, *Proc. 1999 IEEE Workshop on Automatic Identification Advanced Technologies* (Morristown, NJ), Oct. 28–29, 1999, pp. 9–13.
17. Ratha, Nalini K., and Ruud M. Bolle, Fingerprint quality assessment, *Proc. of 4th Conference on Computer Vision*, Jan 8–11, 2000, Taipei, pp. 819–823.
18. Lim, E., X. Jiang, and W. Yau, Fingerprint quality and validity analysis, *IEEE Proc. ICIP*, Rochester, NY, 2002, pp. I-469–I-472.
19. Senior, A. W., and R. Bolle, Improved fingerprint matching by distortion removal, *IEICE Trans. Special Issue on Biometrics*, 2001.
20. Phillips, P. J., Grother, P., Michaels, R., Blackburn, D. M., Elham, T., Bone, J. M., FRVT200: Face Recognition vendor test, http://www.frvt.org, 2003.

Chapter 4

Dynamic Behavior in Fingerprint Videos

Chitra Dorai, Nalini Ratha, and Ruud Bolle

Abstract. Traditional fingerprint acquisition is limited to a single image capture and processing. With the advent of faster capture hardware, faster processors, and advances in video compression standards, newer systems capture and exploit video signals for tasks that are difficult using single images. In this chapter, we propose the use of fingerprint video sequences to investigate dynamic behaviors of fingerprints across multiple frames. In particular, we present a novel approach to detect and estimate distortion occurring in compressed fingerprint video streams. Our approach directly works on MPEG-{1,2} encoded fingerprint video bitstreams to estimate interfield flow without decompression and uses this flow information to investigate temporal characteristics of the behaviors of the fingerprints. The joint temporal and motion analysis leads to a novel technique to detect and characterize distortion reliably. The proposed method has been tested on the NIST-24 database, and the results are very promising. We also describe a new concept called the "resultant biometrics"—a new type of biometrics that has both a physiological, physical (e.g., force, torque, linear motion, rotation) component and/or temporal characteristic, added by a subject to an existing biometrics. This resultant biometric is both desirable and efficient in terms of easy modification of compromised biometrics and is harder to produce with spoof body parts.

4.1. Introduction

In a computer vision system, the process of acquiring or sensing data is, in general, expected to have the least impact on the input signal itself. However, in an automatic fingerprint identification system, the fingerprint acquisition process severely interferes with the quality of input signal captured. With both types of fingerprint input methods, one using inkless touch scanners, also known as "dabs," and the other using ink-based rolled fingerprint acquisition devices, fingerprint images are influenced by different kinds of finger behavior at the time of sensing, notably by distortion. Distortions in fingerprint images arise mainly due to the elasticity of finger skin. The pressure and torque variations in fingers during image acquisition also cause random distortions in structural features used in fingerprint matching. These, sometimes natural and sometimes intended distortions, lead to difficulties in establishing a match between even two images of a single fingerprint. Alternately, if the input quality can be controlled, the matcher performance can be improved significantly.

The process of distortion detection is typically ignored in the acquisition stage. The effects of distortion are handled by the subsequent stages in fingerprint processing such as the feature extraction (representation) or the matching stage. The usual method of handling distortion is to attempt a compensation of the same in the matching stage. The matcher accounts for the shifts of the structural features by using tolerance boxes around minutiae extracted from fingerprint images [1]. Quite often the distortion-tolerance boxes have to be large in order to accommodate large amounts of distortions due to skin elasticity. The goal of our work is to devise a technique to detect and characterize distortions in fingerprints so as to eliminate distorted images from further consideration. A simple approach of merely setting a tighter tolerance box for the matching stage would mean much better accuracy in terms of low false accepts during person recognition and verification. But it may also result in larger false rejects. Hence, detecting distortion is helpful to control the matcher performance.

Detection of distortion in a static fingerprint image is a difficult problem. Active force- and torque-sensing methods have been proposed [2] to improve the matcher performance. However, this method involves additional instrumentation of finger-print sensors and/or extra hardware to measure force and torque. A software-based method is more useful since even the existing systems can directly benefit from it. Senior and Bolle [3] propose a software-based technique for distortion removal from static images. From a single fingerprint image it is often difficult to get any distortion information. Since many live-scan fingerprint scanners are capable of acquiring several frames of the finger and typically provide signal output at a video frame rate, we propose the use of fingerprint video streams to investigate dynamic behaviors of fingerprints across multiple frames in this chapter. Use of video sequences also enables us to characterize distortions arising from specific finger motion patterns (e.g., application of torque to a finger).

In this chapter, we present an approach to estimate the dynamic behavior of fingerprints, especially distortion in fingerprint videos. Our approach is the first to date to process a fingerprint image sequence to extract its temporal behavior along with interframe (or field) motion information in order to detect plastic distortion. Some of the issues under our current study include (i) estimation of appropriate motion model parameters to characterize finger motion across frames in fingerprint videos, (ii) investigation of plastic distortions using interfield flow, and (iii) extraction of key frames based on the degree of distortion to provide *good* frames to the matcher.

Expanding on the theme of dynamic behavior during image capture, we introduce *resultant biometrics* in this chapter, a new type of biometrics that a subject produces through a series of controlled changes to an existing biometrics. This has a physiological, physical (e.g., force, torque, linear motion, rotation), and/or temporal characteristic, thus providing a new means that can be easily modified if the biometrics is compromised and that is harder to produce with spoof body parts.

The chapter is organized as follows. Our approach works on MPEG-{1,2} encoded image sequences. Therefore, a brief description of the MPEG compression standard relevant to our work is provided in Section 4.2. A novel approach to distortion detection is described in Section 4.3. In Section 4.4, the performance of our algorithm on the NIST-24 database is discussed. Section 4.5 introduces the concept of *resultant biometrics*, which adds a behavioral component to existing biometrics. Finally, we provide conclusions in Section 4.6.

4.2. MPEG Compression

The MPEG-2 video standard [4] aims at higher compression rates and contains all the progressive coding features of MPEG-1. In addition, MPEG-2 has a number of techniques for coding interlaced video.

A digital video sequence is a series of one or more images, often referred to as frames. MPEG-2 provides a choice of two picture structures to code a frame [4]. *Field pictures* consist of individual fields (assemblies of alternate lines of a frame) that are each divided into blocks (8×8 blocks of pixels) and macroblocks (MBs) (16×16 blocks), and coded separately [5]. A *frame picture* is one whose interlaced field pair is interleaved together into a frame, which is then divided into blocks and macroblocks, and coded. Thus, a frame can be encoded using two field pictures or a single frame picture. The pictures can be further coded as *I pictures*, *P pictures*, and *B pictures*. MPEG-2 video encoding utilizes five different motion compensation modes to reduce the temporal redundancy between adjacent pictures in an image sequence [5]: (i) frame prediction (just as in MPEG-1) for *frame pictures*; (ii) field prediction for *frame pictures*; (iii) field prediction for *field pictures*; (iv) 16×8 motion compensation for *field pictures*; and (v) dual-prime for P pictures. We refer the reader to [4] for a comprehensive discussion of these prediction schemes.

In order to capture behavioral characteristics in the frames of an MPEG-2 encoded fingerprint video, we exploit the motion vectors (MVs) of the MBs from each frame or field that provide the dynamic information in the bitstream. Especially for extraction of motion from video, direct analysis of compressed data is reasonable, as the motion information has already been encapsulated by the encoding process within the bitstream. However, a major difficulty with MPEG-2 encoded videos is that pictures in the sequences can be of different structures (frame pictures or field pictures); they can be of different types—I, P, or B frames or fields; and they can occur together in a variety of group of pictures (GOP) patterns. This poses difficulties in obtaining MVs directly from any frame in the stream without the knowledge of its frame type and coding specifics. The additional flexibility to predict MVs from different fields or frames (field prediction and frame prediction, to name a few) in MPEG-2 further aggravates the generation of consistent frame-to-frame motion information and comparison of MVs across different frame types. A more uniform set of motion vectors that can be extracted independently of the frame type, the picture structure, and the direction of prediction used during encoding becomes essential for a coherent motion analysis spanning multiple temporally contiguous frames. In Section 4.3.2 we briefly outline our technique to extract *flow*, a frame-type-independent uniform motion representation, reliably from the raw MVs embedded in MPEG-2-encoded video bitstreams.

4.3. Distortion Detection in Fingerprint Videos

Distortion in fingerprint sequences can be viewed as that of adding a dynamic component to static fingerprints, thus imposing a behavioral aspect on the physiological aspect of the finger that is normally captured by a fingerprint scanner. The appearance of a fingerprint image is changed over time by various factors: A user may exert force on the finger with respect to the sensing device that typically results in images with thick ridges. The force may vary at different time instants during the interval when the print is being obtained. Or a user may apply torque, which results in rotated fingerprint frames. Or it could be rolling a fingerprint, which results in frames containing partial views of the finger to full views. One can also envision a fingerprint sequence, in which a user uses a combination of translation, rotation, and force to embody specific patterns of movements across the scanner surface. All these result in sequences, where the fingerprints are continuously elastically deformed according to the force, torque, and roll employed.

Our approach employs a novel flow-based analysis of fingerprint frames in a compressed bitstream to detect distortion in a fingerprint video. Since MPEG-{1,2}-based compression is typically used to compress fingerprint image sequences, our approach directly works with the embedded information in the encoded bitstream, without having to decompress the bitstream into their individual images. This savings can be quite huge when large fingerprint images are sampled at high frame rates.

Our approach consists of the following processing steps:

Acquisition of compressed fingerprint videos (image sequences)
Flow estimation in compressed bitstreams
Selection of candidate distortion subsequences using attributes of flow
Interfield affine motion estimation in candidate frames
Curl estimation in candidate frames
Distortion detection based on curl estimates
A final grouping process to signal *distorted* and *undistorted* intervals for key frame selection

These steps are all described in detail in the following sections.

4.3.1. Acquisition of Fingerprint Video Streams

Fingerprints are obtained as a continuous sample of fingers placed on a scanning surface for a specific time interval, T ($= 10$ sec) and at a frame rate of 30 frames per second. The resultant sequence of gray-scale images are encoded into a video bitstream using MPEG-1 or MPEG-2 video compression standard. Many live-scan fingerprint scanners are capable of producing video frame rate outputs that can be easily directed to a real-time MPEG-2 compression system [6] to result in encoded bitstreams.

4.3.2. Flow Extraction in Compressed Domain

Since raw motion vectors (MVs) from MPEG-{1,2} video can be from different picture structures (frame pictures) in progressive scanning mode or field pictures in interlaced mode) and from different picture coding types (I, P, or B), which can occur in a variety of frame orderings (*IBBPBBPBBPBBI...*, *IPPPP...*, etc.), utilizing them directly in video analysis leads to problems in generation of consistent frame-to-frame motion information and in comparison of motion across different frame types. We make use of a frame-type-independent motion representation called *flow vectors* [7] for a coherent analysis spanning multiple temporally contiguous frames.

Our approach involves representing each MV in an MB in a picture regardless of its frame and picture type, with a backward-predicted vector determined with respect to the *next immediate field*. The set of backward-predicted vectors (called the *flow*) computed for each field in the stream then represents the direction of motion of each MB in the field with respect to the next field in the sequence. Observe that even if the picture in the video was encoded as a frame picture, our approach computes the flow fields for its top and bottom fields; this aids us in characterizing high motion changes that may be present even between fields of the frame. Further observe that not all MBs will necessarily have their associated flow vectors; but the number of such MBs is rarely large enough to affect our aggregate analysis of flow vectors. An input video stream consisting of frame and field pictures is thus transformed into a sequence of flow fields using our efficient flow estimation techniques. As a result of utilizing this frame/picture/motion-type-independent framework, a video stream that has been encoded into different bitstreams with differing IPB patterns can be analyzed easily under a single common framework and compared. We have developed accurate flow estimation procedures, and details relating to generation of reliable flow vectors from MPEG-2 encoded bitsreams are found in [7]. Our flow representation handles MPEG-1- as well as MPEG-2-specific enhancements related to picture structures, picture coding types, and additional motion compensation schemes. Experiments on thousands of frames from standard-definition and high-definition video bitstreams have demonstrated the good performance of our flow estimation process. These experiments also showed that the flow estimates generated from our algorithm were consistent and robust, leading to correct interpretation of motion occurring in video streams.

Thus, the flow of each macroblock present in a field (frame) in an MPEG-2 compressed fingerprint bitstream is computed without decompression. A sequence of three undistorted frames from a video sequence, *pf0_1* (see Section 4.4.1) obtained from the right index finger of a female subject, and their color-encoded flow representations obtained are shown in Figure 4.1. The frame size is 720×480 and the flow field size is 45×30. The dark points in the flow field indicate zero motion of the macroblocks. Likewise, a sequence of three *distorted* frames from the same video stream and their color-encoded flow fields are shown in Figure 4.2.

4.3.3. Detection of Candidate Distorted Frames

Using the flow computed for each frame in a given bitstream, we next determine frames that exhibit a high level of interfield motion activity. This filtering enables us to perform a first-level identification of those frames likely to contain a high degree of distortion. It is based on a novel measure, *Z2NZ* computed for each frame in the

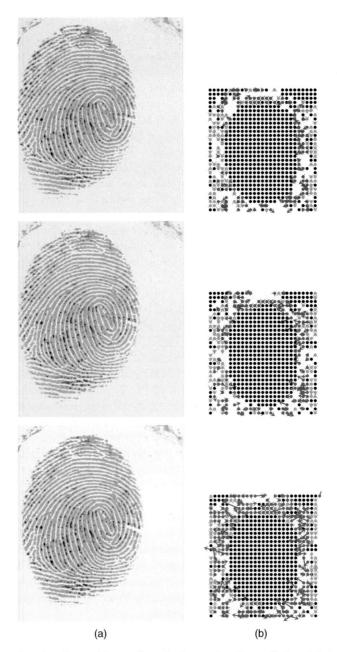

(a)   (b)

Fig. 4.1. Samples of undistorted frames from the fingerprint video, *pf0_1*, and their flow fields are shown in (a) and (b), respectively.

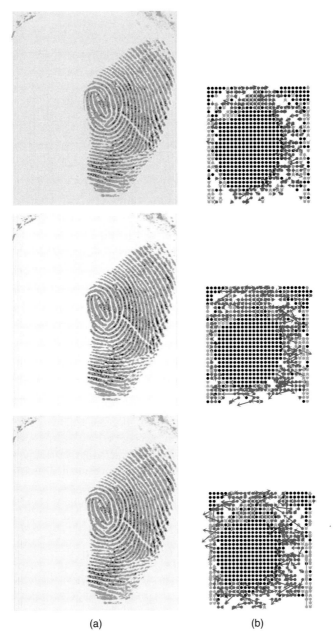

(a)   (b)

Fig. 4.2. Samples of *distorted* frames from *pf0_1*, and their flow fields are shown in (a) and (b), respectively.

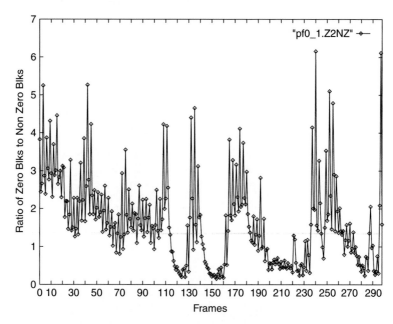

Fig. 4.3. A plot of the *Z2NZ* values for the fingerprint video stream *pf0_1*.

stream, which is defined as the ratio of the number of macroblocks of zero flow vectors to the number of macroblocks exhibiting nonzero flow vectors in a frame. During distortion, while a portion of the finger is held stationary, the rest of the finger is twisted, rolled, or pressed hard on the scanning surface. This results in a flow field in which a few zero flow macroblocks correspond to the stationary part of the finger and a substantial number of surrounding macroblocks show some nonzero flow. Thus, the measure *Z2NZ* provides a quantitative characterization of the flow present in the frame. If *Z2NZ* < 1, implying that macroblocks undergoing nonzero motion exceed those with no motion, the frame is deemed to be a candidate frame for a detailed distortion investigation. In Figure 4.3, the values of *Z2NZ* have been plotted for the sample fingerprint sequence, *pf0_1*.

4.3.4. Stationary Region Detection in Candidate Frames

When a person knowingly or unknowingly attempts to induce distortions in images of his or her fingers during signal capture, a portion of a finger may be held stationary and the rest of the finger around this pivotal unmoving region is pressed, twisted, and moved around to result in distorted frames. Observe that this fixed region need not be the center or the core associated with the fingerprint. Therefore, determining the unmoving region in a fingerprint frame aids in focusing the behavioral study around this region.

With the subset of candidate distorted frames determined above, our analysis proceeds further by identifying the stationary region in the fingerprint present in each frame using the flow field of the frame. A connected component analysis is performed on a candidate frame using zero flow as the basic macroblock merging criterion. This results in connected regions containing macroblocks that show absolutely no motion. The largest (in area) connected component is selected as the unmoving pivotal region around which further processing is carried out. We compute the bounding box of the pivotal region determined in the frame.

4.3.5. Affine Motion Estimation in Candidate Frames

For each candidate frame, we compute motion parameters from the fingerprint region around the pivotal component by imposing an affine motion model on the frame flow and sampling the moving region radially around the bounding box of the pivotal region. A parameterized model of image motion such as an affine motion model is invoked when it can be safely assumed that spatial variations of pixels in a region can be represented by a low-order polynomial [8]. With fingerprint frames, we are especially interested in studying the rotational and translational effects due to force and twist in finger movements; therefore, an affine model is deployed as a first-level approximation of our requirement to estimate rotation, translation, and scale parameters.

Six parameters, $a_1, \ldots, a_6$, are estimated in this process, where a_1 and a_4 represent horizontal and vertical translation, respectively, a_3 and a_5 correspond to rotation, and a_2 and a_6 correspond to scale. Within small regions, in our case, annular regions around the pivotal region in a candidate frame, the affine motion model is used to characterize the flow of a macroblock in the region:

$$u(x, y) = a_1 + a_2 x + a_3 y \tag{1}$$
$$v(x, y) = a_4 + a_5 x + a_6 y \tag{2}$$

where (x, y) denote the coordinates of a macroblock in the frame and (u, v), the flow vector associated with that macroblock.

Let us use the following notation:

$\mathcal{U}$ to denote $\begin{bmatrix} u & v \end{bmatrix}^T$

$\mathcal{X}$ to denote $\begin{bmatrix} 1 & x & y & 0 & 0 & 0 \\ 0 & 0 & 0 & 1 & x & y \end{bmatrix}^T$

$\boldsymbol{a}$ to denote $\begin{bmatrix} a_1 & a_2 & a_3 & a_4 & a_5 & a_6 \end{bmatrix}^T$

We estimate $\boldsymbol{a}$ by minimizing the error between the flow estimated for each macroblock using Eqs. (1) and (2) and its actual flow determined from the encoded bitstream:

$$S(\boldsymbol{a}) = \sum_x \sum_y \left[\left(\hat{u}_{xy} - u_{xy} \right)^2 + \left(\hat{v}_{xy} - v_{xy} \right)^2 \right] \tag{3}$$

where $\begin{bmatrix} \hat{u} & \hat{v} \end{bmatrix}^T$ is the estimated flow vector. We solve for $\boldsymbol{a}$ using the least-squares estimation technique [9]. For details about setting up the equations and their solutions to compute $\boldsymbol{a}$, we refer the reader to [9]. In our process of parameters estimation for each candidate frame, we employ regions of different radii, starting from the periphery of the bounding box of the pivotal region and incrementing the radius in unit step; all valid macroblocks in the region marked by each radius in the frame are used in the estimation.

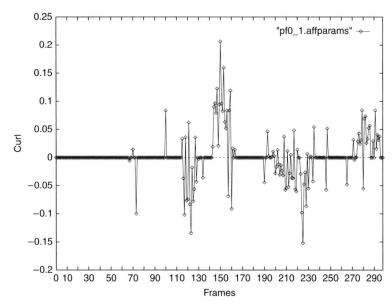

Fig. 4.4. Curl values for the candidate distortion frames in the fingerprint video stream *pf0_1*.

Once the affine transformation vector is determined, characterizing the behavior around the pivotal region, we compute the *curl* [10] in each frame j, $C_j = -a_3 + a_5$. The curl in each frame quantitatively provides the extent of rotation, or the spin of the finger skin around the pivotal region. The rotation about the viewing direction captured by curl proves to be useful in determining and describing the distortion. We also compute the magnitude of the translation vector, $T_j = (a_1, a_4)$ of the frame. Figure 4.4 shows the curl values estimated for the candidate distorted frames in *pf0_1*.

4.3.6. Final Selection of Distorted Frames

For each candidate frame, we next compute smoothed curl and translation magnitude values by computing the average values of curl and translation magnitude over its temporal neighborhood. The temporal window used for smoothing spans one tenth of a second, that is, over three frames. The candidate frames near the beginning and the end of the sequence retain their curl values if an adequate neighborhood cannot be established for smoothing. A sequence of fingerprint frames can be viewed at this juncture as a set of contiguous candidate distorted frames with substantial curl values separated by groups of undistorted frames.

In each group of contiguous candidate distorted frames, a simple thresholding classifier is employed to signal whether this interval contains distorted frames. This classifier takes into account the temporal extent of the distortion interval and the range of the curl values in its final determination of occurrence of distortion. If the temporal extent of a candidate group exceeds a threshold, t_b ($t_b = 0.1$ sec in our implementation), then it is established that the group cannot be a noisy blip but rather that it contains frames that have a low *Z2NZ* ratio and significant smoothed curl values. Therefore, that group is marked to contain distorted frames.

On the other hand, if the temporal length of a group is small (less than t_b), then the classifier investigates more closely to verify whether this small blip is a true distortion event. This is carried out using two sequential tests: (i) The first test checks whether the range of curl values of frames in this group exceeds a certain threshold $\mathcal{C}_v$; this establishes that there are abrupt and large changes in the curl values, which are indicators of distortion due to quick finger twist; (ii) the second test examines whether the maximum translation magnitude in this group of frames is less than a certain threshold, $\mathcal{T}_v$; this is to ensure that the group of frames does not undergo pure translation only, which can be due to the finger being merely moved around from one point on the scanning surface to another without any twist.

Once the group of frames is shown to possess high curl variation and low translation, the classifier labels the group as a true distortion group. If the curl variation is low, it is inferred that there is no strong evidence of distortion and the group is marked as an undistorted interval. Affine parameters of the selected distorted frames characterize the finger movements in frames in the distorted group, thus providing a sense of the dynamic behavior of the finger.

4.3.7. Grouping Distortion Intervals

Finally, a merging process is carried out to group consecutive intervals of frames possessing identical distortion flags to form large, meaningful intervals in the bitstream.

Each frame is given one of two labels, "distorted" or "undistorted." The labels of successive frames are compared to extract a grouped contiguous sequence of frames with identical labels. The presence of a few noisy labels (e.g., over one tenth of a second or three frames) within a sequence is tolerated and handled by assigning them the same label as that of the longer enveloping sequence. Key frames can be chosen for final matching from each "undistorted" interval by selecting the middle frame in the interval or the start, middle, and end frames of the interval, or by using other criteria such as frames containing large and sharp fingerprints. These key frames are expected to yield better matching scores with tighter tolerance values in the matching system.

4.3.8. Highlights of Our Approach

The advantages of our distortion detection scheme are the following: (i) Our technique can work on both compressed bitstreams and uncompressed image sequences. With compressed streams, we have shown that we could estimate the flow reliably using the raw motion vectors encoded in the streams. With uncompressed fingerprint image sequences, the optical flow between successive frames can be estimated using one of many well-established methods from the literature [11, 8]. (ii) With the latest fingerprint scanning systems that directly output compressed data, all our computations are performed directly in the compressed domain without decompressing the stream to generate an image sequence. This leads to less memory requirement and more efficient computations. (iii) Robust interfield flow extraction from raw motion vectors of an MPEG-2 compressed video bitstream is unique to our approach. (iv) Analysis of compressed fingerprint videos has not yet been reported in the literature, our work is the first to report a study of behavioral aspect of fingerprints over time. (v) A novel measure, *Z2NZ* ratio for first-level filtering of distorted frames, and a robust method for locating a nonmoving fingerprint region during distortion using the flow are included in our approach. (vi) It also demonstrates a viable software solution for distortion detection.

4.4. Experimental Results

Our scheme has been implemented and evaluated using several compressed bitstreams from the NIST 24 database [12].

4.4.1. NIST Special Database 24

The NIST Special Database 24 [12] contains MPEG-2 encoded videos of live-scan fingerprints. This collection contains two data sets:

1. The first data set contains 100 MPEG-2 video files obtained from 10 fingers of 5 males and 5 females; each video stream is 10 sec long obtained at 30 fps and a 720×480 frame resolution. The important point about this data set is that the prints are with plastic distortions. The distortions were induced by rolling and twisting each finger. Some blurring is also present in the data.

2. The second set also contains 100 MPEG-2 video files obtained from 10 fingers of 5 males and 5 females; each video stream is again 10 sec long, at 30 fps and a 720×480 frame resolution. This differs from the other set in that the fingerprints are obtained at various rotated angles of fingers. The finger rotation is from the left extreme to the right extreme. Sampling angles might not be uniform across different streams. The goal of this data collection was to create five evenly sampled rotated prints between the two extremes.

4.4.2. Performance

Twenty streams from the first data set, corresponding to 2 different fingers, left and right index fingers of 10 different people (both males and females), were manually analyzed and the frames were marked as those that exhibited distortion and those that did not. This ground truth was then compared with the distortion results obtained from our system to determine both false-positive and missing intervals. The thresholds, C_v and $\mathcal{T}_v$, were set to values, 0.5 and 1.0, respectively. These values were stably and consistently used in processing all 20 compressed bitstreams.

The presence and absence of distortion as detected by our technique are plotted for the video stream, *pf0_1* in Figure 4.5. The reported results completely agree with the ground truth. Table 4.1 summarizes the performance of our automatic distortion

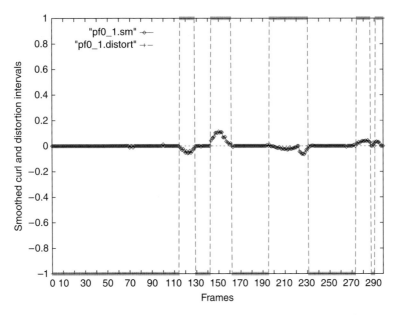

Fig. 4.5. Detected distortion intervals in the fingerprint video stream *pf0_1*.

Table 4.1. Results of Automatic Distortion Detection

Video stream	Correctly detected distortion intervals	Total false positive	Total missed	Ground truth distortion intervals
pf0_1.m2v	5	0	0	5
pf1_1.m2v	5	0	0	5
pf2_1.m2v	1	1	0	1
pf3_1.m2v	5	2	0	5
pf4_1.m2v	3	0	1	4
pm0_1.m2v	4	1	0	4
pm1_1.m2v	5	0	3	8
pm2_1.m2v	4	1	1	5
pm3_1.m2v	2	0	3	5
pm4_1.m2v	3	0	0	3
pf0_6.m2v	0	0	0	0
pf1_6.m2v	3	0	0	3
pf2_6.m2v	0	7	0	0
pf3_6.m2v	8	0	0	8
pf4_6.m2v	1	8	0	1
pm0_6.m2v	2	0	1	3
pm1_6.m2v	4	0	0	4
pm2_6.m2v	3	1	0	3
pm3_6.m2v	1	6	0	1
pm4_6.m2v	4	0	0	4

detection system on the test video streams. The correct detection rate is 87.5%, and the false-positive rate is 37.5% on the data tested. Note that falsely detected intervals are less damaging to the system performance compared to the missed ones. The table shows that the system performs quite well across videos acquired from varying fingers and varying subjects. The false-positive rate can be reduced if we establish thresholds to filter out distortion intervals more strictly. The current settings are on the conservative side to eliminate as many misses as possible. The false-positive distortion intervals help us to be extra cautious in our final selection of frames for matching.

4.5. Dynamic Behavior Modeling

Motivated by the success of the experiments discussed, we generalize the analysis of dynamic behavior in videos to define a new concept called the *resultant biometrics*. A resultant biometrics is a sequence of consecutive physiological or behavioral biometrics signals recorded at some sample rate producing the first biometrics signal plus a second biometric, namely the behavioral biometric, which is the way the physiological or behavioral biometric is transformed over some time interval. This transformation is the result of a series of user-controlled changes to the first biometric.

The core design principles underlying the proposed resultant biometrics are the following:

1. It is a new type of biometrics a subject produces through a series of *controlled* changes to an existing biometric.
2. It is a biometric modified through a series of user-controlled changes, which has a physiological, physical (e.g., force, torque, linear motion, rotation), and/or temporal characteristic.
3. It is an efficient way to modify compromised biometrics.
4. It is a biometric modified through a series of user-controlled changes, a combination of a traditional biometrics with a user-selected behavioral biometric.
5. It is a biometric that is harder to produce with spoof body parts.

These resultant biometrics are sequences of biometric signals over a short interval of time where the signals are modified according to some pattern. Resultant fingerprints or palmprints, for example, are consecutive print images where the subject exerts force, torque, and/or rolling (controlled change) over an image acquisition interval of time. The physical way the subject distorts the images is the behavioral part of the resultant biometrics, and the fingerprint or palmprint is the physiological part of the resultant biometric. An undistorted fingerprint image in combination with an expression of the distortion trajectory, which can be computed from the sequence of distorted fingerprint images, forms a more compact representation of the resultant fingerprint. A template representing the resultant fingerprint biometrics is derived from the traditional template representing the fingerprint or palmprint plus a template representing the behavior trajectory.

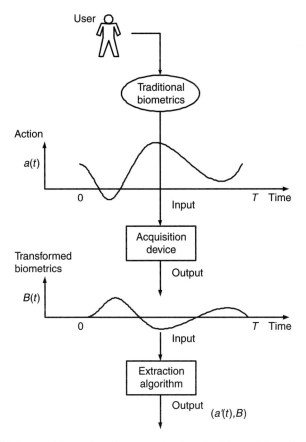

Fig. 4.6. Combining one biometric with user action (another biometric) to obtain a biometric that is modified through a series of user-controlled changes.

4.5.1. Examples of Resultant Biometrics

A generic flow diagram for combining a biometric with a user action, namely, combining biometrics at a subject level, is shown in Figure 4.6. The user action, just like the movement of a pen to produce a signature, is the second behavioral biometric. A user offers a traditional biometric for authentication or identification purposes. Such a biometric could be a fingerprint, iris, or face. However, rather than holding the biometric still, as in the case of a fingerprint or face, or keeping the eyes open, as in the case of iris recognition, the user performs some specific action, $a(t)$, with the biometrics. This action is performed over time, from time 0 to some time T. Hence, the action $a(t)$ is some one-dimensional function of time and acts upon the traditional biometric. Note that this biometric is the actual user's biometric and not a machine-readable biometrics signal (i.e., in the case of fingerprints, it is the three-dimensional finger with the print on it). During image/video acquisition, we can specify the constraints of the action, but within these constraints the user can define the action. That is, the action in some sense transforms the user's biometric over time. This transformed biometric is input to the biometric signal recording device. The output of this device is a sequence (series) of individually transformed biometrics signals $B(t)$ from time 0 to some time T. In the case of fingerprints, these are fingerprint images, in the case of faces, these are face images. This output sequence is the input to some extraction algorithm, which computes from the sequence of transformed biometrics the pair $(a'(t), B)$, which itself is a biometric. The function $a'(t)$ is an estimation of some behavioral way of transforming the biometric B over a time interval $[0, T]$ and is related to the function $a(t)$, which the user chooses (very much like a user would select a signature). The biometric B can be computed from the pair $(a'(t), B)$, that is, where $a(t)$ is zero; where there is no user action, the output is an undistorted digitization of biometrics. In general, it can be computed from the signal, where the biometric is not distorted.

Figure 4.7 is an example of a resultant fingerprint biometric where the user can rotate the finger on the fingerprint reader (without sliding over the glass platen).

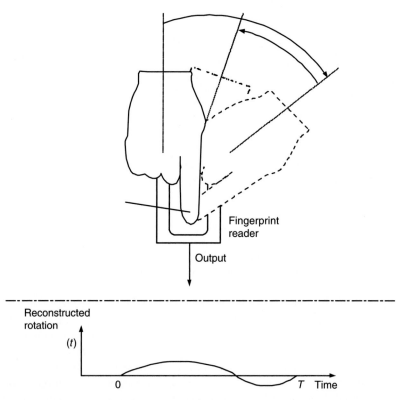

Fig. 4.7. Example of a resultant fingerprint biometrics where the user can rotate the finger on the scanner according to a pattern.

This rotation can be performed according to some user-defined angle as a function of time $a(t)$. The illustrated rotation takes place in the horizontal plane, the plane parallel to the glass platen of the fingerprint reader. The rotation function in this case is the behavioral part of the resultant fingerprint and is user-defined. (If this portion of the resultant biometric is compromised, the user can redefine this behavioral part of the resultant fingerprint.) The resultant fingerprint in this case is $(a(t), F)$ with F the undistorted fingerprint image. The undistorted fingerprint image is found where the rotation angle a is zero.

4.5.2. Extracting the Behavioral Component

In Fig. 4.8, a block diagram of a generic process for extracting the behavioral component from a resultant biometric is shown. The input is a sequence of biometric signals $B(t)$. First, contiguous biometric signals, $B(t+1)$ and $B(t)$, are processed through intersignal analysis. The results are used to extract the change, $a(t+1) - a(t)$, in the behavioral component. In turn, this gives the output $a(t)$ as a function of time, where $a(t)$ is the behavioral component of the resultant biometric $B(t)$. Added in this figure

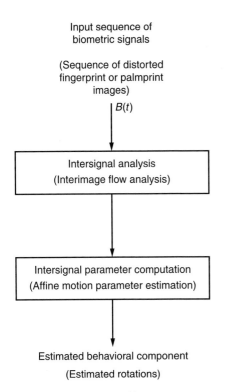

Input sequence of
biometric signals

(Sequence of distorted
fingerprint or palmprint
images)

$B(t)$

Intersignal analysis
(Interimage flow analysis)

Intersignal parameter computation
(Affine motion parameter estimation)

Estimated behavioral component

(Estimated rotations)

$a(t)$

Fig. 4.8. Process for extracting the behavioral component of a resultant biometric.

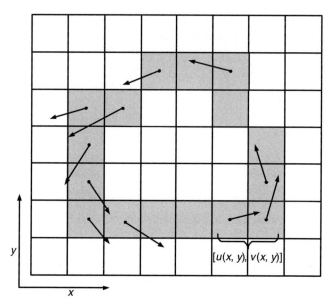

Fig. 4.9. Local flow computation on a block-by-block basis from the input resultant fingerprint image sequence.

are the specific steps (interimage flow analysis and affine motion parameter estimation) for estimating the finger rotation from a sequence of distorted fingerprint images produced as in Fig. 4.7.

Rotation from one fingerprint image to the next can be estimated from both an uncompressed image sequence or an MPEG-1 or MPEG-2 encoded [5] resultant fingerprint biometric video sequence. A flow characterization $[u(x, y), v(x, y)]$ (see Fig. 4.9) computed as a function of (x, y) and t of an image sequence is then a uniform motion representation amenable for consistent interpretation. The flow information between the images can be computed from the raw motion vectors encoded in the MPEG-1 or MPEG-2 image sequences [7]; if the input is uncompressed, the flow field can be estimated using existing motion estimation techniques [8].

By examining the flow $[u(x, y), v(x, y)]$ in the blocks of an image sequence, a largest connected component of zero-motion blocks, pictured by a pivotal region in Fig. 4.10a, is determined as described in Section 4.3. Affine motion A can transform a square shape as shown in Fig. 4.10b and quantifies translation, rotation, and shear of the movement. Further analysis is performed as presented in Section 4.3 to estimate the affine motion parameters from the fingerprint region. The curl computed from each frame quantitatively provides the extent of rotation and is an expression $C(t)$ of the behavioral component of the resultant fingerprint. Based on an analysis of the dynamic behavior as well as the basic biometrics, a better biometrics recognition system can be achieved.

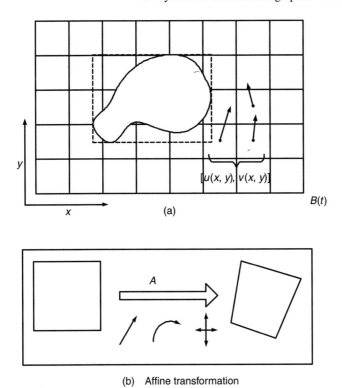

(a)

(b)   Affine transformation

Fig. 4.10. Computation of the curl or the spin of the finger as a function of time, which is the behavioral component of the resultant fingerprint.

4.6. Conclusion

We proposed a flow-based structural distortion detection method for analysis of compressed fingerprint image sequences. This is part of our ongoing study of dynamic behaviors of fingerprints using fingerprint video streams. Our software solution can be used with existing frame rate live-scan fingerprint scanners. Our distortion detection system has been evaluated using streams from the NIST 24 database—a public database of compressed fingerprint videos—and validated against the ground truth marked by us. The results are extremely positive. The underlying techniques can be used to understand and estimate other types of dynamic behavior in biometrics videos. We introduced a new concept called the "resultant biometrics"—a new type of biometrics a subject produces through a series of controlled changes, which has a physiological, physical (e.g., force, torque, linear motion, rotation), and/or temporal characteristic, added to an existing biometric. The proposed resultant biometric is efficient in terms of easy modification of compromised biometrics and is harder to produce with spoof body parts.

References

1. Ratha, N. K., K. Karu, S. Chen, and A. K. Jain, A real-time matching system for large fingerpring database, *IEEE Trans. on Pattern Analysis and Maching Intelligence*, 18:799–813, Aug. 1996.
2. Ratha, N. K., and R. M. Bolle, Effect of controlled image acquisition on fingerprint matching, *Proc. of the 14th IAPR Intl. Conf. on Pattern Recognition*, Brisbane, Australia, A. K. Jain, S. Venkatesh, and B. C. Lovell, eds., Vol. II, pp. 1659–1661, Aug. 1998.
3. Senior, A., and R. Bolle, Improved fingerprint matching by distrotion removal, *IEICE Trans. on Information and Systems, Spl. Issue on Biometrics*, pp. 825–832, July 2001.
4. Joint Technical Committee ISO/IEC JTC 1, ISO/IEC 13818-2. Information technology—generic coding of moving pictures and associated audio information, Video, May 1996.
5. Haskell, B. G., A. Puri, and A. N. Netravali, *Digital Video: An Introduction to MPEG-2*, New York: Chapman and Hill, 1997.
6. Optibase Inc., MPEG fusion, *MPEG-2 Encoder*, 1997.
7. Dorai, C. and V. Kobla, Extracting motion annotations from MPEG-2 compressed video for HDTV content management application, *Proc. Intl. Conference on Multimedia Computing and Systems*, Vol. 1 Florence, Italy, pp. 673–678, June 1999.
8. Bergen, J., P. Anandan, K. Hanna, and R. Hingorani, Hierarchical model-based motion estimation, *2nd European Conference on Computer Vision*, pp. 237–252, 1992.
9. Meng, J. and S.-F. Chang, CVEPS—A compressed video editing and parsing system, *Proc. ACM Multimedia 96 Conference*, Boston, MA, Nov. 1996.
10. Black, M. J. and Y. Yacoob, Tracking and recognizing rigid and non-rigid facial motions using local parametric models of image motion, *ICCV*, Boston, MA, pp. 374–381, 1995.
11. Lucas, B. and T. Kanade, An iterative image registration technique with an application to stereo vision, in *7th Intl. Joint Conference on Artificial Intelligence*, pp. 674–679, April 1981.
12. Watson, C. I., NIST Special Database 24 digital video of live-scan fingerprint data, National Institute of Standards and Technology, July 1998.

Chapter 5

Computer Enhancement and Modeling of Fingerprint Images

B.G. Sherlock

Abstract. The chapter discusses computer enhancement of fingerprint images, as well as the mathematical modeling of fingerprint ridge structure.

Fingerprints have local properties such as ridge orientation and ridge spacing that are well defined in the neighborhood of each point but vary continuously over the image. They are therefore ideal candidates for anisotropic filtering, which is able to adapt to the changing values of these position-dependent local properties, particularly ridge orientation. A detailed description is given of an enhancement technique based on the use of anisotropic, nonstationary Fourier domain filters. Fingerprints are first smoothed using a directional filter whose orientation is everywhere matched to the local ridge orientation. A local average thresholding then yields the enhanced image. Extension of this approach to a general method for performing nonstationary enhancement of images is discussed. A detailed evaluation of the enhancement algorithm in comparison with that contained in a working Automatic Fingerprint Recognition (AFR) system is given.

A mathematical model of the fingerprint local ridge orientation as a function of position within the image is developed. This model expresses the local ridge orientation in terms of the position of the singular (core and delta) points within the image and provides a theoretical framework within which the processing (for example, smoothing and interpolation) of ridge orientation data may be accomplished. This model provides an intelligent tool for resolving ambiguities due to the periodic nature of orientation in algorithms for interpreting fingerprint patterns. It provides a simple, powerful, and accurate means allowing such operations as smoothing of a noisy ridge orientation field and interpolating between spatially separated samples of fingerprint ridge orientation.

5.1. Introduction

Several stages of processing take place when an Automatic Fingerprint Identification System (AFIS) is used to match an unknown fingerprint. The print is first *enhanced* to remove noise and other irrelevant information. The enhanced image is *encoded* into a form suitable for comparison with the records held in the AFIS database. The encoded record consists of information describing the positions of the fingerprint's key attributes, called *minutiae*, and their spatial relationships. *Matching* is then performed by comparing the encoded record against those held in the database, thereby generating a short list of most likely candidate matches. Finally, in the *verification* stage, a fingerprint expert visually compares the unknown print with the short list of candidates, determining which (if any) is the correct match. The enhancement stage provides the only information available to the later stages. Consequently, the performance of an entire AFIS depends critically on the quality of enhancement achieved.

This chapter discusses the topics of fingerprint enhancement and of modeling of fingerprint ridge orientation. The enhancement algorithm described here makes use of directional filtering that is performed in the Fourier domain rather than spatially and over the entire image rather than within small blocks. This reduces noise more effectively, because the value assigned to each pixel is not based solely on a small neighborhood. The enhancement consists of a filtering stage followed by a thresholding stage. The filtering stage produces a directionally smoothed version of the image from which most of the unwanted information ("noise") has been removed but which still contains the desired information (i.e., the ridge structure and minutiae). The thresholding stage produces the binary, enhanced image.

Fingerprints exhibit everywhere a well-defined local ridge orientation (LRO) and a ridge spacing (LRS). The enhancement algorithm takes advantage of this regularity of spatial structure by filtering the image with a position-dependent directional Fourier domain filter whose passband is everywhere matched to the local ridge orientation and spacing.

This chapter also describes a model of fingerprint ridge orientation (LRO, local ridge orientation). The model incorporates an understanding of the topology of fingerprints and is therefore of value in the interpretation of fingerprint images.

Two distinct types of directionality exist, one described by the mathematics of vectors and the other by the direction field of differential geometry. The directionality within fingerprint images is of the type best described by direction fields. The model describes LRO as a direction field having singular points at the cores and deltas of the fingerprint. It correctly represents the pattern of ridge flow around each singular point and exhibits the Poincaré indices characteristic of fingerprint images. Although the model correctly represents the topological behavior of LRO, it does not provide accurate pointwise approximation to the true values. Therefore, its utility lies not in providing accurate orientation values but in providing knowledge about their behavior.

Ambiguities caused by the multivalued nature of orientation can cause difficulty during the processing of orientations. The model is able to resolve these ambiguities. To demonstrate its usefulness we apply it to the problem of two-dimensional interpolation between sampled values of LRO from real fingerprints. The model assists with "unwrapping" the orientations during the interpolation process, thereby removing the ambiguities and allowing us to apply classical interpolation techniques.

Section 5.2 describes the image enhancement algorithm. Section 5.2.2 describes Fourier domain filtering in analog terms, and implementation of the filters for digital processing of fingerprints is covered in Section 5.2.3. Section 5.2.4 discusses the estimation of the LRO parameter for the filters. The enhancement algorithm is presented in full in Section 5.2.5, results presented in Section 5.2.6, and results evaluated in Section 5.2.7.

Section 5.3 describes the mathematical model of fingerprint ridge topology. After an introduction in Section 5.3.1, the model is presented in detail in Section 5.3.2, and Section 5.3.3 discusses its use in resolving ambiguities that occur during orientation unwrapping and interpolation of orientations. Conclusions are provided in Section 5.4, followed by a list of references.

5.2. Enhancing Fingerprint Images by Directional Fourier Filtering

5.2.1. Introduction

This section describes a fingerprint enhancement algorithm [35] for Automated Fingerprint Recognition Systems (AFIS). AFIS systems depend critically on high-quality enhancement. The algorithm is shown here to improve the speed and accuracy of a particular AFIS, namely, that developed by the U.K. Home Office.

5.2.1.1. Background

The importance of ridge orientation in fingerprint image processing is well established; indeed, many results describing directionality in general images have been applied to fingerprints [3, 10, 12, 24, 42]. Applications requiring knowledge of ridge orientation include enhancement/segmentation [17, 18, 21, 22], detection of singular points [38], ridge detection during preprocessing [40], postprocessing to reduce numbers of false minutiae [41], and fingerprint pattern classification [9, 11, 20, 27].

Fingerprint enhancement algorithms sometimes involve little more than local average thresholding [1, 20, 28]. Methods that require higher noise immunity, such as those used operationally in AFIS systems [19, 30], usually precede the thresholding with directional smoothing. By estimating the local ridge orientations in the fingerprint image, one may construct an "orientation image," giving the ridge orientation at each pixel position. Mehtre et al. [17, 18] describe an enhancement algorithm based on statistics derived from the orientation image. O'Gorman and Nickerson [21, 22] enhance fingerprints by applying oriented, matched spatial filter masks, where the mask orientation is determined by the orientation image.

Ratha et al. [29] compute an orientation flow field, picturing the fingerprint as a textured image. From the flow field, adaptive filters are designed for the input image, and a waveform projection-based ridge segmentation algorithm used. Hong et al. [13, 14] describe enhancement techniques using a Gabor filter bank. The filters are characterized by orientation, frequency, and sensitivity. Kamei and Mizoguchi [15] define an energy function for selecting image features from a set of bandpass-filtered images according to a smoothness measure. Kim and Park [16] enhance fingerprints using adaptive normalization determined from the statistics of each image block. Ghosal et al. [5] propose an enhancement where a set of filters is learned using the learn-from-example paradigm, based on ground truth information for ridges in a set of representative fingerprint images. Connell et al. [2] present a model-based fingerprint image enhancement algorithm that makes use of a weak model about the image formation process. The model characterizes the general appearance of the fingerprint image. Park et al. [25] present an enhancement algorithm based on the directional filter bank. This is a maximally decimated, perfect reconstruction filter bank that decomposes wedge-shape frequency components using a 1D filter prototype. Randolph and Smith [26] make use of a binary directional filter bank that outputs a binary image set comprised of directional components. Through manipulation of the subbands, specific features within the fingerprint can be enhanced.

5.2.1.2. Overview of the Enhancement Algorithm

The major difference between the approach presented here and previous techniques is that here the directional filtering is performed in the Fourier domain rather than spatially, over the entire image rather than within small blocks. This reduces noise more effectively, because the value assigned to each pixel is not based solely on a small neighborhood.

The enhancement consists of a filtering stage followed by a thresholding stage. The filtering stage produces a directionally smoothed version of the image from which most of the unwanted information ("noise") has been removed, but that still contains the desired information (i.e., the ridge structure and minutiae). The thresholding stage produces the binary, enhanced image.

Fingerprints exhibit everywhere a well-defined local ridge orientation and ridge spacing. The enhancement algorithm takes advantage of this regularity of spatial structure by filtering the image with a position-dependent directional Fourier domain filter whose passband is everywhere matched to the local ridge orientation and spacing.

Figure 5.1 illustrates the enhancement process. Although the directional filter is position-dependent, it is implemented using several position-independent Fourier filters. Choosing a representative set of quantized directions, we define a set of di-

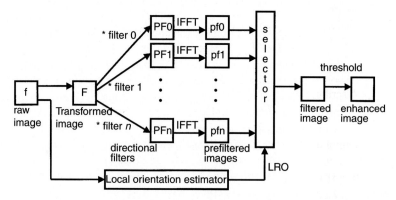

Fig. 5.1. Block diagram of the fingerprint enhancement algorithm.

rectional filters that, when applied to the original image, yield a set of directionally filtered images. We shall call these the "prefiltered images" (see Fig. 5.1).

The filtered image is then built up by selecting, for each pixel position, the pixel value from the prefiltered image whose direction of filtering corresponds most closely to the actual ridge orientation at that position (see Fig. 5.1). In order to perform this selection operation, knowledge of the actual ridge orientation is required, and this is obtained by estimation from the original image. The selection process is indicated in Fig. 5.1 by the box labeled "selector."

Finally, the thresholding stage binarizes the directionally filtered image using a local average as the threshold surface.

5.2.2. Fourier Domain Filtering of Fingerprint Images

This section is presented in terms of infinite-extent analog images and filters. Discretization of the images and filters is deferred to Section 5.2.3.

5.2.2.1. Local Ridge Parameters

Fingerprints consist of a pattern of locally parallel ridges, interrupted by minutiae, the fundamental types of which are ridge endings and bifurcations. The ridge structure defines everywhere a direction of ridge "flow," called the local ridge orientation (LRO). Two types of singular points, cores and deltas, form isolated singularities of the otherwise continuous LRO function. The position and relationship of the minutiae make a fingerprint unique—not the singular points or general classification types [4]. In addition, a local spatial frequency is determined everywhere by the local ridge spacing (LRS). The LRS is constrained within a range of values (typically 2:1 within a single print, or 4.5:1 over all prints).

In fingerprint image processing, one has the advantage of a well-defined local frequency and orientation of information. In forming the Fourier transform of the image, the immediate neighborhood of each point contributes (to first approximation) a single frequency component. The LRS determines its distance from the Fourier origin, and the LRO determines its angular position.

Our approach is to center the passband of a filter over this component. We define in this way an anisotropic, nonstationary bandpass filter that depends parametrically on the LRS and the LRO. This filter is applied at each point of the image, with the LRO and LRS as position-dependent parameters that determine the location of the passband. Values of LRS and LRO at each point are required; these are estimated from the image data. This filter passes the ridge information while eliminating most of the noise, since the noise is not localized in the same way as the ridge information. It is, of course, important that real minutiae are not discarded as noise. We show in our evaluation that this does not occur.

The present section develops the basic bandpass filter. The problem of parameter estimation is deferred to Section 5.4.

5.2.2.2. Directional Bandpass Filters

Using polar coordinates (ρ, φ), express the filter as a separable function:

$H(\rho, \phi) = H_{\text{radial}}(\rho) \cdot H_{\text{angle}}(\phi)$ in order to allow independent manipulation of its directional and radial frequency responses. $H_{\text{radial}}(\rho)$ depends on LRS, and $H_{\text{angle}}(\phi)$ on the LRO.

Any good, classical one-dimensional bandpass filter would be adequate for $H_{\text{radial}}(\rho)$; the Butterworth filter was chosen because its implementation is simpler than such alternatives as the Chebyshev or elliptic filter, especially if one wants to vary the filter order n. The expression for this filter is

$$H_{\text{radial}}(\rho) = \sqrt{\frac{(\rho \, \rho_{BW})^{2n}}{(\rho \, \rho_{BW})^{2n} + (\rho^2 - \rho_0^2)^{2n}}}$$

where ρ_{BW} and ρ_0 are the desired bandwidth and center frequency, respectively. A value of $n = 2$ worked well and was used throughout.

In designing $H_{\text{angle}}(\phi)$, one cannot be guided by analogy to one-dimensional filters, because there is no meaningful one-dimensional concept of orientation. Knutsson et al. [12] use the following function in their development of anisotropic "kernels" for their GOP image processor [8]:

$$H_{\text{angle}}(\phi) = \begin{cases} \cos^2 \dfrac{\pi}{2} \dfrac{(\phi - \phi_c)}{\phi_{BW}} & \text{if } |\phi| < \phi_{BW} \\ 0 & \text{otherwise} \end{cases}$$

where ϕ_{BW} is the "angular bandwidth" of the filter, or the range of angles for which $|H_{\text{angle}}(\phi)| \geq 0.5$. The ϕ_c is its "orientation," that is, the angle at which $|H_{\text{angle}}|$ is maximum.

If $\phi_{BW} = \pi/n$ for some integer n, then we can define n directional filters with equally spaced orientations $\phi_c = i\pi/n, i = 0, \ldots, n - 1$. These filters sum to unity everywhere; therefore, they separate an image into n "directional components," which sum to the original image.

5.2.3. Implementation of the Filter

5.2.3.1. Discretization of the Filter

The previous section is presented in terms of infinite-extent analog images and filters. To implement our filter on a digital computer, the images must be spatially sampled, and the continuous Fourier transform is replaced by the discrete Fourier transform (DFT). All images are sampled at a resolution of 512 by 512 pixels. Edge effects in the DFT were reduced using a separable split-cosine window with a 10% taper.

One method of discretizing an analog filter is the bilinear transform with prewarping of the center and cut-off frequencies [23]. If these frequencies are well below the sampling frequency, the bilinear transform/prewarping design is closely approximated simply by sampling the analog filter. This approach was used because the center frequency of 50 pixel units and bandwidth of 80 units were well below the sampling frequency of 256 units.

5.2.3.2. Obtaining a Set of Prefiltered Images

The position dependence of the filter implies a different filtering action for each pixel position. Direct implementation as an explicit function of position involves considerable computational effort. Noting that the direct dependence of the filter is on LRO and LRS rather than position, an approximation substantially reduces the computation. Choosing a representative set of values for LRO and LRS determines some number n of different stationary filters. Applying these to the image yields n "prefiltered images" (see Fig. 5.1). The filtered fingerprint is then built up by scanning the input fingerprint, selecting at each point the pixel value from whichever prefiltered image corresponds to the LRS and LRO values closest to the true values.

Care must be taken when choosing discrete values of LRS and LRO for generating prefiltered images. Obviously it is desirable to keep the number of prefiltered images small, but this must be done without unacceptable degradation of the final filtered image. Two approaches help to achieve this:

1. *Elimination of the LRS parameter*: As already mentioned, the LRS parameter is constrained in range. By increasing the bandwidth of the filter so that it tolerates variations of LRS within its expected range, LRS may be assumed constant. The wider bandwidth results in lower attenuation of noise, but many fewer prefiltered images are required. This approach also eliminates the need to estimate LRS.

2. *Coarser discretization of LRO*: The number of discrete values of the LRO may be reduced if intermediate values are dealt with by interpolating between pixel values from prefiltered images rather than by selecting the pixel value from one of them. This implementation uses linear interpolation.

With the LRS parameter eliminated, the number of discrete orientations equals the number of prefiltered images. An angular bandwidth of $\pi/8$ was chosen, allowing the LRO to be estimated to the nearest $\pi/16$. This implies a minimum of eight orientations. For the sake of caution, 16 equally spaced orientations were used. This corresponds to 16 prefiltered images organized as 2 sets of 8 directional components. We refer to these 16 prefiltered images as $fp_i(x, y), i = 0, \ldots, 15$. Results produced using eight orientations were found to be almost indistinguishable from those presented here.

5.2.3.3. Regions of High Ridge Curvature

High ridge curvature occurs where the LRO changes rapidly, that is, near cores and deltas. Far from these singular points, ridge curvature tends asymptotically to zero. In regions of higher curvature, a wider range of orientations is present. The angular bandwidth of the directional filter must therefore increase near singular points.

Away from singular points, the angular bandwidth is $\pi/8$, as discussed earlier. The angular bandwidth must equal π at singular points since all orientations are present.

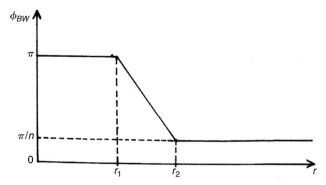

Fig. 5.2. Filter angular bandwidths near singular points. The graph shows the angular bandwidth as a function of the distance r to the nearest core or delta point.

Figure 5.2 shows an empirical piecewise linear relationship giving angular bandwidth as a function of distance from the nearest singular point. Values of $r_1 = 0$ and $r_2 = 20$ pixels are used throughout.

Where necessary, the effect of a filter of wider bandwidth than $\pi/8$ is simulated by an appropriately weighted combination of pixel values from two or more prefiltered images.

5.2.4. Estimation of the LRO Parameter

The value of the LRO at each pixel (i.e., the orientation image) is required as parametric input to the filter. Because determining the LRO reliably can be computationally demanding, it may not be feasible to estimate the LRO directly for every pixel. Our approach is to determine the LRO at a square grid spaced (say) 16 pixels apart and obtain intermediate values by interpolation. An alternative, equally acceptable approach is to use a faster-running but perhaps less reliable algorithm to estimate orientation at every pixel position and to smooth the resultant orientation image [17, 18]. Either approach could, of course, be used in conjunction with our filter.

Other researchers have worked with LRO values determined as one of four [20] or eight [28] possible orientations. This algorithm determines the LRO as one of 16 orientations $\theta_i = i\pi/16$, $i = 0, \ldots, 15$, that is, to a precision of $\pm\pi/32$.

5.2.4.1. Algorithm for Estimating the LRO at a Point

A window of size 32 by 32 pixels is centered at the point where the LRO is to be found. This window is rotated to 16 different orientations, $\theta_i = i\pi/16$, for $i = 0$ to 15. At each orientation a projection along the y-axis of the window is formed:

$$p_i(x) = \frac{1}{32} \sum_{y=0}^{31} W_i(x, y), \qquad x = 0, \ldots, 31$$

where $W_i(x, y)$ is the data inside the window at angle θ_i.

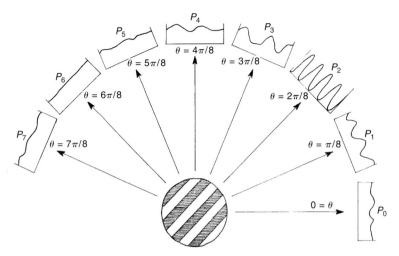

Fig. 5.3. Projections of a window of fingerprint image data. The projection that exhibits the greatest variation corresponds to the orientation of the ridges within the window (here $\theta = 2\pi/8$). For clarity, 8 rather than 16 projections are shown.

When the window is aligned with its x-axis perpendicular to the ridges, one expects maximum variation of the projection (since ridges are crossed as x varies, the gray-scale values will change over a wide range). Alignment of the x-axis along the ridges should lead to minimum variation (no ridges crossed implies smaller changes in gray-scale values). This is illustrated in Fig. 5.3.

A second-order Butterworth bandpass filter removes noise from the projections. The total variation V_i of each filtered projection $fp_i(x)$ is evaluated:

$$V_i = \sum_{x=0}^{31} |fp_i(x+1) - fp_i(x)|$$

The LRO estimate is given by $i_{max}\,\pi/16$, where $V_{i_{max}}$ is the maximum of the 16 variations. This algorithm produces the correct value of the LRO except in the noisiest regions. The typical failure rate for inked fingerprints is approximately 0.5%. Incorrect estimates can be dealt with using the model of the LRO described later in this chapter.

5.2.5. Fingerprint Enhancement by Directional Filtering

Previous sections developed a position-dependent anisotropic filter and means to estimate the LRO parameter, which it requires. This section brings these results together to present an algorithm that produces high-quality enhancements of fingerprint images. The enhancement algorithm consists of directional filtering followed by thresholding. The following description may be understood by reference to Fig. 5.1.

5.2.5.1. Directional Filtering

The input to this first stage consists of a 512 by 512-pixel raw fingerprint image and a 30 by 30 array of LRO values. The filtering algorithm follows:

1. Obtain 16 prefiltered images PF[i] from the raw fingerprint PRINT, as described by the following pseudocode:

       Window the image, to reduce edge effects.
       Take the 2D DFT of the windowed image.
       for i:=0 to 15 do
           Multiply this by the ith filter function, and
           inverse transform this to get the ith
           prefiltered image PF[i].
       endfor

2. Obtain the LRO at each point by interpolation between the 30 by 30 sampled values.

3. Form the output image OUT(x,y) by an appropriate combination of pixel values from the prefiltered images, as follows:

       for x:=0 to 511 do
         for y:=0 to 511 do

           Determine the distance r from (x, y) to the nearest singular point. Using the function in Fig. 5.2, determine the angular bandwidth that is required, and hence the number j of prefiltered images that must be combined.

           Form the output pixel OUT(x, y) as a weighted average of the (x, y) pixels of the j prefiltered images nearest in orientation to the LRO [as determined in step (2) above].

         endfor
       endfor

The result of applying this algorithm is a filtered image that has been smoothed in the direction of the ridges. Additionally, only wavelengths within the permissible range of ridge spacings have been passed. Figures 5.4a and b show a fingerprint image and the filtered image produced by the above algorithm. Some of the 16 prefiltered images are shown in Fig. 5.5.

5.2.5.2. Thresholding

The output of the filtering stage is an image that renders the fingerprint ridge structure in the form of smooth gray-scale "ripples" with very little residual noise. The thresholding stage converts this into a binary image where pixels located on ridges are black, and pixels not on ridges are white. Local average thresholding within 32 by 32-pixel neighborhoods yields the following threshold surface:

$$g_T(x, y) = \frac{1}{32^2} \sum_{i=0}^{31} \sum_{j=0}^{31} f(x - 16 + i, y - 16 + j)$$

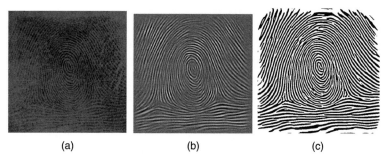

(a)   (b)   (c)

Fig. 5.4. Stages of the fingerprint enhancement process: (a) raw fingerprint; (b) after filtering; (c) after thresholding.

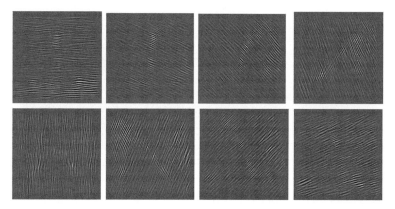

Fig. 5.5. Eight of the 16 directionally filtered versions of Fig. 5.4a. These are the prefiltered images combined to generate Fig. 5.4b.

where $f(x, y)$ is the filtered image, and $g_T(x, y)$ is the value of the threshold at the point (x, y).

The binary image produced as the output of the thresholding stage is the enhanced fingerprint (Fig. 5.4c). This image is intended to be close to the idealized one "imagined" by a trained fingerprint officer when examining a raw print.

5.2.6. Results

The enhancement algorithm was applied to 14 inked fingerprint images of various classification types. Figure 5.6 shows a representative sample of these images, together with their filtered and enhanced versions.

5.2.7. Evaluation of Results

Image enhancement has been defined [7] as the processing of an image so that the enhanced version is more suitable than the original for a specific application. The quality of this fingerprint enhancement technique should therefore be judged in terms of the

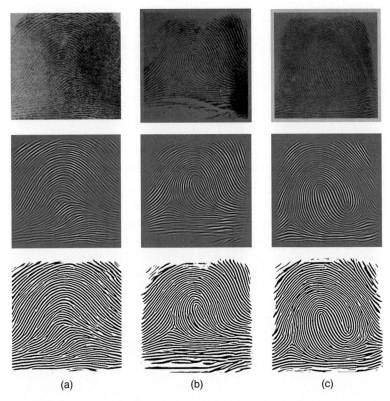

(a)   (b)   (c)

Fig. 5.6. Enhancements of inked fingerprints of (a) plain arch, (b) loop, and (c) double loop classification types. For each fingerprint, the images shown are raw image (top), filtered image (middle), and thresholded enhancement (bottom).

suitability of the enhanced prints for the specific application of personal identification using an AFIS.

To perform the evaluation, use was made of the AFIS developed by the Home Office in the United Kingdom [19]. First, two enhancements of each fingerprint were obtained, one using the Home Office algorithm, and the other using the algorithm presented here. These enhancements were both submitted to the encoding stage of the Home Office AFIS, and the encoded outputs were then compared quantitatively.

The encoding stage of this AFIS consists of two phases:

1. *Minutiae detection.* Analysis of the enhanced image yields a list of candidate minutiae. Among these are usually a large proportion of "false minutiae," that is, points that have been incorrectly identified as minutiae. These are further categorized into "hard" and "soft" false minutiae. Soft false minutiae are caused by noisy imperfections in the enhanced image, such as jagged ridge edges, isolated dots, and small holes in the ridges. Hard false minutiae occur where the enhanced image possesses apparently true minutiae that are not present in the original fingerprint. Distinction between hard and soft minutiae can be done by a human fingerprint expert.

2. *Minutiae reduction.* Further processing of the image and minutiae list removes most of the false minutiae. Unfortunately, this often yields "missed minutiae," in other words, the removal of true minutiae from the list.

Table 5.1 shows numbers of minutiae found by phase (1), numbers of minutiae remaining after phase (2), and processing times for phase (2). A human fingerprint expert determined "ground truth" numbers of minutiae within each print, as well as the numbers of missed and false minutiae remaining after the completion of phase (2). These numbers are presented in Table 5.2, which also includes sensitivities and specificities, defined as follows:

$$\text{Sensitivity} = 1 - \frac{\text{Missed minutiae (after reduction)}}{\text{Ground truth number of minutiae}}$$

$$\text{Specificity} = 1 - \frac{\text{False minutiae (after reduction)}}{\text{Ground truth number of minutiae}}$$

Tables 5.1 and 5.2 yield the following comparisons between the two enhancement algorithms:

1. *Total number of candidate minutiae detected (before reduction).* This indicates the relative degree of noisiness of the two enhancements, since noisy artifacts cause false minutiae. In every case, considerably more minutiae were detected on the Home Office enhancements. The Home Office enhancements generated 319.5 minutiae per image (3.50 times ground truth). The proposed algorithm generated 133.7 minutiae per image (1.43 times ground truth).

Table 5.1. Results of Application of Home Office Minutiae Detection and Reduction Algorithms to Enhanced Fingerprint Images

Fingerprint number	Total minutiae found by minutiae detection		Minutiae remaining after minutiae reduction		Time to perform minutiae reduction (seconds)	
	a	b	a	b	a	b
1	114	402	84	100	35	125
2	113	313	71	78	30	92
3	190	560	79	122	53	200
4	143	355	77	92	45	100
5	165	409	88	122	52	128
6	132	300	80	99	40	87
7	132	243	82	118	44	72
8	125	233	86	122	45	75
9	169	467	78	101	51	164
10	98	310	68	89	28	85
11	95	333	64	82	31	98
12	116	214	89	92	40	61
13	139	226	85	105	38	75
14	158	237	114	135	55	79
15	116	190	74	92	36	57

a. Using enhancement algorithm proposed here.
b. Using Home Office enhancement algorithm.

Table 5.2. Analysis of Enhanced Fingerprints by Fingerprint Expert

Fingerprint number	Ground truth (true number of minutiae)	False minutiae		Missed minutiae		Sensitivity (%)		Specificity (%)	
		a	b	a	b	a	b	a	b
1	87	8	24	9	11	90	87	91	72
2	—	—	—	—	—	—	—	—	—
3	74	18	52	13	4	82	95	76	30
4	—	—	—	—	—	—	—	—	—
5	102	6	29	20	9	80	91	94	72
6	92	9	18	19	9	79	90	90	80
7	113	4	15	27	10	76	91	97	87
8	107	4	24	25	9	77	92	96	78
9	84	17	41	23	24	73	71	80	51
10	83	3	16	18	10	78	88	96	81
11	80	7	16	23	14	71	83	91	80
12	92	6	10	9	10	90	89	94	89
13	108	0	10	23	13	79	88	100	91
14	131	7	13	24	8	82	94	95	90
15	96	0	11	22	15	77	84	100	89

a. Using enhancement algorithm proposed here.
b. Using Home Office enhancement algorithm.
The table gives the "ground truth" numbers of minutiae as well as the numbers of false and missed minutiae.

2. *Time taken for minutiae reduction.* Because of the greater numbers of false minutiae detected on the Home Office enhancements, one expects longer processing times for minutiae reduction. Indeed, the processing times were found to average 2.43 times longer for the Home Office enhancements. Using the proposed enhancements saved an average of 58 sec per image.

3. *False minutiae remaining after minutiae reduction.* Because the minutiae reduction process removes almost all of the "soft" false minutiae, the number of minutiae remaining approximates the number of "hard" errors that have occurred during the enhancement process. Consequently, this number provides an important evaluation of the enhancement algorithm. Averages of 21.5 and 6.9 false minutiae per image were produced using the Home Office and proposed enhancements, respectively. The respective specificities are 76.0% and 92.3%. The proposed method reduces the false minutiae count by a factor of 3.1, again a very favorable figure.

4. *Missing minutiae after minutiae reduction.* The numbers of missing minutiae are 11.2 and 19.6 minutiae per image missed by the Home Office and the proposed enhancements, respectively. The respective sensitivities are 88.0% and 79.6%.

All the above comparisons except (4) strongly favor the proposed algorithm. Because of the disproportionately large numbers of candidate minutiae associated with the Home Office algorithm, the Home Office minutiae reduction algorithm has been made particularly stringent. When applied to the proposed enhancements, therefore, a larger than desirable proportion of the true minutiae are removed. A less severe tuning of this algorithm is likely to reduce the number of missed minutiae without significantly increasing the number of false minutiae. The approach of Ratha et al. [29] provides an alternative to the use of specificities and sensitivities. They calculate a goodness index (GI), for which a large value implies that a good job of feature extraction has been done on the image. The GI provides a greater weighting for mistakes within good-contrast windows than poor-contrast windows.

5.3. A Mathematical Model of Fingerprint Ridge Topology

5.3.1. Background

This part of the chapter describes a model for fingerprint ridge orientation formation. The model incorporates an understanding of the topology of fingerprints and is therefore of value in the interpretation of fingerprint images in Automatic Fingerprint Identification Systems (AFIS) [34]. We resolve here one of the basic issues underlying fingerprint interpretation, namely that of resolving ambiguities in the recognition of ridge orientation.

In a fingerprint the ridge structure defines everywhere a direction of ridge "flow," called the Local Ridge Orientation (LRO). Two types of singular points, cores and deltas (see Fig. 5.7), form isolated singularities of the otherwise continuous LRO function. Ridge orientation has proven to be of fundamental importance in fingerprint image processing. The directional image introduced by Mehtre et al. [18] consists of the LRO evaluated at each pixel position in the image. Applications requiring knowledge of ridge orientation include filtering to enhance fingerprint images [21, 22], detection of singular points [38], fingerprint image segmentation [17, 18], ridge detection during preprocessing [40], postprocessing to reduce numbers of false minutiae [41], and pattern analysis to extract classification types [9, 11, 20, 27].

Several AFIS-based techniques of fingerprint enhancement and pattern analysis require (ideally) a value for fingerprint LRO at every pixel [30]. The most usual approach in commercial AFIS systems has been to determine the LRO accurately

Fig. 5.7. A loop fingerprint, showing two singular points, marked C at the core and D at the delta.

on a coarse, regularly spaced grid, and assume it constant within each rectangular area. This is particularly unsatisfactory in regions near cores and deltas, where the ridge curvature is high. For example, the AFIS developed by the U.K. Home Office [19] directionally enhances images only in low-curvature regions. By incorporating the model, the enhancement can be applied to the entire image, greatly improving the encoding that follows. Another, more satisfactory, approach has been to use the directional image [21, 22]. Our model is also useful here because it can guide the process of LRO determination, yielding a better-quality directional image, particularly for noisier images.

Much work in the description and analysis of orientations in general images has been applied to fingerprint image processing. Kass and Witkin [10] analyze oriented patterns by estimating dominant local orientations and combining these to construct a flow coordinate system. Applied to fingerprints, this approach can determine the LRO pattern and locate the singular points. Zucker [42] describes orientations in terms of tangent vector fields, distinguishing between Type I (contour) and Type II (flow) processes. Fingerprint LRO is an example of a Type II process. Zucker and others have developed techniques of trace inference and curve detection [3, 24] that have successfully detected ridges in fingerprints. This work, and related work for three-dimensional images [31, 32], is of interest because it applies differential geometric concepts such as tangent fields, direction fields, and Poincaré indices to the analysis of image directionality. It is not, however, immediately applicable to the problem of modeling LRO, because the LRO represents a flowlike (two-dimensional) rather than a curvelike (one-dimensional) process. Fingerprint pattern classification techniques in the literature [9, 20, 27] often depend on an analysis of the LRO pattern. While we do not directly address the classification problem, this model incorporates an understanding of LRO topology and can therefore be usefully applied to pattern classification.

As mentioned above, many applications must process ridge orientation information. Ambiguities due to the multivalued nature of orientation modulo π can occur during the analysis of the LRO pattern. Without an intelligent model, which understands the topological behavior of ridge orientation, it is difficult to resolve these ambiguities satisfactorily. The following sections concern the nature of the ambiguities and the use of the model to resolve them. The result is demonstrated in an algorithm for interpolating between sampled values of LRO.

5.3.2. The Model of Ridge Orientation Topology

5.3.2.1. Direction and Orientation

Two distinct types of direction can be defined. One of these, which we shall call simply "direction," is easily described by the elementary mathematics of vectors. The other, called "orientation," is more useful for describing directionality in images, but requires the concept of the "direction field." We adopt the term "direction field" from differential geometry [36] even though "orientation field" might be a less confusing description in view of our distinction between direction and orientation.

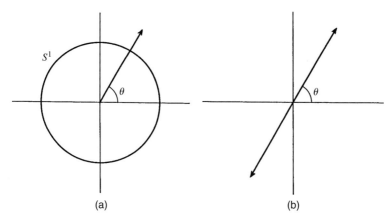

(a)   (b)

Fig. 5.8. Illustrating the difference between (a) direction and (b) orientation.

As we shall see, the direction field is suitable for describing the behavior of fingerprint ridge orientation in the vicinity of cores and deltas, whereas the vector field is not.

A vector in the plane, as shown in Fig. 5.8a, forms some angle θ with the Cartesian x-axis. Angle θ is in the range 0 to 2π radians and is called the *direction* of the vector. Directions of vectors can be naturally represented as elements of the unit circle S^1. Since we are interested only in the directional properties of vectors, all vectors will be assumed to have unit length.

Figure 5.8b shows a straight line through the origin instead of a vector. This line forms some smallest positive angle θ with the positive x-axis. θ is called the *orientation* of the line and lies in the range 0 to π because it is unaffected by rotation through integer multiples of π. Orientations can be represented as elements of the projective circle P^1, which may be thought of as a circle with circumference π and radius 1/2. (Mathematically, the *projective n-space* P^n is obtained by identifying radially opposite points of the unit n-sphere S^n.)

5.3.2.2. Vector Fields and Direction Fields

A vector field can be regarded as a 2D function assigning a direction in S^1 to each point. Analogously, a *direction field* [37] can be regarded as a 2D function taking on values that are orientations in P^1. In both cases the function is defined and continuous everywhere except at a finite number of *singular points*.

The fundamental difference between vector and direction fields is revealed when their integral curves are compared. An *integral curve* of the field is a curve whose tangent has everywhere the same direction (or orientation) as the field. Integral curves of vector fields are by nature *orientable*; that is, it is possible to assign arrows to the curves, indicating a forward sense of "flow" that is consistent and continuous. However, direction fields need not be orientable. Figure 5.9 shows examples of orientable and nonorientable sets of curves. In the nonorientable example, a discontinu-

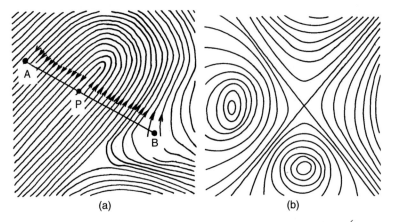

Fig. 5.9. Two sets of curves. The curves in (b) are orientable; those in (a) are not.

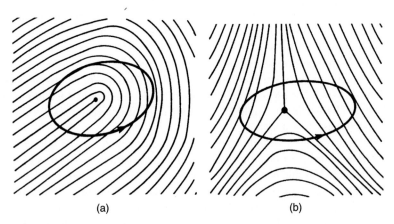

Fig. 5.10. Poincaré indices for direction field singular points: (a) core (index 1/2); (b) delta (index −1/2).

ous change in the sense of the arrows occurs at the point p along the path AB shown in Fig. 5.9a.

It is in the concept of orientability that we find a vector field unsuitable to model realistic fingerprints and a direction field suitable. Note the similarity between the nonorientable example of Fig. 5.9 and the ridge pattern of a loop fingerprint.

The difference between direction and vector fields is also revealed by the Poincaré indices [6] of the singular points of the field. The *Poincaré index* of a singular point p is the net or algebraic number of rotations through 2π made by the direction (or orientation) of the field as a simple closed curve surrounding p and no other singular point is traversed in the counterclockwise sense (see Fig. 5.10). It is well known that Poincaré indices in vector fields are always integers. For direction fields the indices may also be half-integers [37]. Figure 5.10 shows patterns of lines resembling the areas around cores and deltas in fingerprints, showing that the index of a core is $+1/2$ and the index of a delta is $-1/2$, corresponding to changes in LRO of π and $-\pi$, respectively, as the curve is traversed. The center of a circular whorl has an index of $+1$ and can be regarded as two superimposed cores. The values of Poincaré indices for the various LRO singularities are noted in [11]. Sander and Zucker [32] describe these singularity types, their Poincaré indices, and the use of direction fields to describe surfaces in three-dimensional images.

The use of the direction field provides a mathematical basis for describing fingerprints. Without it, the orientation of ridges cannot be modeled in a manner that exhibits the nonorientability and Poincaré index values characteristic of fingerprints.

5.3.2.3. A Model of LRO Topology

It should now be clear that a local ridge orientation function $LRO(x, y)$ can be modeled as a direction field having singular points $d_1, \ldots, d_m$ of index $-1/2$ at delta points and $c_1, \ldots, c_k$ of index $1/2$ at core points.

The model of LRO developed here is the simplest possible model that accounts correctly for the topological behavior of orientation around the singular points. It provides a direction field $\theta(x, y)$ that is continuously deformable onto the true LRO field of a real fingerprint. Any two fingerprints with the same singular points are modeled by the same function, even though their LRO values may differ in detail. Each pattern can, however, be continuously mapped onto the other. Therefore, the $\theta(x, y)$ of the model can be regarded as the LRO of some "ideal" fingerprint having the given core and delta positions. Its relation to the actual LRO of a real fingerprint is discussed in the next section; its usefulness in real applications is described in sections that follow.

We now describe the model. First, regarding the image plane as the complex plane C, consider the rational polynomial function

$$q(z) = \frac{(z - z_1)(z - z_2) \ldots (z - z_k)}{(z - p_1)(z - p_2) \ldots (z - p_m)}$$

with first-order poles and zeroes $p_1, \ldots, p_m$ and $z_1, \ldots, z_k$. It is well known that the Poincaré indices are $+1$ at each zero and -1 at each pole.

We observe empirically that far from the center of the image, the ridge orientation tends toward a constant value, say θ_∞. Noting that the cores and deltas of a fingerprint have Poincaré indices of $1/2$ and $-1/2$, define

$$p(z) = \sqrt{e^{2j\theta_\infty} \cdot \frac{(z - z_{d1})(z - z_{d2}) \ldots (z - z_{dk})}{(z - z_{p_1})(z - z_{p_2}) \ldots (z - z_{p_m})}}$$

where $z_{c1}, \ldots, z_{ck}$ and $z_{d1}, \ldots, z_{dk}$ are the locations of the cores and deltas, respectively, and θ is the ridge slope at infinity. With the usual alignment, $\theta = 0$.

The above equation has the required half-integral Poincaré indices, since taking the square root of a complex number halves its argument.

Thus the model of the LRO is

$$\theta(z) = (\operatorname{Arg} p(z)) \bmod \pi.$$

5.3.2.4. Relationship to the LRO of Real Fingerprints

The actual LRO of a real fingerprint is a direction field with singular points at the cores and deltas. The modeled orientation $\theta(x, y)$ is a direction field with identical singular point positions and types. Therefore, $\mathrm{LRO}(x, y) = \theta(x, y) + \varepsilon(x, y)$, where the error $\varepsilon(x, y)$ is a direction field having indices of value zero at all singular points.

Figure 5.11 shows fingerprints of the plain arch, tented arch, whorl, loop, and double loop classification types. Line segments representing orientations determined by the model are superimposed. The model correctly represents the topological behavior of the ridge structure but does not provide close pointwise approximation to the true values. Therefore, the usefulness of the model lies not in providing accurate orientation values but in providing knowledge about their behavior.

5.3.3. Use of the Model to Resolve Ambiguities in LRO

Applications requiring knowledge of ridge orientation include filtering to enhance fingerprint images and pattern analysis to extract classification types and minute details in AFIS systems.

Traditional methods of real analysis assume that the function being analyzed is continuous and real-valued. Problems arise when processing orientations because this basic assumption is violated. Although the LRO is continuous as a function taking values in P^1, it is usually discontinuous (and indeed multivalued) when viewed as real-valued.

The multivalued nature of orientation leads to ambiguities when processing orientations. Suppose, for example, that interpolated orientation values are required along the line joining points p_1 and p_2, where $\theta(p_1) = 3\pi/4$ and $\theta(p_2) = \pi/4$ (say) as in

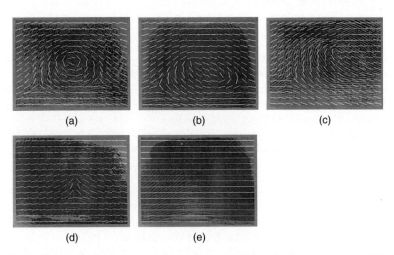

(a)   (b)   (c)

(d)   (e)

Fig. 5.11. LRO patterns determined by the model for the following fingerprint types: (a) whorl; (b) double loop; (c) loop; (d) tented arch; (e) plain arch.

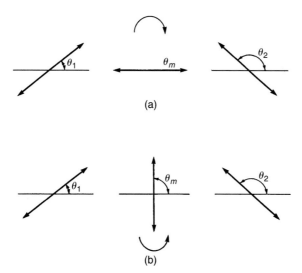

Fig. 5.12. Two orientations $\theta_1 = \pi/4$ and $\theta_2 = 3\pi/4$, with the interpolated midpoint values θ_m: (a) $\theta_m = 0$ obtained assuming clockwise rotation from θ_1 to θ_2; (b) $\theta_m = 0$ obtained assuming counterclockwise rotation.

Fig. 5.12. There are infinitely many ways of reaching $3\pi/4$ from $\pi/4$: P^1 may be circumnavigated any number of times in either sense. The figure shows two of these options, which yield different results.

If the rate of change of θ is known, the ambiguity is resolved. The sign of the derivative indicates whether to move clockwise or counterclockwise around P^1, and its magnitude indicates the number of revolutions required. With a suitable sampling rate, the number of full revolutions is always zero, and the choice is simply between clockwise and counterclockwise rotation. The LRO model provides the information required to make this choice.

5.3.3.1. Orientation Unwrapping

Standard two-dimensional analysis could be applied to the LRO if it were possible to "unwrap" $\theta(x, y)$, converting it into a continuous real-valued function $\theta_u(x, y)$. Unwrapping is performed by adding a suitable multiple of π to each sample, thereby removing the discontinuities. Unfortunately, the following result applies:

Theorem. *A two-dimensional orientation-valued function $\theta(x, y)$ cannot be unwrapped if it has a singular point.*

Proof. Let p be singular. Assume θ can be unwrapped, yielding θ_u. Let C be a simple, closed curve around p, and (x, y) any point on C. As C is traversed counterclockwise from (x, y), θ_u changes through $2\pi.ix(p)$ to its final value $\theta_u(x, y) + 2\pi.ix(p)$. This final value occurs at the same point (x, y), so by continuity of θ_u, $\theta_u(x, y) =$

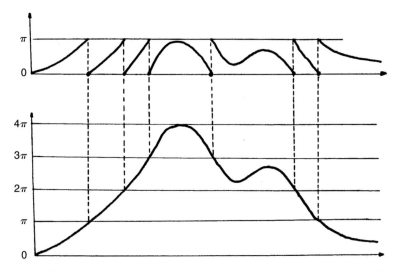

Fig. 5.13. A 1D orientation function (above) and its unwrapped version (below).

$\theta_u(x, y) + 2\pi.ix(p)$. So $ix(p) = 0$, contradicting the statement that p is singular.[QED]

However, unwrapping is always possible in the one-dimensional case. For each x in increasing order, choose an integer $k(x)$ that makes $\theta_u(x) = \theta(x) + k(x)\pi$ continuous from 0 to x. Figure 5.13 shows an orientation function and its unwrapped version.

Phase unwrapping [23, 39] is a related problem where the phase $\theta(\omega)$ of the discrete Fourier transform of some signal $f(x)$ must be unwrapped. The unwrapped phase takes the form $\theta_u(\omega) = \theta(\omega) + k(\omega).2\pi$, where k is integral. Solutions to this problem find $k(\omega)$ by using the signal data $f(x)$ to estimate the phase derivative $\theta'(\omega)$. Phase unwrapping does not apply directly to orientation unwrapping because there is no corresponding signal. However, the same general approach can be applied by using the LRO model to estimate the derivative of the orientation.

The ability to unwrap one-dimensional functions permits a restricted form of analysis of orientations in two dimensions. Given a simple curve $C(t)$ not passing through singularities of $\theta(x, y)$, the one-dimensional function $\theta(C(t))$ can be unwrapped along the curve, yielding $\theta_u(C(t))$. Ordinary analysis can then be applied along C using any classical algorithm. In particular, C could be any straight line parallel to either coordinate axis, and the entire image can be covered by such lines.

5.3.3.2. Use of the LRO Model for Orientation Unwrapping

An estimate of the derivative of the orientation is given by the gradient of the modeled LRO function:

$$\nabla\Theta = \nabla(\arg p(z))$$

$$= \frac{1}{2}\sum_{i=1}^{k}\left\{\frac{(y_{ci} - y, x - x_{ci})}{(x - x_{ci})^2 + (y - y_{ci})^2} - \frac{(y_{dl} - y, x - x_{di})}{(x - x_{di})^2 + (y - y_{di})^2}\right\}$$

With an appropriate sampling rate, the LRO changes by less than π radians between samples. If so, only the sign of the derivative is required. With this simplification, the unwrapping algorithm is

```
procedure unwrap (var x, xdot: array of real)
{x is the data to be unwrapped, and        }
{xdot is the array of derivative values }
const
  maxdiff = π/4
begin
  x[1] := x[1] mod π
  for i:=2 to length of x do
    Restrict x[i] to the range x[i-1]-π/2 .. x[i-1]+π/2 by
    adding or subtracting a suitable multiple of π.
    diff := x[i] - x[i-1]
    if (diff > maxdiff) and (xdot[i] < 0) then
      x[i] := x[i]-π
    elseif (diff < -maxdiff) and (xdot[i] > 0) then
      x[i] := x[i]+π
    endif
  endfor
end
```

5.3.3.3. Application to Interpolation of Orientations

Because determining ridge orientation reliably can be computationally demanding unless special hardware is available, it is often not feasible to evaluate the LRO directly for each pixel. Our approach is to determine the LRO at a square grid spaced (say) 16 pixels apart, and obtain intermediate values by interpolation. During interpolation, the multivalued nature of orientation leads to ambiguities that can be resolved by the model as described earlier. The algorithm for interpolating an n by n array of orientations by a factor **K** is

```
{We have n rows and n columns of data}
for i:=1 to n do
  unwrap row i
  interpolate row i by factor K
endfor

{We now have n rows and n*K columns}
for i:=1 to n*K do
  unwrap column i
  interpolate column i by factor K
  wrap column i
endfor

{We now have n*K rows and n*K columns}
```

Provided that the unwrapping does not fail, the behavior of the above interpolation algorithm is identical to that of the standard interpolation technique incorporated within it.

5.4. Conclusions

The fingerprint enhancement algorithm presented above is of importance because it has been shown to produce significant improvement over the algorithm incorporated in a working AFIS. This demonstrates the usefulness of position-dependent directional Fourier domain filtering in the processing of fingerprint images within AFIS systems.

We saw that fingerprint local ridge orientation can be best described using the direction field concept of differential geometry, rather than the more usually encountered vector field. A simple model of fingerprint local ridge orientation topology in terms of the positions of cores and deltas has been presented and shown to be of practical use in the two-dimensional interpolation of sampled LRO values from real fingerprints. The model emphasizes the fundamental importance of core and delta numbers and positions in determining the topology of the fingerprint LRO structure.

References

1. Chiralo, R.P. and L.L. Berdan, Adaptive digital enhancement of latent fingerprints, in *Proc. 1978 Carnahan Conference on Crime Countermeasures*, Lexington, KY, 1978, pp. 131–135.
2. Connell, J.H., N.K. Ratha, and R.M. Bolle, Fingerprint image enhancement using weak models, in IEEE International Conference on Image Processing, 2002.
3. David, C., and S.W. Zucker, Potentials, valleys, and dynamic global coverings, *Intl. J. of Computer Vision*, 5:219–238, 1990.
4. Federal Bureau of Investigation, *The Science of Fingerprints: Classification and Uses*, Washington, DC: U.S. Government Printing Office, 1984.
5. Ghosal, S, R. Udupa, S. Pankanti, and N.K. Ratha, Learning partitioned least squares filters for fingerprint enhancement, in IEEE Workshop on Applications of Computer Vision, Palm Springs, CA, 2000.
6. Godbillon, C. *Dynamical Systems on Surfaces*, New York: Springer-Verlag, 1983.
7. Gonzalez, R.C. and P. Wintz, *Digital Image Processing*, Reading, MA: Addison-Wesley, Applied Mathematics and Computation Textbooks, no. 13, 1977.
8. Granlund, G.H. and J. Arvidsson, The GOP image computer, in O.D. Faugeras, ed., *Fundamentals in Computer Vision: An Advanced Course*, Cambridge University Press, 1983, pp. 57–67.
9. Grasselli, A. On the automatic classification of fingerprints, in *Methodologies of Pattern Recognition*, S. Watanabe, ed., New York: Academic Press, 1969.
10. Kass, M. and A. Witkin, Analyzing oriented patterns, *Computer Vision, Graphics and Image Processing*, 37:362–385, 1987.
11. Kawagoe, M. and A. Tojo, Fingerprint pattern classification, *Pattern Recognition*, 17:295–303, 1984.

12. Knutsson, H.E., R. Wilson, and G.H. Granlund, Anisotropic nonstationary image estimation and its applications: Part I—Restoration of noisy images, *IEEE Trans. on Communications*, COM-31:388–397, 1983.

13. Hong, L., Y. Wan, and A. Jain, Fingerprint image enhancement: Algorithm and performance evaluation, *IEEE Trans. on Pattern Analysis and Machine Intelligence*, 20:777–789, 1998.

14. Hong, L., A. Jain, S. Pankati, and R. Bolle, Fingerprint enhancement, in IEEE Workshop on Applications of Computer Vision, Sarasota, FL, 1996, pp. 202–207.

15. Kamei, T. and M. Mizoguchi, Image filter design for fingerprint enhancement, in *Proc. of ISCV*, Coral Gables, FL, 1995, pp. 109–114.

16. Kim, B.G. and D.J. Park, Adaptive image normalisation based on block processing for enhancement of fingerprint image, *Electronics Letters*, 38:696–698, 2002.

17. Mehtre, B.M. and B. Chatterjee, Segmentation of fingerprint images—a composite method, *Pattern Recognition*, 22:381–385, 1989.

18. Mehtre, B.M., N.N. Murthy, S. Kapoor, and B. Chatterjee, Segmentation of fingerprint images using the directional image, *Pattern Recognition*, 20:429–435, 1987.

19. Millard, K., Developments on automatic fingerprint recognition, in *Intl. Carnahan Conference on Security Technology*, Zurich, 1983, pp. 173–178.

20. Moayer, B. and K.S. Fu, A syntactic approach to fingerprint pattern recognition, *Pattern Recognition*, 7:1–23, 1975.

21. O'Gorman, L. and J.V. Nickerson, An approach to fingerprint filter design, *Pattern Recognition*, 22:29–38, 1989.

22. O'Gorman, L. and J.V. Nickerson, Matched filter design for fingerprint images enhancement, in *IEEE International Conference on Acoustics, Speech, and Signal Processing*, New York, 1988, pp. 916–919.

23. Oppenheim, A.V. and R.W. Schafer, *Digital Signal Processing*, Englewood Cliffs, NJ: Prentice–Hall, 1975.

24. Parent, P. and S.W. Zucker, Trace inference, curvature consistency, and curve detection. *IEEE Trans. Acoustics, Speech, Signal Processing*, 11:823–839, 1989.

25. Park, S., M.J.T. Smith, and J.J. Lee, Fingerprint enhancement based on the directional filter bank, in *IEEE International Conference on Image Processing*, Vancouver, 2000, pp. 793–795.

26. Randolph, T.R. and M.J.T. Smith, Fingerprint image enhancement using a binary angular representation, in *IEEE International Conference on Acoustics, Speech, and Signal Processing*, Salt Lake City, UT, 2001, pp. 1561–1564.

27. Rao, C.V.K. and K. Balck, Type classification of fingerprints: A syntactic approach, *IEEE Trans. Pattern Anal. Mach. Intell.*, PAMI-2:223–231, 1980.

28. Rao, T.C.M., Feature extraction for fingerprint classification, *Pattern Recognition*, 8:181–192, 1976.

29. Ratha, N.K., S. Chen, and A.K. Jain, Adaptive flow orientation-based feature extraction in fingerprint images, *Pattern Recognition*, 28:1657–1672, 1995.

30. Riganati, J.P., An overview of algorithms employed in automated fingerprint processing, in *Proc. Intl. Conference on Crime Countermeasures*, Lexington, KY, 1977, pp. 125–131.

31. Sander, P.T. and S.W. Zucker, Inferring surface trace and differential structure from 3-D images, *IEEE Trans. Pattern Anal. Mach. Intell.*, 12:833–854, 1990.

32. Sander, P.T. and S.W. Zucker, Singularities of principle direction fields from 3-D images, *IEEE Trans. Pattern Anal. Mach. Intell.*, 14:309–317, 1992.

33. Sherlock, B.G., D.M. Monro, and K. Millard, Algorithm for enhancing fingerprint images, *Electronics Letters*, 28:1720–1721, 1992.

34. Sherlock, B.G. and D.M. Monro, A model for interpreting fingerprint topology, *Pattern Recognition*, 26:1047–1055, 1993.
35. Sherlock, B.G. and D.M. Monro, Fingerprint enhancement by directional Fourier filtering, *IEEE Proc.—Vision, Image and Signal Processing*, 141:87–94, 1994.
36. Spivak, M., A comprehensive introduction to differential geometry, Vol. I, Berkeley, CA: Publish or Perish, 1979.
37. Spivak, M., Singularities of line fields, in Chapter 4, Addendum 2, *A Comprehensive Introduction to Differential Geometry*, Vol. III, Berkeley, CA: Publish or Perish, 1979.
38. Srinivasan, V.S. and N.N. Murthy, Detection of singular points in fingerprint images, *Pattern Recognition*, 25:139–153, 1992.
39. Tribolet, J.M., A new phase unwrapping algorithm, *IEEE Trans. Acoustics, Speech, Signal Processing*, ASSP-25:170, 1977.
40. Verma, M.R., A.K. Majumdar, and B. Chatterjee, Edge detection in fingerprints, *Pattern Recognition*, 20:513–523, 1987.
41. Xiao, Q. and H. Raafat, Fingerprint image postprocessing: A combined statistical and structural approach, *Pattern Recognition*, 24:985–992, 1991.
42. Zucker, S.W., Early orientation selection: Tangent fields and the dimensionality of their support, *Comput. Vision Graphics Image Process.*, 32:74–103, 1985.

Chapter 6

Image Filter Design for Fingerprint Enhancement

Toshio Kamei

Abstract. Fingerprint filter design and a method of enhancing fingerprint images are discussed. Two distinct filters in the Fourier domain are designed, a frequency filter corresponding to ridge frequencies and a direction filter corresponding to ridge directions on the basis of fingerprint ridge characteristics. An energy function for selecting image features (i.e., frequencies and directions) is defined by power of images obtained with the above filters and a measure of smoothness of the features. Using the image features that minimize the energy function, we produce an enhanced image from the filtered images. This image enhancement method is applied to fingerprint matching. In experiments with rolled prints, it is shown that the false identification rate is reduced by about two thirds compared with Asai's method.

6.1. Introduction

Fingerprint recognition has been used for a long time to determine person identify in law enforcement [1], and it has become a more and more important task with increasing demand for person identification in various applications such as online banking, e-commerce, and security control, because fingerprints have significant characteristics such as *exchangeability* and *uniqueness*. A fingerprint consists of ridges separated by valleys, these ridges flow almost parallel to each other, and ridges change their flow at minutiae such as endings and bifurcations of ridges. The relation graph between fingerprint minutiae is unique for each finger and does not change during life.

Although various algorithms and systems have been proposed as means of determining the identity of fingerprints, most fingerprint identification systems adopt a matching based on comparison of fingerprint minutiae [2–4]. However, automatic detection of minutiae tends to be influenced by various noises as caused by dry skin and imprint condition. In order to suppress the influence of noise and enhance signal components of the print, fingerprint enhancement is performed based on fingerprint image properties.

Ridge flow is characterized by local ridge direction and local ridge width. The directional features represent an outline of ridge flow. The ridge width between fingerprint ridges is different according to its location, imprint condition, and finger size. As a consequence, these differences result in a variety of ridge frequencies in the fingerprint. Therefore, these features are important to design image filters and to process fingerprint enhancement according to the local ridge features of the print.

However, most approaches [3, 5–7] proceed with the enhancement based on only directional features and do not pay much attention to the ridge frequency, though it is as important as ridge direction. Since the ridge pattern is a cyclical pattern in a local scope, the Fourier domain is suitable to describe the print. Based on the intrinsic characteristics of fingerprint patterns, we propose two distinct filters designed in the Fourier domain, a frequency filter and a directional filter.

Using these filters, a fingerprint image is filtered, and then the best matched filter is selected to enhance the image. The selected filter indicates the local feature of the region, such as ridge direction or ridge width.

In this filter selection, the energy minimization principle is applied as in the detection of optical flow [8]. An energy function for extracting local image feature (i.e., frequencies and directions) is defined using power of the filtered image and assuming local smoothness in the fingerprint. Using the image features that minimize the energy function, an enhanced image is produced from the filtered images.

Section 6.2 describes characteristics of fingerprint ridges and a fingerprint filter design. Section 6.3 explains an image enhancement using the designed filters. Section 6.4 reports on a fingerprint matching experiment that demonstrates the effectiveness of enhancement with image filters.

6.2. Fingerprint Filter Design

6.2.1. Fourier Features of Fingerprint

The 2D Fourier spectrum of ridge flow in a subregion of a fingerprint image shows two high peaks in addition to the DC component, indicating the presence of parallel ridges. These peaks are symmetrical to the DC components. This is illustrated in Fig. 6.1. Figure 6.1d shows the 2D Fourier spectrum of the fingerprint image in Fig. 6.1a; this spectrum has twin peaks. The location of these peaks in the Fourier domain characterizes two fingerprint features—the frequency and the direction of the ridge flows in the subregion. The frequency of ridges is indicated by the distance between the peaks, and the direction of the ridges is indicated by the direction perpendicular to the line connecting the peaks.

For low-quality images such as those in Fig. 6.1b, and c, however, the peaks are not distinct. In Fig. 6.1b the image is blurred and the peaks in e are also blurred. In Fig. 6.1c, alphabetical letters appear in the image, and as a consequence other peaks appear in f.

In order to enhance the ridges of the fingerprint image, it is necessary to distinguish between fingerprint signal components and noise components and to filter the images to produce a greater contrast between the signal components and the noise components.

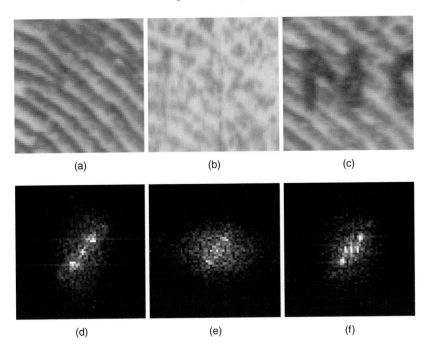

Fig. 6.1. Fourier power spectra of fingerprint images. (a), (b), and (c) are subregions of a fingerprint image, and (d), (e), and (f) are the Fourier power spectra of (a), (b), and (c), respectively.

The signal components of fingerprint ridges in the Fourier domain are localized in peak regions corresponding to the direction and frequency of ridges. This localization can be used to design fingerprint filters and to enhance ridges.

6.2.2. Fingerprint Filter in the Fourier Domain

In our filter design, we use the above-described characteristics of fingerprints in the Fourier domain. The filters described in this chapter are designed in the Fourier domain and are characterized by ridge frequencies ρ_i, ridge directions ϕ_j, and several other parameters.

We designed image filters satisfying the following criteria:

1. A filter is characterized by the ridge frequency and ridge direction since a fingerprint has various ridge frequencies and ridge directions in each subregion.

2. A filter transmits the peak spectra corresponding to ridges and attenuates the other noise spectra. It will increase the contrast between the ridges and valleys in the spatial domain and reduce the noise components.

3. The filter is parameterized. The bandwidth of a filter determines the ridge-to-valley contrast and the degree of difference between the original and the filtered images. In image enhancement, a narrow band is usually effective in producing a

higher ridge-to-valley contrast, but if the wrong type of filter is selected, the narrow bandpass filter produces erroneous ridge connections. A bandpass parameter is therefore desirable.

4. The DC and low-frequency component are eliminated, since they are not relevant to ridge features such as frequencies and directions, and thus interfere with feature extraction, as is described later.

The filter $H(\rho, \phi)$ was designed on the basis of these criteria,

$$H(u, v) = H(\rho, \phi) = H_{\text{frequency}}(\rho) \cdot H_{\text{direction}}(\phi) \tag{1}$$

Here (ρ, ϕ) denotes the polar coordinates in the Fourier domain, and the orthogonal coordinates are expressed as $(u, v) = (\rho \cos \phi, \rho \sin \phi)$. Filter $H(\rho, \phi)$ is separable into ρ and ϕ components. The ρ component $H_{\text{frequency}}(\rho)$ is the frequency filter corresponding to a ridge frequency and the ϕ component $H_{\text{direction}}(\phi)$ is a directional filter corresponding to a ridge direction.

Separability of the filter into $H_{\text{frequency}}(\rho)$ and $H_{\text{direction}}(\phi)$ enables independent treatment of the frequencies and directions in the enhancement process described in Section 6.3.

M. Kass et al. [9] propose a separable filter based on the difference of Gaussian filters in flow detection for oriented patterns. However, this filter was unsuitable for detecting the frequency of fingerprints, because it appeared to be weighted too much toward high frequencies.

Therefore, the following bandpass filter was designed as $H_{\text{frequency}}(\rho)$:

$$H_{\text{frequency}}(\rho \mid \rho_i, \rho_{\min}, \rho_{\max}, \sigma_\rho, c)$$
$$= \begin{cases} f(\rho \mid \rho_i, \sigma_\rho, c) & (\rho_{\min} < |\rho| < \rho_{\max}) \\ 0 & (\text{otherwise}) \end{cases} \tag{2}$$

where

$$f(\rho \mid \rho_i, \sigma_\rho, c) = \frac{1}{Z(\rho + c)} \exp\left(-\frac{(\rho - \rho_i)^2}{2\sigma_\rho^2}\right) \tag{3}$$

$$Z = \int f(\rho \mid \rho_i, \sigma_\rho, c) \, d\rho \tag{4}$$

and ρ_i and σ_ρ are the center frequency and bandwidth parameter of the filter. Frequency $\rho_{\min}$ is a parameter for the low-cut property, which suppresses the effects of low frequency caused by imprint unevenness; $\rho_{\max}$ is a parameter for the high-cut property, which suppresses the effects of high-frequency noise such as sweat gland holes and scratches in the ridges. Z is a normalization factor for the filter output and $1/(\rho + c)$ is a factor that suppresses relatively high-frequency components. c is a constant. The Z and $1/(\rho + c)$ factors are necessary for filter selection, as described later.

As the directional filter $H_{\text{direction}}(\phi)$, the following filter was designed:

$$H_{\text{direction}}(\phi \mid \phi_j, \sigma_\phi)$$
$$= \exp\left(-\frac{\min_n (\phi - \phi_j + n\pi)^2}{2\sigma_\phi^2}\right) \tag{5}$$

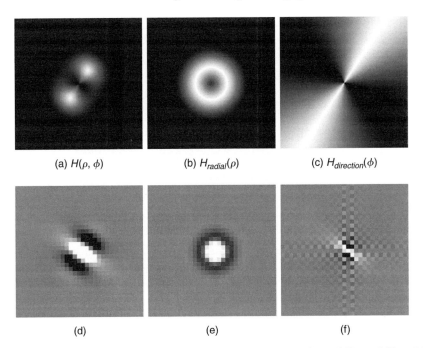

(a) $H(\rho, \phi)$ (b) $H_{radial}(\rho)$ (c) $H_{direction}(\phi)$

(d)   (e)   (f)

Fig. 6.2. Example of filters. (d), (e), and (f) are inverse Fourier transformed filters of filters (a), (b), and (c), respectively.

where ϕ_j is the direction of the filter bandpass and σ_ϕ is the direction bandwidth parameter. Examples of filters designed in the Fourier domain and their inverse Fourier transformation (real component only) are shown in Fig. 6.2. The designed filter is matched to ridge patterns that have the same ridge direction and ridge width as shown in Fig. 6.2d.

Given an original image $g(x, y)$ in the spatial domain, the filtering operation is performed in the 2D Fourier domain under the following equation:

$$g'(x, y) = F^{-1}(H(u, v) \cdot F(g(x, y))) \tag{6}$$

where $g'(x, y)$ is the image filtered by filter $H(u, v)$. $F(\cdot)$ and $F^{-1}(\cdot)$ denote a forward and inverse 2D Fourier transformation, respectively.

Figure 6.4 shows filtered images of an original image in Fig. 6.3. Six filters with various frequency and direction parameters are applied in the filtering. When the filter parameters match the ridge features, the ridge pattern in the subregion of the filtered image have a high contrast between ridges and valleys.

Fig. 6.3. Fingerprint image.

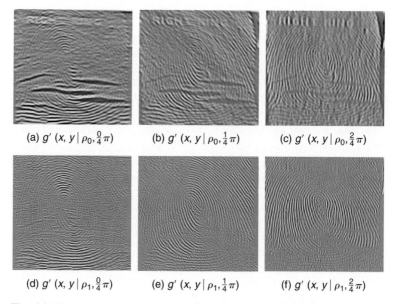

(a) $g'(x, y \mid \rho_0, \frac{0}{4}\pi)$ (b) $g'(x, y \mid \rho_0, \frac{1}{4}\pi)$ (c) $g'(x, y \mid \rho_0, \frac{2}{4}\pi)$

(d) $g'(x, y \mid \rho_1, \frac{0}{4}\pi)$ (e) $g'(x, y \mid \rho_1, \frac{1}{4}\pi)$ (f) $g'(x, y \mid \rho_1, \frac{2}{4}\pi)$

Fig. 6.4. Filtered images by $H(\rho, \phi)$. ρ_0 is a lower frequency than ρ_1 ($\rho_0 < \rho_1$).

6.3. Image Enhancement

If we can select appropriate filters that match ridge features at each region, we can effectively enhance fingerprint ridges. When various filters with parameters (ρ_i, ϕ_j) are processed for one image, the parameters (ρ_i, ϕ_j) of the filter, which give the most enhanced image in each subregion, usually correspond to the ridge features in the region. If there was no effect from noise components, we could produce the whole enhanced image by selecting the most enhanced images in each region.

Due to the effect of noise, however, the best matched filters do not always accurately represent the ridge features. Thus, it is necessary to smooth the image features spatially. We have examined a smoothing method for ridge direction fields, which is based on the energy minimization principle [10]. In this work, a ridge direction in a subregion has a confidence associated with it. However, the measure used for the confidence lacks enough information about the fingerprint image for smoothing. This is because the confidence measure in our previous work was valid only for the initially detected direction and not for the other directions since smoothing was processed after direction extraction. In this work, an image power in each local region is used as confidence for all directions (and frequencies), and the feature extraction and smoothing processes are combined into one process.

In order to obtain locally smoothed features, we take spatial smoothness into consideration in the definition of the energy function for the filter selection scheme. The selected filter set, minimizing the energy function, represents local ridge features, which collectively produces an enhanced image.

The outline of this process is as follows:

1. Representative filters $\{H(\rho, \phi|\rho_i, \phi_j)\}$ with various center frequencies and center directions are prepared.
2. An input image is filtered by the prepared filters. This filtering produces multifiltered images with the various filters.
3. Local image powers of multifiltered images are calculated.
4. Filters at each local region are selected to minimize the energy function.
5. An enhanced image is produced from the multifiltered images by referring to the selected filters at each region.

The frequency and direction features in each region are expressed by filter parameters (ρ_i, ϕ_j) selected in the region. A flowchart of this is shown in Fig. 6.5.

6.3.1. Preparation of Filters

It is desired that (i) a filter set $\{H(\rho, \phi|\rho_i, \phi_j)\}$ should densely cover the region of the Fourier domain where signals of fingerprints are expected to appear, and (ii) each filter should be normalized in order to make sense when comparing filter outputs.

The number of filters is limited in an actual implementation due to requirements such as computer memory and computer processing time. The first requirement may be satisfied by using a large number of filters. Since the normalization is taken into consideration in (2) and (5), the second requirement is satisfied by using the same parameters in the same filter set except for center frequencies ρ_i and center directions ϕ_j.

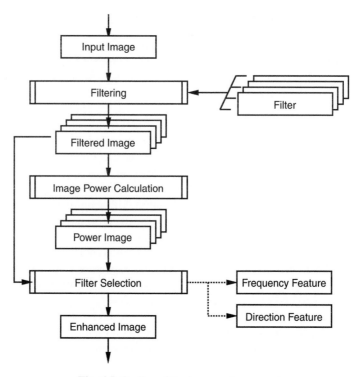

Fig. 6.5. Outline of the image enhancement.

6.3.2. Filtering and Image Power

An input image is filtered using each filter in the filter set $\{H(\rho, \phi|\rho_i, \phi_j)\}$. The following local image powers are used as a measure of the filter output. The local image powers $p(x, y|\rho_i, \phi_j)$ of the image $g'(x, y|\rho_i, \phi_j)$ filtered by $H(\rho, \phi|\rho_i, \phi_j)$ are calculated as follows:

$$p(x, y|\rho_i, \phi_j) = \frac{1}{S} \sum_{b=-h_y}^{h_y} \sum_{a=-h_x}^{h_x} g'(x+a, y+b|\rho_i, \phi_j)^2 \tag{7}$$

where $S = (2h_x + 1)(2h_y + 1)$.

6.3.3. Energy Function for Filter Selection

It is assumed that ridge features such as frequencies and directions are locally smooth. An energy function $E(\rho(x, y), \phi(x, y))$ for filter selection is defined by image powers and smoothness of ridge features as follows:

$$E(\rho(x, y), \phi(x, y)) = - \sum_{\forall(x,y)} p(x, y | \rho(x, y), \phi(x, y))$$

$$+ \alpha_\rho \sum_{\forall(x,y)} \sum_{(x',y')\in C_\rho(x,y)} D_\rho(\rho(x, y), \rho(x', y'))$$

$$+ \alpha_\phi \sum_{\forall(x,y)} \sum_{(x',y')\in C_\phi(x,y)} D_\phi(\phi(x, y), \phi(x', y')) \quad (8)$$

Here, $(\rho(x, y), \phi(x, y))$ represents the parameters (ρ_i, ϕ_j) of the filter, which is selected in each region (x, y). $C_\rho(x, y)$ and $C_\phi(x, y)$ denote neighbors of (x, y). The first term of (8) represents total power of the filtered image. The second and third terms represent smoothness of frequencies and directions, respectively. $D_\rho(\cdot), D_\phi(\cdot)$ are penalty functions for the difference between each feature in neighbors given by the equations

$$D_\rho(\rho(x, y), \rho(x', y')) = ||\rho(x, y) - \rho(x', y')||^2 \quad (9)$$

$$D_\phi(\phi(x, y), \phi(x', y')) = || \exp(j2\phi(x, y)) - \exp(j2\phi(x', y'))||^2 \quad (10)$$

The energy function is minimized using a "greedy algorithm" [11]. Values $(\rho(x, y), \phi(x, y))$ in each region (x, y) are selected to minimize the energy while values in the other regions are fixed. Generally, a minimization by a greedy algorithm is thought to converge slowly. In this work, a fast algorithm is applied to this minimization. Filter parameters $(\rho(x, y), \phi(x, y))$ are selected from a set of discrete values. This discreteness can make the minimization fast. In this algorithm, transitions of the values $(\rho(x, y), \phi(x, y))$ at each region (x, y) are watched. If the values at both the region (x, y) and the neighbor are not changed, renovation of the values at the region (x, y) is judged to be unnecessary and the renovation is omitted. This modified greedy algorithm is about 10–30 times faster than the normal greedy algorithm. Although it is said that the greedy algorithm is more unstable than dynamic programming and tends to fall into a local minimum, our experiment show that this problem is insignificant.

6.3.4. Fast Implementation

In the above image enhancement, given the N_ρ frequency filters and N_ϕ direction filters, $N_\rho \cdot N_\phi$ times filtering is needed. Filter $H(\rho, \phi)$ is designed to be separable into ρ and ϕ as shown in Eq. (1). Making use of the separability of the filters for fast operation, the number of operations is reduced from $N_\rho \cdot N_\phi$ to $N_\rho + N_\phi$. The image enhancement for fast implementation is separated into two steps: directional enhancement and frequency enhancement. The first step enhances an input image using a directional filter set $\{H_{\text{direction}}(\phi|\phi_j)\}$, and the second step enhances the output of the first step using a frequency filter set $\{H_{\text{frequency}}(\rho|\rho_i)\}$. We found from basic experiments that two-step enhancement produces results that are very similar to the one-step enhancement.

Table 6.1. Determined Parameters

Parameter	Values
size of image	256×256 pixel
N_ρ	10
$\rho_i (i = 1, 2, \cdots, 10)$	28.4,34.1,39.8, 45.5,51.2,56.9, 62.3,68.3,74.0, 79.6 cycles
ρ_{min}	22.0 cycles
ρ_{max}	100.0 cycles
σ_ρ	12.0 cycles
c	20.0
α_ρ	0.0
C_ρ	5×5 neighbors
N_ϕ	16
$\phi_j (j = 1, 2, \cdots, 16)$	$0/16\pi, 1/16\pi, 2/16\pi, \cdots, 15/16\pi$ rad
σ_ϕ	0.40 rad
α_ϕ	2.6×10^{-9}
C_ϕ	5×5 neighbors
(h_x, h_y)	(25,25) pixel

6.4. Results and Discussion

A suitable filter set for the image enhancement depends on the image size and the image resolution. A filter set is described here in a case of a rolled fingerprint whose image size is 256×256 and whose resolution is 250 dpi. Ridge width usually distributes in the range from 0.3 mm to 1.0 mm, which corresponds to frequencies in the range from about 25 to 85 cycles in the Fourier domain. The center frequencies ρ_i are set in this range. Here, a unit *cycle* means wave numbers in the image. Since ridge directions of fingerprints may appear in all directions, each direction filter is treated equivalently.

The filter parameters were adjusted by experiments on fingerprint matching [4] with 1000 pairs of rolled fingerprints from the NIST (National Institute of Standards and Technology) database 4 [12]. Since the images in the database were taken in 512×512 pixels with 500 dpi, they were converted into 256×256 pixels with 250 dpi. The minutiae matching accuracy was used to evaluate the parameter setting. The resulting set of parameters is listed in Table 6.1. Ten frequency filters and 16 direction filters were designed in the parameter setting. In the table, α_ρ is set to zero, because it is found from the experiments that the penalty factor of frequency smoothness reduces accuracy of matching. This is why the ridge width of fingerprint changes drastically near minutiae, and this change causes erroneous selection of frequencies. The processing time of the image enhancement is approximately 1.0 sec/finger on a RISC-based workstation (NEC UP4800/890).[1]

Figures 6.6 and 6.7 show an enhanced image and ridge features of the original image in Fig. 6.3. Figure 6.8 compares thinned images by the proposed enhancement with that by a method developed by Asai et al. [3]. As shown in Fig. 6.8b, the proposed method greatly reduces the effect of printed letters, connects breaks in ridges, and finally removes pseudominutiae from low-quality regions.

---

[1] R12000, 300 MHz.

Fig. 6.6. Enhanced image.

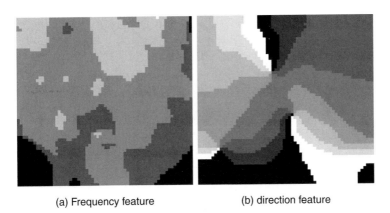

(a) Frequency feature   (b) direction feature

Fig. 6.7. Ridge features. (a) Frequency feature. Brighter values mean higher frequency in frequency feature. (b) Direction feature. Direction coordinate is clockwise, and $\phi_0 = 0/8\pi$ is shown dark and $\phi_7 = 7/8\pi$ is bright in direction feature.

We did a fingerprint matching experiment to evaluate our image enhancement methods. As the fingerprint matching, a minutiae relation algorithm proposed by Asai et al. [4] is implemented. The matching accuracy is evaluated by the false identification rate.

Some 27,000 pairs of rolled fingerprints from the NIST 14 database [13] were used in the evaluation. The experimental result shows that the proposed enhancement

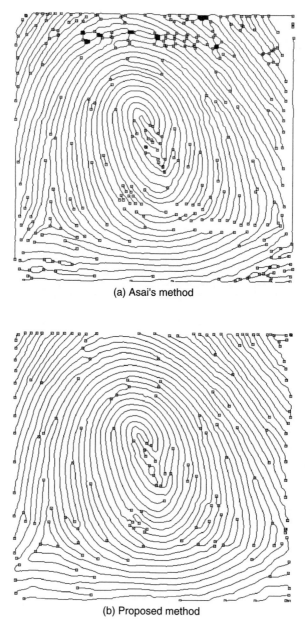

(a) Asai's method

(b) Proposed method

Fig. 6.8. Comparison of thinned images. The proposed method greatly reduces the effect of printed letters and connects breaks in ridges.

reduces the false identification rate by about two thirds compared with Asai's method. This improvement demonstrates the effectiveness of image enhancement with the proposed filters.

6.5. Conclusions

Fingerprint filter design and a method for enhancing fingerprint images are discussed. Filters are designed in the Fourier domain with consideration given to the frequency and direction features of fingerprint ridges. We have introduced two filters, a frequency filter and a directional filter, where the separability of filters decreases the computational complexity of the image enhancement. This image enhancement method is based on an energy minimization principle. Multifiltered images are produced by filtering the image with various filters, which characterize ridge features, and the energy function is used for selecting filters, which match ridge features. Using selected filters, which minimize the energy function, an enhanced image is produced from multifiltered images.

From matching experiments on the NIST 14 fingerprint database, it is found that this method decreases the false identification rate by about two thirds compared to just using Asai's matching method.

Acknowledgments

The author would like to thank Tsutomu Temma for providing the opportunity for this work and Kazuo Kiji and Masanori Hara for the preparation of the NIST database.

References

1. Federal Bureau of Investigation; *The Science of Fingerprints*, Washington DC: U.S. Department of Justice, 1963.
2. Hoshino, Y., K. Asai, Y. Kato, and K. Kiji, Automatic reading and matching for single-fingerprint identification, 65th International Association for Identification Conference, Ottawa, Canada, 1980, 1–7.
3. Asai, K., Y. Hoshino, and K. Kiji, Automated fingerprint identification by minutia-network feature—Feature extraction process, *IEICE Trans.*, J72-D-II(5):724–732, 1989.
4. Asai, K., Y. Hoshino, and K. Kiji, Automated fingerprint identification by minutia-network feature—Matching process, *IEICE Trans.*, J72-D-II(5):733–740, 1989.
5. Danielsson, P. E. and Q. Z. Ye, Rotation-invariant operators applied to enhancement of fingerprints, *Proc. Intl. Conference on Pattern Recognition*, 1988, pp. 329–333.
6. O'Gorman, L. and J. V. Nickerson, An approach to fingerprint filter design, *Pattern Recognition*, 22(1):29–38, 1989.
7. Sherlock, B.G., D.M. Monro, and K. Millard, *Electronics Letters*, 28(18):1720–1721, 1992.
8. Schunck, B. G., The image flow constraint equation, *Computer Vision, Graphics, and Image Processing*, 35:20–46, 1986.

9. Kass, M. and A. Witkin, Analyzing oriented patterns, *Computer Vision, Graphics, and Image Processing*, 37:362–401, 1987.

10. Kamei, T., H. Kawakami, N. Ohta, and J. Tajima, Smoothing method of fingerprint ridge directions on the energy minimization principle, *Record of IEICE Spring Conference*, D-602(7)344, 1992.

11. Williams, D. J. and M. Shah, A fast algorithm for active contours, *Proc. Intl. Conference on Computer Vision*, 1990, pp. 592–595.

12. National Institute of Standards and Technology, NIST Special Database 4—Fingerprint database, 1992.

13. National Institute of Standards and Technology, NIST Special Database 14—Mated Fingerprint Card Pairs 2, 1993.

Chapter 7

Fingerprint Enhancement

Lin Hong and Anil Jain

Abstract. To ensure reliable minutiae extraction is one of the most important issues in automatic fingerprint identification. Fingerprint enhancement is the most widely used technique to achieve such a goal. In this chapter, we describe (1) a spatial domain filtering enhancement algorithm and (2) a frequency decomposition enhancement algorithm. Both algorithms are able to adaptively improve the clarity of ridge and valley structures based on the local ridge orientation and ridge frequency. They also identify the unrecoverable corrupted regions in an input fingerprint image and mask them out, which is a very important property because such unrecoverable regions do appear in some of the corrupted fingerprint images and they are extremely harmful to minutiae extraction.

7.1. Introduction

The uniqueness of a fingerprint is exclusively determined by the ridge characteristics and their relationships [1, 2]. More than 100 different local ridge characteristics (for example, ridge ending, core, delta, islands, short ridges, enclosure, *etc.*) have been identified [2]. Most of these local ridge characteristics are not invariant to acquisition and/or impression conditions. For automatic fingerprint identification, only the two most prominent local ridge characteristics, ridge ending and ridge bifurcation (called *minutiae*), are widely used (see Fig. 7.1). A ridge ending indicates the location where a ridge ends abruptly. A ridge bifurcation indicates a location where a ridge forks or diverges into branch ridges.

Currently the most widely used and the most accurate automatic fingerprint identification techniques use minutiae-based automatic fingerprint matching algorithms. Reliably extracting minutiae from the input fingerprint images is critical to fingerprint matching. The performance of current minutiae extraction algorithms depends heavily on the quality of input fingerprint images. In an ideal fingerprint image, ridges and valleys alternate and flow in a locally constant direction and minutiae are anomalies of ridges, that is, ridge endings and ridge bifurcations. In such situations, the ridges can be easily detected and minutiae can be precisely located from a binary ridge map. Figure 7.3 shows an example of good-quality live-scan fingerprint image. In practice, due to variations in impression conditions, ridge configuration, skin conditions

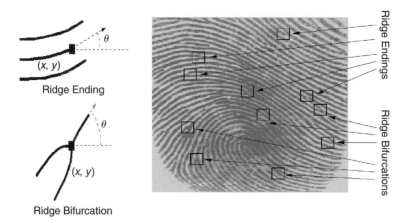

Fig. 7.1. Examples of minutiae: left—a minutia can be characterized by its position and its orientation; right—minutiae in a fingerprint image.

Fig. 7.2. Poor-quality fingerprint images.

(dryness, wet finger, aberrant formations of epidermal ridges of fingerprints, postnatal marks, occupational marks), acquisition devices, and noncooperative attitude of subjects, etc., a significant percentage of acquired fingerprint images (approximately 10% according to our experience) is of poor quality. Figure 7.2 shows examples of poor-quality fingerprint images. The ridge structures in poor-quality fingerprint images are not always well defined and hence they cannot always be correctly detected. This, of course, can result in failures of minutiae extraction algorithms, including (1) a significant number of spurious minutiae may be created, (2) a large percentage of genuine minutiae may be undetected, and (3) a significant amount of error in position and orientation may be introduced. Figure 7.4 shows an example of applying minutiae extraction algorithm to live-scan fingerprint images of poor quality. We can see that the performance of the minutiae extraction algorithm on the poor-quality image is far from desirable; a significant number of spurious minutiae are created and a large percentage of genuine minutiae is undetected by the algorithm.

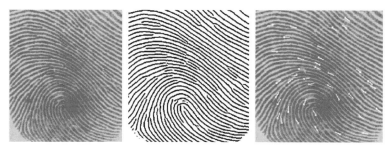

Fig. 7.3. Results of applying a minutiae extraction algorithm to a fingerprint image of good quality: from left to right—input image; extracted ridge map; extracted minutiae superimposed on the input fingerprint image.

Fig. 7.4. Results of applying a minutiae extraction algorithm to a fingerprint image of poor quality: from left to right—input image; extracted ridge map; extracted minutiae superimposed on the input fingerprint image.

To ensure that the performance of the minutiae extraction algorithms are robust with respect to the quality of input fingerprint images, an enhancement algorithm, which can improve the quality of the ridge structures of input fingerprint images, is thus necessary. Ideally, when the ridge structures in a fingerprint image are well defined, each ridge is separated by two parallel narrow furrows, each furrow is separated by two parallel narrow ridges; and minutiae are anomalies of ridges, that is, ridge endings and ridge bifurcations. When a fingerprint image is corrupted by various kinds of noise, such well-defined ridge structures are no longer visible. However, a fingerprint expert is often able to correctly identify the minutiae by using various contextual visual clues such as local ridge orientation, ridge continuity, ridge tendency, *etc.*, as long as the ridge and valley structures are not corrupted completely. Therefore, it should be possible to develop an enhancement algorithm that exploits these visual clues to improve the clarity of ridge structures in corrupted fingerprint images.

Generally, for a given fingerprint image, fingerprint regions can be assigned as one the following three categories (see Fig. 7.5):

1. Well-defined regions, in which ridges and furrows are clearly visible for a minutia extraction algorithm to operate reliably.
2. Recoverable corrupted regions, in which ridges and furrows are corrupted by a small amount of creases, smudges, etc. But they can still be correctly recovered by an enhancement algorithm.

Fig. 7.5. Example of fingerprint region: left to right—well-defined region, recoverable region; unrecoverable region.

3. Unrecoverable corrupted regions, in which ridges and furrows are corrupted by such a severe amount of noise and distortion that it is impossible to recover them from the corrupted image.

We refer to the first two categories of fingerprint regions as recoverable and the last category as unrecoverable. It is impossible to recover the original ridge structures in the unrecoverable regions, since no ridges and furrows are present at all within these regions. Any effort to improve the quality of the fingerprint image in these regions is futile. Therefore, the goal of a reasonable enhancement algorithm is to improve the clarity of ridge structures of fingerprint images in recoverable regions and to mask out the unrecoverable regions. In addition, since the objective of a fingerprint enhancement algorithm is to improve the quality of ridge structures of input fingerprint images to facilitate the extraction of ridges and minutiae, a fingerprint enhancement algorithm should not create any spurious ridge structures. This is very important, because spurious ridge structures may change the individuality of input fingerprints.

Fingerprint enhancement can be performed at either the binary level or the gray level. A binary-level ridge image is an image where all the ridge pixels are assigned a value 1 and nonridge pixels are assigned a value 0. The binary image can be obtained by applying a ridge extraction algorithm on a gray-level image. Since ridges and valleys in a fingerprint image alternate and run parallel to each other in a local neighborhood, a number of simple heuristics can be used to differentiate the spurious ridge configurations from the true ridge configurations in a binary ridge image [4]. However, after applying a ridge extraction algorithm on the original gray-level images, information about the true ridge structures is often lost depending on the performance of the ridge extraction algorithm. Therefore, enhancement of binary ridge images has its inherent limitations.

In gray-level fingerprint images, ridges and valleys in a local neighborhood form a sinusoidal-shaped plane wave, which has a well-defined frequency and orientation. A number of techniques that take advantage of this information have been proposed to enhance gray-level fingerprint images [5, 10–13]. However, these algorithms usually assume that the local ridge orientations can be reliably estimated. For fingerprint images of poor quality, such an assumption cannot be made, due to the existence of noise, creases, smudges, and holes. Figure 7.6 shows two examples of estimated

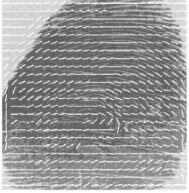

Fig. 7.6. Estimated orientation fields of fingerprint images of poor quality.

local ridge orientation of fingerprint images of poor quality. Therefore, a fingerprint enhancement algorithm should not assume that local ridge orientation could be easily obtained. Instead, it should focus a significant amount of effort on reliable estimation of orientation field.

In this chapter, we introduce two algorithms, a spatial domain filtering algorithm [15] and a frequency decomposition algorithm [14]. The spatial domain filtering algorithm estimates the local ridge orientation and frequency using a multistage approach and then adaptively enhances the ridge and valley structures using the estimated local ridge orientation and local frequency information. The spatial domain filtering algorithm is able, to a certain extent, to tolerate the poor image quality to obtain a reliable local orientation estimation using frequency and continuity characteristics of ridges. The frequency decomposition algorithm uses a decomposition method to estimate the local ridge orientation from a set of filtered images obtained by applying a bank of Gabor filters on the input fingerprint images. It concentrates a large amount of effort on a reliable estimation of the local ridge orientation. It is capable of obtaining a relatively good estimate of the orientation field even if the quality of the input fingerprint image is poor. Both algorithms identify the unrecoverable corrupted regions in the fingerprint and mask them out. This is a very important property because such unrecoverable regions do appear in some of the corrupted fingerprint images and they are extremely harmful to minutiae extraction.

7.2. Spatial Domain Filtering Algorithm

The spatial domain filtering algorithm adaptively enhances the clarity of ridge and valley structures using a bank of Gabor filters that are tuned to the local ridge orientation and ridge frequency. The local ridge orientation and ridge frequency are estimated directly from input images in the spatial domain. The main steps of the enhancement algorithm are shown in Fig. 7.7. In the following, we explain each of these steps.

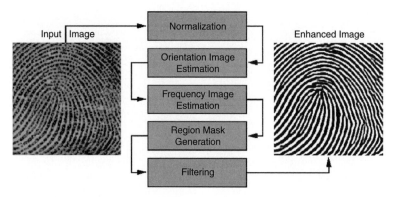

Fig. 7.7. The flowchart of the spatial domain fingerprint enhancement algorithm.

7.2.1. Normalization

An input fingerprint image needs to be normalized so that it has a prespecified mean and variance. Normalization is a pixel-wise operation, in which an output pixel value depends only on the corresponding input pixel. It does not change the clarity of the ridge and valley structures. The main purpose of normalization is to reduce the variations in gray-level values along ridges and valleys, which facilitates the subsequent processing steps.

7.2.2. Local Ridge Orientation Estimation

Local orientation indicates the major ridge orientation tendency in a local neighborhood. It represents an intrinsic property of a fingerprint image and defines an invariant coordinate for ridges and valleys in a local neighborhood. Following ridges, local ridge orientation changes slowly. Therefore, it is usually specified block-wise. In addition, there is no difference between a local ridge orientation of 90° and 270°, since the ridges oriented at 90° and the ridges oriented at 270° in a local neighborhood cannot be differentiated from each other.

By viewing a fingerprint image as an oriented texture, a number of methods have been proposed to estimate the orientation field of fingerprint images [16, 18, 19]. A least mean-square orientation estimation algorithm is used in local orientation estimation [3]. Examples of local ridge orientation estimation are shown in Fig. 7.8.

7.2.3. Local Ridge Frequency Estimation

Local ridge frequency is the frequency of the ridge and valley structures in a local neighborhood along a direction normal to the local ridge orientation. The ridge and valley structures in a local neighborhood where minutiae or singular points appear do not form a well-defined sinusoidal-shaped wave. In such situations, the frequency is defined as the average frequency in the neighborhood. Local ridge frequency represents another intrinsic property of a fingerprint image.

Fig. 7.8. Examples of local ridge orientation estimation.

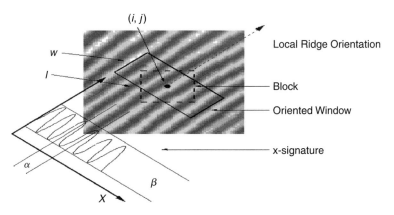

Fig. 7.9. Local ridge frequency estimation.

In a local neighborhood, the x-signature of two-dimensional sinusoidal-shaped wave along a direction normal to the local ridge orientation (see Fig. 7.9) has the same frequency as the ridges and valleys in the oriented local neighborhood. The x-signature is robust to noise and small artifacts. It can be efficiently calculated. The frequency of ridges and valleys can be reliably estimated from the x-signature as the average number of pixels between two consecutive peaks in the x-signature. In some regions of a dry/wet finger, the x-signature may not be reliable enough for robust frequency estimation. However, as long as some regions can provide reliable estimates, the regions with an unreliable x-signature can be easily compensated for by using the low-variation property of local frequency.

7.2.4. Region Mask Estimation

The region mask is used to indicate the category of the pixel. A pixel could be either a non-ridge-and-valley (unrecoverable) pixel or a ridge-and-valley (recoverable) pixel.

As mentioned earlier, a pixel (or a block of pixels) in an input fingerprint image could be either in a recoverable region or in an unrecoverable region. Classification of pixels into recoverable and unrecoverable categories can be performed based on the assessment of the shape of the wave formed by the local ridges and valleys. Three features are used to characterize the sinusoidal-shaped wave: amplitude, frequency, and variance of x-signature (the intensity profile along local ridge orientation in a small local neighborhood). A number of typical fingerprint images where both recoverable and unrecoverable regions were manually labeled and the three features for those regions are computed. The three-dimensional patterns obtained are fed to a squared-error-based clustering algorithm to find representative patterns for the two classes, in which six clusters are identified. Four of these clusters correspond to recoverable regions and the remaining two correspond to unrecoverable regions. The six prototypes (corresponding to the six cluster centers) were used in a one-nearest-neighbor (1NN) classifier to classify each block in an input fingerprint image into a recoverable or an unrecoverable block. The percentage of recoverable regions is also computed as a quality indicator. If the quality indicator is smaller than a threshold, then the input fingerprint image is rejected.

7.2.5. Filtering

A bank of Gabor filters tuned to local ridge orientation and ridge frequency is applied to the ridge-and-valley pixels in the normalized input fingerprint image to obtain an enhanced fingerprint image. The configurations of parallel ridges and valleys with well-defined frequency and orientation in a fingerprint image provide useful information to remove undesired artifacts and noise. The sinusoidal-shaped waves of ridges and valleys vary slowly in a local constant orientation. A bandpass filter tuned to the corresponding frequency and orientation can efficiently remove the undesired artifacts and noise and preserve the true ridge and valley structures. Gabor filters (Fig. 7.10) have both frequency-selective and orientation-selective properties and have optimal joint resolution (i.e., can maintain a maximum filter accuracy in well-defined frequency/spatial range) in spatial and frequency domains [20, 21]. It is appropriate to

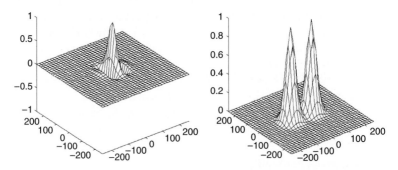

Fig. 7.10. An even-symmetric Gabor filter: left—Gabor filter tuned to 60 cycles/width and 0 orientation; right—the corresponding modulation transfer function (MTF).

Fig. 7.11. Examples of fingerprint enhancement results: left—input images; right—enhanced recoverable regions superimposed on the corresponding input images; unrecoverable regions are marked white.

use Gabor filters as bandpass filters to remove the artifacts and noise and preserve true ridge/valley structures. To apply Gabor filters to an image, three parameters must be specified: (1) the frequency of the sinusoidal plane wave; (2) the filter orientation; and (3) the standard deviations of the Gaussian envelope. Obviously, the frequency characteristic of the filter is completely determined by the local ridge frequency and the orientation is determined by the local ridge orientation. The values of the Gaussian envelope involves a trade-off. The larger the values, the more robust noises are the filters to artifacts and but the more likely the filters will create spurious ridges and valleys. On the other hand, the smaller the values, the less likely the filters will create spurious ridges and valleys; consequently, they will be less effective in removing the noise. Empirical data can provide a good estimation, which is usually 1.5 to 2.5 the interridge distance. Examples of enhanced images are shown in Fig. 7.11.

7.3. Frequency Decomposition Algorithm

An overview of the frequency decomposition algorithm is shown in Fig. 7.12. It consists of two main stages: (1) orientation field estimation, and (2) enhancement. Instead of estimating the orientation field directly from the input fingerprint image, we estimate it from the filtered images in which degradation that is not parallel to the dominant ridge orientation is greatly attenuated. Because our algorithm can obtain a reliable estimate of the orientation field, a better performance can thus be achieved in the enhancement stage. Its main steps are described in the following.

7.3.1. Decomposition

Gabor filters have both frequency-selective and orientation-selective properties and have optimal joint resolution in both spatial and frequency domains [20, 21]. It is

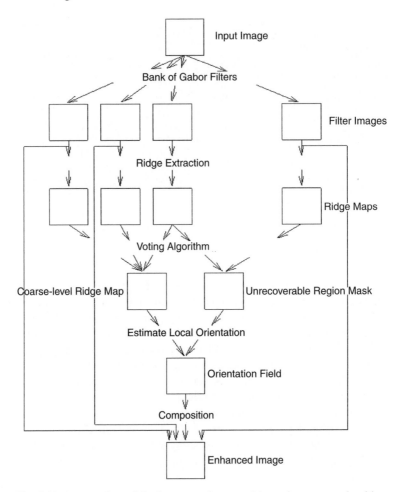

Fig. 7.12. An overview of the frequency decomposition enhancement algorithm.

beneficial to use Gabor filters to decompose an image into a number of subband images, which can preserve true ridge/furrow structures. For a given input fingerprint image, eight Gabor filters are applied to obtain eight filtered images. To obtain a filtered image, an FFT is first performed on the input fingerprint image. Then the corresponding Gabor filters with tuned radial and orientation frequencies are applied to the frequency image and an inverse FFT is performed to obtain the filtered image. Figure 7.13 shows a fingerprint image and the eight filtered images.

7.3.2. Ridge Extraction

The filtered image corresponding to a given Gabor filter mainly preserves the ridges and furrows that are of the same direction as the filter direction. A channel selection algorithm is needed to combine the filtered images to generate an enhanced image.

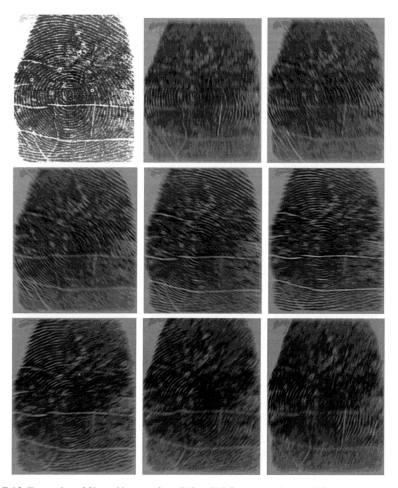

Fig. 7.13. Examples of filtered images for a 512 × 512 fingerprint image: left top—input image; from top to bottom and left to right—filtered images with Gabor filters tuned to 60 cycles/width and orientations of 0°, 22.5°, 45°, 67.5°, 90°, 112.5°, 135°, 157.5°, respectively.

Ideally, a Bayesian evidence integration scheme, which is based on the difference of the orthogonal channel contribution, can be used to select channel(s) corresponding to each block. However, in order to ensure that such an evidence integration scheme be robust to noise, evidence should be collected from a relatively large area of a local neighborhood. Computationally, it is very expensive. Therefore, in the algorithm, a binary ridge map is extracted and is used to select the correct channels, which is computationally inexpensive.

7.3.3. Combine Ridge Map Using Voting

The coarse-level ridge map consists of the ridges extracted from each filtered image that are consistent with one another. It is used to estimate a reliable orientation field.

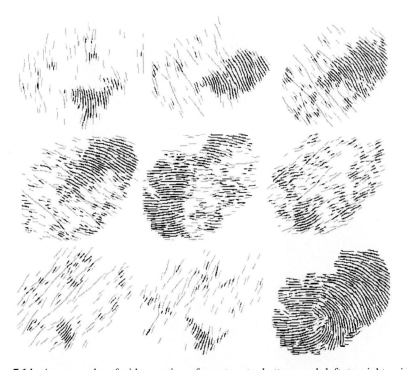

Fig. 7.14. An example of ridge voting: from top to bottom and left to right—ridge map on filtered images with Gabor filters tuned to 60 cycles/width and orientations of 0°, 22.5°, 45°, 67.5°, 90°, 112.5°, 135°, 157.5°, respectively; bottom right—the voting result.

The only requirement for the generated coarse-level ridge map is that it should roughly reflect the orientation of the local ridge structures of the input fingerprint image. It is not necessary to impose a requirement that this coarse-level ridge map be very precise in terms of local ridge structures, since the minutiae will not be extracted from the coarse-level ridge map. Neighboring ridges in a fingerprint image are usually oriented in the same direction (see Fig. 7.14). A filtered image obtained by applying a Gabor filter tuned to a certain direction retains the ridges that are oriented approximately in the same direction as the tuned direction of the Gabor filter. Generally, a ridge is a genuine ridge only if it is in a continuous region of significant size and tends to run parallel to its neighboring ridges. This property can be used as a heuristic to differentiate the genuine ridges from the spurious ridges. In the algorithm, the coarse-level ridge map and unrecoverable region mask are generated from the ridge maps of filtered images by using a voting algorithm, which selects dominant ridges that are consistent in a local neighborhood.

7.3.4. Composition

The coarse-level ridge map generated from the ridge maps of the filtered images preserves the local orientation information of the ridge structures of the input fingerprint image. The orientation field of the input fingerprint image can now be estimated from the coarse-level ridge map by ignoring the unrecoverable regions. The orientation field estimated from the coarse-level ridge map is more reliable than the orientation field estimated directly from the original image, because the steps introduced in the previous sections greatly suppress the harmful effect of noise, speckles, creases, holes, etc.

From the computed orientation field and filtered images, an enhanced image is obtained. The gray-level value at each pixel of the enhanced image can be interpolated from selected filtered images. The major reason for interpolating the enhanced image directly from the limited number of filtered images is that the filtered images are already available and the above interpolation is computationally efficient. Obviously, the quality of the image obtained from such an interpolation scheme is not as good as the quality of the image obtained by adaptively filtering the original image using the Gabor filters. However, it is sufficient for our minutiae extraction algorithm, which, in fact, has the capability of tolerating the boundary effect of the enhanced images due to the limited amount of filtered images being used.

7.4. Evaluation of Fingerprint Enhancement Algorithms

The purpose of a fingerprint enhancement algorithm is to improve the clarity of ridges and valleys of input fingerprint images and make them more suitable for the minutiae extraction algorithm. The ultimate criterion for evaluating an enhancement algorithm is the total amount of "quality" improvement when the algorithm is applied to the noisy input fingerprint images. Improvement can be assessed subjectively by a visual inspection of a number of typical enhancement results. However, a precise and consistent characterization of the quality improvement is beyond the capability of subjective evaluation.

A goal-directed performance evaluation assesses the overall improvement in the system performance that incorporates the enhancement module as a component. Therefore, it is capable of providing a more reliable assessment of the performance benchmark and is directly associated with the ultimate goal of the system [15]. In the following, we present the results of the goal-directed performance evaluation of the enhancement algorithm.

Fig. 7.15. Results of applying the enhancement algorithm to a fingerprint image of poor quality: left to right—input image; unrecoverable region mask; enhanced image.

7.4.1. Evaluation Using Goodness Index

The goodness index indicates the accuracy of minutiae extraction. It could be used to quantitatively assess the performance of our fingerprint enhancement algorithm. Let $M_d = \{f^1, f^2, \ldots, f^n\}$ be the set of n minutiae detected by the minutiae extraction algorithm and $M = \{g^1, g^2, \ldots, g^m\}$ be the set of m minutiae identified by a human expert in an input fingerprint image. Define:

Paired minutiae, p: minutiae f and g are said to be paired if f is located in a tolerance box centered around g (e.g., an 8 by 8 block)

Missing minutiae, a: a minutia that is not detected by the minutiae extraction algorithm

Spurious minutiae, b: a minutia that is detected by the minutiae extraction algorithm, but that is not in the tolerance box of any minutiae, g.

The goodness index (GI) is defined as follows [17]:

$$GI = \frac{\sum_i^r q_i[p_i - a_i - b_i]}{\sum_i^r q_i t_i}$$

where r is the number of 16 by 16 windows in the input fingerprint image, p_i represents the number of minutiae paired in window i, q_i represents the quality factor of the window i (good = 4, medium = 2, poor = 1), a_i represents the number of missing minutiae in window i, b_i represents the number of spurious minutiae in window i, and t_i represents the number of true minutiae in the window i. GI penalizes both the missing minutiae and spurious minutiae. It is a reasonable measure of the quality of the extracted minutiae. The larger the value of GI, the better the minutiae extraction algorithm. The maximum value of GI equals 1, which means there are no missing and spurious minutiae.

The spatial domain filtering algorithm was tested on 50 typical poor fingerprint images obtained from IBM. First, the goodness index of the extracted minutiae without applying the enhancement algorithm was computed and then the goodness index of the extracted minutiae was computed with the enhancement algorithm applied to the input fingerprint images before the minutiae were extracted. The mean and variance of the GI values, 2.4 and 0.05, respectively, before applying the enhancement algorithm are always larger than those, 0.39 and 0.04, respectively, after applying the enhancement algorithm. Thus, it demonstrates that the enhancement algorithm does improve the quality of the fingerprint images, which, in turn, improves the accuracy and reliability of the extracted minutiae.

7.4.2. Evaluation Using Identification Performance

The purpose of a fingerprint enhancement algorithm is to improve the quality of input fingerprint images and make them more suitable for the minutiae extraction module. Therefore, the ultimate criterion for evaluating such an enhancement algorithm is the amount of performance improvement when the algorithm is applied to the noisy

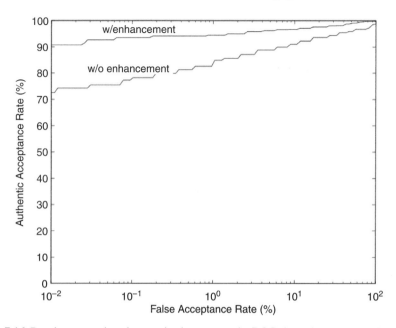

Fig. 7.16. Receiver operating characterization curves; the ROC shows improvement in verification performance of the enhancement algorithm.

fingerprint images. In order to evaluate the performance of the enhancement algorithm, we have conducted experiments using the verification algorithm on a subset of the MSU fingerprint database, which consists of 700 images of 70 individuals. The receiver operating characterization (ROC) curves, which indicate an empirical assessment of the system performance at different operating points, provide a comparison of identification accuracy before enhancement and after enhancement.

First, the fingerprint enhancement algorithm was not applied. Each fingerprint image in the data set was directly matched against the other fingerprint images in the database. Second, the enhancement algorithm was applied to each fingerprint image in the data set. Then, the matching was conducted on the enhanced fingerprint images. The ROC curves resulting from the two tests are shown in Fig. 7.16. From the experimental results, it can be observed that the performance of the fingerprint verification system is significantly improved when the fingerprint enhancement algorithm is applied to the input fingerprint images. In particular, the enhancement algorithm substantially reduced the false-reject rate while maintaining the same false-accept rate.

7.5. Summary

Two fingerprint enhancement algorithms are described in this chapter. Both algorithms are able to improve the quality of a fingerprint image such that more reliable feature extraction can be achieved. Both algorithms identify the unrecoverable corrupted regions in the fingerprint and mask them out. This is a very important property because such unrecoverable regions do appear in some of the corrupted fingerprint images and they are extremely harmful to minutiae extraction.

The spatial domain filtering algorithm adaptively improves the clarity of ridge and valley structures based on the local ridge orientation and ridge frequency estimated from the input image. The performance of the algorithm was evaluated using the goodness index of the extracted minutiae. Experimental results show that the enhancement algorithm is capable of improving the goodness index. Note that, in this algorithm, the local ridge orientation estimation is estimated directly from the input image, which may not be as accurate as the frequency decomposition algorithm. However, it is computationally more efficient.

The frequency decomposition algorithm concentrates a large amount of effort on a reliable estimation of the orientation field, which plays a critical role in the minutiae extraction algorithm. The algorithm is capable of obtaining a relatively good estimate of the orientation field even if the quality of the input fingerprint image is poor. The algorithm does not perform very well around singular regions where ridges and valleys have relatively high curvature values. It tends to mask these regions as unrecoverable regions. However, because minutiae around singular regions are usually assigned lower weights during matching, such a deficiency is not serious.

The global ridge and valley configuration of fingerprint images presents a certain degree of regularity. A global model of the ridges and valleys that can be constructed from partial "valid" regions can be used to correct the errors in the estimated orientation images, which, in turn, will help the enhancement. Currently, we are investigating such a model-based enhancement algorithm.

The configurations of ridges and valleys within a local neighborhood vary with the quality of input fingerprint images, so well-defined sinusoidal-shaped waves of ridges and valleys may not always be observed. Global features are needed for a more precise region mask classification.

References

1. Lee, H. C. and R. E. Gaensslen, *Advances in Fingerprint Technology*, New York: Elsevier, 1991.
2. Moenssens, A., *Fingerprint Techniques*, London: Chilton Book Company, 1971.
3. Jain, A. K., L. Hong, and R. Bolle, On-line Fingerprint Verification, *PAMI*, 19(4):302–314, 1997.
4. Huang, D. C., Enhancement and feature purification of fingerprint images, *Pattern Recognition*, 26(11):1661–1671, 1993.
5. Danielsson, P. E. and Q. Z. Ye, Rotation-invariant operators applied to enhancement of fingerprints, *Proc. 9th ICPR*, Rome, 1988, pp. 329–333.
6. Millard, K., D. Monro, and B. Sherlock, Algorithm for enhancing fingerprint images, *Electronics Letters*, 28(12), 1992.
7. Kaymaz, E. and S. Mitra, A novel approach to Fourier spectral enhancement of laser-luminescent fingerprint images, *J. Forensic Sciences*, 38(3), 1993.

8. Nickerson, J. and L. O'Gorman, Matched filter design for fingerprint image enhancement, *Proc. IEEE Intl. Conf. on Acoustic, Speech and Signal Processing*, New York, 1988, pp. 916–919.

9. Berdan, L. and R. Chiralo, Adaptive digital enhancement of latent fingerprints, *Proc. Intl. Carnahan Conf. on Electronic Crime Countermeasures*, University of Kentucky, Lexington, KY, 1978, pp. 131–135.

10. Kamei, T. and M. Mizoguchi, Image filter design for fingerprint enhancement, *Proc. ISCV 95*, Coral Gables, FL, 1995, pp. 109–114.

11. Sherlock, D., Monro, D. M., and K. Millard, Fingerprint enhancement by directional Fourier filtering, *IEE Proc. Vis. Image Signal Processing*, 141(2):87–94, 1994.

12. Sherstinsky, A. and R. W. Picard, Restoration and enhancement of fingerprint images using M-Lattice: A novel non-linear dynamical system, *Proc. 12th ICPR-B*, Jerusalem, 1994, pp. 195–200.

13. O'Gorman, L. and J. V. Nickerson, An approach to fingerprint filter design, *Pattern Recognition*, 22(1):29–38, 1989.

14. Hong, L., A. K. Jain, S. Pankanti, and R. Bolle, Fingerprint enhancement, *Proc. 1st IEEE WACV*, Sarasota, FL, 1996, pp. 202–207.

15. Hong, L., Y. Wan, and A. K. Jain, Fingerprint image enhancement: Algorithms and performance evaluation, *IEEE Trans. on PAMI*, 20(8):777–789, August 1998.

16. Kawagoe, M. and A. Tojo, Fingerprint pattern classification, *Pattern Recognition*, 17(3):295–303, 1984.

17. Ratha, N., S. Chen, and A. K. Jain, Adaptive flow orientation based feature extraction in fingerprint images, *Pattern Recognition*, 28(11):1657–1672, 1995.

18. Rao, A., *Taxonomy for Texture Description and Identification*, New York: Springer–Verlag, 1990.

19. Kass, M. and A. Witkin, Analyzing oriented patterns, *CVGIP*, 37(4):362–385, 1987.

20. Daugman, J. G., Uncertainty relation for resolution in space, spatial-frequency, and orientation optimized by two-dimensional visual cortical filters, *J. Opt. Soc. Am.*, 2:1160–1169, 1985.

21. Jain, A. K. and F. Farrokhnia, Unsupervised texture segmentation using Gabor filters, *Pattern Recognition*, 24(12):1167–1186, 1991.

Chapter 8

Feature Extraction in Fingerprint Images

Weicheng Shen and M.A. Eshera

Abstract. A fingerprint image is comprised of a spatial map of the friction ridges of the skin and the valleys between them. An automated fingerprint indentification system (AFIS) compares two fingerprints by examining the "landmarks" (or features) of the ridges and valleys in order to decide whether they are a matching pair. Two fingerprint images are called a "matching pair" if it can be determined that they both are produced by the same finger of the same individual regardless of the time and method by which each image is collected. In most of the current fingerprint matching systems, the features used in the matching process are the fingerprint minutiae, mainly ridge bifurcation and ridge ending. However, the features do not necessarily have to be minutiae, as there are several characteristics that can also be utilized in the matching process. Minutiae-based fingerprint matching requires each fingerprint image be transformed into a minutiae map. This transformation generally includes the following steps: preprocessing, ridge direction and ridge width, enhancement, and minutiae detection. This chapter discusses several approaches for extracting the fingerprint feature maps from the spatial-domain images.

8.1. Introduction and Background

Fingerprint images are very rich in information content. There are two main types of information in the fingerprint image. First is the overall ridge flow information, which is defined by the pattern of the ridges and valleys in the fingerprint. This type of information describes the global pattern of the fingerprint and can be utilized for the classification of the fingerprint database into classes either at the global pattern level or furthermore into subpattern levels. The second type of information content is represented by many local points of discontinuities in the ridges and valleys, which are usually referred to as minutiae. Fingerprints are unique in their information content in that the combination of the local and global information forms a topological minutiae map represented by the minutiae, their relative relationships, and their relationship to points of global singularities of the pattern classes. Figure 8.1 shows an example of two different fingerprint images (or impression) of the same finger, while Fig. 8.2 shows several minutiae in each of the fingerprint images of Fig. 8.1.

Humans can manually recognize and identify fingerprint images by matching their corresponding minutia maps, that is, the matching of minutia pairs across both minu-

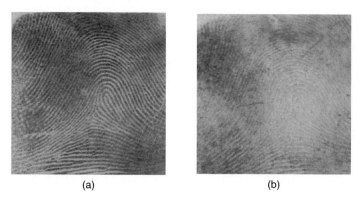

(a)   (b)

Fig. 8.1. Example of two fingerprint images taken from the same finger.

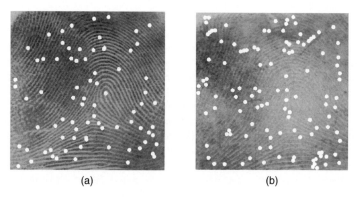

(a)   (b)

Fig. 8.2. Extracted minutiae from the two fingerprint images of Fig. 8.1.

tiae maps, their directions, and their relative topological relationships. The number of minutiae in a fingerprint image may vary widely from one fingerprint to another and from a fingerprint image to another due to many reasons. But, on the average, there are about 70 to 150 minutiae in a typical full fingerprint image. However, humans can make positive identification decisions by matching a much smaller number of minutia pairs, their respective topological relationships, and no unexplainable differences between two fingerprint images.

There are several serious problems with the fingerprint recognition process that arise from the following main reasons:

1. The minutiae map could vary from one image to another for the same fingerprint, due to many reasons; for example, the inking conditions—underinking or overinking could cause the creation of false minutiae or the disappearance of valid minutiae from one fingerprint image to another, unexpected smudges and smears, the sensitivity of the fingerprint live-scan devices, etc.
2. Stretches, changing of scale, rotation, translation, and nonuniform deformation of the fingerprint.

3. Nonuniform noise and distortion.
4. Unexpected natural variations due to personal conditions, extra-dry skin, cuts, aging, etc.

Two fingerprint images are called a "matching pair" if it can be determined that they are both produced by the same finger of the same individual regardless of the time and method by which each of the images was collected. Each of such fingerprints is referred to as the mate of the other. There are two major applications of the concept of a "matching pair," namely, identification and verification. In the case of identification, fingerprints of unknown individuals (search prints) are compared with fingerprints of individuals with known identities (reference prints) in order to positively determine the identity of the unknown individual. In the case of verification, one or more fingerprints of an individual (query prints) are compared with fingerprints of the person on file whose identity is claimed by the individual submitting the query prints, in order to verify the claim of identity. Before the use of computers, both processes used to be performed manually, which is obviously not an efficient way of dealing with a large quantity of data and meeting fast response requirements. Through the utilization of new state-of-the-art computer technology (both software and hardware), several Automated Fingerprint Identification Systems (AFIS) have been built, which are in operation.

How does an AFIS make such a determination of positive identification? In other words, what is the basis for a computer to decide whether two fingerprints are a matching pair? Such a system can automate this time-consuming process in a cost-effective way by closely mimicking the manual process. A fingerprint image is comprised of a map of friction ridges and the valleys between them. An AFIS compares two fingerprints by examining the "landmarks" of the ridges. In most of the current fingerprint matching algorithms, the landmarks are the fingerprint minutiae, mainly ridge bifurcation and ridge ending (see Fig. 8.4). However, the landmarks do not necessary have to be minutiae, as there are several other characteristics, such as pore and ridgelines, that can also be utilized in this process. Our discussion in this chapter is focused on obtaining the characteristics of fingerprint minutiae only, as they are the main type of characteristics most automated systems use.

Many diverse approaches have been proposed in the literature for feature extraction in fingerprint images. Most of these approaches convert the fingerprint image into a binary image and then perform a thinning process that reduces the ridges into one pixel wide. The local minutiae are then located on the binary thinned image. Moayer and Fu [1] propose a binarization technique based on an iterative application of a Laplacian operator and a dynamic thresholding algorithm. Similarly, Verma et al. [2] developed a fuzzy approach that uses an adaptive thresholding to preserve the same number of back and white pixels for each neighborhood. On the other hand, O'Gorman and Nickerson [3] propose an approach to fingerprint image enhancement and binarization based on the convolution of the image with a filter bank oriented according to the directional image of the fingerprint. The directional image of the fingerprint is defined as a matrix whose elements represent the tangent direction to the ridgelines of the corresponding fingerprint image. Sherlock et al. [4] propose an approach to fingerprint image enhancement and binarization by performing frequency-domain filtering through a bank of position-dependent filters. Szekely and Szekely [5] propose a minutiae detection technique based on the computation of divergence of the directional image as extracted from the fingerprint binary image.

A complete automated fingerprint identification system that includes a promising enhancement algorithm to overcome noise in the gray-scale fingerprint images has been proposed by Mehtre [6]. A detailed discussion of noise in fingerprint images is also presented in that work. Weber [7] proposes an approach that uses a frequency-domain bandpass filtering for image enhancement followed by binarization through local thresholds and then detects the minutiae from the thick ridges in the binary image.

There have been several neural network-based approaches; for example, the work of M. T. Leung et al. [8], which uses a multilayer perceptron for minutiae extraction by analyzing the output of a bank of Gabor filters applied to the gray-scale fingerprint images. Also, another neural network approach is presented by W. F. Leung et al. [9] where a three-layer perceptron is trained to extract the minutiae from the thinned binary images. Some neural network-based techniques can provide good results when applied to very high-quality fingerprint images, but most are not robust enough to handle noisy images. Several postprocessing techniques, such as in the work of Hung [10] and Xiao and Raafat [11], have also been presented in the literature to eliminate false minutiae, therefore improving the accuracy and speed of the matching process.

Figure 8.3 shows an image of a fingerprint captured by a live-scan device. The brighter regions in the image represent fingerprint ridges, while the darker regions between the brighter regions represent fingerprint valleys. The fingerprint minutiae ridge ending and ridge bifurcation are shown in more detail in Fig. 8.4. A ridge ending occurs when a ridgeline comes to an end, and no ridge ending with the same orientation is adjacent to it. A ridge bifurcation occurs when a ridgeline comes to a branch point,

Fig. 8.3. A live-scan fingerprint image.

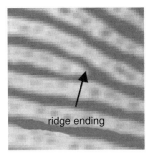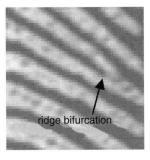

Fig. 8.4. Ridge ending and ridge bifurcation.

that is, where it splits into two ridgelines. A ridge bifurcation can be viewed as a valley ending. Similarly, a ridge ending can be viewed as a valley bifurcation.

This chapter is organized according to the major steps in minutiae extraction algorithms: Section 8.2 preprocessing; Section 8.3 ridges and ridge width; Section 8.4 enhancement; Section 8.5 minutiae detection in binary images; Section 8.6 minutiae detection in gray-scale images; Section 8.7 conclusion, Section 8.8 appendix, and then the references.

8.2. Foreground Detection

Figure 8.5 shows a fingerprint captured by digitizing an ink-rolled fingerprint on a fingerprint card. The digitized fingerprint is 500×500 pixels in size and has a resolution of 500 dpi in both the horizontal and vertical directions. The 500 dpi in resolution meets the current fingerprint image standard established by NIST in 1993 [12]. After the quantization of each pixel value, in the current standard, it has 256 gray levels, 0–255. In this image, the fingerprint ridges are represented by bright pixels, while the valleys are represented by dark pixels. An ideal dark pixel has a value of 0, while an ideal bright pixel has a value of 255. It can be observed that the image has some blank space near its edges, while the image is noisier at the boundary of the fingerprint and the surrounding blank space. It is also observed that the ridges at the boundaries of the image are often corrupted as a result of imperfect fingerprint collection processes. These regions constitute the "undesirable area," and they need to be excluded from further processing. We wish to focus our attention to the "interior" of the fingerprint image. The word "interior" is loosely defined as the portion of the image that is not at the boundary of the fingerprint and the blank space. In other words, it is the region of interest (ROI) and is denoted by R.

In order to find the "interior" of the fingerprint, we partition the image into a number of blocks by a rectangular or a square grid. Each "interior" block is more likely to contain more "bright" areas than the blocks on the boundary and in the blank regions. Let the fingerprint image be denoted by a 2D array G, and the value of the pixel located at the ith row and jth column be denoted by $G(i, j)$. Figure 8.6 shows

Fig. 8.5. An ink-rolled fingerprint image.

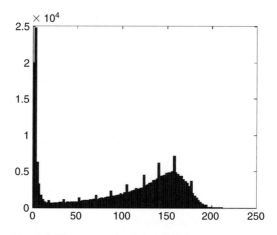

Fig. 8.6. Histogram of an ink-rolled fingerprint image.

the histogram of the gray-scale fingerprint image in Fig. 8.5. It is roughly a bimodal distribution: The center of the gray-scale value of the dark region is near 5, while the center of the gray-scale value of the bright region is near 160. Using the Otsu optimum threshold method [13], we can find a threshold value t (80) upon which the fingerprint image, G, can be segmented. A brief description of the Otsu optimum threshold is given in the appendix. Each pixel of G can be classified into one of two classes: b (bright) and d (dark). A pixel $G(i, j)$ belongs to b if $G(i, j) > t$, and it belongs to d

Fig. 8.7. Thresholded fingerprint image.

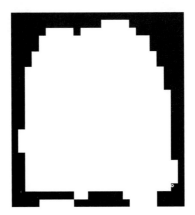

Fig. 8.8. Region of interest (ROI).

otherwise. The segmentation results in a binary map, in which each pixel is either an element of b or d, as shown in Fig 8.7.

Let's partition the image into the union of disjoint blocks, in which each block is a 20×20 pixel square. As the fingerprint image in Fig. 8.5 is 500×500 pixels in size, it is partitioned into 25×25 such squares. Each square is denoted as $block(p, q)$, $0 \leq p, q \leq 24$. Compute the percentage of white area within each block, and let it be z. Compare z with a threshold value t. If $z > t$, set all pixels in the block to white. Otherwise, set all pixels in the block to black. In the resulting image, the white region represents the region of interest (ROI), which is shown in Fig. 8.8. In other words, these are the pixels of interest considered for further processing.

Overlaying Fig. 8.8 on Fig. 8.5, we produce the regions of the fingerprint images to be further processed for feature extraction. The result is shown in Fig. 8.9.

Fig. 8.9. ROI of a fingerprint.

8.3. Ridge Flow and Ridge Width

Two fundamental measures of a digital fingerprint image are discussed in this section. They play key roles in characterizing a fingerprint image. Ridge flow is a description of the local ridge orientation in a fingerprint image. It represents the local ridge orientation for each pixel in the image. It is useful when applying oriented operators in later stages for minutiae detection. The term "oriented operator" is loosely defined as those operations in which the selection of an operator depends on the orientation of underlying data, for instance, the directional filter. The ridge flow calculation described here follows the work of Donahue and Rokhlin [14].

View a gray-scale fingerprint image as a 3D surface plot with image intensity $G(i, j)$ being the height of the surface, as shown in Fig. 8.11. Let the local ridge orientation at each pixel (i, j) be $\overline{O}(i, j)$, let the tangent orientation to $G(i, j)$ be $u(i, j)$, and let the surface normal of $G(i, j)$ be $n(i, j)$. The local ridge orientation $\overline{O}(i, j)$ is obtained by finding the "average" tangent orientation over a moving window centered at (i, j), as shown in Fig. 8.10. The box indicates the window, while the arrow indicates the ridge orientation. Let w be the size of the moving tangent orientation window. The surface normal, $n(i, j)$, of each pixel within the window is first computed. The normal vector $n(i, j)$ is expressed using a four-neighbor system, as illustrated in Fig. 8.11 with neighbor intensity values $a_1 = G(i + 1, j + 1), a_2 = G(i + 1, j - 1), a_3 = G(i - 1, j - 1)$, and $a_4 = G(i - 1, j + 1)$. According to Donahue and Rokhlin [14], the normal vector at (i, j) can be expressed as

$$n(i, j) = ((-a_1 + a_2 + a_3 - a_4)/4, (-a_1 - a_2 + a_3 + a_4)/4, 1)^T = (a_{ij}, b_{ij}, 1)^T$$

$$(1)$$

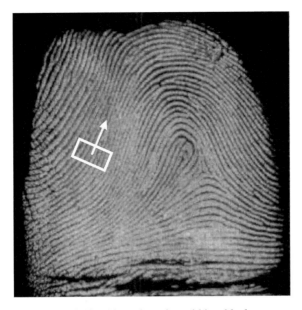

Fig. 8.10. Ridge orientation within a block.

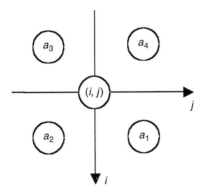

Fig. 8.11. Pixel configurations of a neighborhood.

While the unit tangent vector $u(h, k)$ for each pixel within the tangent orientation window is not expressly calculated, the collection of them contributes to the formulation of the least-square minimization solution of $\overline{O}(i, j)$. Mathematical details of this formulation can be found in Donahue and Rokhlin [14]. The steps for calculating the local ridge orientation for each pixel $G(i, j)$ in the fingerprint G are described below.

1. Determine the set of pixels that are within the window centered at (i, j),

$$S = \{(h, k) \mid -(w-1)/2 \leq h - i \leq (w-1)/2, -(w-1)/2 \leq k - j \leq (w-1)/2\}$$

$$(2)$$

2. Calculate three intermediate terms,

$$A = \sum_{(h,k) \in S} a_{hk}^2 \tag{3a}$$

$$B = \sum_{(h,k) \in S} b_{hk}^2 \tag{3b}$$

$$C = \sum_{(h,k) \in S} a_{hk} b_{hk} \tag{3c}$$

3. Determine the local ridge orientation $\overline{O}(i, j)$ by

$$\overline{O}(i, j) = \begin{cases} \arctan\left(\dfrac{B - A}{2C} - \sqrt{\left(\dfrac{B - A}{2C}\right)^2 + 1}\right) & \text{if } C > 0 \\[3ex] \arctan\left(\dfrac{B - A}{2C} + \sqrt{\left(\dfrac{B - A}{2C}\right)^2 + 1}\right) & \text{if } C > 0 \\[3ex] \dfrac{\pi}{2} & \text{if } C = 0 \end{cases} \tag{4}$$

The result is a local ridge orientation map, $\overline{O}$, which is of the same dimension as that of the fingerprint image G. Each pixel value in $\overline{O}$, denoted as $\overline{O}(i, j)$, represents the local ridge orientation of each pixel (i, j) in G. Figure 8.12 shows the ridge flow map for the fingerprint image shown in Fig. 8.10.

A ridge orientation map $\overline{O}$ provides ridge orientation estimates at each pixel of a fingerprint image. A ridge frequency (or width) map $\overline{W}$ provides a ridge width estimate at each pixel of a fingerprint image. The ridge width at a pixel (i, j) is defined

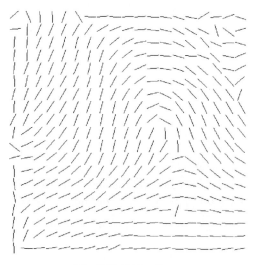

Fig. 8.12. Ridge flow.

as the average distance between two consecutive intensity peaks in the direction perpendicular to its tangential orientation $\overline{O}(i, j)$. The reciprocal of the width of local ridges is defined as the frequency of the local ridges. A ridge frequency map can be built from a fingerprint image and its ridge orientation map. A simple ridge frequency estimation procedure was developed by Hong et al. [15]. Following their work, the key steps of this procedure are outlined below, and the details can be found in Section 2.6 of [15].

1. The normalized gray-scale fingerprint image G is partitioned into blocks of size $W \times W(16 \times 16)$.
2. For each block centered at pixel (i, j), construct an oriented window of size $l \times w$ (32×16), where l and w are, respectively, the number of columns and rows of the window. The orientation of the window centered at (i, j) is decided by the ridge flow map at that pixel, $\overline{O}(i, j)$, as shown in Fig. 8.13. A zoomed-in version of the ridges within the window is shown is Fig. 8.14.

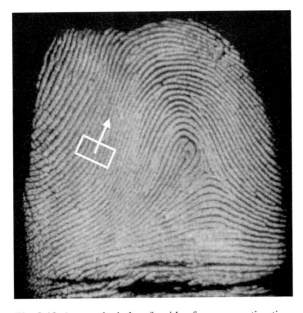

Fig. 8.13. A rotated window for ridge frequency estimation.

Fig. 8.14. Enlarged picture of a ridge frequency estimation window.

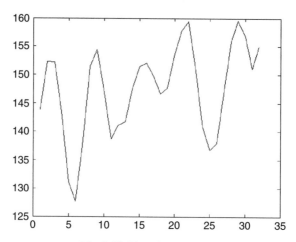

Fig. 8.15. Plot of x-signature.

3. For each block centered at pixel (i, j), compute the *x-signature*, $X[0]$, $X[1], \ldots, X[l-1]$. Each $X[k], k = 0, 1, \ldots, l-1$, is the average of pixel values in the kth column of the window and is calculated as

$$X[k] = \frac{1}{w} \sum_{d=0}^{w-1} G(u, v) \tag{5}$$

where

$$u = i + \left(d - \frac{w}{2}\right) \cos \overline{O}(i, j) + \left(k - \frac{1}{2}\right) \sin \overline{O}(i, j) \tag{6a}$$

$$v = j + \left(d - \frac{w}{2}\right) \sin \overline{O}(i, j) + \left(\frac{1}{2} - k\right) \cos \overline{O}(i, j) \tag{6b}$$

Plotting the *x-signature* X in Fig. 8.15, we observe that it resembles a sinu-soidal. To reduce the noise level, a low-pass filter can be applied to smooth this 1D signal. One way of estimating the frequency corresponding to X is taking the Fourier transform of X and detecting the peak without the DC component, as shown in Fig. 8.16. In this case, the peak occurs at 3 in frequency. That is the indication that the local ridge frequency is approximately 3 for a 32×16 window. If no peak, which is at least β times or higher than the second-highest frequency component, can be detected from the power spectrum, then set $\overline{W}(i, j) = 1$. The factor β is a positive number chosen by the user, and it is usually greater than 2.

4. For a given image resolution, the fingerprint ridge width normally varies within a fixed range. As most fingerprint images are collected at 500 dpi, the frequency of ridges and valleys normally is within the range [1/3, 1/25] [15]. If $\overline{W}(i, j)$ is outside this range, set $\overline{W}(i, j)$ to -1.

5. In some blocks, the corresponding ridge frequency is set to -1, as the occurrences of minutiae, corrupted ridges, or smudges might result in the inability to detect a

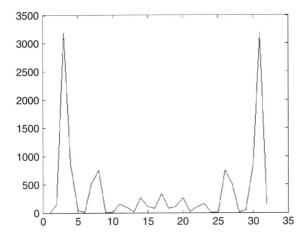

Fig. 8.16. Fourier transform of an x-signature.

power spectrum peak. In other words, these blocks do not provide the information necessary for estimating ridge frequencies. Their corresponding frequencies have to be estimated by interpolation of the frequencies of the neighboring blocks [15] as follows:

a. For each block centered at (i, j), the interpolated ridge frequency map $W(i, j)$ is formulated as

$$
W(i, j) = \begin{cases} \overline{W}(i, j) & \text{if } \overline{W}(i, j) \neq -1 \\[2em] \dfrac{\displaystyle\sum_{u=-w_\Omega/2}^{w_\Omega/2} \sum_{v=-w_\Omega/2}^{w_\Omega/2} w_g(u, v)\mu(\overline{W}(i - uw, j - vw))}{\displaystyle\sum_{u=-w_\Omega/2}^{w_\Omega/2} \sum_{v=-w_\Omega/2}^{w_\Omega/2} w_g(u, v)\delta(\overline{W}(i - uw, j - vw) + 1)} & \text{otherwise} \end{cases} \tag{7}
$$

with

$$
\mu(x) = \begin{cases} 0 & \text{if } x \leq 0 \\ x & \text{otherwise} \end{cases}
$$

and

$$
\delta(x) = \begin{cases} 0 & \text{if } x \leq 0 \\ l & \text{otherwise} \end{cases}
$$

Here w_g is a Gaussian kernel with zero mean and a variance of 9, with $w_\Omega = 7$ the size of the kernel.

b. If there is at least one block of $W(i, j) = -1$ remaining, then copy W into $\overline{W}$ and repeat (a). This process continues until no element of W equals -1.

6. As the ridge width varies slowly in any local region of a fingerprint image, it is assumed that the transitions between $W(i, j)$ and its neighbors do not have

sharp jumps. Hence, a low-pass filtering operation will smooth the noise in the estimation of W. Let the result of the previous step be relabeled as W'.

$$W(i, j) = \sum_{u=-w_i/2}^{w_i/2} \sum_{v=-w_i/2}^{w_i/2} w_l(u, v) W'(i - uw, j - vw) \tag{8}$$

where w_l is a 2D low-pass kernel of size $w_l = 7$, and the sum of all coefficients of w_l equals 1.

In the subsequent discussions, the orientation map is extensively used, while the ridge frequency (or width) map is only used when performing Gabor filtering. However, the ridge frequency map is a useful tool when performing fingerprint identification with "ridge counts." Using ridge counts is a powerful way of improving fingerprint identification accuracy in addition to the coordinates of fingerprint minutiae map.

8.4. Enhancement

Having produced a local ridge direction map (also known as the ridge flow map), we can proceed to decide whether a pixel belongs to a ridge or a valley. First consider a profile of a cross section of ridges and valleys. The cross section of ridges and valleys forms a waveform that resembles a sinusoidal. An ideal form of a number of parallel ridges is shown in Fig. 8.17, which is plotted as a 3D surface. The height of the surface (z) represents the pixel intensity of the image defined on the support represented by a subregion of the xy-plane. For an "ideal ridge" that can be further processed to obtain minutiae, the surface is constant in the tangential direction, while it is approximately a sinusoidal in the direction orthogonal to the tangential direction. The reason why such a ridge is ideal for minutiae extraction will become clear later in the minutiae extraction section. A section of real fingerprint image is shown in Fig. 8.18. In the tangential direction of a ridge, the peaks do not have the same value. Any break in a

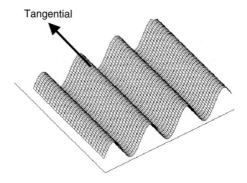

Fig. 8.17. Ideal ridges.

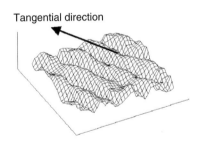

Tangential direction

Fig. 8.18. Three-dimensional plot and image of real ridges.

ridge results in more significant elevation changes in the ridge peaks of the tangential direction. On the other hand, along the orthogonal direction to the ridges, the transition from the peak of a ridge to its adjacent valley is not as smooth as a sinusoidal. It is more like a "bumpy" decaying function. As a result, we need to design a filter that is low pass in the tangential direction, and high pass in the direction orthogonal to the tangential direction. With appropriate rotations, multiple copes of this filter will be produced and form a directional filter bank. We consider three different designs of the filter banks with the above characteristics in the following discussions.

For all filter banks discussed, the number of ridge orientations computed in the ridge flow map determines the number of filters in each filter bank. If the elements of $\overline{O}$ have seven orientations, then the number of filters in a given filter bank will be seven. They overlap with the orientations specified in $\overline{O}$, that is, $\{-90°, -60°, -30°, 0°, 30°, 60°, 90°\}$.

8.4.1. Box Filter

Consider a box filter in the horizontal direction. The width, *filterWidth*, and length, *filterLength*, of the filter are defined as the horizontal size and vertical size, respectively. Let i and j denote the row and column indices of the filter, respectively. Let the maximum and minimum ridge and valley widths be w_{max}, w_{min}, v_{max}, and v_{min}, respectively [15]. These parameters can be estimated from the images under consideration. The filter comprises three types of horizontal bands: center band, transition band, and side band. Following the notations in [3], the locations of these bands are defined as

center band: $-h_m \leq i \leq h_m$

transition band: $-h_l < i < -h_m, \quad h_m < i < h_t$

side band: $-h_f \leq i \leq -h_t, \quad h_t \leq i \leq h_f$

The length of the box filter can be obtained by *filterLength* $= 2h_f + 1$. The center band is designed to enhance the ridge, while side bands are designed to enhance the

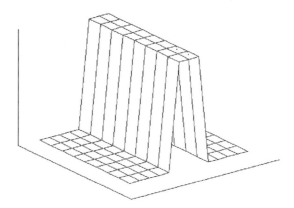

Fig. 8.19. Surface plot of a box filter.

contrast between the ridge and its adjacent valleys. The center band enhances the ridge by a smoothing operation in the ridge tangential direction. Contrast enhancement between the ridges and valleys is achieved by the difference operation implemented along the direction orthogonal to the tangential direction. The magnitude of the impulse response of the box filter is defined as

$$
f(i, j) = \begin{cases} 1.0 & -h_m \le i \le h_m \\ 0 & -h_t < i < -h_m, \quad h_m < i < h_t \\ \dfrac{-(2h_m + 1)}{2(h_f - h_t + 1)} & -h_f \le i \le -h_t, \quad h_t \le i \le h_f \end{cases}
\tag{9}
$$

Note that the sum of all nonzero values of this function is zero, which indicates that it has a zero DC component. The function is constant over index j, the tangential direction. Figure 8.19 is the plot of impulse response of the box filter with the following parameters: *filterWidth* $= 9$, $h_m = 1$, $h_t = 2$, $h_f = 6$, and *filterLength* $= 13$. This only specifies the box filter with horizontal tangential orientation, which is called the base filter. We can construct a directional filter bank by rotating this horizontal oriented filter according to a prespecified number of angles. For example, simple coordinate rotation coupled with interpolation will result in a rotated copy of the box filter. Let us assume that the ridge flow map contains elements of seven orientations. The directional filters in the filter bank are formed by rotating the base filter by -90, -60, -30, 30, 60, and 90 degrees. They are respectively denoted as $\{f_{-90}, f_{-60}, f_{-30}, f_0, f_{30}, f_{60}, f_{90}\}$, where f_0 is the base filter.

Enhancement of a fingerprint image by a box filter bank is obtained by the following 2D convolution:

$$
E(i, j) = \sum_{u=-h_f}^{h_f} \sum_{v=-h_f}^{h_f} G(i - u, j - v) f_p(u, v)
\tag{10}
$$

where $p = \overline{O}(i, j)$. In other words, each output pixel $E(i, j)$ is obtained as a weighted sum of the input pixels within a window centered at $G(i, j)$. The weights are determined by one of the filters in the box filter bank. Which orientation filter is selected for computing $E(i, j)$ depends on the orientation field surrounding the input pixel $G(i, j)$, which can be found in the orientation map $\overline{O}(i, j)$.

8.4.2. O&N Filter

Now consider the filter bank design introduced by O'Gorman and Nickerson [3], and let it be called the O&N directional filter bank. The cross section of fingerprint ridges and valleys is again viewed as slowly varying sinusoidal waves. Consider the horizontal oriented copy of the O&N filter bank, which is developed based on this view. It comprises three bands: the central band, the transition band, and the side band, each of which is defined in the same way as that of the box filter bank described previously. The sizes of the center band, transition bands, and side bands are specified by the following expressions:

$$
h_m = \begin{cases} \dfrac{w_{min}}{2} - 1, & w_{min} \text{ even} \\[2mm] \dfrac{w_{min}-1}{2}, & w_{min} \text{ odd} \end{cases} \tag{11a}
$$

$$
h_t = \begin{cases} \dfrac{w_{max}}{2} + 1, & w_{max} \text{ even} \\[2mm] \dfrac{w_{max}+1}{2}, & w_{max} \text{ odd} \end{cases} \tag{11b}
$$

$$
h_f = \begin{cases} h_t + 1 + \dfrac{v_{min}}{2}, & v_{min} \text{ even} \\[2mm] h_t - 1 + \dfrac{v_{min}+1}{2}, & v_{min} \text{ odd} \end{cases} \tag{11c}
$$

Figure 8.20 shows the different bands of the support of an O&N filter. In the original design of an O&N filter bank, it is assumed that each filter is a square filter of size $k \times k$, where $k = 2 \times h_f + 1$. In practice, it has been demonstrated that the width and length of the filter do not have to be the same—they can be rectangular filters. To calculate the filter coefficients $f(i, j)$, consider the center column of $f(i, j)$, namely $f(i, 0)$. It is a vertical 1D high-pass filter that is orthogonal to the ridge orientation (horizontal). In [3], the coefficients of this center column are defined as

$$
f(i, 0) = f(-i, 0) = \begin{cases} a_0 \cos \dfrac{i\pi}{4h_m}, & 0 \le i \le h_m \\[2mm] 0, & h_m < i < h_t \\[2mm] b_0 \cos \dfrac{\pi(h_f - i)}{4(h_f - h_t)}, & h_t \le i \le h_f \end{cases} \tag{12}
$$

where the value of a_0 is selected by the filter designer. It is set to 1000 in [3]. We have experimented with values from 1 to 5 when processing fingerprints of gray scale

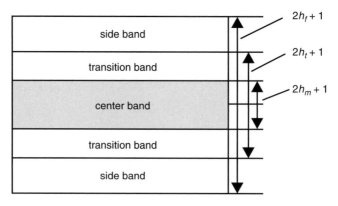

Fig. 8.20. Support of an O&N filter.

0–255, with good results. The magnitude of the filter affects the sharpness of the filter response. It is worthwhile to note that the above expression of $f(i, 0)$ is defined neither for the center band when $h_m = 0$, nor for the side band when $h_f = h_t$. When $h_m = 0$, the center band is defined as $f(i, 0) = f(-i, 0) = a_0/\sqrt{2}$. When $h_f = h_t$, the side band is defined as $f(i, 0) = f(-i, 0) = b_0$. The value of b_0 is obtained by equating the sum of all coefficients in the center column to zero:

$$a_0 + 2 \sum_{i=1}^{h_m} f(i, 0) + 2 \sum_{i=h_t}^{h_f} f(i, 0) = 0 \tag{13}$$

from which b_0 can be directly expressed as [3]

$$b_0 = \frac{-a_0 \left[1 + 2 \sum_{i-1}^{h_m} \frac{i\pi}{4h_m} \right]}{2 \sum_{i=h_t}^{h_f} \cos \left[\frac{\pi(h_f - i)}{4(h_f - h_t)} \right]} \tag{14}$$

After the coefficients of the center column are determined with the above expressions, the coefficients of other columns are obtained as cosine tapered center column. The filter coefficients in the jth column are thus expressed as

$$f(i, j) = f(-i, j) = f(i, 0) \cos \frac{j\pi}{2.383h_f}, \qquad 0 \le |j| \le h_f \tag{15}$$

This construction indicates that the pixel values along the center column within the filter are weighted more than the ones at the columns toward the edges when performing the enhancement filtering. Figure 8.21 shows the 3D plot of the base filter of an O&N filter bank.

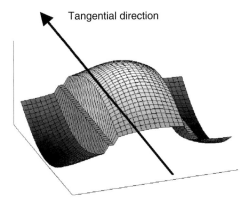

Fig. 8.21. Surface plot of an O&N filter.

Fig. 8.22. Original and enhanced fingerprint.

Enhancement of a fingerprint image using an O&N filter bank is obtained by the following 2D convolution:

$$E(i, j) = \sum_{u=-h_f}^{h_f} \sum_{v=-h_f}^{h_f} G(i - u, j - v) f_p(u, v) \qquad (16)$$

where $p = \overline{O}(i, j)$, the direction index in a filter bank. In other words, each output pixel $E(i, j)$ is obtained as a weighted sum of the input pixels within a window centered at (i, j). The weights are determined by one of the filters in the O&N filter bank. Which orientation filter is selected for computing $E(i, j)$ depends on the orientation field surrounding the input pixel $G(i, j)$, which can be found in the orientation map $O(i, j)$. Figure 8.22 shows the enhanced fingerprint image produced by applying an O&N filter bank followed by Otsu optimum thresholding [13] in each block.

8.4.3. Gabor Filter

Gabor filters were proposed to detect the slowly varying sinusoidal-shaped wave-forms that approximate cross sections of fingerprint ridges and valleys [15]. Gabor filters are widely used in signal detection, as it possesses the unique feature of having optimal joint spatial-frequency localization [16]. Creating orientation-rotated and center frequency-shifted copies of a base filter can construct a Gabor filter bank. The base filter of a Gabor filter bank is a horizontal ($\omega = 0$) sinusoidal wave with a center frequency ω_0 tapered by a Gaussian window with directional variances σ_i^2 and ω_j^2,

$$f(i, j, \phi, \omega) = \exp\left(-\frac{1}{2}\left(\frac{i_\phi^2}{\sigma_i^2} + \frac{j_\phi^2}{\sigma_j^2}\right)\right)\cos(\omega j_\phi)$$

where $i_\phi = -j\sin\phi + i\cos\phi$, $j_\phi = j\cos\phi + i\sin\phi$, $\phi = 0$, and $\omega = \omega_0$. The row index is denoted by i and the column index is denoted by j. The subscripted indices i_ϕ and j_ϕ represent the row and column indices in the rotated copies of the filter. This filter is specified by four parameters: ϕ, ω, σ_i, and σ_j. The angle ϕ represents the orientation of the Gabor filter and ω represents the sinusoidal frequency of the filter. The variances σ_i and σ_j represent the reciprocals of the vertical and horizontal decaying rates of the Gaussian window. Larger values of σ_i and σ_j allow more robust noise removal, but poorer ridge and valley localization. Smaller values allow better ridge and valley localization, but less robust noise removal. The value of ϕ is chosen to closely match the local orientation of the image pixel to which the filter is applied. The value of ω is chosen to closely match the estimated local "sinusoidal" frequency. The estimation of the local "sinusoidal" frequency is discussed in the section on ridge flow and ridge width. Figure 8.23 shows a 3D plot of a Gabor filter. Note its tangential direction is to be lined up against the ridge orientation of the pixel, at which the filter is centered.

Having defined the Gabor filter bank as a set of orientation-rotated and center frequency-shifted copies of a base filter, it follows that using this filter bank in a way similar to the approaches described in the previous sections, one can achieve the goal

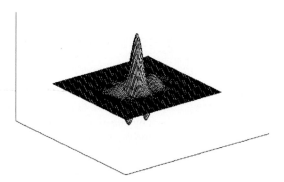

Fig. 8.23. A Gabor base filter.

of image enhancement. A detailed description of how a Gabor filter bank can be used for fingerprint image enhancement is the subject of another chapter in this book.

8.4.4. Postprocessing of Binary Image

Consider an enhanced fingerprint image produced by any one of the above three directional filter banks followed with an optimum thresholding [13] in each block, such as the one shown in Fig. 8.22. It contains both islands and lakes. Islands are the small white fragments completely surrounded by black pixels, while lakes are the black fragments completely surrounded by white pixels. Both of these are likely the results of thresholding noise and will produce spurious minutiae in the minutiae detection process. Therefore, it is highly recommended that they be removed before further processing. To remove the islands, first apply a connected component labeling algorithm [13] to all the white segments in the image. Then count the number of white pixels in each component, and remove the components whose size (number of white pixels) is below a given threshold value. In other words, remove the small connected components by setting their pixels to black. Lakes can be viewed as black islands in a white background. As a result, lakes can be removed in a similar way by first inverting the image, that is, switching white pixels to black pixels and black pixels to white pixels. Then perform the operations for removing islands discussed above. Invert the image back by switching the black and white pixel values. An alternative approach to removing the lakes is the fill algorithm developed by Soille [17].

8.5. Minutiae Detection

The aforementioned directional filter bank-based enhancement operations produce a binary image of the original gray-scale fingerprint image. Each white pixel represents a ridge pixel, while each black pixel represents a valley pixel. There are different approaches to obtain minutiae from such an enhanced binary fingerprint image [4, 10, 15, 18, 19]. Many have suggested applying a thinning operator to the enhanced binary image followed by some postprocessing that will eliminate the spurious minutiae resulting from the thinning operation. We describe an alternative approach using a binary edge detection operation followed by a local edge tracing and a curvature measure. Criteria are established to determine a potential minutia based on the measurements from this mechanism. The advantage of this mechanism is that it avoids the challenges associated with the applications of thinning algorithms.

Although edge detection of a gray-scale image in general is a challenging subject and there is a great body of excellent work on the subject [20–22], edge detection on a binary image is rather straightforward. Consider the following algorithm of edge detection on a binary image. Let the binary image be E and the edge map be T. When an element of E is zero, it indicates a background pixel, while a positive element of E indicates a foreground pixel. For the edge map T, each zero pixel indicates a nonedge pixel, while each positive pixel indicates an edge pixel. The steps of the edge detection algorithm follow:

Fig. 8.24. Edge map of an enhanced fingerprint image.

1. Initially, each pixel of T is set to zero.
2. For each foreground pixel in E, $E(i, j)$, check its 4-connected neighbors. If any of them is a background pixel, set the corresponding pixel in T, $E(i, j)$, to a prespecified value, which indicates an edge pixel.

Figure 8.24 shows the result of this operation applied to an enhanced (bi- narized) fingerprint image similar to the one shown in Fig. 8.22.

Based on the edge map produced above, we develop a local edge trace algorithm followed by a curvature measure for minutiae detection. In the minutiae detection algorithm, arrays T and $\overline{O}$ contain the edge map and orientation map obtained previously. Array M, which has the same size as that of T and whose elements are initially set to zero, contains the bitmap of minutiae. The number of rows and columns in each of these arrays $(T, \overline{O}, M)$ are m and n, respectively. The array *edgeLink* contains the location and direction information about the pixels on an edge link, which is a segment of an edge line. Variable *maxEdgeLinkLength* specifies the maximum length of the edge link to be traced (or followed) by *traceLocalEdgeLink()*. Variable *edgeLinkLength* returns the actual number of pixels in *edgeLink*. The steps to finding a minutiae map are described below.

1. Repeat the following steps for each pixel in the array T.
2. If $T(i, j) > 0$, call an edge tracing function *traceLocalEdgeLink*, which returns the *edgeLinkLength* in terms of pixels on the edge. The function *traceLocalEdgeLink* performs "edge following" on T starting from $T(i, j)$ and records the coordinate and orientation of each subsequent pixel on the linked list *edgeLink* until it reaches *maxEdgeLinkLength* or the end of an edge.

3. If the returned *edgeLinkLength* exceeds a preset threshold value, call a distance and angle computing function, *findDistAndAngleBetweenHeadAndTail*. This function calculates the average distance between the first α elements and the last α elements on *edgeLink* and returns the average distance in parameter *dist*. It also calculates the orientation difference between the first α elements and the last α elements on *edgeLink* and returns the average orientation distance in parameter *angle*.
4. Under the same conditions as (3), if the *edgeLinkLength* exceeds a preset threshold value, call a minutia validation function, *IsThereMinutia*. This function first checks a set of conditions to make sure that the *edgeLink* has the potential of containing a minutia: (*dist*>=minDist) && (*dist*<=maxDist) && (*angle* <=maxAngle), where *minDist* and *maxDist* are the minimum and the maximum allowed *dist*, respectively, and *maxAngle* is the maximum allowed *angle*. If all these conditions are satisfied, it indicates that the curvature in the region is high enough to potentially form a minutia. Choose the pixel in the middle of the *edgeLink* as the minutia, and record its location and orientation as the coordinate and orientation of the minutia. Set all the pixels in T that are also on the *edgeLink* to zero to avoid retracing the edge in the next iteration.

Figure 8.25 illustrates this process applied to a fingerprint ridge segment. The edge of the ridge segment is delineated by dashed lines. Its thicker dashed-line portion indicates the edge link produced by *traceLocalEdgeLink*. The first pixel on the edgeLink is labeled *edgeLink* head, and the last pixel on the *edgeLink* is labeled *edgeLink* tail. Let **x** be the vector from *edgeLink* tail to *edgeLink* head. The length of vector **x** is determined as the average distance between the first three pixels on *edgeLink* and the last three pixels on *edgeLink*. This number is examined to decide whether a ridge ending or bifurcation is reached depending on the types of pixels along **x** (ridge or valley). It is observed that a value of [1, 6] for the length of vector

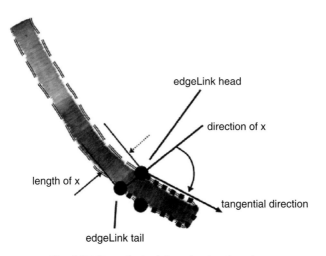

Fig. 8.25. Use *edgeLink* for minutiae detection.

x given a *maxEdgeLinkLength* of [20, 24] produces good minutiae detection results. If the length of **x** is within the tolerance range [1, 6], we estimate that a minutia is detected at the pixel in the middle of the *edgeLink*. The selection of *maxEdgeLinkLength* is influenced by the average ridge width in the neighborhood. A larger value is chosen for *maxEdgeLinkLength* if the ridge width is wide, while a smaller value is used if the ridge width is narrow. An additional constraint for deciding whether any minutiae is detected on the *edgeLink* is the angle between the tangential direction of the edgeLink head and the direction of **x**. The closer this angle is to $\pm\pi/2$, the more likely there is a minutia at the middle of the *edgeLink*. More details about the functions called in *findMinutiaeMap*() are given below.

Note in *findDistAndAngleBetweenHeadAndTail*() α is an integer chosen varying in the range of [1–3]. Let the first α elements on the *edgeLink* be $(i_0, j_0), (i_l, j_l), \ldots, (i_{\alpha-1}, j_{\alpha-1})$, and the last α elements on the *edgeLink* be $(i_{N-\alpha}, j_{N-\alpha}), (i_{N-\alpha+1}, j_{N-\alpha+1}), \ldots, (i_{N-1}, j_{N-1})$. The mass center of the first α elements of the *edgeLink* is at $\sum_{k=0}^{\alpha-1}(i_k, j_k)/\alpha$. The mass center of the last α elements of the *edgeLink* is at $\sum_{k=n-\alpha}^{N-1}(i_k, j_k)/\alpha$.

The average distance between the first α elements and the last α elements on *edgeLink* is defined as $d\left(\sum_{k=0}^{\alpha-1}(i_k, j_k)/\alpha, \sum_{k=n-\alpha}^{N-1}(i_k, j_k)/\alpha\right)$, where $d(\ldots)$ is the Euclidean distance measure. Similarly, let the orientations of the first α elements on the *edgeLink* be $\overline{O}(i_0, j_0), \overline{O}(i_{\alpha-1}, j_{\alpha-1})$, and orientations of the last α elements on the *edgeLink* be $\overline{O}(i_{N-\alpha}, j_{N-\alpha}), \overline{O}(i_{N-\alpha+1}, j_{N-\alpha+1}), \ldots, \overline{O}(i_{N-1}, j_{N-1})$. The average orientation of the first α elements of the *edgeLink* is

$$\theta_h = \tan^{-1}\left\{\frac{\left(\sum_{k=0}^{\alpha-1} 2\sin\left(\overline{O}(i_k, j_k)\right)\cos\left(\overline{O}(i_k, j_k)\right)\right)}{\sum_{k=0}^{\alpha-1}\left(\cos^2\left(\overline{O}(i_k, j_k)\right) - \sin^2\left(\overline{O}(i_k, j_k)\right)\right)}\right\} \tag{17}$$

The average orientation of the last α elements of the *edgeLink* is

$$\theta_h = \tan^{-1}\left\{\frac{\left(\sum_{k=N-\alpha}^{N-1} 2\sin\left(\overline{O}(i_k, j_k)\right)\cos\left(\overline{O}(i_k, j_k)\right)\right)}{\sum_{k=N-\alpha}^{N-1}\left(\cos^2\left(\overline{O}(i_k, j_k)\right) - \sin^2\left(\overline{O}(i_k, j_k)\right)\right)}\right\} \tag{18}$$

In both expressions of the angles θ_h and θ_t, when the numerator is zero, the angle is defined as 0. When the denominator is zero, the angle is defined as $\pi/2$. The difference between the θ_h and θ_t is evaluated as $\mod(|2\theta_h - 2\theta_t|, 2\pi)/2$, where $\mod(\ldots)$ is the modulus operation.

After executing *findMinutiaeMap*(), a minutiae map with a substantial amount of false minutiae is obtained as the breaks in ridges or smudges of fingerprints caused errors in binarization of the fingerprint image. Postprocessing algorithms are applied

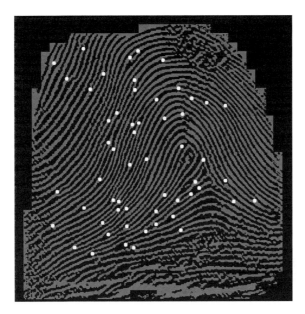

Fig. 8.26. Minutiae map.

to reduce the false minutiae in the minutiae map. These algorithms are summarized in the following rules.

1. For each minutia, $M(i, j)$, check the orientations of its neighborhood within a windowed area centered at (i, j), based on the orientation map $\overline{O}$. If these orientations are not very consistent, it's very likely that the area is noisy, and $M(i, j)$ is excluded from the final minutiae list.

2. For each minutia, $M(i, j)$, check its neighborhood within a windowed area centered at (i, j), based on the minutiae map, M, to find any existing minutiae. The windowed area in this case is usually a disk of radius r, where r is a preselected value by the user. If at least one additional minutiae exists in the neighborhood of $M(i, j)$, remove all the additional minutiae within the window, as they are likely spurious minutiae due to broken ridges.

After the above postprocessing algorithms on Fig. 8.24 are performed, a cleansed version of the minutiae map is shown in Fig. 8.26.

8.6. Minutiae Detection in Gray-Scale Images

Previous sections have discussed methodologies for producing a binarized fingerprint image for minutiae detection. Although the most commonly used approaches to minutiae detection [4, 10, 15, 18, 19] include a fingerprint "binarization" step, it is not surprising to see that such an approach leads to some loss of information about the ridge structures as they are more completely characterized in a gray-scale image before binarization. From an information theory point of view, the number of bits used for representing an image is a measure of information that the representation carries [23]. The "binarization" of a gray-scale image represents a data reduction. From a computational viewpoint, the binarization and thinning steps used in minutiae detection via binarization algorithms are often time-consuming and produce artifacts. Even the aforementioned edge-based minutiae detection often requires extensive computing due to its edge tracing step. And its performance depends greatly on the quality of the binarized fingerprint image. Based on such observations, Maio and Maltoni [24] propose a direct minutiae detection method based on the gray-scale image. This approach provides an efficient way of minutiae detection directly on gray-scale images using a directional filter bank without the binarization step. It consists of two main steps: ridge segment following and minutiae detection. The ridge segment following step approximates each fingerprint ridge by a piecewise linear curve. Each linear segment of the curve is obtained by locating the local maximum of the ridge cross section (orthogonal to the ridge orientation) at both ends of that segment. The minutiae detection step locates the ending points of a curve and the merging points of two curves. The Maio and Maltoni algorithm is outlined below, and its details can be found in [24].

8.6.1. Ridge Segment Following

As the ridge segment following algorithm requires the information of ridge orientation at each pixel, first a ridge orientation map $\overline{O}$ is computed for the fingerprint G using the Donahue and Rokhlin [14] method discussed before. Let (i_s, j_s) be the coordinate for the pixel in G that is a local maximum of a ridge segment of G. Let the ridge orientation at (i, j) be $\varphi_0 = \overline{O}(i_s, j_s)$ as specified in $\overline{O}$. Figure 8.27 shows the relations between the variables used in the ridgeline following algorithm. The pseudocode for the ridgeline following algorithm is given below.

```
ridgeLineFollowing(is, js, φ0)
{
    endFlag = false;
    (ic, jc) = (is, js);
    φc = φ0;
    while (!= endFlag)
    {
        (it, jt) = (ic, jc) + (μ pixels in direction φc);
        Ω = findSectionSet(it, jt, φc, σc);
        (in, jn) = findLocalMax(Ω, h);
        φlocal = average of the directions of the linear segment (ic, jc)(in, jn)
            relative to the last k steps;
        endFlag = checkStopCriteria((ic, jc), (it, jt), (in, jn), φc, φlocal);
        (ic, jc) = (in, jn);
        φc = O(ic, jc);
    }
}
```

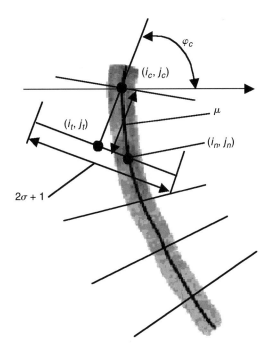

Fig. 8.27. Illustration of *ridgeLineFollowing()*.

The algorithm traces a ridge segment starting at (i, j) until the Boolean variable *endFlag* becomes true, which indicates the end of the ridge segment. Based on the principle of approximating a ridge segment by a piecewise linear curve, it assumes that each linear segment of the ridge segment is at least μ pixels long. Denote the location of the starting pixel of each linear segment as (i_c, j_c). It provides an initial estimate for the end of the linear segment, (i_t, j_t), which is μ pixels away from (i_c, j_c) in direction φ_c. The section set of (i_t, j_t) is the set of pixels along a line segment orthogonal to φ_c and centered at (i_t, j_t). Figure 8.28 shows a section set where each bar represents one pixel value. The length of the segment is approximately $2\sigma - 1$. We can obtain the section set Ω_0 at (i_t, j_t) by calling *findSectionSet()*. From Ω_0, the end of the linear segment starting at (i_c, j_c) is re-estimated as (i_n, j_n). The re-estimation is carried out in *findLocalMax()*. At this stage of the computation, the locations of all three pixels involved, $\{(i_c, j_c), (i_t, j_t), (i_n, j_n)\}$, are passed to the function *checkStopCriteria()* to be checked against the stop criteria. The pseudocode follows.

findSectionSet(i_t, j_t, φ_c, σ)
{
    $\phi = \varphi_c + \pi/2$;
    sectionSetWidth $= 2\sigma + 1$;
    $(i_{start}, j_{start}) = (\text{round}(i_t - \sigma \cos \phi), \text{round}(j_t - \sigma \sin \phi))$;
    $(i_{end}, j_{end}) = (\text{round}(i_t + \sigma \cos \phi), \text{round}(j_t + \sigma \sin \phi))$;
    find all the pixels along the line segment orthogonal to φ_c and centered at
        (i_t, j_t);

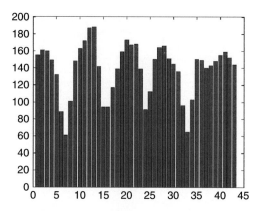

Fig. 8.28. A cross section of ridge segments (section set).

> sort them in the order starting from (i_{start}, j_{start}) to ending at (i_{end}, j_{end})
> so that $(i_1, j_1) = (i_{start}, j_{start})$, (i_2, j_2), (i_3, j_3), ..., (i_m, j_m),
> $= (i_{end}, j_{end})$, and store them in Ω_0;
> return Ω_0;
}

The return of *findSectionSet* is Ω and is mathematically defined as

$$\Omega = \{(i, j) | (i, j) \in G, (i, j) \in segment((i_{start}, j_{start}), (i_{end}, j_{end}))\}$$

where $segment((i_{start}, j_{start}), (i_{end}, j_{end}))$ is the set of pixels along the vector orthogonal to φ_c and centered at (i_t, j_t). The number of pixels in the set is approximately $2\sigma + 1$.

Once the section set is determined, one might attempt to directly search for the maximum-valued pixel and assign it as the re-estimated end point for the linear segment emanating from (i_c, j_c). However, such a direct approach is often not sufficiently robust to provide accurate re-estimation. The function *findLocalMax()* provides a more robust solution for the re-estimation. It first produces $2h$ parallel line segments that are parallel and adjacent to the section set Ω_0. It can be viewed as placing a window of $(2h + 1) \times (2\sigma + 1)$ over the section set, in which the center row overlaps with the section set . As a result, $2h + 1$ adjacent parallel section sets are obtained $\{\Omega_{-h}, \ldots, \Omega_{-1}, \Omega_0, \Omega_1, \ldots \Omega_h\}$. Each is a row of size m. An example of adjacent parallel section sets is shown in Fig. 8.29. An average section set, $\overline{\Omega}$, can thus be calculated by summing these rows with their respective columns and dividing by $2h + 1$. A low-pass filter, or a moving average filter, smooths the average section set. The local maximum over the section set $\overline{\Omega}$ can be determined by finding the "weak" local maximum closest to the center (i, j).

findLocalMax(Ω, h)
{
    winWidth $= m$;
    winHeight $= 2h + 1$;

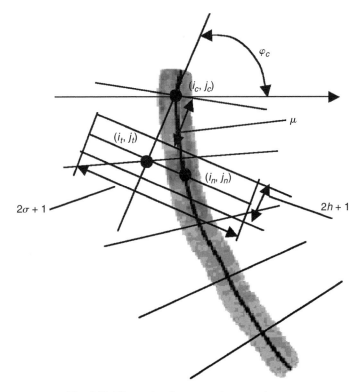

Fig. 8.29. Illustration for computing a section set.

produce $2h$ adjacent section sets to Ω by placing a window
of size $(2h + 1) \times (2\sigma + 1)$ overlapping its center row with Ω, which results in
$\{\Omega_{-h}, \ldots, \Omega_{-1}, \Omega_0, \Omega_1, \ldots \Omega_h\}$;

produce the average section set, $\overline{\Omega} = \dfrac{1}{2h + 1} \displaystyle\sum_{k=-h}^{h} \Omega_k$;

smooth the average section set $\overline{\Omega}$ by convolving it with a Gaussian kernel;
perform "weak" local maximum search over $\overline{\Omega}$, and denote the location of
the pixel with the "weak" local maximum that is closest to (i_t, j_t) as (i_n, j_n);
return (i_n, j_n);
}

The discovery of (i_n, j_n) marks the completion of the description for the linear segment starting from (i_c, j_c) and ending at $i_n, j_n)$. The next step is to decide whether the ridge segment being traced stops at $i_n, j_n)$. That is carried out by
checkStopCriteria(). It checks the triplet $\{(i_c, j_c), (i_t, j_t), (i_n, j_n)$ against a set of
predefined criteria to determine if the end of the ridge segment has been reached. Let
S denote the subimage of G, in which the minutiae are to be detected.

checkStopCriteria(i_c, j_c), (i_t, j_t), (i_n, j_n), φ_c, φ_{local})
{
    if ((i_t, j_t) $\notin$ S) return 1;
    if (no local maximum detected such that the angle formed between the
vector (i_c, j_c) − (i_n, j_n) and φ is less than β (threshold value)) return 2;
    if ((i_n, j_n) is labeled as belonging to another ridge line) return 3;
    if (the angle formed between the vector ($i − c$, j_c) − (i_n, j_n) and the ridge
        line local direction φ_{local} exceeds ψ (threshold value)) return 4;
}

Four stop criteria are proposed in [24]. The first is to check if the estimation of
the linear segment ending point is still within the region of interest S. The second is
to check if vector (i_c, j_c) − (i_n, j_n) is too far deviated from φ_c, which is a condition
for ridge termination independent of the gray level of the local region. The third is
to check if the current ridge segment merges into a previously labeled ridge. The
last is to check if the orientation of vector (i_c, j_c) − (i_n, j_n) is consistent with that of
previous vectors on the same ridge segment.

8.6.2. Minutiae Detection

In order to detect minutiae in fingerprint image G, first create an auxiliary image T of
the same size as G. The auxiliary image T is used as an indicator map for keeping track
of extracted ridge segments. Each pixel in T is initially set to zero. Whenever a ridge
segment is extracted from G, it is approximated by a piecewise linear curve. In the
auxiliary image T, set all the pixels on the piecewise linear curve to a positive integer
number, and dilate that curve by a disk of radius ($\varepsilon − 1$)/2, provided that ε is odd.
As a result, a polygonal of width ε is recorded on T in place of the piecewise linear
curve. A different positive integer is selected for indicating a different ridge segment
for identification purpose; one can simply use the positive integer set {1, 2, 3, ...}.
Let $X(T)$ be the set of positive-valued pixels in T. The location of each pixel in $X(T)$
indicates that the corresponding pixel in G is classified as being on an extracted ridge.

findMinutiae(i_s, j_s)
{
    esc = false;
    (i_c, j_c) = findNearestRidgeLineMax(i_s, j_s);
    if ((i_c, j_c) $\in X(T)$) esc = true;
    if ($\sim$esc)
    {
        $\varphi_c = \overline{O}(i_c, j_c)$;
        //   perform minutiae detection in direction φ_c
        ridgeLineFollowing(i_c, j_c, φ_c);
        if ((endFlag==2) || (endFlag==4))
        {
            //   termination minutia has been found
            store termination minutia (i_n, j_n);
        }

```
        if (endFlag==3)
        {
            //   bifurcation minutia may exist
            if (intersection point is valid)
            {
                store biburcation minutia (i_n, j_n);
            } else {
                delete the false minutia (i_n, j_n);
            }
        }
        store the polygonal specified by ridgeLineFollowing(i_c, j_c, φ_c) in T;

        //   perform minutia detection in direction φ_c + π
        ridgeLineFollowing(i_c, j_c, φ_c + π);
        if ((endFlag==2) || (endFlag==4))
        {
            //   termination minutia has been found
            store termination minutia (i_n, j_n);
        }
        if (endFlag==3)
        {
            //   bifurcation minutia may exist
            if (intersection point is valid)
            {
                store biburcation minutia (i_n, j_n);
            } else {
                delete the false minutia (i_n, j_n);
            }
        }
        store the polygonal specified by ridgeLineFollowing(i_c, j_c, φ_c + π) in
T;
    }
}   //   end of findMinutiae()
```

The algorithm for finding minutiae starts by calling function *findNearestRidgeLineMax*() to determine the nearest ridge-segment maximum pixel location (i_c, j_c). This coordinate is used to check the value at $T(i_c, j_c)$. If $T(i_c, j_c)$ is greater than zero, then $G(i_c, j_c)$ is on a previously labeled ridge, which indicates that no new ridge segment is found and the function terminates. However, if $T(i_c, j_c)$ is not greater than zero, then $G(i_c, j_c)$ is not on any previously labeled ridge, and it can be used as a starting pixel to trace a new ridge segment. Continue tracing the new ridge segment by calling *ridgeLineFollowing*() in the direction of $φ_c$. After the execution of *ridgeLineFollowing*(), check the returning termination code, end-Flag. Based on the value of *endFlag*, we decide the type of the minutia, store a ridge ending (termination) or a bifurcation, or delete a false minutia. Record the polygonal produced in the process in the auxiliary array T; mark the processing of the pixels on the polygonal. Repeat the same process starting from calling ridgeLineFollowing(), but in the direction of $\varphi_c + \pi$. This concludes the process of finding a pair of minutiae on the ridge segment that includes (i_c, j_c).

The algorithm of *findNearestRidgeLineMax*() is similar to that of the *findLocalMax*(). Given a pixel at (i_s, j_s), first find the section set Ω that passes through (i_s, j_s). From the section set Ω, the local maximum can be found by calling *findLocalMax*(). It returns the local maximum closest to (i_s, j_s) and denotes it as (i_c, j_c). The algorithm is outlined below.

findNearestRidgeLineMax(i_s, j_s)
{

$\quad \varphi_s = \overline{O}(i_s, j_s)$;
$\quad \Omega = \text{findSectionSet}(i_s, j_s, \varphi_s, \sigma_s)$;
$\quad h = 0$;
$\quad (i_c, j_c) = \text{findLocalMax}(\Omega, h)$;
$\quad \text{return}(i_c, j_c)$;

}

Function *findMinutiae*() finds all minutiae on the ridge segment emanating from the local maximum closest to (i_s, j_s). Denote the region of interest (ROI) in G by a window R. In order to find all minutiae in window R, partition it into square grids of size v in each side, where $v = 2$. Loop over each square grid inside W, and apply *findMinutiae*() at the upper left corner pixel of each square grid. All minutiae in the fingerprint image can thus be detected. Figure 8.30 [25] shows minutiae maps produced by this method. The larger one is produced from an ink-rolled image, while the smaller one is produced from a live-scan. Both fingerprint images are considered of good quality. Figure 8.31 [25] shows the minutiae maps of another fingerprint. Similar to Fig. 8.30, the larger one is produced from an ink-rolled image, while the smaller one is produced from a live-scan. The markers for different minutiae types are

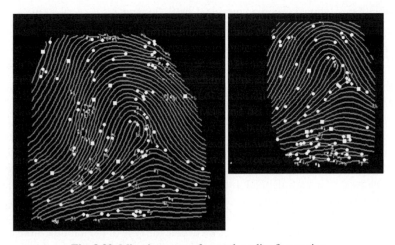

Fig. 8.30. Minutiae maps of a good-quality fingerprint.

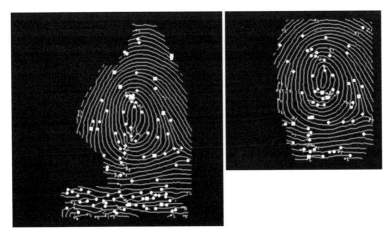

Fig. 8.31. Minutiae maps of medium-quality fingerprint.

disk for ridge ending, square for bifurcation, small box for removed false minutiae, and diamond for minutiae at high curvature region.

8.7. Conclusions

Modern computer technologies have significantly improved the performance of AFIS as they are now able to carry out significantly more computationally intensive algorithms. For example, the current generation of Intel cpus can perform about 100 times more operations per second than an Intel cpus a decade ago. Many algorithms currently employed in large-scale AFIS were not feasible without these state-of-the-art computer facilities. That leads to an explosion in fingerprint matching algorithm research because of the possibility of using additional fingerprint features for high-performance fingerprint matching. Additional features currently being investigated for fingerprint matching include fingerprint ridge pores and ridge segments.

While Maio and Maltoni's paper presents a way of detecting minutiae by first finding ridge segments, it provides a robust way of extracting ridge segments, which themselves can be used for identifications. The main difference between the traditional minutiae-based fingerprint matching algorithms and the ridge-segment-based matching algorithm is that the former is a point matching problem and the latter is a curve matching problem. A key issue here is the development of curve-based matching algorithms.

An excellent paper on the topic of fingerprint ridge pores for identification is by Roddy and Stosz [26]. Fingerprint matching algorithms based on ridge pores can be similar to the minutiae-based algorithms as they are both point matching problems. The challenges here include the collection of fingerprints at higher resolution and the development of robust pore detection algorithms. The fingerprints analyzed are collected at 1100 dpi, which is significantly higher than the current standard (500 dpi). It is interesting to note that if pores are viewed as "generalized" minutiae, the number of points upon which fingerprint comparisons are made is increased. As a result, the computational complexity is increased, and the corresponding hardware requirements are also increased.

Pores are most likely to show up on ridges. As a result, the detection of pores can be performed on the ridges. Following the detection and validation of pores, their locations can be viewed as forming a secondary minutiae map. Overlaying this secondary minutiae map on the original minutiae map formed with ridge endings and bifurcations, one can thus form a mixed minutiae map. It increases the number of comparison points for fingerprints, which leads to higher discrimination power, especially when only a partial print is available.

Another trend in fingerprint matching system development is the data acquisition methods. In addition to the traditional digitization of scanned ink-rolled fingerprint images, live-scan fingerprint images are becoming more available. Most live-scan images are collected using optical scanners. Matching fingerprint images collected from digitization of scanned ink-rolled fingerprint images with the live-scanned flat fingerprint images have demonstrated new challenges in fingerprint matching. It has been observed that the rolled fingerprints normally have fuzzier image regions near the rolling areas, while the live-scanned flat fingerprint images often do not have clear image detail on the side of a fingerprint. Nonoptical live-scan devices are being developed to overcome some of the weaknesses in fingerprint image collection using optical scanners. For example, the ultrasound-based fingerprint image scanner does not rely on the reflection of light for imaging. It uses an ultrasound transducer to receive the reflected ultrasound signal and reconstructs the fingerprint image from the received ultrasound signal. It has been demonstrated that this approach can overcome some of the image-quality problems due to unclean fingers, fingers with too dry or too oily skins, or the fingers with some degrees of skin damage. For the fingers with skin damage, as long as the tissue immediately under the skin is not damaged, an ultrasound fingerprint scanner can often reconstruct its fingerprint image. These advantages of the ultrasound imaging lead to better minutiae extraction quality.

8.8. Appendix

Segmentation of a fingerprint image can be viewed as finding an "optimum" threshold, t, for a two-mode histogram. According to a given t, pixels in the image are partitioned into two groups depending on whether or not it is greater than t. One group consists of those on ridges, while another consists of those in valleys. The criteria for selecting the "optimum" threshold value can be specified differently for different applications. Otsu [27] choose maximizing the between-group variance or minimizing the within-group variance as the criterion for selecting the "optimum" threshold. As the sum of between-group variance and within-group variance is fixed for a gray-scale image, maximizing the between-group variance is equivalent to minimizing the within-group variance. The following algorithm [13] iteratively searches over the entire range of t for the t_0 that minimizes the within-group variance, thus the "optimum" threshold.

Let the variance of the group 1, whose pixels have values less than or equal to t, be denoted as $\sigma_1^2(t)$, and the variance of the group 2, whose pixels have values greater than t, group 2, be denoted as $\sigma_1^2(t)$. The proportion of pixels of value i in the image is denoted by $P(i)$, where $P(i)$ is the probability of a pixel having value i. The variances for the two groups of pixels are defined as

$$\sigma_1^2(t) = \sum_{i=0}^{t} [i - \mu_1(t)]^2 P(i)/q_1(t) \tag{A1}$$

$$\sigma_2^2(t) = \sum_{i=t+1}^{I} [i - \mu_2(t)]^2 P(i)/q_2(t) \tag{A2}$$

The estimated means of group 1 and group 2 are respectively defined as

$$\mu_1(t) = \sum_{i=0}^{t} i P(i)/q_1(t) \tag{A3}$$

$$\mu_2(t) = \sum_{i=t+1}^{I} i P(i)/q_2(t) \tag{A4}$$

Let the proportion of pixels belonging to group 1 be $q_1(t)$, and the proportion of pixels belonging to group 2 be $q_2(t)$:

$$q_1(t) = \sum_{i=0}^{t} P(i) \tag{A5}$$

$$q_2(t) = \sum_{i=t+1}^{I} P(i) \tag{A6}$$

The within-group variance can thus be expressed as

$$\sigma_w^2(t) = q_1(t)\sigma_1^2(t) + q_2(t)\sigma_2^2(t) \tag{A7}$$

The "optimum" threshold t can be obtained by calculating $\sigma_w^2(t)$ for all values of t, $t \in [0, I]$, and finding the minimum $\sigma_w^2(t_0)$. Label t_0 as the "optimum threshold." To reduce the computation complexity, one can use the following recurrence relations:

$$\mu = \sum_{i=0}^{I} i P(i) \tag{A8}$$

$$q_1(0) = 0 \tag{A9}$$

$$q_1(t+1) = q_1(t) + P(t+1) \tag{A10}$$

$$\mu_1(0) = 0 \tag{A11}$$

$$\mu_1(t+1) = \frac{q_1(t)\mu_1(t) + (t+1)P(t+1)}{q_1(t+1)} \tag{A12}$$

$$\mu_2(t+1) = \frac{\mu - q_1(t+1)\mu_1(t+1)}{1 - q_1(t+1)} \tag{A13}$$

$$\sigma_1^2(t+1) = \sum_{i=0}^{t+1} [i - \mu_1(t+1)]^2 P(i)/q_1(t+1) \tag{A14}$$

$$\sigma_2^2(t+1) = \sum_{i=t+2}^{I} [i - \mu_2(t+1)]^2 P(i)/[1 - q_1(t+1)] \tag{A15}$$

Otsu's work provides an "optimum" threshold finding method based on formal pattern classification methodology. It works fine when the numbers of pixels in two groups are of the same order of magnitude. But it may not provide an "optimum" threshold when the numbers of pixels in the two groups are very diverse. Kittler and Illingworth developed a different criteria for finding the "optimum" threshold [28]. Their approach sometimes performs better than Otsu's.

References

1. Moayer, B. and K.S. Fu, A tree system approach for fingerprint pattern recognition, *IEEE Trans. Pattern Analysis and Machine Intelligence*, 8(3):376–388, 1986.
2. Verma, M.R., A.K. Majumdar, and B. Chatterjee, Edge detection in fingerprints, *Pattern Recognition*, 20(5):513–523, 1987.
3. O'Gorman, L. and J. Nickerson, An approach to fingerprint filter design, *Pattern Recognition*, 22:29–38, 1989.
4. Sherlock, B.G., D.M. Monro, and K. Millard, Fingerprint enhancement by directional Fourier filtering, *IEE Proc. Vis. Image Signal Processing*, 141:87–94, 1994.
5. Szekely, E.N. and V. Szekely, Image recognition problems of fingerprint identification, *Microprocessor and Microsystems*, 17(4):215, 1993.
6. Mehtre, B.M., Fingerprint image analysis for automatic identification, *Machine Vision and Applications*, 6(2–3):124–139, 1993.
7. Weber, D.M., A cost effect verification algorithm for commercial application, *Proc. 1992 South African Symposium on Communications and Signal Processing*, pp. 99–104, 1992.
8. Leung, M.T., W.E. Engeler, and P. Frank, Fingerprint image processing using neural network, *Proc. Tenth Conf. Computer and Communication Systems*, pp. 582–586, 1990.
9. Leung, W.F., S.H. Leung, W.H. Lau, and A. Luk, Fingerprint recognition using neural network, *Proc. IEEE Workshop Neural Network for Signal Processing*, pp. 226–235, 1991.
10. Hung. D.C.D. Enhancement and feature purification of fingerprint image, *Pattern Recognition*, 26:1661–1671, 1993.
11. Xiao, Q. and H. Raafat, Fingerprint image postprocessing: A combined statistical and structural approach, *Pattern Recognition*, 24(10):985–992, 1991.
12. NIST, Data format for the interchange of fingerprint, facial & SMT information, ANSI/NIST-CSL-1-1993, National Institute of Standards and Technology, 1993.
13. Haralick, R.M. and L.G. Shapiro, *Computer and Robot Vision*, Vol 1, Reading, MA: Addison-Wesley, 1992, pp 20–23.
14. Donahue, M.J. and S.I. Rokhlin, On the use of level curves in image analysis, *CVGIP: Image Understanding*, 57:185–203, 1993.

15. Hong, L., Y. Wan, and A. Jain, Fingerprint image enhancement: Algorithm and performance evaluation, *IEEE Trans. Pattern Analysis and Machine Intelligence*, 20:777–789, 1998.

16. Jain, A. and F. Farrokhnia, Unsupervised texture segmentation using Gabor filters, *Pattern Recognition*, 24:1167–1186, 1991.

17. Soille, P., *Morphological Image Analysis: Principles and Applications*, New York: Springer-Verlag, 1999, pp. 173–174.

18. Coetzee, L, and E.C. Botha, Fingerprint recognition in low quality images, *Pattern Recognition*, 26:1441–1460, 1993.

19. Ratha, N.K., S. Chen, A. Jain, Adaptive flow orientation-based feature extraction in fingerprint images, *Pattern Recognition*, 28:1657–1672.

20. Canny, J. A computational approach to edge detection, *IEEE Trans. Pattern Analysis and Machine Intelligence*, 8:679–698, 1986.

21. Marr, D. and E. Hildreth, Theory of edge detection, *Proc. Royal Society of London B*, 207:187–217, 1980.

22. Perona, P., Steerable-scalable kernels for edge detection and junction analysis, *Image Vision Comput.*, 10:663–672, 1992.

23. Gallager, R.G., *Information Theory and Reliable Communication*, New York: John Wiley and Sons, 1968.

24. Maio, D. and D. Maltoni, Direct gray-scale minutia detection in fingerprints, *IEEE Trans. Pattern Analysis and Machine Intelligence*, 19:27–40, 1997.

25. Maio, D. and D. Maltoni, Private Communications, 2002.

26. Roddy, A.R. and J.D. Stosz, Fingerprint features—statistical analysis and system performance estimates, *Proc. IEEE*, 85:1390–1421, 1997.

27. Otsu, N., A threshold selection method from gray-level histogram, *IEEE Trans. Sys., Man, and Cybernetics*, 9:62–66, 1979.

28. Kittler, J. and J. Illingworth, On the thresholdselection using clustering criteria, *IEEE Trans. Sys., Man, and Cybernetics*, 15:652–655, 1985.

Chapter 9

The State of the Art in Fingerprint Classification

R. Cappelli and D. Maio

Abstract. Fingerprint classification is an effective technique that allows the number of comparisons necessary to retrieve a fingerprint in a large database to be strongly reduced: In fact, if a reliable and accurate classification is performed, an unknown fingerprint needs to be compared only to the fingerprints belonging to the same class. Automatic fingerprint classification is a very difficult pattern recognition task, due to the small interclass variability, the large intraclass variability, and the presence of noise. This chapter surveys the main approaches presented in the literature and introduces a fingerprint classification method based on a multispace generalization of the Karhunen–Loève transform (MKL), which is particularly promising and achieves very good classification accuracy. Results on NIST DB4 and NIST DB14 are reported and compared with those published in the literature.

9.1. Introduction

Automated Fingerprint Identification Systems (AFIS) are increasingly adopted for both forensic (e.g., *latent fingerprint recognition, 10-print based identification*) and civil applications (e.g., *welfare benefit collection, driver license registration*) [33]. The identification of a person requires the comparison of his or her fingerprint with all the fingerprints in a database, which in many applications may be very large (several million fingerprints). A common strategy to reduce the number of comparisons during fingerprint retrieval and, consequently, to improve the response time of the identification process is to divide the fingerprints into some predefined classes.

Fingerprint classification means assigning each fingerprint to a class in a consistent and reliable way, such that an unknown fingerprint to be searched needs to be compared only with the subset of fingerprints in the database belonging to the same class. While fingerprint matching is usually performed according to fingerprint microfeatures, such as ridge terminations and bifurcations (*minutiae*), fingerprint classification is usually based on macrofeatures, such as global ridge structure.

The first scientific studies on fingerprint classification were made by Francis Galton (1822–1916) [19], who divided the fingerprints into three major classes. Later, Edward Henry (1850–1931) [22] refined Galton's classification by increasing the number of the classes. All the classification schemes currently used by police agencies are variants of the so-called Henry's classification scheme. Figure 9.1 shows the

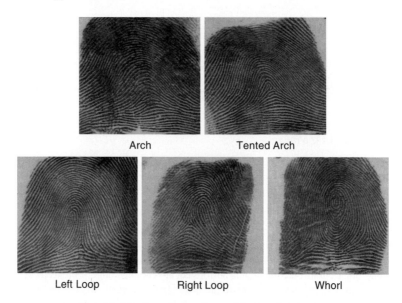

Arch   Tented Arch

Left Loop   Right Loop   Whorl

Fig. 9.1. The five commonly used fingerprint classes.

five classes (*arch, tented arch, left loop, right loop,* and *whorl*) commonly used by today's fingerprint classification techniques. In reality, fingerprints are not uniformly distributed among these five classes: The proportions, as estimated in [53], are 3.7%, 2.9%, 33.8%, 31.7%, and 27.9% for arch, tented arch, left loop, right loop, and whorl, respectively.

Automated fingerprint classification into these five classes is a difficult pattern recognition problem, due to the small interclass variability and the large intraclass variability (Fig. 9.2); moreover, fingerprint images are often affected by noise, which makes the classification task even more difficult (Fig. 9.3). Several methods have been proposed by the scientific community to deal with this problem: Section 9.2 presents a survey of the main approaches found in the literature, roughly categorized according to the features exploited and the classification strategies adopted. The rest of this chapter is organized as follows: Section 9.3 introduces a fingerprint classification approach that (although quite simple in design) is able to achieve a very good accuracy; a technique for combining different instances of the classifier, trained on disjoint data sets, is also proposed, and the results of both the single and the combined classifiers are compared with several approaches proposed in the literature. Finally, Section 9.4 draws some conclusions.

9.2. Literature Review

Great interest in the fingerprint classification problem aroused in the scientific community due to its importance and intrinsic difficulty, and many papers have been published on this topic during the last 30 years. This section briefly introduces the

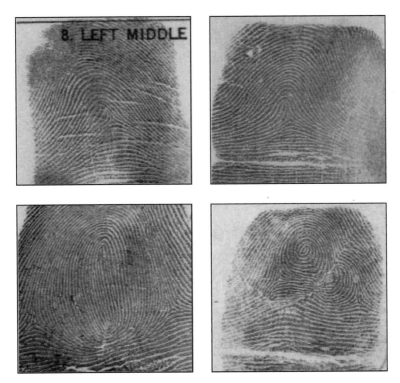

Fig. 9.2. Top: two fingerprints belonging to different classes (left loop and a tented arch) that have similar appearance (small interclass variability). Bottom: two fingerprints belonging to the same class (whorl) that have quite different characteristics (large intraclass variability).

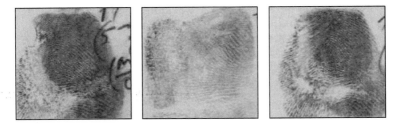

Fig. 9.3. Examples of noisy fingerprint images.

main fingerprint features used for classification and presents a review of the main approaches proposed in the literature.

9.2.1. Feature Extraction

Although a wide variety of classification algorithms has been experimented with, a relatively small number of features extracted from fingerprint images have been used

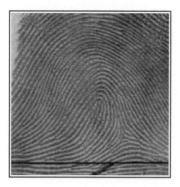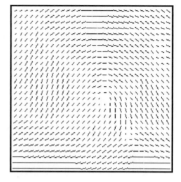

Fig. 9.4. A fingerprint image and the corresponding directional image, calculated over a 32×32 grid.

by most of the works in the literature. In particular, almost all the methods are based on one or more of the following features: *directional image, singular points, ridge flow*, and *Gabor-filter responses*.

9.2.1.1. Directional Image

A directional image is a discrete matrix whose elements represent the local average directions of the fingerprint ridges (Fig. 9.4) [20, 47]. A directional image effectively summarizes the information contained in a fingerprint pattern and it can be reliably computed from noisy fingerprints. Furthermore, the local directions within a damaged area can be restored by means of a regularization process. For the above reasons, most of the existing classification methods make use of fingerprint directional images.

Various techniques have been proposed for calculating the directional image: See, for instance, [47, 20], and [36]. In order to reduce the effect of noise, directional images are often smoothed (for instance, by applying a 3×3 averaging filter). To this purpose, a useful representation is proposed in [5] and adopted in several successive works: Each directional element is denoted by a vector $\mathbf{v} = \xi[\cos 2\theta, \sin 2\theta]$, where $\theta \in [0°, 180°)$ represents the orientation and $|\mathbf{v}| = \xi$ gives a confidence value of the direction reliability. This encoding allows the problems induced by the orientation discontinuity ($180° \leftrightarrow 0°$) to be avoided and enables orientation elements to be simply averaged. Without using such a representation, averaging orientations is not straightforward: For instance, the average orientation between $10°$ and $170°$ is not $90°$ (as simple average would suggest) but $0°$.

9.2.1.2. Singular Points

The ridge lines of a fingerprint often flow parallel, but sometimes produce local singularities called the *core* and *delta* (Fig. 9.5). A core is present when there is at least one ridge that enters from one side and then curves back, leaving the fingerprint

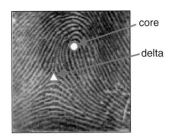

Fig. 9.5. Core and delta points in a fingerprint image.

core

delta

on the same side: The core is defined as the point at the top of the innermost curving ridge. At the other side of a core, ridges enter the fingerprint and meet the curving ridges; some of these flow above the core and some below: The delta is defined as the point where those ridges diverge that is closest to the core.

Finding the singular points in a fingerprint image is not an easy task, especially if the image is of poor quality; on the other hand, singularity positions can be very useful for aligning fingerprints with respect to a fixed point and for classification (see Section 9.2.2.3).

The most widely adopted technique for detecting singularities is based on the Poincaré index [30], which is calculated along a small closed curve around a particular point; this is usually performed on the directional image, rather than on the original image [29, 30].

9.2.1.3. Ridgeline Flow

The flow of the ridges is an important discriminating characteristic; although not always easy to be reliably extracted from noisy fingerprints, it is a feature more robust than singular points.

The ridgelines are typically extracted directly from the directional image, or by binarizing the image and performing a thinning operation, so that each ridge is represented by a single-pixel line [13, 45] (Fig. 9.6). Often, before extracting the ridgelines, the image is enhanced by applying directional filters, to reduce the presence of noise.

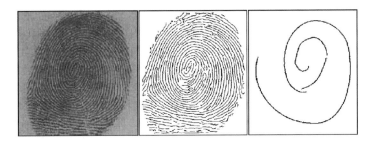

Fig. 9.6. From left to right: a fingerprint image, the ridgelines extracted from the fingerprint, and a representative flow-line trace.

Fig. 9.7. Left: the spatial tessellation of the fingerprint pattern; right: the four Gabor filters used to extract the Finger-Code [27] (only the real part is shown).

Some approaches [5, 13], after finding the ridgelines, analyze their shape and extract one or more representative curves (not necessarily corresponding to a single ridgeline), which are called *flow-line traces* or *pseudoridges* (Fig. 9.6).

9.2.1.4. Gabor-Filter Responses

Gabor filters [14] have been used in some works for enhancing fingerprint images [24, 17], due to their orientation-selective and frequency-selective properties [14]. More recently, Jain et al. [26, 27] proposed a Gabor-based representation of fingerprints (called *FingerCode*, for its analogies with the well-known IrisCode introduced by Daugman [15]), which can be used both for classifying and matching fingerprints. In [27] the feature extraction is carried out as follows (Fig. 9.7): First a center point is found, by searching for the topmost core (with a Poincaré-based algorithm) and the region of interest of the image is defined as a circular region around the center point. Subsequently a spatial tessellation (into a collection of sectors) of the region of interest is performed; then the image is decomposed into a set of component images by applying Gabor filters with different orientations ($0°, 45°, 90°$, and $135°$), and finally the standard deviation of gray-level values in each sector is computed to form the FingerCode feature vector.

9.2.2. Classification Techniques

Most of the existing fingerprint classification methods can be coarsely assigned to one of the following categories: *syntactic methods, structural methods, approaches based on singularities, neural approaches, approaches based on ridgeline shape,* and *combined approaches.*

9.2.2.1. Syntactic Methods

A syntactic method describes patterns by means of terminal symbols and production rules; a grammar is defined for each class and a parsing process is responsible for classifying each unknown pattern. Moayer and Fu [40, 41] propose a syntactic approach

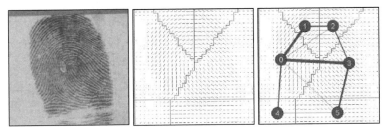

Fig. 9.8. From left to right: a fingerprint image, the partitioning of its directional image, and the corresponding relational graph [37].

where terminal symbols are associated to small groups of directional elements within the fingerprint directional image (calculated on a 16 × 16 grid); a class of context-free grammars is used to describe the fingerprint patterns, which are divided into seven classes. The approach introduced by Rao and Balck [44] is based on the analysis of ridge traces, which are labeled according to the direction changes, thus obtaining a set of strings that can be processed (through ad-hoc grammars or string-matching techniques) to derive the final classification.

9.2.2.2. Structural Methods

Fingerprint patterns are partitioned into "homogeneous" connected regions according to their topology; relational graphs are constructed in order to compactly summarize the fingerprint macrostructures resulting from the partitioning process. Maio and Maltoni [37] partition the directional image into regions by minimizing a cost function that takes into account the variance of the element orientations within each region (Fig. 9.8).

In [35] an inexact graph matching technique is applied to compare the relational graphs with prototype graphs corresponding to the main fingerprint classes. In [6] a template-based matching is performed to guide the partitioning of the directional images (Fig. 9.9): The main advantage of the approach is that, since it relies only on global structural information, it can work on very noisy images, where the singular points or other local features cannot be exploited.

9.2.2.3. Approaches Based on Singularities

A fingerprint can be simply classified according to the number and the position of the singular points (see Table 9.1 and Fig. 9.10). Several classification approaches that use heuristic criteria based on the number and the position of the singularities have been proposed in the literature [1, 12, 23, 29, 30].

Since these methods heavily rely on singularities, some problems arise in the presence of noisy or partial fingerprints, where singularity detection can be misleading. In [29] an iterative regularization is carried out, until a valid number of singular points is detected, to reduce noise and consequently to improve the classification accuracy.

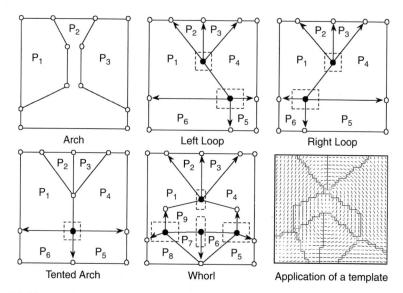

Fig. 9.9. The templates corresponding to the five classes used in [6] and an example of application of the whorl template to the directional image of a fingerprint belonging to the whorl class.

Table 9.1. Singular Points in the Five Fingerprint Classes (See Fig. 9.10)

Fingerprint class	Singular points
Arch	No singular points
Tented arch, left loop, right loop	One core and one delta
Whorl	Two cores and two deltas

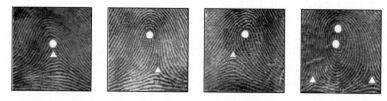

Fig. 9.10. From left to right: a tented arch, a left loop, a right loop, and a whorl fingerprint, marked with core and delta points.

In [30] and [23], the flow-line trace is also exploited to improve the performance; in particular, in [23] Hong and Jain propose a rule-based classification algorithm that uses the number of core and delta points together with the number of recurring ridges found in the image.

A further problem with approaches based on singularities is that, while they work reasonably well on *rolled* (nail to nail) fingerprint impressions, they are not suitable to be used on *dab* (acquired by just pressing the finger) fingerprints, since delta points are often missing in this kind of images. In [12] Cho et al. propose a method that uses only the core points and classifies fingerprints according to the curvature and the orientation of the fingerprint area near the cores.

9.2.2.4. Neural Network Approaches

Several neural network approaches have been proposed in the literature: Most are based on multilayer perceptrons and use the elements of the directional image as input features [4, 25, 28]. In [28], Kamijo presents an interesting pyramidal architecture constituted by several multilayer perceptrons, each of which is trained to recognize fingerprints belonging to different classes. In [4], the position of the singularities, and the relationship between them, is used together with a 20×20 directional map to train two different neural networks, whose outputs are passed to a third network, which produces the final classification. In [43], a feed-forward neural network is trained to classify fingerprints on the basis of a discrete wavelet transform applied to the image: The feature vector is assembled from the 64 coefficients from subbands 0, 1, 2, and 3 of the transform. Wilson et al. [53] apply a dimensionality-reduction technique to the feature vectors, in order to reduce the complexity (and thus the training time) of the network. First, a 28×30 directional image is calculated and aligned with respect to the core position; then the dimensionality of the directional image (considered as a single vector of 1680 elements) is reduced to 64 elements by using the principal component analysis (KL transform) [18]. Finally, a multilayer perceptron is used for assigning each 64-element vector to a fingerprint class. Self-organizing networks are used in [2, 21, 42]; in [42], a Kohonen map is trained to find delta points, and a rule-based approach is applied for the classification; in [21], core-aligned directional images are reduced by using the KL transform (with some analogies to [53]), then a multilayer self-organizing map provides the classification.

9.2.2.5. Approaches Based on Ridgeline Shape

Chong et al. [13] base the classification on the ridge geometrical shape. B-splines are used to model fingerprint ridgelines; adjacent curves are merged to limit noise artifacts. Classification is performed by tracing the resulting curves in order to detect turns (i.e., complete direction changes). Senior proposes in [46] a hidden Markov Model classifier, whose input features are the measurements (ridge angle, separation, curvature, etc.) taken at the intersection points between some horizontal/vertical *fiducial lines* and the fingerprint ridgelines. The fiducial lines are parallel lines located at fixed and equal intervals along the image; the appropriate number of fiducial lines has been empirically determined by the author.

9.2.2.6. Combined Approaches

Different classifier designs potentially offer complementary information about the patterns to be classified, which may be exploited to improve the performance; in fact, in a number of pattern classification studies it has been observed that the sets of patterns misclassified by different classifiers do not necessarily overlap [31, 48]. This motivates the recent interest in combining different approaches for the fingerprint classification task, in order to achieve better results. In the PCASYS system [5], an evolution of the method proposed in [53] is coupled with an auxiliary ridge-tracing module, which is specifically designed to detect whorl fingerprints.

Jain et al. [26, 27] adopt a two-stage classification strategy: A K-nearest-neighbor classifier is used to find the two most likely classes from a FingerCode feature vector; then a specific neural network, trained to distinguish between the two classes, is exploited to obtain the final decision. A total of 10 neural networks is trained to distinguish between each possible pair of classes.

Senior [45] proposes a combination of three classifiers: the hidden Markov Model classifier introduced in [46]; PCASYS [5]; and an approach based on ridgeshape features classified by means of decision trees. PCASYS is also used in [52], where a feedback method based on a genetic algorithm is added to the classifier, to automatically select the best input parameters of the system and improve its accuracy.

In [8], six classifiers based on the MKL [10] transform, trained on different data sets, are combined (see also [7]); Section 9.4 of this chapter discusses this approach in more detail.

Other recent attempts of fingerprint classifier combinations can be found in [39] and [54]. In [39], a structural approach similar to [38] is combined to a neural network classifier that uses FingerCode feature vectors; in [54], the authors combine multiple Support Vector Machines trained to classify FingerCode feature vectors.

9.2.2.7. Continuous Classification

To complete the survey, a further group of approaches has to be mentioned: the fingerprint retrieval techniques that are not based on exclusive classification schemes. For applications where it is not necessary to comply with an existing classification scheme, some researches propose performing a "continuous classification" [9, 16, 34]. In continuous classification, each fingerprint is associated to a point in a multidimensional space through a similarity-preserving transformation, such that similar fingerprints correspond to close points. During the retrieval, the fingerprints considered are only those whose corresponding points are within a given radius from the query fingerprint: This allows the problems due to ambiguous fingerprints (Fig. 9.2) to be avoided and the trade-off between accuracy and efficiency to be adjusted according to the application requirements (by changing the search radius). Obviously, these approaches cannot work with existing systems based on Henry's classes, but if the aim is only to minimize the number of comparisons during fingerprint retrieval in a large database, they seem promising [16].

9.3. An MKL-based Fingerprint Classifier

In this section a fingerprint classification approach based on the MKL transform [10] is described; its performance is evaluated on NIST databases and compared to other results published in the literature. The MKL-based fingerprint classifier relies on a generalization of the KL transform called MKL (which is introduced in a more

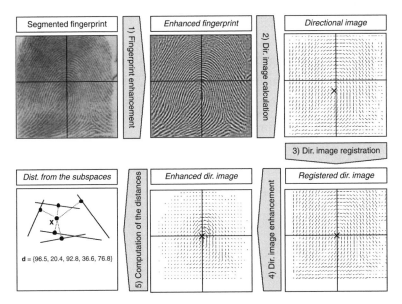

Fig. 9.11. Functional schema of the MKL-based classifier.

general context in [10, 11]), where multiple subspaces are used for representing and classifying patterns, hence the term multispace KL transform. Figure 9.11 shows a functional schema of the approach: Steps 1–4 concern the feature extraction and enhancement, step 5 the classification using MKL.

9.3.1. Feature Extraction

The fingerprint image is initially separated from the background (segmentation) and its quality is enhanced through a filtering in the frequency domain; these two steps are performed as in [5]. Then, the *directional image* is calculated using the Stock and Swonger method [47] over a 28 × 30 grid. The directional image is registered with respect to the *core point*, which is determined by using the Poincaré method [30] and by iteratively smoothing the directional image until a valid number of cores is found (as in [29]). In case the core point is not found with the above method, the R92 algorithm [51] is used for its detection.

The displacement-normalized directional image is then enhanced as follows (Fig. 9.12):

1. In order to reduce the effects of noise (which usually greatly affects the border elements), a Gaussian function *att* is applied, to progressively reduce the element magnitude moving from the center toward the borders:

$$\mathbf{v}' = \mathbf{v} \cdot att(\mathbf{v}, \sigma_1)$$

where $att(\mathbf{v}, \sigma) = (1/\sqrt{2\pi \cdot \sigma})e^{-distc(\mathbf{v})^2/2\sigma^2}$, $distc(\mathbf{v})$ returns the distance of $\mathbf{v}$ from the center of the image and σ is the scale of the Gaussian function.

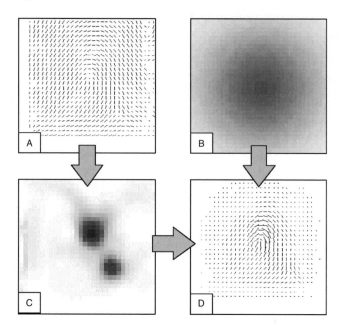

Fig. 9.12. Directional image enhancement. (A) registered directional image; (B) Gaussian map obtained by applying the function att; (C) irregularity map $str_{\mathbf{v}'}$; (D) enhanced directional image.

2. To increase the importance of the discriminant elements, the vectors located in the irregular regions are strengthened by calculating, for each $\mathbf{v}'$:

$$str_{\mathbf{v}'} = 1 - \frac{\left| \displaystyle\sum_{\mathbf{v}' \in W_{5\times5}} \mathbf{v}' \right|}{\displaystyle\sum_{\mathbf{v}' \in W_{5\times5}} |\mathbf{v}'|}$$

The function $str_{\mathbf{v}'}$ takes into account the irregularity degree in the 5×5 neighborhood of $\mathbf{v}'$ (denoted by $W_{5\times5}$): Its value is close to zero if the directional elements in $W_{5\times5}$ have similar orientation and it tends to 1 if the orientations are discordant.

3. The final enhanced directional image is made up of vectors $\mathbf{v}''$ such that

$$\mathbf{v}'' = \mathbf{v}' \cdot \left(1 + R_m \cdot \overline{str_{\mathbf{v}'}} \cdot att(\mathbf{v}', \sigma_2) \right)$$

where R_m is a weighting factor empirically determined and $\overline{str_{\mathbf{v}'}}$ is the local average of $str_{\mathbf{v}'}$ on a 3×3 window.

9.3.2. MKL-based Classification

The enhanced directional image is treated as a single vector of n elements (by simply concatenating its rows); in the following, we indicate with $\mathbf{x}_i$ the n-dimensional vector obtained from a generic fingerprint i.

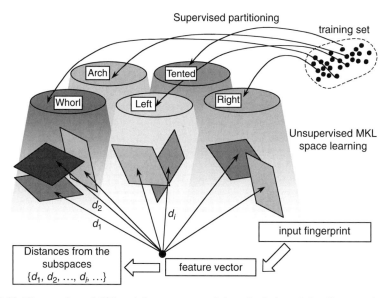

Fig. 9.13. The two-layer MKL training process and the calculation of the distances from an input fingerprint.

The underlying idea of the approach is to find, for each class, one or more KL subspaces, which are well suited for representing the fingerprints belonging to the class. These subspaces are created according to an optimization criterion, which attempts to minimize the average mean-square reconstruction error over a representative training set; the reader should refer to [10] for a formal discussion of the MKL-related concepts. With respect to the general MKL formulation, which is an unsupervised technique over a global training set, the MKL classifier is implemented here in a two-layer way (Fig. 9.13): First, a "supervised" MKL transform partitions the training set according to the class information; then for each partition an "unsupervised" MKL is applied to calculate a set of KL subspaces.

The number of subspaces for each class is fixed a priori according to the class "complexity"; in particular, more subspaces are created for complex classes (e.g., whorl), where the MKL ability to handle nonlinear spaces allows a more effective indexing to be achieved.

The classification of an unknown pattern is performed according to its distances from all the KL subspaces. For example, in Fig. 9.14, three KL subspaces (S_1, S_2, S_3) have been calculated from a training set containing elements from the two classes A and B: subspaces S_1 and S_2 have been obtained from the elements in A, while S_3 has been obtained from those in B. Given a new pattern **x**, the distances from the three subspaces (d_1, d_2, and d_3) contain useful information for its classification.

More formally, let P be a training set of fingerprints, $P \subset \Re^n$, whose classes (A, L, R, W, and T) induce a partitioning of P into five subsets: P_A, P_L, P_R, P_W, P_T; let $K = \{k_A, k_L, k_R, k_W, k_T\}$ be a set of scalars specifying, for each class, the dimen-

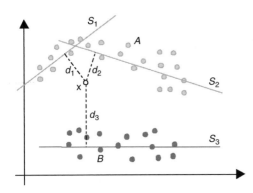

Fig. 9.14. A two-dimensional example of MKL transform, where two subspaces (S_1, S_2) and one subspace (S_3) are used to represent classes A and B, respectively.

sionality of the subspaces associated to that class and let $N = \{n_A, n_L, n_R, n_W, n_T\}$ be a set of scalars determining the number of subspaces to be created for each class; then the set of KL subspaces $S = \{S_A(1), \ldots, S_A(n_A), S_L(1), \ldots, S_L(n_L), S_R(1), \ldots, S_R(n_R), S_W(1), \ldots, S_W(n_W), S_T(1), \ldots, S_T(n_T)\}$ are obtained by generating, for each training subset $P_c(c \in \{A, L, R, W, T\})$, the set of n_c KL subspaces $\{S_c(1), \ldots, S_c(n_c)\}$ through the MKL optimization procedure described in [10].

Given a vector **x** corresponding to an unknown fingerprint, the feature vector (of dimensionality $n_A + n_L + n_R + n_W + n_T$) used for the classification is

$$\mathbf{d} = [d_{FS}(\mathbf{x}, S_A(1)), \ldots, d_{FS}(\mathbf{x}, S_A(n_A)), \ldots, d_{FS}(\mathbf{x}, S_T(1)), \ldots, d_{FS}(\mathbf{x}, S_T(n_T))]$$

where $d_{FS}(\mathbf{x}, S_i)$ denotes the distance between the vector **x** and the subspace S_i. In order to assign a fingerprint to a class, given a feature vector **d**, we adopt the following two simple approaches:

1. Minimum-distance classifier (MKL-MIN): The fingerprint is assigned to the class c' corresponding to the closest subspace:

$$c^* = \arg \min_{c \in \{A, L, R, W, T\}} \left(\min_{i=1..n_c} d_{FS}(\mathbf{x}, S_c(i)) \right)$$

2. k-nearest-neighbor classifier (MKL-KNN): The fingerprint is classified according to the k-NN rule.

In order to provide a rejection option, a confidence value in [0,1] is associated to each fingerprint by the above classifiers:

1. MKL-MIN: The confidence is the normalized difference between the two smallest distances d_1 and d_2:

$$\text{conf} = \frac{|d_1 - d_2|}{(d_1 + d_2)}$$

2. MKL-KNN: The confidence is the normalized difference between the number of occurrences (n_1 and n_2) of the two most frequent classes among the k nearest neighbors:

$$\text{conf} = \frac{|n_1 - n_2|}{(n_1 + n_2)}$$

9.3.3. Experimental Results

The experimentation has been performed on NIST Special Database 4 (DB4) [49] and NIST Special Database 14 (DB14) [50]. Both databases consist of 256 gray-level images; two different fingerprint instances (F = first, S = second) are present for each finger. Each fingerprint was manually analyzed by a human expert and assigned to one of the five classes: arch (A), left loop (L), right loop (R), tented arch (T), and whorl (W). Actually, some ambiguous fingerprints have an additional reference to one or more classes.

DB4 contains 2000 fingerprint pairs, uniformly distributed over the five classes; the images are numbered from F0001 to F2000 and from S0001 to S2000. In accordance with the testing rules adopted in [27], we use the 2000 images from the first 1000 fingers (F0001–F1000 and S0001–S1000) as a training set and we test the classifiers on the remaining 2000 images (F1001–F2000 and S1001–S2000).

DB14 contains 27,000 fingerprint pairs randomly taken, thus approximating the real fingerprint distribution: The images are numbered from F00001 to F27000 and from S00001 to S27000. In accordance with the testing rules adopted in PCASYS [5], we test the classifiers on the last 2700 fingerprints (S24301-S27000). Fingerprints F00001–F24300 and S00001–S24300 (48,600 images) can be used for training the classifiers; we do not use fingerprints F24301–F27000 for training, because they are impressions of the same fingers used in the test set.

9.3.3.1. Results on NIST DB4

It has been experimentally found that the performance of the k-nearest-neighbor classifier (MKL-KNN) on DB4 is always lower than that of the simple minimum-distance classifier (MKL-MIN), probably because the size of the DB4 training set is too small to take advantage of the k-nearest-neighbor rule; thus, only the results of MKL-MIN are reported here.

The MKL-MIN classifier achieves an accuracy of 93.1% for the five-class problem; the confusion matrix is reported in Table 9.2. Please note that the rows of the table do not sum up to 400; in fact, some ambiguous fingerprints are assigned to two classes in the database; in such cases, when any one of the two labels matches the output of the classifier, the result is assumed to be correct.

Table 9.2. Confusion Matrix for the Five-Class Problem

True class	Assigned class				
	A	**L**	**R**	**W**	**T**
A	**422**	5	0	0	12
L	2	**375**	3	5	14
R	5	2	**394**	1	17
W	3	6	10	**378**	1
T	32	12	8	1	**292**

It is worth noting that many errors are due to the classification of some tented arch fingerprints as arch: In fact, these two classes have a substantial overlap and it is very difficult to separate them, even for human experts. By merging arch and tented arch into a single class (four-class problem), the accuracy increases to 95.4%.

By using the rejection criterion, the following results are obtained for the five-class problem (Table 9.3).

The parameter values used in the experimentation are $\sigma_1 = 0.6$, $\sigma_2 = 0.5$, $R_m = 8.2$, and $K = \{19, 27, 27, 28, 26\}$, $N = \{1, 2, 2, 3, 1\}$.

9.3.3.2. Results on NIST DB14

Both MKL-MIN and MKL-KNN have been tested on DB14. Three disjoint training sets (TR1, TR2, and TR3), each 9,720 fingerprints wide, were assembled from a subset (3/5) of the available 48,600 images; the remaining two fifths were used as a validation set for parameter tuning. The results reported in this section have been obtained by training MKL-MIN and MKL-KNN on the set TR1; the other two sets (TR2 and TR3) have been used for classifier combination experiments, as described in Section 9.3.4.

Tables 9.4 and 9.5 report the confusion matrices of the MKL-MIN and MKL-KNN classifiers, respectively. The last row in both tables is related to some fingerprints that

Table 9.3. Accuracy Versus Rejection Percentage

Rejection	0%	6.4%	12.6%	18.1%	22.9%	28.3%
Accuracy	93.1%	94.4%	95.7%	96.8%	97.5%	98.3%

Table 9.4. Confusion Matrix for the MKL-MIN Classifier

True class	Assigned class				
	A	L	R	W	T
A	51	2	0	0	1
L	0	773	3	27	7
R	6	9	696	22	7
W	2	33	24	968	2
T	11	7	4	2	38
S	1	1	3	0	0

Table 9.5. Confusion matrix for the MKL-MIN Classifier

True class	Assigned class				
	A	L	R	W	T
A	49	0	2	1	2
L	3	798	3	11	1
R	6	15	718	4	1
W	2	42	40	942	0
T	17	15	7	0	16
S	0	2	3	0	0

Table 9.6. MKL-MIN: Accuracy Versus Rejection Percentage

Rejection	0%	4.9%	12.4%	19.1%	24.6%
Accuracy	93.6%	95.4%	97.2%	98.4%	99.1%

Table 9.7. MKL-KNN: Accuracy Versus Rejection Percentage

Rejection	0%	5.8%	11.1%	20.0%
Accuracy	93.4%	96.2%	97.5%	98.7%

the human expert was not able to classify; obviously, these fingerprints are always counted as errors. The accuracy is 93.6% for MKL-MIN and 93.4% for MKL-KNN.

By using the rejection criteria defined in Section 9.3.2, the following results are obtained (Tables 9.6 and 9.7). The parameter values used in the experimentation are $\sigma_1 = 0.6$, $\sigma_2 = 0.5$, $R_m = 8.2$, and $K = \{26, 28, 28, 29, 28\}$, $N = \{1, 2, 2, 3, 1\}$; the number of neighbors for the MKL-KNN classifiers is $k = 5$.

9.3.4. Combining MKL-based Fingerprint Classifiers

In this section we investigate how a combination of MKL-based classifiers, trained on different learning sets, can be adopted to improve fingerprint classification accuracy.

Several classification schemes may be adopted for combining classifier outputs [3, 31, 32, 48]; some of the most popular are simple and weighted averaging, voting schemes [55], and nonlinear combinations using rank-based estimators such as the median. In our experimentation, a simple *majority-vote rule* proved to be an effective technique:

Let $C = \{C_1, C_2, \ldots, C_{NC}\}$ be a set of NC classifiers and

$$\theta_{ij} = \begin{cases} 1 & \text{if } j \text{ is the class hypothesized by } C_i \\ 0 & \text{otherwise} \end{cases} \qquad (1 \le i \le NC, 1 \le j \le 5)$$

then the fingerprint is assigned to the class t such that

$$t = \max_{j=1}^{5} \left(\sum_{i=1}^{NC} \theta_{ij} \right)$$

In order to provide a rejection criterion, the confidence of the combined classifier is defined as the average of the individual classifier confidences:

$$\text{conf} = \frac{1}{NC} \sum_{i=1}^{NC} \text{conf}_i$$

The rejection criterion simply consists of discarding fingerprints whose confidence is lower than a fixed threshold.

Table 9.8. Errors of the Different Classifiers

Classifier	Error
MKL-KNN 1	6.6%
MKL-KNN 2	6.7%
MKL-KNN 3	7.0%
MKL-MIN 1	6.4%
MKL-MIN 2	7.0%
MKL-MIN 3	7.1%

Note: The average error is 6.8%.

9.3.4.1. Experimental Results

The experimentation was performed on DB14, by using the same training and test sets as described in Section 9.3.3. In particular, the training set is partitioned into three disjoint subsets: TR1, TR2, and TR3. Both MKL-MIN and MKL-KNN classifiers were trained over TR1, TR2, and TR3, thus obtaining six different classifiers (see Table 9.8). The classifier MKL-COMB is obtained by coupling the six classifiers according to the majority-vote rule. The parameters used are $\sigma_1 = 0.6$, $\sigma_2 = 0.5$, $R_m = 8.2$, $K = \{26, 28, 28, 29, 28\}$, $N = \{1, 2, 2, 3, 1\}$; the number k of neighbors for the MKL-KNN classifiers is five. In Table 9.8, the error rates of the different classifiers are reported; it should be noted that the MKL-COMB error rate is 5.6%, which constitutes an 18% improvement with respect to the average error of the individual classifiers (6.8%).

9.3.5. Comparison with Previous Results

The first fingerprint classification systems proposed in the literature (years 1970–1990) were tested on small databases, usually collected by the authors themselves. Although the results reported on these internal databases provided an initial overview of the difficulty of the classification problem, a comparison among the various techniques was impossible and the results are not useful to track advances in the field. For example, in [40] and in [4], the test sets are two internally collected databases of 92 and 47 fingerprints, respectively: It is very difficult to deduce any conclusion from results reported on such different and small data sets.

In the beginning of the 1990s, NIST released two fingerprint databases well suited for development and testing of fingerprint classification systems: NIST Special Database 4 [49] and NIST Special Database 14 [50] (see Section 9.3.3). NIST DB4 and DB14 have become de facto standard benchmarks for fingerprint classification, and most of the works published in the last decade report results on one or both of these databases. In the following sections, the results of the MKL-based classifiers are compared with those of the main fingerprint classification approaches for which results on DB4 or DB14 are available.

9.3.5.1. Comparison on NIST DB4

Table 9.9 reports the error rates on DB4 of 10 different approaches: Most were obtained by using the first half of the database for training and the second for testing,

Table 9.9. Error Rates on NIST DB4

Method	Data set	5 classes	Weighted	4 classes	Weighted
Candela et al. 1995 [5]	Second half	—	—	11.4%	6.1%
Karu and Jain 1996 [29]	Whole DB	14.6%	11.9%	8.6%	9.4%
Senior 1997 [46]	Random 542	—	—	—	8.4%
Jain et al. 1999 [27]	Second half	10.0%	7.0%	5.2%	—
Hong and Jain 1999 [23]	Whole DB	12.5%	10.6%	7.7%	—
Cappelli et al. 1999 [9]	Second half	7.9%	6.5%	5.5%	—
Marcialis et al. 2001 [39]	Second half	12.1%	9.6%	—	—
Yao et al. 2001 [54]	Second half	10.7%	9.0%	6.9%	—
Senior 2001 [45]	Second half	—	—	—	5.1%
MKL-MIN	Second half	7.0%	5.9%	4.7%	5.4%

as explained in Section 9.3.3; two methods [23, 29] do not require a training set, thus they were tested on the whole database; Senior [46] reports results on 542 randomly selected fingerprints. All the results are reported at 0% rejection rate, with the exception of the approaches based on FingerCode feature vectors [27, 46, 54], where 1.8% fingerprints are rejected during the feature extraction stage. The results of the PCASYS system [5] on DB4 are not reported by the authors in [5], but by Senior in [45]. When available, both results of the five-class problem and four-class problem (Section 9.3.3.1) are reported for the various methods. Furthermore, since DB4 contains an equal number of fingerprints for each class, some authors prefer to weight the results according to the natural class distribution (Section 9.1): Weighted results, when published by the authors or derivable from the confusion matrices, are reported both for the five-class and four-class cases.

Despite its simple classification rule (a minimum-distance criterion), MKL-MIN exhibits very good accuracy: Its error rate is lower than that of more sophisticated classifiers, such as the combination of support vector machines proposed in [54] and the two-stage classifiers (a k-NN and 10 neural networks) presented in [27]. The only better result previously reported in the literature is a 5.1% error for the four-class problem with weighted results. This is achieved by the combination of three classifiers (PCASYS, hidden Markov model, and decision trees) proposed in [45]. On the other hand, it should be noted that MKL-MIN does not exploit any additional information (such as the class prior probabilities) to enhance the classification accuracy for the natural distribution case; therefore, the better result is obtained in case of uniform-distributed classes (4.7% error rate).

9.3.5.2. Comparison on NIST DB14

Table 9.10 reports the error rates on DB14 of the PCASYS system [5] and the MKL-based classifiers; all the results are obtained on the test set defined in Section 9.3.3.

The graph in Fig. 9.15 shows the accuracy of the classifiers as a function of the percentage of rejected fingerprints; the results of MKL-COMB and of the best MKL-MIN and the best MKL-KNN classifiers are reported; the remaining two curves

Table 9.10. Error Rates on NIST DB14

Method	Error
Candela et al. 1995 [5]	7.8%
MKL-MIN	6.4%
MKL-KNN	6.6%
MKL-COMB	5.6%

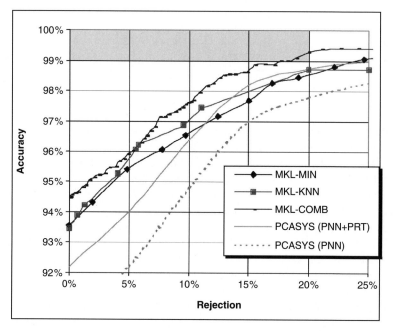

Fig. 9.15. Accuracy versus rejection curves. PCASYS performance was manually sampled from the graph printed in [5].

show the accuracy of the PCASYS system, when used with and without the auxiliary pseudoridge tracer (PRT), respectively. The gray area of the graph highlights the region where the FBI requirement [29] (99% accuracy at 20% rejection rate) is met. It should be noted that MKL-COMB crosses this region; in particular, a 99% accuracy is achieved at a 17.5% rejection rate.

9.4. Summary

Fingerprint classification is a challenging pattern recognition task that has captured the interest of several researches during the last 30 years. A number of approaches and various feature extraction strategies have been proposed to solve this problem: from rule-based methods, to neural networks and multiple-classifier systems, from directional image to Gabor-filter responses.

To date, no definitive solution has been proposed: Some of the most promising approaches seem to be the PCASYS system [5], the FingerCode-based methods [27], and the MKL-based classifiers introduced in Section 9.3. A strength of the MKL approach is its relative simplicity: In fact, after an initial fingerprint processing and normalization, the effectiveness of the MKL transform [10] yields very good accuracy to be achieved both on NIST DB4 and NIST DB14. In particular, the error rate of the MKL-MIN classifier on NIST DB4 is 7% without rejection: To the best of our knowledge, these are the best accuracy results reported in the literature for the for the five-class problem on NIST DB4. On NIST DB14, a combination of MKL-based classifiers achieves 5.6% error rate without rejection and 1% error rate at 17.5% rejection, thus meeting the FBI requirement [29] (99% accuracy at 20% rejection rate).

References

1. Ballan, M., F.A. Sakarya, and B.L. Evans, A fingerprint classification technique using directional images, Asilomar Conference on Signals, Systems, and Computers, 1997.
2. Bernard, S., N. Boujemaa, D. Vitale, and C. Bricot, Fingerprint classification using Kohonen topologic map", *Proc. International Conference on Image Processing ICIP'2001*, Thessaloniki, Greece, 2001.
3. Bigun, E.S., J. Bigun, B. Duc, and S. Fisher, Expert conciliation for multi modal person authentication systems by Bayesian statistics, in *Proc. First Int'l Conf. Audio Video-Based Personal Authentication*, Crans-Montant, Switzerland, March 1997, pp. 327–334.
4. Bowen, J.D., The Home Office automatic fingerprint pattern classification project, in *Proc. IEE Coll. on Neural Network for Image Processing Applications*, 1992.
5. Candela, G.T. et al., PCASYS—A pattern-level classification automation system for fingerprints, NIST Tech. Report NISTIR 5647, August 1995.
6. Cappelli, R., A. Lumini, D. Maio, and D. Maltoni, Fingerprint classification by directional image partitioning", *IEEE Trans. on Pattern Analysis Machine Intelligence*, 21(5):402–421, May 1999.
7. Cappelli, R., D. Maio, and D. Maltoni, A multi-classifier approach to fingerprint classification, *Pattern Analysis and Applications Special Issue on Fusion of Multiple Classifiers*, 5(2):136–144, May 2002.
8. Cappelli, R., D. Maio, and D. Maltoni, Combining fingerprint classifiers, in *Proc. First International Workshop on Multiple Classifier Systems (MCS2000)*, Cagliari, 2000, pp.351–361.
9. Cappelli, R., D. Maio, and D. Maltoni, Fingerprint classification based on multi-space KL, in *Proc. Workshop on Automatic Identification Advances Technologies (AutoID'99)*, Summit, NJ, 1999, pp. 117–120.
10. Cappelli, R., D. Maio, and D. Maltoni, Multi-space KL for pattern representation and classification, *IEEE Trans. on Pattern Analysis Machine Intelligence*, 23(9):977–996, Sept. 2001.
11. Cappelli, R., D. Maio, and D. Maltoni, Similarity search using multi-space KL, in *Proc. International Workshop on Similarity Search—DEXA'99 (IWOSS'99)*, Florence, Italy, 1999, pp. 155–160.
12. Cho, B.H., J.S. Kim, J.H. Bae, I.G. Bae, and K.Y. Yoo, Core-based fingerprint image classification, *Intl. Conf. Pattern Recognition* (15th), 2:863–866, 2000.

13. Chong, M.M.S. et al., Geometric framework for fingerprint image classification, *Pattern Recognition*, 30(9):1475–1488, 1997.
14. Daugman, J.G., Complete discrete 2-d Gabor transforms by neural networks for image analysis and compression, *IEEE Trans. Acoustics, Speech, and Signal Processing*, 36:1169–1179, 1988.
15. Daugman, J.G., High confidence visual recognition of persons by a test of statistical independence, *IEEE Trans. on Pattern Analysis and Machine Intelligence*, 15(11):1148–1161, 1993.
16. De Boer, J., A.M. Bazen, and S.H. Gerez, Indexing fingerprint databases based on multiple features, ProRISC2001, Workshop on Circuits, Systems and Signal Processing, Veldhoven, Netherlands, Nov. 2000.
17. Erol, A., U. Halici, and G. Ongun, Feature selective filtering for ridge extraction, in L.C. Jain, U. Halici, I. Hayashi, and S.B. Lee, *Intelligent Biometric Techniques in Fingerprint & Face Recognition*, Boca Raton, FL: CRC Press, 1999.
18. Fukunaga, K., *Statistical Pattern Recognition*, San Diego: Academic Press, 1990.
19. Galton, F., *Finger Prints*, London: Mcmillan, 1892.
20. Grasselli, A., On the automatic classification of fingerprint—Some consideration of the linguistic interpretation of pictures, in *Methodologies of Pattern Recognition*, S. Watanabe, ed., Academic Press, 1969, pp. 253–273.
21. Halici, U. and G. Ongun, Fingerprint classification through selforganizing feature maps modified to treat uncertainties, *Proc. IEEE*, 84(10):pp. 1497–1512, 1996.
22. Henry, E.R., *Classification and Uses of Finger Prints*, London: Routledge, 1900.
23. Hong, L. and A.K. Jain, Classification of fingerprint images, Scandinavian Conf. (11th) on Image Analysis, June 7–11, Kangerlussuaq, Greenland, 1999.
24. Hong, L., Y. Wan, and A.K. Jain, Fingerprint image enhancement: Algorithms and performance evaluation, *IEEE Trans. on Pattern Analysis Machine Intelligence*, 20(8):777–789, 1998.
25. Hughes, P.A. and A.D.P. Green, The use of neural network for fingerprint classification, in *Proc. 2nd Intl. Conf. on Neural Network*, 1991, pp. 79–81.
26. Jain, A.K., S. Prabhakar, and L. Hong, A multichannel approach to fingerprint classification, ICCVGIP'98, Dec. 21–23, Delhi, India, 1998, pp. 153–158.
27. Jain, A.K., S. Prabhakar, and L. Hong, A multichannel approach to fingerprint classification, *IEEE Trans. on Pattern Analysis Machine Intelligence*, 21(4):348–359, April 1999.
28. Kamijo, M., Classifying fingerprint images using neural network: Deriving the classification state, in *Proc. 3rd Intl. Conf. on Neural Network*, 1993, pp. 1932–1937.
29. Karu, K. and A.K. Jain, Fingerprint classification, *Pattern Recognition*, 29(3):389–404, 1996.
30. Kawagoe, M. and A. Tojo, Fingerprint pattern classification, *Pattern Recognition*, 17(3):295–303, 1984.
31. Kittler, J., On combining classifiers", *IEEE Trans. on Pattern Analysis Machine Intelligence*, 20(3):226–239, 1998.
32. Kittler, J., M. Hatef, and R.P.W. Duin, Combining classifiers, in *Proc. 13th ICPR*, Vienna 96, August 1996, pp. 897–901.
33. Lee, H.C. and R.E. Gaensslen, *Advances in Fingerprint Technology*, Elsevier Publishing, 1991.
34. Lumini, A., D. Maio, and D. Maltoni, Continuous vs. exclusive classification for fingerprint retrieval, *Pattern Recognition Letters*, 18(10):1027–1034, 1997.
35. Lumini, A., D. Maio, and D. Maltoni, Inexact graph matching for fingerprint classification, *Machine graphics & vision Special Issue on Graph Trasformations in Pattern Generation and CAD*, 8(2):231–248, Sept. 1999.

36. M. J. Donahue and S. I. Rokhlin, On the use of level curves in image analysis, *Image Understanding*, 57:185–203, 1993.
37. Maio, D. and D. Maltoni, A structural approach to fingerprint classification, Intl. Conf. (23th) on Pattern Recognition, Vienna, Aug. 1996.
38. Maio, D. and D. Maltoni, A structural approach to fingerprint classification, in *Proc. 13th ICPR*, Vienna 96, August 1996.
39. Marcialis, G.L., F. Roli, and P. Frasconi, Fingerprint classification by combination of flat and structural approaches, Intl. Conf. (3rd) on Audio-and Video-Based Biometric Person Authentication, Sweden, June 6–8, 2001, pp. 241–246.
40. Moayer, B. and K.S. Fu, A syntactic approach to fingerprint pattern recognition, *Pattern Recognition*, 7:1–23, 1975.
41. Moayer, B. and K.S. Fu, An application of stochastic languages to fingerprint pattern recognition, *Pattern Recognition*, 8:173–179, 1976.
42. Moscinska, K. and G. Tyma, Neural network based fingerprint classification, in *Proc. 3rd Intl. Conf. on Neural Network*, 1993, pp. 229–232.
43. Neto, H.V. and D.L. Borges, Fingerprint classification with neural networks, IVth Brazilian Symposium on Neural Networks, 1997, pp. 66–72.
44. Rao, K. and K. Balck, Type classification of fingerprints: A syntactic approach, *IEEE Trans. on Pattern Analysis Machine Intelligence*, 2(3):223–231, 1980.
45. Senior, A., A combination fingerprint classifier, *IEEE Trans. on Pattern Analysis Machine Intelligence*, 23(10):1165–1174, 2001.
46. Senior, A., A hidden Markov model fingerprint classifier, Asilomar Conf. (31st) on Signals, Systems and Computers, 1997, pp. 306–310.
47. Stock, R.M. and C.W. Swonger, Development and evaluation of a reader of fingerprint minutiae, Cornell Aeronautical Laboratory, Technical Report CAL no. XM-2478-X-1:13–17, 1969.
48. Suen, C.Y. and L. Lam, Multiple classifiers combination methodologies for different output levels, in *Proc. First International Workshop on Multiple Classifier Systems (MCS2000)*, Cagliari, June 2000, pp. 52–66.
49. Watson, C.I. and C.L. Wilson, Nist Special Database 4, Fingerprint Database, U.S. National Institute of Standards and Technology, 1992.
50. Watson, C.I., Nist Special Database 14, Fingerprint Database, U.S. National Institute of Standards and Technology, 1993.
51. Wegstein, J.H., An automated fingerprint identification system, U.S. National Institute of Standards and Technology, *NBS Special Publication* 500-89, Feb. 1982.
52. Wei, D., Q. Yuan, and T. Jie, Fingerprint classification system with feedback mechanism based on genetic algorithm, Intl. Conf. Pattern Recognition (14th), 1998.
53. Wilson, C.L., G.T. Candela, and C.I. Watson, Neural network fingerprint classification, *J. Artificial Neural Networks*, 1(2):203–228, 1994.
54. Yao, Y., P. Frasconi, and M. Pontil, Fingerprint classification with combination of support vector machines, Intl. Conf. (3rd) on Audio- and Video-Based Biometric Person Authentication, Sweden, June 6–8, 2001, pp. 253–258.
55. Zuev, Y.A. and S.K. Ivanonv, The voting as a way to increase the decision reliability, in *Proc. Foundations of Information/Decision Fusion with Applications to Eng. Problems*, Washington, DC, Aug. 1996, pp. 206–210.

Chapter 10

Fingerprint Classification by Decision Fusion

Andrew Senior and Ruud Bolle

Abstract. Fingerprint classification is an important indexing method for any large-scale fingerprint recognition system or database, as a method for reducing the number of fingerprints that need to be searched when looking for a matching print. Fingerprints are generally classified into broad categories based on global characteristics. This paper describes novel methods of classification using hidden Markov models (HMMs) and decision trees to recognize the ridge structure of the print, without needing to detect singular points. The methods are compared and combined with a standard fingerprint classification algorithm, and results for the combination are presented using a standard database of fingerprint images. The paper also describes a method for achieving any level of accuracy required of the system, by sacrificing the efficiency of the classifier. The accuracy of the combination classifier is shown to be higher than that of two state-of-the-art systems tested under the same conditions.

10.1. Introduction

The classification of fingerprints has long been an important part of any fingerprint identification system. A partition of fingerprints into groups of broadly similar patterns allows filing and retrieval of large databases of fingerprints for quick reference. Currently interest in fingerprint classification is stimulated by its use in automatic fingerprint identification systems (AFIS). In an AFIS, the goal is to find a match for a probe fingerprint in the database of enrolled prints, possibly numbering many millions. Classification is used in an AFIS to reduce the size of the search space to fingerprints of the same class before attempting exact matching.

The most widely used system of fingerprint classification is the Henry system and its variants [1]. Examples from five of the main classes of the Henry system are shown in Fig. 10.1. An indexing method widely used in manual fingerprint systems identifies a person with a 10-digit binary number wherein each digit indicates whether or not the corresponding fingerprint is a whorl. This allows the population to be divided into 1024 (unequal) groups to narrow a search.

This paper describes a combination of novel approaches to fingerprint classification using the Henry system. The system described has been designed to operate on both rolled and "dab" fingerprints, where some of the structural information other

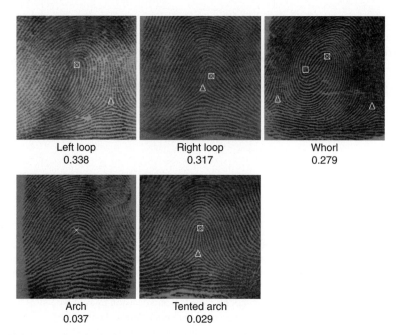

Left loop   Right loop   Whorl
0.338   0.317   0.279

Arch   Tented arch
0.037   0.029

Fig. 10.1. Examples of five fingerprint categories, marked with core and delta points, with their frequencies of occurrence.

systems use (such as the delta position) may not be available in the fingerprint image. The system described has been tested on the NIST Special Database 4 [2] of fingerprint images and results are presented. Further, a method of measuring the efficiency of a classification algorithm is described, allowing a principled comparison of this algorithm with previous published works. Finally, a method for achieving arbitrary accuracy is described, allowing the Henry classifier to be used with the flexibility of continuous classifiers. This method trades off accuracy against classifier efficiency, allowing an imperfect classifier to be used in a real-world system while retaining all the advantages of a traditional Henry system.

The approach taken here is of a combination of classifiers each using different features and with different errors on test data. Two novel classifiers are described, using two-dimensional hidden Markov models (HMMs) and decision trees. In addition to showing that these classifiers perform well on the classification problem, this paper shows that the combination of classifiers provides a way forward for the improvement of fingerprint classification, in the same way as recent improvements in isolated handwritten character recognition performance have been largely brought about not by better classifiers but by combinations of different classifiers. The classifiers are tested in isolation and in combination with the probabilistic neural network classifier and pseudoridge tracer from the PCASYS system described by Candela et al. [3] (Section 10.2.1). The experiments are all performed on discrete, Henry classification, but the system could be extended to continuous classification or classification with unsupervised clustering, using such techniques as unsupervised K-means HMM clustering [4].

The following section reviews previous fingerprint classification systems, including the PCASYS system that we use as a component in our joint classifier. Section 10.3 describes the processing of the fingerprint images to extract the ridges and the extraction of features for recognition. Then Sections 10.4 and 10.5 describe the hidden Markov model classifier and the decision tree classifier, respectively; the latter are discussed in Section 10.6 also. In Section 10.7, classification based on the outputs of these classifiers is described as well as methods of combining the classifiers to improve accuracy. Section 10.8 describes a measure of efficiency of the classifier and shows how arbitrary efficiency can be achieved. Section 10.9 presents results for the classifiers and their combinations, and results are compared with previously published results in Section 10.10.

10.2. Previous Work

Many previous authors have developed automated systems to classify fingerprints, using a wide variety of techniques. Cappelli et al. [5] provide a review of a number of methods that have been used. We summarize these briefly and in Section 10.10, we present results from other authors.

Most automatic systems use the Henry classes, and these are important for existing AFIS databases and systems that require compatibility with human classifications, either because of legacy data or because some manual intervention is necessary in the process, requiring the use of human-interpretable classes. A variety of approaches to classification has been tried, the most fundamental being a syntactic analysis of the relative positions and number of core and delta points in the print [6, 7]. The core and delta points, shown in Fig. 10.1, are the singular points in the flow of the ridges. Finding these points in the image is a difficult image processing task, particularly with poor-quality images, but if found reliably, the classification is simple. Maio and Maltoni [8] use a structural analysis of the direction of ridges in the print, without needing to find core and delta points. Blue et al. [27] and Candela et al. [3] use the core location to center their representation scheme, which is based on a principal components analysis (PCA) of ridge directions, and they then use a variety of classifiers. Halici and Ongun [9] similarly use PCA-projected, core-centered ridge directions, but classified with a self-organizing map; and Jain et al. [10] also use the core for translation invariance, using a Gabor-filter representation and a k-nearest neighbor classifier.

For situations where there is no need to use existing classes, some researchers have developed systems that rely on machine-generated classes, or dispense with classes all together, and use "continuous" classification [5, 9, 11, 12]. Here the criterion is not adherence to the Henry classes, but merely consistency among classifications of different prints from the same finger. Fingerprints are represented by points in a feature space on which some distance measure is defined. Test fingerprints are matched against all those in the database falling within some radius of the test print. By increasing the radius, classification can be made arbitrarily accurate, reducing errors by increasing the size of the search space and hence search time. Continuous classification holds the prospect of circumventing the difficult and restrictive Henry classification problem and has produced the best results of recent years, but has disadvantages, besides the uninterpretability mentioned above. With Henry classes, the portions of the database that must be searched are always the same, allowing for rigid segmentation of the database and a priori design of the search strategy. A continuous system presents an entirely different subset of the database for every matching operation, complicating and slowing the matching.

More recently Yao et al. [13] have described systems that use and support vector machines to classify fingerprints represented by the features of [10] and an additional set of features derived by using recursive neural networks.

10.2.1. PCASYS

Candela et al. [3] describe a fingerprint classifier called PCASYS, which is based on a probabilistic neural network (PNN) classifying features consisting of principal component projected orientation vectors. The orientations of the ridges taken in a 28×30 grid of points around the core are reduced in dimensionality with principal components analysis. The resulting 64-dimensional vectors are classified with the PNN. They have published results and made their software available, making possible a realistic comparison with this system. Lumini et al. [11] use this software and extend it to provide continuous classification. To provide an alternative classification method and an enhanced combination classifier, PCASYS has been tested on the same testing data as classified by our HMM and decision tree classifiers. Results are presented for PCASYS alone and in combination with the other classifiers.

PCASYS incorporates a *pseudoridge tracer*, which detects upward curving ridges and is able to correctly identify some whorl prints, but provides no information to distinguish among the other classes. This effectively penalizes the other classes when returning a "yes" answer. PCASYS also exploits prior information to improve its accuracy (see Section 10.7.1).

10.3. Ridge Extraction

The system deals with fingerprint images stored as arrays of gray levels and obtained with a scanner or camera device—either from an inked fingerprint on paper or as a "live scan" directly from the finger. For much of the work in this paper, the NIST-4 [2] database of rolled fingerprint images has been used, since this provides a large number (4000) of fingerprints with associated class labels. In addition, part of the NIST-9 database has been used.

The features provided to the recognizer are based on the characteristics of the intersections of ridges with a set of fiducial lines that are laid across the fingerprint image. To find the ridge locations, a number of image processing techniques are used [14], summarized as follows:

1. Initial segmentation; The PCASYS algorithm for extracting a central fingerprint region from a full rolled print is used on prints from the NIST-9 database. NIST-4 is already segmented at this level.
2. Smoothing.
3. Finding the predominant direction in each of an array of blocks covering the image.
4. Segmenting the image into the area of the print (*foreground*) and the unwanted background, based on the strength of directionality found in each block.
5. Applying directional filters to highlight the ridges and detect pixels that are parts of ridges.
6. Thinning the ridge image so that each ridge is left represented by an eight-connected, one-pixel-wide line termed the *skeleton*.

From this ridge representation, two sets of features are extracted as concise expressions of the fingerprint shape suitable for classification. The first, described in the next section, is recognized by HMM, and the second, described in Section 10.5.1, is classified by decision trees.

10.3.1. Feature Extraction

Given the skeleton image of the ridges, parallel fiducial lines are laid across the image at an angle ϕ, as shown in Fig. 10.2, and each one followed in turn. For each intersection of a fiducial line with a ridge, a feature is generated. Each feature consists of a number of measurements, chosen to characterize the ridge behavior and its development at the intersection point:

1. The distance since the last intersection
2. The angle of intersection
3. The change in angle since the last intersection
4. The curvature of the ridge at the intersection

The angle features (2) can be seen to contain similar information to the coarse direction field calculated in the preprocessing stages of this system and used by other

Fig. 10.2. A sample fingerprint showing horizontal fiducial lines ($\phi = 0$).

systems as the feature set for classification [3]. However, this representation allows a higher-resolution representation of the fingerprints and allows more information to be represented (e.g., ridge spacing and curvature). Further measurements could also be taken at each point.

The measurements of each feature are termed a frame, and the frames, R_{i_k}, for the ith fiducial line are collectively termed a row, R_i, whose ordering is preserved. For each orientation ϕ of fiducial lines, a separate representation $\mathcal{R}^\phi = \{R_i, \forall i\}$ of the print is obtained. In this work, only horizontal and vertical lines have been used, giving features $\mathcal{R}^h$ and $\mathcal{R}^v$, respectively, but other angles may allow further information to be captured.

10.4. Fingerprint Recognition by Hidden Markov Models

Hidden Markov models are a form of stochastic finite-state automaton well suited to pattern recognition and successfully applied to speech recognition [15, 16] and other problems. They are appropriate to the problem posed here because of their ability to classify patterns based on a large quantity of features, whose number is variable and which have certain types of an underlying structure, especially if that structure results in stationarity of the feature distributions over some spatial or temporal period. Such a structure is found in fingerprints, where ridge orientations, spacings, and curvatures are, for the most part, only slowly varying across the print. In a fingerprint the basic class information can be inferred from syntactic analysis of singular points, but can also be seen in the general pattern of the ridges—the way a nonexpert human would classify prints. The HMM is able to statistically model the different structures of the ridge patterns by accumulations of evidence across the whole print, without relying on singular point extraction.

Typically HMMs are one-dimensional structures suitable for analyzing temporal data. Here, the data are two-dimensional, but the process of feature extraction can also be described as a one-dimensional array of one-dimensional row processes. Thus we can apply a "two-dimensional hidden Markov model," similar to that of Agazzi et al. [17], which consists of a nesting of row models within whole-print models as shown in Fig. 10.3.

For classification, a model $\mathcal{M}_c$ is constructed for each class, c, and the maximum-likelihood class is chosen after calculating the probability of the data $\mathcal{R}$ given the model $\mathrm{argmax}_c P(\mathcal{R}|\mathcal{M}_c)$.

Row Modeling

To simplify the analysis of the model, first consider a row model modeling a single row of the fingerprint data of Section 10.3.1. Each row model M_i is a conventional HMM and consists of a number of states, which model the small, stationary regions in a row. Any row R_i is assumed to have been generated by the row automaton transitioning from state to state, producing the frames in the observed order at each transition, with $S_{i_j k}$ being the kth state in the sequence whereby M_i produces R_i (k corresponds

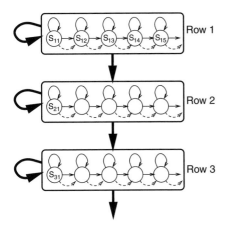

Fig. 10.3. A schematic of the two-dimensional structure of the HMM, showing three row models of five states each, forming a global model for a single class.

to time in a temporal HMM). The state transitions are controlled by probabilities $P(S_{ij_k}|S_{ij_{k-1}})$ trained with certain constraints: The state must monotonically increase $S_{ij_k} \geq S_{ij_{k'}}$ for $k > k'$, and it is possible to skip states at the edge of the print. Because of the nature of the printing process whereby, especially for dabs, it is to be expected that edge regions of the fingerprint will be missing but the central regions will always be present, only states at the edge of the print may be skipped. This effectively constrains the initial state distribution $P(S_{ij_0})$.

The frame emission probabilities are modeled with mixtures of diagonal covariance, multivariate Gaussian distributions. Thus for any frame R_{i_k}, it is possible to calculate the likelihood $P(R_{i_k}|S_{ij_k})$ of it occurring in any state S_{ij_k}. With these likelihoods, for any row model, the likelihood of any row can be approximated by the maximum likelihood of any state sequence aligning the features and states calculated as a product of frame likelihoods and transition probabilities for the state sequence:

$$P(R_i|M_j) \approx \max_{S_{ij}} P(R_{i_0}|S_{ij_0})P(S_{ij_0}) \prod_k P(R_{i_k}|S_{ij_k})P(S_{ij_k}|S_{ij_{k-1}})$$

The models are initialized by using an equal-length alignment with the frames evenly distributed across the states of the model. After estimating the initial parameter values, using smooth equal-length alignment [18], Viterbi alignment is used to find the maximum-likelihood alignment of frames with states, which is used for retraining. Around two iterations of training are necessary to achieve good classification performance.

Global Model

The global model is the same as a row model, except that its states are row models, and its frames are whole rows. Thus for each model c:

$$P(\mathcal{R}|\mathcal{M}_c) \approx \max_{S'} P(R_0|M_{S'_0})P(M_{S'_0}) \prod_k P(R_k|M_{S'_k})P(S'_k|S'_{k-1})$$

where S' is an alignment specifying which row model $M_{S'_k}$ models the row of data R_k.

10.4.1. Multiple HMM Classifiers

For each orientation of fiducial lines, a separate classifier can be made. Since the errors of the different classifiers will be different, a combination of their scores may yield a better accuracy. Denoting by $\mathcal{M}_c^h$, $\mathcal{M}_c^v$ the class c models trained with vertical and horizontal features, respectively, and assuming independence, the likelihood of the data is written as

$$P(\mathcal{R}^h, \mathcal{R}^v | C_c) \approx P(\mathcal{R}^h | \mathcal{M}_c^h) P(\mathcal{R}^v | \mathcal{M}_c^v) \tag{1}$$

Fusion of multiple classifiers is treated in more detail in Section 10.7.3.

10.5. Decision Tree Classifiers

To provide a supplementary classification, hopefully giving uncorrellated errors, another type of feature has been extracted and classified with a decision tree approach. Such decision trees are built using techniques based on those of Amit et al. [19]. These authors tackled a number of problems including that of digit recognition—classifying images of the digits 0 to 9.

The technique used by Amit et al. for constructing decision trees involves the generation of a large number of simple features. Each feature in isolation provides little information about the classification decision; for example, the existence of an edge at a particular location in an image may give little clue as to the digit's identity. However, combinations of such features can represent much important information needed to make an accurate classification decision. Amit et al. describe a procedure for making decision trees by growing questions based on such combinations of simple features.

The procedure has been adopted here for fingerprint classification and involves an initial feature extraction phase, followed by question building, which creates informative questions assisting in classification. These complex questions are combined in a hierarchical manner to form decision trees, which are used for classification. Because the trees are constructed stochastically, trees constructed for the same problem have different performances, and, as is common with decision tree classifiers, multiple trees are combined to give the final classification.

10.5.1. Feature Extraction

This second classifier was designed to give a second opinion on the classification of a fingerprint image. For this purpose, the errors in classification should be as uncorrelated as possible with those made by the HMM; thus a different set of features was generated for this classification method. Again the motivation is to consider distributed information from across the fingerprint without extraction of singular points. Because the class information is implicit in the shapes of ridges, features that are easily and reliably extracted and that encode the ridge shape in a simple, concise manner were chosen.

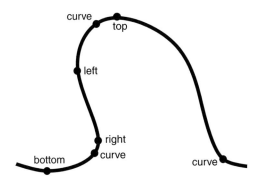

Fig. 10.4. A single ridge showing the extracted features for the decision tree: curvature maximum and left, right, bottom, and top turning points.

The initial preprocessing used is identical to that of the HMM classifier, up to the extraction of ridges (Section 10.3), but instead of taking features at intersections with fiducial lines, features are generated at salient points on the ridges. The features consist of curvature maxima and four axis-parallel turning points [$dx/ds = 0$ or $dy/ds = 0$ for a ridge represented as the parametric curve $(x(s), y(s))$, and distinguished by the sign of the second derivative]. Some example features are shown in Fig. 10.4. For each feature the feature type and location (in pixels at 500 dpi) are recorded. These features are all based on local computations on the ridges and again avoid the extraction of global features such as core and delta points. Again they are invariant to translation and to small amounts of rotation. These features are also appropriate for the classification of dabs, since the majority of features in a rolled print also occurs in the region typically imaged in a dab.

10.6. Fingerprint Classification by Decision Trees

A binary decision tree is constructed as a hierarchy of binary questions [20]. Questions are logical statements about the features that may be present in the fingerprint and about the relations between those features; for a given fingerprint a question is either true or false. At the "top" level, each test sample is asked the first question. According to the test sample data, the question returns either true or false, and the branch to the second-level is determined. On whichever branch is chosen, a second-level question is asked, and a further bifurcation is induced. In this way, each test sample descends the tree, by a route dependent on its features, and arrives at a leaf node. Leaf nodes are labeled according to the classes of the test data that arrived there. In a simple classification problem, leaf nodes will be pure—that is, they receive only training samples from a single class, and the unambiguous classification of any test sample arriving there would be the class of the training data at that node. For more complex problems, the leaf nodes contain mixed data, and the test data is labeled with a probability distribution across the classes.

Figure 10.5 shows a small decision tree with two levels. Each of the three nodes of the tree contains a question of the form specified in Section 10.6.1. At each node,

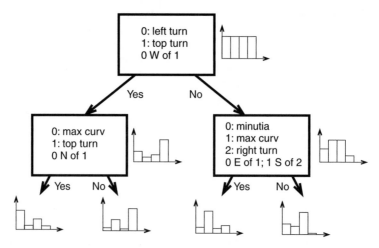

Fig. 10.5. A two-level decision tree, showing hypothetical class distributions at each node. Each node has a question formed of a list of feature types that must be present and a list of relationships between them that must be true for the question to return "yes".

and at the leaves, a class histogram with four classes is shown, indicating the reduction in entropy as the tree is traversed. The root node has all classes equally likely, with no discrimination, and the other nodes have successively stronger discrimination between the classes.

10.6.1. Questions

A question consists of a list of required features and a set of relations between them, in the same manner as those of Amit et al. Each feature is specified as one of the five features described above (four turning points and a curvature maximum). Relations are all of the form "x is <*direction*> of y", where <*direction*> is one of North, South, East, and West. Optionally a question can also impose a distance limit—that the feature must be within a certain distance. Experimentation led us to use two distance bands: features within 0.1" and features within 0.2". An example question may specify that there is a maximum of curvature East of a lower turning point that itself is East of, and within 0.2" of, a maximum of curvature. Other questions are shown in the nodes of Fig. 10.5. Questions are constructed in such a way that every feature is related to at least one feature in the feature list, and so every pair of features can have at most one relation.

Given a new print, the print can be tested by a search that determines if the question can be fulfilled by the features of the print.

10.6.2. Question Construction

During tree construction, questions are constructed randomly as follows:

1. Select any feature class as the first feature.

2. Test the data separation. If more than 2/3 of the training data at this node replies yes, refine the question and repeat this step. If less than 1/3 replies yes, discard this question and construct a new question. Otherwise, evaluate the question.

Refining the question consists of adding extra restrictions, which inevitably make a "yes" answer less likely. The proportion of samples answering "yes" can be reduced in one of two ways. First, a feature can be added. In this case, a random feature type is chosen and added to the list. A random relation is chosen to relate it to a randomly chosen feature already in the list. Second, if there are two or more features in the question, and some pair has no relation between them, then an additional relation can be added to the question between any pair of features that are as yet unrelated.

When adding a relation is not possible, a feature is added. Otherwise, a random choice is made, biased toward adding a relation, since this keeps the number of features lower, limiting the dimensionality of the search space for answering questions, and making testing faster.

Having arrived at a question that channels between one and two thirds of the data to each of the "yes" and "no" sides, the question is evaluated. The measure of the effectiveness of a question is the change of entropy in the distributions before and after applying the question. Classes at the root node have high entropy, but the leaf nodes should have very low entropy (be "purer"). The relative entropy of the output distributions for a node is computed for many randomly constructed, candidate questions; the question with the highest entropy change is chosen.

A tree is recursively constructed until the leaves are pure or until a maximum depth (typically 7) is reached. Figure 10.6 shows the effect of varying the depth of

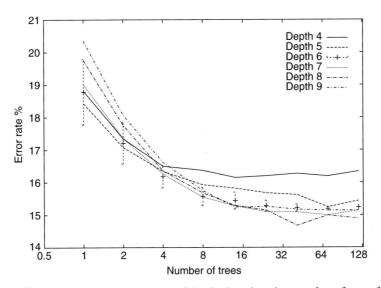

Fig. 10.6. Raw error rates (no priors, unweighted) plotted against number of trees for the decision tree classifier tested on the NIST-4 test set, using averages of different numbers of trees, for trees built to different depths. Error bars in the error rate estimate are shown for the depth 6 case.

the trees and the number of trees used. Multiple trees are merged by multiplying the leaf node distributions class by class as in Section 10.4.1.

10.7. Postprocessing and Classifier Combination

Given the raw classifiers presented above, a number of steps must be taken to apply the classifiers to a test set. The following sections describe using class priors to enhance classifier accuracy, weighting the results to predict behavior on true test sets and methods for the combination of multiple classifiers.

10.7.1. Class Priors

Because the classes that are used are not equal in frequency of occurrence, calculating the posterior probability of a class given the data requires the product of the data likelihood given the class c and the prior probability of the class:

$$P(c|\mathcal{R}) \propto P(\mathcal{R}|\mathcal{M}_c)P(c) \tag{2}$$

The class priors have been estimated by Wilson et al. [21] on 222 million fingerprints. (The proportions are 0.037, 0.338, 0.317, 0.029, 0.279 for arch, left loop, right loop, tented arch, and whorl, respectively.)

10.7.2. Class Weighting

Since the NIST-4 database (and correspondingly the test set used here) has equal numbers of prints from each class, to obtain a good estimate of the true test-condition accuracy, the results must be weighted according to the true frequencies of occurrence, using the same procedure as Wilson et al. [21]. Otherwise, a classifier good at recognizing arches, which are rare, would appear better on this test set than in the real world or on a representative test set where this ability is rarely called upon.

10.7.3. Classifier Combination

Four classifiers (counting the PCASYS pseudoridge classifier) are available in this work. Each by itself is capable of classifying fingerprints with a limited accuracy. However, each classifier uses different features and methods, so the errors produced by each classifier should be somewhat uncorrelated. In this situation, combining the results of the classifiers should produce an improved classifier with a lower error rate. Many other authors have tackled the problems of decision fusion, and here we take two simple approaches.

Linear Likelihood Fusion

The first method of combination is a probabilistic approach since the output of each classifier is a probability distribution $P(c|\mathcal{R}^i)$ across the classes c.

Strictly speaking, if each classifier gave a true probability out, and with N independent classifiers operating on features $\mathcal{R}^i$, the posterior probability would be

$$P(c|\mathcal{R}^1, \ldots, \mathcal{R}^N) \propto P(c) \prod_i P(\mathcal{R}^i|c) \tag{3}$$

However, in practice, the probabilities are correlated and have varying reliabilities. The HMM probabilities are the product of many correlated probabilities, and the PNN already incorporates prior information. To correct for these effects, weights w_i are introduced to balance the classifier combination. Working in the log domain, with normalization constant k:

$$\log P(c|\mathcal{R}^1, \ldots, \mathcal{R}^N) = k + \log P(c) + \sum_i w_i P(\mathcal{R}^i|c) \tag{4}$$

For simple classification, the class $\text{argmax}_c \log P(c|\mathcal{R}^1, \ldots, \mathcal{R}^N)$ is chosen as the correct answer. Finding the weights w_i, however, is a difficult problem. Estimation of weights by line searches on the training set fails to generalize well to the test set, so the following trained approach was used, which is found to achieve accuracies close to those obtained when optimizing linear weights by line search on the *test* set.

Neural Network Fusion

The second fusion approach is to use a backpropagation neural network. Here the class probabilities for all the classifiers are combined in a neural network, trained to output the true class on the training set. Additionally, four estimates of the fingerprint quality [22] are supplied to the network, though their effect is not significant. Training uses a momentum-based weight update scheme and Softmax outputs [23], giving an output class probability distribution. Training samples are weighted to simulate a uniform prior, and the output probabilities are multiplied by the class prior 10.7.1 when testing. Separate networks are trained to combine the HMM and decision tree, or to combine all four classifiers. To generate enough training data for the neural network, the first half of the NIST-4 database was supplemented with 5400 prints from the NIST-9 database (Vol. 2, CDs 1, 2, and 3).

10.8. Classifier Efficiency

Since the purpose of a fingerprint classifier is to partition large fingerprint databases, in addition to the classification accuracy—the proportion of classifications that give the correct class—the classification efficiency must also be considered. Since many authors use different classes, a consistent measure of efficiency, as described here, is essential for the comparison of results. An efficiency measure also permits the evaluation of rejection and backing-off strategies described in Section 10.8.2.

The classification efficiency can be considered as a measure of the reduction of search space. In practice, the proportion of the database to be searched will vary with each query, so over a test set, the average efficiency can be calculated as

$$\frac{\text{Number of matches required with no classifier}}{\text{Number of matches required when classifier is used}} \tag{5}$$

where an exhaustive one-to-many match against a database of N prints is counted as N matches. If a perfect classifier is used to classify M prints prior to matching against a database of N prints, any of the MP_c test prints in class c (which occurs with probability P_c) need only be tested against the NP_c database prints of class c. Thus the total number of matches required is now $\sum_c NMP_c^2$ instead of NM. The efficiency of a perfect classifier using these classes is thus $1/\sum_c P_c^2$. Using the five NIST-4 classes and the frequencies of Section 10.7.1, this gives an efficiency of 3.39. Merging arch and tented arch classes only reduces the efficiency to 3.37, since this distinction so rarely needs to be made. As can be seen, the imbalance of the class priors makes the efficiency significantly lower than would be obtained with five equally frequent classes (an efficiency of 5). In practice the efficiency of a fallible classifier will deviate from this value—for instance, a classifier that consistently mistakes all prints for arches will have an efficiency of 15 (1/0.066).

10.8.1. Alternate Classes

NIST-4 provides alternate class labels for 17.5% of the prints [2, p. 8], but these are ignored in this work, a classification being deemed correct only if it matches the primary class label. Allowing matches with the alternate label too would increase the recognition rates but would lower the efficiency of the classifier, since such prints when enrolled would have to be stored twice (under both classes) in our database, resulting in extra searches every time the secondary class was searched.

10.8.2. Backing Off

Previous classification works have quoted error rates that would be unacceptable in real-world systems. However, it is clear that accuracy can be traded off for efficiency— searching more than just the top one class will give higher accuracy but lower efficiency [24]. If a reliable measure of confidence in the classifier's answer is available, it is possible to devise methods to adjust the reliance on the classifier answer, when that classification is uncertain, and thus reducing the number of errors made. Some classifiers [3] have used a rejection mechanism, which improves the accuracy at the cost of not pruning the search with those prints that are rejected. This section proposes a more complex scheme to allow graceful and efficient "backing off" of classifier reliance based on a likelihood ratio confidence measure.

It is clear that if the likelihoods for the top two classes are very different, then the classifier can be considered to be more "confident" in its answer than if the two likelihoods are similar (when it would only take a small perturbation to change the ranks of the answers). Thus, the likelihood ratio of the top two answers is examined. If this is less than an empirically determined threshold, then the top choice is deemed not to be confident and the top two classes are jointly returned as the answer (increasing the proportion of the database subsequently searched by the one-to-many matcher). Similarly, the likelihood ratio of the second and third choices is compared to a threshold to allow backing off to three classes. Repeating the procedure, if all the likelihoods are similar, the classifier will return a "don't know" answer, and all classes must be searched. More traditional rejection strategies (e.g., [21]) use a criterion to back off directly from the "top-choice only" to the "don't know" answer without allowing as rich a classification.

The efficiency of the classifier when allowing backing off is now

$$\frac{MN}{\sum_{m=1}^{M} \pi_m N} \tag{6}$$

where π_m, $1 \geq \pi_m \geq 0$, is the proportion of the database searched for query print m.class c.

Adjusting the likelihood ratio threshold allows arbitrary accuracy to be obtained. A large threshold would give a null classifier with 100% accuracy but an efficiency of 1. A threshold of zero would give the basic top-one accuracy and maximum efficiency (3.37 for the four-class problem). Adjusting the threshold allows us to set the overall classifier accuracy to that deemed necessary for the whole system. However, it should be noted that this arbitrary classification accuracy is achieved within the context of a Henry classification system where the portions of the database to be searched will always conform to the Henry classifications, and thus allow the database partitioning and search to be designed to operate on prior knowledge, not having to cope with dynamically changing subsets as in continuous classification.

In fact, the efficiency loss (i.e., extra search time) of searching the next class is dependent on the frequency of that class, so a more advanced backing-off algorithm should take this into account to achieve a better trade-off of accuracy for efficiency.

10.9. Results

Following the practice of Jain et al. [10], the system has been trained and tested on the NIST-4 database of fingerprint images. The training set was composed of the first 2000 prints, and the test set was the remaining 2000 prints from NIST-4 (1000 pairs, so no test prints had corresponding prints in the training data). The primary class labels given with the databases were used, but since the efficiency is hardly affected,

Table 10.1. Error Rates, Testing Different Combinations of the Classifiers Described in This Paper.

Classifier	Error (%)
HMM horizontal ($\mathcal{R}^h$) features	20.8
HMM vertical ($\mathcal{R}^v$) features	13.8
HMM both with prior	12.8
DT with prior	14.4
HMM + DT + prior	9.0
PCASYS (PNN only)	8.5
PCASYS (PNN + pseudoridge)	6.1
HMM + DT + PCASYS (no prior)	6.8
HMM + DT + PCASYS (prior)	5.1

Note: The HMM classifier used here has 8 rows of 8 states each and uses a shared pool of 200 Gaussians with four-dimensional features. The decision tree (DT) classifier is a mixture of 30 trees, each with 7 levels. The three combination results use a neural network. The PCASYS PNN + Pseudoridge classifier result uses a heuristic combination [3], which incorporates the priors.

Table 10.2. Confusion Matrix for the NIST-4 Test Set (Without Reweighting).

True class	Assigned class				Error rate
	A/T	W	L	R	
A/T	637	5	66	112	22.3%
W	0	384	4	14	4.5%
L	10	2	370	4	4.2%
R	8	2	2	380	3.1%

Note: The table shows the assigned classes for fingerprints falling into each of the true classes, and a per-class error rate.

the classifier was only trained to distinguish four classes, treating arch and tented arch as identical. Table 10.1 shows the error rates for various combinations of classifiers. All results presented in this table are weighted, as in Section 10.7.2, to simulate the natural frequencies of occurrence of the fingerprint classes.

Table 10.2 shows the confusion matrix for the four-classifier neural network fusion with priors, but without the class weighting, and shows the distribution of misclassifications and the error rate for each of the four classes used.

Figure 10.7 shows the trade-off between error rate and efficiency obtainable by varying the likelihood ratio used for backing off.

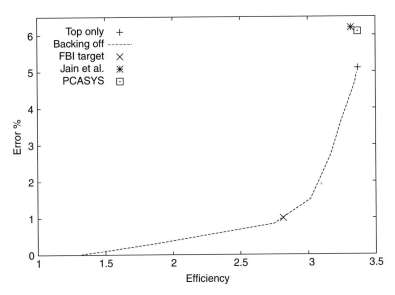

Fig. 10.7. A graph of error rate against efficiency, for the combination described here. The curve shows the trade-off of efficiency against error rate for a variety of likelihood ratio thresholds. Other algorithms tested under the same conditions are also plotted, along with the FBI performance target.

10.10. Previous Results

Table 10.3 shows the results achieved by a number of fingerprint classification systems that have previously been published. These points are plotted in Fig. 10.8 along with the curve of possible operating points for the combination presented here and the continuous systems of Lumini et al. [5, 11] and Halici and Ongun [9]. For each system the efficiency of the classifier is shown with the corresponding error rate. In some cases, authors have used rejection strategies where a proportion π of prints is rejected, making the identification system search the whole database (with an efficiency of 1). Assuming these rejected prints are uniformly distributed across the database, the efficiency of the combined system is

$$E_r = E(1 - \pi) + \pi \tag{7}$$

where E is the natural efficiency using a classifier returning a single class. (This is the value plotted in Fig. 10.8 where appropriate.)

10.10.1. Comparison

Because of the estimation of efficiency in the case of rejection, and because of the wide range of testing conditions previously used, the figure and table present results

Table 10.3. A Comparison of Published Fingerprint Classification Methods

Authors and year	Classes	Efficiency	Error %	Reject	Test set
Ohteru et al. 1974 [6]	3	1.95	14	—	102 good quality
Rao & Balck 1980 [25]	6	3.9	8.3	—	60
Kawagoe & Tojo 1984 [26]	7	2.6	8.5	—	94
Wilson et al. 1993 [21]	5	3.39	4.6	10	weighted 2000 NIST-4
Blue et al. 1994 [27]	5	3.39	7.2	—	weighted 2000 NIST-4
Candela et al. 1995 [3]	5	3.39	7.8	—	2700 NIST-14
	5	3.39	3.6	10	2700 NIST-14
PNN only	5	3.39	9.5	—	2700 NIST-14
Pal & Mitra 1996 [28]	5	3.6	18+	—	45 (training set)
Fitz & Green 1996 [29]	3	1.95	15	—	40
Karu & Jain 1996 [7]	4	3.37	7.0	10%	4000 NIST-4 (priors)
	4	3.37	9.4	—	4000 NIST-4 (priors)
	4	3.37	6.1	10%	4000 NIST-4
	4	3.37	8.6	10%	4000 NIST-9
Halici & Ongun 1996 [9]	continuous	3.33	4.0	—	250 NIST
Jain et al. 1999 [10]	4	3.37	5.2	1.8%	second half of NIST 4
Yao et al. 2001 [13]	4	3.37	5.3	1.8%	NIST 4
	4	2.816	1.6	20%	NIST 4

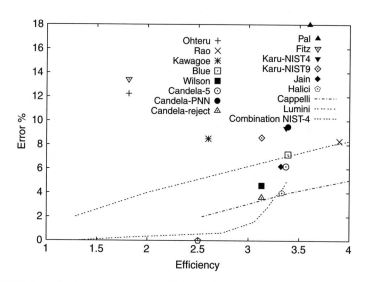

Fig. 10.8. A graph of error rate against efficiency for a number of published algorithms.

Table 10.4. Comparative Error Rates and Efficiencies for Three Systems on the Second Half of the NIST-4 Data Using True Class Frequency Weightings

System	Error (%)	Efficiency
Combination classifier	5.1	3.37
PCASYS	6.1	3.37
Jain et al.	6.2	3.32

that are not always directly comparable. In particular, the error rate of the PCASYS system is 7.8% under the conditions described by Candela et al. [3]. However, when their software is run on this test set and scoring in a manner consistent with the results presented here, with class weighting, the error rate was 6.1% (11.4% without weighting), a figure to which the results of the combined classifier here should be compared. Similarly Jain et al. quote an accuracy of 5.2% with 1.8% rejection, but if the data from the confusion matrix [10, Table 3] are scored using the class frequencies found in real data (Fig. 10.1), the accuracy is 6.2%. [1] These two are the only systems for which truly comparable results were available. Table 10.4 shows the error rates for the uniform testing conditions, which are plotted in Fig. 10.7.

One limitation of some previous works is simply that little can be inferred from the results presented when the test sets are so small or where the test set is not truly independent of the training set. For example, [28] derives the test set from the training set using artificial noise processes. Although [21] and [27] use the NIST-4 database, they test on second imprints of the same fingers that were used for training, an unrealistic scenario for which classification could be achieved by recognition of the fingerprints, resulting in much lower error rates, and efficiencies of the order of many thousands. Fitz and Green [29] average over five samples of a fingerprint before attempting classification.

A final problem with previous work is that the accuracies of the systems are simply not high enough. If one is to get the full filtering effect of the classification, only the top class must be chosen, and it has been seen that the classification accuracies for the top class (no paper presents any other accuracy, such as top 2, etc.) are never high enough to be used in a real system. The higher accuracies obtained are achieved by rejecting difficult prints, so the filtering achieved is even lower. Karu and Jain [7] quote the acceptable error rate for the FBI as being 1% at 20% rejection rate. With four classes, using Eq. (7), this is equivalent to a filtering efficiency of 2.816, a performance achieved by the combination classifier described here and by no previous system, as shown in Fig. 10.7.

---

[1] A weighted average of the class error rates 7.4%, 7.3%, 5.0%, 1.4%, 6.0%, counting arch/tented arch confusions as correct. For these results, however, where an alternate class label is given (cf. Section 10.8.1), either answer is considered to be correct, giving a higher accuracy than would be obtained under the same conditions we have used.

10.11. Conclusions

This paper proposes two new, effective methods for fingerprint classification that do not require core and delta information and that have been designed to work on both dabs and rolled prints. The combination of classifiers described here produces significantly better results than any of the component classifiers. Existing Henry fingerprint classifier accuracies fall short of what is required to make a significant contribution to an AFI system.

This paper proposes a method for comparing the efficiencies of different classification schemes and describes a system for achieving an arbitrary degree of accuracy from a classification system while evaluating the effect of the trade-off. By this means, current fingerprint classifiers can be rendered of use in an AFI system. The new classification combination can achieve a filtering efficiency of 2.8, with an error rate of only 1.0%, meeting the FBI requirements for a classification system, and is the first system known to the authors to acheive this. Performance for this Henry system is comparable to the performance of continuous classifiers and extensions are envisaged to adapt the methods here for non-Henry and continuous classification.[2]

References

1. Federal Bureau of Investigations, *The Science of Fingerprints (Classification and Uses)*, U.S. Department of Justice, Superintendant of Documents, Washington, DC: U.S. Government Printing Office, 12–84 edition, 1984.
2. Watson, C. I. and C. L. Wilson, NIST special database 4: Fingerprint database, Tech. Rep., National Institute of Standards and Technology, March 1992.
3. Candela, G. T., P. J. Grother, C. I. Watson, R. A. Wilkinson, and C. L. Wilson, PCASYS—A pattern-level classification automation system for fingerprints, Tech. Rep. NISTIR 5647, NIST, April 1995.
4. Perrone, Michael P., and Scott D. Connell, K-means clustering for hidden Markov models, in *Proc. International Workshop on Frontiers in Handwriting Recognition*, 2000, 7:229–238.
5. Cappelli, Raffaele, Alessandra Lumini, Dario Maio, and Davide Maltoni, Fingerprint classification by directional image partitioning, *IEEE Trans. Pattern Analysis and Machine Intelligence*, 21(5):402–421, May 1999.
6. Ohteru, S., H. Kobayashi, T. Kato, F. Noda, and H. Kimura, Automated fingerprint classifier, in *International Conference on Pattern Recognition*, 1974, pp. 185–189.
7. Karu, Kalle and Anil K. Jain, Fingerprint classification, *Pattern Recognition*, 29(3):389–404, 1996.
8. Maio, Dario and Davide Maltoni, A structural approach to fingerprint classification, in *Proc. 13th International Conference on Pattern Recognition*. 1996, 3:578–585.
9. Halici, Ugur and Güçlü Ongun, Fingerprint classification through self-organizing feature maps modified to treat uncertainties, *Proceedings of the IEEE*, 84(10):1497–1512, Oct. 1996.
10. Jain, Anil K., Salil Prabhakar, and Lin Hong, A multichannel approach to fingerprint classification, *IEEE Trans. on Pattern Analysis and Machine Intelligence*, 21(4):348–359, April 1999.

---

[2] The authors would like to thank the reviewers for their suggestions, and Sharath Pankanti and Nalini Ratha at IBM for assistance throughout this work.

11. Lumini, Alessandra, Dario Maio, and Davide Maltoni, Continuous versus exclusive classification for fingerprint retrieval, *Pattern Recognition Letters*, 18:1027–1034, 1997.

12. Kamei, Toshio and Masanori Mizoguchi, Fingerprint preselection using eigenfeatures, in *Proc. of Computer Vision and Pattern Recognition*, 1998, pp. 918–923.

13. Yao, Y., G. L. Marcialis, M. Pontil, P. Frasconi, and F. Roli, A new machine learning approach to fingerprint classification, *Lecture Notes in Computer Science*, 2175:57–63, 2001.

14. Ratha, N. K., K. Karu, S. Chen, and A. K. Jain, A real-time matching system for large fingerprint databases, *IEEE Trans. on Pattern Analysis and Machine Intelligence*, 18(8):799–813, Aug. 1996.

15. Rabiner, L. R. and B. H. Juang, An introduction to hidden Markov models, *IEEE ASSP Magazine*, 3(1):4–16, Jan. 1986.

16. Woodland, P. C., J. J. Odell, V. V. Valtchev, and S. J. Young, Large vocabulary continuous speech recognition using HTK, in *Proc. IEEE International Conference on Acoustics, Speech, and Signal Processing*, Apr. 1994, 2:125–128.

17. Agazzi, Oscar E., Shyh-shiaw Kuo, Esther Levin, and Roberto Pieraccini, Connected and degraded text recognition using planar hidden markov models, in *Proc. IEEE International Conference on Acoustics, Speech, and Signal Processing*, 1993, V:113–116.

18. Nathan, Krishna S., Andrew Senior, and Jayashree Subrahmonia, Initialization of hidden Markov models for unconstrained on-line handwriting recognition, in *Proc. IEEE International Conference on Acoustics, Speech, and Signal Processing*, 1996, 6:3503–3506.

19. Amit, Y., D. Geman, and K. Wilder, Joint induction of shape features and tree classifiers, *IEEE Trans. on Pattern Analysis and Machine Intelligence*, 19(11):1300–1305, Nov. 1997.

20. Breiman,Leo, *Classification and Regression Trees*, Belmont, CA: Wadsworth International Group, 1984.

21. Wilson, C. L., G. T. Candela, and Watson C. I., Neural network fingerprint classification, *J. Artificial Neural Networks*, 1(2):203–228, 1993.

22. Bolle, R.M., S. Pankanti, and Y.-S. Yao, System and method for determining the quality of fingerprint images, U.S. Patent: 5963656, Oct. 1999.

23. Senior, Andrew and Tony Robinson, An off-line cursive handwriting recognition system, *IEEE Trans. on Pattern Analysis and Machine Intelligence*, 20(3):309–321, March 1998.

24. Mandal, Deba Prasad, C. A. Murthy, and Sankar K. Pal, Formulation of a multivalued recognition system, *IEEE Trans. on Systems, Man, and Cybernetics*, 22(4):607–620, July/Aug. 1992.

25. Rao, Kameswara and Kenneth Balck, Type classification of fingerprints: A syntactic approach, *IEEE Trans. on Pattern Analysis and Machine Intelligence*, 2(3):223–231, May 1980.

26. Kawagoe, Masahiro and Akio Tojo, Fingerprint pattern classification, *Pattern Recognition*, 17(3):295–303, 1984.

27. Blue, J. L., G. T. Candela, P. J. Grother, R. Chellappa, C. L. Wilson, and J. D. Blue, Evaluation of pattern classifiers for fingerprint and OCR application, *Pattern Recognition*, 27:485–501, 1994.

28. Pal, Sankar K. and Sushmita Mitra, Noisy fingerprint classification using multilayer perceptron with fuzzy geometrical and textural features, *Fuzzy Sets and Systems*, 80:121–132, 1996.

29. Fitz, A. P. and R. J. Green, Fingerprint classification using a hexagonal fast Fourier transform, *Pattern Recognition*, 29(10):1587–1597, 1996.

Chapter 11

Fingerprint Matching

Salil Prabhakar and Anil K. Jain

Abstract. Fingerprint matching refers to finding the similarity between two given fingerprint images. The choice of the matching algorithm depends on which fingerprint representation is being used. Typically, a matching algorithm first attempts to recover the translation, rotation, and deformation parameters between the given image pair and then determines the similarity between the two images. Due to noise and distortion introduced during fingerprint capture and the inexact nature of feature extraction, the fingerprint representation often has missing, spurious, or noisy features. Therefore, the matching algorithm should be robust to these errors in the representation. The matching algorithm outputs a similarity value that indicates its confidence in the decision that the two images come from the same finger. We review and compare various fingerprint matching algorithms and show that a combination of different matching algorithms can improve the overall matching performance. Fingerprint matching is a challenging problem due to the large intraclass variation between different impressions of the same finger, noise in the fingerprint images, and small interclass variations in fingerprint images from different fingers. Each verification application has a different system performance requirement. Therefore, for fingerprint verification to be useful in a wide variety of applications, there is a need to continually improve the matching performance of the current systems.

11.1. Introduction

A fingerprint recognition system is essentially a pattern recognition system that can be deployed in two different modes: (1) verification and (2) identification. Verification refers to authenticating the *claimed* identity of a user, while identification refers to establishing the identity of a user. Identification (one-to-N matching) is inherently a more difficult pattern recognition problem as it involves an N-class classification problem, where N is the number of users enrolled in the system. Verification (one-to-one matching) is a relatively easier problem that can be formulated as a simple two-class hypothesis testing problem (accept or reject). We focus only on the verification problem in this chapter and use the words verification, authentication, and recognition interchangeably.

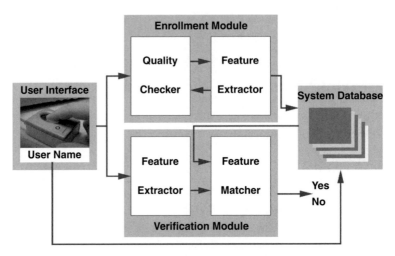

Fig. 11.1. Architecture of a typical automatic fingerprint verification system.

11.2. Fingerprint Verification System

A typical fingerprint verification system (see Fig. 11.1) logically consists of four major components: (1) user interface, (2) system database, (3) enrollment module, and (4) verification module. The user interface provides a mechanism for a user to indicate her identity and present her fingerprints to the system. The user interface can be designed to fit the application domain.

The system database consists of a collection of records, one for each of the authorized individuals who has access to the system. Each record contains the following fields, which are used for authentication purposes: (1) the profile (e.g., name, access privileges, etc.) of the individual and (2) fingerprint template(s) of the individual. Depending on the application, the system database may be either a physical database that resides in the verification system server or a virtual database with the record of each individual being stored on a smartcard[1] issued to the individual. For example, in an access control system, the system database may be used to store the records of authorized individuals. At the point of access, the individual indicates her identity by entering her user name, and the system then retrieves the corresponding record from the database for authentication. In ATM card authentication, it may not be advisable to have a central database that stores all the records, since a large template database may become the "point of failure." As a result, it is more efficient to store records on smartcards, which users carry. At the point of access, the individual presents her smartcard to indicate her identity and provides the system her fingerprints. In this case, the template database is only a virtual database and there is no physical central database in the system. Also, note that the fingerprint matcher resides at the point of access instead of at a server. In fact, the most secure method for authentication on

---

[1] A smartcard looks and feels like a credit card but has an integrated microprocessor chip to store much larger amount of information (http://www.scia.org/).

smartcard involves an "on-chip" fingerprint matching where the template as well as the fingerprint matcher reside on the smartcard. The number of templates per individual is an important design parameter of the verification system. On the one hand, the larger the number of templates, the better the expected accuracy of the verification system. On the other hand, the larger the number of templates stored for each individual, the more resources (computational and memory) are required.

The task of the enrollment module is to register each individual into the system database. When the fingerprint images and the profile of a perspective user are entered into the enrollment module, a feature extraction algorithm is first applied to the fingerprint images and a valid fingerprint representation is extracted. A quality-checking algorithm is usually used to ensure that the records in the system database only consist of fingerprints of good quality. If a fingerprint image is of poor quality, it may be enhanced to improve the clarity of ridge/valley structures; regions where features cannot be reliably extracted may be masked out.

The task of the verification module is to authenticate the identity of the individual who intends to access the system. The individual to be authenticated indicates her identity and places her finger on the scanner; a digital image of her fingerprint is captured; a representation is extracted from the captured fingerprint image and fed to a matching algorithm, which matches it against the individual's template(s) to authenticate the identity.

From a design perspective, the fingerprint verification problem can be formulated as follows. Let the stored fingerprint signal (template) of a person be represented as T and the acquired signal (input) for authentication be represented by I. Then the null and alternate hypotheses are

$H_0: I = T$, input fingerprint comes from
the same finger as the template

$H_1: I \neq T$, input fingerprint does not come from
the same finger as the template

The associated decisions are as follows:

D_0: person is who she claims to be

D_1: person is not who she claims to be

The verification involves matching T and I using a similarity measure. If the matching score is greater than some decision threshold θ, then decide D_0, else decide D_1. The above terminology is borrowed from communication theory, where the goal is to detect a message in the presence of noise. H_0 is the hypothesis that the received signal is message plus the noise, and H_1 is the hypothesis that the received signal is noise alone. Such a hypothesis testing formulation inherently gives two types of errors: type I: false rejection (D_1 is decided when H_0 is true) and type II: false acceptance (D_0 is decided when H_1 is true). False rejection rate (FRR) is the probability of type I errors, and false acceptance rate (FAR) is the probability of type II errors.

$$\text{FRR} = P(D_1|H_0 = \text{true})$$
$$\text{FAR} = P(D_0|H_1 = \text{true})$$

There is a trade-off between the two types of errors (FRR and FAR) in a fingerprint authentication system. Different applications may have different requirements on these two types of error rates. For example, high security access applications have stricter requirements on the FAR than, say, banking applications. A system designer may not know in advance the particular application for which the system may be used (or a single system may be designed for a wide variety of applications). So, it is a common practice to report the system performance at all operating points (threshold, θ). This is done by plotting a *receiver operating characteristic (ROC)* curve. An ROC curve is a plot of relation between FAR and FRR for various decision thresholds. The system designer's challenge is to minimize both the FRRs and FARs for various decision thresholds.

11.3. Fingerprint Representation

Fingerprint representation constitutes the essence of algorithm-level design and determines almost all aspects of the matching mechanism. A good representation should have the following two properties: (1) *saliency* and (2) *suitability*. Saliency means that a representation should contain enough class-specific (individual user) information about the fingerprint. Suitability means that the representation can be easily extracted and stored in a compact fashion and is useful for matching. Saliency and suitability properties are not generally correlated. A salient representation is not necessarily a suitable representation.

Which machine-readable representation completely captures the invariant and discriminatory information in a fingerprint image? This representation issue constitutes the essence of fingerprint verification design. Currently, the three major representation types for automatic fingerprint identification are (1) *image-based representation*, (2) *landmark-based representation*, and (3) *texture-based representation*.

11.3.1. Image-based Representation

It is well known that a fingerprint image has a sufficient amount of redundancy and, further, it tends to have large intraclass variations. The gray-scale values of the fingerprint images are not invariant over the time of capture. Still, representations based on the entire gray-scale profile of a fingerprint image are prevalent among the verification systems using optical matching [1–4]. However, the utility of the systems using such representation schemes may be limited due to factors like brightness variations, image quality variations, scars, and large global distortions present in the fingerprint image, because they rely on template matching strategies for verification. Therefore, in our opinion, the fingerprint image itself is not a desirable representation. Some system designers attempt to circumvent this problem by imposing a restriction that the representation be derived from a *small* (but consistent) part of the finger [1]. However, if this same representation is also being used for identification applications, then there is a risk of restricting the number of unique identities that could be handled, simply because of the fact that the number of distinguishable templates is limited.

On the other hand, an image-based representation makes fewer assumptions about the fingerprints and, therefore, has the potential to be robust to a larger class of distortions and sources of noise. For instance, it is extremely difficult to extract a landmark-based representation from a (degenerate) finger devoid of any ridge structure. The image-based representation assumes that the *individuality* of fingerprints can be exclusively determined in either the spatial or the frequency domain. For example, due to orientation-specific flow pattern of ridges in the fingerprints, a concise representation may be obtained using the Fourier spectrum. The image-based representations usually require that the input image be registered with the template image. In practice, registering an input image is as difficult as matching itself. Although several image-based fingerprint representations have been proposed in the literature [1–9], the validity of these representations is still far from established.

11.3.2. Landmark-based Representation

There are a large number of landmark-based representations, which extract different types of minute details in the fingerprints, including minutiae, singular points, ridge counts, and ridge pores [10–23]. The common hypothesis underlying the landmark-based representations is the belief that the *individuality* of fingerprints is captured by the local ridge structures (minute details) and their spatial distributions [24, 25]. Fingerprint verification involves matching these minute details. Even though a large number of different types of local ridge structures have been identified [24], all of these cannot be reliably extracted because (1) some of them are very similar to each other and (2) their characterization depends on the fine details of the ridge structure, which are difficult to obtain from fingerprint images of poor quality. As a result, most automatic fingerprint authentication systems extract only the two most prominent structures: ridge endings and ridge bifurcations. Many of the other ridge structures could be described as a combination of ridge endings and bifurcations [24]. Figure 11.2 shows an example of ridge ending and ridge bifurcation. These two structures are "background–foreground" dual of each other, that is, taking negative of one converts it to the other. Finger-pressure variations could convert one type of structure into the other during fingerprint acquisition. Therefore, many common representation schemes do not even distinguish between ridge endings and bifurcations, which are collectively called minutiae.

The simplest of the minutiae-based representations constitutes a list of points defined by their spatial coordinates with respect to a fixed imagecentric coordinate system. Typically, these minimal minutiae-based representations are further enhanced by tagging each minutia (or each combination of minutiae subset, e.g., pairs, triplets [14]) with additional features. For instance, each minutia could be associated with the orientation of the ridge at that minutia; or each pair of the minutiae could be associated with the ridge count: the number of ridges visited during the linear traversal between the two minutiae. The ANSI-NIST standard representation of a fingerprint is based on minutiae location and orientation [26]. The minutiae-based representation might also include one or more global attributes like orientation of the finger, locations of core or delta (see Fig. 11.2), etc. Landmark-based representations are also used

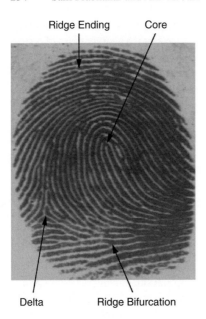

Ridge Ending   Core

Delta   Ridge Bifurcation

Fig. 11.2. A fingerprint image of type "right loop." The overall ridge structure, core, delta, a ridge ending, and a ridge bifurcation are marked.

for privacy reasons—one cannot reconstruct the entire fingerprint image from the landmark information alone.

A typical minutiae extraction technique performs the following sequential operations on the fingerprint image: (1) fingerprint image enhancement, (2) binarization (segmentation into ridges and valleys), (3) thinning, and (4) minutiae detection. A large number of fingerprint matching algorithms [11, 20, 21] follow this sequential approach to minutiae detection. Alternative techniques for minutiae detection directly operate on the gray-scale fingerprint image itself and detect minutiae by adaptively tracing the gray-scale ridges in the fingerprint images [22, 23].

11.3.3. Texture-based Representation

For a fraction of the population, the automatic extraction of representations based on an explicit detection of complete ridge structures in the fingerprint is difficult. The widely used minutiae-based representation does not utilize a significant component of the rich discriminatory information available in the fingerprints as local ridge structures cannot be completely characterized by minutiae.

The smooth flow pattern of ridges and valleys in a fingerprint can be viewed as an oriented texture field. The image intensity surface in fingerprint images is comprised of ridges whose directions vary continuously, and it constitutes an oriented texture. Most textured images contain a limited range of spatial frequencies, and mutually distinct textures differ significantly in their dominant frequencies [27, 28]. Textured regions possessing different spatial frequency, orientation, or phase can be easily discriminated by decomposing the image into several spatial frequency and orientation channels. For typical fingerprint images scanned at 500 dpi, there is only limited variation in the spatial frequencies (determined by interridge distances) among different fingerprints of adults [29]. This implies that there is an optimal scale (spatial frequency) for analyzing the fingerprint texture. Every pixel in a fingerprint image is associated with a dominant local orientation and a local measure of coherence of the flow pattern. A symbolic description of a fingerprint image can be derived by computing the angle and coherence at each pixel in the image. Fingerprints can be represented/matched by using quantitative measures associated with the flow pattern (oriented texture) as features.

A typical scheme for representing fingerprint texture [30] relies on extracting one (or more) invariant points of reference [typically, the core point(s)] of the fingerprint texture based on an analysis of its orientation field. A predetermined region of interest (typically, circular) around the reference point is tessellated into cells. Each cell is then examined for the information in one or more different, orientation-specific, spatial frequency channels (typically, using a bank of Gabor filters). An ordered enumeration of the features (typically, average absolute deviation from the mean of the gray values in the filtered images) thus extracted from each cell is used as the representation of the fingerprint (called the FingerCode [30]; similar to the IrisCode introduced by Daugman [31]). Thus, the representation captures both the local information and the invariant global relationships among the local patterns (see Fig. 11.3). A disadvantage

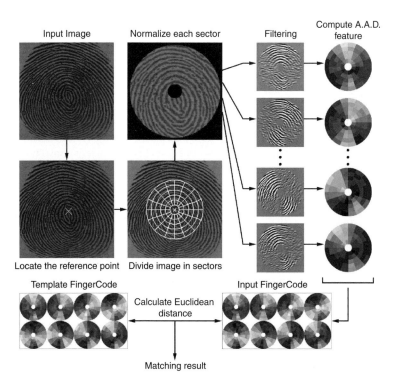

Fig. 11.3. A typical scheme for texture-based fingerprint representation extraction and Euclidean distance-based matching. @IEEE.

of the FingerCode representation is that it is dependent on a very small number of reference points [e.g., core point(s)] that are difficult to reliably extract in poor-quality fingerprints. Moreover, due to variations in placement of the finger on the sensor, the core point may not always be imaged. This problem is avoided by a variant of this algorithm that estimates the alignment between the input and the template fingerprints based on the minutiae points and tessellates the overlapping area into rectangular cells for feature extraction [32].

11.4. Fingerprint Matching

Given two (input and template) representations, the matching module determines whether the associated prints are impressions of the same finger. The matching phase typically defines a similarity measure between two fingerprint representations. For a given representation, choosing a similarity function is a very difficult problem because of large intraclass and small interclass variations (see Fig. 11.4). Once the similarity value has been computed, it is compared to a threshold to determine whether the given pair of representations is from the same finger (mated-pair) or not. The choice of threshold is determined by the desired FAR or FRR of the system.

In the ideal case, where (1) the correspondence between the input and template representations is known, (2) there are no deformations such as translation, rotation, and distortions between them, and (3) features in a fingerprint image can be reliably extracted (correctly localized), fingerprint verification is a relatively simple task of finding the similarity between the two representations. In general, determining whether two representations of a finger extracted from its two impressions, possibly separated by a long duration of time, are indeed representing the same finger is an extremely challenging problem. The difficulty can be attributed to two primary reasons. First, the correspondence between the test and reference minutiae in the two representations is not known. Second, the fingerprint imaging system introduces the following distortions and noise in the two images: (1) inconsistent contact: the act of sensing distorts the finger. The pressure and contact of the finger on the sensor surface determine how the three-dimensional shape of the finger gets mapped onto the two-dimensional image. Typically, this mapping function is uncontrolled and results in different inconsistently mapped fingerprint images across impressions. (2) Nonuniform contact: The ridge structure of a finger would be completely captured if ridges on the finger are in complete contact with the sensor surface. However, the dryness of the skin, skin disease, sweat, dirt, humidity in the air all confound the situation, resulting in a nonideal contact. This results in "noisy" low-contrast images, leading to errors in the representation (e.g., spurious minutiae or missing minutiae in the case of landmark-based representation). (3) Irreproducible contact: manual work, accidents, etc. inflict cuts and bruises on the finger, thereby changing the ridge structure of the finger either permanently or semi-permanently. This may introduce additional spurious minutiae. (4) Feature extraction artifacts: The feature extraction algorithm introduces measurement errors. (5) The act of sensing itself adds noise to the image. For example, residues may be leftover from the previous fingerprint capture.

(a)   (b)

(c)   (d)

Fig. 11.4. Two fingerprint impressions [(a) and (b)] from the same finger may look significantly different (large intraclass variation); impressions [(c) and (d)] from different fingers may look similar to an untrained eye (small interclass variation). The goal of fingerprint matching is to design a similarity metric in such a way that (a) and (b) are recognized as similar (matcher yields a large similarity value) without erroneously associating (c) and (d) (matcher yields a small similarity value). @IEEE.

In light of the operational environments mentioned above, the design of a matching algorithm needs to utilize a realistic model of the variations among the representations of mated pairs. This model should take into consideration the following factors:

1. The finger may be placed at different locations on the sensor, introducing (global) translation between the input and the template representations.
2. The finger may be placed in different orientations on the sensor, introducing a (global) rotation between the input and the template representations.
3. The finger may exert a different (average) downward normal pressure on the sensor, introducing a (global) spatial scaling between the input and the template representations.

4. The finger may exert a different (average) shear force on the sensor, introducing a (global) shear transformation (characterized by a shear direction and magnitude) between the input and the template representations.
5. Spurious features may be present in both the input and the template representations.
6. Genuine features may be absent in both the input and the template representations.
7. Minutiae-based features may be locally perturbed from their "true" location, and the perturbation may be different for each individual feature.
8. The individual perturbations among the corresponding features could be relatively large (with respect to ridge spacings), but the perturbations among pairs of the features could be linear or nonlinear.
9. Only a (ridge) connectivity-preserving transformation could characterize the relationship between the input and the template representations.

A fingerprint matcher may take into account one or more of the above factors, resulting in a wide spectrum of algorithms. At the one end of the spectrum, we have the "Euclidean" matchers that allow only rigid transformations among the test and reference representations. At the other extreme, we have a "topological" matcher that may allow the most general transformations including, say, order reversals (order reversal means that the feature set in the input representation is in a totally different spatial order with respect to template representation). A number of the matchers in the literature assume *similarity* transformation; they tolerate both spurious features as well as missing features. "Elastic" matchers [11] accommodate a small, bounded local perturbation of minutiae features from their true location but cannot handle large displacements.

Figure 11.5 illustrates a typical situation of aligned ridge structures of mated pairs. Note that the best alignment in one part (center) of the image may result in a large amount of displacements between the corresponding ridges in the other regions (bottom right). In addition, observe that the distortion is nonlinear: Given distortions at two arbitrary locations on the finger, it is not possible to predict the distortion at all the intervening points on the line joining the two points. In our opinion, a good matcher needs to accommodate not only global similarity transformations but also shear transformation, and linear and nonlinear differential distortions. In our experience, it is extremely difficult to extract connectivity information from fingerprint images of poor quality, and its use in matcher design may compromise the efficiency and discriminatory power of the matcher. The available fingerprint matching techniques can be broadly classified into three categories depending on the types of features used: (1) *correlation-based matching*, (2) *point-based matching*, and (3) *Euclidean distance-based matching*. Table 11.1 compares some recently published fingerprint matching algorithms.

11.4.1. Correlation-based Matching

The simplest correlation-based technique is to align the two fingerprint images and subtract the input image from the template image to see if the ridges correspond. However, such a simplistic approach suffers from many problems, including

Fig. 11.5. Aligned ridge structures of mated pairs. Note that the best alignment in one part (center) of the image results in a large displacements between the corresponding minutiae in the other regions (bottom right). @IEEE.

Table 11.1. Fingerprint Matching Approaches

Author (Year)	Alignment	Features used
Bhanu and Tan [14] (2001)	nonlinear	minutiae
Bazen et al. [9] (2000)	R (up to 10°) + T + local S	minutiae and 24 × 24 gray-scale templates
Kovacs-Vajna [15] (2000)	nonlinear	minutiae and its 16 × 16 gray-scale neighborhood
Jiang and Yau [18] (2000)	R + T + S	minutiae
Almansa and Cohen [17] (2000)	nonlinear	minutiae
Jain et al. [30] (2000)	R + T	texture features
O'Gorman [20] (1999)	R + T in local regions	minutiae
Jain et al. [21] (1997)	R + T + nonlinear	thin ridges, minutiae
Sibbald [5] (1997)	R + T	gray-scale intensity
Ratha et al. [11] (1996)	R + T + S	minutiae
Maio et al. [16] (1995)	R + T	minutiae, core, delta
Coetzee and Botha [7] (1993)	R + T	minutiae and frequency-domain features
Marsh and Petty [3] (1991)	R + T	gray-scale intensity
Driscoll et al. [6] (1991)	R + T	gray-scale intensity

Note: The fingerprint matching algorithms are classified based on the alignment assumed between the template and the input fingerprint features. The rotation is denoted by R, the translation is denoted by T, and the scale is denoted by S.

the errors in estimation of alignment, nonlinear deformation in fingerprint images, and noise. An autocorrelation technique has been proposed by Sibbald [5] that computes the correlation between the input and the template at fixed translation and rotation increments. If the correlation exceeds a certain threshold, the two fingerprints are declared to originate from the same finger. A variant of the correlation technique is to perform the correlation in the frequency domain instead of the spatial domain. The sum of the pixel-to-pixel multiplication of the frequency-domain representations of the input and the template fingerprint images is then compared to a threshold to make a decision. One of the advantages of performing correlation in the frequency domain is that it is translation-invariant. One of the major disadvantages, however, is the extra computation time required to convert the spatial image to a frequency representation. The frequency-domain correlation matching can also be performed optically [1–3]. The input and the template fingerprints are projected via laser light through a lens to produce their Fourier transform; their superposition leads to a correlation peak whose magnitude is high for the matching pair and low otherwise. The main advantage of performing optical correlation is its speed; the main disadvantage is that optical processors have very limited versatility (programmability) (cf. [20]). A modification of the spatial correlation-based techniques is to divide the fingerprint images into grids and determine the correlation in each sector instead of the whole image [6, 7]. Another modification of the spatial correlation-based technique is to use texture-based features instead of image gray-scales for correlation [8]. The correlation of texture-based features is expected to be more stable under brightness variations, image quality variations, scars, and global distortions. The correlation-based technique overcomes some of the limitations of minutiae-based approach. For example, the minutiae extraction algorithm detects a large number of spurious minutiae and misses genuine minutiae in very noisy fingerprint images. However, they have several disadvantages. For example, correlation-based techniques are more sensitive to an error in estimation of the alignment between the two fingerprints. Also, the correlation-based techniques cannot easily deal with the nonlinear deformation present in the fingerprint images. Additionally, the correlation-based techniques typically require more resources (matching time and template size).

11.4.2. Point-based Matching

The minutia points-based techniques typically match the input and the template minutia point sets by first aligning them and then counting the number of matched minutiae. The alignment between the input and the template fingerprints can be obtained using the orientation field of the fingerprints, the location of singular points such as the core and the delta, ridges [21], inexact graph matching on the minutiae graphs [12, 13], Hough transform [11], shape represented by points, etc. The number of matched minutiae, given some tolerances, is typically normalized by the total number of minutiae in the two sets to account for falsely detected and missed minutiae during feature extraction. One of the main difficulties in the minutiae-based approach is that it is very challenging to reliably extract minutiae in poor-quality fingerprint images. A number of image enhancement techniques can be used to improve the quality of the fingerprint image prior to minutiae extraction (e.g., [33]).

11.4.3. Euclidean Distance-based Matching

The filterbank-based representations described in [30, 32] do not fall into either the minutiae-based or the correlation-based categories. They are feature-based techniques that capture both the local and the global details in a fingerprint as a compact, fixed-length feature vector (FingerCode). In [30], the matching algorithm assumes that the representations are translation-invariant. It further assumes that the representations are invariant to small amounts of rotation due to the nature of the tessellation and handle large amounts of rotation in discrete multiples of $11.25°$ (up to a maximum of $±45°$) by rotating the FingerCode itself. The matching is based on simply computing the Euclidean distance between the two corresponding FingerCodes and hence is extremely fast. In [32], the translation and rotation parameters are estimated from the minutiae points in the two fingerprints before extracting the FingerCode representation from the input fingerprint. Although the FingerCode representation is invariant to small amounts of deformation due to the nature of the tessellation, the matching algorithm has difficulty in matching fingerprints with large, nonlinear deformations.

11.4.4. Typical Matching Algorithms

Hough Transform-based Minutiae Matching (Algorithm Hough)

The major steps of this algorithm are (1) Estimate the transformation parameters $δ_x$, $δ_y$, $θ$, and s between the two representations, where $δ_x$ and $δ_y$ are translations along x- and y-directions, respectively, $θ$ is the rotation angle, and s is the scaling factor (2) Align the two sets of minutiae points with the estimated parameters and count the matched pairs within a bounding box. (3) Repeat the previous two steps for the set of discretized allowed transformations. The transformation that results in the highest matching score is believed to be the correct one. Note that the Hough transform is used at two different scales to account for the nonlinear distortion between the fingerprints. The final matching score is scaled between 0 and 99. Details of the algorithm can be found in [11].

String Distance-based Minutiae Matching (Algorithm String)

Each set of extracted minutia features is first converted into polar coordinates with respect to an anchor point. The two-dimensional (2D) minutia features are, therefore, reduced to a one-dimensional (1D) string by concatenating points in an increasing order of radial angle in polar coordinates. The string matching algorithm is applied to compute the edit distance between the two strings. The edit distance is normalized and converted into a matching score.

This algorithm [21] can be summarized as follows: (1) A small ridge segment (represented as a planar curve) associated with each minutiae is available in the fingerprint representation. Each ridge segment in the input fingerprint representation is rotated and translated to align with each ridge segment in the template fingerprint representation. The number of matching minutiae pairs are counted for each alignment. The rotation and translation that result in the maximum number of matched minutiae pairs is considered to be the correct transformation and the corresponding minutiae are labeled as anchor minutiae, A_1 and A_2, respectively. (2) Convert each set of minutiae into a 1D string using polar coordinates anchored at A_1 and A_2, respectively. (3) Compute the edit distance between the two 1D strings. The matched pairs are retrieved based on the minimal edit distance between the two strings. (4) Output the normalized matching score, which is the ratio of the number of matched pairs to the number of minutiae points.

2D Dynamic Programming-based Minutiae Matching (Algorithm Dynamic*)*

This matching algorithm is a generalization of the above-mentioned string algorithm. The transformation of a 2D pattern into a 1D pattern usually results in a loss of information. Chen and Jain [19] show that fingerprint matching using 2D dynamic time warping can be done as efficiently as 1D string editing while avoiding the loss of information in converting the 2D patterns to 1D. The 2D dynamic time-warping algorithm can be characterized by the following steps: (1) Estimate the rotation between the two sets of minutiae features as in Step 1 of algorithm *String*. (2) Align the two minutiae sets using the estimated parameters from Step 1, (3) Compute the maximally matched minutiae pairs using 2D dynamic programming technique. The intuitive interpretation of this step is to warp one set of minutiae to align with the other so that the number of matched minutiae is maximized. (4) Output the normalized matching score, which is based on only those minutiae that lie within the overlapping region. A penalty term is added to deal with unmatched minutiae features.

Euclidean Distance-based FingerCode Matching (Algorithm Filter*)*

The FingerCode representation is based on the location of a reference point and so it is invariant to translation of the image. Further, it is assumed that the fingerprint is captured in an upright position and the rotation invariance is achieved by storing 10 representations corresponding to the various quantized rotations ($-45.0°$, $-33.75°$, $-22.5°$, $-11.25°$, $0°$, $11.25°$, $22.5°$, $33.75°$, $45.0°$, 56.25) of the image. Euclidean distance is computed between the input representation and the 10 templates to generate 10 matching distances. Finally, the minimum of the 10 distances is inverted to give a matching score. The matching score is scaled between 0 and 99 and can be regarded as a confidence value of the matcher.

11.5. Experimental Performance Evaluation

Fingerprint images were collected at Michigan State University from 167 subjects using an optical sensor manufactured by Digital Biometrics, Inc. (image size = 508×480, resolution = 500 dpi). A single impression each of the right index, right middle, left index, and left middle fingers for each subject was taken in that order. This process was then repeated to acquire a second impression. The fingerprint images were collected again from the same subjects after an interval of approximately six weeks in a similar fashion. Thus, we have four impressions for each of the four fingers of a subject. This resulted in a total of 2672 ($167 \times 4 \times 4$) fingerprint images. We call this database MSU_DBI. A live feedback of the sensed image was provided, and the subjects were guided to place their fingers in the center of the sensor in an upright position. A total of 100 images (about 4% of the database) was removed from the MSU_DBI because the filter-based fingerprint matching algorithm rejected these images either due to failure in locating the core point or due to poor quality of the images. We matched all the remaining $2,572$ fingerprint images with each other to obtain $3,306,306$ ($2572 \times 2571/2$) pairs and called the matchings genuine only if the pair corresponded to different impressions of the same finger. Thus, we have a total of $7,472$ genuine matchings and $3,298,834$ ($3,306,306 - 7,472$) imposter matching for each of the four matchers under consideration.

It is well known in the pattern recognition literature that different matchers often misclassify different patterns [34, 35]. This suggests that different matchers offer complementary information about the given matching task. A combination of independent matchers is likely to improve the overall matching performance. The outputs of various matchers can be combined to obtain a decision that is more accurate than the decisions made by any one of the individual matchers. Prabhakar and Jain [36] combined the above-mentioned four matchers. To demonstrate the usefulness of this combination, we randomly selected half the imposter matching scores (i.e., $1,649,417$) and half the genuine matching scores (i.e., $3,736$) for training and the remaining samples for test. This process was repeated 10 times to give 10 different training sets and 10 corresponding independent test sets. All performances are reported in terms of ROC curves computed as an average of the 10 ROC curves corresponding to the 10 different training and test sets.

In the combination scheme of Prabhakar and Jain [36], the feature selection scheme selects the (*String, Dynamic, Filter*) subset out of the four matchers (*String, Dynamic, Filter,* and *Hough*) for the combination. Thus, the feature selection schemes decides not to use the matcher *Hough* in the combination. This is consistent with the nature of the *Hough* algorithm, which is basically the linear pairing step in algorithms *String* and *Dynamic*, without the capability of dealing with elastic distortions. Therefore, *Hough* does not provide "independent" information with respect to *String* and *Dynamic* and its inclusion in the combination is not expected to improve the overall performance. The performance of the (*String, Dynamic, Filter*) combination is more than 3% better than the best individual matcher at low FARs (see Table 11.2). The equal error rate of the combination is ~1.4%. Thus, it is approximately 2% better than the best individual matcher. The matcher combination takes about 0.02 sec on an Sun Ultra 1 in the test phase. In an authentication system, this increase in time will have almost no effect on the overall matching time, which is still bounded by the slowest individual matcher.

The ROC curves computed from the test data for the four individual fingerprint matchers described in the previous section are shown in Fig. 11.6. Note that matcher *Filter* is better than the other three matchers at high FARs while it is the worst at

Table 11.2. Comparison of the Performance of the Combination of Matchers with the Best Individual Matcher

FAR	GAR *Dynamic* Mean (Var)	GAR *String + Dynamic + Filter* Mean (Var)	GAR Improvement
1.00%	95.53 (0.08)%	98.23 (0.02)%	2.70%
0.10%	92.96 (0.05)%	96.16 (0.04)%	3.20%
0.01%	90.25 (0.04)%	93.72 (0.05)%	3.47%

Note: GAR refers to the genuine acceptance rate that is plotted on the ordinate of the ROC curves.

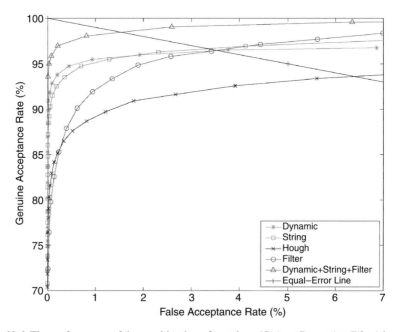

Fig. 11.6. The performance of the combination of matchers (*String+Dynamic+Filter*) is compared with the individual matchers.

very low FARs. Matcher *Hough* is the worst at most operating points except at very low FARs. At an equal error rate of about 3.5%, the matchers *Dynamic*, *String*, and *Filter* are equivalent, while the matcher *Hough* has an equal error rate of about 6.4%. Matcher *Filter* has a much slower texture-based feature extraction but a much faster Euclidean distance-based matching when compared to the minutiae-based matchers *Hough, Dynamic*, and *String*. The minutiae-based matchers have the same feature extraction time and differ only slightly in their matching speed. The fastest matcher is *Hough*, followed by *String*, and *Dynamic*, respectively.

11.6. Conclusions

Fingerprint matching is a difficult problem due to (1) the large intraclass variability in different impressions of the same finger, (2) small interclass variability in different fingers, (3) noise and distortion introduced during the sensing process, (4) difficulty in extracting reliable features from poor-quality fingerprint images, and (5) difficulty in finding correspondence between features in two representations in the presence of missing and spurious features. The true model of the intraclass variations (especially the nonlinear deformation of fingerprints due to finger-pressure differences) is not known. Different researchers have assumed different alignment models for matching a pair of fingerprints. Cappelli et al. [37] have proposed a model for the nonlinear deformation in fingerprints, but it is not known if its use in estimating the alignment between the input and the template representations improves the performance of the verification system. However, this is a step in the right direction. More work and validation are required to establish the "best" alignment model for fingerprint matching.

A number of fingerprint representations and matching algorithms have been developed in the last few years both by academic institutions (e.g, algorithms Hough, String, Dynamic, Filter described in this chapter) and commercial vendors. To determine which fingerprint matching algorithm is the best, third-party benchmarking such as the FVC2000 and FVC2002 [38] should be performed, where various algorithms are evaluated on standard databases. In FVC2000 comparative testing, the minutiae-based algorithms performed better than the correlation-based algorithms in general. In our opinion, the reason for the superiority of minutiae-based algorithms is the stability and large signal capacity [39] of the minutiae representation. FVC2002 also demonstrates that the current state-of-the-art fingerprint matchers perform very well on the majority of fingerprint images. The main difficulty remains in successfully matching extremely poor-quality fingerprints originating from a small fraction of the population.

This is because minutiae extraction in poor-quality fingerprint images is a very challenging problem. In poor-quality images where minutiae cannot be reliably extracted, correlation-based algorithms are expected to perform better. Although correlation-based matchers use the more discriminatory information present in the gray-scale fingerprint images, their performance is expected to deteriorate as the time duration between enrollment and verification increases. In our opinion, this is because the intensity-based features are not as stable as the minutiae features. Since fingerprint matching algorithms based on different representations provide "independent" information, a combination of multiple algorithms is expected to perform better than any individual algorithm. In fact, the best way to improve performance is to use an appropriate alignment model and combine multiple features, multiple alignment hypotheses, and multiple matching algorithms. We expect that future matching algorithms will increasingly focus on the issues specifically related to successfully matching very poor-quality fingerprints.

Even with their shortcomings, the current commercially available fingerprint verification systems are ready for large-scale deployment in a number of civilian, governmental, and law enforcement applications. Ongoing research to further improve the accuracy of the fingerprint matching algorithms will largely benefit the one-to-N identification systems. We expect that the very high security applications, large-scale systems, and negative identification applications will increasingly use multimodal biometric systems while the personal low-cost applications, conscious of the cost and user convenience, will probably continue striving to improve the unimodal systems. It is important to point out that an accurate fingerprint matching algorithm alone does not necessarily result in a good authentication system; a large number of system level issues such as sensor quality, automatic image capture, enrollment procedure, speed of feature extraction and matching, security and integrity of the system, etc. contribute to the success of the deployed systems. Further, the verification performance is expected to improve with habituation through user training and user feedback (e.g., an appropriate GUI can provide quality and finger placement feedback to the user during verification).

References

1. Access Control Applications Using Optical Computing, Mytec Corp. (now Bioscrypt www.bioscrypt.com), 1994.
2. Bahuguna, R., Fingerprint verification using hologram matched filterings, *Proc. Biometric Consortium Eighth Meeting*, San Jose, CA, 1996.
3. Marsh, R.A. and G.S. Petty, Optical fingerprint correlator, U.S. Patent 5050220, 1991.
4. Fielding, K., J. Homer, C. Makekau, Optical fingerprint identification by binary joint transform correlation. *Optical Engineering* 30:1958, 1991.
5. Sibbald, A., Method and Apparatus for Fingerprint Characterization and Recognition Using Auto-correlation Pattern. US Patent 5633947, 1997.
6. Driscoll, E.C., C.O. Martin, K. Ruby, J.J. Russel, and J.G. Watson, Method and apparatus for verifying identity using image correlation, U.S. Patent 5067162, 1991.
7. Coetzee, L. and E.C. Botha, Fingerprint recognition in low quality images, *Pattern Recognition*, 26(10):1141–1460, 1993.
8. Ross, A., J. Reisman, and A.K. Jain, Fingerprint matching using feature space correlation, *Proc. ECCV Workshop on Biometric Authentication*, Copenhagen, 2002.
9. Bazen, A.M., G.T.B. Verwaaijen, and S.H. Gerez, A correlation-based fingerprint verification system, *Proc. ProRISC 2000 Workshop on Circuits, Systems and Signal Processing*, Veldhoven, The Netherlands, 2000.
10. Roddy, A. and J. Stosz, Fingerprint features—statistical analysis and system performance estimates, *Proc. IEEE* 85(9):1390–1421, 1997.
11. Ratha, N., K. Karu, S. Chen, and A.K. Jain, A real-time matching system for large fingerprint database, *IEEE Trans. on PAMI* 18(8):799–813, 1996.
12. Hrechak, A. and J. McHugh, Automated fingerprint recognition using structural matching, *Pattern Recognition* 23(8):893–904, 1990.
13. Isenor, D. and S. Zaky, Fingerprint identification using graph matching, *Pattern Recognition*, 19:113–122, 1986.
14. Bhanu B. and X. Tan, Triplet based approach for indexing of fingerprint database for identification, *Proc. Third International Conference on Audio- and Video-Based Biometric Person Authentication*, 2001, pp. 205–210.

15. Kovacs-Vajna, Z.M., A fingerprint verification system based on triangular matching and dynamic time warping, *IEEE Trans. on Pattern Anal. and Machine Intell.*, 22(11), 2000.

16. Maio, D., D. Maltoni, and S. Rizzi, An efficient approach to on-line fingerprint verification. *Proc. International Symposium on Artificial Intelligence*, Mexico, 1995, pp. 132–138.

17. Almansa, A., and L. Cohen, Fingerprint image matching by minimization of a thin-plate energy using a two-step iterative algorithm with auxiliary variables. Workshop on the Application of Computer Vision, Palm Springs, CA, 2000, pp. 35–40,

18. Jiang, A., and W.Y. Yau, Fingerprint minutiae matching based on the local and global structures. *Proc. 15th International Confererence on Pattern Recognition*, 2:1042–1045, Barcelona, Spain, 2000.

19. Chen, S., and A.K. Jain, A fingerprint matching algorithm using dynamic programming, Technical report, Department of Computer Science and Engineering, Michigan State University, 1999.

20. O'Gorman, L., Fingerprint verification, in *Biometrics: Personal Identification in a Networked Society*, A.K. Jain, R. Bolle, and S.Pankanti, eds., Kluwer Academic Publishers, 1999, pp. 43–64.

21. Jain, A.K., L. Hong, S. Pankanti, and R. Bolle, An identity authentication system using fingerprints, *Proc. IEEE*, 85(9):1365–1388, 1997.

22. Maio, D. and D. Maltoni, Direct gray-scale minutiae detection in fingerprints, *IEEE Trans. Pattern Anal. and Machine Intell.*, 19(1):27–40, 1997.

23. Jiang, X., W.Y. Yau, and W. Ser, Detecting the fingerprint minutiae by adaptive tracing the gray-level ridge, *Pattern Recognition*, 34(5):999–1013, 2001.

24. Lee, H.C. and R.E. Gaensslen, *Advances in Fingerprint Technology*, 2nd ed., New York: Elsevier, 2001.

25. Federal Bureau of Investigation, *The Science of Fingerprints: Classification and Uses*, Washington, DC: U.S. Government Printing Office, 1984.

26. American National Standard for Information Systems, Data format for the interchange of fingerprint information, Doc# ANSI/NIST-CSL 1-1993, New York: American National Standards Institute, 1993.

27. Bigun, J., G.H. Granlund, and J. Wiklund, Multidimensional orientation estimation with applications to texture analysis and optical flow, *IEEE Trans. Pattern Anal. and Machine Intell.*, 13(8):775–790, 1991.

28. Jain, A.K. and F. Farrokhnia, Unsupervised texture segmentation using Gabor filters, *Pattern Recognition*, 24(12):1167–1186, 1991.

29. D. A. Stoney, Distribution of epidermal ridge minutiae, *American J. of Physical Anthropology*, 77:367–376, 1988.

30. Jain, A.K., S. Prabhakar, L. Hong, and S. Pankanti, Filterbank-based fingerprint matching, *IEEE Trans. Image Processing*, 9(5):846–859, 2000.

31. Daugman, J.G., High confidence recognition of persons by a test of statistical independence, *IEEE Trans. Pattern Anal. and Machine Intell.*, 15(11):1148–1161, 1993.

32. Jain, A.K., A. Ross, and S. Prabhakar, Fingerprint matching using minutiae and texture features, *Proc. International Conference on Image Processing (ICIP)*, Greece, 2001, pp. 282–285.

33. Hong, L., Y. Wan, and A.K. Jain, Fingerprint image enhancement: Algorithm and performance evaluation, *IEEE Trans. Pattern Anal. and Machine Intell.*, 20(8):777–789, 1998.

34. Ho, T.K., J.J. Hull, and S.N. Srihari, On multiple classifier systems for pattern recognition, *IEEE Trans. on Pattern Analysis and Machine Intelligence*, 16(1):66–75, 1994.

35. Kittler, J., M. Hatef, R.P.W. Duin, and J. Matas, On combining classifiers, *IEEE Trans. on Pattern Analysis and Machine Intelligence*, 20(3):226–239, 1998.

36. Prabhakar, S. and A.K. Jain, Decision-level fusion in fingerprint verification, *Pattern Recognition*, 35(4):861–874, 2002.
37. Cappelli, R., D. Maio, and D. Maltoni, Modelling plastic distortion in fingerprint images, *Proc. Second International Conference on Advances in Pattern Recognition (ICAPR2001)*, Rio de Janeiro, 2001, pp. 369–376.
38. Maio, D., D. Maltoni, R. Cappelli, J.L. Wayman, and A.K. Jain, FVC2000: Fingerprint verification competition, *IEEE Trans. on Pattern Analysis and Machine Intelligence*, 24(2):402–412, 2002.
39. Pankanti, S., S. Prabhakar, and A.K. Jain, On the individuality of fingerprints, *IEEE Trans. on Pattern Analysis and Machine Intelligence*, 24(8), 2002.

Chapter 12

Fingerprint Matching Using Distortion-Tolerant Filters

Craig Watson and David Casasent

Abstract. This chapter shows how using distortion-tolerant filters can significantly improve correlation fingerprint matchers. Filters are built by combining several elastic distorted variations of the fingerprint into a single matched filter. The three techniques tested for making the distortion-tolerant filters are averaging, synthetic discriminate function, and minimum average noise and correlation plane energy filters. A data set containing 200 fingers is used for evaluation. Receiver operator curves show that distortion-tolerant filters are a significant improvement compared to a single-finger filter in correlation matching.

12.1. Introduction

The purpose of this chapter is to discuss the use of distortion-tolerant filters to improve the performance of fingerprint correlation matching. Previous work has shown that correlation matching of fingerprints is susceptible to larger false-alarm rates than more traditional minutiae-based methods [12, 14]. The elasticity of the fingerprint creates enough distortion to produce poor results in correlation matching, because the correlation matcher uses the global ridge structure of the fingerprint image. A way to improve correlation matcher performance is to create filters that combine several elastic distorted versions of the fingerprint images. In this work three different distortion-tolerant filters are tested: average, synthetic discriminate function (SDF), and minimum average noise and correlation plane energy (MINACE).

The correlation function is performed in the frequency domain:

$$I_1 \text{ o } I_2 = F(I_1)F^*(I_2) \tag{1}$$

I_1 and I_2 are the images being correlated, $F(I_1)$ is the Fourier transform of I_1 and $F^*(I_2)$ is the conjugate of the Fourier transform of I_2. A correlation matcher computes the inverse Fourier transform of the correlation function and searches that result for the peak magnitude value. A feature of the correlation matcher is its translation independence, so the location of the correlation peak magnitude value gives the offset of I_2 from I_1. The peak magnitude value is also used to determine a confidence level in the match, with larger values being more confident of a match.

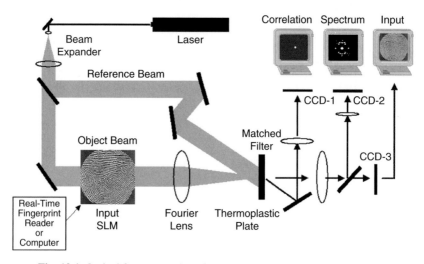

Fig. 12.1. Optical frequency-plane fingerprint correlation matching system.

A real attraction of fingerprint correlation matching is for use in optical systems. In fact, the idea for this work on distortion-tolerant filters started as an optical fingerprint matcher demonstration [12]. An optical frequency-plane correlation system was designed that performed real-time matching of a fingerprint input image from a live-scan fingerprint reading device against a fingerprint stored in optical memory (see Fig. 12.1). The system allowed only one fingerprint to be stored in memory, but by using other optical memory components it could potentially store thousands. It was discovered that optical correlation fingerprint matching performed significantly better if the fingerprint stored in memory was actually a composite filter, which stored several variations of the fingerprint into a single matched filter. The composite filter was built by recording 10 seconds from a live-scan device into the optical memory. During that 10 seconds the individual would change the pressure of his or her finger on the input device to create elastic distortions of the fingerprint, which were stored in the optical memory. The demonstration system worked very well and did not produce false alarms in over 30 demonstrations. The testing for this present work is done digitally, but this optical demonstration system shows a real application for optical frequency-plane correlator architectures.

Generally, optical recognition systems emphasize the use of distortion-tolerant filters intended for implementation on devices with binary phase levels. The work in this chapter uses filters with multiple amplitude and complex frequency-plane values. These filters are of use in both digital applications and advanced optical realizations that allow other encoding methods to convert complex data to real data for encoding on a real-value optical device [1, 13]. There are many different variations of distortion-tolerant filters [6] beyond those addressed here, several of which [3–5, 7, 9, 10] have been applied to fingerprint recognition.

12.2. Filter Types

The three distortion-tolerant filters tested in this chapter are the average, synthetic discriminate function (SDF), , and minimum average noise and correlation plane energy (MINACE) [8]. The average filter idea came directly from the optical demonstration work previously described [12], although it is not intended to be an exact simulation of the optics work. The other two filters provide more complex techniques for creating the distortion-tolerant filters that improve on deficiencies in the average filter technique.

When building all three types of filters, an iterative technique would be used in which one image is used to initially make the filter. The next image is correlated with the filter, and if the correlation peak is below a set threshold that image is added to the filter. The input image is shifted and rotated so that the correlation peak value is maximized and centered, thereby removing alignment differences between the filter and the image being added. Aligning the training image that is added to the filter significantly improves the overall performance of the filter. This process is continued until all the training images have been processed. In this work, the training image sets were small enough that all the training images were used in building the filters. This technique would not be used if a user controlled the data input environment and could limit the expected elastic distortions of future test fingerprints; such a filter would be built from just a few training fingerprint images.

12.2.1. Average Filter

The first filter tested is the average filter. The filter $\mathbf{H}$ is the summation of the Fourier transforms $\mathbf{F}(I_n)$ of the training set images divided by the number N of training set images. A scaling factor c is applied to limit the largest correlation peak value for the training images to 1. The scaling factor c is 1/(maximum correlation peak of the training images) and $n = 1, \ldots, N$.

$$\mathbf{H} = c(\text{Sum}[\mathbf{F}(I_n)]/N) \tag{2}$$

A deficiency in the average filter is that it uses equal weights for all training set images, which assumes that all the training images are of equal importance when building the filter. This could cause problems if several fingerprints in the training set have a similar distortion, as the filter will be weighted more toward that distortion and diminish the effectiveness of other training images.

12.2.2. SDF Filter

The second filter considered is the synthetic discriminate function (SDF) filter. This improves on the average filter by using a combination of weights in vector $\mathbf{a}$, whose elements $a(n)$ are chosen to satisfy

$$\mathbf{a} = \mathbf{V}^{-1}\mathbf{u} \tag{3}$$

Matrix $\mathbf{V}$ is composed of the vector inner products of each pair of training set images, and vector $\mathbf{u}$ is all elements equal to 1. The filter is the summation of the training set images with the individual weights $a(n)$ applied where $n = 1, \ldots, N$ and N is the number of training images.

$$\mathbf{H} = \text{Sum}[a(n)F(I_n)] \tag{4}$$

The SDF filter is designed to provide correlation peak values of 1 for all training set images and not just to scale the largest correlation peak to 1. The combination weights now depend on the similarity of the different training set images. The elements of $\mathbf{V}$ denote this similarity. While this filter should improve over the average filter, it is still deficient because a single weight $a(n)$ is used for each spatial frequency in training set image n.

12.2.3. MINACE Filter

The MINACE distortion-invariant filter improves on the average and SDF filter designs by creating weights at each frequency in the image. The MINACE filter [8] algorithm designs the filter $\mathbf{H}$ to satisfy the peak constraints

$$\mathbf{X}^H \mathbf{H} = \mathbf{u} \tag{5}$$

where $\mathbf{u}$ is an all-1's vector and the rows of the transpose conjugate data matrix $\mathbf{X}^H$ are the conjugate Fourier transforms of the training set images included in the filter. The peak constraint requires the correlation peak of any training image compared to the filter to be 1. The MINACE filter is required to minimize the correlation plane's overall energy for each training set image; this reduces low spatial frequency fingerprint data, improves rejection of other nonmatching fingerprints, and produces narrower correlation peaks (since the spectrum of the fingerprint is enhanced by this operation). To provide better recognition of distorted and noisy versions of the true fingerprint, the filter also minimizes the correlation-plane energy due to white Gaussian noise as characterized by a diagonal matrix $\mathbf{S}_n(0, 0)$. This also minimizes correlation-plane energy due to input image distortions. These objective functions are combined and minimized by forming the matrix

$$\mathbf{T}(u, v) = \max[\mathbf{S}_1(u, v), \ldots, \mathbf{S}_N(u, v), c\mathbf{S}_n(0, 0)] \tag{6}$$

at each spatial frequency (u, v), where $\mathbf{S}_1$ to $\mathbf{S}_N$ are diagonal matrices whose diagonal elements are the magnitude Fourier transform squared of each training set image included in the filter and describe the minimization of correlation-plane energy. Minimization of the last term $\mathbf{S}_n$ minimizes correlation-plane energy due to input image distortions. The constant value of each training image is normalized to 1. The solution for the filter $\mathbf{H}$ that satisfies the peak constraints and minimizes the combined objective function has been shown [8] to be

$$\mathbf{H} = \mathbf{T}^{-1}\mathbf{X}(\mathbf{X}^H\mathbf{T}^{-1}\mathbf{X})^{-1}\mathbf{u} \tag{7}$$

The parameter c included in $\mathbf{T}$ is a free parameter chosen for a given application. Large c-values emphasize recognition and low c-values emphasize rejection of false alarms. Minimizing the objective functions and hence the choice of c and $\mathbf{T}$ provides a spatial filter preprocessing of the input test data and of the training set data included in the filter. This preprocessing attenuates low frequencies and emphasizes high frequencies, with the c choice determining the amount of emphasis. This preprocessing

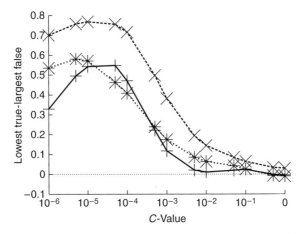

Fig. 12.2. Choosing the optimal c parameter for the MINACE filter.

is vital to reject false fingerprint inputs. All fingerprints have similar constant and low spatial frequency values, and thus these frequencies must be reduced to improve rejection of false fingerprint inputs.

The selection of c in the MINACE filter determines the type of high-pass filtering performed on the data set with lower c-values suppressing lower spatial frequencies. To select c, a set of three fingerprints, all whorls pattern type, was used with each containing nine training set images. A MINACE filter was made for each fingerprint using the training set images. Then the filters were tested against the three test images for the filters and six other test inputs from other whorl class-type fingerprints to determine the best c choice for rejection of other fingerprints. All fingerprints were of the same class type, which should make it more difficult to discriminate between matching and nonmatching fingerprints. For each of the three fingerprint sets, 13 filters were formed, each with a different c-value ranging from 1 (no high-pass filter preprocessing) to 10^{-6}. At each choice of c for the three filters, the difference between the smallest true fingerprint correlation peak and largest false correlation peak are plotted versus c (see Fig. 12.2). In all cases, large differences (above 0.3) occur for all filters over a c range from 10^{-4} to 10^{-6}. Thus, the choice of c in this range does not appear critical and a value of 10^{-5} was chosen. The same c-value was used for all MINACE filters in these tests.

12.3. Data Set Processing

The data set used for creating and testing the filters came from NIST Special Database 24 [11]. Special Database 24 contains 10-sec video segments of subjects putting their fingerprint on a live-scan fingerprint reader at various angles. The 10 sec of video were processed and still-image frames were captured at various angles and with various elastic deformations for each subject. This produced a set of 100 fingers with between 4–13 occurrences of each fingerprint. Figure 12.3 shows examples of the fingerprints.

This work addresses only the effects of elastic distortion on the correlation matcher; so all fingerprints were rotated to a canonical orientation by using a set of common points on the images. The points used were the fingerprint core about which all other pixels were rotated and another common minutiae point. Using digital rotation on the images caused a drop of about 7.5%, independent of the amount of rotation, in the autocorrelation peak; but since this will occur in all images, the overall effects of digital rotation on matching results should be negligible.

When rotating the images to align to a common angle, any pixels shifted into the image from outside the original image edges are set to black. Figure 12.4 shows an example of this rotation correction.

Before rotating the image all the white background pixels are set to black so they do not contribute energy to the correlation peak value. This is done through several morphological processing steps (see Fig. 12.5a–h). First, the image is binarized using a threshold of 180 (Fig. 12.5b). Next, the binary image is dilated and eroded to fill any white spaces that occur in the fingerprint's foreground area (Fig. 12.5c–d). This produces a binary image mask that is inverted and used to set all background

Fig. 12.3. Fingerprints from NIST Special Database 24.

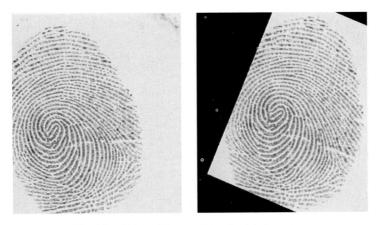

Fig. 12.4. Original fingerprint and rotated version.

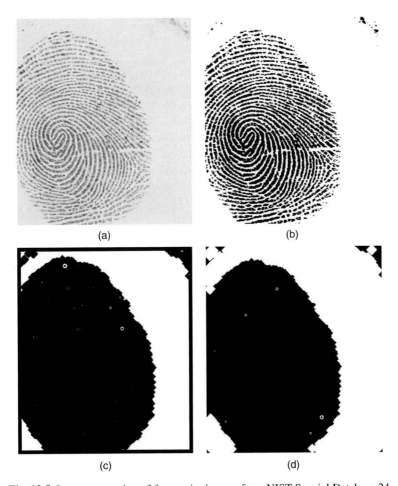

Fig. 12.5. Image processing of fingerprint images from NIST Special Database 24.

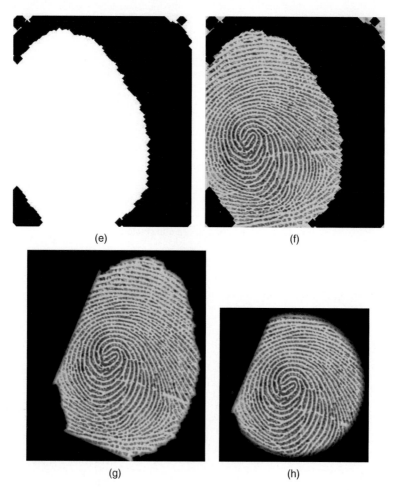

(e)

(f)

(g)

(h)

Fig. 12.5. (*Continued*) Image processing of fingerprint images from NIST Special Database 24.

pixels in the fingerprint image to black (Fig. 12.5e–f). The transition region from the foreground fingerprint area to background is tapered between 1 and 0, producing a smooth cutoff region and fewer artifacts in the Fourier domain.

After setting the background pixels to black and removing rotation differences (Fig. 12.5g), a 350-pixel-diameter circular window is applied to the image centered around the core of the fingerprint image (Fig. 12.5h). The circular window isolated the most significant ridge structure around the fingerprint core that is needed for correlation matching and eliminated some of the edge problems created when rotationally aligning the images. Again, the transition region at the edge of the circular window was tapered to produce a smoother cutoff and fewer artifacts in the Fourier domain.

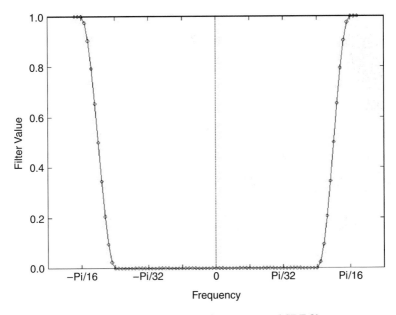

Fig. 12.6. High-pass filter used for average and SDF filters.

Two of the most important steps to make the correlation matching work for the average and SDF filters is to high-pass-filter the image, removing the constant value and low-frequency information and then energy-normalize the data. Otherwise, the constant value and low frequencies will dominate the correlation and all the images will appear similar; by eliminating this information, the higher frequencies containing the ridge structure information are used to help discriminate between matched and nonmatched fingerprints. This is similar to the filtering provided by the selection of c in the MINACE filter.

The high-pass filter used is shown in Fig. 12.6 and was selected by using a validation set of images. For each set of training images in the validation set, a filter was built using various radii of low-frequency blocking. Each filter was then tested versus its matching test finger and several not-matching fingerprints of the same pattern class. The filter that produced the best discrimination between the matching fingerprint and nonmatched fingerprints was used to filter the data for the average and SDF filters.

The final step in processing the data is to energy-normalize to negate the effects of partial images created by rotational alignment or fingerprints not filling the 350-pixel-diameter of the circular window (Fig. 12.7). If the fingerprint only fills a portion of the circular window, its overall energy in the correlation plane will be less than a complete fingerprint; energy-normalizing the fingerprint data makes partial fingerprints contribute the same amount of energy information as complete images.

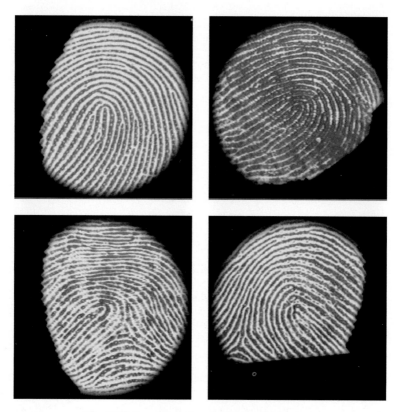

Fig. 12.7. Examples of partial fingerprint images.

12.4. Results

The two scenarios used to evaluate the distortion-tolerant filters are verification and identification (Fig. 12.8). Verification is determining if the subject is the identity she claims to be and identification is defined as determining if the subject is contained in the database. Receiver operating characteristic (ROC) plots are generated for both cases. In verification, to obtain false accepts, all test images were compared to each filter and any correlation peaks over a certain threshold were accepted as matches to that filter. Ideally, only the matching fingerprint would be over the threshold and all others would be rejected. A false alarm occurs when a nonmatching fingerprint is accepted.

In identification, each test fingerprint is compared to all the filters; the filter with the largest correlation peak is assumed to be the match in the database. If the largest correlation peak is below a certain threshold, it is rejected and the fingerprint is assumed not to match any filter in the database. False alarms occur when the largest correlation peak above the threshold is not the matching fingerprint. Some identification scoring considered a valid match as long as the matching fingerprint is in the top

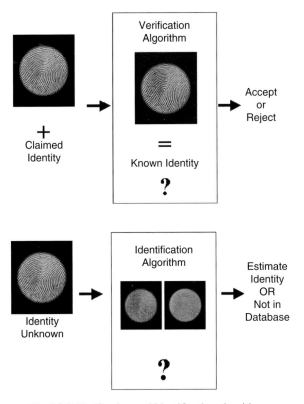

Fig. 12.8. Verification and identification algorithms.

5, 10, etc. correlation peak values, but for this identification scoring the match had to be the top correlation peak value.

The initial testing of the filters used only fingers that had 8 or more fingerprints in the training data set. This limited the data set to 55 fingers. Figure 12.9 shows the results for the verification scoring for the average, SDF, and MINACE filters. Also included in the scoring is the best result possible when using only one-to-one matching of fingerprints. For one-to-one results, each training image was scored versus each test image and the best matching score was kept. The results clearly show that all distortion-tolerant filters perform better than the one-to-one matching. As expected, the MINACE filter was the best-performing distortion-tolerant filter. A little surprising was that the SDF and average filters performed basically the same; it was expected that the SDF would do better. This seems to support the fact that the high-pass filtering used in both was more important than applying a single global weight to each of the training set images as done in the SDF case. The more complex filtering used by the MINACE filter was superior in performance to the simple high-pass filtering used in the average and SDF filters, since all 55 fingers were correct, with no false alarms.

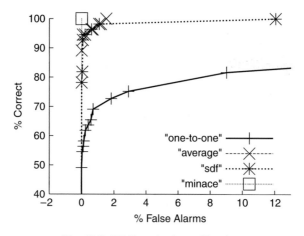

Fig. 12.9. ROC results for verification.

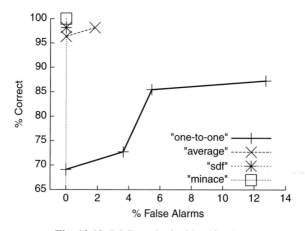

Fig. 12.10. ROC results for identification.

Identification scores (Fig. 12.10) again proved that the MINACE filter is superior to the others and that all three distortion-tolerant filters performed significantly better than one-to-one matching. A larger data set would be useful to improve the accuracy of the identification evaluation curves. Although the MINACE filter was perfect on this data set, testing on a larger data set is needed to solidify these results.

One final test was done using only the MINACE filter since it performed the best of the three filters. The rest of the fingers from the data set with only four to seven training set images were evaluated. The verification results clearly show a drop in performance with smaller training set sizes (Fig. 12.11). Improvement in the percent correct would be possible by adjusting the c parameter when building the MINACE filter, but most likely at the cost of a larger false-alarm rate.

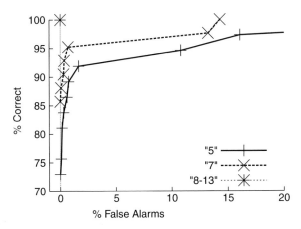

Fig. 12.11. Verification results for MINACE filters with only four to seven training images.

12.5. Conclusions

The results show that distortion-tolerant filters are clearly superior to one-to-one correlation fingerprint matching. Also, the more complex filtering scheme the MINACE filter uses provides better discrimination between matched and nonmatched fingerprints. For these particular data, a larger training set (8 or more images per finger) is desirable, but that could probably be reduced by having better controls placed on the fingerprint capture process; for example, eliminating the rotation of the input fingerprint and trying to limit the amount of distortion present by having a method to repeat the fingerprint capture under similar conditions each time a fingerprint is captured. It is anticipated that improving the quality of the input data would only improve the results shown here. Also, these filters have realizations in both digital and advanced optical systems but are most suited to take advantage of the speed that optical systems can provide-especially in performing a large number of matches. Results show that distortion-tolerant filters can produce a very good percent-correct recognition rate with low false-alarm rates, which should compare well with minutiae-based matchers. Correlation filter methods are also attractive since they provide fewer rejected fingerprints and minutiae-based systems require high-quality images, while correlation-based systems do not.

References

1. Chao, T.H., H. Zhou, and G. Reyes. 512×512 High-speed grayscale optical correlator, *SPIE, Optical Pattern Recognition*, XI:4043:40–45, 2000.
2. Fielding, K., and J.L. Horner, Optical fingerprint identification by joint transform correlation, *Optical Engineering*, 30:1958, 1991.
3. Gamble, F., L.M. Frye, and D.R. Greiser, Real-time fingerprint verification system, *Applied Optics*, 31:652–655, 1992.

4. T. Grycewicz, Fingerprint identification with the joint transform correlator using multiple reference fingerprints, *SPIE*, 2490:249–254, 1995.
5. T. Grycewicz, Fingerprint recognition using binary nonlinear joint transform correlators, *SPIE, Critical Review*, 65:57–77, 1997.
6. B.V.K. Kumar, Tutorial survey of composite filter designs for optical correlators, *Applied Optics*, 31:4773–4801, 1992.
7. H. Rajbenbach, Fingerprint database search by optical correlation, *SPIE*, 2752:214–223, 1996.
8. G. Ravichandran and D. Casasent, Minimum noise and correlation energy (MINACE) optical correlation filter, *Applied Optics*, 31:1823–1833, 1992.
9. D. Roberge, C. Soutar, and B.V.K. Kumar, Optimal correlation filter for fingerprint verification, *SPIE*, 3386:123–133, 1998.
10. A. Stoianov, C. Soutar, and A. Graham, High-speed fingerprint verification using an optical correlator, *SPIE*, 3386:242–252, 1998.
11. C. Watson, NIST Special Database 24: Digital video of live-scan fingerprint data, www.itl.nist.gov/iad/894.03/databases/defs/dbases.html#finglist, 1998.
12. C. Watson, P. Grother, E.G. Paek, and C. Wilson, Composite filter for VanderLugt Correlator, *SPIE Optical Pattern Recognition*, X:3715:53–59, 1999.
13. H. Zhou, T.H. Chao, G. Reyes, Practical filter dynamic range compression for grayscale optical correlator using bipolar-amplitude SLM, *SPIE, Optical Pattern Recognition* XI:4043:90–95, 2000.
14. C. Wilson, C. Watson, E.G. Paek, Combined optical and neural network fingerprint matching, *SPIE Optical Pattern Recognition*, VIII:3073:373–382, 1997.
15. R. Gonzalez and P. Wintz, *Digital Image Processing*, Reading, MA: Addison-Wesley, 1977.

Chapter 13

Fingerprint Preselection Using Eigenfeatures for a Large-Size Database

Toshio Kamei

Abstract. We describe fingerprint preselection using eigenfeatures for automated fingerprint identification systems in large-size, 10-print card databases. As preprocessing for minutiae matching, the preselection reduces minutiae matching candidates. Eigenfeatures and confidence factors are extracted for the preselection from the fingerprints in the 10-print cards. The eigenfeatures are calculated by the KL (Karhunen–Loève) expansion of the ridge directional pattern of the fingerprint, and the confidence factors are extracted as confidence of the eigenfeatures. Using the confidence factors, we can adaptively calculate a matching distance according to variances of the features under the confidence. This adaptation significantly improves preselection accuracy and achieves 1/1,500 to 1/10,000 reduction of minutiae matching candidates. The average number of instructions needed to compare a pair of cards is approximately 90 and is 10^5 times faster than minutiae matching computation. This preselection scheme enables the realization of fingerprint identification systems of high computational performance.

13.1. Introduction

Automated Fingerprint Identification Systems (AFIS) have been widely used in law enforcement for more than 20 years [1]. One of the major objectives is to determine, given a card with 10 fingerprint impressions to be searched (10-print card), if there is a corresponding card from the same person in a collection of enrolled cards.

Although various algorithms and systems have been proposed as means of determining the identify of fingerprints, most AFIS matchings adopt algorithms based on comparison of fingerprint minutiae (endings and bifurcations of finger ridgelines). However, minutiae matching is a time-consuming process, especially when the system is to retrieve fingerprints from a huge database consisting of several million 10-print cards. In order to expedite the process, it is necessary to have a mechanism that extracts a much smaller number of 10-print cards having the largest similarity to the given query card, as candidates for minutiae matching.

Conventional fingerprint classification has been performed by human experts according to Henry's classification scheme [2] to reduce matching candidates in the database. In this scheme, 10-print cards are separately stored into one group ("bins") according to a combination of fingerprint classes such as "arch," "loop," and "whorl."

To automate this conventional classification, many approaches have been proposed. Candela et al. [3] apply probabilistic neural networks to directional patterns, and Karu and Jain [4] detect singularities (cores and deltas) and perform classification based on the number and locations of the detected singularities. Kamei et al. [5] analyze structures of ridge flows around the singularities and integrate the structure-based classifier with a neural network classifier. However, these classification approaches are not very effective at reducing the number of candidate matches, even if an accurate pattern classifier is developed.

One reason is that reduction of matching candidates strongly depends on the number of classes and on the distribution of fingerprints in the classes. The classes are generally defined as four or five major classes in the traditional classification scheme, and the natural occurrence of pattern classes is unevenly distributed. For example, the natural percentage of an "ulnar loop"(a loop that flows in the direction of the unla bone, i.e., toward the little finger) is about 60%, much greater than $1/4 = 25\%$. Furthermore, 10-print cards having all 10 ulnar loops are about 8%, which is far greater than $(1/4)^{10} \simeq 10^{-6}$, and even much greater than $(60\%)^{10} \simeq 0.6\%$. Likewise, cards with nine or more ulnars are 17%, and those with eight or more ulnars is 32%. This nonuniform distribution inevitably makes some classification bins much larger than others, thus causing insufficient candidate reduction.

Another reason is that, in the process of Henry categorization, either manual or automated, there are a considerable number of inherently ambiguous patterns and also unavoidable recognition errors (sometimes because of low image quality, e.g., blurred impressions). Therefore, a mechanism to incorporate decision ambiguity and errors has to be implemented (otherwise, we have to assign ambiguous cards to multiple bins, which also evidently degrades candidate reduction performance).

Toward solving this binning problem and improving the retrieval performance, a "preselection" approach is proposed instead of a traditional binning database in [6, 7]. For instance, in [7], 10-print cards are characterized with feature vectors, which express pattern classes and structural characteristics such as core–delta distance and the number of ridgelines crossing between cores and deltas. Then, a query 10-print feature is compared with all enrolled data in the database, and the 10-print cards having the closest similarity with the query cards are extracted as candidates for minutiae matching.

There are two important aspects to a preselection scheme: One is how efficiently the number of candidates is reduced (selectivity); the other is how fast it compares query data with all of the enrolled data (computation complexity). In consideration of this, new features should be investigated for card preselection in addition to Henry classification features. Eigenfeatures of fingerprint flow pattern are an option for a new feature representation.

Eigenfeature techniques have been widely studied in many fields such as face recognition [8, 9], character recognition [10], and fingerprint recognition [11]. Because the eigenfeatures are extracted as a subset of the Karhunen–Loève (KL) expansion of the original features, which exploits correlation in the features to represent the original features effectively, the eigenfeatures become compact and its data size is tiny compared with the original features. The KL transform enables high-speed computation of 10-print card preselection. As the original features for KL expansion, the ridge directional pattern of a fingerprint is applied, because it represents holistic characteristics of ridge flow in the print.

In order to further improve the selectivity of the preselection, we introduce an adaptive distance by using confidence factors the preselection scheme. Fingerprint cards are often degraded by ink blur, scratches, and dry skin, and some of them are very low-quality images, which even human experts can hardly identify. Because these low-quality images influence the selectivity of the preselection, we propose using the confidence factors, which reflect the image quality in a matching distance to reduce the influence of quality degradation. Introducing the confidence of the eigenfeatures into the matching distance, we can adjust the matching according to the confidence. We demonstrate in this chapter that this adaptation in the matching distance significantly improves preselection accuracy.

In Section 13.2, we outline the configuration and process of the fingerprint identification system using fingerprint preselection. In Section 13.3, an adaptive discriminant distance with confidence is introduced as a key technology to achieve high-performance preselection. Section 13.4 describes extraction of eigenfeatures and confidence factors. Section 13.5 is devoted to a matching scheme using confidence factors. Section 13.6 discusses experimental results of fingerprint preselection on an NIST database.

13.2. Fingerprint Preselection

As a preprocessing to fingerprint minutiae matching, a fingerprint preselector selects the most similar cards to the given query card from a 10-print card database. The design goals are as follows:

An enrolled card from the same person as the query card, if there is one, should be selected.

The number of the selected cards should be as small as possible.

The computation needed in the preselection processing should be much smaller than minutiae matching.

Given n enrolled cards in a 10-print card database and a query card to be identified, the fingerprint identification system performs as follows (see Fig. 13.1):

1. Card profile database preparation: Preselection features are extracted from 10 fingerprints for all the n enrolled cards in the 10-print card database and are stored in advance as "card profiles."

2. Query profile generation: At the time of identification, the same set of features is extracted from the given query card, and the query card profile is generated.

3. Card comparison: A file card's similarity to the query card is evaluated by comparing the features from both card profiles; the result is used to determine whether the enrolled card should be accepted as a minutiae matching candidate.

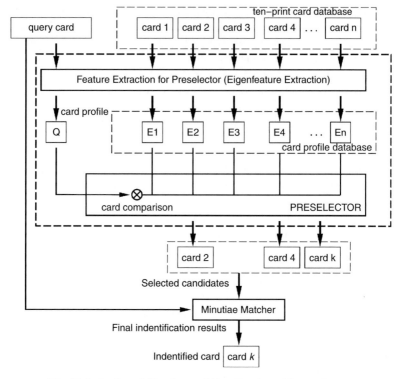

Fig. 13.1. Outline of 10-print card identification with preselector.

4. Card preselection: Preselection is the process of extracting the most similar m matching candidates from n cards, by repeating the card comparison for all n enrolled cards.

5. Final identification: Last, after the card classification reduces the candidate set size from n to m ($\ll n$), detailed minutiae matching of the search card against each of the m candidates is carried out, precisely determining whether or not there is a matching card.

The preselection process obviously involves much less computation than executing the fingerprint minutiae matching for all enrolled cards. The 10-print card identification system is shown in Fig. 13.1.

13.3. Adaptive Discriminant Distance with Confidence

In this section, an adaptive discriminant distance with confidence is introduced as a key technology to achieve high-performance preselection. At first, the discriminant distance is derived from a decision rule for person identity, and Karhunen–Loève expansion is applied to the distance to reduce computational complexity. Finally, the discriminant distance is modified to become adaptive to variances of features by using confidence factors of the features.

13.3.1. Distance Based on a Decision Rule

Consider two N-dimensional feature vectors x^q and x^e, where x^q denotes a feature vector of a query card, and x^e denotes a feature vector of an enrolled card in a database. In a preselection problem, it is necessary to determine whether the enrolled data x^e should be selected as the candidate corresponding to the query data x^q.

The decision problem to decide the identity of x^q and x^e can be expressed as the following decision rule:

$$\frac{P(W|s)}{P(B|s)} > 1 \Rightarrow \text{identical} \tag{1}$$

$$\frac{P(W|s)}{P(B|s)} < 1 \Rightarrow \text{not identical} \tag{2}$$

where s denotes a difference vector between x^q and x^e ($s = x^q - x^e$), W denotes an event that x^q and x^e are extracted from the same person (within-class), and B denotes an event that x^q and x^e are extracted from the different persons (between-class), respectively.

A distance function $d(s)$ to decide the identity of the two vectors is defined using a discriminant function expressed as a likelihood ratio:

$$d(s) = -\ln \frac{P(W|s)}{P(B|s)} \tag{3}$$

Using the Bayes theorem,

$$d(s) = -\ln \frac{P(W)P(s|W)/P(s)}{P(B)P(s|B)/P(s)} \tag{4}$$

$$= -\ln \frac{P(W)P(s|W)}{P(B)P(s|B)} \tag{5}$$

$$= -\ln \frac{P(s|W)}{P(s|B)} - \ln \frac{P(W)}{P(B)} \tag{6}$$

Because 10-print cards are not duplicated in the fingerprint card database, the a priori probability of the enrolled card corresponding to the query is constant for each person. Therefore, a priori probabilities $P(W)$ and $P(B)[= 1 - P(W)]$ are considered as constant, and the distance between two vectors can be calculated from $P(s|W)$ and $P(s|B)$. $P(s|W)$ is the probability density of the difference vector s between two vectors within the identical person and is recognized as an error distribution. $P(s|B)$ is the probability density of the difference vector between the different persons.

Suppose that x^q and x^e belong to the same Gaussian distribution with covariance Σ, and error distribution of x^q and x^e, that is, $P(s|W)$, is Gaussian with covariance Σ_W and zero mean. We can obtain

$$P(x^q) = \frac{1}{(2\pi)^{\frac{N}{2}}|\Sigma|^{\frac{1}{2}}} \exp\left(-\frac{1}{2}x^{q\top}\Sigma^{-1}x^q\right) \tag{7}$$

$$P(x^e) = \frac{1}{(2\pi)^{\frac{N}{2}}|\Sigma|^{\frac{1}{2}}} \exp\left(-\frac{1}{2}x^{e\top}\Sigma^{-1}x^e\right) \tag{8}$$

$$P(s|W) = \frac{1}{(2\pi)^{\frac{N}{2}}|\Sigma_W|^{\frac{1}{2}}} \exp\left(-\frac{1}{2}s^{\top}\Sigma_W^{-1}s\right) \tag{9}$$

where N denotes the number of dimensions of x^q and x^e. The distribution of s can be expressed as

$$P(s) = P(x^q - x^e)$$
$$= \frac{1}{(2\pi)^{\frac{N}{2}}|2\Sigma|^{\frac{1}{2}}} \exp\left(-\frac{1}{2}s^{\top}(2\Sigma)^{-1}s\right) \tag{10}$$

As for probabilities of the vector s, there is the following relationship:

$$P(W|s) + P(B|s) = 1$$
$$P(s|W)P(W) + P(s|B)P(B) = P(s) \tag{11}$$

A priori probability $P(W)$ is $1/n$, where n is the number of cards in the database, and $P(B) = 1 - P(W) = 1 - 1/n$. In a large-size database, $P(W)$ is regarded as 0, and $P(B)$ becomes almost 1. Approximating the above equation using this relationship and Eq. 10,

$$P(s|B) \simeq P(s)$$
$$= \frac{1}{(2\pi)^{\frac{N}{2}}|2\Sigma|^{\frac{1}{2}}} \exp\left(-\frac{1}{2}s^{\top}(2\Sigma)^{-1}s\right) \tag{12}$$
$$= \frac{1}{(2\pi)^{\frac{N}{2}}|\Sigma_B|^{\frac{1}{2}}} \exp\left(-\frac{1}{2}s^{\top}\Sigma_B^{-1}s\right) \tag{13}$$

Here, $\Sigma_B(=2\Sigma)$ is the covariance of the distribution of s in a class B.

Substituting (9) and (13) in (6), we obtain

$$d(s) = \frac{1}{2}s^{\top}\left(\Sigma_W^{-1} - \Sigma_B^{-1}\right)s + \frac{1}{2}\ln\frac{|\Sigma_W|}{|\Sigma_B|} \tag{14}$$

This equation is the similar formula to the Bayes discriminant function in classification on the assumption of Gaussian distribution. When the errors for all data belong to the same Gaussian distribution, the second term of (14) becomes constant. Ignoring the second term of Eq. 14 and a constant coefficient $1/2$, we obtain

$$d(s) = s^{\top}\left(\Sigma_W^{-1} - \Sigma_B^{-1}\right)s \tag{15}$$

13.3.2. Karhunen–Loève Expansion

For high-speed calculations, we apply Karhunen–Loève expansion to the discriminant distance, and omit calculations of insignificant components. Let Φ and λ_i be an eigenvector matrix and eigenvalues of covariance Σ of the pattern distribution of x^q and x^e, respectively.

The eigenvector matrix Φ and eigenvalues λ_i are obtained by solving an eigenvalue problem:

$$\Lambda = \Phi^{\top} \Sigma \, \Phi \tag{16}$$

where Λ is a diagonal matrix that consists of eigenvalues λ_i as diagonal elements.

Suppose the distribution of Σ_W has the same principal axes that the distribution of Σ has, and both Σ and Σ_W can be diagonalized by the same matrix, that is:

$$\Phi^{\top} \Sigma_W \Phi \equiv K \Lambda (= \Lambda_W) \tag{17}$$

where K is a diagonal matrix. Although this assumption is not true in general, this is necessary to apply the KL expansion to the discriminant distance for reducing calculations.

From the above assumption, we rewrite (15) in the diagonalized form:

$$
\begin{aligned}
d(s) &= s^{\top} \left(\Phi (K\Lambda)^{-1} \Phi^{\top} \right) s - s^{\top} \left(\Phi (2\Lambda)^{-1} \Phi^{\top} \right) s \\
&= v^{\top} (K\Lambda)^{-1} v - v^{\top} (2\Lambda)^{-1} v \\
&= \sum_{i=1}^{N} \left(\frac{1}{\kappa_i \lambda_i} - \frac{1}{2\lambda_i} \right) v_i^2 \\
&= \sum_{i=1}^{N} \left(\frac{1}{\lambda_{i,W}} - \frac{1}{\lambda_{i,B}} \right) v_i^2
\end{aligned}
\tag{18}
$$

where $v = \Phi^{\top} s$ is a vector projected onto the principal axis, a so-called eigenfeature. The factor $\lambda_{i,W} (= \kappa_i \lambda_i)$ is a diagonal element of the eigenvalue matrix Λ_W, and $\lambda_{i,B} (= 2\lambda_i)$ is the corresponding eigenvalue of Σ_B. This means that $\lambda_{i,W}$ and $\lambda_{i,B}$ are the error variance (within-class variance) of v_i and the total variance (between-class variance) of v_i, respectively.

Approximating (18) with M principal components of v ($1 \le M \le N$), we have

$$d(s) \simeq \sum_{i=1}^{M} \left(\frac{1}{\lambda_{i,W}} - \frac{1}{\lambda_{i,B}} \right) v_i^2 \tag{19}$$

In general, higher-order principal components are noisier than lower-order components. When a component i has only noise and no information on pattern discrimination, $\lambda_{i,B}$ will get close to $\lambda_{i,W}$, so that the component i becomes ineffective. The term $\left(1/\lambda_{i,W} - 1/\lambda_{i,B} \right)$ could be considered as an evaluation factor to measure the effectiveness of each principal component.

13.3.3. Confidence Factor

In the above discussion, we have assumed that errors of feature vectors belong to the same distribution of Σ_W. This assumption, however, is wrong for fingerprint images, because fingerprint impressions on images are degraded according to ink blur, dry skin, and other conditions; and some fingerprints are unrecognizable, even for human experts. In order to treat this problem, the covariance of the error distribution is supposed to be dependent on the confidence factor ρ of a feature vector. The matrix $\Sigma_W(\rho)$ denotes the within-class covariance as a function of the confidence factor ρ.

By substituting $\Sigma_W(\rho)$ in (14), we derive the following equation on the similar assumption for (19):

$$d(s, \rho) = \sum_{i=1}^{M} \left(\frac{1}{\lambda_{i,W}(\rho)} - \frac{1}{\lambda_{i,B}(\rho)} \right) v_i^2$$

$$+ \sum_{i=1}^{M} \left(\ln \lambda_{i,W}(\rho) - \ln \lambda_{i,B}(\rho) \right) \tag{20}$$

Here, $\lambda_{i,W}(\rho)$ is the diagonal element of eigenvalue matrix $\Lambda_W(\rho)$ of $\Sigma_W(\rho)$ at confidence ρ, and it is a variance of v_i for class W (within-class). $\lambda_{i,B}(\rho)$ corresponds to the diagonal element of eigenvalue matrix $\Lambda_B(\rho)$ at ρ, and it is a variance of v_i for class B (between-class).

13.4. Feature Extraction

Preselection features in a card profile are extracted from 10 fingerprints on a 10-print card. The features consist of eigenfeatures of ridge directional pattern of each fingerprint and confidence factors that express confidence of the eigenfeatures.

13.4.1. Ridge Directional Pattern

Since the ridge directional pattern expresses the major characteristics of fingerprint ridge flow, eigenfeature technique are applied to this feature to effectively represent the fingerprint flow. At first, a ridge directional pattern is extracted from an original fingerprint image by using a method described in [13]. Here, the image is enhanced by using multiple filters that correspond to fingerprint ridge directions and ridge frequencies. Since the best-matched filter in each region represents the ridge directions and frequencies in the local region, the direction of the matched filter is extracted in each region as the ridge directional pattern. The local image powers of the filtered image are used as confidence of the directions, described in Section 13.4.3.

Then, the extracted directional pattern is translationally positioned using a center point of a fingerprint [15]. The center point of a fingerprint is almost the same as the "core" of the fingerprint. It is detected by matching of direction histograms projected vertically and horizontally. The center point is used for an initial positioning, and then the pattern is adjusted translationally and rotationally by template-

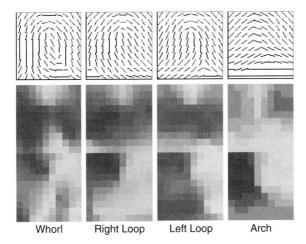

| Whorl | Right Loop | Left Loop | Arch |

Fig. 13.2. Ridge directional patterns. The upper row uses line segments to express directionality and the lower rows are gray-scale image expressions of cosine components (middle) and sine components (bottom) of the directional patterns.

matching with the reference pattern. After the directional pattern is cropped and subsampled, the final pattern size becomes 10×10 for image size 320×320 pixels in a 500-dpi resolution. The directional pattern x is expressed by a set of 100 unit vectors of orientations $\theta(m, n)$ $(0 \le \theta < \pi)$ in each block (m, n) $(1 \le m, n \le 10)$. Each unit vector is denoted by $(\cos 2\theta(m, n), \sin 2\theta(m, n))$. Finally, the directional vector x has 200 elements, which is used as an input vector for KL expansion. Figure 13.2 shows some examples of 10×10 direction patterns.

13.4.2. Eigenfeatures

As a preselection feature, eigenfeatures of ridge directional pattern x are extracted from each fingerprint on the 10-print card. The eigenfeatures are calculated by projecting the directional vector x onto the subspace specified by a set of eigenvectors $\{\phi_i\}$ of covariance matrix Σ. The covariance matrix Σ of x is calculated from a set of x in a training data set.

$$\Sigma = \frac{1}{N-1} \sum_i (x_i - \bar{x})(x_i - \bar{x})^{\top} \tag{21}$$

where $\bar{x}$ denotes the mean vector of the directional vectors x_i. The set of eigenvectors $\{\phi_i | i = 1, 2, \ldots, M\}$ of Σ corresponding to the M largest eigenvalues $\{\lambda_i | i = 1, 2, \ldots, M\}$ is used as the basis vectors. The projected vector v is calculated as follows:

$$v = \Phi^{\top} x \tag{22}$$

where Φ is the basis matrix consisting of the eigenvectors ϕ_i.

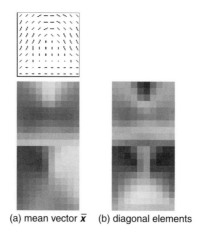

(a) mean vector $\bar{x}$ (b) diagonal elements

Fig. 13.3. Average vector $\bar{x}$ and diagonal elements of covariance matrix Σ.

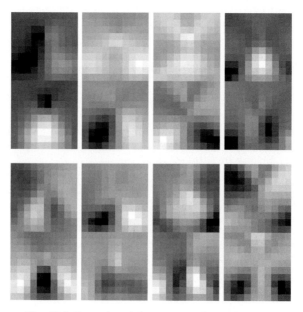

Fig. 13.4. Examples of eigenvectors of covariance Σ.

The 27,000 fingerprints in NIST Special Database 14 [12] are used to calculate the covariance matrix Σ of the directional patterns x. The mean vector $\bar{x}$ and diagonal elements of covariance matrix Σ are shown in Fig. 13.3, each element reflecting the variance of the corresponding pattern element. The eigenvectors of Σ are shown in Fig. 13.4.

As seen in Fig. 13.3b, variances in the lower region of a fingerprint are larger than those of the upper region. In the lower region, loop and whorl patterns have delta(s),

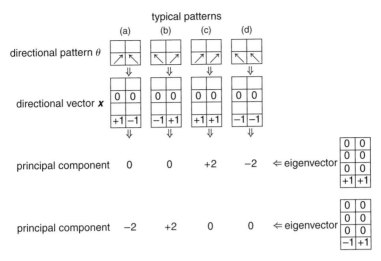

Fig. 13.5. Relation between eigenvectors and principal components. In this figure, directional patterns are simplified into four local blocks, and a direction θ takes only two values, $1/4\pi$ and $3/4\pi$.

which do not appear in an arch pattern. Thus, this region is important for fingerprint classification.

Figure 13.4 shows eigenvectors of covariance matrix Σ in decreasing order of eigenvalue magnitude. The eigenvectors that have larger eigenvalues represent lower-frequency characteristics than those of smaller eigenvalues as often seen in the principal component analysis of face images [8].

Figure 13.5 depicts a relation between eigenvectors and principal components. In this figure, directional patterns are simplified into four local blocks, and a direction θ takes only two values, $1/4\pi$ and $3/4\pi$. The typical pattern (a)–(d) symbolize arch, whorl, left, and right loop, respectively. The upper elements of the directional vector x are $\cos(2\theta)$ and the lower elements are $\sin(2\theta)$. As seen in Fig. 13.4, the first eigenvector has large values in sine components of the directional vector and represents horizontal symmetry of the sine components. As patterns (c) and (d) in Fig. 13.5 are symmetrical in the sine components, the first principal component discriminates between the left flow and right flow. Asymmetry of the sine components is extracted using the second eigenvector as seen in Fig. 13.5 and discriminates between whorl and arch.

As said above, the major principal components, especially the first and the second ones, represent typical characteristics of fingerprint ridge flow. The first components and the second components represent the typical characteristics such as flow direction (left $\leftrightarrow$ right) and prominence degree (prominent $\leftrightarrow$ plain), respectively.

Figure 13.6 shows plots of correlation between the first and the second components of the eigenfeatures in each categories; whorl, right loop, left loop, tented arch, and plain arch. The figure shows that the first component indicates whether fingerprint

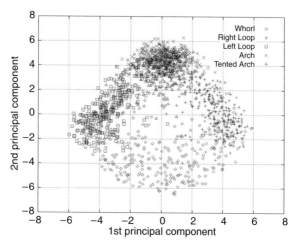

Fig. 13.6. Correlation between the first principal component and the second principal component plotted for the categories: right loop, left loop, whorl, and (tented) arch.

pattern is left loop or right loop and the second component discriminates whether the pattern is whorllike or archlike.

13.4.3. Confidence Factor

We introduce an adaptive matching scheme for exploiting confidence factors in eigenfeature techniques [14]. In this scheme, the matching distance is adjusted according to confidence in the feature vectors as noisy components of the eigenfeatures are weighted less. In order to apply this scheme to fingerprint preselection, confidence factors are extracted for each fingerprint.

As a confidence factor, any measure may be effective if the measure strongly correlates with variance of the eigenfeatures. We evaluated 30 measures such as pixel value statistics extracted from local subregion, template-matching score in positioning of directional pattern. As a result, we selected the following three measures as confidence factors:

1. Weighted distance from mean directional pattern ρ_{MDP}: The weighted distance ρ_{MDP} is a weighted distance between an input directional pattern x and the mean directional pattern $\bar{x}$ using direction confidence $r = (r_{i,1}, r_{i,2}, \dots)$ and $\bar{r}$, which are the confidence of x and $\bar{x}$, respectively. Direction confidence r is calculated in extraction of directional pattern [13].

$$\rho_{MDP} = \frac{\sum r_i \bar{r}_i (x_i - \bar{x}_i)^2}{\sum r_i \bar{r}_i} \tag{23}$$

This calculation is performed using a directional pattern and its confidence in 64×64 resolution before subsampling and cropping into 10×10 resolution.

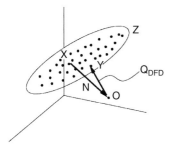

Fig. 13.7. Confidence ρ_{DFD}. A noiseless vector X is observed as O due to a noise N. Confidence ρ_{DFD} is defined as the minimum distance of $||O - Y||$ among the sample Y in a good-quality sample set Z.

2. Weighted direction confidence in eigenspace ρ_{WDC}: The weighted direction confidence ρ_{WDC} is a weighted confidence of the direction confidence in eigenspace. Using eigenvector $\boldsymbol{\phi}_i = (\phi_{i,1}, \phi_{i,2}, \ldots)$, which is one of the elements of eigenvector matrix Φ of covariance Σ, we calculated confidence ρ_{WDC}^i as follows:

$$\rho_{WDC}^i = \sqrt{\sum_j r_j^2 \phi_{i,j}^2} \qquad (24)$$

ρ_{WDC}^i means a direction confidence that is weighted according to its contribution $\phi_{i,j}$ of each block j. The resolution of the directional pattern is 10×10.

3. Distance from high-quality pattern ρ_{DFD}: The distance from the high-quality pattern is a distance from a surface enclosing the distribution of a "high-quality pattern." The closed space is represented by a set of sample vectors whose quality is "high." The distance between an input vector and the nearest sample vector is calculated as a confidence (see Fig. 13.7):

$$\rho_{DFD} = \min_i ||x_t^i - x|| \qquad (25)$$

where x_t^i are fingerprint sample vectors and x is the input vector. Some 10,000 "good-quality" fingers were selected among 13,500 fingers in the NIST database to compute a confidence factor.

13.5. Matching

13.5.1. Adaptive Distance Using Confidence Factors

The adaptive discriminant distance described in Section 13.3 is applied to matching in the preselection. The confidence factors adjust the distance adaptively according to the confidence in the eigenfeatures.

The distance between the eigenfeature v^q and v^e is calculated using confidence factors ρ as follows:

$$d(v^q, v^e) = \sum_{i=1}^{M} \left(\frac{1}{\sigma_{i,W}^2(\rho)} - \frac{1}{\sigma_{i,B}^2(\rho)} \right) |v_i^q - v_i^e|^2 \qquad (26)$$

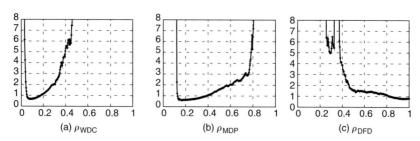

Fig. 13.8. Standard deviations $\sigma_{i,W}(\rho)$ for between-class variation corresponding to each confidence. The horizontal axis denotes value of confidence factor, and the vertical axis denotes standard deviation.

Here, $\sigma_{i,W}^2(\rho)$ is a within-class variance of vector component v_i conditioned under confidence ρ; likewise $\sigma_{i,B}^2(\rho)$ is a between-class variance of v_i under the confidence ρ. Using the adaptive distance, weighting factors of each component are adjusted through variances under confidence ρ. The second term of (20) is omitted to reduce computational complexity.

13.5.2. Training

The variances $\sigma_{i,W}^2(\rho)$ and $\sigma_{i,B}^2(\rho)$ are calculated using a training data set. Figure 13.8 shows examples of the within-class standard deviation of the first principal component corresponding to confidence ρ_{WDC}, ρ_{MDP}, and ρ_{DFD}, respectively. The horizontal axis denotes value of confidence factor and the vertical axis denotes standard deviation. A large within-class variance (error variance) indicates that the input features are degraded. The confidence is an indicator, because error variances are strongly dependent on the confidence, as seen in the figure.

13.5.3. Integration of Variances

There are three pairs of variances, $\sigma_{i,W}^2(\rho)$ and $\sigma_{i,B}^2(\rho)$, for three confidence factors: ρ_{WDC}, ρ_{DFD}, ρ_{MDP}. We re-estimate the variance by selecting the maximun value among the three variances instead of averaging three variances. From basic experiments, it was confirmed that the maximum variance performs better than the average of the variances. So the maximum variances are selected among the three variances:

$$\sigma_{i,W}^2(\rho) = \max \sigma_{i,W}^2(\rho_k) \tag{27}$$

$$\sigma_{i,B}^2(\rho) = \max \sigma_{i,B}^2(\rho_k) \tag{28}$$

When the distribution is a normal distribution, the average of the variances yields a better estimate than the maximum variance. However, the maximum variance gives the better results. It means that the distribution is different from a normal distribution, and the difference in variance estimation is compensated for by taking the maximum value.

13.5.4. For Ten-Print Card

When feature vectors v^q and v^e are extracted from each finger on a 10-print card, respectively, we obtain a distance for the 10-print card, d_{card}, by summing the distances $d_i(v^q, v^e)$ over 10 fingers assuming independence between the fingers:

$$d_{card} = \sum_{i=1}^{10} d_i(v^q, v^e) \qquad (29)$$

13.6. Experiment and Discussion

We implemented a prototype preselection system based on the proposed feature extraction and matching algorithms. The performance is evaluated using the NIST 14 fingerprint database consisting of mated 2,700 card pairs (54,000 fingerprints) [12].

Half of the 2,700 card pairs is used as the training set to calculate a basis matrix Φ and variances used in the matching. The other half of the database (1,350 pairs) is used as a test set. One of each pair in the test set is stored in a card profile database, thus containing 1,350 cards. The remaining cards (1,350 cards) are used as query cards.

The preselection capability is evaluated from the standpoint of both its reliability and its selectivity. The reliability is measured by the false rejection rate (FRR), namely, the percentage of erroneously rejected mated pairs. The selectivity is measured by the false acceptance rate (FAR), namely, the percentage of erroneously accepted nonmated pairs, and it expresses how much the preselection reduces the number of matching candidates. A lower FRR means higher reliability, and a lower FAR means higher selectivity.

The false rejection at the preselection stage is not possible to fix later, whereas the false acceptance can be rejected in the detailed minutiae matching stage. However, the minutiae matching requires high computational costs. Therefore, both high reliability and high selectivity are required in the preselection.

Figure 13.9 and Fig. 13.10 respectively show the dependency of the false acceptance rate and the false rejection rate on the number of eigenfeatures components, where the principal components are selected in decreasing order of eigenvalue magnitude. The false rejection rate is kept constant at 2% in Figure 13.9, and the false acceptance rate is set at 2% in Figure 13.10 by adjusting a decision threshold, respectively. For comparison, results of the preselectors replacing the adaptive discriminant distance with the Mahalanobis distance or the discriminant distance are also shown.

For all distances, the preselector achieves the maximum accuracy when 4–10 components are used. Including the higher-order components increases recognition error. Though the basis vectors used of the KL expansion are calculated without any prior knowledge of discriminant information, the KL expansion is as effective as fingerprint feature representation. It indicates that important features of fingerprint directional pattern are effectively condensed in primary components of the eigenfeatures, and most higher-order components are ineffective for recognition purposes.

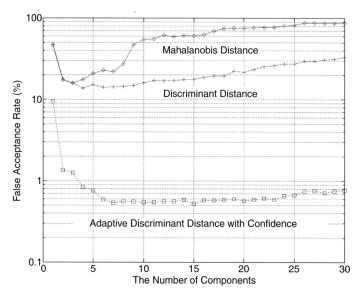

Fig. 13.9. Dependency of false acceptance rate on the number of eigenfeature components. The best FAR of adaptive distance with confidence factor (0.52%) is 1/30 of that of the Mahalanobis distance (15.8%). The FRR is kept constant at FRR = 2%.

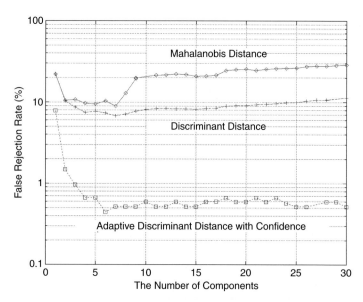

Fig. 13.10. Dependency of false rejection rate on the number of eigenfeature components. The best FRR of adaptive distance with confidence factor (0.44%) is 1/20 of that of the Mahalanobis distance (8.9%). The FAR is kept constant at FAR = 2%.

The preselection using discriminant distance produces better results than those using the Mahalanobis distance, especially when the number of components is large. The reason is that discriminant distance reduces the effects of ineffective higher-order components, which cause recognition error when using the Mahalanobis distance. This effect is obtained through a weighting coefficient $(1/\sigma_{i,W}^2 - 1/\sigma_{i,B}^2)$ for each component by compensating for within-class variances and for between-class variances.

The adaptive discriminant distance with confidence factor shows much better accuracy than the other distances. The adaptation by the confidence factor improves the FAR to 1/30 of that obtained by the Mahalanobis distance and reduces the FRR to 1/20. This significant improvement demonstrates the effectiveness of the adaptive matching scheme.

Figured 13.11 shows receiver operating characteristic curves of preselection based on eigenfeatures and preselection based on classification features developed in [7]. Table 13.1 shows the selectivity (FAR) at typical FRR operating points, 2% FRR and 5% FRR. In the eigenfeature-based preselection, 7 components of eigenfeatures are extracted for each finger, and a size of the card profile is 140 bytes for each card. The classification-based preselection uses 21 components for each finger and 420 bytes for each card. The classification features consist of probability of primary classes (arch, left loop, right loop, and whorl) and structural features such as core–delta distance. The accuracy of the eigenfeature-based preselection and the classification-based preselection are better than the 3% FAR of the traditional binning classification, which is estimated from class distribution of the NIST 14 database based on manual

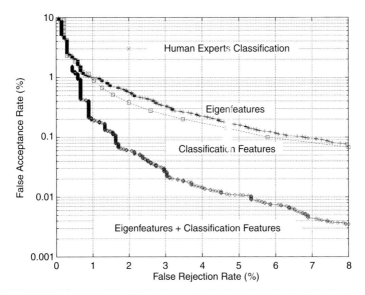

Fig. 13.11. FAR/FRR curves. The FAR of preselection based on the traditional classification by human experts is about 3% at 2% FRR.

Table 13.1. Selectivity of the Preselectors

	2% FRR	5% FRR
Eigenfeature-based preselector	1/178 (0.56%)	1/625 (0.16%)
Classification-based preselector	1/263 (0.38%)	1/714 (0.14%)
Integrated preselector	1/1666 (0.06%)	1/10000 (0.01%)
Integrated preselector(4 fingers)	1/73 (1.37%)	1/141 (0.71%)

The FAR in parentheses. The upper three preselectors use 10 fingers for each card. The last preselector uses four fingers per card, which are index and middle fingers for both hands.

classification by human experts. If the category is classified automatically, the FAR becomes about 9.7% at 2% FRR, even when 10% of the images are rejected and the classification is a manually assigned class.

In addition, selecting the most effective 18 features among the eigenfeatures and classification features (card profile size is 360 bytes), the preselection selectivity improves from 0.6% FAR to 0.06% FAR at 2.0% FRR as seen in Figure 13.11. The 0.06% FAR means a 0.0006 (= 1/1666) reduction of matching candidates. Since selectivity of card classification is only 3% at 2% FRR in conventional manual classification, selectivity of the integrated preselector is approximately 50 times more accurate than that of the conventional classification scheme and the integrated preselector is considered far superior to manual classification.

In recent years, some civil database systems have adopted fingerprint identification to identify the person. These databases do not use 10-print cards, but they enroll only four fingers for each person. For instance, index and middle fingers for both hands are used. The results of the integrated preselector that uses four fingers are also shown in Table 13.1. Since the selectivity is about 1/100, it is high enough for the civil databases.

As a preprocessing of minutiae matching to select matching candidates from a database, the preselection speed should be fast enough in comparison with minutiae matching. We evaluated the average number of instructions needed to compare a pair of cards as the preselection speed, which is 90 instructions using a RISC-based workstation. It means the preselector is more than 10^5 times faster than card comparison of minutiae matching. As for reduction of minutiae matching candidates, the preselector achieves approximately 1/1,500 to 1/10,000 reduction. The high selectivity and high speed of the preselector make it possible to realize a high-performance fingerprint identification system.

13.7. Conclusions

In this chapter, we describe fingerprint preselection techniques using eigenfeatures for automated fingerprint identification systems using large-size, 10-print card databases. As a preprocessing to minutiae matching, the preselection reduces the number of candidates for minutiae matching. Eigenfeatures and confidence factors are extracted by the preselector from the fingerprints on each card. Eigenfeatures are calculated by a KL expansion of the ridge directional pattern of a fingerprint; confidence factors are extracted from variances of the eigenfeatures. Using the confidence factors, the matching distance is adaptively calculated according to variances of the features under the confidence. This adaptation significantly improves preselection accuracy and achieves 1/1,500 to 1/10,000 computational reduction compared to minutiae matching of candidate cards. The average number of instructions needed to compare a pair of cards is 90 instructions/card and is 10^5 times faster than minutiae matching computation. By this preselection, it is possible to realize high-performance fingerprint identification systems with large databases consisting of more than 10 million fingerprint cards.

Acknowledgments

The author would like to thank Tsutomu Temma for providing the opportunity for this work, Kazuo Kiji and Masanori Hara for the arrangement of fingerprint databases, and Kaoru Uchida and Seiji Yoshimoto for their significant advice.

References

1. Asai, K., Y. Kato, Y. Hoshino, and K. Kiji, Automatic fingerprint identification, *Proc. Society of Photo-Optical Instrumentation Engineers—Imaging Applications for Automated Industrial Inspection & Assembly*, 182:49–56, 1979.
2. Federal Bureau of Investigation, *The Science of Fingerprints*, Washington, DC: U.S. Department of Justice, 1963.
3. Candela, G.T., P.J. Grother, C.I. Watson, R.A. Wilkinson, and C.L. Wilson, PCASYS—A pattern-level classification automation system for fingerprints, National Institute of Standards and Technology, NISTIR 5647, 1995.
4. Karu, K. and A.K. Jain, Fingerprint classification, *Pattern Recognition*, 29(3):389–404, 1996.
5. Kamei, T., H. Shinbata, K. Uchida, A. Sato, M. Mizoguchi, and T. Temma, Automated fingerprint classification, IEICE Technical Report, PRU95(200):17–24, 1996.
6. Uchida, K., T. Kamei, M. Mizoguchi, and T. Temma, Fingerprint card classification for identification with a large-size database, IEICE Technical Report, PRU95(201):25–32, 1996.
7. Uchida, K., T. Kamei, M. Mizoguchi, and T. Temma, Fingerprint card classification with statistical feature integration, *Proc. 14th International Conf. on Pattern Recognition*, 2:1833–1839, 1998.
8. Turk, M. and A. Pentland, Face recognition using eigenfaces, *Proc. 1991 IEEE Computer Society Conference on Computer Vision and Pattern Recognition*, pp. 586–591, 1991.
9. Moghaddam, B. and A. Pentland Probabilistic visual learning for object detection, *Proc. 5th International Conference on Computer Vision*, pp. 786–793, 1995.
10. Kato, N., M. Abe, and Y. Nemoto, A handwritten character recognition system using modified Mahalanobis distance, *IEICE Transactions*, J79-D-II(1):45–51, 1996.
11. Wilson, C.L., G. Candela, P.J. Grother, C.I. Watson, and R.A. Wilkinson, Massively Parallel Neural Network Fingerprint Classification System, National Institute of Standards and Technology, NISTIR 4880, 1992.

12. National Institute of Standards and Technology, NIST Special Database 14—Mated Fingerprint Card Pairs 2, 1993.

13. Kamei, T. and M. Mizoguchi, Image filter design for fingerprint enhancement, *Proc. International Symposium on Computer Vision*, pp. 109–114, 1995.

14. Kamei, T. and M. Mizoguchi, Fingerprint preselection using eigenfeatures, *Proc. 1998 IEEE Computer Society Conference on Computer Vision and Pattern Recognition*, pp. 918–923, 1998.

15. Hara, M., K. Morita, I. Suzuki, and Y. Hoshino, A method for positioning fingerprints using ridge directions and center points, Record of 1990 IEICE Spring Conference, pp. 7–285, 1990.

Chapter 14

Systems Engineering for Large-Scale Fingerprint Systems

Rajiv Khanna

Abstract. Systems engineering for large-scale Automated Fingerprint Recognition Systems (AFIS) involves system planning, specification, design, development, testing, and operational support. Testing these systems includes the complex activity of measuring the system's performance. The desired system performance, however, affects each of the system's engineering functions. For large-scale systems, estimating the performance of the full-scale operational system and planning for its development are critical to developing effective systems. It is inefficient and risky to build or buy a large-scale AFIS and then measure its performance, only to find that it does not meet expectations. Measuring performance of the internal technologies supports system planning, design, development, and testing and provides the potential for system performance improvement. Quantitative fingerprint system evaluation requires measurement of missed detection and false-alarm error rates. Two parameters are derived from these error rates, *reliability* and *selectivity*. Reliability is the probability that the system will report a matching fingerprint given that one is in the database. Selectivity is the average number of false candidates per search that the system will report. A third parameter, *filter rate*, is the percent file size reduction provided by a system component. It is related to selectivity and supports the constructive framework for systems engineering. These three parameters provide a basis for system engineering from requirement specification through operations. Equations are derived for these parameters to describe interrelationships and provide insight into system behavior.

14.1. Introduction

14.1.1. Background

Fingerprint systems are used to identify individuals within a population or verify the identity of an individual within the population. Systems vary in size depending on the application, ranging from relatively small populations of less than 1000 to large populations that may be in the millions. Large-scale fingerprint systems are characterized by large file sizes (large numbers of fileprints) and demanding performance requirements. Currently, larger systems retain fingerprint files on about 40 million people and process tens of thousands of search requests each day. As technology improves, our definition of large scale may change, but the systems engineering methods developed in this chapter can still be applied.

Fingerprint system applications can be classified into one of two types: (1) identification systems or (2) verification systems. Identification systems match an individual to his or her unique identity within a population using fingerprints. These systems have been used by law enforcement organizations for over 100 years (although computers have only been used for the last 30 years). As the name might imply, verification systems check the identity of an individual (i.e., *verify* identity) using fingerprints and a unique identifier. Verification systems are enabled by new fingerprint sensors and are driven by authentication, access control, and other applications where we need to verify that a person is who he or she claims to be.

Law enforcement organizations use systems to identify people who are reported missing, are wanted, require background investigation, or need a criminal records check. These systems typically contain an identification system because fingerprint information has traditionally been more reliable than other identifying information and the subject of investigation may not cooperate in providing identifying information. Law enforcement applications have supported automated fingerprint system development over the past 30 years. The future promises both improved performance for existing applications and possibilities for new ones.

Fingerprint systems compare time-invariant features in fingerprints. There are three well- established types of fingerprint features: Galton features or minutiae; finger classification features; and ridge topology. Galton features are natural ridge endings and bifurcations in ridges that are formed before birth and last after death. The classification features consist of cores, or points of high curvature; deltas, the divergence of parallel ridges; and ridge counts between cores and deltas. Ridge topology is the structural relationship of ridges. On the leading edge of research are systems that use sweat pores and ridge shape as automated matching features [1].

While fingerprint features are time-invariant, they are not spatially invariant. The skin on fingertips is elastic. It conforms to the shape of touched objects and deforms with sheer force. Fingerprint systems incorporate techniques to correctly match fingerprints even though they are spatially varying across samples.

Fingerprints were originally collected using ink on paper. Two types of fingerprints are collected. First is the rolled fingerprint. This involves rolling the finger on ink and then rolling it on a paper card. The rolling technique is typically nail-to-nail because the ridge pattern extends to nearly the edge of the fingernail. The second is a flat impression. This technique involves pressing the finger on ink and pressing it on the paper card. Traditionally, multiple fingerprints were taken at once using this method and captured at the bottom of the fingerprint card.

The Henry system of fingerprint classification reduces the effort required to search the fingerprint file by partitioning it into logical bins. This method of classification involves identifying patterns using cores and deltas and counting ridges between them [2].

Early fingerprint systems used manual data entry of fingerprint features and classifications. Today, card scanners convert paper cards to digital images, and automated image processing techniques extract features. Fingerprint files consist of features and fingerprint images. A standard wavelet scalar quantization (WSQ) image compression method facilitates their storage and transmission.

Live-scan technology allows for capturing fingerprint images directly without ink and paper. This technology is capable of capturing both rolled and flat fingerprints. Devices employ optical, ultrasound, and electronic sensors. Livescanners reduce the need for fingerprint cards and scanners in many fingerprint systems by allowing for paperless transfer of images.

Live-scan imaging facilitates many new applications including e-commerce and web-based financial transactions, access to electronic medical records, and entry and access control for facilities, computers, and countries. These new applications differ from the traditional ones used in law enforcement; they verify the identity of an individual. The fingerprint systems that support these applications can be considered subsets of the more complex systems that have unique requirements involving specialized design and development. Within this context, this chapter addresses fundamental elements of engineering design and development of large-scale fingerprint identification systems.

14.1.2. Survey of Related Literature

There has been a significant development of published work relating to the testing and evaluation of fingerprint and other biometric systems. Early literature was published by the author and his colleagues and used during development of several large automated fingerprint identification systems [3–6]. A comprehensive development of benchmark testing was published in the *Proceedings of the IEEE Special Issue on Biometrics* [7]. A best-practices document, available from the Centre for Mathematics and Scientific Computing, defines testing, evaluation, and reporting of biometric technologies [8].

14.1.3. Chapter Overview

This chapter is organized as follows: Section 14.2 describes systems engineering as applied to fingerprint systems; Section 14.3 describes performance measurement and benchmarking; and Section 14.4 provides a summary and conclusions.

14.2. Fingerprint Systems Engineering

Systems engineering begins with determining what stakeholders need and want; the systems engineer formulates system requirements based on these needs and wants. The requirements are the specification of the system. For complex systems, engineers develop architectures and design subsystems to support practical implementations of the system. They decompose system functions into smaller parts. They assess how these parts will work together to satisfy system requirements. Throughout the development process, the systems engineer supports the system design, implementation, testing, and deployment.

This section develops a systems view of fingerprint systems. We start with a black-box description of fingerprint systems and then define internal component functions. We follow with a reference architecture that shows how internal component functions can be used to support the end-to-end system.

14.2.1. System Description

Two types of fingerprint systems are discussed in this section: one-to-one systems and one-to-many systems. The fingerprints submitted to the system for identification or verification are called *searchprints*. The fingerprints retained by the system for reference are called *fileprints*. The terms "searchprint" and "fileprint" refer to fingerprint information from one or more fingers on an individual and are intentionally ambiguous with regard to the number of fingers because the developed theory does not require further definition. Searchprints and fileprints that originate from one person are called *mates* regardless of the time and method of collection.

A one-to-one system compares a searchprint presented by an individual to a corresponding fileprint and decides whether or not they match. The individual using the system asserts his or her identity using a unique identifier, allowing the system to retrieve a fileprint from the database. The fileprints are collected from individuals prior to the comparison and are stored in the system. This type of system is a *verification system*.

A one-to-many system attempts to match the searchprint with all similar fileprints in the system and decides whether any of them match. This type of system is an *identification system*.

The terms "one-to-one" and "one-to-many" refer to comparison of information about the numbers of individuals, as opposed to the number of fingerprints.

Large fingerprint systems use a file entry process with the objective of retaining only *one* fileprint per person. This process searches the file prior to storing a fileprint to ensure duplicates are not entered. In practice, some duplicate fileprints are entered because of missed detection. The systems use *consolidation* processes when duplicate fileprints are discovered. Consolidation removes one of the duplicate fileprints, eliminates the unique identifier, and updates relational links between the remaining fileprint and other related information.

Identification and verification systems produce similar responses. The system reports one or more *matches* (and unique identifiers if needed) if it finds one or more fileprints that correspond to the searchprint, or *no match* if it does not. In the operational system, the unique identifier is the index to other information such as a criminal record or an access control list.

Identification systems typically require more powerful computers than verification systems because more comparisons are required. For verification systems, the unique identifier is descriptive information that reduces the number of comparisons per searchprint to a single fileprint. In subsequent sections, we develop an approach that supports analysis of both types of systems. Some of the systems engineering methods need not be applied to verification systems.

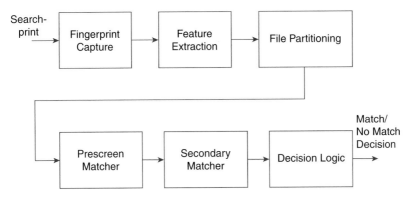

Fig. 14.1. Fingerprint system reference architecture.

14.2.2. Component Technologies

The internal components of a fingerprint system vary depending on the requirements and design. The designer may select the functions for implementation and determine how the information needs to flow to achieve the requirements. The reference architecture and its internal functions provide insight into the inner workings.

A fingerprint system reference architecture is shown in Fig. 14.1. The components contain the subordinate components and data elements (like fileprints) used to perform the function. The architecture represents both identification and verification systems if it allows for entering the identity claim.

The system strategy is to winnow the file at each processing stage. The set of possible matches at each stage is the *candidate list*. The goal is keeping the correct match in the candidate list while removing nonmatches at each processing stage. This reduces the downstream workload and improves the chance of finding a match.

The fingerprint system is decomposed into the following functional components:

Fingerprint image capture: captures one or more fingerprints and produces gray-scale images.

Feature extraction: extracts fingerprint features from images. These features are used in all downstream processes.

File partitioning: partitions the file into classes designed to limit searching. Each fileprint is indexed to one or more classes using extracted features. The search and file indices are compared using quick string comparisons. Downstream matching is performed only if the indices match.

Prescreen matcher: uses a coarse matcher to winnow the candidate list for downstream matchers, reducing workload for downstream matchers. The prescreen matcher eliminates candidates that are not likely to match prior to using secondary matchers that require more computer resources.

Secondary matcher: detail matcher designed to select the matching candidates from the winnowed candidate list.

Decision logic: combines results from distributed matchers and decides which candidates to report as matching fileprints.

14.3. Performance Evaluation and Benchmarking

The performance of an operational fingerprint system describes how well it correctly identifies or verifies an individual. This corresponds to how well the system matches searchprints with fileprints. First consider a case where the system responds with only one match. In this case, the output is a binary *Match/No Match* decision that may be *correct* or *incorrect*. There are four possible outcomes:

1. The system *correctly* reports a searchprint and fileprint *Match*.
2. The system *correctly* reports *No Match*.
3. The system *incorrectly* reports *No Match*.
4. The system *incorrectly* reports that a searchprint and fileprint *Match*.

The first two outcomes are correct results. The third outcome is typically called a *Type I Error, miss,* or *false reject*. The *false reject rate (FRR)* is the probability of a false reject [8]. The system failed to identify the individual when it contained his or her fileprints. In the fourth outcome, the system mistook one individual with the identity of another. This case is called a *Type II Error, false alarm,* or *false accept*. The *false accept rate (FAR)* is the probability of a false accept.

For statistical analysis of performance, the outcomes are considered the result of Bernoulli trials under the following conditions:

1. The trial results in one of two outcomes, typically called "success" and "failure."
2. The trials are identical and independent.
3. The probability of success, and hence failure also, is constant over all trials.

The correct outcomes are Bernoulli successes and the incorrect outcomes are failures. Evaluating system performance is reduced to estimating the probabilities of failures: the probability of miss and the probability of false alarm. We estimate the confidence interval around the estimate of these parameters, to describe the certainty of our estimate.

Reliability is the probability that the system will report the true fileprint if it is in the file. Reliability is related to the probability of miss by the following equation:

$$R = \Pr[TrueMatch] = 1 - \Pr[Miss] \tag{1}$$

Consider the second case, where the system may report more than one match for a searchprint. This type of system is more common in large-scale applications because it is challenging to maintain a consolidated file. Under ideal conditions, there would be no probability of miss. The process of searching the file prior to entry would maintain a fully consolidated file. There would be no need to report more than one match because it would be an error condition to do so. In practice, however, the file is not consolidated and there is a measurable miss probability. Under these conditions, the system is designed to report all matches.

When the system can report more than one match, the possible outcomes become more complex. For example, the system may correctly report a match and incorrectly report a match for a single searchprint. To allow for these cases, we introduce another commonly used performance parameter, selectivity. *Selectivity* is the average number of incorrect matches the system reports per search.

Reliability, probability of false alarm, and selectivity are parameters that characterize fingerprint system matching performance without regard to internal components. We could measure these parameters by treating the system as a black box and exercising the system as people intend to use it. However, the stakeholders often require additional functionality to facilitate testing, including bulk entry of data and reports oriented toward performance measurements.

14.3.1. Benchmarking Fingerprint Systems

A *benchmark test* is a standard test for quantitative performance measurement. Benchmarks may be applied to more than one system for comparative analysis or to one system during development phases to mark improvement. It is important to use a standard test because test results depend on the test data, the procedures, and the system design. The test data, procedure, and evaluation of the results should be consistent to ensure that performance measurements are comparable.

14.3.1.1. Benchmark Design

Three test data sets are required to conduct a benchmark: (1) searchprints with corresponding mated fileprints (mated pairs); (2) a background file that does not contain matches to the searchprints; and (3) searchprints without mates. The background file represents the operational file. The mated searchprint/fileprint pairs are expected to match and form the basis for reliability measurements. The unmated searchprints and background file are expected not to match and form the basis for false-alarm and selectivity measurements.

The number of mated pairs needed in the benchmark is calculated from our reliability requirement and the confidence interval requirement. The following equation is used to compute the number of mated pairs that are required [7]:

$$n \approx \left(\frac{z_{\alpha/2}}{\varepsilon}\right)^2 R_E(1 - R_E) \tag{2}$$

where n is the number of mated pairs, R_E is the expected reliability, ε is size of the confidence interval, and $z_{\alpha/2}$ is the number of standard deviations from the mean in the standard normal distribution that corresponds to the confidence interval. For example, if we expect the system reliability to be 0.98 ± 0.01 with a confidence of 0.95, we would use a value of $z_{\alpha/2}$ of 1.96 and find that we need approximately 750 mated pairs.

We use a similar equation to calculate the number of needed fileprints and unmated searchprints [7]:

$$(uf) \approx \left(\frac{z_{\alpha/2}}{\varepsilon}\right)^2 P_E(1 - P_E) \tag{3}$$

where u is the number of unmated searchprints, f is the number of fileprints, P_E is the expected false-alarm rate or stakeholder requirement, ε is size of the confidence interval, and $z_{\alpha/2}$ is the number of standard deviations from the mean in the standard normal distribution that corresponds to the confidence interval. In this case there is a trade-off between the number of unmated searchprints and fileprints that provides some latitude in our design. If we select u, then f is determined, and vice versa. To provide an example, let both the expected false-alarm rate and the confidence interval be 10^{-8}, let the confidence be 0.95, and let the file size be 128,000; then we would require approximately 3000 unmated searchprints.

If the system is designed to search fingerprints and report matches during the fileprint entry process, the file is consolidated, and we observe this process as part of the benchmark test, then we can consider the file entries as unmated searches. For large files, we can use the following equation to estimate the file size:

$$f' = \sqrt{2uf} \tag{4}$$

where u and f are defined as above and f' is a new estimate of file size. Under this scenario, the example we have been considering would now need a file of approximately 28,000 fileprints to observe about 3 false alarms. No unmated searchprints would be required.

A few words of caution are in order. We developed these engineering equations by modeling the system processes as statistical experiments and using the associated theory to generate the needed results. Test results and test data needs may vary if the implemented system differs from the statistical models. For example, there may be characteristics within the system that skew results. An implementation error may inadvertently retain information about one searchprint and use it with the next one. This error would violate the assumption of independent trials. To compensate for unexpected effects, we typically overspecify the amount of required data to provide better information about the system.

14.3.1.2. Benchmark Data

The objective is to use test data that are representative of operational data and that do not bias the test results. We typically develop a random selection process for test data to ensure that they contain the natural distribution of characteristics of the operational data. For new systems that do not have legacy data, a data collection process needs to be established. For systems that will operate using existing data, random sampling from operational data streams can be used, although care must be taken to avoid bias from the legacy system.

A key part of the collection process is verifying that the test data conform to specifications. Fingerprint examiners should verify mated pairs. As part of this process, the fingerprint examiners create a *truth table* that lists pairs of corresponding unique identifiers for each mated pair. Processes are developed to check, to the extent practical, that unmated searchprints and background fileprints are unique.

Multiple fingerprint samples from certain individuals should be avoided in both the file and search data since this creates a situation where the searches are not independent. This will skew the measurements. Systems engineers can take two steps to make the data representative and unbiased: (1) Use a sufficient number of data samples for the desired confidence; and (2) use independent samples that are not correlated. These samples are selected at random from a large pool, without any subjective selection criteria.

During the data collection process, system engineers collect sufficient data to support both development and testing. The same process is used to collect both data sets. The development data are shared with system developers so that they understand the characteristics and quality of the data. The test data are reserved for benchmarks to provide performance information that is independent from the development process.

14.3.1.3. Test Procedures

The benchmark test procedure is a standard process that can be repeated for all systems under test. It has standard parameter definitions similar to the ones developed here. It observes the same types of outcomes, consistently recording results for evaluation. Typically the test uses much of the operational functionality of the system. However, for convenience, we sometimes use backdoor methods to execute batches of transactions and record results. In these cases, the evaluator needs to ensure that the functionality under test is exercised appropriately.

During the development of the test procedures, one should take care to ensure that all systems under test have appropriate functionality that will be tested in the same way. For example, if the planned test procedure involves using fileprint entry as the mechanism for estimating the false-alarm rate, then the tests for all systems should use the same method.

The following are the typical benchmark test steps:

1. Insert fileprints from the set of mated pairs into random sequence positions in the background file. The resulting data set is called the *seeded background file*. Seeding reduces risks associated with clumped groups of fingerprints in the system.
2. Load the seeded background file into the system. Record reports of matched fingerprints during the file load. Record fingerprints that the system rejects or cannot store.
3. Run the searchprints through the system. Record the results for each searchprint.
4. The following steps are used during evaluations:
   a. Have a fingerprint examiner check matches reported during the file load.
      i. Update the truth table with correct matches.
      ii. Incorrect matches can be used to estimate the probability of false alarm or selectivity.
   b. Use the truth table and standard methods to estimate the performance measures.

c. Keep rejected fingerprints in the truth table. Count misses caused by rejected fingerprints, because they correspond to misses caused by rejected data in the operational scenario. A large amount of rejected data will bias results and is not desirable.

The test procedure should account for all data used in the test. Entered fileprints should be verified by entry statistics, and the amount of rejected data should be verified. Each searchprint should have a recorded outcome, either *Match* with the identifier, or *No Match*.

14.3.1.4. Evaluation Methods

Evaluation of test results involves counting the number of correctly reported matches and incorrectly reported matches and calculating performance in a standard way. Equations for these calculations are provided in the following sections. This is usually sufficient to distinguish relative matching performance among systems. If the performance of two systems is close, we may use a hypothesis test to help determine if the difference is significant.

14.3.2. System Performance Measures

We now develop the external system performance measures and the methods used to calculate them. These are the metrics we will use to characterize the system without regard to internal components.

14.3.2.1. Reliability Estimation

The reliability estimator, denoted as $\hat{R}$, is the average number of correct matches per mated searchprint. As with all estimators, our estimate is not *true* reliability, but it is probable that the true value is in an interval around our estimate. To the extent that the system and benchmark test comply with the conditions of Bernoulli trials, the reliability can be considered the probability of observing a correct match under the conditions of the test. Under all conditions, reliability is a measure of performance for the benchmark test.

The benchmark result is a set of reported matches. We extract the set of correct matches using the truth table and count the number of correct matches for each searchprint that has a mate in the file. The reliability estimate is computed using the following equation:

$$\hat{R} = \overline{R} = \frac{1}{n}\sum_{i=1}^{n} R_i \tag{5}$$

where n is the number of mated pairs and R_i is the number of correct matches for the ith searchprint. If the file is consolidated to contain only one set of fingerprints from each subject, then each search will return at most one mate.

The variance in the reliability estimate is calculated using the following equation:

$$\sigma_{\hat{R}}^2 = \frac{\hat{R}(1-\hat{R})}{n} \tag{6}$$

For a sufficiently large number of mated searchprints, $n \geq 30$, we can use the following equation to estimate a confidence interval for the true reliability R:

$$\hat{R} - z_{\alpha/2}\sqrt{\frac{\hat{R}(1-\hat{R})}{n}} \leq R \leq \hat{R} + z_{\alpha/2}\sqrt{\frac{\hat{R}(1-\hat{R})}{n}} \tag{7}$$

where $z_{\alpha/2}$ is the number of standard deviations from the mean in a standard normal distribution that corresponds to our confidence interval. By using this equation, we can be fairly certain, as specified by the confidence, of the lower and upper bounds of the measured reliability.

14.3.2.2. Selectivity Estimation

Estimating Selectivity Using Probability of False Alarm

Selectivity—the average number of incorrect matches per search—is proportional to file size and the probability of false alarm, denoted by f and P_{FA}, respectively. If the probability of false alarm can be estimated, an estimate of selectivity, $\hat{S}$, can be calculated using the following equation:

$$\hat{S} = f \cdot P_{FA} \quad \text{if } P_{FA} = 1 \tag{8}$$

In the following sections, we discuss estimation methods for selectivity and the probability of false alarms.

Estimating Selectivity Using Searchprints

The benchmark result is a list of reported matches. We extract the list of incorrect matches using the truth table and count the number for each searchprint. The selectivity estimate is computed by dividing the sum of incorrect matches by the total number of searches:

$$\hat{S} = \overline{S} = \frac{1}{u+n}\sum_{i=1}^{u+n} S_i \tag{9}$$

where u is the number of unmated searches, n is the number of mated ones, and $\hat{S}_i$ is the number of false matches for query i.

The following equation can be used to compute the variance in the test results:

$$\hat{\sigma}_S^2 = \frac{1}{u+n-1}\sum_{i=1}^{u+n}(S_i - \overline{S})^2 \tag{10}$$

As $\hat{S}$ is an average, its measurement variance is the variance $\hat{\sigma}_S^2$ divided by the number of searches, $u+n$:

$$\hat{\sigma}_{\hat{S}}^2 = \frac{\hat{\sigma}_S^2}{u+n} \tag{11}$$

The confidence interval for the measurement specifies an interval around $\hat{S}$ and the probability that the true value is within the range. For large $N = u+n(N > 30)$, $\hat{S}$ has a normal distribution. The confidence interval is estimated by solving the following equation:

$$-z_{\alpha/2} \le \frac{\hat{S} - S}{\sigma_{\hat{S}}} \le z_{\alpha/2} \tag{12}$$

Solving for S yields the following equation:

$$\hat{S} - \frac{\sigma_{\hat{S}} \cdot z_{\alpha/2}}{\sqrt{u+n}} \le S \le \hat{S} + \frac{\sigma_{\hat{S}} \cdot z_{\alpha/2}}{\sqrt{u+n}} \tag{13}$$

This equation provides the lower and upper confidence interval bounds of the true selectivity S, given $\hat{S}$.

Estimating Selectivity Using File Load

We can estimate the selectivity from results recorded during the benchmark file load process [9]. We do this by estimating the probability of false alarm and then using it to calculate the expected selectivity. The key to this estimation is that the number of nonmate comparisons is an arithmetic series during file load. The number of comparisons is computed using the following equation:

$$C = \frac{f(f-1)}{2} \tag{14}$$

Let the total number of observed false alarms during the file load be O. An estimate of the false-alarm probability can be computed as

$$P_{FA} = \frac{O}{C} \tag{15}$$

The confidence interval for P_{FA} specifies an interval around the estimate and the chance that the true value is within the range. The size of the confidence interval can be computed using the following equation:

$$\varepsilon = z_{\alpha/2} \sqrt{\frac{P_{FA}(1 - P_{FA})}{C}} \tag{16}$$

The interval is calculated by the following equation:

$$[P_{FA} - \varepsilon, P_{FA} + \varepsilon] \tag{17}$$

The selectivity for the test is estimated by multiplying the results by the file size f as shown in Eq. 8.

14.3.3. Internal Component Performance Measures

There are two performance parameters for measuring performance of internal components:

1. *Filter rate* is the percent reduction in candidate list size for a matching stage.
2. *Conditional reliability* is the probability that a stage will pass the correct candidate given that it was passed by previous stages.

These parameters help us understand mechanisms within the fingerprint system.

14.3.3.1. Filter Rate

The following set denotes the filter rate observed on each of N searches, with or without mates in the file, during testing:

$$\{F_1, F_2, \cdots, F_i, \cdots, F_N\} \tag{18}$$

The estimated filter rate is the average and is computed with the following equation:

$$\hat{F} = \overline{F} = \frac{1}{N} \sum_{i=1}^{N} F_i \tag{19}$$

The estimator is denoted by $\hat{F}$ and average is denoted by $\overline{F}$. The filter rate variance is computed with the following equation:

$$\hat{\sigma}_F^2 = \frac{1}{N-1} \sum_{i=1}^{N} (F_i - \overline{F})^2 \tag{20}$$

The confidence interval is similar to that for selectivity and is computed from the following equation:

$$\hat{F} - \frac{\hat{\sigma}_F \cdot z_{\alpha/2}}{\sqrt{N}} \leq F \leq \hat{F} + \frac{\hat{\sigma}_F \cdot z_{\alpha/2}}{\sqrt{N}} \tag{21}$$

14.3.3.2. Conditional Reliability

For a typical multistage fingerprint system, the *conditional reliability* of the kth stage, R_k, is the chance that the stage will pass the mated fingerprint given that it was passed by the previous stage:

$$R_k = Pr(Pass\,Stage_K | Pass\,Stage_{k-1}) \tag{22}$$

Passing at stage $k - 1$ implies passing stage $k - 2$, which implies passing stage $k - 3$, etc. The conditional probability of stage k has a dependency on all the previous stages. Therefore, all previous stages of the system must be applied when the value of R_k is measured. If stage k is tested independently from the previous stages, then the measurement may be skewed too high because this stage may not lose a matched pair that would have been lost by one of the earlier stages, or it may be skewed too low because this stage is now losing matched pairs that would have been lost in the previous stages.

Let n be the number of searchprints with mates in the file and L_k be the number of searchprint mates lost by the kth matcher stage. The number of mated pairs lost by all stages preceding stage $k - 1$ is equal to $\sum_{i=1}^{k-1} L_i$. The number of mated pairs presented to stage k is equal to $n - \sum_{i=1}^{k-1} L_i$. The conditional reliability at the kth stage is the number of mated pairs passed (or not lost) by the stage divided by the number of mated pairs presented to it. The following formula can be used to compute the conditional reliability of the kth stage, R_k:

$$R_k = \frac{\left(n - \sum_{i=1}^{k-1} L_i\right) - L_k}{\left(n - \sum_{i=1}^{k-1} L_i\right)} = \frac{n - \sum_{i=1}^{k} L_i}{n - \sum_{i=1}^{k-1} L_i} \tag{23}$$

14.3.3.3. Systems Engineering Parameter Relationships

There are three key system equations for fingerprint systems. The first two equations relate the performance of two or more stages to system performance, allowing for combination of multiple stages. The third relates selectivity to filter rate. This equation simplifies performance evaluation and provides a method for relating technical component or stage filter rates to system selectivity.

Since the conditional reliability specifies an output–input relationship, it can be used to evaluate the reliability of a matching process thread. Consider a process thread made by serially combining two or more matching stages. The system reliability of multiple stages can be computed by multiplying the conditional reliabilities of each stage:

$$R_{System} = R_1 \cdot R_2 \cdots R_k \tag{24}$$

The subscript notation above can be used to map system stages to the integers 1 through k in the above equation.

Stage filter rates can be combined in a similar way because they, too, specify output–input relationships:

$$F_{System} = F_1 \cdot F_2 \cdots F_k \tag{25}$$

where each subscript can be mapped to a system stage.

The output–input filter rate definition is used to relate filter to selectivity. Recall that f is the size of the file. If the input to the first stage is the consolidated file, the system selectivity can be computed from stage filter rates and the file size:

$$S_{System} = (f - 1) \cdot F_{System} = (f - 1) \cdot (F_1 \cdot F_2 \cdots F_k) \approx f \cdot F_{System} \tag{26}$$

For large consolidated files, the mated candidate is insignificant and the selectivity is calculated by multiplying filter rate and file size. If the system consists of internal stages within a larger system, the input candidate list size can be substituted for f in Eq. 26 although care must taken when using the approximation to ensure that mated candidates do not bias the result.

14.3.4. Performance Factors and Trade-offs

Many fingerprint systems use a match score that is a similarity measurement between two fingerprints. Match scores can be combined to provide similarity measurements between multiple sets of fingerprints and other biometric information to create a single match score, or they can be considered separately in multiple dimensions. First we consider a single match score and then consider multiple scores.

14.3.4.1. Thresholds

A histogram of match scores typically has two modes: One corresponds to nonmate comparisons and the other to mates. Figure 14.2 shows two normal distributions corresponding to mate and nonmate comparison match scores that serve as an example. Setting a match score threshold provides a decision criterion; if the match score is greater than the threshold, declare a match. Match scores for nonmate pairs greater than the threshold, represented by darker shading, are false alarms or contribute to selectivity. Match scores for mated pairs that are less than the threshold, represented with darker shading, are misses.

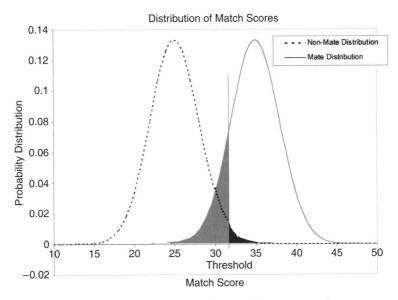

Fig. 14.2. Probability distributions of mate and nonmate match scores.

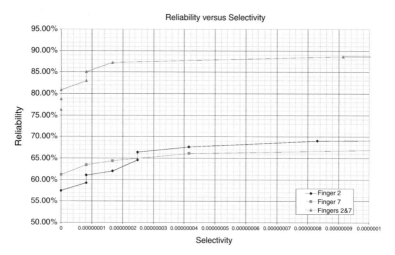

Fig. 14.3. Reliability versus selectivity.

The threshold offers an opportunity to trade-off misses and false alarms, or selectivity depending on the type of system. Increasing the threshold reduces false alarms at the expense of missing more true matches. Decreasing it has the opposite effect; we get more true matches and more false alarms (i.e., higher selectivity).

14.3.4.2. Reliability and Selectivity

Figure 14.3 shows reliability as a function of selectivity. We created this chart by estimating the reliability and selectivity at various thresholds and plotting the results. The figure contains discontinuous jumps because it was generated from empirical results on a small-scale matcher. Figure 14.3 quantitatively shows the relationship described in the previous section without the intermediary threshold. It shows reliability increases as the value of selectivity increases for each of the index fingers, indicated as finger 2 and finger 7. A lower value of selectivity indicates better system performance, but there is a trade-off in reliability, as shown in the figure. It also shows performance improvement when the system used both fingers 2 and 7 for identification, the topic of the next section.

14.3.4.3. Multiple Fingerprints

Figure 14.4 shows reliability versus threshold scores for a system using only finger 2, only finger 7, and both fingers 2 and 7. The figure shows reliability decreasing as the threshold increases, providing a quantitative view of the statistical model in Fig. 14.2.

When combining fingerprint matching information, the system uses decision criteria created by combining match scores from individual fingers. The decision logic is complex, but the results are clear. The system improved reliability by between

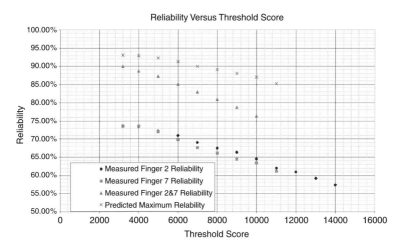

Fig. 14.4. Reliability versus threshold score.

13 and 16 percentage points depending on the threshold. In order to understand its performance, we can compare it to a predicted maximum.

The maximum is predicted by assuming that a match could be declared if one fingerprint or the other is greater than the threshold and that the measured reliabilities are independent of each other. The maximum predicted reliability is computed using the following equation:

$$R_{Max} = R_A + R_B - R_A R_B \qquad (27)$$

Figure 14.4 shows that the measured reliability is closer to the predicted maximum at lower thresholds, lagging it by about 3%. At higher thresholds, the measured reliability lags the predicted maximum by approximately 11%, indicating that there may be room for improvement in these operating regions.

14.3.4.4. Parallel Matchers

In a previous section, we examined the case of serial matchers where one matcher is a prefilter for another matcher. Since the first matcher limits the number of fingerprint pairs compared by the second matcher, we developed the conditional reliability measurement to gauge performance.

Parallel matchers combine the matching information from two or more different matchers to make the Match/No match decision. The term "parallel" is a logical distinction. The computation can be either sequential on one processor with stored results, or simultaneous by using two different processors, or some combination depending on workload distribution. In all cases, the match results are combined to improve performance over using a single matcher.

Figure 14.5 contains a scatterplot of mate (O) and non-mate (X) scores from two matchers, called the primary and secondary matchers. We can partition the coordinate

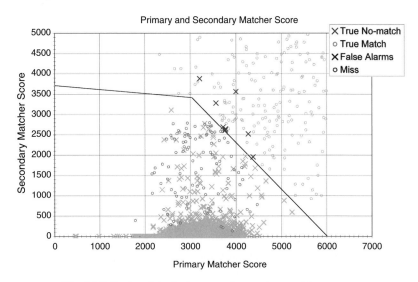

Fig. 14.5. Scatterplot of primary and secondary matcher scores.

system into regions corresponding to our Match and No match decision. Figure 14.5 shows a trapezoid bounded by the axes and two linear functions. The interior of the trapezoid is the No match region; the exterior is the Match region.

In Figure 14.5, the decision regions were designed and developed prior to the benchmark. The scatterplot shows results from the benchmark test. The Xs are non-mate pairs that scored high enough on both matchers to be in the Match decision region. They are false alarms. The Os are mated pairs that scored too low on both matchers to be declared a match, representing misses.

The design objective is to select a geometry that satisfies the requirements using operational data. The system that generated the data in Figure 14.5 was required to make no false-alarm errors, a challenging goal. During development, the decision regions were adjusted to minimize the probability of false alarm by adding a guard band above the highest-scoring false alarm. During more extensive benchmark testing using the file load method, a few false alarms were discovered.

Figure 14.5 shows the challenge in satisfying the original requirement. Any convex geometry that eliminates false alarms would also reduce reliability (increase false rejects). Complex geometries involving concavities or multiple decision regions would not be likely to perform well when using operational data. The stakeholders must make the trade-off between false alarms and reliability.

Figure 14.5 illustrates the need for separate development and test data. The figure shows that the developer can advertently or inadvertently tailor the number of false alarms in the benchmark test by changing the decision regions, or training the system to the test data. To avoid training to the test data, we create a data set for development and create a separate one for benchmarks. The development data provide useful statistical information to the developer, and the test data set provides unbiased performance information.

14.3.4.5. File Size

The probability of observing a false alarm increases as the file size increases. The implication for systems engineering is that the performance measured on the small-scale development system does not correspond to operational performance on the large-scale system. To resolve this problem, we discuss *performance projection*. Projecting performance involves predicting reliability and selectivity at the expected operational file size. We thus create a performance model that uses test results from the small-scale system and produces estimates for the large-scale system.

The approach is to closely examine what occurs in the tail of the nonmate distribution. Researchers may apply extreme-value statistics because of the sparse data in the tail. We will discuss a more traditional method. Perfromance projection with both methods had consistent results in our testing.

Assume that the tail of the nonmate match score distribution drops off exponentially. The probability of reporting a nonmate is the integral from the threshold over the tail that is also an exponential function of score. Represented on a logarithmic scale, the function is linear.

We can compute the system filter rate for the development system using Eq. 26 by dividing the measured selectivity by the file size over a series of threshold values. Each computed filter rate corresponds to the probability of false alarm at the given threshold. Again using Eq. 26, we compute the expected selectivity at each threshold by multiplying the filter rate by the expected operational file size. Results of these calculations from a development system are shown in Fig. 14.6 as triangles.

The best-fit log-linear function forms the basis of the selectivity model. We can use it to predict the selectivity given a threshold value. We use linear regression methods

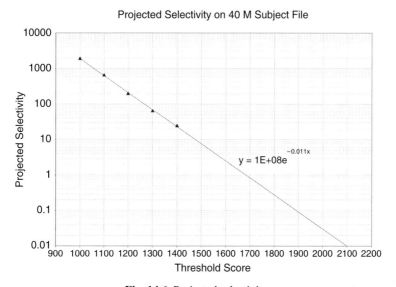

Fig. 14.6. Projected selectivity.

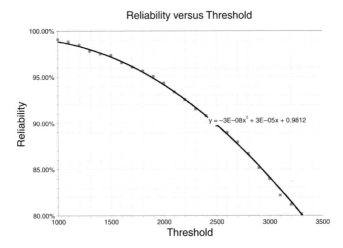

Fig. 14.7. Reliability projection.

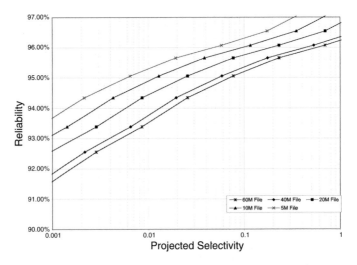

Fig. 14.8. Reliability and selectivity projected to operational file sizes.

to fit the parameters a and b in an equation of the following form:

$$y = ae^{-bx} \qquad (28)$$

Results of a linear regression are shown in Fig. 14.6.

Figure 14.7 shows the reliability projection formula. We fit a function to the reliability measurements at each threshold. In this case we used a quadratic function.

We can combine the reliability and selectivity projections into a single chart as shown in Fig. 14.8. In this figure, we show projections to various operational file sizes to help develop requirements for a new system.

14.4. Summary and Conclusions

In this chapter we develop systems engineering methods for fingerprint systems. We provide the system description for a model system, introducing basic functional elements that can be applied in a variety of configurations for specific applications. The functional elements span those used in contemporary systems and provide insight into applicable technologies.

The second element of fingerprint systems engineering is to specify and develop system performance for the operational environment. The functional elements create a structural foundation for performance measurement. We develop performance evaluation and benchmarking methods for measuring end-to-end performance; defining reliability, selectivity, and filter rate metrics to complement standard false-accept and false-reject rates. Standard benchmark test methods are provided to help ensure valid test results.

We examine performance measures for internal components and develop relationships among them. The benefits and challenges of serial components are presented; using multiple components can reduce the filter rate, but the system reliability must be less than that of the weakest component.

When evaluating performance, we review the trade-off between reliability and selectivity (or false-alarm rate). In examining this trade-off, we show that increasing selectivity can increase reliability. Introducing additional information, such as using more fingerprints, can improve the reliability–selectivity curve, providing better reliability at each selectivity operating point. This can be compared to the theoretical maximum to provide an indication of room for improvement.

Expanding a small-scale system to use a larger file implies that there will be some performance loss. We present a method for estimating large-scale system performance when benchmark testing is conducted on a small-scale system. The method involves fitting selectivity and reliability to modeling functions and scaling them to the projected file size.

Overall, this chapter provides a comprehensive view of the systems engineering associated with fingerprint systems. It provides a set of tools that can be used in the acquisition, development, and testing of fingerprint systems. The tools can be applied to a variety of applications, from traditional law enforcement to new verification applications. The technology within fingerprint systems has historically improved, and it looks like the trend will continue. The changes in both the use and technology of fingerprint systems will require the ability to evaluate and understand system performance and its impact on the desired application. This chapter provides the foundation for our evaluation and understanding of fingerprint systems.

References

1. Roddy, A. and J. D. Stosz, Fingerprint features—Statistical analysis and system performance estimates, *Proc. IEEE Special Issue on Automated Biometric Systems*, New Jersey, Sept. 1997.

2. FBI, *The Science of Fingerprints*, U.S. Dept. of Justice, Federal Bureau of Investigation, Washington, DC.

3. Khanna, R., D. E. Lake, and C. G. Bates, AFIS benchmarking with an identification technology testbed, Criminal Justice Technology Symposium Poster Presentation, Gaithersburg, MD, Sept. 9, 1993.

4. Khanna, R., D. E. Lake, and C. G. Bates, Evaluation methods for identification systems, SPIE Advanced Imaging and Pattern Recognition Conference, Washington, DC, Oct. 13, 1993.

5. Khanna, R., D. E. Lake, and C. G. Bates, The identification technology laboratory, Biometric Authentication Consortium Presentation, Albuquerque, NM, Oct. 25, 1993.

6. Khanna, R., and W. Shen, AFIS benchmark using NIST Special Database 4, International Association of Identification—Chesapeake Bay Division Annual Spring Conference Presentation, Richmond, VA, March 12, 1994.

7. Shen, W., M. Surette, and R. Khanna, Evaluation of automated biometrics-based identification and verification systems, *Proc. IEEE Special Issue on Automated Biometric Systems*, New Jersey, Sept. 1997.

8. Mansfield, A. J. and J. L. Wayman, *Best Practices in Testing and Reporting Performance of Biometric Devices*, Centre for Mathematics and Scientific Computing, National Physical Laboratory, Aug. 2002.

9. Khanna, R. and K. Miller, False alarm estimation in an automated fingerprint identification system (AFIS), 34th Annual Carnahan Conference on Security Technology, Oct. 23, 2000.

Chapter 15

Multifinger Penetration Rate and ROC Variability for Automatic Fingerprint Identification Systems

James L. Wayman

Abstract. AFIS system design and performance is heavily impacted by data correlations and error rate variability both within and across individual fingerprint records, but little is known about these issues. In this paper, we report on experiments done with the best algorithms from six major AFIS vendors tested using a 4128×4080 database of electronically collected flat prints. We obtain Receiver Operating Characteristic curves for thumb through ring finger on right and left hands, as well as experimental penetration and binning error rates for one-, two-, four-, and eight-print systems. Impact of binning on the overall ROC curve is measured. "Zero-effort" impostor error rate variability ("lambs" and "wolves") is observed across the data.

15.1. Introduction

In previous papers [1–7] we consider performance estimation of biometric identification systems based on assumptions of measurement independence between measures. We note in those papers that such assumptions are generally incorrect, but lacking any data on measure correlations, no quantitative estimates of the effect on system performance are offered. Although measurement correlations affect error rates and throughput of all biometric systems, it is the performance of large-scale identification systems that is most critically affected by data correlations because of the large number of measurement comparisons generally made.

Currently operational, large-scale biometric identification is restricted to Automatic Fingerprint Identification Systems (AFIS). In this paper we estimate various measure correlations for AFIS from new fingerprint test data. The multifinger test data are available for both false-match/false-nonmatch comparison errors and binning error/penetration rate estimation. Specifically, in this paper we estimate penetration rates for single-finger systems based on thumb, index, middle, and ring fingers, and multifinger systems for two thumb, two index finger, and combined four thumb–index finger systems. Penetration rates calculated from test data are compared to theoretical calculations based on recent finger-dependent pattern classification statistics from the FBI [8].

We show receiver operating characteristic (ROC) curves computed with nonmatching comparisons differentiated between fingers in communicating and noncommunicating bins. Further, we develop different ROC curves for thumb, index, middle, and ring fingers of both right and left hands. Finally, the variability of the "impostor" distribution across test samples is discussed.

15.2. Test Data

The electronically "live" scanned Philippine fingerprint test database [3] was used in this test. The data consisted of two sets, enrollment, or "training," and "test" data. The training set, consisting of 4080 distinct fingerprints, was taken from 510 individual adult volunteers, each giving 8 fingerprints (thumb through ring fingers on both hands). All volunteers were employees of the Social Security System of the Republic of the Philippines. Most were office and administrative workers, and 55% were women. The test set of 4128 prints was collected one to six weeks after the training set from 506 individual volunteers. Of these 506 volunteers, 409 were common to both test and training data sets. Ten volunteers in the test set donated two sets of eight prints each. Ninety-seven volunteers in the training set were not represented in the test set.

A third "practice" set of 80 images from 10 volunteers, whose images were in both test and training sets, was taken 6 weeks after the test database was completed.

Prints were imaged with an Identicator DF-90 "flat" scanner, believed to be "Appendix G"-compliant and an "MRT" frame grabber in a laptop computer. Front-end quality-control software from Identicator was employed. The Identicator "Biometric Enrollment System" collection and database management software was used for this project. The prints were stored, using lossless compression, as "TIFF" images. Some image quality loss, attributable to frame-grabber noise during collection, was noticed in the upper right-hand quadrant of most images.

15.3. Vendor Testing

To date, six AFIS vendors have had their algorithms evaluated against these data. The current test procedure is to send any requesting vendor training, test and practice data sets. The ordering of the test data image files has been randomly scrambled, but the practice images are clearly linked to their corresponding training set images. These practice images allow the vendors to tune any internal parameters our data quality or format requires. Any vendor can request testing of matching and/or binning algorithms.

For the matching test, the vendor returns a 4128×4080 matrix of comparison scores for all test prints compared to all training prints. For the binning test, the vendor returns the bin assignments for all test and training prints, and the rules by which bins are determined to be "communicating" or "noncommunicating." In large-scale AFIS system, prints in "communicating" bins are similar enough that they must be compared for possible matching. Upon receipt of all these data, we release to the vendor the "key" linking the test and training sets.

In this analysis, we used the score matrix from the "best" matching vendor tested to date, meaning the score matrix that produced generally the lowest ROC. We used the binning results from the "best" binning vendor tested to date, meaning the data that we judged presented the best trade-off between penetration and bin error rates. Binning and matching data used here were not from the same vendor. To protect the identity of the vendors, precise matching values and binning assignments are not discussed here.

15.4. Finger Dependency of Penetration Rate

It is well known that print classification statistics are finger-dependent. Table 15.1 shows classification statistics by finger from recent FBI data [8].

When each print can be classified only into a single bin, the equation for calculating penetration rate from classification statistics is given in [1] as

$$Pn = p_K + \sum_{i=1}^{K-1}(p_i + p_K)p_i \qquad (1)$$

where Pn is the penetration rate, p_i is the probability that the print is of the ith classification, and the kth classification is considered as "unknown." This equation was applied to the data of Table 15.1. Scarred fingers were considered of "unknown" classification, and the data were renormalized after removal of the amputated finger statistics. Table 15.2 shows the resulting penetration rates for this approach when fingers in each position are compared to corresponding fingers, right to right, left to left, right to left (or left to right), or all to all.

By Eq. 1, the penetration rate will generally decrease with an increasing number of classifications of nonzero probability. The five-type classification system of Table 15.1 does not represent an optimal approach by any measure, and AFIS classification algorithms do not generally use this system. Further, AFIS can place prints in multiple classifications, so the penetration rate cannot be determined from classification probabilities using Eq. 1. The values in Tables 15.1 and 15.2 simply make for an interesting comparison when testing AFIS classification algorithms.

Table 15.1. Single-Finger Classification Statistics

Pattern type	Finger position (%)										
	1	2	3	4	5	6	7	8	9	10	Avg.
Arch	3.01	6.09	4.43	1.24	0.86	5.19	6.29	5.88	1.78	1.15	3.59
Tented arch	0.40	7.72	3.20	1.03	0.72	0.58	7.96	4.53	1.45	1.10	2.87
Right loop	51.26	36.41	73.38	51.20	83.03	0.63	16.48	1.66	0.51	0.12	31.47
Left loop	0.46	16.96	1.47	1.10	0.26	58.44	39.00	70.30	61.47	86.11	33.56
Whorl	44.77	32.45	17.21	45.24	14.98	35.04	29.93	17.30	34.57	11.33	28.28
Scar	0.03	0.17	0.13	0.06	0.06	0.04	0.14	0.12	0.06	0.06	0.09
Amp	0.07	0.20	0.18	0.14	0.12	0.09	0.20	0.20	0.16	0.13	0.15
Sum	100.00	100.00	100.00	100.01	100.01	100.01	100.00	99.99	100.00	100.00	100.00

Table 15.2. Single-Finger Penetration Rates from FBI Statistics

Finger	Penetration rate			
	Right-> Right	Left-> Left	Right->Left	All -> All
Thumb	0.54	0.56	0.20	0.37
Index	0.44	0.44	0.37	0.40
Middle	0.85	0.83	0.09	0.47
Ring	0.63	0.70	0.23	0.45
Little	0.92	1.0	0.03	0.49

Table 15.3. Single-Finger Binning Error and Penetration Rates from Test Data

Finger	Error rate		Penetration rate			
	Right	Left	Right-> Right	Left-> Left	Right->Left	All -> All
Thumb	0.002	0.002	0.70	0.67	0.26	0.47
Index	0.005	0.002	0.46	0.43	0.40	0.42
Middle	0.012	0.007	0.74	0.66	0.29	0.49
Ring	0.010	0.007	0.74	0.66	0.40	0.55

To test the AFIS penetration rate, we compared the classifications of each training print to those of all other training prints. Using the vendor's rules of "communication," we calculated the percentage of all comparisons that showed communicating bins. Results were differentiated by finger. As mentioned, 409 volunteers were represented in both training and test data sets. Because of errors in the data collection process, there were only about 404 training test pairs for any particular finger. All comparisons are symmetric. Therefore, there were about $404 \times 403/2 = 81,406$ nonindependent comparisons made for the penetration rate.

The penetration-rate benefits of fingerprint classification come at the cost of classification errors. If the individual test and training prints of a matching pair are placed in noncommunicating bins, the prints will not be matched. To test bin error using the AFIS binning algorithm, we compared binning assignments for each training test pair based on the bin communication rules. There were about 404 matching pairs for each finger.

Table 15.3 shows the bin error and penetration rates individually for thumb, index, middle, and ring fingers. The binning error rate is best for thumbs and left index fingers and worst for right middle and ring fingers. None of the error rate differences between fingers is statistically significant at even the 90% confidence level.[1]

15.5. Penetration Rates of Multifinger Systems

In [1], the prediction of penetration and bin error rate performance for systems using multiple fingerprints is discussed under the assumption that the errors and penetration rates are independent. The general equation for multiple-finger penetration rate

---

[1] This is established by testing with a cumulative binomial distribution the null hypothesis that observed errors for each finger could have come from the same error probability.

can be written as

$$P_{\text{ensemble}} = \prod_{i=1}^{T} P_i \tag{2}$$

where P_i is the penetration rate of the ith finger and P_{ensemble} is the total penetration rate of the multifinger "ensemble." In reality, the binning assignments for thumb, index, middle, or ring fingers of a person are not independent but are highly positively correlated. Therefore, we would expect a true penetration rate less than that calculated from Eq. 2.

Binning error rate for the multifinger case, again under the assumption of error independence, is given in [1] by

$$1 - \varepsilon_{\text{ensemble}} = \prod_{i=1}^{T}(1 - \varepsilon_i) \tag{3}$$

where ε_i is the bin error rate of the ith finger and $\varepsilon_{\text{ensemble}}$ is the total error rate for the ensemble. If errors are positively correlated, the value $\varepsilon_{\text{ensemble}}$ of will be smaller than that calculated using 3.

Using the same AFIS binning algorithm, we tested about 404 finger pairs for left and right thumb, index, middle, and ring fingers with every other similar pair in the training data set. Again, these were symmetric comparisons, so there were about 81,406 nonindependent comparisons. Both binning errors and penetration rates were measured and are given as Table 15.4. Included in Table 15.4 are the error rates calculated from the test data in Table 15.3 by Eq. 3 under the assumption of error independence. Test and calculated error rates are identical except for the case of middle fingers. The middle finger test error rate is slightly smaller than that calculated by 3. In the test data of about 404 pairs, there were two instances of classification errors occurring on both left and right middle fingers of the same volunteer. Again, the error rate differences between fingers are not statistically significant.

Also included in Table 15.4 are the penetration rates calculated from both test and FBI data in Tables 15.2 and 15.3 by Eq. 2 under the assumption of classification independence. Test penetration rates are somewhat (10–20%) higher for all fingers than those calculated using Eq. 2 from the test data of Table 15.3, indicating some positive classification correlations between left and right fingers. Test penetration rates are also higher than calculated using 2 with the FBI data from Table 15.2, except for the middle finger.

Table 15.5 shows error and penetration rates for four-finger (both thumbs and both index) and eight-finger binning systems. While binning error rates behave as though

Table 15.4. Two-Finger Binning Statistics

Finger	Error rate	Error if independent	Penetration rate	Penetration if independent FBI data	Test data
Thumb	0.005	0.005	0.52	0.30	0.47
Index	0.007	0.007	0.25	0.19	0.20
Middle	0.015	0.019	0.55	0.71	0.49
Ring	0.017	0.017	0.55	0.44	0.49

Table 15.5. Multiple-Finger Binning Statistics

Fingers	Error rate	Error if independent	Penetration rate	Penetration if independent	
				FBI data	Test data
Four: Thumb and index	0.012	0.012	0.15	0.059	0.093
Eight: Thumb, index, middle, ring	0.040	0.048	0.08	0.018	0.022

independent, penetration rates do not. The penetration rate on the four-finger system was found to be 15%, while an assumption of finger classification independence would have led to a 9% penetration rate based on the single-finger values. The eight-finger system showed a penetration rate of 8%, with a predicted value of 2%.

15.6. ROC Curves for Communicating and Noncommunicating Impostor Comparisons

In an AFIS system, submitted fingerprints are binned and then compared only to enrolled prints placed in similar (communicating) bins. We might hypothesize that there is a greater probability for prints in communicating bins to be falsely matched than for prints in noncommunicating bins. We computed the ROC for the test fingerprints in three ways: comparing communicating impostors only; comparing noncommunicating impostors only; and comparing all impostors. Figures 15.1 and 15.2 show three ROCs each for right and left thumb comparisons. We note that the false-match rate for the communicating comparisons is almost an order of magnitude greater than for the noncommunicating comparisons at some points in the ROC.

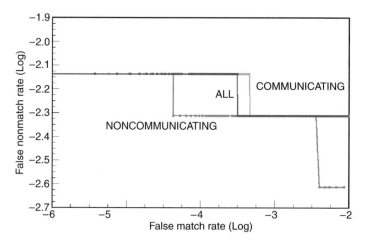

Fig. 15.1. Right thumb ROC.

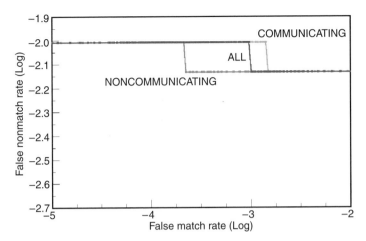

Fig. 15.2. Left thumb ROC.

15.7. Finger Dependency of ROC

Does the ROC vary depending on which finger is used? We calculated the ROC for thumbs, index, middle, and ring fingers using impostor comparisons only with the same fingers from communicating bins. For example, impostor scores for thumbs were developed by comparing right thumbs only to other right thumbs, and left thumbs only to other left thumbs, with communicating classifications. In all, about 410 genuine comparisons and between 100,000 and 200,000 impostor comparisons were made for each finger. Figures 15.3 and 15.4 show right- and left-hand ROCs for each finger

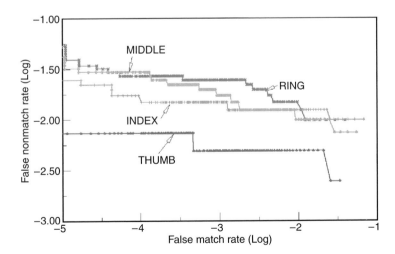

Fig. 15.3. Right-hand ROC.

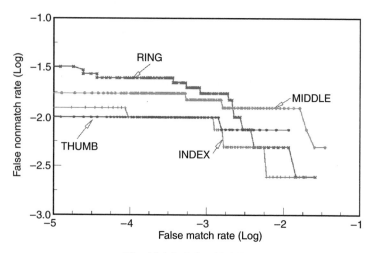

Fig. 15.4. Left-hand ROC.

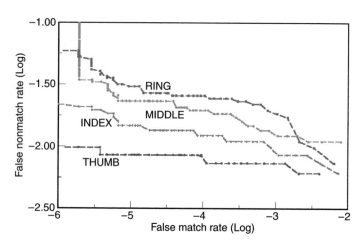

Fig. 15.5. ROC by finger.

position. Both graphs show generally increasing error rates as we move from thumbs through ring fingers.

The most notable difference between the right- and left-hand ROC curves is the difference in thumb error rates, with left thumbs showing worse performance than right thumbs. Figure 15.5 combines ROCs of both left and right for each finger position and clearly shows increasing errors as we move from thumbs through ring fingers.

We also tested to see if a correlation exists between left and right finger scores for thumb and index fingers of the individual users. Using the nonparametric Kendall's Tau test [9] over 409 volunteers with 8 fingers in both enrollment and test sets, $\tau = 0.33$ and 0.26 for thumbs and index fingers, respectively. Comparing ranks of right thumbs to right index fingers, $\tau = 0.28$. None of these measures is statistically significant at any significance level, indicating that individual users do not generally have correlated finger scores.

15.8. Impostor Distribution Variation Across Test Samples

Researchers in biometric identification talk about "sheep," "goats," "wolves," and "lambs" to indicate the variability of error rates of a specific biometric system across various users [10]. Most users are "sheep" who can use the system consistently well and are not easily impersonated. "Goats" are those users who cannot consistently be identified. "Wolves" are users who can be easily mistaken for another user in a "zero effort"[2] attack. "Lambs" are users easily preyed upon by "wolves."

In the comparison matrix, the fingerprints in the rows can be considered as attempted attacks on the fingerprints of the columns. Because we have only two samples of each finger, we cannot test for "goats," those consistently not matched to their own enrollment template. We can, however, test for "wolves" and "lambs." Because of the lack of score correlation between prints of an individual user, we have chosen to test for "wolves" and "lambs" at the single-print level. A "wolf" row will have consistently higher scores across the columns of enrollment prints, not considering, of course, the genuinely matching enrollment image, while a "lamb" column will have higher scores across the rows. Again, we limited our comparisons to prints in communicating bins. Therefore, for each row we summed the scores across all columns that communicated with the row print, and for each column we summed scores across the rows. Because the number of communicating comparisons will vary, these results must be normalized against the number of comparison scores used for each "wolf" row or "lamb" column. This produces the mean communicating impostor score.

If the comparison matrix were symmetric, each "wolf" row mean would be identical to the matching print's "lamb" column mean. The comparison matrix is not symmetric, however, for two reasons. First, the prints represented in the columns are images acquired at a different time from the prints represented in the rows. Second, fingerprint comparison scores are not symmetric. The score of the comparison of print A to print B is generally not equal to the score of the comparison of print B to print A. Therefore, we computed both the row and the column sums.

Using a one-way analysis of variance [11], we tested the null hypothesis that all the communicating scores in the matrix came from the same distribution against the opposing hypothesis that the distribution was row-dependent. Combining results for right and left thumbs, 1,420 thumbs were in about 336,000 communicating comparisons . The "F" statistic was calculated at 6.7, which is much larger than the critical value of nearly 1 for this number of "degrees of freedom." Thus, the alternate hypothesis was accepted. This shows that there are "wolves."

Then we repeated this test for column dependency in the thumb data, calculating the "F" statistic as 9.0, with 1,437 columns in about 278,000 comparisons. We again

---

[2] The term "zero effort attack" means that the attack is passive and does not involve active efforts at impersonation.

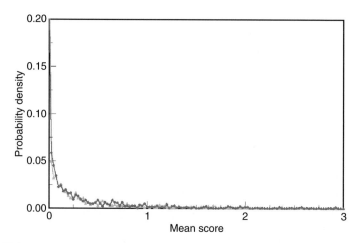

Fig. 15.6. Mean communicating thumb inpostor score probability distribution function.

accept the alternate hypothesis that the data are column-dependent, showing that there are also "lamb" fingerprints.

Figure 15.6 shows a histogram of the mean row impostor thumb scores. Also graphed is the histogram of the mean column thumb scores. Because these distributions are nearly identical, they are not individually labeled. If all the means were nearly identical, Fig. 15.6 would show a sharp spike. If there were strictly "sheep" and "wolves," there would be two spikes, one at a low and one at a high score value. Figure 15.6 shows both "lamb" and "wolf" distributions to be smoothly spread. This indicates that there are "sheep" and "wolves," and "sheep" and "lambs," but the boundary between them is not well defined.

Figure 15.7 shows the same study done on index fingerprints. Results are seen to be the same. Analysis of variance of the index finger rows gave an "F" statistic of 7.5. The "F" statistic for index finger columns was 10.1. With the 1,420 relevant rows or columns and the 232,000 communicating comparisons, both of these "F" statistics are significant at all reasonable significance levels.

The existence of lambs and wolves calls into question the suitability of system false-match error rate equations [1] based on the assumption that all stored templates have the same probability of being falsely matched. Equations of the type

$$\text{FMR}_{\text{sys}} = 1 - (1 - \text{FM})^N \qquad (4)$$

where FMR_{sys} is the system false match rate, FM is the false match rate of a single comparison (assumed to be uniform), and N is the number of stored templates, should be more reasonably replaced with the form

$$\text{FMR}_{\text{sys}} = 1 - \prod_{i=1}^{N}(1 - \text{FM}_i) \qquad (5)$$

yielding higher estimates for the system false-match rate, FMR_{sys}, if $\text{FM}_i \neq \text{constant}$.

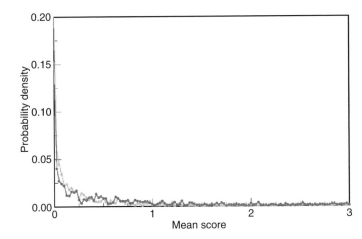

Fig. 15.7. Mean communicating index impostor score probability distribution function.

15.9. Conclusions

We can make the following conclusions:

1. ROCs developed from images in communicating bins show worse performance than those developed without consideration of the binning.
2. Thumbs have lower binning and comparison error rates, but index fingers have better penetration rate.
3. Both binning and comparison error rates increase as we move from thumb, through index, to ring fingers.
4. Because of pattern correlations across individual users, penetration rates for multiple-finger systems cannot be accurately estimated from single-finger penetration rates.
5. Matching scores and binning errors are not correlated across the fingers in the general individual user.
6. "Wolves" and "lambs" exist, but there is a gradual transition between sheep and these populations.
7. The existence of population variability in error rates calls into question the validity of system false-match rate equations based on the assumption that error probabilities are consistent across the population.

References

1. Wayman, J.L., Error rate equations for the general biometric system, *IEEE Robotics and Automation Magazine*, March 1999.
2. Wayman, J.L., A scientific approach to evaluating biometric systems using a mathematical methodology, *Proc. CTST'97*, pp. 477–492, 1997.

3. Wayman, J.L., Benchmarking large-scale biometric system: Issues and feasibility, *Proc. CTST Government'97*, Sept. 1997.
4. Wayman, J.L., The science of biometric technologies: Testing, classifying, evaluating, *Proc. CTST'97*, pp. 385–394, 1997.
5. Wayman, J.L., Testing and evaluating biometric technologies: What the customer needs to know, *Proc. CTST'98*, pp. 385–394, 1998.
6. Wayman, J.L., A generalized biometric identification system model, *Proc. of the IEEE Asilomar Conference on Signals, Systems, and Computers*, Nov. 1997.
7. Wayman, J. L., Technical testing and evaluation of biometric devices, in A. Jain et al., eds. *Biometrics: Information Security in a Networked Society*, New York: Kluwer Academic Press, 1999.
8. Unpublished 1995 report by Frank Torpey of Mitre Corporation using data extracted from the FBI's Identification Division Automated Services database of 22 million human-classified fingerprint records.
9. Press, W.H. et al., *Numerical Recipes in C*, 2nd ed., New York: Cambridge University Press, 1992.
10. Doddington, G. et al., Sheep, goats, lambs and wolves: An analysis of individual differences in speaker recognition performance, ICSLP'98, Sidney, Australia, Nov. 1998.
11. Edwards, A.L., *Experimental Design in Psychological Research*, 4th ed., New York: Holt, Reinhart, and Winston, 1972.

Chapter 16

Latent Fingerprint Analysis Using an AM-FM Model

Marios Pattichis and Alan Bovik

Abstract. We adapt a novel AM-FM (amplitude-modulation, frequency-modulation) image representation to process latent fingerprint images. The AM-FM representation captures, in a very natural way, the global flow of fingerprint patterns. Discontinuities in this flow are easily detectable as potential fingerprint minutiae. We demonstrate application of an AM-FM-based system to actual latent fingerprints and make comparison to expert human analysis.

16.1. Introduction

The problem of classifying, analyzing and recognizing latent fingerprints is a difficult task that currently requires the service of highly trained human experts [1, 2]. In particular, the identification of latent fingerprints (lifted from the actual scene of a crime, as opposed to ink-rolled fingerprints) is a challenging goal that requires special skills and training in finding, developing, enhancing and, especially, in analyzing the latent fingerprints. Recently, the availability of high-speed computing, database and networking technologies, and increasingly sophisticated image processing methods have increased the topical significance of research into the development of Automatic Fingerprint Identification Systems (AFIS). Most of this work has been applied to 10-print and single-print identification/classification, usually employing optimal or adaptive classifiers, such as artificial neural networks (ANNs) [3, 4]. However, very little work has been reported on the automated identification of latent prints, which present special challenges due to the unpredictability of latent fingerprint quality, the variability of fingerprint conditions, and the sheer size of the potential database comparison.

Progress in developing digital systems for latent fingerprint identification and analysis has been slow, although it is desirable to develop systems that assist law enforcement agencies in identifying latent prints in a timely manner, and under a variety of conditions, and even in the field. Until now, fingerprint analysis systems have invariably been designed to operate on digitized fingerprint images without first physically modeling these images. Generally, these have utilized standard image processing or pattern recognition techniques, such as edge detection and ridge following [5].

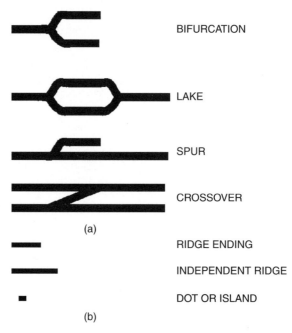

BIFURCATION

LAKE

SPUR

CROSSOVER

(a)

RIDGE ENDING

INDEPENDENT RIDGE

DOT OR ISLAND

(b)

Fig. 16.1. FBI models for minutiae points. In (a), we have minutiae points associated with ridge splitting. In (b), we have minutiae points associated with ridge breaks.

Currently, no existing system uses physical models of the morphogenic processes giving rise to the fingerprint pattern. For example, an important study that we are looking into would be to develop a model based on reaction diffusion (RD) partial differential equations (RD-PDEs), which successfully describe biological morphogenesis and the natural pattern formation, such as, the stripes on a zebra, etc. [6–9]. Interestingly, the solutions of certain RD-PDEs have the form of AM-FM functions [9].

In this chapter, we model fingerprints as AM-FM functions and use these models to extract minutiae points. Minutiae points are topological points where ridges terminate, bifurcate into two ridges, bifurcate into a short and a long ridge, sometimes reuniting into another ridge, or crossover into another ridge [2] (see Fig. 16.1). Thus, minutiae points are the result of local changes in the ridge structure. In certain cases, it is well understood that minutiae points arise due to the physical constraints of the underlying morphogenic process that is responsible for the pattern formation [10].

For example, at bifurcation points, the local ridge separation (which can be thought of as an instantaneous wavelength) undergoes an abrupt change. However, in the vicinity of the minutiae point, the ridge has grown in such a way as to preserve continuity of the ridges. This local–global characteristic of the fingerprint pattern flow is effectively captured using the AM-FM image model.

We develop and test our model on a unique, real-life digitized latent fingerprint that was acquired (courtesy of agent Tom Hopper) from the FBI latent fingerprint lab at FBI Headquarters in Quantico, VA (Fig. 16.2). More recently, the NIST-27 latent fingerprint database has been available, but this database was not available to us at

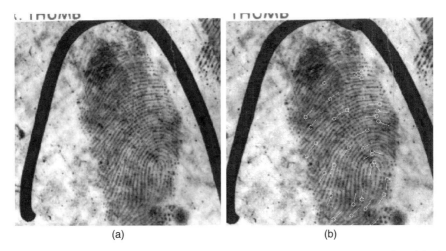

(a)   (b)

Fig. 16.2. The original latent print and the identified minutiae points. In (a), we show the original latent print. In (b), we show the original minutiae as labeled by an FBI team of latent-fingerprint experts. Note the large ink variations in upper-left part of the print. Such ink variations obscure the underlying fingerprint structure.

the time of our study [24]. The particular latent fingerprint that we used is particularly challenging since it does not maintain much continuity along its ridges, making the task of identifying minutiae points particularly demanding. As a basis of comparison, we do have the minutiae points identified by the FBI latent fingerprint team. As it was explained to us, latent fingerprints present challenging aspects, and hence usually not all of the minutiae points are agreed upon by all experts. Likewise, any automated algorithm that is developed is unlikely to deliver results identical to any particular expert. This, a system such as the one we describe here must be regarded as a tool for semi-automated expert analysis, perhaps supplying candidate minutiae points for expert verification, thus speeding the analysis process.

We organize the rest of the chapter into five sections. In Section 16.2, we introduce the AM-FM image expansion and then develop a simplified AM-FM expansion for fingerprint images. In Section 16.3, we show how the extracted AM-FM image representation can be used to segment the latent fingerprint from the background. In Section 16.4, we develop AM-FM techniques for detecting potential fingerprint minutiae points from the extracted AM-FM representation. In Section 16.4.4, we present and summarize the results of the various minutiae extraction algorithms. The chapter concludes with Section 16.5.

16.2. An AM-FM Model for Fingerprints

We model the fingerprint image as a product $I(x_1, x_2) = a(x_1, x_2) f(\phi_1(x_1, x_2), \phi_2(x_1, x_2))$, where $a(x_1, x_2)$ denotes a slowly varying amplitude function that is used to capture variations in the maximum (ridge peak) and minimum (ridge valley) fingerprint intensities. The new curvilinear coordinate system $(x_1, x_2) \rightarrow$

$(\phi_1(x_1, x_2), \phi_2(x_1, x_2))$ is used for describing the image intensity variation along the ridge orientation $\phi_1(x_1, x_2)$, and the constant image intensity along the ridges $\phi_2(x_1, x_2)$. It is important to note that the two curvilinear coordinates introduced here will be continuous away from most minutiae points and corrupted ink areas. However, these discontinuities can be incorporated into the coordinate transformation. We next comment on the curvilinear coordinate system and use it to derive an AM-FM series expansion for the fingerprint.

Along the ϕ_2-coordinate curve, we expect that the image intensity of $I(x_1, x_2)/a(x_1, x_2)$ remains constant. We express the image intensity as only a function of the first curvilinear coordinate:

$$f(\phi_1(x_1, x_2), \phi_2(x_1, x_2)) = f(\phi_1(x_1, x_2))$$

by abuse of notation. We note that we can always approximate $\phi_2(x_1, x_2)$ for any image by simply solving $I(x_1, x_2) = C$ for different values for C. For example, in ridge extraction, valleys are described by ϕ_2 coordinate curves for which $I(x_1, x_2) = C_{min}$, while peaks are described by ϕ_2-coordinate curves for which $I(x_1, x_2) = C_{max}$.

For the second set of coordinate curves, we consider ϕ_1-curves that are orthogonal to the ridge curves. By definition, a curve S is orthogonal to a set of coordinate curves if at every image point the tangent vector of S is orthogonal to the tangent vector of the coordinate curve through the same point. In the NIST standard, examples of such curves are computed by following the ridge orientation vectors. By definition, for any image, $\nabla I(x_1, x_2)$ will always be orthogonal to the $I(x_1, x_2) = C$ curves, and hence will approximate the ϕ_1-curves.

Along the ϕ_1-coordinate, we meet a peak, a valley, followed by another peak, a valley, and so on. We assume that the peaks and valleys will recur at the same slowly varying maximum and minimum intensity levels, where the amplitude function $a(x_1, x_2)$ is used to capture the variation. Under this assumption, we can provide the scale of the ϕ_1-coordinate to be proportional to the change in image intensity $\delta\phi_1 = \alpha\|\delta I\|$ for some constant α. For example, in wavelength units, the distance between a valley and a peak is 0.5, while the distance between any two valleys is 1.0. It is unrealistic to expect that the image intensity between peaks will follow a nice sinusoidal pattern. Instead, we only assume that the image intensity values repeat themselves from peak to peak, so that if $T = 2\pi$ denotes the normalized period, we have the important approximation: $f(\phi_1(x_1, x_2) + T) \approx f(\phi_1(x_1, x_2))$.

Using this approximation, we arrive at a Fourier series expansion approximation for f:

$$f(\phi_1, \phi_2) \approx \sum_n H_n \exp[jn\phi_1]$$

Then, for $I(x_1, x_2)$, we have

$$I(x_1, x_2) \approx a(x_1, x_2) \sum_n H_n \exp[jn\phi(x_1, x_2)]$$

where the subscript has been dropped from the phase function.

16.3. Extracting the Dominant AM-FM Fingerprint Component

In this section, we describe methods for (1) extracting the fundamental AM-FM component of a latent fingerprint and (2) computing AM-FM parameters that are useful for analyzing the fingerprint, and (3) we develop an algorithm that uses the AM-FM parameters to segment the fundamental component from the background of the fingerprint. The computed AM-FM parameters prove useful later in the chapter.

16.3.1. Dominant Component Analysis

Here we summarize the dominant component analysis (DCA) algorithm, which has been carefully developed elsewhere [11–14]. In the current application, the DCA is actually applied twice. In the first application, it is used to obtain an estimate of the distribution of instantaneous frequencies in the fingerprint image. This is used to design an isotropic bandpass filter that captures the main fingerprint region. DCA is then applied again on the bandpass-filtered image to obtain improved AM-FM estimates. The entire AM-FM analysis system has been summarized in Fig. 16.3, where we summarize the various stages of the system and also reference the associated figures and sections in the text.

The DCA algorithm comprises several steps, as follows. First, the fingerprint image I is passed through a bank of Gabor (bandpass) channel filters $g_1, g_2, \ldots, g_M$, yielding output images $t_1, t_2, \ldots, t_M$, satisfying $t_i = I^*g$, where * is convolution. We use the same standard Gabor filter bank as described in several other sources on AM-FM analysis [11, 14, 15, 22].

Let $G_1, G_2, \ldots, G_M$ denote the frequency responses of the Gabor channel filters. Using the *quasi-eigenfunction approximation (QEA)* [11, 14, 15, 22], the filter outputs are approximately given by $t_i(\mathbf{x}) \cong a(\mathbf{x})|G_i[\omega(\mathbf{x})]| \exp\{j\phi(\mathbf{x}) + j\angle G_i[\omega(\mathbf{x})]\}$, where $\omega(\mathbf{x}) = \nabla\phi(\mathbf{x})$.

The Gabor filters are "noncausally" sampled so as to preserve their circular symmetry and obtain $\angle G_i = 0$ for all channel filters. Furthermore, the Gabor filters are arranged to cover the entire frequency plane while intersecting at points no lower than

---

Step 1. Apply bandpass filter to isolate fundamental AM-FM harmonic (see Figs. 16.4–16.6, Section 16.3.1).

Step 2. Apply dominant component analysis to estimate AM-FM model (see Figs. 16.7, 16.8, Section 16.3.1)

Step 3. Apply fingerprint segmentation algorithm (see Figs. 16.9–16.11, Section 16.3.3).

Step 4. Apply zero-amplitude (ZAMP) (see Figs. 16.12, 16.15, Section 16.4.1), Low-instantaneous frequency (LIF) magnitude (see Figs. 16.13, 16.16, Section 16.4.2), and high-instantaneous frequency (HIF) magnitude (see Figs. 16.14, 16.17, Section 16.4.3) models to detect minutiae points (also see Fig. 16.18).

Fig. 16.3. An outline of the AM-FM system for latent fingerprint image analysis.

half the peak response of any channel filter. For the demodulation to be successful, we assume that at each pixel only one of the Gabor channels G_j yields a maximizing response $|G_i(\omega)| > |G_j(\omega)|$ for $u \neq j$. Estimates of the AM-FM functions can then be obtained from each channel, using [11–14]

$$\omega(\mathbf{x}) \cong \hat{\omega}_i(\mathbf{x}) = \text{Real} \left\{ \frac{\nabla t_i(\mathbf{x})}{j t_i(\mathbf{x})} \right\}$$

$$\phi(\mathbf{x}) \cong \hat{\phi}_i(\mathbf{x}) = \arctan \left\{ \frac{\text{Imaginary}\{t_i(\mathbf{x})\}}{\text{Real}\{t_i(\mathbf{x})\}} \right\}$$

Using the instantaneous frequency estimate $\hat{\omega}_i(\mathbf{x})$, we can estimate the AM function using

$$a(\mathbf{x}) \cong \hat{a}_i(\mathbf{x}) = \left| \frac{t_i(\mathbf{x})}{G_i[\hat{\omega}_i(\mathbf{x})]} \right|$$

As estimates are obtained from every channel, we should either combine the estimates into a more reliable one or select the estimate that is most robust. Over most of the latent fingerprint region, we expect the emergent AM-FM component Fig. 16.10 to elicit the strongest response among the Gabor channels at each pixel. A theoretical analysis that supports the use of this algorithm has been described elsewhere [11–13]. Hence at each coordinate the Gabor channel with the maximum response

$$c_{\max}(\mathbf{x}) = \underset{i}{\text{argmax}} \left| \frac{t_i(\mathbf{x})}{G_i(\hat{\omega}_i)} \right|$$

is used to provide the initial estimates for the dominant AM-FM fingerprint component. This concludes the brief description of DCA, which is applied to the fingerprint image.

We then use this initial estimate to design a bandpass filter for isolating the dominant component and improving our estimate. The bandpass filter is designed with passband cutoff frequencies that are taken from the histogram of the image instantaneous frequencies computed by the DCA algorithm, as depicted in Fig. 16.4. For the fingerprints that we have encountered, the instantaneous frequency histogram is invariably multimodal, with the lowest and largest modes being due to low-frequency ink variations and background variation. The upper band limit of the bandpass filter is taken to be beyond any of the apparent modes, while the lower band limit is taken just outside the large low-frequency mode. Currently, the selection of these two frequency thresholds is accomplished manually, which is one of two places in the algorithm where interactive participation is required (both involving threshold selection).

The bandpass filter was designed in Matlab by using a 511-point windowed approximation of an ideal one-dimensional prototype [constructed using **Matlab's fir1(.)** command] and extended to be a two-dimensional circularly symmetric filter [using **Matlab's ftrans2(.)** command], as shown in Figs. 16.5 and 16.6. For the passband, the innermost radius was set to 0.050π rad, and the outermost radius was set to 0.420π rad. The bandpass filter is then applied to the latent fingerprint image and, finally, DCA is applied to the resulting bandpass-filtered image, as shown in Fig. 16.7b and 16.8.

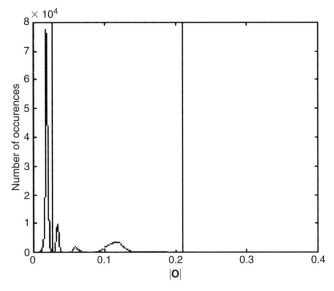

Fig. 16.4. The distribution of the instantaneous frequency magnitude. When |**O**| is less than the low threshold, we assume that this value is due to low ink variations, not due to the fundamental AM-FM component. When |**O**| is more than the high threshold, we assume that this value is due to noise, scars, or other AM-FM harmonics. So, we bandpass filter within the two thresholds.

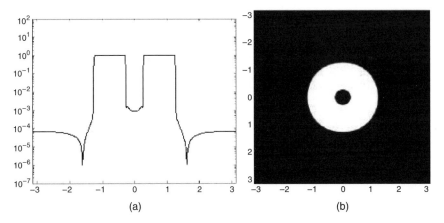

Fig. 16.5. The design of a bandpass filter for selecting the fundamental harmonic. In (a), we show the frequency response of the one-dimensional prototype. In (b), we show the frequency response over the entire two-dimensional frequency plane.

16.3.2. Estimating the Global AM-FM Parameters

We now describe methods of estimating the AM-FM parameters required for the minutiae extraction algorithms. The values of all the parameters are given in this

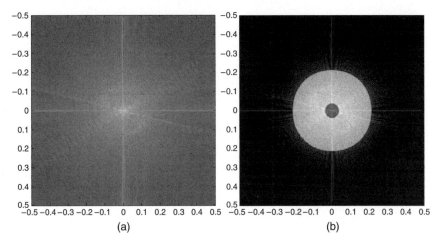

Fig. 16.6. Bandpass filtering results. In (a), we show the log-amplitude plot of the FFT of the original image. In (b), we show the log-amplitude plot of the FFT of the bandpassed image.

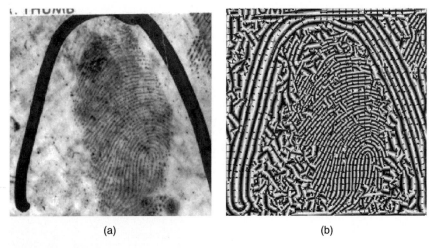

Fig. 16.7. The computation of the first AM-FM harmonic. After bandpass-filtering the image, computed AM-FM image appears to be the fundamental harmonic. On the AM-FM image, we plot the subsampled instantaneous frequency vectors (only one every 16 pixels is shown).

section. AM-FM parameters that are used include a_{min}, which is the minimum value of $a(\mathbf{x})$ assumed to be associated with the dominant fingerprint component; ω_{min} and ω_{max}, which are the minimum and maximum instantaneous frequency magnitudes associated with the fingerprint dominant component; and λ, the average number of pixels in a perpendicular distance between neighboring ridges. Values of $a(\mathbf{x}) < a_{min}$ and $\omega(\mathbf{x}) < \omega_{min}$ are assumed to be associated with areas external to the fingerprint (background), while values $\omega(\mathbf{x}) > \omega_{max}(\mathbf{x})$ are assumed to be associated with minutiae, noise, or other sudden occurrences.

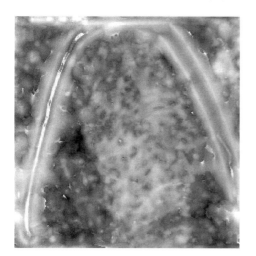

Fig. 16.8. The estimated amplitude image. The results are for the bandpass image. The amplitude values were first clipped to a maximum of 60, and then the logarithm of the result was taken.

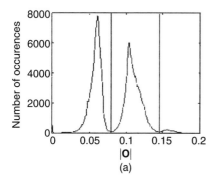 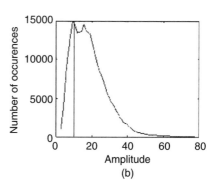

(a)   (b)

Fig. 16.9. Computation of the amplitude and instantaneous frequency magnitude thresholds based on the distribution of their values. The results shown here are for the image after it has been bandpassed. In (a), we show the vertical lines that define what we interpret as the instantaneous frequency magnitude of the main fingerprint area. They correspond to local minima. The values are at $f = 0.080$ and $f = 0.145$ cycles per unit image distance. In (b), we show the distribution of the amplitude. The vertical line goes through the value of 9.86. It corresponds to a local maximum. We consider everything to the left of 9.86 as near-zero amplitude, while everything to the right of 9.86 is taken as nonzero amplitude.

The steps involved in finding the parameters a_{min}, ω_{min}, and ω_{max} are as follows. (See also Fig. 16.9.) The values ω_{min} and ω_{max} denote the instantaneous frequency magnitude bounds of the main fingerprint distribution. We have observed that the instantaneous frequency distribution falls into three bins: one corresponding to low frequencies associated with the background; another associated with high frequencies arising from noise, minutiae, and discontinuities; and a middle mode, associated with the main fingerprint distribution. In our current implementation the middle mode is marked by the two thresholds ω_{min} and ω_{max} corresponding to the between-mode local minima, as shown in the figure. These are found interactively, although it is likely that this step could be automated. The values found there are $\omega_{min} = 0.08$ and $\omega_{max} = 0.145$. Within this range, we computed the average (mean) instantaneous frequency magnitude, returning a value of 0.125. The reciprocal of this we take to be $\lambda \approx 8$. We take the threshold a_{min}, the zero-amplitude threshold, simply to be the first steep peak of the amplitude distribution (also see Fig. 16.9b).

16.3.3. Latent Fingerprint Segmentation

Given an arbitrary image of a latent print, only a portion of it will correspond to the actual fingerprint region. The rest of the image will correspond to the background, which in a latent print could contain just about any kind of markings. The analysis is thus improved if we are able to segment the latent print from its background.

In most situations, for example, as in Fig. 16.7, the background will contain relatively low instantaneous frequencies compared to the print region. We also observe that in most situations, the latent fingerprint region will occupy a connected, contiguous region, although there might be exceptions in difficult prints. The amplitude image is shown in Fig. 16.8. For the amplitude image, we note the strong amplitude estimates at the arches of the fingerprint. These are due to the amplitude modulation resulting from the large contrast of the arch against the background. On the other hand, the uniform background between the arch and the fingerprint results in lower amplitude estimates.

Segmentation of the fingerprint region is accomplished as follows. A bi-valued (zero–one, or indicator) image is created, taking value 0 wherever $\omega(\mathbf{x}) < \omega_{min}$, and

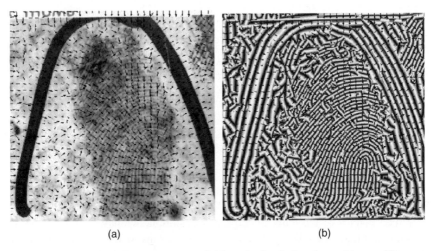

(a)   (b)

Fig. 16.10. Instantaneous frequency vector field results for the bandpassed image. The vector field has been subsampled to show 1 vector every 16 pixels. In (a), we show the instantaneous vector field over the original image. In (b), we show the instantaneous vector field over the FM image $I(x_1, x_2) = \cos\phi(x_1, x_2)$.

value 1 elsewhere. Since thresholding errors are inevitable, we then smooth the resulting binary image using morphological operators. First, the image is smoothed by applying an *open-close(.)* operation using a circularly symmetric window or structuring element having a diameter of 2λ. The result is then smoothed with another *open-close(.)* operator, this time of diameter 4λ. The largest 8-connected region covering values of 1 is then taken to be the fingerprint region. If this region contains any holes, they are removed. Identification of the largest fingerprint area and removal of holes are accomplished using basic connected components analysis [23]. As shown in Fig. 16.11, this algorithm produces a good approximation to the actual latent fingerprint region.

16.4. AM-FM Analysis of Minutiae Points

The principal goal of our latent fingerprint analysis method is the identification of possible minutiae that could be used for print identification. No claim is made here that the points found are true minutiae, or that the approach given here could eventually lead to a replacement for expert human analysts. These are probably not possible goals in the near-term time horizon, since minutiae points are often quite subtle occurrences that are difficult for even trained experts to characterize in a completely quantitative way. Rather, we view the system described here as the basis for a possible semi-automated analysis tool that could be used as a digital assistant to the expert. However, we believe that our technique could be automated to work with "cleaner" images such as rolled fingerprints.

The algorithms described next for finding potential minutiae points are applied only to the segmented fingerprint region. To develop models for minutiae points, we focus on how the location of a minutiae point reflects changes in the ridges and the local instantaneous frequency structure of the fingerprint. Figure 16.11 depicts the types of minutiae points ordinarily studied. There appear to be two general, distinct types of minutiae points requiring different approaches: (1) minutiae points associated with ridge splitting or bifurcation points; and (2) minutiae points associated with ridge breaks or terminations.

Hence we develop models of ridge bifurcation points and ridge terminations. In fact, these types of points are closely related, since there is a duality between fingerprint ridges and fingerprint valleys. The ridges (valleys) of a fingerprint $I(\mathbf{x})$ are actually the valleys (ridges) of its negative $-I(\mathbf{x})$. Likewise, it is clear that a ridge bifurcation corresponds to valley terminations, and ridge terminations occur at valley bifurcations. As $I(\mathbf{x})$ and $-I(\mathbf{x})$ share the same instantaneous frequency magnitudes, we can use a single-frequency modulation model to detect minutiae points associated with bifurcations and terminations.

We note that minutiae points characterize local phenomena (Figs. 16.12–16.14). Away from minutiae points, the average number of pixels between the ridges has a strong tendency to remain relatively constant. At occurrences of minutiae points (ridge/valley bifurcations), either (1) the amplitude tends to zero or (2) the instantaneous frequency magnitude tends to be either larger or smaller than the average over

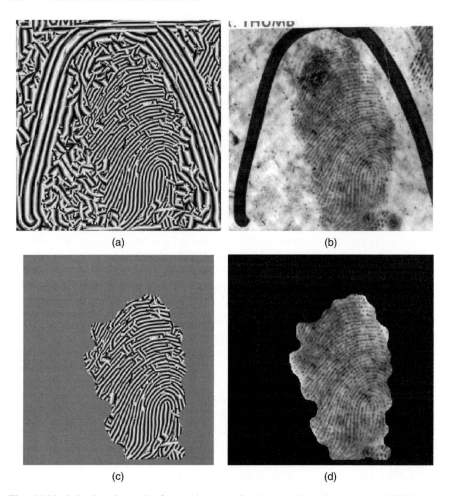

Fig. 16.11. Selecting the main fingerprint area. In (a), we show the computed FM-image $I(x_1, x_2) = \cos\phi(x_1, x_2)$. In (b), we show the original latent fingerprint. In (c), we show the selected main area of the FM image. In (d), we show the selected main area of the latent fingerprint.

the fingerprint. This happens because the ridge density spatially adjusts on a highly localized basis. We have developed three models for describing minutiae points.

The zero-amplitude model (ZAMP) find points where the amplitude $a(\mathbf{x})$ falls nearly to, or to, zero. A numerical simulation of how this happens is given in Figs. 16.12a–c. In Fig. 16.12b, the instantaneous frequency is kept constant throughout the image. Yet, the right half of the image is "delayed" by half a period with respect to the left half of the image. As a result, a near-zero amplitude around the bifurcation point allows the transition to occur smoothly. The ZAMP algorithm is described in Section 16.4.1.

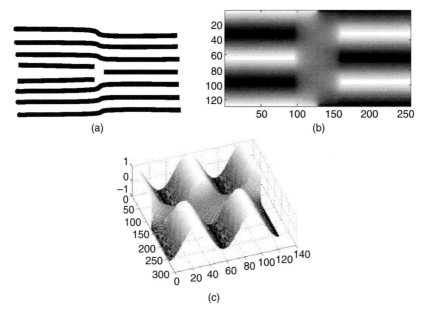

(a)   (b)

(c)

Fig. 16.12. The zero-amplitude model. In this model, the distance between the ridges remains relatively constant. In (b) and (c), a simulation of what happens at the bifurcation point is shown. The simulated image was prepared in three steps. First, the left half of the image was created by a unit amplitude sinusoid [see (b) and (c)]. Second, the right half of the image was created by delaying the left sinusoid by half a period. Third, in the center of the image, around the bifurcation point, all the pixels were removed, and their intensity values were interpolated from the surrounding pixels (using Matlab's roifill() function). In (b) and (c), we see that the interpolated pixels (around the bifurcation point) maintain very low amplitude without any noticeable oscillation. For the location of the bifurcation point, we look for the point with the minimum amplitude.

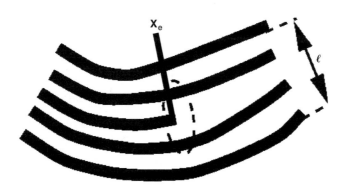

Fig. 16.13. The instantaneous wavelength $\lambda(\cdot)$ is maximized at the ridge ending $\mathbf{X}_e$. At this point, the instantaneous frequency magnitude is minimized.

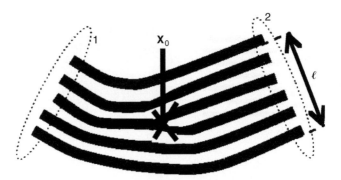

Fig. 16.14. At the bifurcation point, there is a "jump" in the instantaneous wavelength. We use the fact that $\lambda(\cdot)$ is minimized at the bifurcation point $\mathbf{X}_0$. At this point, the instantaneous frequency magnitude is maximized.

The idea behind the low-instantaneous frequency (LIF) model is demonstrated in Fig. 16.13. A ridge ending yields a smaller instantaneous frequency magnitude at a ridge termination (valley bifurcation) minutiae point (around coordinate $\mathbf{x}_e$). At the sudden ridge ending $\mathbf{x}_e$, the region immediately to the right of $\mathbf{x}_e$ has fewer ridges/valleys within a small area. Away from $\mathbf{x}_e$, the ridge density returns to the average value in all directions. Because the number or ridges/valleys per unit length (in the direction orthogonal to the ridges) coincides with the local instantaneous frequency magnitude, it may be seen that the instantaneous frequency magnitude will fall to a local minimum near $\mathbf{x}_e$.

Similarly, the high-instantaneous frequency (HIF) magnitude model is demonstrated in Fig. 16.13 for a bifurcation point. To the right of the bifurcation point $\mathbf{x}_o$, the ridge/valleys density locally increases compared with regions away from $\mathbf{x}_o$. Furthermore, there are more ridges/valleys per unit length in the direction orthogonal to the ridges; hence the instantaneous frequency magnitude will rise to a local maximum at $\mathbf{x}_o$.

The astute reader will, of course, recognize that the LIF and HIF models are duals of one another. A sudden increase in instantaneous frequency due to a ridge bifurcation should, ideally, be accompanied by a sudden decrease in instantaneous frequency due to the equally present valley termination. In other words, there should be local occurrences of both lower-than-average and higher-than-average instantaneous frequencies at ordinary latent fingerprint minutiae points. We choose to use both modes separately, however, because of to the imperfect structure of fingerprints.

The algorithms based on the LIF and HIF models are described in Sections 16.4.2 and 16.4.3, respectively. We also present results of the algorithms in these sections.

16.4.1. The Zero-Amplitude Model (ZAMP)

The ZAMP algorithm seeks points within the segmented fingerprint where the measured AM function falls below a threshold level: $a(\mathbf{x}) < a_{\min}$. As such points might be clustered, some additional processing other than thresholding is involved, as described next.

Let $\mathbf{Q}$ denote the segmented fingerprint region. Given a threshold level $a_{\min}$ (the same one used in the segmentation module has been found to suffice), identify the set of coordinates where the amplitude is low: $S = \{\mathbf{x} \in \mathbf{Q} : a(\mathbf{x}) < a_{\min}\}$. Naturally, not all points in S correspond to distinct minutiae points. Rather, minutiae points will fall within neighborhoods of low-amplitude points. Assuming that minutiae points are well separated, which they ordinarily are, then we can expect the algorithm to return some number M of separate image regions S_i, $i = 1, 2, \ldots, M$, each corresponding to a separate minutiae point and associated low-amplitude neighborhood, and such that $S = S_1 \cup S_2 \cup \cdots \cup S_M$.

Of course, not all of the S_i, $i = 1, 2, \ldots, M$, will correspond to valid minutiae points, due to fingerprint variations, smears or breaks in the latent print, errors in recording the fingerprint, etc. To reject noisy components, we use an area constraint to reject very large or very small regions S_i. All regions S_i containing fewer than $\lambda^2/20$ pixels are removed as likely arising from noise. Likewise, regions containing more than $\lambda^2/8$ pixels are also removed, since they may correspond to large smeared regions where the AM-FM model will poorly match the print, and the estimated AM component might be small. We note that such large regions are relatively rare. The region size thresholds $\lambda^2/20$ and $\lambda^2/8$ were determined empirically.

Suppose that M^* regions S_i^*, $i = 1, 2, \ldots, M^*$, remain following the removal of the too-large and too-small regions. Then, for each S_i^*, extract the coordinates of the point having the minimum amplitude:

$$\mathbf{x} = \operatorname*{argmin}_{\mathbf{x} \in S_i^*} a(\mathbf{x}), \, i = 1, 2, \ldots, M^*$$

In the latent fingerprint shown in Fig. 16.15, the ZAMP algorithm detects six minutiae points (including the core point within the innermost ridge). Out of the six minutiae points, three closely agree with the minutiae points determined by human experts, while two appear to be good candidates to be minutiae points (yet were not picked in this noisy latent print). This is not meant to imply that they are missed minutiae, but rather that they are points of potential interest to an expert latent fingerprint interpreter. Finally, the potential minutiae plotted at the upper left appears likely to be a faulty detection.

16.4.2. Low-Instantaneous Frequency Model (LIF)

In this algorithm we use the same instantaneous frequency parameter, $\omega_{\min}$, used in the segmentation approach. Overall, the LIF algorithm for detecting low-instantaneous frequency magnitude minutiae is quite similar to the zero-amplitude minutiae algorithm. First, all points having sufficiently low-instantaneous frequency magnitude are found: $R = \{\mathbf{x} \in \mathbf{Q} : \omega(\mathbf{x}) < \omega_{\min}\}$, and $R = R_1 \cup R_2 \cup \cdots \cup R_P$, where the R_i, $i = 1, 2, \ldots, P$, are separate and distinct region components. Then, as in the ZAMP algorithm, too-small regions of areas less than $\lambda^2/12$ pixels are removed

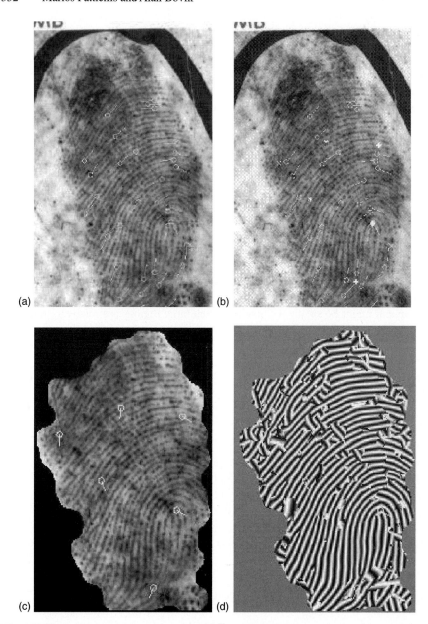

Fig. 16.15. Minutiae results for the low-amplitude model. In (a), we show the original minutiae as labeled by an FBI team of latent fingerprint experts. In (b), we show the low-amplitude minutiae together with the FBI minutiae. There are three low-amplitude minutiae points that match the FBI minutiae (plotted using +). Note that the core point (second from below) was correctly detected with re-assuring accuracy. There are two low-amplitude minutiae that appear to correspond to possible minutiae that were not picked as legitimate minutiae points (plotted using *). There is one minutiae point that is definitely a false detection (plotted using x). In (c), we show all the detected minutiae points plotted on the original print. In (d), we show all the detected minutiae points plotted on the FM print.

as are, all components that contain any pixels with low amplitude (less than a_{min}). This ensures that we do not detect any duplicate minutiae points, namely, points detected by the ZAMP algorithm. For each of the remaining region components R_i^*, $i = 1, 2, \ldots, P^*$, the algorithm returns the coordinates of the point having the least instantaneous frequency magnitude:

$$\mathbf{y_i} = \arg \min_{\mathbf{x} \in R_i^*} \omega(\mathbf{x}), i = 1, 2, \ldots, P^*$$

These coordinates are taken to be potential low-instantaneous frequency minutiae points.

The results of the LIF algorithm as applied to the same latent fingerprint are shown in Fig. 16.16. As can be seen, the algorithm detected seven minutiae points that are in good agreement with those suggested by the FBI experts (see the + points in Fig. 16.16b). However, the difficult conditions under which the latent print was taken have created some errors. An example is the false detection of a ridge termination marked as an x, located near the lower right of the core point of the fingerprint. It looks like a legitimate ridge termination, except for the fact that ridges above and below the presumed ridge ending appear to be perfectly aligned. Hence, we take this as evidence that the apparent termination is not valid. As seen in Fig. 16.16d, the gap between these two ridges was almost removed by DCA, but not completely. There was a total of seven clearly false detections (appearing as x points), all seeming to share similar characteristics. Finally, a total of five suggested minutiae points do not correspond to those found by the experts, but appear to be sufficiently interesting as to be possibly legitimate (marked as * points).

16.4.3. High-Instantaneous Frequency Model (HIF)

The algorithm for detecting minutiae points corresponding to high-instantaneous frequency magnitudes is entirely analogous to the LIF algorithm. First, in the HIF algorithm, all points with sufficiently high-instantaneous frequency magnitude are found: $T = \{\mathbf{x} \in \mathbf{Q} : \omega(\mathbf{x}) > \omega_{max}\}$, and $T = T_1 \cup T_2 \cup \cdots \cup T_L$, where the T_i, $i = 1, 2, \ldots, L$, are again separate and distinct region components. Second, instead of rejecting area components containing fewer than $\lambda^2/12$ pixels, area components containing fewer than $\lambda^2/4$ pixels are removed. Again, regions containing low-amplitude points are deleted as well. Denote the remaining regions as T_i^*, $i = 1, 2, \ldots, L^*$. Finally, in each remaining region, the point having the largest instantaneous frequency is selected as the potential minutiae point:

$$\mathbf{z_i} = \arg\max_{\mathbf{x} \in T_i^*} \omega(\mathbf{x}), i = 1, 2, \ldots, L^*$$

Figure 16.17 depicts the results of applying the HIF algorithm to the latent print. The HIF algorithm managed to detect 11 minutiae that strongly correlate with the FBI-suggested minutiae points (see the + points in Fig. 16.17b). Many of these points have been located with astonishing accuracy. Nevertheless, there appear to be

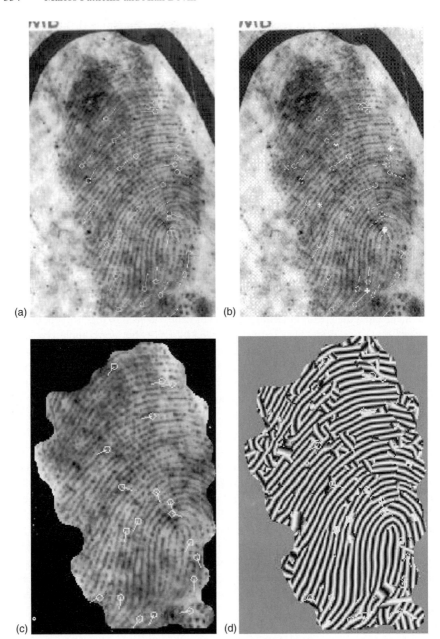

Fig. 16.16. Minutiae results for the low-instantaneous frequency magnitude model. In (a), we show the original minutiae as labeled by an FBI team of latent fingerprint experts. In (b), we show the detected minutiae together with the FBI minutiae. Seven minutiae are in agreement (plotted using +), five are suggested minutiae candidates that might be correct (plotted using *), and seven are most likely to be false detections (plotted using x). In (c), we show the detected minutiae points plotted on the original print. In (d), we show the detected minutiae points plotted on the FM print.

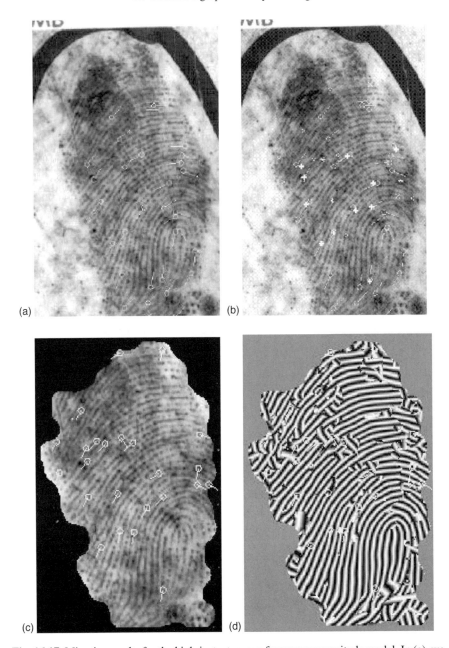

Fig. 16.17. Minutiae results for the high-instantaneous frequency magnitude model. In (a), we show the original minutiae as labeled by an FBI team of latent-fingerprint experts. In (b), we show the detected minutiae points together with the FBI minutiae points. There are 11 minutiae points that are in agreement (plotted using +), 3 candidate minutiae points (plotted using *), and 10 minutiae points that are most likely to be wrong detections (plotted using x). In (c), we show the detected minutiae points plotted on the original print. In (d), we show the detected minutiae points plotted on the FM print.

10 detected potential minutiae points that are in error, mostly concentrated around dark, poorly defined regions of the fingerprint. Also, three points appear as possible positive candidate minutiae points that were not selected by the FBI team. Again, we emphasize that the system we are demonstrating is intended to serve as the basis for a digital assistant, rather than an automated standalone latent fingerprint analyzer.

16.4.4. Summary of the Results

Overall, the aggregate system composed of the ZAMP, LIF, and HIF algorithms discovered 21 minutiae points that strongly correspond to the 31 suggested by the FBI experts (plotted as + points in Fig. 16.18). It is also encouraging that most of the missed minutiae points were extremely close to detected minutiae points.

Hence, we postulate that the algorithms proposed here can at least direct the attention of the human experts toward highly plausible fingerprint minutiae. Furthermore, it is rather encouraging that for most minutiae that are in agreement, the suggested locations were found with near-perfect accuracy. Many of the 11 minutiae points that are not part of the suggested minutiae points also appear to be strong candidates for being actual minutiae points, although the nontrivial conditions of the latent print might actually prohibit them from being identified as such (plotted as * points).

Most of the 18 points that were described as false detections can be seen as being influenced by local ink variations, or by scars. Possibly a more conservative approach would help eliminate many of the false detections, but conversely, such an approach might lead to the failure to identify some of the interesting or legitimate minutiae points. Given the poor quality of the original latent fingerprint (see Fig. 16.2), we believe that this initial study of using FM-derived image features for latent fingerprint analysis is a significant step toward creating new models and paradigms having a physically significant basis for fingerprint analysis. An important step in this direction would be the availability of more latent prints, with corresponding expert analysis results for comparison, from the FBI. Thus far, we have been able to obtain just the one print.

16.5. Conclusion

We presented a novel AM-FM model for latent fingerprint analysis and developed new algorithms for minutiae point detection. We showed the efficacy of the new model and associated algorithms for the detection of potential minutiae points on an actual (real-life) latent fingerprint.

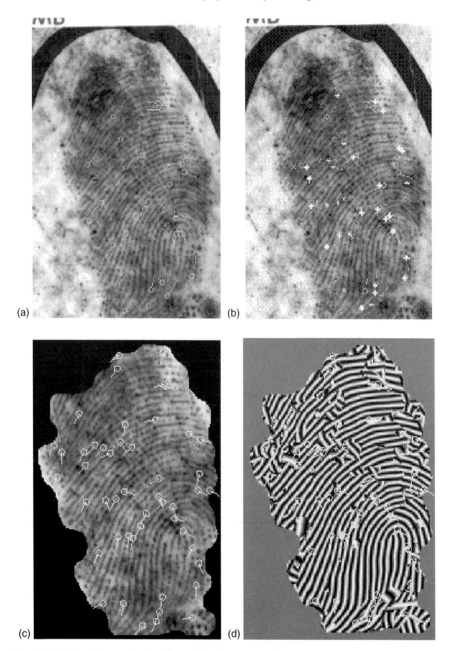

Fig. 16.18. Minutiae results for all models. In (a), we show the original minutiae as labeled by an FBI team of latent fingerprint experts. In (b), we show all the detected minutiae points, together with the FBI minutiae. In (c), we show all the detected minutiae points plotted on the original print. In (d), we show all the detected minutiae points plotted on the FM print.

References

1. FBI, *The Science of Fingerprints*, Washington, DC: U.S. Department of Justice, 1984, 1974.
2. Lee, H.C. and R.E. Gaensslen, *Advances in Fingerprint Technology*, Boca Raton, FL: CRC Press, 1994.
3. Ratha, N.K., S. Chen, and A.K. Jain, Adaptive flow orientation-based feature extraction in fingerprint images, *Pattern Recognition*, 28(11):1657–1672, 1995.
4. Halici, U. and G. Ongun, Fingerprint classification through self-organizing feature maps modified to treat uncertainties, *Proc. of the IEEE*, 84:1497–1512, 1996.
5. Maio, D. and D. Maltoni, Direct gray-scale minutiae detection in fingerprints, *IEEE Trans. on Pattern Analysis and Machine Intelligence*, 1997.
6. Turing, A.M., The chemical basis of morphogenesis, *Philosophical Trans. Royal Society London*, pp. 37–72, 1952.
7. Murray, J.D., A pre-pattern formation mechanism for mammalian coat markings, *J. Theor. Biology*, 88:161–199, 1981.
8. Zhu, S.C. and D. Mumford, Prior learning and gibbs reaction-diffusion, *IEEE Trans. on Pattern Analysis and Machine Intelligence*, 19:1236–1250, Nov. 1997.
9. Murray, J.D., *Mathematical Biology*, 2nd ed., New York: Springer Verlag, 1993.
10. Cross, M.C. and P.C. Hohenberg, Pattern formation outside equilibrium, *Reviews of Modern Physics*, 65(3):851–1112, July 1993.
11. Havlicek, J.P., *AM-FM image models*, Ph.D. dissertation, The University of Texas at Austin, 1996.
12. Bovik, A.C., N. Gopal, T. Emmoth, and A. Restrepo, Localized measurement of emergent image frequencies by Gabor wavelets, *IEEE Trans. on Information Theory*, 38(2):691–712, Mar. 1992, special issue on wavelet transforms and multiresolution signal analysis.
13. Bovik, A.C., P. Maragos, and T.F. Quatieri, Measuring amplitude and frequency modulations in noise using multiband energy operators, *Proc. IEEE Intl. Symp. Time-Frequency and Time-Scale Analysis*, Victoria, BC, Canada, Oct. 1992.
14. Bovik, A.C., J.P. Havlicek, M.D. Desai, and D.S. Harding, Limits on discrete modulated signals, *IEEE Trans. on Signal Processing*, 45(4):867–879, Apr. 1997.
15. Havlicek, J.P., D.S. Harding, and A.C. Bovik, The multi-component AM-FM image representation, *IEEE Trans. on Image Processing*, pp. 1094–1100, June 1996.
16. Ziemer, R.E. and W.H. Tranter, *Principles of Communications Systems, Modulation, and Noise*, 4th ed., Boston: Houghton Mifflin Company, 1995.
17. Stein, E.M. and G. Weiss, *Introduction to Fourier Analysis on Euclidean Spaces*, 1st ed., Princeton, NJ: Princeton Univ. Press, 1971.
18. Cohen, L., *Time-Frequency Analysis*, Englewood Cliffs, NJ: Prentice Hall, 1995.
19. Papoulis, A., *Signal Analysis*, New York: McGraw-Hill, 1977.
20. Kreyszig, E., *Advanced Engineering Mathematics*, 6th ed., New York: John Wiley, 1988.
21. Newell, A.C., The dynamics and analysis of patterns, in *Pattern Formation in the Physical and Biological Sciences*, H.F. Nijhout, L. Nadel, and D.L. Stein, eds., Vol. V of Lecture Notes in the Santa Fe Institute Studies in Sciences of Complexity, pp. 201–268, New York: Addison-Wesley, 1997.
22. Havlicek, J.P., D.S. Harding, and A.C. Bovik, Multidimensional quasi-eigenfunction approximations and multicomponent AM-FM models, *IEEE Trans. on Image Processing*, 9(2):227–242, Feb. 2000.
23. Bovik, A.C. and M.D. Desai, Basic binary image processing, in *The Handbook of Image and Video Processing*, New York: Academic Press, 2000.
24. NIST Special Database 27, Fingerprint Minutiae from Latent and Matching Ten-Print Images, http://www.nist.gov/srd/nistsd27.htm.

Chapter 17

Error Rates for Human Latent Fingerprint Examiners

Lyn Haber and Ralph Norman Haber

Abstract. Fingerprint comparison evidence has been used in criminal courts for almost 100 years to identify defendants as perpetrators of crimes. Until very recently, this evidence has been accepted by the courts as infallibly accurate. We review four kinds of available data about the accuracy of fingerprint comparisons made by human latent fingerprint examiners: anecdotal FBI data; published data on the accuracy of consensus fingerprint comparisons made by groups of examiners working in crime laboratories; the proficiency and certification test scores of latent fingerprint examiners tested individually; and the results of controlled experiments on the accuracy of fingerprint comparisons. We conclude that anecdotal data are useless and misleading; consensus judgments of fingerprint comparisons show either indeterminant or quite large error rates; the proficiency and certification procedures in current use lack validity and cannot serve to specify the accuracy or skill level of individual fingerprint examiners; and there is no published research evidence on error rates. It is impossible to determine from existing data whether true error rates are miniscule or substantial.

17.1. Introduction

A fingerprint expert on television who asserts that the prints on the murder weapon match those of the villain is believed, and the bad guy is convicted. This is equally true in a real-life courtroom. For almost 100 years, fingerprint evidence has been accepted as fact in court in the United States and other countries. Until very recently, when the fingerprint expert declared an identification—a match between the defendant's prints and trace prints associated with the crime—this assertion went unquestioned by judge, jury, and defense attorney.

The fingerprint examiner believes this judgment is fact. Consider the fingerprint expert's testimony in this section of transcript from a trial in 1911:

> Q: In comparing these fingers it is your opinion that the lines in those photographs were made by the same person?
> A: I am positive. It is not my opinion [1].

Today, nearly 100 years later, practicing fingerprint examiners continue to believe they never could make a mistake, based on their "exact science," and they believe they never do make a mistake. For example: "The fingerprint expert is unique among forensic specialists. Because fingerprint science is objective and exact, conclusions reached by fingerprint experts are absolute and final" [2].

A growing number of researchers, the press, and legal scholars are questioning the field of fingerprint matching, from its underlying premises to whether there is any scientific rigor whatsoever in the methodology for making the comparisons. For example, "In fingerprint comparison, judgments of correspondence and the assessment of differences are wholly subjective: there are no objective criteria for determining when a difference may be explainable or not" [3].

The concerns about error rates and scientific rigor have arisen very recently with respect to the fingerprint profession. Court decisions on the scientific requirements for the presentation of expert opinion in court (e.g., [4] and [5]) have made two novel demands on experts who present testimony. First, experts are required to demonstrate that their opinions are derived from a scientific base, a science documented in a research literature and accepted by peers. Second, experts are required to demonstrate knowledge of the error rate associated with the methodology on which their opinions are based. At present, the fingerprint profession insists that fingerprint comparisons are based on an exact science and that competent fingerprint examiners have a zero percent error rate.

In this chapter, we briefly touch on the scientific basis for fingerprint comparisons; then we describe in detail the available data on error rates in making comparisons.

17.2. Forensic Science of Fingerprint Comparison

Researchers and scientists have raised two general concerns about whether fingerprint comparison is a science. The first stems from the fingerprint profession's focus on the details on actual fingers in ascribing a science to the comparison of prints: the problems presented by latent prints, those found at crime scenes, are blurrily addressed, if at all. The second concern is the profession's failure to develop an explicit forensic science of fingerprint comparisons; specifically, one that defines the transformations that occur in fingerprint patterns when fingers touch surfaces, and defines methodologies for making comparisons.

17.2.1. Problems with Latent Prints

A typical latent print associated with a crime differs in many ways from the finger itself, and from the fingerprint image taken by trained technicians under controlled conditions in the police station. Each one of these differences serves to diminish, obscure, distort, or eliminate information necessary to the comparison process.

1. Size: The latent print is partial, not complete. Typical latent prints contain only about one fifth of the finger surface contained in an inked or scanned print.
2. Location: Some parts of a finger's surface are more informative than others, and the latent print's smaller area may contain little useful detail.

3. The latent print may be deposited on a dirty surface, which obscures critical features.
4. The latent print may be smudged or smeared.
5. The latent print may be overlaid or underlaid by other prints.
6. The latent print may be deposited on a noisy surface, such as wood, which itself consists of ridges and grooves that may be confused with those contributed from a finger.
7. The medium in which the latent print was deposited, such as sweat, water, blood, or oil, may interfere with its definition.
8. The amount of pressure and the direction of the pressure between finger and surface produce distortion in the latent print.
9. A curved or irregular surface distorts the patterns of the finger.
10. The procedure used in lifting the latent print usually causes some loss in print detail.

The result of all these factors is that latent prints almost always contain less clarity, less content, and less undistorted information than a fingerprint taken under controlled conditions, and much, much less detail compared to the actual patterns of ridges and grooves of a finger. These transformations between inked or scanned fingerprints and latent prints must be understood, described, and addressed in the methodology for making comparisons (see [6] for further discussion of the problems with latent prints). Further, the impoverished quality of latent prints must be recognized as an inevitable source of error in making comparisons. As one example, the fingerprint examiner profession must explicitly adhere to the practice that more points of agreement be used to make an identification in court when the quality of the latent print is poor, as compared to rich. This follows from common practice throughout all other areas of scientific comparison. When the quality of the stimulus decreases, the likelihood of error increases, so that *more* data are needed to justify a match.

At present, the fingerprint profession neither describes these transformations systematically (but see [6], for an excellent beginning) nor recognizes the loss of information inherent in the latent print as a critical problem in the assessment of comparison accuracy. The profession persists in the nonresponsive claims that fingers are unique and fingerprint examiners do not make errors. This gap between the professional's claims and the problems inherent in the fingerprint comparison task has led researchers, the press, and the legal system to challenge the assertions of an exact science and of a zero error rate.

17.2.2. The Status of a Forensic Science of Fingerprint Comparisons

Every forensic science requires five components in order to achieve individuation [7]: (1) a description of the patterns of the objects being used to individuate (in this case the patterns of ridges and grooves of fingers); (2) evidence that those descriptions of the patterns can be used to individuate (a demonstration of a uniqueness assumption); (3) descriptions of how the patterns are transformed when deposited in a crime scene, and how each change can be related back to the original pattern; (4) evidence that the descriptions of the trace crime scene patterns (in this case, the latent prints) are also unique to every individual, so that two different people would never leave patterns that could be confused; and (5) descriptions of a tested methodology to carry out comparisons between pattern traces associated with a crime and the object itself (in this case, between latent prints and inked or scanned prints), one that spells out the sequence of steps to be followed, rules to rank the relative importance of different parts of the patterns, the rules to decide when a crime trace does not contain enough reliable information to be used for comparison purposes, and the rules to decide when a difference must be an elimination of an individual rather than a distortion that has arisen from a transformation.

When this forensic science of fingerprint comparison is well described, tested, and verified, then the sources of errors in making fingerprint comparisons can be understood, error rates can be determined for different kinds of latent prints and different procedures for making comparisons, and improvements in technology, training, and comparison procedures can be made to reduce the rate of errors. However, at present, a forensic science of fingerprint comparison is neither well described, nor well tested [8].

For these reasons as well, researchers, the press, and the legal system are questioning the magnitude of error rates in fingerprint comparisons.

17.2.3. Sources of an Error Rate for Forensic Fingerprint Comparisons

When an examiner testifies in court that the latent fingerprint found at the crime scene matches one of the fingerprints of the defendant, the examiner can be correct, or the examiner can be wrong. If he is wrong, the error could have arisen for one of several reasons:

1. Uniqueness: Some nonzero probability exists that a second person could have left a latent print that also matches the fingerprint of the defendant, and such an instance occurred in this case. This probability varies as a function of the quality and quantity of detail present. No research has been carried out to demonstrate whether latent prints are unique.
2. Methodology: The procedures followed by the well-trained examiner permits an erroneous identification between the crime scene latent print and the defendant's fingerprint, and that occurred in this case. No research has been carried out to demonstrate whether a latent print from one source finger would be misidentified to an inked print from a different source finger by all competent examiners following a specified method.
3. Human error: The latent print examiner made a human error through inattention, poor judgment, lack of training, etc. (We ignore for this discussion instances of police falsification of evidence (see [9], for examples), or errors in the chain of custody resulting in the examiner comparing a mislabeled latent.).

For legal purposes, only the overall error rate for fingerprint comparisons is of importance. The source does not matter. For a forensic science, it is of critical importance to identify and understand the sources of errors.

The fingerprint profession, represented by the International Association for Identification (IAI), attempts to guard against human error, as the only possible source of error, since the profession denies the possibility of any uniqueness failures, or of a less-than-perfect methodology. The IAI has suggested standards of admissibility to the profession, standards of training adequacy, standards of years of experience, individual certification of examiners, certification of laboratories in which fingerprint examiners work, and individual proficiency testing of examiners [10]. The IAI also recommends that any comparison an examiner judges to be an identification should be verified by a second examiner before the identification is presented in court. Unfortunately, all these standards are advisory, and there is little enforcement in practice.

In this chapter we draw on four areas of evidence and data on human error rates in fingerprint comparisons: anecdotal FBI evidence of a zero error rate; the accuracy of identifications made by examiners working together in crime laboratories; results from proficiency and certification tests of individual examiners; and results of controlled experiments on the accuracy of comparing fingerprints.

17.3. Anecdotal FBI Evidence of a Courtroom Zero Error Rate

A senior supervisor in the FBI fingerprint examination crime laboratory recently testified under oath in United States Federal Court [11] that he had never heard of a single instance of an erroneous identification made in court by an FBI examiner. He observed that it would be headline news, and he offered his lack of such knowledge as evidence that during the 35 years of his experience, no FBI examiner had *ever made* an erroneous identification in court.

"Not hearing about an erroneous identification" can be treated as evidence about the frequency of erroneous identifications if, and only if, these errors would be discovered and made available to the public if they occur. As we will show, the entire legal system conjoins to make erroneous identifications undiscoverable. The belief that fingerprint examiners never make erroneous identifications is so strongly held by every party in the criminal justice system that only a concatenation of extremely unlikely circumstances can uncover such a mistake. Defense attorneys, defendants, police investigators, examiners, jurors, and our society at large all believe that fingerprint evidence is infallible.

As a consequence of this belief, each party in the criminal justice system contributes to the difficulty of exposing an erroneous identification.

Historically, fingerprint evidence has been perceived as unassailable by *defense attorneys*, who until very recently did not consider challenging it. This is one reason that there has been little chance of discovering an erroneous identification during trial.

The *defendant* believes that fingerprint evidence will lead to his or her conviction. An innocent defendant, counseled by his attorney who knows that the prosecution plans to introduce fingerprint evidence, may avail himself of the opportunity to plead guilty to a lesser crime in order to avoid a more severe sentence. Once the guilty plea is recorded, only a fluke can expose the erroneous identification.

Police investigators believe that fingerprint evidence is sufficient to convict the defendant. Once the police have received a report from their crime laboratory that the crime scene prints match a potential suspect, the focus of the investigation switches to collecting further evidence to demonstrate the guilt of the now-identified perpetrator. Other potential leads are ignored and other suspects are not pursued. This switch in focus all but removes the chances that an erroneous identification will be uncovered by further investigation.

The *profession*, represented by the IAI and by the FBI, supports this aura of absolute certainty: "Friction ridge identifications are absolute conclusions. Probable, possible, or likely identifications are outside the acceptable limits of the science of friction ridge identifications" [10]. As a result, the profession as a whole has resisted attempts to collect evidence about accuracy. From their point of view, there is no reason to do so: Ridge and groove identifications are absolute conclusions and accuracy is always perfect; accuracy is always 100%. The absence of data about accuracy reduces opportunities for both exposure of errors and self-correction.

Jurors believe fingerprint evidence is true. Illsey [12] shows that jurors place great weight on the testimony of fingerprint experts and rank fingerprint evidence as the most important scientific reason why they vote for conviction. Mr. Meagher [11] could not remember an instance in which an FBI examiner made a positive identification and the jury set the identification aside and acquitted the defendant. This widely held belief in the accuracy of fingerprint comparisons does not provide any scientific evidence whatsoever that the fingerprint testimony is correct. The jury's conviction does preclude discovery of any further evidence of a possible error.

Our *society* makes it difficult for a convicted but innocent prison inmate to conduct an investigation into the "solved" crime, to enlist law enforcement agencies for assistance, or to engage legal help. These obstacles reduce the chances for an erroneous identification to be exposed once it has been used to convict.

For all of these reasons, if an erroneous identification has been made based on fingerprint evidence, it is extremely unlikely that it will ever be discovered. Mr. Meagher correctly could testify that in his memory, not a single instance of an erroneous identification made in court by an FBI examiner has ever been *discovered*. This more reasonable claim provides no evidence that mistakes are never made; only that if mistakes occur, they are never unearthed.

17.4. Crime Laboratory Consensus Accuracy

Much of the data on fingerprint comparison accuracy comes from joint decisions made by two or more examiners working together in a crime laboratory. Crime laboratories, including the FBI fingerprint crime laboratory, may require that an identification to be presented in court be verified by another examiner of equal or greater experience or rank.

In the accreditation and proficiency testing described below, many laboratories mirror their routine work procedures and have two or more examiners respond jointly to the test comparisons. The response form returned for scoring, like the identification made in court, represents the consensus of several examiners. We present consensus data from four sources.

17.4.1. Crime Laboratory Accreditation and Proficiency Test Results

In 1977 the American Society of Crime Laboratory Directors (ASCLD) began work on a program to evaluate and improve the quality of crime laboratory operations. An accreditation program was developed, and in 1982 the first laboratories were accredited. As of 1999, 182 laboratories had been accredited, including several abroad [13]. One requirement of the accreditation process was that examiners working in the laboratory pass an external proficiency test. Beginning in 1983, ASCLD constructed and administered by mail an annual proficiency test. Each year, each laboratory requesting accreditation was sent a dozen or more latent prints, along with some number of 10-print cards. The latent prints either were selected from actual cases or were constructed to represent the range of quality found in typical latent prints. The 10-print cards were also selected to be of typical quality. The examiners in the laboratory had to judge whether each latent print was scorable, and if scorable, whether it matched a fingerprint on one of the 10-print cards, or could be eliminated as matching none of them.

Table 17.1, taken from [14], shows the percent of erroneous responses by year for 1983–1991 on the ASCLD proficiency test used in their accreditation program. The average error rates over these nine years are shown at the bottom of the table.

The number of laboratories that returned a response form increased from 24 to 88 over this period. This was a proficiency test of the laboratory as a whole, so the response for each latent presumably was the "laboratory" response. If two latent print examiners worked in the laboratory, the judgment was made by those two examiners working together. If five examiners worked there, all five may have participated together. One or more examiners may have reached a decision and then shown their

Table 17.1. Crime Laboratory Proficiency Test Results for Fingerprint Examiners from 1983–1991.

Year	Number labs	Percent scorable?		% Identification?	
		Yes	No	Yes	No
1983	24	9	0	15	0
1984	28	3	7	5	2
1985	37	3	—	7	3
1986	43	1	0	7	2
1987	52	3	—	8	2
1988	62	1	6	2	2
1989	56	1	43	3	0
1990	74	1	1	15	2
1991	88	4	—	—	—
Average error scores		**2**	**8**	**8**	**2**

Source: From Peterson and Markham, 1995).
Scores are the percent of erroneous responses. Note: Blank entries occurred in years in which the response was not requested on the test. Percent of respondents who were completely correct was not reported.

work to a supervisor, who may have corrected any errors. No information is available as to how many examiners these response forms include, or as to how the examiners reached consensus.

The numbers reported in Table 17.1 are the percent of erroneous responses for each category of test item (there is no way to determine how many response forms were perfect). The results are fairly consistent over the nine years, so the average scores are representative (bottom row of Table 17.1). On average, only 2% of the scorable latent prints were erroneously judged to be unscorable, and so were not examined further when they should have been. Only 8% of the unscorable latent prints were erroneously judged to be scorable and were examined further when they should not have been. (No data were reported on the outcome of these erroneously scored prints: whether they resulted in erroneous eliminations or erroneous identifications.) With respect to eliminations and identifications, only 8% of the identifiable latent prints were eliminated (that is, could have been identified but were not), and only 2% of the elimination prints were scored as identifications (that is, were erroneous identifications).

These 2% findings are extremely troublesome. While an individual 2% erroneous identification rate or an individual 2% erroneous unscorable rate may seem negligible, they assume serious proportions in these tests, because the errors result from consensus and not individual, independent judgments. To illustrate, assume that two examiners participated in the certification test, performed the comparisons separately, compared their results, and reported an identification only when they both agreed—that is, reached a consensus. Further, assume (as the data show) that 2% of the time they both agreed on an identification when, in fact, the two prints did not match. Under these conditions, to have a consensus error rate of 2%, each individual examiner acting alone has an average independent error rate of 14% ($0.14 \times 0.14 = 0.02$). If three examiners participate and agree, a 2% consensus error rate implies that each examiner acting alone has an average independent error rate of 27%. The same observations pertain to the 2% scorable latent prints that were not examined when they could have been.

The proficiency tests used by crime laboratories for their ASCLD certification are taken with full knowledge that the fingerprint examiners and the lab as a whole are being tested. Research on double-blind testing procedures (see below) show that test score results are inflated when people know they are being tested, and when they and their supervisors know of the importance of the test results. Test takers are more attentive, follow instructions better, and check and review their work more carefully, all of which improves their scores, compared to their normal level of performance. The 2% consensus error rate for erroneous identifications underestimates the error rates that actually occur in court.

These apparently good results involving consensus in fact reveal substantial individual error rates for examiners working in crime laboratories.

In 1994 the ASCLD Proficiency Advisory Committee contacted the IAI and asked for assistance in the manufacture and review of future testing materials. The IAI contracted with the Collaborative Testing Services (CTS), and, from 1995 to the present, the external latent fingerprint examiner proficiency test used by ASCLD has been administered by CTS, and designed, assembled, reviewed, and authorized by the

Table 17.2. Results for Seven Years of the Collaborative Testing Service Proficiency Examination for Latent Print Examiners.

Year of test	Number taking test	% All correct responses	% one or more erroneous ID	% One or More missed ID
1995	156	44	20	37
1996	184	16	3	80
1997	204	61	6	28
1998	219	58	6	35
1999	228	62	5	33
2000	278	91	4	5
2001	296	80	3	18
2001	120	80	2	18

Note: Two separate tests were given in 2001. (A year may not add to 100% if a respondent made more than one kind of error.)

IAI. Its format still consists of a number of latent prints and 10-print cards. However, all the latent prints are scorable, so the only responses required are identification or elimination. Also, individual examiners who wish to take this test can do so. The summary responses reported by CTS combine consensus reports from laboratories and from individual examiners.

The overall results for the seven years from 1995 to 2001 are listed in Table 17.2. We constructed the table from the annual summary reports issued by CTS for these seven years (CTS publications 9508, 9608, 9708, 9908, 0008, 0108, 01-516, and 01-517). These are the only reports available, and they do not provide breakdowns by item type. Therefore, it is not possible, for example, to determine the percent of latent prints that should have been eliminated, but were identified (erroneous identifications): Only the percent of respondents who made one or more erroneous identifications is reported.

The third column of Table 17.2 reports the percent of respondents who made no errors. For example, of the 156 respondents to the proficiency test in 1995, 44% made no errors at all. Of the 56% who made errors, 37% failed to make at least one of the identifications. This 37% includes 4% who failed to make even one identification ([15], CTS 9508). More seriously, 20% made one or more erroneous identifications, averaging 1.6 such errors per respondent. If these comparisons had been presented in court as testimony, one in five latent print examiners would have provided damning evidence against the wrong person. If these are consensus reports, more than half would have testified erroneously.

The 1996 proficiency test results remained poor. Of the 184 respondents, only 16% correctly identified all nine of the identifiable latent prints while also eliminating the two remaining latent prints. The only improvement over the 1995 results was that fewer erroneous identifications were made (3%)—rather, 80% of the erroneous responses were misses—failures to make correct identifications.

The results for 1997 through 2001 are also reported in Table 17.2. In general, the number of respondents who achieve perfect performance increases, and the number of erroneous identifications remains small, though 3% to 6% of the respondents continue to make one or more.

These test results, though extremely poor in their own right, are useless to the profession and useless to the criminal justice system, especially the courts, in trying to evaluate erroneous identification rates. There is no control on how the test is administered or timed (it is still distributed and returned by mail); and the only information retained on who takes the test each year is whether the respondent is foreign or from the United States, and if from the United States, whether associated with an accredited crime laboratory. The anonymous results published each year still do not include any information as to whether the responses came from a consensus or an individual examiner, or the years of experience or amount of training of those who took the test.

The difficulty level of each test, along with its reliability and validity, are not reported. The difficulty level is not even knowable, because a metric of the difficulty of a print has never been developed and tested. Further, the CTS proficiency tests assess only a small portion of an examiner's typical job. If these tests are to measure proficiency in a way that generalizes to performance accuracy in court, they must include an assessment of handling AFIS search outputs, of eliminations as well as identifications, of prints that cannot be scored at all, and of 10-prints that do not match the latent prints.

The CTS, when reporting its test results, now carefully and properly acknowledge that its proficiency tests do not represent the performance accuracy of print examiners in the field:

> "This report contains the data received from participants in this test. Since it is their option how the samples are to be used (e.g., training exercise, known or blind proficiency testing, research and development of new techniques, etc.), the results compiled in the Summary Report are not intended to be an overview of the quality of work performed in the profession and cannot be interpreted as such. . . . These Comments are not intended to reflect the general state of the art within the profession." ([15], CTS, 01-516)

17.4.2. Crime Laboratory Verification Testing

Meagher [11] provides some information about verification procedures in the FBI fingerprint crime laboratory. However, crime laboratories in general never reveal how many of the identifications made by an examiner working in the laboratory are given to another examiner to verify. More importantly, crime laboratories, including the FBI's, never reveal how many disagreements occur during the verification process, and what happens when one arises. Hence, while the profession claims that verification procedures reduce the chance of erroneous identifications, there are no data to support or refute this claim.

Moreover, the verification procedures described by the IAI [10], to which the FBI adheres, are not followed by all crime laboratories in the United States. Some laboratories have no verification procedure for identifications they offer in court.

There are serious problems with these verification procedures in their present form. In response to Meagher's [11] testimony in *United States of America vs. Plaza et al.* [16], Arvizu [17] and Haber [18] testified that the FBI's procedures were fundamentally flawed as a means to detect errors.

Verifying the accuracy of a result produced by an examiner in a crime laboratory is comparable to auditing the quality-control procedures of a water testing laboratory, or to an experimental test of the efficacy of a new drug compared to a placebo. In general, accurate results are obtained if the person being verified, audited, or tested does not know that a verification, audit, or test is being performed, does not know the specific purposes of the test, and does not know the expected or desired outcome by whoever is administering the procedure. In addition, the persons administering the verification, audit, or test should have no stake in its success or outcome and should not know the correct, expected, or required answers. Finally, the verification, audit, or test results should be scored and interpreted by an external and neutral body. When any of these procedures is violated, biased outcomes and inflated scores result.

These procedures, widely known as *blind testing* in the scientific research literature, are currently required for all federal drug testing programs, and for virtually all peer-reviewed, published scientific experiments. To illustrate why verification procedures in crime laboratories are inadequate, Table 17.3, taken from Haber and Haber [19] differentiates three levels of blind testing for verification tasks.

The research on blind testing demonstrates that double-blind test procedures uncover significantly more errors than single blind, and single-blind procedures uncover significantly more errors than zero blind [17]. Unfortunately, crime laboratories that do verify identifications follow zero blind procedures exclusively [11]. Applying those results to verification of fingerprint examiner's identifications, the conclusion reached by the verifier is more likely to agree with the conclusion reached by the initial examiner who first made the identification than if he had done all of the examination himself from the beginning, in ignorance that anyone else had worked on the case. The research is clear: Under zero-blind conditions, if the first examiner has made an identification that is erroneous, the second examiner is likely to *ratify* the error, rather than discover it.

Double-blind comparisons for verification take more time and increase costs. They are difficult, if not impossible, to implement under the normal operating procedures of crime laboratories today. Crime laboratories need to understand that their present zero-blind verification procedures do not eliminate human examiner error from fingerprint comparison testimony, and courts need to understand that zero-blind verification does not provide demonstrated amounts of protection for the innocent.

17.4.3. Results from the FBI External Crime Laboratory Mitchell Comparison Test

In the trial of *United States of America v. Byron Mitchell [20]*, a latent print examiner testified to an identification between two latent prints lifted from a getaway car and the 10-print card of the defendant. The defendant claimed innocence and challenged the accuracy of the fingerprint evidence. The FBI attempted to demonstrate the scientific certainty of the identification between the defendant's 10-print and the two latent prints found in the car. As part of the demonstration presented at trial, the FBI sent the two latent prints, together with the defendant's 10-print, to 53 different law enforcement agencies around the United States, told them that this request was very important, and asked that their most "highly experienced" examiners determine whether any

Table 17.3. Three Levels of Blind Testing Described by Haber and Haber [19].

Zero Blind Procedures

The fingerprint examiner who has made the initial identification:
  Knows he is being tested
  Knows what he is being tested on
  Knows the person who will verify his result
  Knows there are penalties for his poor performance

The second print examiner doing the verification:
  Knows he is also being tested
  Knows the first examiner
  Knows what the first examiner concluded and why
  Has a stake in the outcome of the test

The Supervisor:
  Knows that a verification is required
  Knows who made the initial identification
  Knows who did the verification
  Knows the outcome desired
  Has a stake in the outcome

Single Blind

The Fingerprint Examiner who made the initial identification:
  Does not know he is the first one to make this identification
  Does not know whether his work will be verified
  Does not know who will verify his work

The Second Print Examiner doing the verification:
  Knows the same as under Zero Blind

The Supervisor:
  Knows the same as under Zero Blind

Double Blind

The fingerprint examiner who made the initial identification:
  Knows the same as under Single Blind

The Second Print Examiner doing the Verification:
  Does not know another examiner made an identification
  Does not have any access to the work of any other examiner on this case
  Does not know he is being asked to verify
  Has no unusual stake in the outcome of his work

The Supervisor:
  Does not know a verification is underway
  Does not participate in the analysis of the verification

identifications could be made (see [21], for the detailed instructions and results). This was a unique opportunity for a demonstration of concurrence among experienced examiners.

Thirty-nine agencies returned analyses of the prints to the FBI. Nine of them (23%) found that either one or both of the latent prints did *not* match any of the prints from the defendant's 10-print card.

Two issues are embedded in the FBI's failure to find consensus among the highly experienced examiners in the crime laboratories that responded. First, if fingerprint comparison is a "scientific certainty," as the FBI and the IAI claim, then every competent examiner should reach the same conclusion. Here, 30 laboratories found the latent prints were an identification, but 9 found they were not an identification. Where is scientific certainty in the identification of Mr. Mitchell as the person leaving those prints (who, by the way, is still in prison)?

Second, given the nature and the extreme wording of the FBI request, it is most unlikely that the difference of opinion among these highly skilled examiners was due to human error. From our previous discussion, it must therefore be due to either failure of the latent print uniqueness assumption, or that the methodology followed by crime laboratories allows different results for the same comparisons.

The results of the FBI external crime laboratory [20] comparison test indicate a lack of a forensic science of fingerprint identification.

17.4.4. Documented Examples of Erroneous identifications

A substantial number of cases in the United States and in England [9, 22] have exposed instances of identification errors made by latent print examiners in court. Epstein [21] lists more than a dozen. Because England requires three verifications before an identification can be presented in court, and SWGFAST guidelines suggest at least two in the United States, we include the data on erroneous identifications presented in court as data on the accuracy of consensus judgments.

Discovery of identification error, thus far, has been a matter of chance: Someone else confessed, or other irrefutable forensic evidence came to light. Because identifications made by a latent print examiner have not even been questioned until recently, these uncovered errors represent but a few planets in a galaxy.

In each such case in the United States, the IAI has removed certification from the latent print examiner who made the error in court, claiming that any examiner who makes an error isn't competent. Certification has also been removed from the verifier. A "good" examiner never makes a mistake [9]. This punitive practice by the IAI ignores fundamental principles of science: No procedure in itself is errorless, and no human being following a procedure is errorless. The IAI, in maintaining that the science of fingerprint comparison is without error, is hindering the profession's capacity to uncover sources of error, to improve performance, and to allow the legal system and society as a whole to make informed decisions about error rates associated with fingerprint evidence.

The documented cases of erroneous identifications in England suggest significant examiner error rates, because, in each one, three verifications of the identification had been made by highly experienced print examiners using the 16-point comparison standard. These cases further demonstrate that a zero-blind verification procedure fails to prevent errors even when three skilled examiners check the comparison. Further, given the high level of examiner experience, these errors again implicate methodological problems rather than human error.

The 1999 case against Shirley McKie [9] glaringly illustrated the fallibility of identifications made by expert examiners. Fingerprint examiners from the Scottish Criminal Records Office testified that McKie's 10-print matched a latent recovered at a murder suspect's home; McKie, who was a Detective Constable investigating the murder, claimed she had never entered the home and that therefore the print could not have been hers. Two American fingerprint experts testified in her defense: experts against experts, in a field where an identification is held to be a certainty!

We have discussed the reasons why documentation of relatively few erroneous identifications made in court cannot stand as evidence that these errors do not occur. We have presented several lines of evidence that fingerprint examiners, working together, do make erroneous identifications. None of the evidence available permits an estimate of the magnitude of the error rates for consensus comparisons. Further, none of these data provides evidence as to the magnitude of these error rates for individual examiners.

17.5. Individual Proficiency and Certification Tests

We turn now to results from tests administered to individual fingerprint examiners.

17.5.1. FBI Internal Examiner Proficiency Test Results

Since 1995, the FBI has mandated annual proficiency testing of every latent fingerprint examiner in their employ. The FBI constructs, administers, scores, and interprets their own examinations. The seven years of results (1995–2001) have never been published, but were acknowledged and produced for the first time in a motion the FBI submitted in *United States of America v. Plaza et al.* [16]. The FBI contended in that hearing [11] that the results of these yearly proficiency tests show that their examiners do not make errors in court.

Approximately 60 fingerprint examiners took the test each year. The contents of the test varied somewhat from year to year, but always included between 5 and 10 latent fingerprints to be compared to 2 to 4 10-print cards. The results showed that none of the examiners taking the tests each year over the seven-year period made an erroneous identification: The erroneous identification rate was 0%. Three different examiners each missed an identification once in the seven years, a miss rate of less than 1%.

However, contrary to the FBI's contention, these results should not be interpreted as indicating virtually perfect accuracy by FBI examiners when they testify in court. The FBI proficiency test procedures are so fraught with problems that the results are uninterpretable. These problems include difficulty level, unrealistic tasks, and lack of peer review.

The latent prints were of very high quality: clear, distinct, and rich in information content. A leading fingerprint expert and instructor also testified in the same hearing [23] that the latent prints in the FBI proficiency tests were so easy to identify that his students would pass these tests with only six weeks of training. In the absence of an independent measure of difficulty, a result that nearly everyone gets a high score is vacuous in meaning. There is no way to establish any measure of validity for these results, because the results have no variation. These scores have a zero correlation with supervisory ratings, number of prints examined in the past, years of training, or years of experience.

The tests sampled only a narrow portion of a typical FBI print examiner's workload: None of the latent prints was unscorable; virtually all comparisons were identifications; there were very, very few eliminations; and there were no comparisons made to AFIS search outputs. As the FBI testified [11] that most of the latent prints sent to the FBI and seen by examiners are unscorable, that most comparisons made in their laboratory were eliminations, and not identifications, and that at least half of all comparisons were produced by AFIS outputs, the proficiency tests neither mirrored the normal workload of FBI examiners, nor sampled the kinds of cases that end up in court.

Finally, great caution should always be exercised in interpreting "in-house" data that are not collected by an independent testing service and are not submitted to peer review in the publication process. As we mentioned in our discussion of blind testing, the research literature shows that test performance is inflated when examiners know they are being tested, when those administering the tests know the correct answers to the test, and when it is their supervisors who run the testing program and have a stake in its success.

The problems discussed here were reviewed in detail in the defense testimony at the pretrial hearing of the *USA v. Plaza* [16–18, 23]. The results of the FBI proficiency tests do not generalize either to an FBI fingerprint examiner's performance on his job, or to the accuracy of the identifications to which attests in court. Their test results, like those of the ASCLD crime laboratory certification test results, are useless to the profession and useless to the courts as an index of erroneous identification error rates.

17.5.2. Certification Test Results for Individual Examiners from the IAI Latent Print Certification Board

In 1993 the IAI, through its Latent Print Certification Board, began offering certification (and re-certification) to individual latent print examiners. To be eligible to take the certification test, then and now, an examiner must have a minimum of 40 hours of formal training in classification, filing, and searching of inked fingerprints, and a minimum of 40 hours of formal training in latent print matters; a minimum of one year's full-time experience in classification, filing, and searching inked fingerprints; and a minimum of two years' full-time experience in the comparison of latent print material. The latent print examiners who take the certification test have both considerable formal training and experience on the job.

Most latent print examiners working in the United States today have not taken the certification test [24].

Each year, the certification test contains a number of practical knowledge sections and 15 latent prints that must be compared to a number of 10-prints. To pass the fingerprint comparison part of the test, the test-taker must identify 12 or more of the 15 latent prints correctly, without making a single false identification. In 1993, only 48% of the 762 applicants passed the test. The pass rate has remained around 50% through 2001 [15]. According to the IAI, the section on latent to 10-print comparisons accounted for nearly all of the failures. No data are available as to what percent of the failures resulted from false identifications.

Given the facts that the majority of working fingerprint examiners have never taken the test, that the latent print examiners who do seek certification are already trained and are working full-time with latent prints, and that about half the applicants for certification fail the test on the basis of poor fingerprint matching skills, the profession simply cannot claim to be performing without error.

A proper proficiency and certification test performs two functions: It permits quantitative assessment of the individual examiner's skill (in this context, accuracy) on the particular tasks examiners perform in their job setting; and it measures examiner skill on the tasks required for their "bottom line," that is, their accuracy when they testify in court. To fulfill the first function, test results must be demonstrably valid: They correlate with years on the job, with supervisory ratings, etc. To fulfill the second, the proficiency test must include the range of tasks the examiners typically perform in the course of their work, including elimination prints, unscorable prints, and AFIS outputs. Like the FBI internal proficiency test, the IAI certification test fails to meet either criterion.

17.5.3. Results from the United Kingdom Review of the 16-Point Comparison Standard

The practice of requiring a threshold number of corresponding matching points for an in-court identification was abandoned officially in the United States in 1973. It prevails in most European countries, and was in use until 2001 in the United Kingdom, where a threshold number of 16 points of comparison was required. In 1988, the Home Office commissioned a review to establish whether the 16-point standard was necessary. Evett and Williams [26] report the individual examiner accuracy data collected as part of this review.

Photographs of 10 pairs of prints, each pair consisting of a latent print and a 10-print card, were sent to fingerprint bureaus in England and Wales. Each bureau was requested to have latent print examiners of 10 or more years' experience do the comparisons and do them independently. Each of the examiners was asked to make one of four responses for every pair: (1) a full identification, that is, 16 or more points of correspondence; (2) a nonprovable (though probable) identification, that is, 8 to 15 points of correspondence; (3) insufficient for an opinion, that is, a latent print that could not be scored; and (4) an elimination, that is, a latent print that did not match the paired 10-print.

The 10 pairs were selected from previous Scotland Yard cases. The experts who chose the pairs had decided that all 10 latent prints could be scored. They decided that 9 of the 10 latent prints matched their respective 10-print, of which 6 pairs were full identifications, sufficient for court testimony, 2 were nonprovable identifications, and 1 was either a full or a nonprovable identification (the experts were split). Only one pair was an elimination.

Of the 130 anonymous responses returned, not one examiner made a single erroneous identification. Of course, there was only 1 opportunity out of 10 to make such an error, so this result by itself does not mean that erroneous identifications are rare among highly experienced examiners. The respondents missed a surprising number of identifications. Half of the respondents judged at least one of the full identification pairs to be nonprovable. Even more surprisingly, one of the two nonprovable identifications produced only 54% correct (nonprovable) responses, with 38% responding that it was unscorable, and 8% declaring an elimination. The authors point out that the results for this latter pair are "puzzling," given that 8% of the examiners declared an elimination, whereas 54% declared a nonprovable (that is, probable) identification. Here was a latent print that some examiners declared was an identification (probable) and some an elimination. Yet, "Examiners consider any identification, provable or probable, as a moral certainty." ([26], 1996, p. 61).

The most startling result found in this study was the tremendous variability in the number of points of correspondence that the examiners reported for each of the nine pairs that matched. Figure 17.1 shows the results for three pairs for which the correct response was a full identification. If the number of corresponding points between a pair of images of the same finger is based on science, then each of these three line graphs should have all the experts piled up on a common number.

Consider pair F: only one examiner incorrectly judged it as nonprovable, finding only 14 points of comparison; all the other 129 examiners correctly reported it as a full identification, with 16 or more points of comparison. However, the number of corresponding points for the full identification reported by the examiners ranged from a low of 16 to a high of 56. How can some examiners find only 16 points of correspondence while others find as many as 56, if the selection of points for comparison is scientific? Evett and Williams [26] conclude that the determination of the individual points for comparison is subjective.

More serious still are the implications to be drawn from pairs B and E in Fig. 17.1. While the correct answer is Identification, 10% of these highly experienced examiners concluded that pair B was not an identification to which they would testify in court. For pair E, the lack of agreement is even more pronounced: Half of the examiners failed to score this as an identification. These results are comparable to those of the FBI Mitchell survey, in which highly experienced examiners, who knew they were being tested, came to disparate conclusions. Human error does not seem to be a likely cause of the lack of agreement. The FBI Mitchell survey and the United Kingdom study both suggest that the comparison procedure itself is unreliable, and is applied inconsistently by highly experienced examiners. Because individual experienced examiners reached

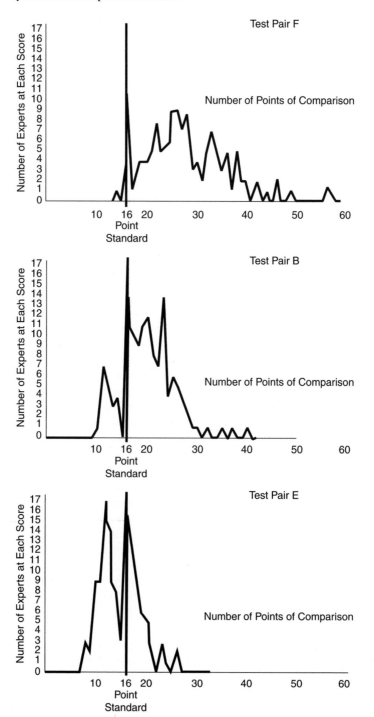

Fig. 17.1. The number of correspondences reported by the 130 expert examiners (data taken from [26]), for 3 of the 10 comparison pairs tested.

different conclusions about the same comparisons, the profession cannot claim an "objective and exact science" in which the conclusions presented are "absolute and final."

The Evett and Williams study is the only published example that assesses the accuracy with which highly skilled examiners made comparisons independently. However, it cannot be used as data about true error rates, nor as a basis from which to generalize to examiner accuracy in court. Four shortcomings are present. The latent prints in this study were judged by experts to be of sufficient quality so they were all usable for comparisons (so examiner accuracy in determining whether a print was scorable was not assessed); 9 of the 10 comparisons were identifications, with only 1 an elimination (so little assessment of erroneous identification rates was possible); each latent print was presented already paired with a single known 10-print card (no search was required); and there were no AFIS outputs or other multiply presented candidates to compare. Each of these lacks makes the study nonrepresentative of the normal kinds of comparisons carried out by latent print examiners.

For these reasons, the Evett and Williams [26] report does not provide information about individual examiner error rates of identifications made in court.

17.6. Experimental Test Results

17.6.1. Results of Published Experiments on Examiner Accuracy Using AFIS Outputs

There are no published experimental tests on the accuracy with which human examiners compare latent prints to AFIS outputs, nor any on the effect of the number of candidates produced by AFIS on the accuracy of comparison. This is the case even though the FBI estimated [11] that at least half of all fingerprint comparisons made by examiners involve AFIS outputs.

When a latent print is submitted to a search of a database by AFIS, the typical output consists of fingerprint images of a number of candidates the AFIS has found to share the greatest similarity to the latent print. The AFIS output also rates or ranks the similarity of each candidate to the target latent. The examiner, presumably having already analyzed the latent, compares it to each of the AFIS candidates. Examiners typically begin with the highest ranked candidate and continue through the remaining ones, until they find an identification or until they eliminate all the candidates.

Some comparison problems are unique to AFIS output tasks. First, most of the candidates displayed in the AFIS output share a number of similarities by virtue of the AFIS search and comparison algorithms, even though only one, at best, can be a correct identification, and all the rest must be erroneous. While the human examiner can usually exclude some candidates as obvious eliminations, many require full analysis and comparison to the latent to eliminate them. When an examiner starts with the highest ranked candidate and does not complete a full analysis and comparison procedure for the other possibilities, there is a greater chance that an erroneous identification will be made. Second, some examiners, especially inexperienced ones, ignore proper use of AFIS as a search device only, and rely on the AFIS rankings rather than on their own judgment. This improper procedure can lead to erroneous identifications. Third, to the extent that the candidate prints produced by AFIS are quite similar to one another, the difficulty of the examiner's task is increased. This has two consequences: The examiner may be more likely to rely on the AFIS ranking; and the examiner is more likely to make an error.

For these reasons, experimental tests are needed to demonstrate the accuracy with which examiners make identifications and eliminations using AFIS outputs. Until such data are available, identifications made in court based on AFIS search outputs will continue to pose special concerns about error rates. At present, there are no data.

17.6.2. Results of Published Experiments on Human Latent Fingerprint Examiner Accuracy and Error Rates

No such experiments have ever been published.

17.7. Summary

The FBI anecdotal evidence of zero error rates should be rejected in light of all the factors that make such exposures virtually impossible. The data on examiner consensus accuracy suggest, on the surface, high error rates for individual examiners. However, the proficiency data from ASCLD and CTS are flawed in such fundamental ways that no conclusions whatsoever on examiner accuracy should be drawn from them. The results from the Mitchell case indicate great variability in judgments of comparison. This variability must be addressed: It suggests a lack of rigorous methodology and/or a failure of the uniqueness assumption with respect to latent prints. Most decisive is the evidence that fingerprint comparison errors have been discovered and erroneous identifications have been attested to in court. The error rate is not zero, but its magnitude is unknown.

The data from the tests of individual examiners, like the consensus data, suggest that examiners may err, but do not permit any estimate whatsoever of the magnitude of the error rate. Nor do the test results generalize to comparisons examiners normally make on the job.

Our careful search of all the professional research literature turned up not a single experiment on examiner accuracy, either when comparing latent prints to AFIS outputs or when comparing latent prints to 10-prints. Such data simply do not exist, even though examiners have testified in court about their infallible accuracy in making fingerprint comparisons for almost 100 years.

We conclude from this review of the data on fingerprint examiner accuracy that the error rate is greater than zero and that no estimate of the magnitude of the error rate can be determined. It would be a gross injustice to the profession to draw any conclusions whatsoever on the basis of these data, taken singly or in combination. It is an even graver injustice to convict a defendant on the basis of a comparison technique for which the magnitude of the error rate is unknown. Research is needed to demonstrate the true accuracy levels for the kinds of tasks print examiners have performed when they testify to an identification in court.

Acknowledgment

The world of highly trained, very experienced fingerprint examiners is a small one, and the examiners work under great pressure and overwhelming demands. Several, nevertheless, gave us many hours of their time. We gratefully acknowledge the help and education they provided us. We are profoundly impressed by their professionalism, level of expertise, and commitment to accurate performance.

References

1. *People of Illinois v. Jennings*, 252 Illinois, 534, 96, NE 1077 (Illinois, 1911).
2. Hazen, R.J. and C.E. Phillips, The expert fingerprint witness, in H.C. Lee & R.E. Gaensslen, eds., *Advances in Fingerprint Technology*, 2nd ed., Boca Raton, FL: CRC Press, 2001.
3. Stoney, David A., Fingerprint Identification, in David L. Faigman, David H. Kaye, Michael J. Saks, and Joseph Sanders, eds., *Modern Scientific Evidence: The Law and Science of Expert Testimony*, St. Paul, MN: West, 1997.
4. *Daubert v. Merrell Dow Pharmaceuticals*, United States Supreme Court, 509, US, 574, 1993.
5. *Kumho Tire Co., Ltd. v. Carmichael*, 236 U.S. 137, 1999.
6. Ashbaugh, D.R., Quantitative-Qualitative Friction Ridge Analysis: An Introduction to Basic and Advanced Ridgeology, Boca Raton, FL: The CRC Press, 1999.
7. Haber, R.N. and L. Haber (in preparation), Forensic scientific theories of identification: The case for a fingerprint identification science. To be submitted for publication, winter, 2002–03.
8. Haber, L. and R.N. Haber (in preparation), The accuracy of fingerprint evidence. To be submitted for publication, winter, 2002–03.
9. Cole, S.A., *Suspect Identities: A History of Fingerprinting and Criminal Investigations*, Cambridge: Harvard University Press, 2001.
10. Scientific Working Group on Friction Ridge Analysis Study and Technology (SWGFAST), Proposed SWGFAST guidelines, *J. Forensic Identification* 47:425–437, 1997.
11. Meagher, S., Testimony on Mr. Plaza's motion to exclude the government's latent fingerprint identification evidence, hearing before Judge Louis Pollak, *USA v. Plaza, et al.*, U.S. District Court for the Eastern District of Pennsylvania, Feb. 24, 2002.
12. Illsley, C., Juries, fingerprints and the expert fingerprint witness. Paper presented at the International Symposium on Latent Prints, FBI Academy, Quantico, VA., July 1987.
13. American Society of Crime Laboratory Directors, Report of the Laboratory Accreditation Board, www.ascld-lab.org, 2001.
14. Peterson, J.L. and P.N. Markham, Crime laboratory proficiency testing results 1978–1991. II: Resolving questions of common origin, *J. Forensic Science*, 40:1009–1029, 1995.
15. Collaborative Testing Services, Certification Examination Testing Program for 1995, Report # 9508; 9608; 9708; 9808; 9908; 0008; 01-517; 01-518, 1995.
16. *United States of America v. Plaza et al.*, U.S. District Court of the Eastern District of Pennsylvania, 2002.
17. Arvizu, J., Testimony on Mr. Plaza's motion to exclude the government's latent fingerprint identification evidence, hearing before Judge Louis Pollak, *USA v. Plaza, et al.*, U.S. District Court for the Eastern District of Pennsylvania, Feb. 24, 2002.

18. Haber, R.N., Testimony on Mr. Plaza's motion to exclude the government's latent fingerprint identification evidence, hearing before Judge Louis Pollak, *USA v. Plaza, et al.*, U.S. District Court for the Eastern District of Pennsylvania, Feb. 24, 2002.

19. Haber, L. and R.N. Haber (in preparation), The importance of double-blind procedures in forensic identification and verification. To be submitted for publication, winter, 2002–03.

20. *United States of America v. Byron Mitchell*, U.S. District Court of the Eastern District of Pennsylvania, 1999.

21. Epstein, R., Reply memo of law in support of Mr. Ramsey's motion to exclude the government's latent fingerprint identification evidence. *USA v. Ramsey*, U.S. District Court for the Eastern District of Pennsylvania, 2001.

22. Starrs, J., More saltimbancos on the loose?: Fingerprint experts caught in a whorl of error, *Scientific Sleuthing Newsletter*, Winter, 1998.

23. Bayle, A., Testimony on Mr. Plaza's motion to exclude the government's latent fingerprint identification evidence, hearing before Judge Louis Pollak, *USA v. Plaza, et al.*, U.S. District Court for the Eastern District of Pennsylvania, Feb. 24, 2002.

24. Newman, A., Fingerprinting's reliability draws growing court challenges, *The New York Times*, April 7, 2001.

25. International Association of Identification, Advanced ridgeology comparison techniques course, www.scafo.org, 2001.

26. Evett, Z.W. and R.L. Williams, Review of the sixteen point fingerprint standard in England and Wales, *J. Forensic Identification*, 46:49–73, 1996.

Chapter 18

Generation of Synthetic Fingerprint Image Databases

Davide Maltoni

Abstract. Collecting large databases of fingerprint images is problematic due to the great amount of time and money required and due to privacy legislation, which in some countries prohibits the diffusion of such personal information. This chapter describes the SFINGE (acronym for Synthetic FINgerprint GEnerator) approach, developed by the BIOLAB team, which can be used to create, at zero cost, large fingerprint databases. The synthesis of each master fingerprint relies on a directional-image model, which determines the underlying ridgeline orientation, and on Gaborlike space-variant filters, which iteratively expand an initially empty image containing just one or a few seeds. From each master fingerprint several finger impressions (fingerprints) can be derived by controlling displacement, rotation, distortion, skin condition, and noise. In particular, an accurate plastic distortion model is employed to deal with the distortion resulting by pressing a finger against the flat surface of an online sensor. SFINGE produces very realistic fingerprint images, which can be used for training, testing, and optimizing fingerprint recognition algorithms. This approach has been validated by proving that several third-party recognition algorithms behave similarly on real and on SFINGE-generated databases.

18.1. Introduction

Fingerprint recognition is one of the most important biometric techniques: The largely accepted uniqueness of fingerprints and the availability of low-cost acquisition devices make it well suited for a wide range of applications [10]. Great efforts are continually spent on designing new fingerprint recognition algorithms, in both academic and industrial environments [14], but not enough care is usually dedicated to performance evaluation. In fact, testing a fingerprint recognition algorithm requires a large database of samples (thousands or tens of thousands), due to the small errors that have to be estimated [21]. Unfortunately, collecting large databases of fingerprint images is (1) expensive in terms of both money and time, (2) boring for both the people involved and the volunteers, (3) problematic due to the privacy legislation that protects such personal data.

FVC2000 [13] and FVC2002 [14] are examples of technology evaluations, where real fingerprint databases were collected to test and compare different algorithms;

unfortunately, these data sets do not constitute lasting solutions since they expire once "used" and new databases have to be collected for future evaluations.

This chapter descripes the SFINGE approach. SFINGE has been developed by the BIOLAB team, in particular, by Raffaele Cappelli, Dario Maio, and Davide Maltoni. SFINGE can be used to create, at zero cost, large databases of fingerprints, thus allowing fingerprint recognition algorithms to be effectively trained, tested, and optimized. The artificial fingerprints generated emulate fingerprints acquired with electronic scanners, since most of today's applications require acquiring fingerprints online. On the other hand, with a few changes, the generation of impressions produced by the classic "ink technique" is also possible.

Very few studies on synthetic fingerprint generation are available in the literature. In [17], with the aim of robustly binarizing a gray-scale fingerprint image, a complex method, which employs a dynamic nonlinear system called "M-lattice," is introduced; the method is based on the reaction-diffusion model first proposed by Turing in 1952 to explain the formation of visual patterns on animals, such as zebra stripes. D. Kosz of the Polish company Optel sp. published some interesting results [11] concerning artificial fingerprint generation based on a novel mathematical model of ridge patterns and minutiae; unfortunately, to protect the commercial exploitation of his idea, the author does not provide any technical details. Novikov and Glushchenko [15] propose a ridge generation technique operating in the frequency domain. For each pixel p of an initial random image, the 2D Fourier spectrum of a local window, centered at p, is computed. The highest energy harmonic (i.e., a pure 2D sinusoid in the spatial domain) is chosen from the Fourier spectrum along the normal to the local ridge orientation in p (according to an a priori artificially generated directional image). All the obtained sinusoids are summed and the result is binarized; the procedure is iteratively repeated until a sufficiently smooth result is obtained. This method has some analogies with the iterative application of Gabor space-variant filters in the spatial domain as discussed in Section 18.4.4; in fact, the MTF (modulation transfer function) of a Gabor filter is characterized by two symmetric peaks along the normal to the filter orientation [5]. Finally, a constructive approach was recently proposed [9] where a fingerprint pattern is generated starting from a given set of minutiae points; the work is aimed at proving that a masquerade attack can be carried out against a fingerprint-based biometric system, by "fraudulently" accessing and deciphering the content of a stored template and by recreating an artificial clone (either digital or synthetic). Unfortunately, the algorithm proposed to draw ridge patterns (starting from minutiae positions and then iteratively filling empty spaces) produces images that are visually not realistic.

This chapter is organized as follows: Section 18.2 introduces fingerprint characteristics and terminology. Section 18.3 presents a basic scheme of the SFINGE approach, which points out the different steps involved in the generation of a *master fingerprint* and its derived *fingerprint impression*. A master fingerprint is a pattern that encodes the unique and immutable characteristics of a "synthetic finger" independently of the variations (displacement, rotation, pressure, skin condition, distortion, noise, etc.) that cause successive acquisitions to differ from one another. Sections 18.4 and 18.5 describe in detail the generation of a master fingerprint and the derivation of fingerprint impressions, respectively. Section 18.6 introduces the experimentation performed to validate SFINGE. Finally, Section 18.7 discusses possible uses and provides some concluding remarks.

18.2. Fingerprint Anatomy

A fingerprint is the representation of the epidermis of a finger. At a macroscopic analysis, a fingerprint is composed of a set of *ridgelines*, which often flow parallel and sometimes produce local macrosingularities called the *core* and *delta*, respectively (Fig. 18.1).

A core is defined by having at least one ridge that enters the fingerprint and curves back, leaving the fingerprint on the same side. The top of the innermost curving ridge is defined as the core. At the other side of a core, there are ridges that enter the fingerprint and meet the curving ridges: Some of these rise above the core and some fall below; the point where they diverge that is closest to the curving ridges is called the delta.

The number of cores and deltas in a single fingerprint is regulated in nature by some stringent rules: In particular, each core has a corresponding delta. Fingerprints are usually partitioned into five main classes (*arch, tented arch, left loop, right loop, whorl*) according to their macrosingularities (Fig. 18.2).

An arch fingerprint has ridges that enter from one side, rise to a slight bump, and go out the opposite side from which they entered. Arches do not have cores or deltas.

A tented arch fingerprint is similar to the (plain) arch, except that at least one ridge exhibits a high curvature and one core and one delta are present.

A loop fingerprint has one or more ridges that enter from one side, curve back, and go out the same side they entered. A core and a delta singularity are present. Loops can be further subdivided: Loops that have ridges that enter and leave from the left side are called left loops, and loops that have ridges that enter and leave from the right side are called right loops.

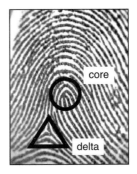

Fig. 18.1. Fingerprint ridgelines (left); fingerprint macrosingularities (right).

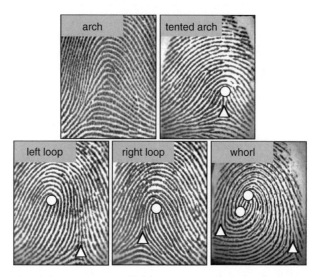

Fig. 18.2. A fingerprint for each of the five main classes: White circles denote core singularities, whereas white triangles denote delta singularities.

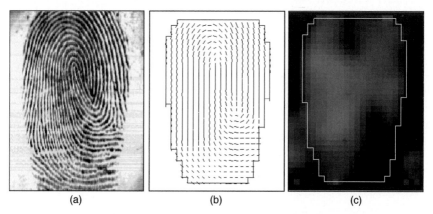

Fig. 18.3. In (b) the directional image of (a) is shown; (c) shows the local density map of (a), where the light blocks denote higher-density regions.

A whorl fingerprint contains at least one ridge that makes a complete 360° circuit around the center of the fingerprint. Two cores and two deltas can be found in whorl fingerprints.

The ridgeline flow can be effectively described by a structure called a *directional map* (or *directional image*), which is a discrete matrix whose elements denote the orientation of the tangent to the ridgelines (Fig. 18.3b). Analogously, the ridgeline density (or frequency) can be represented by using a *density map* (Figure 18.3c).

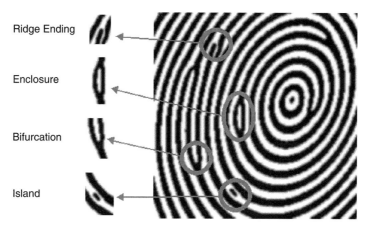

Fig. 18.4. Four kinds of minutiae.

At a finer analysis, other very important features, named *minutiae*, may be discovered in the fingerprint patterns. Minutia means "small detail"; in the context of fingerprints, the term refers to various discontinuities of the ridges. For example, a ridge can suddenly come to an end (*ridge ending*) or can fork into two ridges (*bifurcation*). Sir Francis Galton (1822–1911) was the first person to categorize minutiae and to observe that they remain unchanged over an individual lifetime [12]. Minutiae are sometimes called "Galton points" in his honor. Figure 18.4 identifies 4 kinds of minutiae; fingerprint experts can distinguish up to 19 different types, however, most automatic fingerprint recognition systems consider only two kinds: bifurcations and ridge endings.

18.3. How SFINGE Works

The basic idea behind SFINGE is quite simple (Fig. 18.5): A fingerprint shape, a directional map, and a density map, generated independently from one another, are the inputs of a ridge-generation process; the resulting binary ridge pattern is then rendered by adding fingerprint-specific noise.

In order to generate more impressions of the same finger, a more complicated schema has to be introduced: a *master fingerprint* (i.e., a ridge pattern, which represents the unique and immutable characteristics of a "synthetic finger") must first be generated; then several synthetic fingerprints can be derived from the master fingerprint, by explicitly tuning displacement, rotation, distortion, skin condition, and noise. Figure 18.6 shows the complete generation process: Steps 1–4 create a master fingerprint; steps 5–10 are performed for each fingerprint impression derived from the master fingerprint.

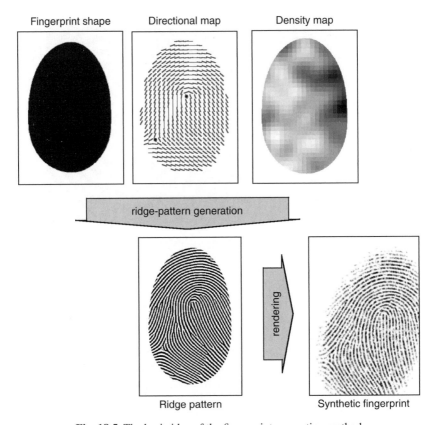

Fig. 18.5. The basic idea of the fingerprint generation method.

18.4. Master-Fingerprint Generation

Creating a master fingerprint involves the following steps:

1. Fingerprint shape generation
2. Directional map generation
3. Density map generation
4. Ridge pattern generation

Step 1 defines the external silhouette of the fingerprint; step 2, starting from the positions of cores and deltas, exploits a mathematical flow model to generate a consistent directional map. Step 3 creates a density map on the basis of some heuristic criteria inferred by the visual inspection of several real fingerprints. In step 4, the ridgeline pattern and the minutiae are created through a space-variant iterative filtering; the output is a near-binary fingerprint image. A separate subsection is dedicated to each of the above steps.

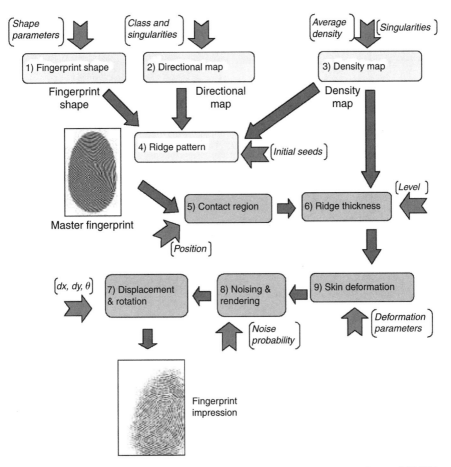

Fig. 18.6. A functional schema of the synthetic fingerprint generation according to SFINGE: Each rounded box represents a generation step; the main input parameters that control each step are reported between brackets. Steps 1–4 create a master fingerprint; steps 5–9 derive from the master fingerprint a fingerprint impression.

18.4.1. Generation of the Fingerprint Shape

Depending on the finger size, position, and pressure on the acquisition sensor, the acquired fingerprint images can have different sizes and external shapes (Fig. 18.7).

The visual examination of several fingerprint images suggests that a simple model, based on four elliptical arcs and a rectangle and controlled by five parameters (Fig. 18.8), can handle most of the variations present in real fingerprint shapes. Figure 18.8 shows some examples of fingerprint shapes generated by this model, varying the five parameters.

Fig. 18.7. Examples of fingerprint images with different sizes and shapes.

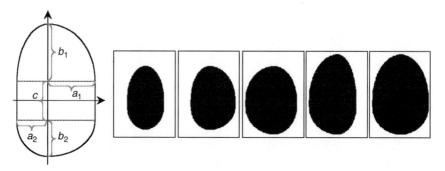

Fig. 18.8. The fingerprint shape model (on the left) and some examples of fingerprint silhouettes generated by this model (on the right).

18.4.2. Directional Map Generation

The orientation model proposed by Sherlock and Monro [16] allows a consistent directional map to be calculated from the position of cores and deltas only. In this model the image is located in the complex plane and the local ridge orientation is the phase of the square root of a complex rational function whose singularities (poles and zeroes) are located at the same place as the fingerprint macrosingularities (cores and deltas). Let c_i, $i = 1, \ldots, n_c$, and d_i, $i = 1, \ldots, n_d$ be the coordinates of the cores and deltas, respectively. The orientation O at each point z is calculated as

$$O(z) = \frac{1}{2} \left[\sum_{i=1}^{n_d} \arg(z - d_i) - \sum_{i=1}^{n_c} \arg(z - c_i) \right]$$

where the function $\arg(z)$ returns the argument of the complex number z.

The Sherlock and Monro model can be exploited for generating synthetic directional maps as follows: First, the fingerprint class is randomly chosen; then the positions of the macrosingularities are randomly selected, according to the class-specific constraints (for instance, in a left loop, the delta must be on the right side of the core). Figure 18.9 shows some examples of directional maps generated by this model. Unfortunately, arch-type patterns, which do not contain any macrosingularities, are not supported and must be considered separately. However, this does not

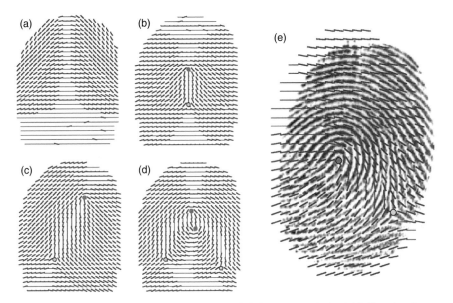

Fig. 18.9. An example of arch (a), tented arch (b), right loop (c), and whorl (d) directional maps as generated by the Sherlock and Monro model. In (e) is an example of a left loop directional image superimposed over a left loop fingerprint with coincident singularity positions.

constitute a big problem since arch directional map generation is straightforward: We use a sinusoidal function whose frequency and amplitude are changed to control the arch shape.

In nature the ridgeline flow is determined by the macrosingularity type and position, hence the Sherlock and Monro model; and although being a good starting point, it is not satisfactory. Figure 18.9e shows a fingerprint image (belonging to the left loop class) and the directional image generated by the above model, with the same position of the core and delta. Evident differences exist between the real ridgeline orientations and the corresponding orientations in the directional image: In particular, the regions above the core and between the core and the delta are not well modeled.

Vizcaya and Gerhardt [18] propose a variant of the Sherlock and Monro model that introduces more degrees of freedom to cope with the orientation variability that may characterize directional images with coincident singularities. The orientation O at each point z is calculated as

$$O(z) = \frac{1}{2}\left[\sum_{i=1}^{n_d} g_{d_i}(\arg(z - d_i)) - \sum_{i=1}^{n_c} g_{c_i}(\arg(z - c_i))\right] \qquad (1)$$

where $g_k(\theta)$, for $k \in \{c_1, \ldots, c_{n_c}, d_1, \ldots, d_{n_d}\}$, are piecewise linear functions capable of locally correcting the orientation field with respect to the value given by the Sherlock and Monro model:

$$g_k(\theta) = \overline{g}_k(\theta_i) + \frac{\theta - \theta_i}{2\pi/L}(\overline{g}_k(\theta_{i+1}) - \overline{g}_k(\theta_i)), \quad \text{for } \theta_i \le \theta \le \theta_{i+1}, \theta_i = -\pi + \frac{2\pi i}{L}$$

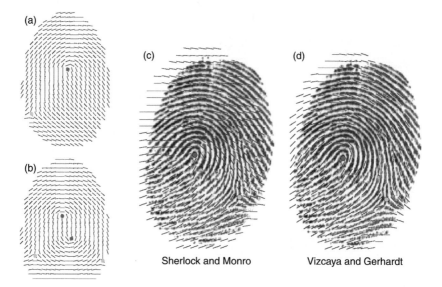

Sherlock and Monro   Vizcaya and Gerhardt

Fig. 18.10. An example of right loop (a) and whorl (b) directional maps as generated by the Vizcaya and Gerhardt model. In (c) and (d) the directional maps produced by the two models, for a given fingerprint, are compared.

Each function $g_k(\theta)$ is defined by the set of values $\{\overline{g}_k(\theta_i)|i = 0, \ldots, L - 1\}$, where each value is the amount of correction of the orientation field at a given angle (in a set of L angles uniformly distributed between $-\pi$ and π). Because the aim of the work by Vizcaya and Gerhardt [18] is approximating a real directional image, given a specific fingerprint, the authors derive the values $\overline{g}_k(\theta_i)$ through an optimization procedure. Our synthetic generation does not need to approximate any given directional map, and the additional degrees of freedom given by the Vizcaya and Gerhardt model are exploited to provide more variations. In particular, we set $L = 8$ and derived appropriate ranges for the parameters from the analysis of real fingerprints; during the directional map generation, random values are selected within such ranges. Figure 18.10a and b show two examples of directional maps generated according to the Vizcaya and Gerhardt model; these maps are definitely more realistic than those in Fig. 18.9. The superiority of the Vizcaya and Gerhardt model in approximating existing ridge patterns is also evident from the comparison of Fig. 18.10c and d.

18.4.3. Density Map Generation

The visual inspection of several fingerprint images leads us to immediately discard the possibility of generating the density map in a completely random way. In fact, we noted that usually in the region above the northernmost core and in the region below the southernmost delta, the ridgeline density is lower than in the rest of the fingerprint. Therefore, the density map generation is performed as follows:

1. Randomly select a feasible overall background density

Fig. 18.11. Some examples of generated density maps.

2. Slightly increase the density in the above-described regions according to the singularity locations
3. Randomly perturb the density map and perform a local smoothing Figure 18.11 reports some examples of density maps generated by this approach.

18.4.4. Ridge Pattern Generation

Given a directional map and a density map as input, a deterministic generation of a ridgeline pattern, including consistent minutiae, is not an easy task. One could try to fix a priori the number, type, and location of the minutiae, and by means of an explicit model, generate the gray-scale fingerprint image starting from the minutiae neighborhoods and expanding to connect different regions until the whole image is covered [9]. Such a constructive approach requires several complex rules and "tricks" to be implemented, in order to deal with the complexity of fingerprint ridgeline patterns. A more "elegant" approach could be based on the use of a syntactic approach that generates fingerprints according to some starting symbols and a set of production rules.

The method SFINGE uses is very simple, but at the same time surprisingly powerful: By iteratively enhancing an initial image (containing one or more isolated spikes[1]) through Gaborlike filters [5] adjusted according to the local ridge orientation and density, a consistent and very realistic ridgeline pattern "magically" appears; in particular, fingerprint minutiae of different types (endings, bifurcations, islands, etc.) are automatically generated at random positions.

Formally, the filter is obtained as the product of a Gaussian by a cosine plane wave; a correction term is included to make the filter DC free (i.e., to eliminate the constant term) [5]:

$$f(\mathbf{v}) = \frac{1}{\sigma^2} e^{-\frac{\|\mathbf{v}\|^2}{2\sigma^2}} \left(cos(\mathbf{k} \cdot \mathbf{v}) - e^{-\frac{(\sigma\|\mathbf{k}\|)^2}{2}} \right)$$

where σ is the variance of the Gaussian and $\mathbf{k}$ is the wave vector of the plane wave. A graphical representation of the filter is shown in Fig. 18.12. The parameters σ and $\mathbf{k}$ are adjusted using local ridge orientation and density. Let $\mathbf{z}$ be a point of the image where the filters have to be applied; then the vector $\mathbf{k} = [k_x, k_y]^T$ is determined by the solution of the following two equations:

$$D(\mathbf{z}) = \sqrt{k_x^2 + k_y^2}, \qquad \tan(O(\mathbf{z})) = -\frac{k_x}{k_y}$$

---

[1] In a digital image with a white background, a spike is represented by a single black pixel.

Fig. 18.12. A representation of the Gaborlike filter used to create ridgeline patterns.

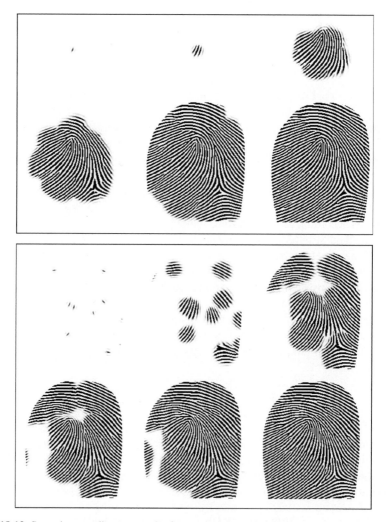

Fig. 18.13. Some intermediate steps of a fingerprint generation process starting from a single central spike (top) and from a number of randomly located spikes (bottom). Usually, increasing the number of initial spikes determines a more irregular ridge pattern richer of minutiae.

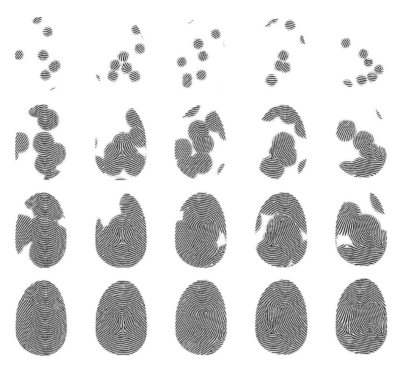

Fig. 18.14. Each column shows an example of a fingerprint generation process for a different fingerprint class; from the left to the right: arch, tented arch, left loop, right loop, and whorl.

where $O(\mathbf{z})$ is the local ridgeline orientation in $\mathbf{z}$ (Eq. 1) and $D(\mathbf{z})$ is the local ridge density (as computed in Section 18.4.3). The parameter σ, which determines the bandwidth of the filter, is adjusted in the time domain according to $D(\mathbf{z})$ so that the filter does not contain more than three effective peaks (as shown in Figure 18.12). The filter is then clipped to get an FIR filter and is designed with the constraint that the maximum possible response is larger than 1. When such a filter is applied repeatedly, the dynamic range of the output increases and becomes numerically unstable, but the generation algorithm exploits this fact. When the output values are clipped to fit into a constant range, it is possible to obtain a near-binary image. The above filter equation satisfies this requirement without any normalization.

While one could reasonably expect that iteratively applying "striped" filters to random images would produce striped images, the generation of very realistic minutiae at random positions is somewhat unpredictable. During our experimentation we argued that minutiae primarily originate from the ridgeline disparity produced by local convergence/divergence of the orientation field and by density changes. In Figs. 18.13 and 18.14, some examples of the iterative ridgeline generation process are shown. We experimentally found that increasing the number of initial spikes determines a more irregular ridge pattern richer of minutiae (Fig. 18.13): This is not surprising, since expanding distinct image regions causes interference where a region collapses, thus favoring the creation of minutiae.

18.5. Generation of Synthetic Fingerprint Impressions

Several factors contribute to make substantially different impressions of a given finger as captured through an online acquisition sensor:

Displacement in X- and Y-direction and rotation

Different touching area

Nonlinear distortion produced by nonorthogonal pressure of the finger against the sensor

Variations in the ridgeline thickness given by pressure intensity or by skin dampness (wet or dry)

Small cuts or abrasions on the fingertip

Background noise and other random noise

For each fingerprint impression to be generated from a given master fingerprint, SFINGE sequentially performs the following steps (the numbering continues from Section 18.4 as specified in Fig. 18.6):

5. Definition of the fingerprint portion that is in contact with the sensor (this is simply performed by shifting the fingerprint pattern with respect to the fixed external silhouette)
6. Variation of the ridge average thickness (skin condition)
7. Distortion
8. Noising and rendering
9. Global translation/rotation

18.5.1. Variation of the Ridge Thickness

Skin dampness and finger pressure against the sensor platen have similar effects on the acquired images: When the skin is dry or the pressure is low, ridges appear thinner; whereas when the skin is wet or the pressure is high, ridges appear thicker (Fig. 18.15).

Morphological operators [8] are applied to the master fingerprint, to simulate different degrees of dampness/pressure. In particular, the erosion operator is applied

Fig. 18.15. Three impressions of the same real finger as captured when the finger is dry, normal, and wet.

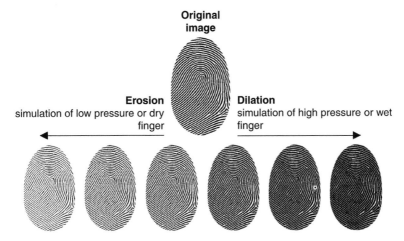

Fig. 18.16. Application of different levels of erosion/dilation to the same master fingerprint is illustrated.

to simulate low pressure or dry skin, while the dilation operator is adopted to simulate high pressure or wet skin (Fig. 18.16). The structuring element used is a square box; its size varies from 2×2 to 4×4 to modulate the magnitude of the ridge thickness variation.

18.5.2. Distortion

One of the main aspects that distinguish different impressions of the same finger is the presence of nonlinear distortions, mainly due to skin deformations according to different finger placements over the sensing element (Fig. 18.17). In fact, due to the skin plasticity, the application of forces, some of whose components are not orthogonal to the sensor surface, produces nonlinear distortions (compression or stretching) in the acquired fingerprints.

In [3] we introduced a skin distortion model to cope with the nonlinear distortion caused by nonorthogonal pressure of the finger against the sensor surface. By noting that the finger pressure against the sensor is not uniform but decreases moving from the center toward the borders, the distortion model defines three distinct regions (see Fig. 18.18):

- *a.* A close-contact region where the high pressure and the surface friction do not allow any skin slippage
- *c.* An external region, whose boundary delimits the fingerprint visible area, where the light pressure allows the finger skin to be dragged by the finger movement
- *b.* A transitional region where an elastic distortion is produced to smoothly combine regions *a* and *c*. The skin compression and stretching are restricted to region *b*, since points in *a* remain almost fixed and points in *c* rigidly move together with the rest of the finger.

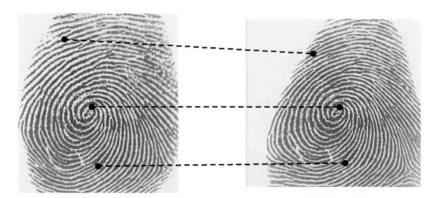

Fig. 18.17. Two impressions of the same real finger where corresponding points are marked to highlight distortions.

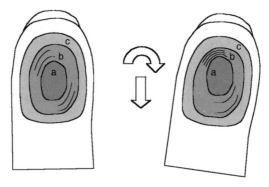

Fig. 18.18. Bottom view of a finger before and after the application of traction and torsion forces. In both cases the fingerprint area detected by the sensor (i.e., the finger touching area) is delimited by the external boundary of region c.

The distortion model is defined by a mapping $\Re^2 \to \Re^2$ that can be viewed as an affine transformation (with no scale change) that is progressively annihilated as it moves from c toward a. Each point $\mathbf{v}$ is mapped into distortion($\mathbf{v}$) such that

$$\text{distortion}(\mathbf{v}) = \mathbf{v} + \Delta(\mathbf{v}) \cdot \text{brake}(\text{shapedist}_a(\mathbf{v}), k)$$

where Δ specifies the affine transformation of the external region c; shapedist(.) is a shape function describing the boundary of region a; brake(.) is a monotonically increasing function that rules the gradual transition from region a toward region c; and the input parameter k regulates the skin plasticity. Figure 18.19 shows some examples of distortion varying the parameters.

Unlike in [3], where the distortion model is applied to remap minutiae points in order to improve fingerprint matching, in SFINGE the mapping has to be applied to the whole master fingerprint image. Therefore, Lagrangian interpolation is employed

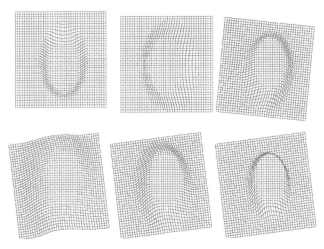

Fig. 18.19. Distortions of a square mesh obtained by applying the above model with different parameter settings. The black square denotes the initial mesh position, and its movement with respect to the mesh boundary indicates the amount of displacement and rotation that occurred. In the first row, different transformations are shown [from the left to the right: a vertical displacement ($dy = -21$), a horizontal displacement ($dx = 18$), and a combined displacement + rotation ($dx = -6$, $dy = 27$, $\theta = -6°$)]; the second row shows the effect of varying the skin plasticity coefficient k (2.0, 1.0, and 0.5, respectively) for a given transformation.

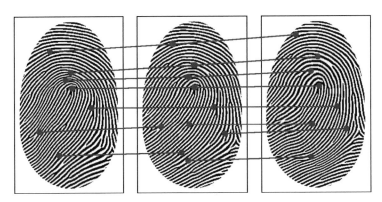

Fig. 18.20. Two distorted images of the same master fingerprint (central image): Some corresponding minutiae are connected to highlight the nonlinear deformations.

to obtain a smoothed gray-scale target image. Performing Lagrangian interpolation requires the inverse mapping function distortion^{-1}(.) to be computed, but unfortunately this function cannot be analytically derived. Therefore, for each pixel involved in the mapping, the Newton–Raphson method [20] is used for numerically calculating the inverse. In Fig. 18.20, two distorted images generated from the same master fingerprint are shown.

Fig. 18.21. An example of noising and rendering with the intermediate images produced after steps 2, 4, and 5.

18.5.3. Noising, Rendering, and Global Translation/Rotation

During fingerprint acquisition, several factors contribute to deteriorate the original signal, thus producing a gray-scale noisy image: irregularity of the ridges and their different contact with the sensor surface; presence of small pores within the ridges; presence of very small prominence ridges; and gaps and cluttering noise due to nonuniform pressure of the finger against the sensor. Furthermore, the fingerprint is usually not perfectly centered in the image and can present a certain amount of rotation.

The noising and rendering phase sequentially performs the following steps:

1. Isolate the valley white pixels into a separate layer. This is simply performed by copying the pixels brighter than a fixed threshold to a temporary image.
2. Add noise in the form of small white blobs of variable size and shape. The amount of noise increases with the inverse of the fingerprint border distance.
3. Smooth the image over a 3 × 3 window.
4. Superimpose the valley layer to the image obtained.
5. Rotate and translate the image.

Steps 1 and 4 are necessary to avoid an excessive overall image smoothing. Figure 18.21 shows an example where the intermediate images produced after steps 2, 4, and 5 are reported.

18.6. Experimental Results and Validation

We developed an automated tool for generating fingerprint images according to the SFINGE method described in this chapter. A demo version of this tool can be downloaded from http://bias.csr.unibo.it/research/biolab/sfinge.html. This software allows a database to be batch-generated given a relatively small set of input parameters (number of fingers, impressions per finger, image size, seed for the random num-

Fig. 18.22. Two synthetic fingerprint images (first row) are compared with two real fingerprints captured with an online sensor.

ber generator, maximum amount of translation/rotation, maximum amount of noise, maximum amount of deformation, global database difficulty).

In our experimentation, on a Pentium IV PC, a fingerprint database of 10,000 images (240 × 336 pixels) was generated in 11 hours. Figures 18.22 and 18.23 show some samples.

Several experimentations have been carried out to validate SFINGE. In particular:

During ICPR 2000, about 90 people, most having an excellent or good background in fingerprint analysis, have been asked to find a synthetic fingerprint image among four images (three of which were real fingerprints). Just 23% of them (refer to Fig. 18.24 and to Table 18.1) identified the artificial image.

Two important tests have been performed in conjunction with the First and Second International Fingerprint Verification Competition (FVC2000 and FVC2002) [13, 14], where one of the four databases used (DB4) was synthetically generated by SFINGE. Not only are the participant algorithms performed on DB4 similar to the other DBs, but the genuine/impostor distributions and the FMR/FNMR curves are also surprisingly close. Figure 18.25 reports the performance of the PA02 and PA24 algorithms over the four databases. A detailed explanation of these graphs is beyond the scope of this chapter (the reader should refer to [13] for a formal treatment); of note here is that the graphs computed on the synthetic database (fourth column) have a very similar trend to the others. This means that fingerprints generated by SFINGE are realistic from the point of view of the two matching algorithms, PA02 and PA24. All other algorithms that took part in the competitions exhibited similar behaviors.

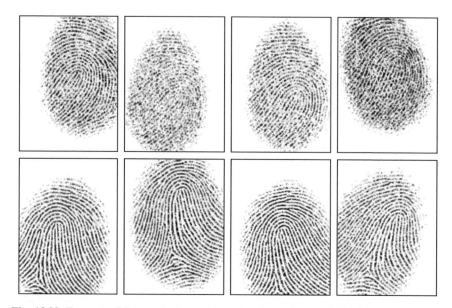

Fig. 18.23. Two sets of fingerprint impressions (one for each row) derived from two master fingerprints (not shown).

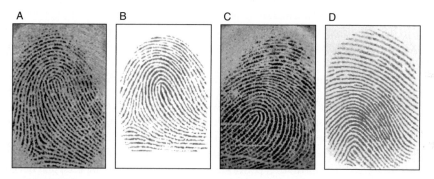

Fig. 18.24. Three real fingerprints (B, C, and D), acquired with different sensors and a synthetic fingerprint (A).

Table 18.1. For Each Fingerprint in Fig. 18.24, the Percentage of People That Chose It as the Synthetic One

Survey result	
A	23%
B	27%
C	21%
D	29%

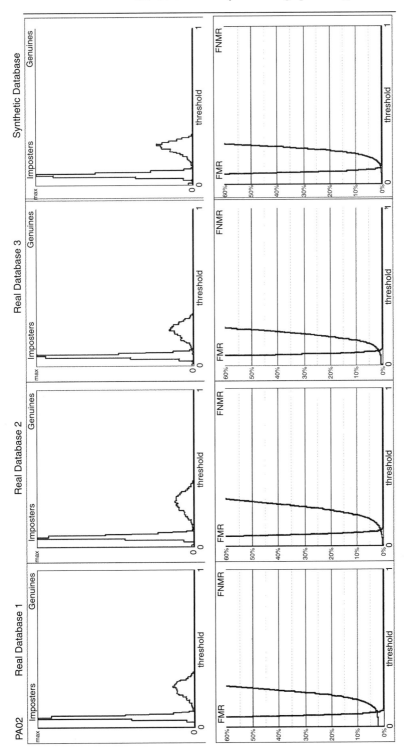

Fig. 18.25. Algorithms PA02 and PA24: impostor/genuine distribution and FMR/FNMR graph, for the four databases used in FVC2002.

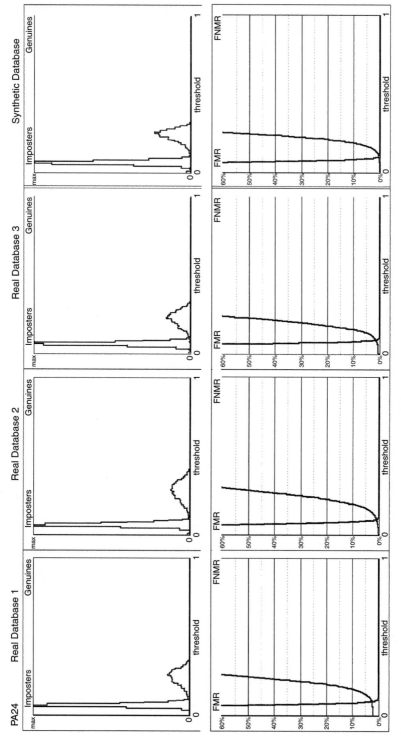

Fig. 18.25. *Continued*

18.7. Conclusions

Synthetic fingerprint generation is an effective technique to overcome the problem of collecting large fingerprint databases for test purposes. Obviously, real-fingerprint databases cannot be completely substituted, especially when performance has to be measured referring to a given real environment/application.

The use of synthetic fingerprints is not only limited to the problem of performance evaluation:

Many classifiers and pattern recognition techniques (i.e., neural network, principal component analysis, and support vector machines.) require a large training set for an accurate learning stage. Synthetic fingerprint images are very well suited to this purpose: In fact, the generator input parameters allow one to explicitly control the type and features of the generated sets (e.g., class, type of noise, distortion, etc.), and this can be exploited in conjunction with boosting techniques to drive the learning process. In [2] we successfully use a large synthetic training set to derive optimal multispace Karhunen–Loève subspaces for fingerprint indexing.

We are currently investigating the use of synthetic fingerprint images to study the robustness of matching algorithms with respect to fake fingerprints. In this case, SFINGE allows us to generate large sets of fingerprints whose features (e.g., minutiae distribution) can be varied independently of other fingerprint characteristics (e.g., directional image), and therefore it is well suited to study the robustness with respect to "hill-climbing" attacks.[2]

As to future improvements, the main aspects we will consider are as follows:

An ad-hoc stage aimed at creating realistic (sensor-dependent) backgrounds. We are currently investigating the use of a supervised technique to learn background variations produced by a set of online sensors.

The ridge thickness is now constant throughout the fingerprint image; this is not true in reality, where this feature may vary across the same fingerprint.

The noise is now uniformly distributed over the fingerprint area (except for the borders, where it gradually increases); in reality, the noise can be clustered in certain regions and in the same fingerprint we can encounter both high-quality and poor-quality regions.

Intraridge noise, which in nature is partially produced by finger pores, is randomly generated by SFINGE. While this is not a problem when generating fingerprints from different fingers, this is not very realistic for impressions of the same finger, where a certain correlation should be kept into account.

References

1. Cappelli, R., A. Erol, D. Maio, and D. Maltoni, Synthetic fingerprint-image generation, *Proc. 15th International Conference on Pattern Recognition (ICPR2000)*, Barcelona, Vol. 3, pp. 475–478, Sept. 2000.

[2] In a hill-climbing attack the response of the system is exploited to guess the key. At each step, the neighborhood of the current solution is explored according to the previous responses.

2. Cappelli, R., D. Maio, and D. Maltoni, Indexing fingerprint databases for efficient 1:N matching, *Proc. 6th International Conference on Control, Automation, Robotics and Vision (ICARCV2000)*, Singapore, Dec. 2000.
3. Cappelli, R., D. Maio, and D. Maltoni, Modelling plastic distortion in fingerprint images, *Proc. ICAPR2001*, Rio de Janeiro, pp. 369–376, March 2001.
4. Cappelli, R., D. Maio, and D. Maltoni, Synthetic fingerprint-database generation, *Proc. 16th International Conference on Pattern Recognition (ICPR2002)*, Québec City, Aug. 2002.
5. Daugman, J.D., Complete discrete 2-d Gabor transforms by neural networks for image analysis and compression, *IEEE Trans. Acoustics, Speech, and Signal Processing*, 36:1169–1179, 1988.
6. Dorai, C., N.K. Ratha, and R.M. Bolle, Detecting dynamic behaviour in compressed fingerprint videos: Distortion, *Proc. CVPR 2000*, Hilton Head, SC, Vol. II, pp. 320–326, June 2000.
7. Duda, R.O. and P.E. Hart, *Pattern Classification and Scene Analysis*, New York: Wiley, 1974.
8. Gonzalez, R.C. and E.R. Woods, *Digital Image Processing*, Reading, MA: Addison-Wesley, 1992.
9. Hill, C.J., Risk of masquerade arising from the storage of biometrics, B.Sc. thesis, Department of Computer Science, Australian National University, Nov. 2001.
10. Jain, A.K., S. Pankanti, and R. Bolle, eds., *BIOMETRICS: Personal Identification in Networked Society*, New York: Kluwer, 1999.
11. Kosz, D., New numerical methods of fingerprint recognition based on mathematical description, *Biometric in Human Service User Group Newsletter*, 15th issue, Aug. 1999.
12. Galton, F., *Finger Prints*, London: Macmillan, 1892.
13. Maio, D., D. Maltoni, R. Cappelli, J.L. Wayman, and A.K. Jain, FVC2000: Fingerprint verification competition, *IEEE Trans. Pattern Analysis Machine Intelligence*, 24(3):402–412, 2002.
14. Maio, D., D. Maltoni, R. Cappelli, J.L. Wayman, and A.K. Jain, FVC2002: Second fingerprint verification competition, *Proc. 16th International Conference on Pattern Recognition (ICPR2002)*, Québec City, Aug. 2002.
15. Novikov, S.O. and G.N. Glushchenko, Fingerprint ridges structure generation models, Intl. Workshop (6th) on Digital Image Processing and Computer Graphics: Applications in Humanities and Natural Sciences, *SPIE Proc.* 3346:270–274, 1998.
16. Sherlock, B. and D. Monro, A model for interpreting fingerprint topology, *Pattern Recognition*, 26(7):1047–1095, 1993.
17. Sherstinsky, A. and R.W. Picard, Restoration and enhancement of fingerprint images using M-lattice-A novel non-linear dynamical system, *Proc. 12th International Conference on Pattern Recognition (ICPR1994)*, Jerusalem, 1994.
18. Vizcaya, P. and L. Gerhardt, A nonlinear orientation model for global description of fingerprints, *Pattern Recognition*, 29(7):1221–1231, 1996.
19. Watson, C.I., *NIST Special Database 24 Digital Video of Live-Scan Fingerprint Data*, U.S. National Institute of Standards and Technology, 1998.
20. Press, W.H., S.A. Teukolsky, W.T. Vetterling, and B.P. Flannery, *Numerical Recipes in C*, Cambridge, UK: Cambridge University Press, 1992.
21. Wayman, J.L., Technical testing and evaluation of biometric devices, in A. Jain et. al. *Biometrics: Personal Identification in Networked Society*, New York: Kluwer Academic Publisher, 1999.

Chapter 19

Fingerprint Image Compression and the Wavelet Scalar Quantization Specification

Remigius Onyshczak and Abdou Youssef

Abstract. Due to the large number and size of fingerprint images, data compression has to be applied to reduce the storage and communication bandwidth requirements of those images. In response to this need, the FBI developed a fingerprint compression specification, called the wavelet scalar quantization (WSQ). As the name suggests, the specification is based on wavelet compression. In this chapter, we review the WSQ specification and discuss its most important theoretical and practical underpinnings. In particular, we present the way wavelet compression generally works and address the choice of the wavelet, the structure of the subbands, the different quantizations of the various subbands, and the entropy coding of the quantized data. The performance of the WSQ is addressed as well.

19.1. Introduction

In the early 1990s, the U.S. Department of Justice, Federal Bureau of Investigation, was confronted with a challenge. It had a rapidly growing collection of 35 million inked fingerprint cards in its repository, a considerable backlog of fingerprint cards needing to be classified, and a steadily increasing volume of fingerprint identification requests. The FBI needed a modern system to capture, classify, and identify fingerprints. It called upon other federal government agencies and private companies to help it create a system capable of gathering fingerprints at state and local law enforcement agencies, transmitting the digital fingerprint images to a central location where they could be classified in real time, matched to known fingerprints in a central database, and stored for future reference. The most current techniques in digital image capture and fingerprint pattern matching promised to make such a system possible, but one other critical piece in such a system had to be developed: image compression.

Digital fingerprint images of sufficient resolution for use in legal proceedings are quite large, presenting problems in rapidly transmitting and economically storing the images. In addition, there are 500 million such images to be stored in and retrieved from a central database and possibly transmitted to state, local, and other federal government law enforcement agencies. To address these issues of transmission speed, bandwidth, and storage capacity, image compression is the logical approach [27].

A crucial question in such situations is the kind of compression to employ. Considering the high demand on reconstruction quality in fingerprint identification, lossless compression may seem the only option. However, lossless image compression techniques offer at most a 2-to-1 or 3-to-1 compression ratio, not sufficient to ease the transmission bandwidth requirements or reduce the amount of media needed to store the volume of fingerprint images at the FBI's central processing facility. A lossy image compression technique had to be developed that could achieve greater than 10-to-1 compression ratios while preserving the essential characteristics of the fingerprint image for both mechanized pattern matching and fingerprint identification by human examiners. The compression technique had to be nonproprietary, allowing it to be used by vendors supplying fingerprint image gathering, storage, retrieval, and processing hardware to local, state, and federal law enforcement agencies.

The FBI, together with the help and cooperation of the other agencies and private firms, developed a lossy compression technique for fingerprint images, which it described in a document entitled "WSQ gray-scale fingerprint image compression specification" [3–5, 12]. This chapter presents the theory behind, a description of, and practical implementation considerations of WSQ.

It should be noted that there are several techniques and standards for compressing general images, including fingerprints. Among the most widely used image compression standards are JPEG [20] and JPEG 2000 [24], and examples of well-known compression techniques include transform coding [7], DCT-based compression [21], subband coding [33], and fractal compression [2]. Also, there have been studies and development of compression techniques for fingerprint images specifically, such as model-based compression [15, 11] and JPEG adapted to fingerprint images [29]. However, none of those standards and techniques has been officially adopted by law enforcement for fingerprint compression. Instead, WSQ is now the primary specification for fingerprint compression, used by the FBI and other law enforcement agencies and departments. Therefore, we focus primarily on WSQ, and compare its performance with JPEG.

This chapter is organized as follows. The next section discusses the general framework of wavelet compression, which is the theory underlying WSQ. Section 19.3 addresses the various choices to be made by the designer for a complete wavelet compression system and identifies briefly the choices made by WSQ. Section 19.4 elaborates more on the WSQ specification, and Section 19.5 discusses the WSQ implementation experience of the first author. The last section concludes the chapter.

19.2. The General Framework of Wavelet Compression

Wavelet-based compression has received considerable attention in the 1990s [1, 31] and has been adopted by various important standards such as JPEG 2000 [24] and MPEG4 [8]. The reasons for the high interest in wavelet compression are largely due to the competitive compression ratios that can be achieved at high quality without the bothersome blocking artifacts of the JPEG-style discrete-cosine-transform (DCT) compression [7, 21].

Like any transform-based compression algorithm, wavelet compression works in three stages: transform, quantization, and entropy coding. In quantization and entropy coding, one can use the same techniques applied in other transform-based compression. For quantization, one can choose between scalar [13] and vector quantizers [14], and from each category one can select from several types that are discussed later. Similarly, for entropy coding, a variety of lossless bit-packing techniques can be used, such as run-length encoding (RLE) [23], Huffman coding [16], RLE+Huffman, or arithmetic coding [26], to name a few of the most commonly used ones. The choices made by WSQ are discussed later in the chapter.

In the transform stage, wavelet compression differs significantly from other compression techniques. Specifically, in standard transform-based compression such as DCT, the transform is a matrix-vector multiplication, where the vector represents the signal to be transformed and compressed, while the matrix is fixed for any given signal size. In wavelet compression, on the other hand, the transform is a pair of filters, where one is low-pass and the other is high-pass, and the output of each filter is downsampled by two. Each of those two output signals can be further transformed similarly, and this process can be repeated recursively several times, resulting in a tree structure, called the *decomposition tree*. Unlike in DCT compression, where the transform matrix is fixed, in wavelet transform the designer has the choice of what filter pair to use and what decomposition tree structure to follow.

To aid the reader in understanding wavelet compression, the basic concepts of filters and downsampling are reviewed in the next subsection. (For additional details, the reader can refer to any digital signal processing text such as [18].) The rest of the section defines wavelets and wavelet transforms, and outlines the wavelet-based compression scheme.

19.2.1. Linear Filters

A (linear) filter is a process characterized by a (finite or infinite) sequence (f_k), called the *filter coefficients*. The filter takes as input any sequence (signal) (x_k) and outputs another sequence (y_k), which is *the convolution* of the (x_k) and (f_k). That is, for all index values k, $y_k = \sum_r f_{k-r} x_r$, where r ranges over all values for which f_{k-r} is nonzero.

To understand the effect of a filter, it is better to view it from the frequency-domain perspective using the z-transform and the Fourier transform. The *z-transform* of any sequence (a_k) is the complex function $A(z) = \sum_k a_k z^k$, where k ranges over all values for which a_k is nonzero, and z is a complex variable. The *Fourier transform* of (a_k) is the function $A(e^{-i\theta})$, where θ is a real variable. Note that $A(e^{-i\theta})$ is periodic of period 2π. The value $A(e^{i\theta})$ is referred to as *the frequency content of the signal* (a_k) at *frequency* θ. In the range from $-\pi$ to π, the values of $A(e^{i\theta})$ at θ near 0 are typically referred to as the *low-frequency contents* (or simply the low frequencies) of the signal, and those at θ away from 0 and near $\pm\pi$ are referred to as the *high-frequency contents* (or simply the high frequencies) of the signal. Note also that if the signal sequence (a_k) is finite (say that $k = 0, 1, \ldots, N-1$), then the *discrete Fourier transform* of (a_k) is a new sequence (A_k) where $A_k = A(e^{-i\frac{2k\pi}{N}})$, for $k = 0, 1, \ldots, N-1$.

The relationship between the input (x_k) and the output (y_k) of a filter (f_k) can be easily expressed using the z-transform: $Y(z) = F(z)X(z)$, that is, the z-transform of (y_k) is the product of the z-transforms of (f_k) and (x_k). In particular, $Y(e^{-i\theta}) = F(e^{-i\theta})X(e^{-i\theta})$, that is, the Fourier transform of the output is the product of the Fourier transforms of the input and the filter.

Therefore, the frequencies in the output signal (y_k) of a filter are the frequencies of the input signal (x_k) but scaled (i.e., multiplied) by the frequencies of the filter coefficients (f_k). In particular, if the low frequencies of the filter are equal to 1 and the high frequencies are all equal to 0, then the filter effect is the preservation of the low frequencies of the input (x_k) and the zeroing out of the high frequencies of the input. In such a case, the filter is called a *low-pass filter*. Conversely, if the low frequencies of the filter are 0 and the high frequencies are all 1, then the effect of the filter is to zero out the low frequencies of the input and preserve the high frequencies. In this case, the filter is called a *high-pass filter*.

In intuitive terms, the low frequencies of a signal generally represent the overall outline of the shape of the signal, while the high frequencies represent the fine details of the signal shape. Thus, a low-pass filter preserves the broad features of a signal (such as an image) but eliminates much of the details, whereas a high-pass filter eliminates much of the texture and preserves the outlines (edges) of an image.

In addition to filtering, the wavelet transform and inverse transform involve downsampling by 2 and upsampling by 2. The *downsampling by 2 of a signal* (u'_k) is simply the dropping of the odd-index terms of the sequence, resulting in a sequence (u'_{2k}) consisting of the terms of even index. Thus, the output of filtering (x_k) into (u'_k) and then downsampling by 2 is $(u_k) = (u'_{2k})$ where $u_k = u'_{2k} = \sum_i f_{2k-i}x_i$. The *upsampling by 2 of a signal* (u_k) is achieved by interspersing a zero between every two consecutive sample values of the signal. That is, the upsampling by 2 of (u_k) results in a signal (w_k) where $w_{2k} = u_k$ and $w_{2k+1} = 0$ for all k. In particular, if (u_k) was the result of downsampling by 2 of (u'_k), then the upsampling by 2 of (u_k) is (w_k) where $w_{2k} = u'_{2k}$ and $w_{2k+1} = 0$ for all k.

19.2.2. Definition of Wavelets

A function $\psi(t)$ is called a *wavelet* if there exists a corresponding function $\phi(t)$, called a *scaling function*, and four sequences of real (or complex) numbers (g_k), (h_k), (p_k) and (q_k), all satisfying the following equations:

$$\phi(t) = \sum_k p_k \phi(2t - k) \quad \text{and} \quad \psi(t) = \sum_k q_k \phi(2t - k) \tag{1}$$

$$\phi(2t - n) = \frac{1}{2} \sum_k [g_{2k-n}\phi(t - k) + h_{2k-n}\psi(t - k)] \tag{2}$$

where for most wavelets of interest to compression the four sequences are real and finite. In addition, for ϕ and ψ to form a legitimate wavelet system, certain constraints have to be satisfied by the four sequences. Some of these constraints are

$$\sum_k g_k = \sum_k p_k = 2 \quad \text{and} \quad \sum_k h_k = \sum_k q_k = 0$$

Other, more stringent constraints are known as the perfect reconstruction (PR) conditions in the subband coding community [30, 31, 33]. The PR conditions can be stated succinctly by means of the z-transform:

$$G(z)P(z) + H(z)Q(z) = 4 \quad \text{and} \quad G(-z)P(z) + H(-z)Q(z) = 0$$

where $G(z)$, $H(z)$, $P(z)$, and $Q(z)$ are the z-transforms of (g_k), (h_k), (p_k), and (q_k).

19.2.3. Wavelet Transforms

Given a wavelet defined through the four sequences (g_k), (h_k), (p_k), and (q_k), the wavelet transform of an input data sequence (x_k) of length N transforms the sequence (x_k) into another sequence (y_k) of the same length N. The first $\lceil \frac{N}{2} \rceil$ terms of (y_k) form a sequence (u_k) called a low-frequency subband, and the remaining $\lfloor \frac{N}{2} \rfloor$ terms of (y_k) form a second sequence (v_k) called a high-frequency subband, computed as follows:

$$u_k = \sum_n \frac{g_{2k-n}}{\sqrt{2}} x_n \quad \text{and} \quad v_k = \sum_n \frac{h_{2k-n}}{\sqrt{2}} x_n$$

That is, (u_k) is derived by first passing the (x_k) through a linear filter of coefficients $(\frac{g_k}{\sqrt{2}})$, yielding a sequence (u'_k), where $u'_k = \sum_n (g_{k-n}/\sqrt{2}) x_n$, and then downsampling (u'_k) by 2, i.e., $u_k = u'_{2k}$. The subband (v_k) is derived similarly using the filter $(h_k/\sqrt{2})$. Note that the first filter is low-pass because $\sum_k g_k$ is nonzero, while the second filter is high-pass because $\sum_k h_k = 0$.

Because of the equations of the PR conditions, the original sequence (x_k) can be perfectly reconstructed from the two subbands (u_k) and (v_k) by the following equation:

$$x_k = \sum_n \left[\frac{p_{k-2n}}{\sqrt{2}} u_n + \frac{q_{k-2n}}{\sqrt{2}} v_n \right]$$

which is equivalent to the following three steps: (1) upsampling (u_k) by 2 and then filtering through a linear filter of coefficients $(p_k/\sqrt{2})$; (2) upsampling (v_k) by 2 and then filtering through a linear filter of coefficients $(q_k/\sqrt{2})$; and finally, (3) adding the two resulting sequences. This whole reconstruction process implements the inverse wavelet transform. Figure 19.1 shows graphically both the transform (or analysis) stage and the reconstruction (or synthesis) stage. The dotted lines, labeled "process" in the figure, refer in our context to the other stages of compression, that is, quantization and entropy coding, which are discussed later.

Note that the low-pass subband (u_k) contains basically the same features as the original signal, albeit with slightly fewer details. Those missing details are indeed what is stored in the high-frequency subband (v_k). Since the subband (u_k) still has most of the original features, its data elements must still carry considerable correlation. This warrants further transforms on (u_k). Indeed, in actual wavelet-based compression systems, the wavelet transform is applied several times on the subbands, resulting in many subbands, which are then quantized and entropy-coded. Figure 19.2 shows a typical wavelet coding/decoding structure.

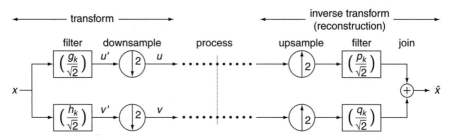

Fig. 19.1. The subband coding scheme corresponding to wavelets.

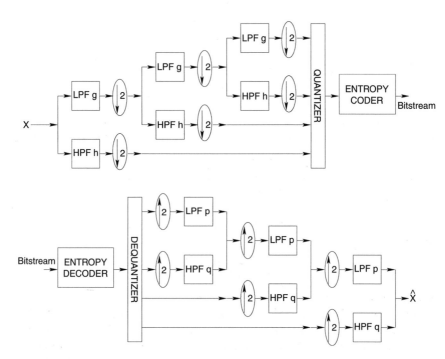

Fig. 19.2. An example structure of a typical wavelet coder (above) and its corresponding decoder (below).

In the case of multidimensional data (e.g., images), the transforms are typically performed on the various dimensions independently. The reconstruction (i.e., decompression) follows the exact reverse process: entropy decoding, dequantization, and inverse wavelet transforms applied as many times as, and in the opposite order of, the direct transform.

19.3. Choices and Trade-offs in Wavelet Compression

Clearly, many different decomposition tree structures can be followed. Also, many different choices of wavelets (i.e., wavelet filters) are available to choose from. Similarly, for the next two stages of the compression scheme, namely, quantization and entropy coding, the designer can choose from a variety of techniques. These choices and some of the trade-offs are discussed in this section, and the choices made by WSQ are identified.

19.3.1. Choice of Good Wavelets

As mentioned earlier, the designer has the choice of which wavelet to use, that is, which set of filters to employ. One of the earliest questions addressed in wavelet compression was which wavelets yield good compression performance [9, 25, 32, 34]. This subsection briefly addresses this question.

First of all, bi-orthogonal wavelets are better than nonbi-orthogonal ones for compression because the corresponding filters have the very desirable property of being linear-phase filters, that is, symmetric or asymmetric. In other terms, bi-orthogonal wavelets do not exhibit frequency aliasing artifacts, while other wavelets do.

Still, there is an unlimited number of bi-orthogonal wavelets, and many families have been defined and shown to yield good compression performance. One of the extensive studies of best-wavelet selection was conducted by one of the authors on a very large set of wavelets [34]. This large set and the wavelet evaluation process and findings are outlined next.

To start, it is worthwhile to mathematically characterize bi-orthogonal wavelets. The perfect reconstruction equations, the standard choice of $P(z) = zH(-z)$ and $Q(z) = -zG(-z)$, and the linear-phase (symmetry) property of the filters together imply that for $z = e^{-i\omega}$,

$$P(z)G(z) = \cos^{2N}\left(\frac{\omega}{2}\right)\left[\sum_{k=0}^{N-1}\binom{N-k+1}{k}\sin^{2k}\left(\frac{\omega}{2}\right) + \sin^{2N}\left(\frac{\omega}{2}\right)T(\cos(\omega))\right]$$

where N is an arbitrary positive integer and T is an arbitrary odd polynomial $[T(-x) = -T(x)]$ [6, 10]. Wavelet designers have many choices for $T(x)$ and N, and, even for a fixed T and N, the designer can find many choices for P and G that satisfy the equations just stated.

In [34], $T(x)$ was taken to be simply 0, in which case the filters (g_k) and (h_k) have a total of $4N$ coefficients. All bi-orthogonal filters where the total number of coefficients of (g_k) and (h_k) ranges from 4 to 56, corresponding to $N = 1, 2, \ldots, 14$, were generated and evaluated. The total number of those wavelets is 4297. The total filter length was capped at 56 because longer filters incur high computation cost. The evaluation was based on the frequency response of the filters as well as on direct experimentation, that is, each 4-filter set was tested by compressing several test images and evaluating the reconstruction quality at various compression ratios.

The findings of this extensive study revealed that out of the 4297 wavelets tested, only about 18 of them were good for compression. The rest had inferior reconstruction quality, and in most cases the quality was very unacceptable. Interestingly, the wavelet specified in WSQ turned up among the 18 good wavelets. Furthermore, although the WSQ wavelet was not the absolute best, its filter lengths were the shortest (thus most efficient) and its performance was very close to the best wavelet.

19.3.2. Choices of Decomposition Trees

As just mentioned, many different tree structures can be followed. For example, the tree depth can vary depending on the size of the signal, the amount of correlation of the data, and the desired speed of the system, among other factors. Also, the high-frequency subband can be transformed further, although its tree need not be so elaborate because high-frequency subbands do not have much correlation left in them to warrant many additional decompositions.

In images, as in 1D signals, various tree structures can be used. Figure 19.3 shows two tree structures for wavelet image compression. The first structure, due to Mallat [19], is well known, and the second is the structure used in the FBI's WSQ specification.

The structure of the decomposition tree can be determined dynamically at compression time. The general approach is to measure the level of "energy" in each subband generated after each application of the transform. The term "energy" is often used in this context as a metaphor for the amount of details and variations present in the subband: the more variations and the finer the details, the more energy. This can be measured in various ways, such as the spectrum and the statistical variance of the subband. If the energy level of a subband is found to be above a certain threshold, that subband is transformed further (i.e., decomposed into smaller subbands), and then

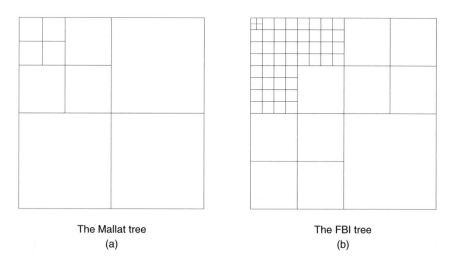

The Mallat tree   The FBI tree

(a)   (b)

Fig. 19.3. Examples of tree decompositions of images.

the same energy test is applied on the smaller subbands. While this dynamic approach can yield high compression ratios, its advantage is offset by the overhead of (1) extra execution time to measure the energy level and (2) the extra bits needed to represent the shape of the resulting decomposition tree.

The logical alternative is to perform tests on several benchmark images in the intended application domain, such as fingerprints. From those tests, a reasonably optimal decomposition (on average) can be deduced and used thereafter on all images in the application. This has the advantage of avoiding the overhead of dynamic decisions, while still producing nearly optimal results. This was the route taken in WSQ.

19.3.3. Quantization in Wavelet Compression

Roughly speaking, quantization is a process of further discretization of the data and can be done at the individual data element (e.g., pixel) level or at a vector (or block) level. In the first case, it is called *scalar* quantization [13], and in the second case *vector* quantization [14].

A scalar quantizer is specified by (1) subdividing the entire range of the data to be quantized into intervals labeled with integer values and (2) designating a reconstruction value for each interval. If interval i is denoted $(d_i, d_{i+1}]$, and its reconstruction value r_i, where $d_i < r_i \leq d_{i+1}$, then quantizing a value x is nothing more than replacing x by the integer label i of the interval in which x falls ($d_i < x \leq d_{i+1}$). Dequantizing i amounts to replacing it by the reconstruction value r_i.

Different classes of scalar quantizers have been defined, most notably uniform quantizers and optimal Max–Lloyd quantizers [17]. In uniform quantizers, all the intervals have the same length, and the reconstruction values are the exact middle points of their respective intervals. Clearly, uniform quantizers are efficient to specify and efficient to quantize with. In optimal Max–Lloyd quantizers [17], the end points of the intervals and the reconstruction values are determined so that the error between the original data and the reconstructed (i.e., quantized then dequantized) data is minimized, where the error measure is the Euclidean distance (or mean-square error). Max–Lloyd quantizers optimize reconstruction quality and are fairly efficient to derive and apply. Nevertheless, they are not always used because they do incur additional overhead over uniform quantizers.

Scalar quantization works very well when the data elements are rather independent (i.e., uncorrelated). If, however, the data elements are correlated, scalar quantization causes serious distortions because it quantizes the various elements independently, that is, irrespective of interelement relations. When data are correlated, vector quantization is preferable because it better maintains the correlations and thus the patterns and features represented thereof.

Vector quantization is specified by a dictionary of patterns (vectors), which are relatively small 2D $n \times m$ blocks in the case of images. Quantizing an image involves subdividing it into contiguous, nonoverlapping $n \times m$ blocks, and coding each block by the index of the best-matching block in the dictionary. Dequantizing is simply replacing each index in the quantized image by the corresponding dictionary block.

A typical block size is 4×4 or 8×8, and the number of blocks in a dictionary ranges from a few hundred to a few thousand. Various clustering techniques are used to construct good dictionaries [14].

In the context of wavelet compression, the coefficients of a low-frequency subband may still be quite correlated, and thus a vector quantizer may yield better performance than a scalar quantizer. However, in practice, the decomposition tree is so deep that the low-frequency subband size is so small that little gain can be derived from vector quantization, in which case scalar quantization of that subband is adequate. As for all other (high-frequency) subbands, if the wavelet chosen is a very good wavelet, the coefficients in all those subbands are highly decorrelated, making the use of vector quantization unnecessary and even undesirable because of the high overhead as compared to scalar quantization. Therefore, scalar quantization of the high-frequency subbands is the quantizer of choice.

Of course, not all the subbands have to be quantized with the same scalar quantizer. Rather, each subband is better processed with a quantizer whose specifications are tailored to that subband's statistics. (Note that more intervals are used and the smaller the intervals are, the less the error is, but of course the less the compression ratio is.)

The FBI WSQ specification opted for subband-adaptive scalar quantization. The quantizer of each subband is nearly a uniform quantizer: All intervals are of the same length except for the middle interval centered at 0, which is 40% larger than the other intervals. The reconstruction values are all near the middle points of their intervals. Those quantizers are subband-adaptive in that the length of most of the intervals is inversely proportional to the logarithm of the variance of the subband. The length of the intervals depends also on a scalar multiplicative value, which is set depending on the desired compression ratio: smaller factors for higher compression ratios.

19.3.4. Entropy Coding

Entropy coding is the process of representing information efficiently but losslessly. Many entropy coding techniques have been developed over the last several decades, such as run-length encoding (RLE) [23], Huffman coding [16], arithmetic coding [26], and Lempil–Ziv [35], among others. Entropy coders are used either as standalone lossless compression systems or as the last stage of lossy compression. In the latter case, which is the one of interest to us here, the entropy coder is used to represent the quantized data. Among the many entropy coders, the most commonly used ones in lossy compression are arithmetic coding and RLE+Huffman.

Arithmetic coding encodes binary decisions as well as data bits using a probabilistic model of the information to be coded. It achieves optimal compression performance (in terms of bit rate or compression ratio). As a result, it has been adopted in many standards such as JPEG 2000, MPEG4, and JBIG. It is also an option in JPEG. However, there are numerous patents on arithmetic coding. This complicates matters for many users and hinders their ability to utilize arithmetic coding.

The situation with RLE and Huffman coding is much simpler as users are free to use them at will. Furthermore, they are easy to implement, are fast to run, and yield very good compression performance. Therefore, they have been adopted in standards such as JPEG and MPEG-2, as well as in the FBI WSQ specification.

RLE works well when the data to be coded consist of relatively long sequences of repeated values. Such sequences are called *runs*. RLE represents each run by a pair (n, v) where n is the length of the run, and v is the repeated value. In applications where only one type of runs is represented (e.g., runs of zeroes only), the runs are coded simply by their lengths since the repeated value is implicit.

Huffman coding represents a data set of symbols by coding each symbol with a binary string whose length depends on the probability (or frequency) of occurrence of that symbol in the data set. The individual symbol codes are constructed in such a way that (1) the more frequently occurring a symbol is, the shorter its binary code is, and (2) no symbol binary code is a prefix of another symbol code. The alphabet symbol codes are derived as follows.

Suppose the symbols used in the data set are drawn from an alphabet of m distinct symbols $\{a_1, a_1, \ldots, a_m\}$, and let p_i be the probability of occurrence of symbol a_i, for $i = 1, 2, \ldots, m$. The Huffman coding algorithm for coding the alphabet is a greedy algorithm that builds a binary tree. First, a node is created for each alphabet symbol; afterwards, the algorithm repeatedly selects two unparented nodes of smallest probabilities, creates a new parent node for them, and makes the probability of the new node to be the sum of the probabilities of its two children. Once the root is created, each left-pointing edge of the tree is labeled with 0, and each right-pointing edge is labeled with 1. Finally, each symbol is coded with the binary sequence that labels the path from the root to the leaf node of that symbol.

In WSQ, each quantized subband is turned into a one-dimensional sequence, then RLE is applied to code runs of zeroes, and finally the run lengths and other remaining data are coded with Huffman.

19.3.5. Other Approaches to Wavelet Compression

In recent years, wavelet techniques for lossless compression and lossy-to-lossless compression have been developed [28, 22]. Prior to this development, the filter coefficients of the wavelets used in compression were noninteger numbers that make their use lossy because of the limited precision of computer hardware. Later on, integer wavelets were developed, especially what is called the *lifting scheme* [22], allowing for lossless compression.

Furthermore, because of the multiresolution nature of wavelet representations, they can be used for progressive transmission, also called lossy-to-lossless. The idea is to format the bitstream in such a way that any number of leading bits in it allows for a reconstruction of the whole image at a resolution level that depends on the number of those leading bits. This allows the user to control the trade-off between image quality and amount of bits transmitted. It also allows for error tolerance and data loss in image transmission. For example, if some bits of the transmitted bitstream are lost or corrupted by noise, the receiver-decoder can use the bits that preceded the error/loss to reconstruct the whole image at whatever resolution affordable by those bits.

JPEG 2000 uses this scheme of wavelet compression for still images. WSQ, however, does not have provisions for lossless or lossy-to-lossless coding. The initial intent of WSQ, namely, to save not only on transmission bandwidth but also on storage, makes both of these modes undesirable because the resulting compression ratio would still be too modest as compared to the WSQ target compression ratios of at least 10 to 1 and above.

19.4. Fingerprint Image Compression: The WSQ Specification

19.4.1. Intended Use of WSQ Compression

The WSQ compression technique developed by the FBI and other entities was designed to compress source fingerprint images between ratios of 10 to 1 and 20 to 1. At these compression ratios, sufficient friction ridge and pore detail is retained for the purposes of identification, by fingerprint matching hardware and by human latent fingerprint examiners. The technique is designed to discard information that is not necessary for the reconstruction of a fingerprint image usable by a latent fingerprint examiner to make a positive identification and by devices that classify the fingerprint pattern and extract minutiae by mechanized means. Minutiae, that is, the friction ridge endings and bifurcations, are the features by which fingerprint patterns are distinguished from one another.

19.4.2. The Source Fingerprint Image

This lossy compression technique produces best results when the source fingerprint image is a result of scanning an inked or chemical process fingerprint image from a card, or the output image produced by a live-scan fingerprint capture device with a spatial resolution from 500 to 520 samples per inch in both the vertical and horizontal directions and an intensity resolution of 8 bits. The source image is also required to be continuous tone [i.e., having a reasonably diverse intensity histogram with significant contribution from pixel values other than white (integer value 255) and black (integer value 0)]. The reasons for these requirements are

Using less than the required spatial resolution results in a source image with features too small to produce a significant result in the wavelet analysis, resulting in loss of these features in the quantization step of the WSQ encoding process.

A source image with less than 8 bits per pixel in intensity resolution will also suffer from high loss of information in the quantization step of the WSQ encoding process.

Source images with most of their pixel intensities consisting of white and black exhibit too much "ringing" or "echos" in the reconstructed image, again resulting from information discarded in the quantization step of WSQ encoding.

Using a source fingerprint image with the correct characteristics will produce a reconstructed fingerprint image remarkably similar to the source fingerprint image.

Before wavelet analysis, the 8-bit image pixel values must be shifted and scaled, in that order. The statistical mean of the pixel data is obtained, then subtracted from all of the pixel values in the source image. Finally, the shifted image pixel data are divided by a value equal to the absolute furthest shifted pixel value from 0. This ensures no input data to the wavelet analysis process extends beyond the -1.0 to 1.0 range.

19.4.3. Wavelet Transform and Quantization in WSQ

The WSQ wavelet is a bi-orthogonal wavelet. The low-pass analysis filter has nine coefficients, and the high-pass analysis filter has seven coefficients. These short filters make the transform rather fast. The coefficients of these filters are as follows:

Low-pass filter coefficients	High-pass filter coefficients
0.037828455506995	
−0.02384946501938	0.064538882628938
−0.11062440441842	−0.040689417609558
0.37740285561265	−0.41809227322221
0.85269867900940	0.78848561640566
0.37740285561265	−0.41809227322221
−0.11062440441842	−0.040689417609558
−0.02384946501938	0.064538882628938
0.037828455506995	

The wavelet transform is as described in Section 19.2.3. The decomposition tree with labeled subbands is shown in Fig. 19.4.

The quantization is uniform scalar quantization of the subbands except that the interval centered at 0 is 40% larger than the rest of the intervals, and the reconstruction value of each interval $(d_i, d_{i+1}]$ is $d_i + 0.56(d_{i+1} - d_i)$ rather than $d_i + 0.5(d_{i+1} - d_i)$. The precise length of the intervals varies from subband to subband and depends on the variance of the subband.

19.4.4. Run-Length Encoding and Decoding in WSQ

This encoding scheme uses integers, either 8-bit or 16-bit, to represent long sequences of zeroes (called runs) in a subband which result from scalar quantization. Only sequences of zeroes are coded with RLE. The lengths of these runs of zeroes are encoded with Huffman encoding, as described in the next subsection. During the run-length decoding process, the integers that indicate a zero run are decoded from the Huffman encoded bitstream and zeroes are deposited in the subband in preparation for wavelet synthesis. More information about this is found in the section about Huffman coding.

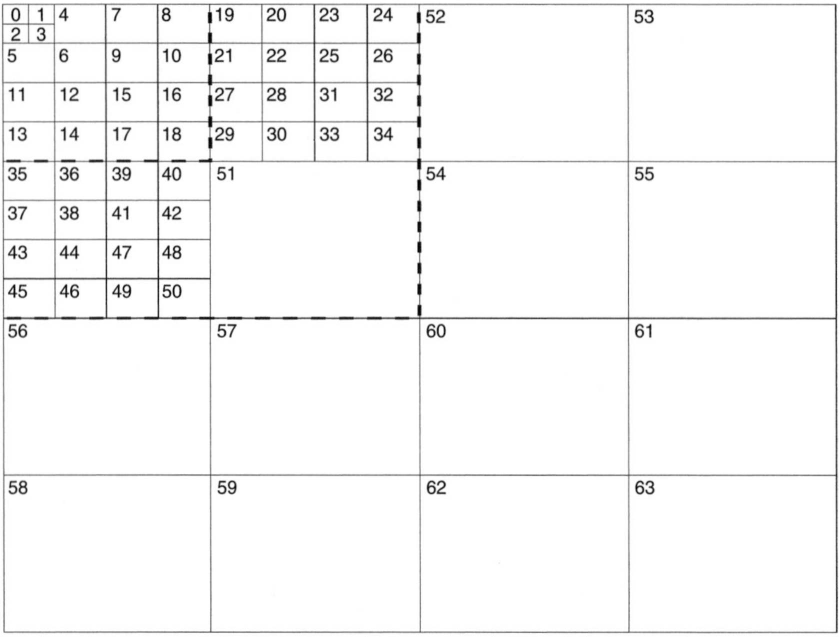

0 1 2 3	4	7	8	19	20	23	24	52	53
5	6	9	10	21	22	25	26		
11	12	15	16	27	28	31	32		
13	14	17	18	29	30	33	34		
35	36	39	40	51				54	55
37	38	41	42						
43	44	47	48						
45	46	49	50						
56				57				60	61
58				59				62	63

Fig. 19.4. The WSQ decomposition tree with labeled subbands.

19.4.5. Huffman Coding and Decoding

Huffman encoding, used as the last step in WSQ lossy compression, is based on assigning the shortest binary codes to the most frequently occurring symbols in the Huffman input table, which is derived by a process described in Subsection 19.3.4. Table 19.1 shows the codes of each of the 254 valid input symbols for the Huffman coder. These input symbols are fixed in the WSQ specification. A Huffman table transmitted with the entropy coded bitstream consists of the number of each code length (1 through 16) and the Huffman input symbol order. This is sufficient to generate the decoding table at the decoder. A maximum of eight Huffman tables may be included with each WSQ compressed file.

Huffman coding is simply the concatenation of variable-length codes, each representing a symbol, to create a bitstream. The boundaries of codes can, and most often will, occur within bytes in a WSQ file. No Huffman code can begin with any other Huffman code. This makes decoding analogous to traversing a binary tree, concluding at a leaf containing the symbol the code represents. The code associated with each symbol is generated using the population distribution of the input symbols.

Huffman coding starts at the upper-left corner of subband 1, proceeds left to right then top to bottom, exhausting all bin index values in subband 1. Subbands 2 through 64 are processed in turn. At the end of Huffman coding, the rest of the byte is filled with "1" bits to signal the end of the bitstream to the decoder. As Huffman coding proceeds in the encoder, any byte consisting of all 1 bits is immediately succeeded by

Table 19.1. Huffman Coder Input Symbols

Symbol	Description
1	Zero run of length 1
2	Zero run of length 2
⋮	
99	Zero run of length 99
100	Zero run of length 100
101	Escape for positive 8-bit coefficient index
102	Escape for negative 8-bit coefficient index
103	Escape for positive 16-bit coefficient index
104	Escape for negative 16-bit coefficient index
105	Escape for 8-bit zero run
106	Escape for 16-bit zero run
107	Coefficient index value -73
108	Coefficient index value -72
⋮	
180	(same as symbol 1)
⋮	
253	Coefficient index value 73
254	Coefficient index value 74

a byte consisting of all 0 bits. This eliminates any confusion between these Huffman generated all-1 bytes and valid marker codes. (See the subsection on markers to further explain the makeup and use of markers.)

19.4.6. Progressive Transmission

To facilitate the possibility of transmitting a half-resolution or quarter-resolution image using the WSQ specification, frequency subbands have been separated into three groups. Decoding the first group to completion yields an image one quarter the resolution of the original source image. A half-resolution image can be obtained by decoding the first two subband groups. Decoding all subband groups to completion reconstructs the full-sized image. This feature is thought to find application when a human is looking through many images to find candidate matches.

The fact that a smaller portion of the total data is transmitted and processed to produce fractional resolution images quickens the search process and reduces processing and transmission bandwidth usage. This segmentation also allows the calculation of three independent Huffman coding tables to further optimize the compression performance of WSQ.

19.4.7. Marker Codes

Marker codes are two-byte sequences, the first of which is a byte with all bits set to 1, ending with a byte indicating the type of marker. Some marker codes allow the

Table 19.2. WSQ Marker Codes

Second byte	Description
1010 0000	Start of image
1010 0001	End of image
1010 0010	Start frame
1010 0011	Start subband group
1010 0100	Start wavelet filter tap table
1010 0101	Start quantization tables
1010 0110	Start Huffman tables
1010 0111	Restart interval
1010 1000	Comment

WSQ encoded file to be quickly searched for items of interest such as the Huffman tables, wavelet filter coefficients (i.e., tap values), and image dimensions. Others allow recovery from bit or byte errors encountered as a result of bad storage media, or interference during transmission.

A description of the marker secondary byte contents and their meaning appears in Table 19.2. Note that the second byte will never be all 0 bits because this sequence is reserved for the purpose of indicating an all-1 byte generated by the Huffman coder. Some of the more useful marker codes are Start Frame, Start Subband Group, Start Wavelet Filter Tap Table, Start Quantization Tables, and Start Huffman Tables.

It is necessary to include information in the WSQ compressed file to enable the decoder to reconstruct an image with the same dimensions, brightness, and contrast as the original source image. The Start Frame marker indicates the point after which these data are found. Figure 19.5 shows the Start Frame header information content and sequence.

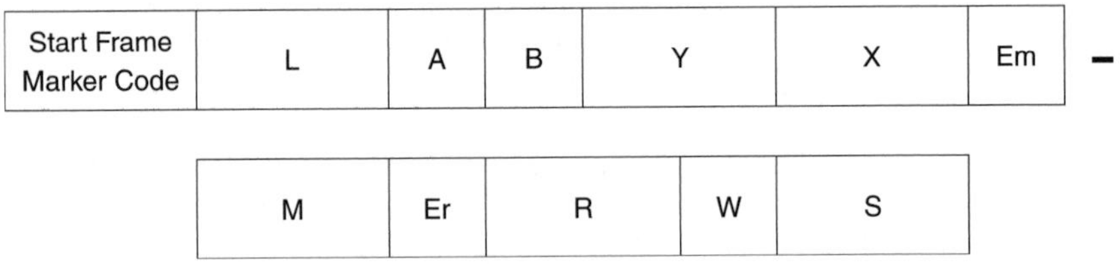

Start Frame Marker Code	L	A	B	Y	X	Em	–

M	Er	R	W	S

L - indicated the length of the rest of the information
A - scanner BLACK calibration value
B - scanner WHITE calibration value
Y - number of lines in the source image
X - number of columns in the source image
Em - the decimal point in M is shifted left Em places
M - source image pixel value mean subracted before scaling
Er - the decimal point in R is shifted left Er places
R - the source image was divided by R before transformation
W - specifies the WSQ encoder algorithm used on this image
S - specifies the software implementation that encoded this image

Fig. 19.5. Start of frame information.

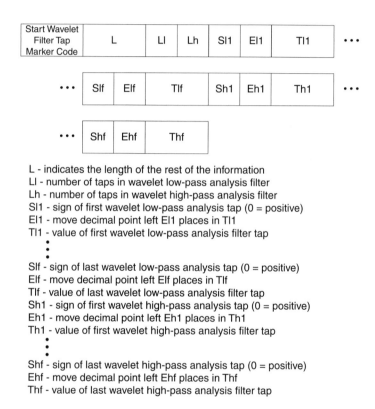

Start Subband Group Marker Code	L	H

L - length of Start Subband Group marker header
H - Huffman code table number used in this subband group

Fig. 19.6. Subband group information.

L - indicates the length of the rest of the information
Ll - number of taps in wavelet low-pass analysis filter
Lh - number of taps in wavelet high-pass analysis filter
Sl1 - sign of first wavelet low-pass analysis tap (0 = positive)
El1 - move decimal point left El1 places in Tl1
Tl1 - value of first wavelet low-pass analysis filter tap
    ·
    ·
    ·
Slf - sign of last wavelet low-pass analysis tap (0 = positive)
Elf - move decimal point left Elf places in Tlf
Tlf - value of last wavelet low-pass analysis filter tap
Sh1 - sign of first wavelet high-pass analysis tap (0 = positive)
Eh1 - move decimal point left Eh1 places in Th1
Th1 - value of first wavelet high-pass analysis filter tap
    ·
    ·
    ·
Shf - sign of last wavelet high-pass analysis tap (0 = positive)
Ehf - move decimal point left Ehf places in Thf
Thf - value of last wavelet high-pass analysis filter tap

Fig. 19.7. Wavelet filter tap information.

Each subband group is marked by a Start Subband Group marker code to enable progressive transmission and reconstruction, and allows for multiple Huffman code tables to be used, one for each subband group. Figure 19.6 details the content of the Start Subband header.

The Wavelet Filter Tap information must be provided with the encoded bitstream to provide some indication of the synthesis high-pass and low-pass filter tap values needed to reconstruct the image. A Start Wavelet Filter Tap Table marker signals the start of this group of information. Figure 19.7 shows the content of this header.

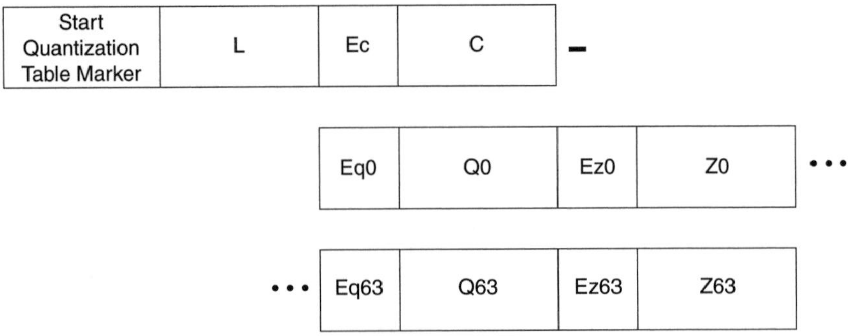

Start Quantization Table Marker	L	Ec	C	—

	Eq0	Q0	Ez0	Z0	•••

•••	Eq63	Q63	Ez63	Z63

L - Total length of information in this header
Ec - decimal point shift left Ec0 digits in C
C - quantizer bin center parameter
Eq0 - decimal point shifts left Eq0 digits in Q0
Q0 - quantization bin size for subband 0
Ez0 - decimal point shifts left Ez0 digits in Z0
Z0 - quantization zero bin size for subband 0
•
•
•
Eq63 - decimal point shifts left Eq63 digits in Q63
Q63 - quantizer bin size for subband 63
Ez63 - decimal point shifts left Ez63 digits in Z63
Z63 - quantizer bin size for subband 63

Fig. 19.8. Quantization table information

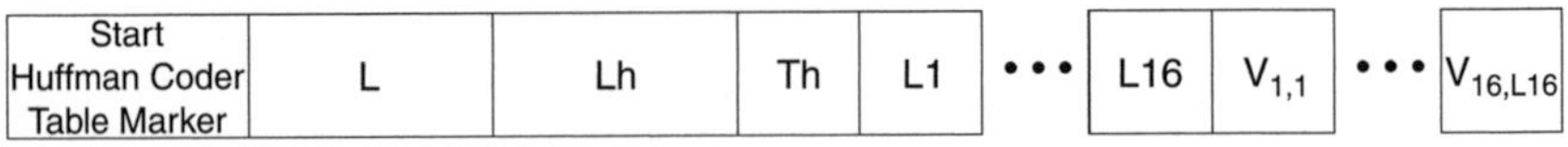

Start Huffman Coder Table Marker	L	Lh	Th	L1	•••	L16	$V_{1,1}$	•••	$V_{16,L16}$

L - Total length of information in this header
Th - Huffman Table Identifier
L1 - Number of 1-bit Huffman codes
•
•
•
L16 - number of 16-bit Huffman codes
$V_{1,1}$ - symbol associated with this Huffman code
•
•
•
$V_{16,L16}$ - symbol associated with last Huffman code

Fig. 19.9. Start Huffman table header.

The quantization bin centers and sizes used in the WSQ encoder must be supplied to the decoder to enable the recovered integer bin index values to be converted to approximate wavelet coefficients for processing by the wavelet synthesis stage. Figure 19.8 shows how these bin centers and sizes are transmitted using the Start Quantization Table marker code.

Figure 19.9 shows the the Start Huffman Table header. This header enables Huffman decoder tables to be constructed at the WSQ Decoder and is crucial to extracting bin index integers from the entropy coded bitstream.

19.5. Implementation of WSQ

The performance evaluation of WSQ, presented in this chapter, is based on experience with the reference WSQ encoder/decoder pair, which was designed and tested by the first author at the National Institute of Standards and Technology (NIST) in Gaithersburg, Maryland. The encoder/decoder pair was implemented in the C programming language.

19.5.1. Processing Speed

The coding process consists of the transform stage, the determination of the quantizer parameter value, the quantization stage, and the entropy coding stage. To estimate the time it takes to code an $N \times M$ fingerprint image at the transform stage, let

$t_* =$ the time for a single floating-point multiplication operation,
$t_+ =$ the time for a single floating-point addition/subtraction operation,
$t_d =$ the time for a single floating-point division operation,
$t_c =$ the time for a single floating-point comparison operation,
$t_l =$ the time for computing the natural logarithm.

The transform stage takes time equal to

$$T_{\text{transform}} = (34t_* + 30t_+)NM$$

and the quantization stage takes time equal to

$$T_{\text{quantization}} = (10.5t_+ + 5.25t_* + 2.62t_c)NM + 284t_d + 184t_* - 56t_+ + 56t_l$$

The entropy coding stage involves scanning the quantized image and finding runs of zeroes, and then Huffman-coding the run lengths and the nonzero coefficients. The scanning time is proportional to NM, but the number of runs encountered varies from image to image and, within the same image, varies depending on the target bit rate. Due to this variability, it is hard to come up with a quantified time formula for the entropy coding stage. Rather, empirical time measurements are provided below.

For the determination of the value of the quantizer parameter that would meet the target bit rate, the implementors of WSQ are free to follow any method they choose. The correctness of the decoder depends on the value of the parameter, not on the method of derivation of that value. Therefore, it is hard to give a time formula for this part of WSQ as well, but empirical performance measures are provided instead.

The decoding process consists of the entropy decoding stage, the dequantization stage, and the inverser transform stage. The entropy decoding stage takes time proportional to NM. The dequantization stage takes time equal to

$$T_{\text{dequantization}} = (t_* + 3t_+)NM$$

and the inverse transform stage takes time equal to

$$T_{\text{inverse transform}} = (17t_* + 13.77t_+)NM$$

Table 19.3. WSQ Speed on a Pentium 733 MHz at Compression Ratio of 15:1

Image dimensions	Encoding speed	Decoding speed
768×768	0.635 sec	0.994 sec
800×856	0.741 sec	1.061 sec

In terms of real time, WSQ is quite fast. We ran WSQ on various images on a Pentium II 733 MHz and measured the speed. Table 19.3 gives representative figures of encoding and decoding speeds for two fingerprint images of typical sizes, at compression ratio of 15:1.

19.5.2. Compression Performance of WSQ: Compression Ratio Versus Quality

The compression ratio range of the WSQ specification is 10:1 to 20:1. In this range, studies have shown that the visual quality of the reconstructed images is very good: adequate for fingerprint identification. Figure 19.10 illustrates the WSQ performance at compression of 15:1, and Figs. 19.11 and 19.12 show the performance at much higher compression ratios (60:1 and 120:1). As the figures show, the quality is very good at 15:1; it also holds up well at much higher compression ratios, although echoing and smearing effects begin to appear and adversely limit fingerprint identification.

Examining the performance limits of WSQ at high and low ends of compression ratios is, indeed, of interest. At very high compression ratios in the mid-hundreds, the limit was reached when the size of the additional information included in the WSQ file (e.g., Huffman tables, etc.) dwarfed the encoded bitstream information and the compression ratio could not be achieved. Near this compression rate upper limit, the reconstructed image showed ringing or echoing at edges and blurring within the fingerprint image, as already apparent in Fig. 19.12. The blurring within the fingerprint obscured minutiae and made even classification impossible. The echoing at edges created the opportunity for false minutia detection by automated methods.

At the low end of compression ratios, the limit was noted when, during scalar quantization, large wavelet coefficients in the lower subbands needed to be represented by integers larger than the 16-bit maximum the WSQ specification allows. Near this low compression ratio limit, the image, as expected, showed very little difference from the source image. These differences were only detectable using a pixel-by-pixel comparison of the two images. Because this low compression ratio limit is lower than compression ratios achieved by other lossless compression techniques (e.g., the lossless mode of JPEG), the WSQ technique is unsuitable for lossless compression.

To appreciate the performance of WSQ relative to other lossy compression systems, we compare the performance of WSQ with that of JPEG, which is one of the most widely used lossy image compression standards. Figures 19.13, 19.14, and 19.15 show the same fingerprint image reconstructed by both compression systems at compression ratios of 15:1, 30:1, and 45:1. To the untrained eye, JPEG seems to give the same performance at 15:1; however, the FBI latent examiners found that even at this

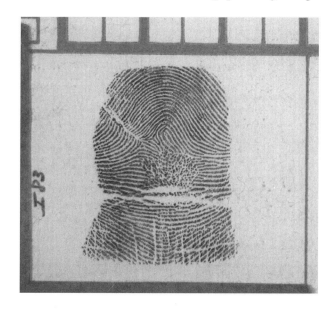

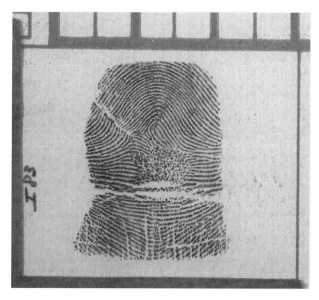

Fig. 19.10. An original fingerprint image (above) and its WSQ-reconstructed at 15:1 (below).

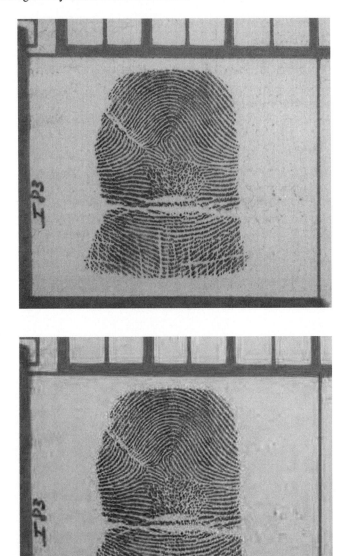

Fig. 19.11. Original (above) and WSQ-reconstructed at 60:1 (below).

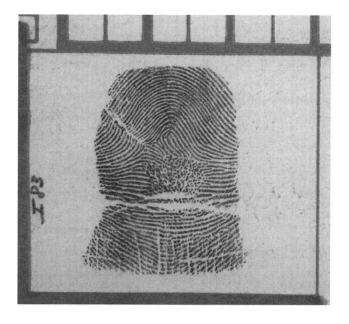

Fig. 19.12. Original (above) and WSQ-reconstructed at 120:1 (below).

Fig. 19.13. JPEG at 15:1 (above) and WSQ at 15:1 (below).

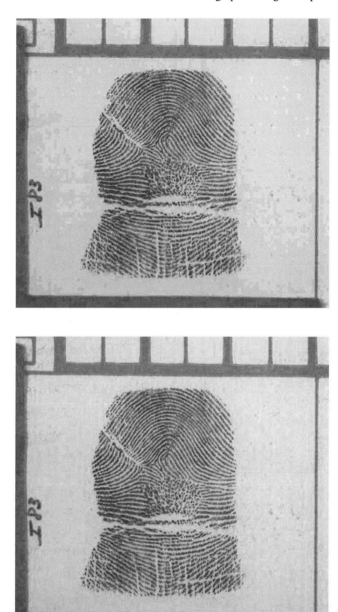

Fig. 19.14. JPEG at 30:1 (above) and WSQ at 30:1 (below).

Fig. 19.15. JPEG at 45:1 (above) and WSQ at 45:1 (below).

relatively modest compression ratio, JPEG images hindered fingerprint identification. At higher compression ratios (e.g., 45:1), the blocking artifacts and loss of details in JPEG become more evident, as can be seen in Fig. 19.15.

19.5.3. Compliance Testing Using the WSQ Coder/Decoder

Vendors wishing to produce WSQ implementations must show compliance with the FBI's WSQ specification by participating in a compliance testing program set up by Michael McCabe, NIST. The vendor obtains test files from NIST, processes them using his own implementation of the WSQ specification, and submits the files he produces to NIST for evaluation. The results are sent to the FBI for review, and the FBI issues the Certificate of Compliance to the vendor for that implementation. The reference WSQ encoder/decoder software is used at NIST to review a vendor's submissions for WSQ implementation certification.

19.6. Summary

This chapter has addressed wavelet compression of images in general, and the FBI wavelet scalar quantization specification in particular. Choices for the wavelet filters, the decomposition trees, quantization, and entropy coding are discussed, and comparisons and trade-offs between those choices are examined. In light of those considerations and the underlying theory of wavelet compression, the chapter sheds some light on the careful choices made in WSQ. In addition, practical implementation aspects of WSQ are presented, and performance findings are briefly reported.

Much has developed in wavelet compression since the release of the WSQ specification. Integer wavelet, lifting schemes, and quantization and bit-packing methods have been devised and shown to yield improved lossy compression performance and to allow for lossless as well as lossy-to-lossless modes of compression. JPEG 2000, which incorporates those ideas and more, has been finalized and released. It will be interesting to test those new methods, and especially JPEG 2000 on fingerprint compression, and determine their performance improvement while preserving the ability to do fingerprint identification.

References

1. Antonini, M., M. Barlaud, P. Mathieu, and I. Daubechies, Image coding using wavelet transform, *IEEE Trans. on Image Processing*, 1(2): 205–220, April 1992.
2. Barnsley, M. F. and L. P. Hurd, *Fractal Image Compression*, Wellesley, MA: AK Peters, 1993.
3. Bradley, J., C. Brislawn, and H. Topper, The FBI wavelet/scalar quatization standard for fingerprint image compression, *Proc. SPIE*, 1961: 293–304, Orlando, FL, 1993.
4. Brislawn, C., Fingerprints go digital, *Notices American Mathematical Society*, 42: 1278–1283, 1995

5. Brislawn, C., J. Bradley, R. Onyshczak, and H. Topper, The FBI compression standard for digitized fingerprint images, *Proc. SPIE*, 2847, 344–355, Denver, CO, Aug. 1996.

6. Chui, C. K., *An Introduction to Wavelets*, Cambridge, MA: Academic Press, 1992.

7. Clarke, R. J., *Transform Coding of Images*, London: Academic Press, 1985.

8. MPEG-4: Coding of moving pictures and audio, ISO/IEC 14496, 1999.

9. Coifman, R. R. and M. V. Wickerhauser, Entropy-based algorithms for best basis selection, *IEEE Trans. Info. Theory*, 38(2): 713–718, Mar. 1992.

10. Daubechies, I., *Ten Lectures on Wavelets*, Philadelphia: Society for Industrial and Applied Mathematics, 1992.

11. Ersoy, I., F. Ercal, and M. Gokmen, A model-based approach for compression of fingerprint images, *Proc. IEEE Intl. Conf. on Image Processing, ICIP'99*, Kobe, Oct. 1999, 2: 973–977.

12. FBI, *WSQ Gray-Scale Fingerprint Image Compression Specification*, Standard IAFIS-IC-0110v2, Criminal Justice Information Services, 1993.

13. Gersho, A., Quantization, *IEEE Communications Magazine*, 15, Sept. 1977.

14. Gersho, A. and R. M. Gray, *Vector Quantization and Signal Compression*, Norwell, MA: Kluwer Academic Publishers, 1991.

15. Gokmen, M., I. Ersoy, and A.K. Jain, Compression of fingerprint images using hybrid image model, *Proc. IEEE Intl. Conf. on Image Processing, ICIP'96*, Lausanne, 1996, Vol. III, 395–398.

16. Huffman, D. A., A method for the reconstruction of minimum redundancy codes, *Proc. IRE*, 40:1098–1101, 1951.

17. Lloyd, S. P., Least squares quantization in PCM, *IEEE Trans. on Information Theory*, IT-28: 127–135, 1982.

18. Lyons, R. G., *Understanding Digital Signal Processing*, Reading, MA: Addison-Wesley, 1996.

19. Mallat, S.G., A theory for multiresolution signal decomposition: The wavelet representation, *IEEE Trans. on Pattern Analysis and Machine Intelligence*, 674–693, July 1989.

20. Pennebaker, B. and J. L. Mitchell, *JPEG Still Image Data Compression Standard*, New York: Van Nostrand Reinhold, 1993.

21. Rao, K. R. and P. Yip, *Discrete Cosine Transform—Algorithms, Advantages and Applications*, New York: Academic Press, 1990.

22. Sweldens, W., The lifting scheme: Construction of second generation wavelets, *SIAM J. Math. Anal.*, 29(2): 511–546, 1997.

23. Tanaka, H. and A. Leon-Garcia, Efficient run-length encoding, *IEEE Trans. Info. Theory*, IT-28(6): 880–890, 1987.

24. Taubman, D. S. and M. W. Marcellin, *JPEG 2000: Image Compression Fundamentals, Standards, and Practice*, New York: Kluwer International Series in Engineering and Computer Science, Nov. 2001.

25. Tewfik, A. H., D. Sinha, and P. Jorgensen, On the optimal choice of a wavelet for signal representation, *IEEE Trans. Info. Theory*, 38(2):747–765, 1992.

26. Rissanen, J. and G. Langdon, Arithmetic coding, *IBM J. Res. Develop.* 23:149–162, Mar. 1979. Also in *IEEE Trans. Comm.*, COM-29(6):858–867, June 1981.

27. Sayood, K., *Introduction to Data Compression*, San Fransisco: Morgan Kauffmann Publishers, 1996.

28. Shapiro, J. M., Embedded image coding using zerotrees of wavelet coefficients, *IEEE Trans. on Signal Processing*, 41(12): 3445–3462, 1993.

29. Srikanth, S. and N.N. Murthy, Adapting JPEG to fingerprint images, *Criminal Justice Information Services Technology Symposium (CJISTS'93)*, sponsored by Federal Bureau

of Investigation and National Institute of Standards And Technology, Gaithersburg, MD, 1993.

30. Vaidayanathan, P. P., *Multirate Systems and Filter Banks*, Englewood Cliffs, NJ: Prentice Hall, 1993.

31. Vetterli, M. and J. Kovacevic, *Wavelets and Subband Coding*, Englewood Cliffs, NJ: Prentice Hall, 1993.

32. Villasenor, J., B. Belzer, and J. Liao, Wavelet filter evaluation for efficient image compression, *IEEE Trans. on Image Processing*, (4):1053–1060, 1995.

33. Woods, J. W. and S. D. O'Neal, Subband coding of images, *IEEE Trans. Acous. Speech Signal Processing*, ASSP-34(5):1278–1288, 1986.

34. Youssef, A., Selection of good biorthogonal wavelets for data compression, *International Conference on Imaging, Science, Systems, and Technology, CISST '97*, Las Vegas, pp. 323–330, June 1997.

35. Ziv, J. and A. Lempel, Compression of individual sequences via variable rate coding, *IEEE Trans. Info. Theory*, IT-24:530–536, 1978.

Chapter 20

Security Considerations for the Implementation of Biometric Systems

Colin Soutar

Abstract. Biometric systems serve as a component in security systems—they identify individuals to support strong user authentication. As such, the interface between the biometric system and the other components in a security system, as well as potential vulnerabilities inherent within the biometric system, need to be fully understood to avoid introducing points at which an attacker can mount an attack. This has become even more important as the biometrics industry adopts standardized Application Programming Interface definitions, such as BioAPI [1], to allow the interchange of different biometric components, as these interfaces, by definition, are available to developers and attackers alike.

This chapter reviews some of the implementation issues that relate to biometric systems within security systems and presents details of steps that can be taken to mitigate potential vulnerabilities. API-specific issues are discussed in Section 20.2; more general system design issues are discussed in Section 20.3; the relationship with privacy issues is covered in Section 20.4; a discussion of the Common Criteria framework appears in Section 20.5; and conclusions are stated in Section 20.6. This chapter presents these issues within the general context of biometrics—all issues are relevant to fingerprints and other types of biometric systems. See [2] for further discussion on fingerprint verification issues on personal digital assistants (PDAs).

20.1. Introduction

The role that biometric systems play within the context of a security system is generally to provide evidence (herein referred to as "verification") that an individual is who he or she claims to be. This claim is based on an established persona or user that the individual has within the security system. In this chapter, we distinguish between the individual's *identity*; an *identifier* (see [3]) by which he or she is known to a security system; and the *verification* process, which simply verifies that he or she is the valid owner of the identifier. We also distinguish between authentication (accomplished here via biometric verification) and authorization. Authentication verifies the individual's identity and authorization permits him or her to continue with a service or transaction, based on status within the security system.

As background, consider the various steps comprising the *registration* of a new user within a security system (for example, an operating system, or a passport issuance process).

- An administrator of the system will establish the unique *identity* of the individual. This is typically achieved through the use of so-called breeder documents such as birth certificate, passport, etc. This step may also include a search over a biometric database to establish the uniqueness of the individual's claim according to the range of that database.
- If the individual is identified as unique, the security system will establish the individual as a new *user* of the system and assign a unique *identifier* by which he or she is known to the system. An example of an identifier would be a passport number.
- The individual will be instructed to *enroll* his or her biometric, and the biometric system will create a biometric *template* that is associated with the user.
- The template will be *bound* to the identifier, either by physically storing them in related locations in the biometric or security system, or by binding them together using encryption or a digital signature mechanism, to create a *user record*.

Subsequently, when the user requests to use a service or initiate a transaction, the following steps are undertaken:

- An individual establishes a *claim* to the system that he or she is a valid user of the system. This is usually achieved either by inputting the username associated with the user, or by presenting a card or other credential to the system to make the claim.
- The security system ensures that the user record of the claimed user is available to the biometric system (either by transmitting it to the biometric system or by selecting it within the biometric system), where it will be *unbound* to produce the template and identifier. The unbinding will reflect the binding process used above; that is, when binding occurred by encryption, the unbinding process will comprise decryption of the user record. Note that as part of the unbinding process, either the security system or the biometric system (or both) may verify the authenticity of the user record, by, for example, checking a digital signature.
- The individual is requested to *verify* that he or she is the valid owner of the user record, by comparing a live biometric sample with that represented by the template in the user record.
- If a successful match occurs, the identifier stored in the user record is relayed to the security system, where the user is *authorized*, according to his or her security system rights and privileges, to complete the service or transaction.

This separation between the verification of the individual and the authorization of the user is critical for successful integration of biometric systems into general security systems. It provides an explicit segregation between the verification process in the biometric system and the rights and privileges that the user is assigned by the security system. This is especially important when considering issues such as the revocation of a user's rights and privileges, and the fact that any individual may appear as multiple users to the security system (for example, as a normal user and as an administrator).

Note that while the discussion above relates to the verification of a single user, it could equally well apply to the identification from a group of users. However, in a positive verification system, as is normally used in a security context (i.e., where users prove that they are valid users of the system rather than negative verification, where users are screened for uniqueness), the objective of an identification operation is generally to reduce the list of candidates to a single user. The claim that the user is one of a list of authorized users in this case is implicit in providing a sample to the biometric system. Therefore, for clarity, verification is used throughout the remainder of this chapter.

Some examples of identifiers that can be mapped to the above discussion include passwords, passport numbers, social security numbers, and a user's private key. We can generalize the concept of identifier to one of a set of *user credentials* that may be associated with the user's biometric template.

20.2. API Discussions

Within biometrics standards such as BioAPI [1] and X9.84 [4], there is some discussion of potential security vulnerabilities if biometric devices are not deployed appropriately (Appendix E in X9.84 gives a good summary of these issues). More specifically, due to the public definition of an Application Programming Interface (API), such as BioAPI, it must be assumed that an attacker potentially has access to all data that are passed across the API interface (the API definition specifies the data format and flow across the API boundary and so we assume that an attacker can also use this definition). In this section we review the security implications of passing these data across the API, and we recommend methods that can be used to protect the data.

20.2.1. Biometric System

Consider the general diagram of a biometric system as shown in Fig. 20.1.
The basic components of a biometric system are [1]

- Capture: capture of a raw biometric sample.
- Process: conversion of the raw sample into a set of features or image sections (this component is also sometimes known as extract).
- Create template: creation of the biometric template. This step may include conformance with a standard such as CBEFF [5] and/or addition of *user credentials* as "payload" [1].
- Match: matching (verify or identify) of the candidate (live) sample with a reference template.
- Decision: comparison of the score output from match with a predefined threshold.

Note that capture, process, and create template may be compiled by the biometric system developer into a convenience function known as *enroll* and that capture, process, match, and decision may be correspondingly compiled into a convenience function, *verify* (or *identify*). The templates may be stored on the biometric device, or they may be stored by the security system, as shown in Fig. 20.1.

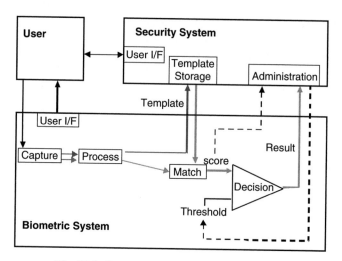

Fig. 20.1. General biometric system architecture.

It is obvious from Fig. 20.1 that there are two main areas where security considerations are important. The first area is the interconnection of the components within the biometric system. The second area is the interfaces (biometric system–user and biometric system–security system).

20.2.1.1. Interconnection of Components

The mechanism for the interconnection of the various components will depend largely on the implementation method used for the biometric system. For example, all the components may be compiled together as a single static or dynamic library, or they may all be implemented with a single physical device. On the other hand, they may be separated either logically (on the same client machine, for example) and/or physically (for example, capture, process, and create template may run on a client, and match and decision may run on a server, or on a portable device, such as a smart card). Whenever components are fragmented in this manner, there is the potential for an attacker to inject a "rogue application" that fools a component of the biometric system into releasing important security information, or falsely initiating a service or transaction. Therefore, it is important to ensure that a secure channel is established; for example, through mutual authentication between the various components. Mutual authentication can be achieved by embedding a shared secret (for example, a key for a cryptographic algorithm) within the two components to establish "trust" between them [6]. Another method of achieving mutual authentication of components is to use a third party to establish trust, such as a security architecture; for example, The Open Group's Common Data Security Architecture (CDSA) [7]. Of particular importance in the operation of the biometric system are the areas relating to match and decision. Particular attention should be paid to the capability of an attacker to access, modify, or circumvent these components.

20.2.1.2. Interfaces

Biometric System to User Interface

Two areas of significance in this interface are the user–sensor interface and the feedback the user attains through the User I/F [typically via graphical user interface (GUI)]. There has been much discussion relating to the detection of liveness in the biometric sensor. This process is key to the successful deployment of a biometric system, and the ability to detect a live finger mitigates much of the risk associated with this issue. Relating to the second issue of User I/F, this is an area where careful design of the feedback to the user must consider the misuse of such information. In general, the appropriate question for an integrator of a biometric system to ask is, "How much of the information relayed to a user will assist an attacker?" For example, if the User I/F returns an indication of the success of a match (perhaps on an LED scale), then this would certainly help a user to correctly position his or her biometric. However, in general, this advantage would be outweighed by the vulnerability that is exposed as a result of an attacker's having feedback on optimizing the placement or modification of a fake or distorted biometric.

Biometric System to Security System Interface

At this interface the main consideration is the passing of data, such as threshold, score, audit data [1] (raw biometric sample), and the result of the biometric operation.

Threshold. The security relating to the threshold setting is, of course, an obvious area where potential vulnerabilities can arise. An attacker could wreak havoc within a security system if he or she is able to modify the threshold setting. The threshold in some biometric systems can be configurable by an administrator, either for individual templates or globally for all templates. The attacker could set an individual threshold setting (if applicable) for his or her own or an associate's template to a very low setting; they could set the global threshold to a very low setting allowing a complete breach of security; or the attacker could set the global threshold to a very high setting, achieving a complete denial of service attack. Methods used to mitigate the threat of threshold modification include hardware factory setting of the threshold, establishment of limits within the biometric system for different operations (for example, the threshold required to be exceeded to release a positive verification signal may be lower than that required to permit the release of user credentials), and the use of access control by biometric verification prior to an adjustment of the threshold's being initiated.

Score. The return of the score to the application provides useful information in the construction of, for example, fused biometric systems. In fact, this is one of the primary reasons that APIs such as BioAPI support the return of the score in an operational biometric system. A particular attack using the score information uses a rogue application to address the biometric system and is described in detail in [8]; it is referred to as a hill-climbing attack. Basically, a hill-climbing attack can occur when an attacker has

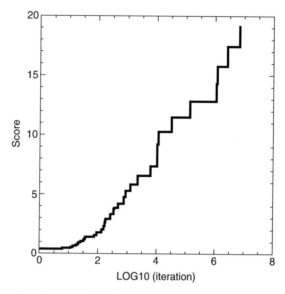

Fig. 20.2. Plot of the effect of the biometric system returns granular scores in response to inputs.

access to the biometric system and the user's template upon which he or she wishes to mount a masquerade attack. The attacker creates a simple rogue application that inputs the template along with a randomly generated image as input to the biometric system. The score the biometric system returns is saved and the attacker randomly perturbs the image, retaining only those samples that positively increase the score. In this manner, the attacker can iteratively synthesize an image that produces a score that exceeds the threshold of the biometric system and use that image as input to the security system that the original template belongs to. Potential solutions to this problem include (1) the biometric system can limit the number of sequential attempts (not necessarily consecutive) against any particular template without a success, (2) the biometric system and the application can be forced to mutually authenticate to each other, or to a third party, such as the Common Data Security Architecture (CDSA) [7], (3) and the biometric system can provide the scores with a level of granularity that will prohibit the attacker from being successful on any particular perturbation. This solution is demonstrated in Fig. 20.2, where the scores were returned with a granularity of 2.5 (arbitrary units), which for this particular biometric system makes the probability that an attacker can introduce a perturbation and thus a score change that is able to "climbs the stairs" becomes prohibitively small. Note that extrapolation of the graph demonstrates that a score that exceeds the threshold, 50 (arbitrary units), is 10^{16} iterations. For further details, see Ref. [8].

Audit Data. The output of audit data can present an immediate security threat if it is output erroneously to a rogue application, which can later input the audit data to the same or different security system. Some biometric systems cite detection of identical samples as a method to mitigate this particular form of replay attack, but in most cases the attacker could easily modify the acquired sample sufficiently to distinguish it from the original sample and still meet the threshold requirements. The most straightforward method to mitigate such attacks is to provide mutual authentication between the biometric components and the security system, prior to outputting any audit data.

Result. The attacks relating to the returned result from the biometric system again relate to the potential of an attacker's using this result to replay at a later date or location. Of course, if the result is simply a yes/no, then access to the score implies that the attacker has circumvented the process in any event. The case where the decision is more detailed than a simple yes/no is covered in more detail ahead.

As a summary of API issues, it can be observed that the majority of potential vulnerabilities with biometric system component interconnections can be resolved with a sound mutual authentication strategy.

20.3. General System Design

This section demonstrates how a biometric system can be enhanced by the complementary use of cryptography to eliminate potential vulnerabilities. Specifically, encryption is used in two concepts: a trusted device and a user record to facilitate the integration of biometric devices into existing security systems.

20.3.1. Trusted Biometric System

Figure 20.3 demonstrates the general concept of a trusted biometric system. In this definition, the trusted biometric system is comprised of a secured (physically and/or logically) biometric system within which all relevant biometric security operations will take place, along with a trusted path between the biometric system and the security system. Note that although the various components of the biometric system may be in different physical locations (i.e., a client and server model), they may be "bound" together logically using mutual authentication between the components.

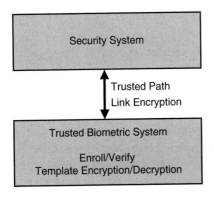

Fig. 20.3. Trusted biometric device.

20.3.1.1. Template Encryption

Encrypting/decrypting the template inside the trusted biometric system has the advantage that once it has been encrypted, it can be freely moved around or stored; for example, on a portable medium. It should be borne in mind, however, that encryption of a template alone does not mitigate template substitution attacks, as each commensurate template in the system will share the same encryption mechanism and so will appear equivalently to the biometric and security systems. The requirements for mitigating identity theft are more appropriately covered by the user record format described in the Section 20.3.2.

20.3.1.2. Link Encryption

Although the data passed across the template can be protected for confidentiality and integrity across the link, a unique session data or a session key must also be used to prevent a replay attack. This is typically accomplished by establishing a unique session key each time a critical piece of information is passed across the link, using a key exchange protocol such as Diffie–Hellman [6].

20.3.1.3. Digital Signatures

Similar functionality of link encryption can be accomplished by using a public private key system to mutually authenticate between the host and the biometric system. This has the added benefit of also potentially using a certification process to help eliminate attacks by rogue applications.

Also, if the user credential is the user's private key and is only released after a successful verification—and then used to generate a digital signature based on a random string sent from the host—then this is a powerful connection between user and system. Also, if the device contains the public key of "registered" security systems to use, this provides mutual authentication. This process is particularly attractive for portable devices using infrared, or RF, communications as the transmission mechanism.

20.3.2. Template Encryption and User Records

Template encryption can be used to protect the confidentiality of the biometric template. Confidentiality of a biometric template is a multifaceted concept. First, it safeguards against the reuse of templates for secondary applications (this is also addressed by the use of proprietary transformations, as discussed in [9]). This is one of the core concerns of privacy principles: that user data is unintentionally available for secondary applications ("function creep"). Second, encryption of the template can mitigate identity theft. Third, the use of encryption can prevent the unwanted investigation of template structures that can assist an attacker in compiling an attack using a synthetic template or biometric sample.

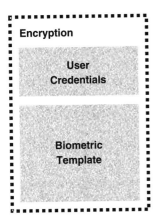

Fig. 20.4. User record.

Encryption also inherently provides an integrity check of the data (modification of the cyphertext would result in a corrupted decrypted template, which would be evident by an incorrect checksum or header information).

As described in Section 20.1, user credentials, such as an identifier, may be added to the biometric template (for example, as payload data using the enroll function as defined by BioAPI) to produce a user record (see Fig. 20.4).

20.3.2.1. Benefits of User Record

The use of the user record in the manner described above provides the following features:

1. As seen in Fig. 20.5, the user credentials, or identifier, provide a link between the user verification and the security system authorization. This segregates the biometric process from the attribution of rights and privileges through the security system.

2. It provides a complex verification "answer" from the biometric system to the security system. This helps to mitigate attacks related to the injection of a match signal.

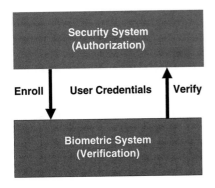

Fig. 20.5. The interaction of user credentials between user verification and system authorization.

For example, in an operating system application, the user credential may be the user's password (although note that the user credential is not constrained by having to be remembered). If an attacker were to inject a signal in this system, he or she would need to know the password. On the contrary, if the output is a simple yes/no, then this is much more easier to attack.

3. A single user can be associated with a number of user credentials, or identifiers, which may comprise multiple roles on a single system, or single roles on multiple systems.

4. It prevents identity theft. Reviewing Fig. 20.4, it can be seen that an attacker cannot simply overwrite a legitimate user record with his or her own (if he or she has access to both on a portable medium such as a smart card), as he or she would also need to have a valid user credential on the system—which would make the "attack" redundant—because the biometric template and the user credential are bound together, the attacker cannot "steal" someone else's user credential by linking his or her template to it.

20.3.2.2. Other Methods for Binding Identifier and Template

While the methods for linking an identifier to the biometric template thus far have been based on the use of traditional cryptography or secure storage, there has also been some work on using proprietary techniques to inextricably link the identifier with the biometric to form a composite template. Such an implementation is described in Refs. [10]–[13]. This method has the advantage not only of providing reconstruction of the key, but also of providing protection of the biometric data without the need for the distribution or storage of encryption keys. This is an attractive solution when biometric systems are deployed on devices such as PDAs or cellular telephones with no areas of protected memory.

20.3.3. System Layout

Applying the concepts of a trusted device and user record allows the general system depicted in Fig. 20.1 to be extended, to that presented in Fig. 20.6 above. Such a system possesses the following features:

1. Encryption of user record: provides confidentiality and integrity of the biometric template; mitigates identity theft.
2. Unique session key: mitigates replay attack.
3. Use of user credentials/identifier: mitigates attack on the biometric system result.
4. Internally set threshold: avoids threshold-based attacks.

Other factors that should be considered include

1. The storage of the user record on a smart card can provide two-factor authentication (smart card and biometric).
2. The provision of audit trail capability can greatly enhance the potential of security attack detection and prevention.

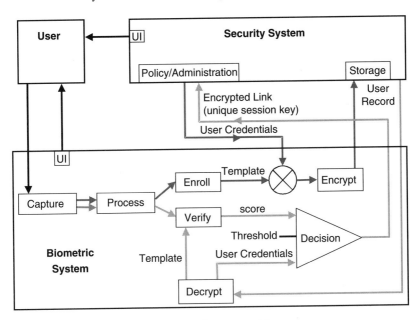

Fig. 20.6. General system architecture.

20.4. Relationship with Privacy Principles

Traditionally, systems are viewed as either providing security or ensuring privacy. However, when implemented appropriately, biometric systems can address both security and privacy concerns. For example, consider that a primary organization may issue a biometric template and associate it with user credentials, known as primary credentials (for example, demographic data such as name, address, etc.), as shown in Fig. 20.7. Two forms of user record are depicted in the figure, using encryption to bind the biometric template and primary credentials and using a digital signature to bind the two entities together. These two scenarios would have different privacy impacts and uses. As examples, the primary credential in Fig. 20.7a may be a piece of data the user expects to remain private (credit rating, for example), and in Fig. 20.7b the credential may be a public piece of information, such as a passport number, where the important issue is that the user is bound to the credential, not that it is private.

We can consider the following commonly accepted privacy principles developed by the Canadian Standards Association as a Model Code for the Protection of Personal Information [14]:

1. Accountability
2. Identifying purposes*—verification or identification
3. Consent*—Express or implied
4. Limiting collection
5. Limiting use*, disclosure, and retention—only for stated purpose
6. Accuracy*

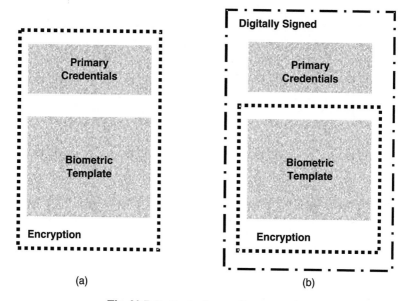

Fig. 20.7. Particular forms of user record.

7. Safeguards*—confidentiality
8. Openness
9. Individual access
10. Challenging compliance

The principles marked with an asterisk are worth special consideration with respect to biometric systems:

Identifying Purposes. A biometric template plays significantly different roles when used for verification or identification purposes. The purpose of the enrollment can be clearly stated at the time that the biometric sample is obtained.

Consent. The user can be requested to provide express consent at the time of enrollment/registration. Furthermore, the user can be requested to provide express or implied consent at the time of verification, perhaps through cooperation (i.e., a system where the user must know that he or she is using a biometric), or through user interface.

Limiting Use. The limiting use is also a consideration for the primary organization in terms of the primary credential. Encryption of the biometric template provides a mechanism to limit use.

Accuracy. The use of encryption or digital signatures for either the biometric data or the associated user data can be used to maintain integrity of the data—thus ensuring that the data have not been tampered with. This has the important consequence of knowing that the primary credential has not been tampered with, nor has the binding of the primary credential with the correct template. These are important trust considerations in terms of knowing that an attacker has not interjected his or her template to mount an "identity theft" to masquerade as a valid user of the system (strictly speaking, according to the definitions above, this prevents an *identifier* theft).

Safeguards. The provision of confidentiality through the use of cryptography can be used as a mechanism to ensure safeguarding of the data.

Segregation of Identifiers. One of the issues for which biometrics receives a lot of attention is the potential for "function creep." Once an individual's biometric has been enrolled in a number of security systems, there is a tendency to assume that the identifiers from all the security systems are "linked together" and the individual's private data have been compromised. However, it can be seen that an extension of the processes shown in Fig. 20.7 can be used to establish a series of independent links between a biometric template and a security system identifier. This series of links can be used to maintain segregation between purposes of the biometric template; for example, at an immigration checkpoint, an individual simply has to prove that he is the valid holder of a passport number (which is authorized by the issuing party)—he does not have to demonstrate that he is the valid holder of a driver's license number, which may also be bound to the same biometric template in a segregated user record.

20.5. Common Criteria

20.5.1. Background

The Common Criteria Scheme was established in 1998 [15] to provide a mutually recognizable basis for the evaluation of IT security products. The Common Criteria was designed to replace the existing National Body schemes for security evaluations and to provide a mechanism whereby products evaluated in any signatory nation in the scheme would be valid in those nations that recognize the scheme. The Common Criteria comprises three components:

1. Common Evaluation Methodology
2. Protection Profile
3. Security Target

The common evaluation methodology (CEM) is the method by which a product or system is evaluated. It describes how evaluators should assess threats and vulnerabilities and provide *assurance* that the product developer has addressed those issues by providing suitable security functionality or environment recommendations. The evaluation is conducted against a security target (ST) that precisely defines the security capabilities of a product. The ST essentially demonstrates how the vendor's security claims are mapped onto security functionality defined by the ST. The ST may also claim compliance with a protection profile (PP). A protection profile essentially lists the security requirements as collected by a group of customers or systems integrators.

20.5.2. Biometric Evaluation Methodology

The common evaluation methodology is defined for general IT security devices. Issues that are specific to biometrics are not adequately covered in the existing CEM. Such issues are the environmental effects related to the usage of biometrics, the particular vulnerabilities, and the performance of the system as a security parameter. The extension to biometric evaluation was first contemplated in 1999 within the Canadian National Body of the Scheme, which led to completion of an evaluation of a biometric product in 2001 [16] and the general discussion of a biometric evaluation methodology (BEM) [17]. This BEM has been extended to include contributions from other members, including the U.K., Germany, the United States, and Italy, with the U.K. taking the lead in generalizing the concepts. The current draft of this evaluation methodology is posted at [18].

Some of the following assumptions, vulnerabilities, and performance characteristics relate to the evaluation of biometric devices:

Assumptions:
> Controlled administrative conditions for registration/enrollment or a user.
> A nonhostile administrator is typically assumed.

Vulnerabilities:
> In addition to the issues addressed in the general system design in Section 20.3, other considerations that relate to the common criteria evaluation of a biometric device include
>> Reverse engineering of device firmware
>> Memory exploitation of residual biometric information
>> Latent image tests
>> Fake biometric tests

20.5.2.1. System Configuration Issues

A unique point of attack for a biometric system is the finite probability that a user will be erroneously accepted by the biometric system. This, of course, is defined as a false acceptance, and a biometric system is characterized by the false acceptance rate (FAR). From a security perspective, the FAR has much more relevance than the FRR. In fact, it can be argued that the FRR is not security relevant at all and is just a convenience parameter. However, the FRR does relate to security functionality in that it affects the rate at which a fallback system (something other than the biometric system that is used in the event of a failure) is used. Therefore, the FRR must be at an appropriate level such that the use of the fallback mechanism is both secure and practical.

The FAR is related to the security of the biometric system in a nonstraightforward manner. There is an excellent description of how to appropriately determine the FAR and FRR in Refs. [18] and [19]. There is also a concept in the Common Criteria known as strength of function. The strength of function is a probabilistic measure of the security strength of a system and as such relates proportionally to the FAR, albeit in a nontrivial manner.

Note also that an interesting aspect of biometric systems is that a single false acceptance is not equivalent to a single attempt at a user's PIN. The significance of this is often overlooked, and there is a tendency to equate a 4-digit PIN (with 10^4 permutations) to a biometric system with a FAR of 10^{-4}. However, these situations should not be equated for the following reason: an attacker attacking a 4-digit PIN system would establish a means for generating the 10^4 permutation of the PIN and present each permutation sequentially as input to the security system. On average, it would take half, or 5000, of these permutations before the correct combination was achieved and the system was breached. With a biometric system, on the other hand, an attacker needs to somehow acquire a candidate input sample (either from a database, or synthetically generated), input it to the system, and receive the result. Therefore, there are three issues:

1. The attacker has to have available a method for generating or acquiring a large number of images.
2. There is a level of computational complexity in attempting each of the candidate samples that comprises the components of process, match, and decision, as described in Section 20.2.
3. It is not clear that the attack would expect to be successful, on average, in half the search space, as is the case for a PIN. The difference is that in a PIN attack, the attacker can sequentially step through all the available PIN space, as all the permutations are sequentially defined. In the case of a biometric, however, the biometric feature space may be much larger than the steps indicated by the accuracy of the system, that is, an attacker can't simply change a bit in the input sample and examine the result—he or she would need to modify the input sample in a logical manner. For example, if the biometric input is sampled at 128×128 pixels of a byte each, the attacker could not feasibly run through all the permutations, instead he or she would need to cycle through only appropriate permutations of the images. This, of course, is a nontrivial exercise.

For these reasons, equating the inverse of the number of permutations of a PIN to the FAR is not a valid process (see also [20] and [21] for further discussion).

20.5.3. Biometric Protection Profile

A protection profile (PP) states the security requirements of a "collection" of customers. At the time of writing, there are two protection profiles under review—U.S. and U.K. protection profiles, Refs. [22] and [23], respectively. There are steps under way to harmonize these PPs, and it is anticipated that a single protection profile will be registered with the Common Criteria Scheme for future biometric system evaluations.

20.5.4. Biometric Security Target

A security target defines the security claims that a vendor makes with respect to its particular product. The evaluation provides a degree of assurance (evaluation assurance level, ranging from 1–7) that the product meets those claims [15]. The security target may also be mapped to a particular protection profile (if it exists).

20.5.5. Common Criteria and Privacy

The Common Criteria provides for the treatment of user data. Currently some international activity is under way to more explicitly relate to the protection of biometric data. An overview of this is in given in Appendix C of [18].

The Common Criteria will provide a very important platform for the evolution of biometric systems. The Common Criteria provides an objective framework against which vendor claims of security functionality, performance, and privacy awareness can be assessed. As such, it will play a valuable role in providing assurance to potential customers that the claims of the vendor are valid and will therefore establish appropriate customer expectations.

20.6. Conclusions

Biometrics can play an important part of an overall security system. Their role is not to replace the security system, but rather to complement it by facilitating strong user authentication. The relationship between user verification and system authorization should be clearly delineated through the use of user credentials. The use of cryptography was seen to enable the secure integration of a biometric system into a security system and to minimize the privacy impact of the resulting system. Finally, the Common Criteria is seen as an important step in providing an objective mechanism for assessing the security functionality, performance, and privacy awareness of biometric systems.

References

1. ANSI INCITS 358-2002, Information technology—BioAPI specification (Version 1.1).
2. Kansala, I. and P. Tikkanen, Security risk analysis of fingerprint based verification in PDAs, *AutoID '02 Proc.*, 2002.
3. Kent, S. T. and L. I. Millett, *Ids—Not That Easy*, National Academy Press, 2002.
4. Biometric information management and security, American National Standards Institute, X9.84-2001, 2001.
5. Common Biometric Exchange File Format (CBEFF), National Institute of Standards and Technology (NIST), NISTIR 6529, 2001, http://www.nist.gov/cbeff.
6. Stinson, D. R., *Cryptography—Theory and Practice*, Boca Raton, FL: CRC Press, 1995.
7. Common data security architecture, http://www.opengroup.org/security/cdsa.
8. Soutar, C., Biometric system performance and security, *Auto ID '99 Proc.*, 1999.
9. Cambier, J. et al., Application-specific biometric templates, *AutoID '02 Proc.*, 2002.
10. Tomko, G. J., C. Soutar, and G. J. Schmidt, Biometric controlled key generation, U.S. Patent 5,680,460, 1997.
11. Bjorn, V., Cryptographic key generation using biometric data, U.S. Patent 6,035,39, 2000.
12. Soutar, C. et al, Method for secure key management using a biometric, U.S. Patent 6,219,794, 2001.
13. ICSA guide to cryptography, Ch. 22 in *Biometric Encryption*, R. K. Nichols, ed., New York: McGraw-Hill, 1999.

14. Canadian Standards Association Model Code for the Protection of Personal Information, http://www.csa.ca/standards/privacy/code/Default.asp?articleID=5286&language= English.
15. http://www.commoncriteria.org/.
16. http://www.cse.dnd.ca/en/services/ccs/bioscrypt.html.
17. Biometric Technology Security Evaluation under the Common Criteria, Version 1.2, 2001, http://www.cse.cst.gc.ca/en/documents/services/ccs/ccs_biometrics121.pdf.
18. Biometric Evaluation Methodology Supplement, http://www.cesg.gov.uk/technology/ biometrics/index.htm.
19. Mansfield, T. and J. Wayman, Best practices in testing and reporting performance of biometric devices, NPL Report CMSC 1402, Version 2, Aug. 2002, http://www.cesg.gov.uk/technology/biometrics/media/Best Practice.pdf.
20. Ratha, N., J. Connell, and R. Bolle, An analysis of minutiae matching strength, *Audio- and Video-based Personal Identification* (AVBPA-2001), 2001.
21. Pankanti, S., S. Prabhakar, and A. K. Jain, On the individuality of fingerprints, *IEEE Trans. PAMI*, 24(8):1010–1025, 2002.
22. http://www.c3i.osd.mil/biometrics/init/bpp_annc.htm.
23. http://www.cesg.gov.uk/technology/biometrics/media/bdpp082.pdf.

Chapter 21

Fingerprint Interoperability Standards

R. Michael McCabe

Abstract. The commercialization of the Automatic Fingerprint Identification System (AFIS) began in the mid-1970s with the installation of five systems at the FBI. In subsequent years additional vendors developed competing AFIS without considering any aspects of fingerprint data exchange between the systems. This chapter describes and reviews the standards created to effect interoperability between dissimilar systems, the certification procedure for the WSQ compression algorithm, image quality issues, and the reference databases developed to assist manufacturers and researchers.

21.1. Background

Fingerprints as a means for identification and verification have a long history traceable back to before the third century B.C. A Chinese clay seal provides evidence of the belief that the patterns and ridge details found on the finger had at least some degree of uniqueness and could be used as an identifying or authorship mark. The seal contains a left thumbprint embedded on one side and Chinese script identifying the owner of the print on the other side. Although the fingerprint image was too deliberate to have been made accidentally, there is nothing to suggest that the Chinese believed that every fingerprint was unique [13].

In the mid-1800s, the British had recognized the individuality of fingerprints and began using them as a means for civil identification even though they lacked an indexing system for efficient retrieval. But by the late 1890s, Sir Edward Henry began the development of a system based on the combination of pattern classes found on the 10 fingers. His classification system would facilitate the identification and retrieval of a single set of fingerprints against a large master file. In 1901 Scotland Yard adopted this system and within a few years it was introduced to other countries [2]. The Federal Bureau of Investigation (FBI) also adopted the system and in 1924 established its Identification Division with 810,000 10-print fingerprint cards. Each card contained 10 inked images that were rolled in a manner that captured all the friction skin area on each finger from one side of a fingernail to the other. Each card was filed according to the Henry system [[18]. Classification of fingerprint cards that used this system gained so much support worldwide that it could be considered as the earliest de facto fingerprint standard.

21.2. Introduction

Ten-print cards received by the FBI for searching against their master criminal file were first assigned a Henry classification. This classification code and other physical descriptors were used to effectively reduce the size of the criminal master file by filtering it down to a select subset of candidate 10-print records to be searched. A fingerprint examiner would then visually compare the fingerprint images on the search 10-print card to the images on each of the selected candidate fingerprint cards. Use of filtering parameters greatly reduced the number of candidate cards that had to be sent to a human examiner for detailed visual comparison. This approach worked well, but as time went on, the daily workload increased, as did the number of records in the master file. By 1963 the FBI's file had grown to 15 million subjects and 10,000 daily searches were being performed. Their fingerprint identification operation was becoming overwhelming, as the manual procedures required were very time-consuming and labor-intensive. It became apparent that the matching procedures in place would eventually become inefficient and ineffective as the daily workload grew and the number of records to be searched increased. Furthermore, at that time it was not even imagined that by 2002 the file size would grow to 45 million and the daily workload to 80,000 transactions [1]. In response to this problem, the FBI sought the assistance of R. T. Moore at the National Bureau of Standards (NBS)—currently the National Institute of Standards and Technology (NIST)—to help develop an automated solution for fingerprint matching. Research contracts were issued to private laboratories to develop methods for electronically scanning and capturing fingerprint images. Meanwhile the NBS worked on techniques for computerizing the comparison of minutiae details from one set of fingerprints against the FBI's criminal master file in order to identify matching subjects. Both research efforts were successful, and by 1981 the FBI had deployed five operational Automated Fingerprint Identification Systems (AFIS) [13].

The FBI was not the only agency developing an AFIS capability. In subsequent years, other manufacturers developed competing AFIS systems, including those from Great Britain, France, and Japan. By the mid-1980s, independent standalone AFIS systems had been installed not only in federal, but also in state, city, and county agencies. This was in addition to the operational systems located at Scotland Yard in London and the Royal Canadian Mounted Police (RCMP) in Canada.

During this AFIS evolution, communication and exchange of quality fingerprint information between the different or dissimilar systems were never considered. Built-in communications did not exist between the systems, nor were there any provisions for interoperability. Each system was a standalone entity. As a consequence, fingerprint information read on one system could not be searched directly against the fingerprint files on another system. To run a 10-print search on more than one system required physically processing the card on each system to be searched. Not only was this approach inefficient and costly, but often it was not even possible. It became apparent that this void had to be filled. Standards were needed that would specify methods for interchanging fingerprint information and provide a solution to the problem of data conversion between systems in the law enforcement arena.

In 1985 a meeting was held between scientists from NIST and officers of the International Association for Identification (IAI). The purpose of this meeting was to initiate a program for establishing interoperability among AFIS vendors. To accomplish this, an effort was begun to develop a set of standards and specifications to ensure a common format for the exchange of high-quality fingerprint information and images. Eventually, these data exchange standards would address aspects of image capture, compression, and exchange principles.

The first standard developed specified a common method for formatting fingerprint feature information. It was believed that use of this format would enable all vendors to effectively exchange processed fingerprint image data captured by dissimilar AFIS systems. Within a few years the need for an image-based standard was recognized. As the development of this standard matured, the need for an image compression specification and a certification procedure was identified. Work began to develop a common detailed algorithmic approach to be followed for compressing fingerprint images. An additional specification was developed, comprised of a set of engineering requirements and a corresponding test method to be used for qualifying individual hardware components. This was to ensure that AFIS systems and their peripherals were capturing, displaying, and printing the fingerprint images properly. Finally, in order to provide test data to researchers and to assist vendors in testing new products, several databases of scanned fingerprint images were compiled and made available as standard data reference materials.

21.3. Fingerprint Format Standard

21.3.1. Need for a Standard

Early commercial AFIS systems developed from 1975 to 1985, produced by different manufacturers, all operated in the same general manner. All used a vidicon or flying spot scanner to capture the fingerprint image from which the same general type of information relating to discrete features of each image was extracted and used for determining the similarity and potential match between two fingerprints. However, the presentation formats each vendor used were different and precluded interoperability.

During this period the matcher algorithms were minutiae-based, although there were some advocates for topological approaches [19]. Matching algorithms used in these systems were all based on the comparison of minutiae information. In fingerprint terminology, minutiae are generally defined as small, precise minor details occurring along the friction ridges of a fingerprint. Although there are several types that can be defined, AFIS algorithms that are minutiae-based generally rely upon and limit themselves to ridge endings and bifurcations. A *ridge endings* is defined as the point on a fingerprint at which a ridge abruptly begins or terminates. A *bifurcation* is the point at which an existing ridge splits into two separate ridges. The relative positions

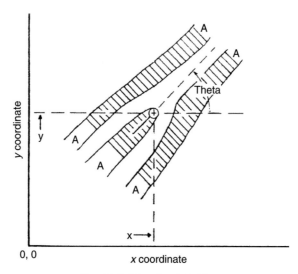

Fig. 21.1. Minutiae definition.

and orientations of the minutiae, as well as the ridge count information between neighboring minutiae are recorded. This information, in addition to the fingerprint core (approximate center of the fingerprint) and delta (approximate point of ridge divergence) information extracted from the image [18], is used in the decision-making process of the matching algorithms.

Figure 21.1 illustrates the method of defining the position and orientation of a minutia [16]. Assume the enclosed areas labeled A are ridges. The middle A area is a ridge ending having x and y positional values in the coordinate system. Its orientation *Theta* provides the minutia's positional relationship with the coordinate system. If the unmarked area between the areas labeled A is considered to be a ridge, then a bifurcation occurs at the same position and orientation as the ridge ending. It will also be assigned the same x-, y-, and *Theta* values as the ridge ending. Using the same method to describe both types of minutiae has the advantage that no minutia will be lost as a result of an overinked ridge ending (resulting in a bifurcation) or underinked bifurcation (resulting in a ridge ending). Both situations will be recorded with essentially the same position and orientation.

There are many similarities as well as differences among the AFIS manufacturers regarding the data and the algorithm used to match fingerprints. All minutiae-based AFIS systems recorded the data from each minutia as a tuplet consisting of an x-coordinate, a y-coordinate, and a minutia direction *Theta*. This is the angle measured from the system's x-axis to the projection of the tail of the marked minutia that is in the direction that a ridge points. The tuplets from a search print were compared to those from each candidate print and a metric indicating the closeness between the two prints was calculated. Two fingerprint images (and their sets of minutiae) will never align exactly, due to the inherent nature of friction skin that causes it to expand, compress, twist, and contort. For this reason, AFIS matchers rely on a closeness or similarity measure for identification rather than requiring an exact match.

Details for precisely locating the minutiae, and the conventions used for these measurements, have always been AFIS-dependent. Although similarities existed among the systems, there were never two systems, produced by different manufacturers, that recorded all the minutiae information in exactly the same manner. Each vendor extracted and recorded the data in a manner compliant with its own system. For example, of the five major vendors in the mid-1980s, three different coordinate system origins were used. One was located at the upper left corner, another in the lower left corner, and a third in the center. Four different units of measurement existed for reporting the coordinates of a minutia. There were also four different units of measurement for the angular orientation of the minutiae in addition to indicating a clockwise and counterclockwise rotation. Two systems reported the number of ridge crossings between minutiae, but each system used different minutiae and slightly different rules for counting ridges [13].

Of the AFIS systems available, it was not possible to find two systems that could interchange the data directly without a conversion step that was required for every combination of two AFIS systems. In other words, for a set of data to be fully operable among four systems, each system required a bidirectional conversion program to each of the other three, or a total of 12 programs. As additional vendors were added, each of the other vendor systems would be required to generate another pair of conversion programs.

One solution for coping with this conversion problem was the creation of a voluntary standard to specify a common format for the exchange of fingerprint and other demographic and physical information. Then only one interface would be required by each vendor for converting information to and from the common format. The requirement for a unique interface between every combination of two systems would be eliminated. NIST was tasked with the responsibility for developing this standard.

21.3.2. ANSI Standards

For such a "standards" solution to be effective requires that all parties involved have an equal voice in the participation and development of the standard. For this reason, NIST decided to use the American National Standards Institute (ANSI) process for the development of this format standard and thereby have it registered as an ANSI standard. Since ANSI is a well-respected standards approval body, use of their rules and procedures to achieve consensus could ensure a standard's adoption. Although some of its members are federal, state, or local employees, ANSI is a private organization independently financed, controlled, and operated by its members. Being responsible for the identification of a single set of voluntary standards, they verify that principles of openness, due process, and consensus are followed during the approval process. As a private organization it is responsible for ensuring that standards are developed without conflict or duplication.

NIST is accredited by ANSI to develop standards for data interchange using the "canvass method" for attaining consensus. Using this approach, the first step is to develop a canvass list. This entails contacting all parties identified as having a direct or material interest in the development of the standard and offering them the opportunity to participate as canvassees in the development process. As a canvassee, there is no financial commitment for participation, but each must agree to review the drafts of the standard and vote on its acceptability. Drafts of proposed standards that are developed are transmitted to all parties on the canvass list with appropriate supplemental information and a letter ballot. The ballot form provides the opportunity for the canvassee to indicate concurrence, objection, or abstinence with the proposed standard.

The canvass list may not be dominated by any single interest category. Dominance means a position of dominant influence, by reason of superior leverage, to the exclusion of other viewpoints. The canvassee list should have a balanced representation of interest categories. At a minimum it should include manufacturers, users, system integrators, consultants, etc. This ensures that no single interest is responsible for the contents of the standard [17].

21.3.3. Fingerprint Minutiae Standard, 1986

In the spring of 1985, solicitation letters were sent to all identified manufacturers and users of AFIS equipment who could be affected by the development of a standard. This was in addition to other consultants and system developers. These letters announced the development of a proposed format standard, described the "canvass method," and invited each recipient to register as an official canvassee. An initial working draft was developed by NIST staff members and circulated for review and comment to the registered canvassees and others with an interest in the development of the standard. The draft defined the content, format, and units of measurement for the exchange of a subject's physical descriptive and fingerprint information that would be used in the identification process of a subject. The proposed standard would promote interoperability between dissimilar AFIS systems by allowing each vendor to convert its proprietary data into and out of a common format, acceptable to the canvassees, that could be usable by other vendors to identify fingerprints.

In addition to the proposed draft, each recipient received an invitation to attend a jointly sponsored IAI/NIST workshop that was held at NIST on October 22–24, 1985. The workshop was to serve as a forum to discuss comments and changes to the draft of the proposed standard, to resolve differences, and to make alterations to the document before it was mailed for balloting by members of the canvassee list. The initial draft of this proposed standard defined a file structure consisting of a single Type-1 logical data record and up to 10 Type-2 logical data records. The Type-1 record was associated with a given subject. Fields within this record contained information related to the identity of the agency or organization in possession of the fingerprint card. Additionally, there was descriptive information regarding the subject such as name, date of birth, gender, etc. The Type-2 record contained geometric minutiae-based fingerprint information together with other supplementary information such as pattern type. Each Type-2 record recorded all the information pertaining to a single fingerprint. Figure 21.2 illustrates the coordinate system and the units of measurement used for describing the minutiae. The system of measurement units chosen was

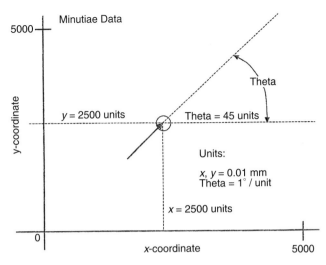

Fig. 21.2. Minutiae description.

designed not only to accommodate the common systems in operation, but also to provide compatibility with future systems that would use more precise measurements for describing minutiae.

Approximately 50 participants attended the invitational workshop. During the course of the workshop, participants debated different issues relating to the proposed format standard while considering changes and additions to it. The consensus of the group was that the format standard should be expanded to include fingerprint image information. This would enable vendors to use their own proprietary algorithms to process the fingerprint image information. As a result, two additional fingerprint image record types were developed as part of the standard. The Type-3 record defined a format to be used for exchanging 10 pixels/mm (250 pixels/in.) low-resolution images, while the Type-4 record defined a format for 20 pixels/mm (500 pixels/in.) high-resolution images. Although the definition of these additional record types could have been developed more thoroughly to fully address the need for image exchange, fields were inserted to specify the offsets between the coordinate system of the minutiae and that of the fingerprint images [15]. The canvass list for this standard was comprised of 43 organizations and consultants who unanimously approved the standard by a letter ballot. The ANSI standard was certified as the Data Format for the Interchange of Fingerprint Information on August 25, 1986 [3].

21.4. FBI Modernization and Image-based Systems

Although approved by vendors and users, the minutiae standard was never operationally implemented. For interoperability purposes, new procurements of AFIS systems often required the capability of compliance with the 1986 standard. Despite acceptance of the compatibility requirement, vendors claimed that their systems would not operate optimally using minutiae extracted by other systems. During the 1980s the exchange of Type-3 or Type-4 image records over communication lines was also impractical due to bandwidth limitations. Furthermore, although one AFIS producer claimed compliance with the standard, the vendors argued that unless there were at least two vendors willing to design and implement a minutiae exchange program, it would be a waste of the user and company resources to develop the required conversion software unilaterally. As a result, the 1986 standard went untested, untried, and unused. However, the standard itself and the experience gained from implementing the procedures required to develop an ANSI standard provided a framework for the development of future standards and specifications.

By 1989 the FBI had begun a modernization program with the objective of updating its AFIS capabilities and the revamping of the traditional methods used to process 10-print card submissions. The FBI's fingerprint Identification Division was to be relocated from the Washington, DC, headquarters to a new facility in Clarksburg, West Virginia. Long-range plans called for replacing the card-based AFIS with a modern image-based system capable of handling its daily workload in a timely manner. The size of the criminal fingerprint card file and the number of search requests submitted to the FBI were increasing daily at an unprecedented rate, resulting in a growing processing backlog and an unacceptable delay in response time. Furthermore, the FBI was being called on to perform additional noncriminal background checks for targeted jobs, volunteer organizations, etc.

Additional factors that contributed to the decision of converting the FBI operation to an image-based AFIS approach were the rapid advances being made in communication and storage technologies. Communication speeds and bandwidth were increasing. Devices capable of storing and retrieving millions of fingerprint images were becoming practical and available. Meanwhile, associated costs for communication facilities and storage were steadily decreasing while system processing speeds were increasing. Finally, live-scan technology with its many advantages was being greatly improved, and jurisdictions were converting to this new technology rather than adhering to the traditional inked-card approach. Eventually live-scan capture would be accepted as an alternative to the inked card. Using live-scan technology, the captured fingerprint images could then be directly transmitted to a remote AFIS.

Transactions containing fingerprint images captured directly from live-scan equipment or scanned from a 10-print card would be submitted to the FBI electronically. Eventually, these electronic submissions would replace the traditional burdensome tracking, handling, and processing of the 10-print cards. Fingerprint images used for verifying candidate identifications resulting from AFIS searches would be stored online and could be called up and displayed at an examiner's terminal. Previous requirements to physically locate each candidate 10-print card and provide it to an examiner for verification were eliminated. Online storage of the fingerprints also provided the advantage of allowing copies of the same record to be viewed simultaneously by more than one examiner.

The modernization of the FBI's fingerprint identification operation to an online image-based AFIS system was the largest AFIS procurement ever attempted. Original specifications required that by 2006 the system had to be capable of storing at least 40 million 10-print records online and have the processing power to handle up to 65,000 transactions a day with a 2- to 24-hour response time, depending on the system request priority. The system would be required to electronically communicate and exchange data with all the state systems installed by the major AFIS vendors. A high-speed network capable of handling the large number of daily image transmissions was required for communication between the FBI and its law enforcement customers at the state, local, and federal government agency levels. Additional networking facilities were required within the AFIS environment to handle the flow of internal data between the databases. Control of the flow of images between the AFIS and fingerprint examiners was also required.

Although some states had installed image-based AFISs, none compared in size, capability, or complexity to that required by the FBI. For the proposed system to be successful, an unprecedented amount of cooperation and coordination would be required among the FBI, AFIS vendors, live-scan vendors, and FBI customers located throughout the country. Standards and specifications related to the submission of electronic images and related data over a wide area network had to be developed and implemented in order to facilitate and control the flow of data between the FBI and its customers. The original format standard developed in 1986 would not be adequate for the proposed system, as it was primarily minutiae-based and specified a minimum amount of descriptive and demographic subject data. An updated system would need to be capable of handling detailed information items contained on subject rap sheets and all the images normally found on a 10-print card. New standards, specifications, and compliance programs were required to address the issues of image capture, quality, compression, and formatting of both the rolled and plain fingerprint images customarily found on 10-print cards.

21.4.1. Fingerprint Image Standard, 1993

It was imperative that the FBI, AFIS manufacturers, FBI users, and other parties affected have input into the creation and operation of the new image-based system. Being responsible for the 1986 standard, NIST was familiar with the ANSI procedures and requirements for standards development. The agency was also regarded as a neutral party that could act as a negotiator on points of disagreement. For these reasons, NIST's assistance was requested to coordinate and develop the expanded format standard for image exchange. To accomplish this, NIST sponsored three workshops between 1990 and 1992. These workshops were held to discuss issues and review results of experiments that had been performed. There were over 150 participants at each of the workshops. As was done for the 1986 standard, a "strawman" draft of a proposed image-based standard was written and circulated to the registered participants prior to the first workshop. This document was designed as a starting point, to be discussed, redesigned, and improved on by the agreements made at each of the workshops. Several drafts of the proposed standard were developed and circulated to the 100 organizations that registered as canvassees. After more than three years of development, testing, and refinement, the Data Format for the Interchange of Finger-

Table 21.1. Logical Record Types

Logical record identifier	Logical record contents	Type of data
1	Transaction information	ASCII
2	Descriptive text (user-defined)	ASCII
3	Fingerprint image data (low-resolution gray-scale)	Binary
4	Fingerprint image data (high-resolution gray-scale)	Binary
5	Fingerprint image data (low-resolution binary)	Binary
6	Fingerprint image data (high-resolution binary)	Binary
7	Image data (user-defined)	Binary
8	Signature image data	Binary
9	Minutiae data	ASCII

print Information was accredited as an ANSI standard on November 22, 1993 [4]. In its final approved form nine record types were defined to satisfy the various transactions acceptable to the IAFIS. Table 21.1 provides a brief description of each of the nine types.

Like the 1986 standard, the first record type provided information describing the use and originator of the transaction. The second type provided a physical description of the subject together with his or her demographic information. Although user-defined, the majority of the fields recorded in the Type-2 record is specified and described by the FBI's transmission specification [7]. Both of these records are recorded using ASCII text. The next four record types are fixed-field binary records used to convey the required scanning parameters and the physical image data for the 10 rolled and 4 plain impressions from a 10-print record. Three of the four fingerprint image records were included to fulfill specific vender application requirements. The Type-4 record is the image foundation of this standard and of the current FBI operation. It records the 19.69 ppmm 8-bit gray-scale data scanned from each of 14 possible fingerprint images. The Type-7 record is user-defined and designed primarily for the exchange of latent fingerprint and palmprint images not addressed in the standard. The Type-8 record is also a fixed-field binary record used to transmit both the arresting officer's and the subject's scanned written signature. The Type-9 was a carryover of the minutiae exchange record from the 1986 standard.

Of all the aspects of the standard discussed during the workshops, three major issues of contention focused on the quality of the captured image and processed data. To a great extent it was the latent examiners who participated in the workshops that campaigned for the highest possible rendition of gray-scale pixel data for FBI usage. The first issue was the nature of the scanned data—binary versus gray-scale. Significant savings in both transmission bandwidth and storage could be realized by restricting the values of each pixel to either a 1 or 0. This would allow a single byte to contain data from eight pixels. The argument made was that a recorded binary image scanned with a high resolution and without any lossy compression would produce an image that would be visually equivalent to an eight-bit gray-scale image. Live-scan vendors developing binary solutions up to 47.24 ppmm (1200 ppi) and AFIS vendors relying on binarized skeletal images for their search algorithms favored this approach. The latent examiners argued that the binary images could not supply all the visual information they needed to make a confident decision regarding a match. The second issue was the scan resolution required. Although the major AFIS vendors were scanning 10-print cards at a nominal 20 pixels/mm (500 ppi), live-scan vendors were scanning images from as low as 11.8 ppm (300 ppi) to as high as 23.6 ppm (600 ppi). Eventually, consensus was achieved that the FBI would only accept images that were scanned at a nominal resolution of 19.68 ppmm (500 ppi), with each pixel quantized to 8 bits or 256 levels of gray-scale.

The third issue dealt with the compression algorithm and the compression rate to be used for storing and transmitting the image data. Achieving consensus on this issue proved to be the most difficult of the issues. In the early 1990s, although band-width was increasing and the price for a megabyte of storage was decreasing, the amount of scanned fingerprint image data was still too great to handle without some form of data compression. The uncompressed data from 10 rolled images and the 4 plain impressions required 10 megabytes of storage. Since the scanned fingerprint image usually contains a significant amount of white background, and the very high-frequency pixel data in a fingerprint image provides little visual information, these sources of data easily lend themselves to a lossy form of data compression with min-imal visual degradation. In the same timeframe that the NIST workshops were being conducted, the JPEG [11] algorithm was also being developed. Being essentially free of patent issues it was considered as a possible candidate for image compression. But in order to satisfy projected system requirements it would be necessary to achieve a data compression ratio of approximately 15:1. The JPEG algorithm achieves its compression by operating on 8×8 tiles of pixels. However, reconstructed fingerprint images that had been JPEG compressed with compression ratios greater than 8:1 il-lustrated blocking effect degradations at the borders of the 8×8 tiles. In an effort to overcome this problem, the FBI developed its own wavelet scalar quantization (WSQ) compression algorithm that globally compressed the entire image and achieved the 15:1 compression ratio with minimal visual degradation [16]. The details of the WSQ algorithm have already been described in a previous chapter of this book and can also be found in the specification itself. Consensus was finally achieved to use the WSQ algorithm at 15:1 for the exchange of fingerprint images with the FBI, but the specifi-cation was never included as part of the standard. It was thought that eventually better compression schemes would be developed for use with fingerprints and the standard should be open enough to accommodate future advances.

21.4.2. WSQ Compliance Program

The WSQ specification document [22] provides a comprehensive description of the steps required for compressing gray-scale fingerprint images using the wavelet scalar quantization technique. To ensure adherence to the specification, NIST established a WSQ implementation compliance-testing program for vendors and researchers. The intention of this accreditation program was to ensure that interoperability, proper numerical precision, and image fidelity were consistent among different implementations. The compliance program determined if a vendor's compressed image files were created in accordance with the requirements stated in the WSQ Gray-scale Fingerprint Image Compression Specification.

The encoder function of an implementation was required to produce a syntactically and numerically correct compressed file that could be properly decoded without any errors by an independent decoder implementation. A decoder implementation had to be capable of correctly reconstructing an image file from a syntactically correct WSQ compressed file. Compared to the original image file, the reconstructed image file was required to be numerically accurate to within closely specified tolerances.

Validation of a specific vendor implementation was based on compressing and reconstructing test images in accordance with the WSQ specification [10]. The images used were from a reference set of test files. The tests specified and images used for encoders and decoders were not exhaustive tests of interoperability, numerical precision, or image fidelity. The testing only guarantees the correctness for those images tested. Compliance with the WSQ specification was determined by comparing the output from the candidate implementation with the output from a double-precision reference implementation developed by NIST's Information Technology Laboratory (ITL). The same reference implementation was and is still being used for accreditation. The comparison of test results between a candidate implementation and the ITL reference implementation determines if acceptable tolerance limits have been met.

Accreditation for a WSQ encoder/decoder implementation required the product developer to download the NIST reference test set of 17 fingerprint images. Each image was scanned at a resolution of 19.69 pixels/mm (500 pixels/in.) and quantized to 8 bits of gray-scale (256 levels). Image dimensions ranged from 375×526 to 832×768 pixels. In addition to the original scanned image file, NIST provided its reference implementation of the WSQ-encoded image file, and the reconstructed image file for each of the original fingerprint images. For each image file supplied, the vendor was required to return a WSQ file compressed using their implementation. For each WSQ file compressed by the NIST reference implementation, the vendor was to return an image file reconstructed by its implementation.

The compliance procedures require that the output data sets generated by a vendor's candidate implementation match the output data sets from the NIST reference implementation to within the stated accuracy levels. The encoder compliance measures include compressed file sizes and intermediate numerical results calculated and recorded during the quantization phase of the algorithm. The only decoder compliance measure used is a comparison of the reconstructed images. All the individual gray-scale pixel values from each image of the vendor and NIST sets are compared to each other. At least 99.9% of the pixels must match exactly, and no pixel can differ in intensity by more than one level of gray-scale value. Figure 21.3 is an illustration of the checks performed on WSQ encoder/decoder implementations.

All federal, state, and local agencies transmitting fingerprint images to the FBI are required to transmit and receive fingerprints as WSQ compressed fingerprint image files. As a result of this WSQ implementation accreditation program, testing for proper

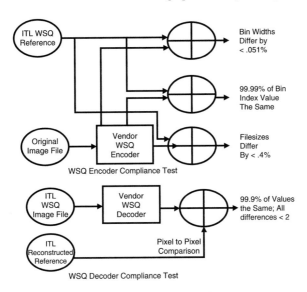

Fig. 21.3. WSQ compliance requirements.

image compression performance has achieved reliable interoperability between the FBI and different agencies using dissimilar AFIS systems.

21.4.3. Facial Image Standard, 1997

In 1997 an addendum describing the Type-10 logical record was approved by ANSI and added to the ANSI/NIST-CSL 1-1993 exchange standard [5]. This was the product of the NIST Mugshot Workshop, held in 1995, that addressed the exchange of facial images and also provided a vehicle for describing and transmitting scar, mark, and tattoo (SMT) images found on a subject. The Type-10 logical record encoded this information as part of the data exchange standard to accommodate the long-term plan that called for mugshots, SMT information, fingerprint, and other descriptive information to be included as parts of an FBI submission. This new record type introduced the concept of the tagged-field image to the standard. It provides for both ASCII and binary data to be included in the same logical record. This concept was used extensively in the 2000 revision of the standard.

21.4.4. Fingerprint Image Standard Revision, 2000

According to ANSI procedures, every five years each ANSI-certified standard must be reviewed and a decision made to withdraw the standard, reaffirm it in its current form, or modify it with additions, corrections, and/or deletions [17]. Accordingly, a review of the 1993 ANSI/NIST standard was required to be started in 1998. In addition to this mandatory regulation, it was also a logical time to reevaluate the requirements of the standard in light of technological advances that had occurred in the previous five years.

As with the previous standards, a workshop was convened at NIST in September 1998 to discuss the existing standard and submit suggestions for its modification. There were 180 registered participants at the workshop representing 10 different countries. By 1998, implementations of the "ANSI/NIST Standard," as it had come to be known as, had been adopted for use by both the United Kingdom and INTERPOL. Foreign countries represented at the workshop were interested in the future revision of the standard due to the increasing international adoption and its potential for foreign communication with the FBI. Several enhancements to the standard were suggested during the three-day workshop. Most were approved by the group and subsequently incorporated into the ANSI/NIST-ITL 1-2000 revision [6]. Those participating in the development of the revision included 108 canvassees from 9 countries. Foreign interests were represented by 13 of these canvassees. The 2000 revision of the standard received ANSI approval on July 27, 2000.

The major issues discussed during the workshop addressed the current limit on the scanning resolution for fingerprint images, lack of unique record types for specific applications, and mechanisms for the exchange of palmprint images. In the 1993 version of the standard, the Type-4 logical record defined a binary record containing eight-bit gray-scale information from a fingerprint image scanned at 19.69 ppmm. The latent fingerprint examiner community in attendance at the workshop campaigned for the removal of this cap on the scanning resolution. They argued that retaining this artificial limit had the effect of freezing AFIS technology and limiting their ability to verify identifications of latent fingerprints found at the scene of a crime. At that time, there were agencies planning for the procurement of new AFIS systems or updates to existing ones. These procurements could take advantage of new advances in AFIS technology including increases scanning resolution. Higher-resolution scanners were available, and the cost for storing the extra data had dropped dramatically over the previous few years. Therefore, a recommendation for the adoption of 39.37 ppmm (1000 ppi) as the scanning resolution for the next-generation AFIS procurements was added to the standard. This recommendation is implemented in the 2000 version with the use of tagged fields to express the value of the scanning resolution. Using this technique, any variable scanning resolutions can be used and expressed as information items in the record.

The 1993 standard did not associate logical record types with specific applications such as latent print or palmprint processing. In response to this need, attendees at the workshop developed four additional tagged-field records and defined information fields for each of these record types. Table 21.2 lists the additional record types to the 1993 version that have been approved for inclusion in the standard.

The Type-13 and Type-14 are basically tagged-field update records for the previous Type-4 10-print and Type-7 user-defined record for exchanging latent images. The Type-15 record was developed to exchange required palmprint information, including the writer's palm located on the side of the hand. All of these added record types provided for the use of variable scanning resolutions including the Type-16 record used for user-defined testing purposes.

Another major addition to the standard was the introduction of a method for handling international character sets to reflect the increased use of the standard in non-

Table 21.2. Additional Logical Record Types

Logical record identifier	Logical record contents	Type of data
10	Facial and scar, mark, and tattoo (SMT) data	ASCII/Binary
11	Reserved for future use	—
12	Reserved for future use	—
13	Latent image data (variable-resolution)	ASCII/Binary
14	10-print image data (variable-resolution)	ASCII/Binary
15	Palmprint image data (variable-resolution)	ASCII/Binary
16	User-defined testing image data (variable-resolution)	ASCII/Binary

English-speaking countries. This allowed for backward compatibility with existing readers. It also supported multiple character sets in a single text string and handled text-ordered conventions such as ISO character sets and Unicode.

21.5. Image Quality Specifications

The quality of captured fingerprint images has always been an issue dating back to before the advent of the live-scan devices when inked 10-print cards were used to record the images. Law enforcement officials were constantly being encouraged to use care to capture all the deltas present on a finger and to ensure the recorded ridge structure contained relatively clear ridges, valleys, and minutiae.

With the introduction of live-scan technology [9], the operator had the opportunity to review an image before recording it on a 10-print card record for subsequent processing by an AFIS. Despite the advantages offered by live-scan technology, there were also quality issues associated with this new approach. In an effort to control the quality of the input, an initial requirements document was developed that addressed issues associated with area of coverage, image color, number of gray levels, contrast, resolution, and repeatability. These issues were not always adequately considered in the early models of live-scan systems [14]. As the electronic live-scan images replaced the 10-print card as the primary input to AFIS, this requirements document became outdated. In response, an updated specification was developed that addressed the capabilities of the equipment rather than the characteristics of the cards [7]. Emphasis was placed not only on the quality of the image but also on the equipment used to capture the image. Capture devices were required to comply to several performance criteria that included achieving specified levels of geometric accuracy, meeting modulation transfer function requirements, and demonstrating the required pixel gray-scale dynamic range. These specifications are still in force and are used for evaluating new products.

Table 21.3. NIST Special Databases

ID	Description	Size
4	Image pairs—distributed by classification	2000 pairs—JPEG lossless
9	Image pairs—distributed by frequency of occurrence	2700 pairs—JPEG lossless
10	Supplemental single images—less frequent classification	5520 images—JPEG lossless
14	Image pairs—distributed by frequency of occurrence	27,000 pairs—WSQ lossy
24	Digital video live-scan	200 MPEG-2 video files
27	Latent & matching 10-print images	258 cases—JPEG lossless
29	Rolled & plain images from 10-print cards	216 card pairs—WSQ lossy
30	Dual resolution (19.68 & 39.37 ppmm) rolled & plain images	36 card pairs—JPEG lossless

21.6. Fingerprint Research Databases

Before 1992 there were no publicly available fingerprint databases. Researchers and vendors wanting to test new products or designs had difficulty acquiring the data they needed. When they did get data, it was not enough to perform a proper test. Often fingerprint images could only be voluntarily obtained from employees at their own company. Privacy issues associated with the data prevented law enforcement agencies from releasing fingerprint images or personal data to private companies, researchers, or universities not actively involved in a system procurement project. Since that time, several databases of scanned fingerprint images have been compiled and made available as Special Databases under the NIST Standard Reference Data Program [21]. The majority of the images were derived from 10-print cards scanned at 19.69 ppmm (500 ppi) and recorded as 8-bit gray-scale pixels.

These publicly available Special Databases have been used for evaluating fingerprint classification and matching systems. They have also proven to be useful tools for algorithm development, system training, and system testing, including fingerprint verification systems. Each database was created to fulfill a special need. The first one provided a data set evenly distributed by fingerprint classification type. To investigate characteristics of compression schemes, the last data set provides samples of flat and corresponding rolled images scanned at two different resolutions. Many of the databases consisted of mated fingerprint pairs—two distinct fingerprint image captures separated by a relatively long period of time. Table 21.3 provides a brief description and size of each Special Database.

21.7. Future Directions and Trends

For the past 20 years, the primary uses for fingerprint identification has been for law enforcement and background clearance applications. Both were based on the 10-print card or electronic record as input. During this time standards and specifications have been developed. For quality assurance purposes, specifications and evaluation procedures have been designed to ensure that the physical components of AFIS and live-scan systems meet engineering specifications. Fingerprint images are scanned in accordance with mutually agreed-upon parameters. A compliance testing program has been developed to ensure that fingerprint images compressed using the WSQ algorithm comply with established accuracy requirements. For interoperability purposes, ANSI standards have been developed that specify the data format to use for the interchange of fingerprint and other information. As in the case of the FBI, these specifications, procedures, and standards enable the use and exchange of data between similar and multivendor systems. Every state either has an AFIS or belongs to a consortium network that shares the use of one or more systems. Many agencies are planning on upgrading to, or have already upgraded to, their next-generation AFIS installation. The availability of the standards has made this feasible without the need for a massive retooling effort. The established standards have also provided agencies the opportunity to negotiate their most favorable contract by choosing an alternate AFIS vendor.

The traditional use of fingerprint identification for criminal checks will continue to thrive. But as the technology used to capture these images improves, existing standards will have to be upgraded to account for the changes. For example, images are currently scanned at 19.69 ppmm (500 ppi) and compressed using the WSQ algorithm with a nominal compression ratio of 15:1. Doubling the scanning resolution to 39.37 ppmm (1000 ppi) will require a new approach to image compression. The JPEG 2000 algorithm [12] is being considered as a replacement for the WSQ algorithm for these higher-resolution images. This wavelet-based algorithm is now capable of compressing these higher-resolution images to the same or better quality achieved by the WSQ algorithm.

An additional demand for AFIS resources is the result of a growing number of professions that now require a civilian applicant fingerprint background check. Volunteer organizations that interact with the youth or elderly add to the daily workload by requiring the same checks for their staff and volunteers. New standards, specifications, and guidelines will be needed to accommodate this increased demand for service. Methods used to deliver these services are also changing, as is the demand for faster response times. One state is using the Internet not only to submit web-based applications for civilian jobs, but also to submit applicant fingerprints for civilian background checks against the state's repositories. Tests are in progress to extend this concept to check the FBI files. For this application, the plain or flat impressions from an applicant's index fingers are used rather than the 10 rolled prints formerly required. This use of the web has drastically reduced the turnaround time for these civilian job applications and allowed job openings to be filled faster. Developmental work to extend these concepts for searching the FBI's repository is also underway.

Identification is the process of matching a subject's fingerprint record against an entire database in order to establish the identity of the owner of the fingerprint record— a one-to-many comparison. Criminal and civil applicant background checks are examples of this identification function. It is probable, that in the future, background-checking applications will put more reliance on the use of two or more flat images (rather than rolled images) for identification purposes. Verification is the process of confirming that a person is who he or she claims to be by matching their fingerprint record against that of the claimed identity. Fingerprints are gaining widespread popularity as verification checks for access control applications. Verification functions include the use of the fingerprint for physical access to a locked area or as a substitute for a password or authenticator in order to gain access to a computer or network.

As a result of the attack on the World Trade Centers on September 11, 2001, the Patriot Act of 2001 [20] and the Enhanced Border Security and Visa Entry Reform Act of 2002 [8] were passed. These acts are aimed at denying visas to undesirable foreign nationals identified as having a criminal record, who may be wanted under an arrest warrant, or who are on "watch lists." Individuals seeking to enter the United States with a valid visa will also be expected to verify their identity on entry to the United States. Appropriate tools are to be provided to the State Department and Department of Justice to intercept and obstruct terrorism in the United States.

Both acts mandate the use of biometrics as part of the visa control systems. They also set forth the requirement that accuracy standards be established for different types of biometrics. Efforts to develop standards for this application began during the first quarter of 2002. Plans have been developed and tests initiated to determine the current accuracy rates for fingerprint comparison using FBI and INS systems. Although other biometrics such as the face are being evaluated for the verification function, fingerprints are considered as one of the leading biometrics for use for both the identification and verification requirements.

Another effort directed toward biometric standardization began in November of 2001 with the formation of the ANSI/INCITS M1 biometric committee. It was formed to develop data format exchange standards and protocols to effect interoperability among systems. Current projects within the committee address the exchange of fingerprint image information, and minutiae and pattern template information. One of the main applications for these standards is in the area of border-crossing operations. The minutiae standard is also being considered by the American Association of Motor Vehicle Administrators (AAMVA) for use as part of the driver's license requirements. As of June of 2002, the M1 committee has expanded its influence to become part of an international standards body. In addition to fingerprint standards, this committee is developing face and iris standards aimed at verification applications. Aspects of performance measurement and reporting, and the development of biometric profiles are also being addressed by M1 and its international counterpart ISO/IEC JTC1/SC37.

References

1. Biometric Consortium 2002 Conference Proceedings, Washington, DC.
2. Cole, S., *Suspect Identities*, Cambridge MA: Harvard University Press, 2001.
3. Data Format for the Information Interchange—Fingerprint Identification, ANSI/NBS-ICST 1-1986, 1986.
4. Data Format for the Interchange of Fingerprint Information, ANSI/NIST-CSL 1-1993, 1993.
5. Data Format for the Interchange of Fingerprint, Facial & SMT Information, ANSI/NIST-ITL 1a-1997, 1997.
6. Data Format for the Interchange of Fingerprint, Facial & Scar Mark & Tattoo (SMT) Information, ANSI/NIST-ITL 1-2000; NIST Special Publication 500-245, 2000, ftp://sequoyah.nist.gov/pub/nist_internal_reports/sp500-245-a16.pdf.

7. Electronic Fingerprint Transmission Specification, FBI CJIS-RS-0010(V7), 1999.
8. Enhanced Border Security and Visa Entry Reform Act of 2002, P.L. #107-173, signed May 2002.
9. Gerhardt, L. et al., Fingerprint imagery using frustrated total internal reflection, *Proc. 1986 International Carnahan Conference on Security Technology*, 1986, pp. 251–255.
10. Hogan, M.D. et al., Information technology measurement and testing activities at NIST, *J. Research of the National Institute of Standards and Technology*, 106:241–370, 2001.
11. ISO/IEC 10918, Information Technology—Digital Compression and Coding of Continuous-Tone Still Pictures, 1992.
12. ISO/IEC 15444, Information Technology—Coding of Still Pictures, 2000.
13. Lee, H. C. and R.E. Gaensslen, *Advances in Fingerprint Technology*, New York: Elsevier Science, 1991.
14. Minimum Image Quality Requirement for Live-Scan, Electronically Produced, Fingerprint Cards, Washington, D.C: FBI, 1988.
15. Moore, R.T. and R.M. McCabe, Standard format for the exchange of fingerprint information, *Proc. 1986 International Carnahan Conference on Security Technology*, 1986, pp. 13–16.
16. Phillips, P.J. et al., Biometric image processing and recognition, *Proc. IX European Signal Processing Conference (EUSIPCO-98)*, Island of Rhodes, 1998.
17. Procedures for the Development and Coordination of American National Standards, 2002, http://www.ansi.org/public/library/std_proc/default.htm.
18. *The Science of Fingerprints Classification and Uses*, Washington, DC: U.S. Department of Justice, FBI, 1984.
19. Sparrow, M.K. and P.J. Sparrow, A topological approach to the matching of single fingerprints: Development of algorithms for use on rolled impressions, National Bureau of Standards Special Publication 500-124, 1985.
20. Uniting and Strengthening America by Providing Appropriate Tools Required to Intercept and Obstruct Terrorism (USA PATRIOT ACT) Act of 2001, P.L. #107-56, signed October 2001.
21. Watson, C.I. and C.L. Wilson, NIST Special Database 4 Fingerprint Database, 1992, www.itl.nist.gov/iad/894.03/databases/defs/databass/defs/dbases.html#finglist.
22. WSQ Gray-Scale Fingerprint Image Compression Specification, IAFIS-IC-0110, Washington, DC: FBI, 1997.

Index